UTAH: A Guide to the State

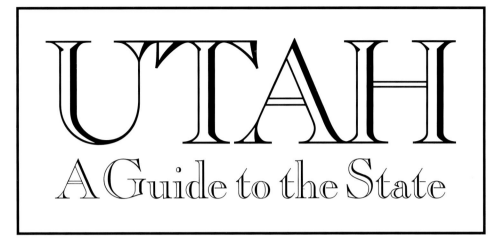

UTAH
A Guide to the State

REVISED TRAVEL GUIDE

– by –

Barry Scholl and François Camoin

with an Introduction by Larry Clarkson

Based on the original 1941 Guide
Compiled by Workers of the Writers' Program of the Work Projects Administration for the State of Utah
under the direction of Dale L. Morgan; and on the 1982 revision by Ward J. Roylance

Sponsored by the Utah Arts Council with support from the Utah Centennial Commission

UTAH: A GUIDE TO THE STATE FOUNDATION · GIBBS SMITH, PUBLISHER

SALT LAKE CITY

Revised Edition

02 01 00 99 98   5 4 3 2 1

This is a PEREGRINE SMITH BOOK, published by
   UTAH: A GUIDE TO THE STATE FOUNDATION, Utah Arts Council, 617 East South Temple, Salt Lake City, Utah 84102
   and
   GIBBS SMITH, PUBLISHER, P.O. Box 667, Layton, Utah 84041

Book design by Larry Clarkson, production by Brian Glissmeyer, Clarkson Creative, Salt Lake City, Utah
Woodcut illustrations by Tom Olson, © Clarkson Creative, Inc.
Maps design by Larry Clarkson, production by Brian Glissmeyer, © Clarkson Creative, Inc.
Photography by François Camoin, Stephen Trimble, Steve Midgley, and Scott Smith, © individual photographers
Photography by John P. George, Frank Jensen, Mel Lewis, and Tom Till, courtesy of the Utah Travel Council,
   © individual photographers and the Utah Travel Council
Essays by Deenise Becenti, Katharine Coles, Edward A. Geary, Lyman Hafen, Margaret Pettis, Gregory C. Thompson,
   and Stephen Trimble, © individual authors

Printed in Hong Kong

Library of Congress Cataloging-in-Publication Data
Scholl, Barry, 1962–
   Utah, a guide to the state : revised travel guide / by Barry Scholl, François Camoin. — Rev. ed.
   p. cm.
   "Based on the original 1941 guide 'compiled by workers of the Writers' Program of the Works Projects Administration
for the State of Utah' under the direction of Dale L. Morgan; and on the 1982 revision by Ward J. Roylance."
   "Sponsored by the Utah Arts Council with support from the Utah Statehood Centennial Commission."
   Includes index.
   ISBN 0-87905-836-6
   1. Utah—Guidebooks. I. Camoin, François André, 1939–. II. Roylance, Ward Jay, 1920–. Utah, a guide to the state.
III. Utah Arts Council. IV. Utah Statehood Centennial Commission. V. Title.
F824.3.S36 1998
917.9204'33—dc21   97-35532
                                                                                CIP

DEDICATION

In Memory

- WARD JAY ROYLANCE -

This edition of *Utah: A Guide to the State* is respectfully dedicated to Ward Jay Roylance.
Ward loved the West—its open spaces, its mountains and deserts—and he loved the place we call Utah.
He died before he could undertake this, the third edition of the guide.
He was a writer, a photographer, a man of the land, and our friend. We miss him.

ACKNOWLEDGMENTS

No book exists by itself, no book is an original work. This one began as a collective effort, and the present editors have done no more than add their piece to an already complex structure that has now spanned some fifty-seven years. We have brought the text up to date, attempted to have it reflect some of the changes Utah has undergone since the last edition. We have reorganized the information, written some new text where it seemed necessary, added illustrations, put in new photographs and new maps. But the heart and soul of this book came from the writers of the 1941 edition, and from Ward Jay Roylance.

Primary editing was a collaboration by three individuals: writer and editor Barry Scholl, author and photographer François Camoin, and graphic designer and writer Larry Clarkson. As close friends of Mr. Roylance we were familiar with *Utah: A Guide to the State*, and shortly before his untimely death, Ward asked if we would assist with the third edition. Upon his passing, the Utah Ars Council and Utah: A Guide to the State Foundation concerted and we began our work, sadly without our mentor and friend.

Funded by an arts foundation created specifically for the publication of this book, *Utah: A Guide to the State* is more than just an information and travel guide. It is, as Clarkson states in his introduction, "a celebration of the art of living in Utah." The third edition includes work from many of Utah's best writers, designers, artists, and photographers.

We began editing the third edition by dividing the state of Utah into six provinces along geographic, historical, and cultural boundaries. The second edition manuscript was reorganized accordingly and six new chapters were written by Scholl and Camoin for each area. A chapter highlighting Utah's monuments and parks was added by Scholl, and Camoin wrote an overview of the state as chapter one.

The book design, created by Clarkson, reflects the WPA heritage of the first edition of *Utah: A Guide to the State*. Design style, page layout, and typefaces of the 1940s were incorporated. Typefaces include Caslon Open Face for the heads, Copperplate for the initial caps and introductory quotes, and Goudy Oldstyle for the body copy.

The entire book was digitally composed. Maps for each province were created electronically using Illustrator by Clarkson and his design assistant Brain Glissmeyer. Illustrations were conceived by Clarkson, then drawn and cut into woodblock prints by graphic artist Tom Olson. Artist proofs were then digitally scanned, edited, and colored using Photoshop by Clarkson and Glissmeyer.

Camoin commissioned four Utah photographers to shoot photographs for the third edition, including himself, Steve Midgley, Scott T. Smith, and author and photographer Stephen Trimble.

Additional photography was contributed by the Utah Travel Council, courtesy of Dean Reeder, director, and Janice Carpenter, photo editor. Photographers include John P. George, Frank Jensen, Mel Lewis, and Tom Till.

Consequently, Scholl commissioned six authors to write personal travel vignettes highlighting each of the geographic provinces and chapters, including himself, Deenise Becenti, Katharine Coles, Edward Geary, Lyman Hafen, Margaret Pettis, Greg Thompson, and Stephen Trimble.

Clarkson selected the introductory quotes for each chapter, featuring journal entries or contemporary musings about Utah from historic personalities and contemporary writers, including Edward Abbey, Warren A. Ferris, Zane Grey, Virginia Sorenson, Wallace Stegner, Maurine Whipple, and Terry Tempest Williams.

Stacey Clark read the final manuscript and checked our Utah facts. Gibbs Smith, along with in-house editors Madge Baird and Linda Nimori, of Gibbs Smith, Publisher, turned our collective creativity into an actual book.

To all of them we give our heartfelt thanks. Moreover, a special thank you is in order for Bonnie Stephens of the Utah Arts Council, the gracious members of the Utah: A Guide to the State Foundation, including Chairman Edward Geary, board member Guy Lebeda of the Utah Humanities Council, Sam Weller and his son Tony of Zion Books, and especially to Terrie Buhler for her smile and loving persistence.

- Barry Scholl - François Camoin - Larry Clarkson -

TABLE OF CONTENTS

Foreword by Edward A. Geary ix

Introduction by Larry Clarkson x

Chapter 1 Utah: An Overview 1
State Map: *Geographical Provinces* 2
- Landscape 3
- Culture 3
- Traveling in Utah 6
Essay: "The Indians of Utah," by Gregory C. Thompson 10

Chapter 2 Utah's Treasures: Parks and Monuments 15
State Map: *National and State Parks, Wilderness Areas* 16
- National Park and Monuments 17
Vignette: *Lake Powell* 42
- State Parks 56
- National Forests 57
- Bureau of Land Management 58
- Wilderness Areas 58
- Scenic Byways and Backways 59
Essay: "The Last Frontier of Loneliness," by Barry Scholl 60

Chapter 3 Bright Lights: Utah's Urban Corridor 63
Province Map: *Davis, Salt Lake, Summit, Wasatch, Weber, Morgan, and Utah Counties* 64
- Central Corridor: Salt Lake Valley 65
- Southern Corridor: Utah Valley 83
- Northern Corridor: Weber, Morgan, and Davis Counties 92
Essay: "The Right Place," by Katharine Coles 100

Chapter 4 Utah's Great Basin and Range 103
Province Map: *Box Elder, Morgan, Weber, Tooele, Juab, Millard, Beaver, and Iron Counties* 104
- Great Salt Lake Desert North 105
- Great Salt Lake Desert South 107
Vignette: *The Great Salt Lake* 117
- Great Salt Lake Desert West 120
Essay: "Captain Bonneville's Desert," by Stephen Trimble 126

Chapter 5 O Ye Mountains High: Utah's Mountain Province 129
Province Map: *Cache, Summit, Wasatch, Duchesne, Uintah, Rich, and Daggett Counties* 130
- Cache Valley: Logan and Bear Lake Areas 131
- The Wasatch Range 137
- The Uinta Mountains 143
Essay: "Utah's Northern Tier," by Margaret Pettis 153

Chapter 6   The Central Valleys: Utah's Heartland 155
             Province Map: *Utah, Carbon, Emery, Sanpete, Sevier, Piute, Beaver, Millard, Iron, and Garfield* 156
             - Coal Country: Price Area 157
             - Mormon Country: Castle, Sanpete, and Sevier Valleys 159
             - The High Plateaus: Sevier and Fishlake Plateaus 166
             - Juab and Pahvant Valleys: Fillmore Area 172
             Essay: "The People of the Valley," by Edward A. Geary 176

Chapter 7   Utah's Canyonlands and the Colorado Plateau 179
             Province Map: *Carbon, Emery, Garfield, Grand, San Juan, Unitah, and Wayne Counties* 180
             - The Green and Colorado Rivers 181
             - The Uinta Basin 182
             - The Book Cliffs 182
             - The San Rafael Swell 184
             - Spanish Valley: Moab Area 188
             - San Juan Country: Four Corners Area 194
             - Robbers Roost: Hanksville Area 205
             Essay: "Beauty All Around," by Deenise Becenti 208

Chapter 8   Utah's Dixie and the Grand Staircase 211
             Province Map: *Kane, Washington, Iron, Garfield, and Wayne Counties* 212
             - Cedar City Environs 213
             - Virgin River Valley: St. George Area 215
             - Long Valley and Sevier Valley South: Kanab and Points North 221
             - Grand Staircase: Lake Powell, Bryce Canyon, Escalante 224
             - Boulder Country 233
             Essay: "Landscape and Story," by Lyman Hafen 235

Biographical Sketches 237

Index 238

FOREWORD

The first edition of *Utah: A Guide to the State* was compiled from extensive field research by the Utah Writers project, a depression-era federal works program directed by Dale L. Morgan, and published in 1941 under the sponsorship of the Utah State Institute of Fine Arts. In the late 1970s, Salt Lake City bookseller Sam Weller initiated work on a second edition by hiring Ward J. Roylance to revise and update the original text. The efforts of Weller and Roylance attracted the attention of Ruth R. Draper, director of the Utah Arts Council, successor-agency to the Institute of Fine Arts and holder of the copyright to the guide. Mrs. Draper set in motion discussions that led to the incorporation of the non-profit UTAH: A GUIDE TO THE STATE FOUNDATION in 1980 with Edward L. Hart as chairman of the board of trustees, Ruth R. Draper as director, Terrie DeMill Buhler as assistant director and secretary-treasurer, and a distinguished board. With the assistance of the Utah Arts Council, the Utah Travel Council, and several private donors, the revised edition was published in 1982 with Ward J. Roylance as author, Eugene E. Campbell as consulting editor, and Margaret D. Lester as picture editor.

With the passing of another decade, it once again became apparent that the touring section of the guide, in particular, needed to be revised if it was to retain its usefulness. Proposals for a third edition received strong support from Bonnie H. Stephens, current director of the Utah Arts Council, and from the guide foundation board, including original trustees Ruth R. Draper, Edward L. Hart, Terrie Buhler, Sam Weller, Anthony L. Rampton, Everett L. Cooley, and more recent appointees Carol H. Nixon, Edward A. Geary, Aden Ross, and Guy Lebeda. The goal was to produce an up-to-date guide in a more attractive and accessible format while preserving and enlarging upon the virtues of the earlier editions, including a sense of history and an informed appreciation of the Utah landscape that goes well beyond the superficialities of the typical tourist guidebook. Ward Roylance was eager to take up the revision but died shortly before it began, leaving the task in the able hands of his friends and colleagues Larry Clarkson, François Camoin, and Barry Scholl. Special thanks are due to Terrie Buhler for keeping the project on track and pushing it to its conclusion, and to the many contributors who have shared our vision of this new edition.

- EDWARD A. GEARY -
Director, Utah: A Guide to the State Foundation

Introduction

Imagine for a moment that you are an artist—a painter of landscapes of epic proportion.

Cut a frame of molten mantle from deep in the earth. Lift it to the surface and let it cool, forming a dense igneous foundation. Cover the frame with siltstone and shale, and apply heat and pressure until the crust begins to break and fold, twist and buckle. Lace with dikes and sills—veins of hot lava fusing frame and crust together. Add more heat until it melts into a canvas of metamorphic schist, speckled with flakes of black-and-white mica, feldspar and crystal quartz. Take your time, millions of years if necessary. Build it strong.

Your canvas will be large, four hundred by three hundred miles wide. Prime it with layer upon layer of geologic sediment, the remnants of ancient seabeds flooding and receding. Color the sands burgundy for wingate, ochre for navajo dunes, shades of gray for mancos shale—both warm and cool—with bentonite bands of ivory and the blackest indigo. Buildup the surface of the canvas, color upon clay, sand upon stone, epoch upon eon, until it is thick and textured like the skin of an ancient beast. Leave a trace or two of the last great body of water: a splash of salty brine in the upper left-hand corner, a smaller freshwater stroke of ultramarine shimmering on the top edge of the canvas.

Grasp the sides of your frame, applying pressure again, this time pushing inward until the surface buckles and ripples, and a long angular crease protrudes like a spine running lengthwise north and south, with a shorter but higher spur jutting off to the east. Call these rocky folds "mountains"; name them Wasatch, Uinta, and Abajo.

Take the long flat surface of a giant pallette knife and spread a thin crust of salt and clay over the vast empty void west of the mountainous crease, punctuating it haphazardly with solitary peaks and juniper parklands, plains of sage and saltbush. Call these rambling peaks and valleys "basin and range"; name them Topaz, Hogup, and Wah Wah.

Use the knife's razor edge and slice a long parallel cut east of the crease, meandering down the canvas, gouging through layers of colored sandstone. Fill the canyon with spring runoff and august rains, and color it green. Gouge another cut to the right and connect the two, forming a third canyon—deeper and more grand; color it red. These will be the paths of great rivers, whose countless tributaries will expose and erode a maze of rincons and hoodoos, labyrinths of blowing sand and red rock, stone windows and arches, and natural bridges the likes of which the world has never seen. Call this enchanted wilderness "canyonlands"; name the mesas and buttes Wild Horse, Kapairowits, and The Maze.

Paint the canvas with earth tones, umber and sienna, both burnt and raw. Juxtapose patterns of rabbitbrush with pigmy forests of pinyon. Mix aspen and fir with wildflowers in season and a blanket of white in the winter months. Add strokes of cerulean for high alpine lakes and wild cascading rivers. Tint the foothills cadmium and magenta with the breath of autumn winds. Sew patchwork quilts of spring grasses and alfalfa, thalo green and viridian, in the lower valleys.

Accent your landscape with the hues of civilization: the chaotic color of shopping malls, the dazzle of downtown districts, the fluorescent neon of cafes and coffee shops. Draw long straight lines for highways, heavy and bold, crisscrossing the canvas north and south, east and west; skirting the high peaks, the lonely wastelands, the deep canyons.

Render complex patterns of urban life along the foothils of the Wasatch in the north, trickling south to merge with the checkered textures of the central rural valleys, to reappear at the bottom left of the canvas. Add these final creative touches, but temper the growing patterns with prudence. Monitor the feats of mankind so that the rivers might still run wild and the deep cobalt blue of the Utah sky will not turn a muddy gray.

Contrast the bright colors and sharp angles of modern man with the sensuous contours of nature and the fading tones of indigenous cultures and pioneers past. Let the sketchy paths of the anasazi, the explorers, the pioneers and outlaws faintly show through. Create and plan carefully, so the promise of technology will not obscure the values of the people who have and will inhabit this desert wasteland—this place it was once said no one wanted—where gentile and chosen alike have wrested a living from the land, cultivated a garden in the midst of the wilderness.

Step back and admire the art you have created. Title it "Utah" after the proud people who once roamed the high plateaus and fertile valleys. You've created a symphony of landscape and community, a place unlike any other on earth. Visitors from around the world will come to view your landscape, tour the treasures of your canvas: the parks and the monuments, the bright modern cities, the quaint rural towns, the purple mountain cirques, the red desert trails. And this book will help guide them.

An artistic legacy itself, *Utah: A Guide to the State* has always been more than just a guidebook. For the authors and artists, photographers and writers, and the foundation that has nourished its creation, the book is a celebration of the art of living in the West.

At present, Utah has left a legacy for its children. Whether by insight or tyranny of circumstance, our state is still a master-piece, at least for the moment. Owing much perhaps to our ancestors, federal politics, or maybe to the tenacity of the land itself, much of our state is as it was when democracy was but a hope to Jefferson. Controlled growth of our cities and towns, conservation of our parks, prudent efforts to manage the forests and public lands, and protection of wilderness—these things testify that Utah is a place where man is a respecter of God's handiwork, and can be an example to the rest of the world that the needs of a people and the values of their homeland *will* be balanced.

In times past, the wind and rain, the ice and snow have sculpted and shaped the mountains and deserts of Utah. And not unlike our painting, their future will now be shaped by us, the people of Utah.

- LARRY CLARKSON -
A Utahn

Cabin in the Pines – Tom Olson

Utah: An Overview

THE VISION OF UTAH DEEPLY ENTRENCHED IN THE AMERICAN PSYCHE IS THAT OF A RUGGED LAND, SCORED BY CANYONS, BROKEN BY RED-ROCK CLIFFS, A DESERT COUNTRY WITH LITTLE VEGETATION AND FEWER INHABITANTS. WE'VE ALL SEEN THE JOHN FORD MOVIES—STAGECOACHES AND HORSE-SOLDIERS MAKING THEIR WAY BETWEEN THE PINNACLES AND BUTTES OF MONUMENT VALLEY. THE RED-ROCK DESERT COUNTRY OF THE COWBOY MOVIES IS A PART OF THE GEOGRAPHY OF UTAH, JUST AS THE EXPLOITS OF OUTLAW BUTCH CASSIDY, THE PONY EXPRESS TRAIL, AND THE URANIUM BOOM

Sunset reflections over Monument Valley – Frank Jensen, UTC

OF THE FIFTIES ARE PART OF ITS HISTORY. BUT UTAH IS A COMPLICATED PLACE, NOT EASY TO SUM UP IN A FEW WORDS OR A FEW FILMS.

THERE IS THE ALPINE COUNTRY OF THE HIGH UINTAS, WITH ITS MOUNTAIN LAKES AND CONIFERS; THERE ARE FERTILE VALLEYS; THERE IS THE WEST DESERT, MORE BARREN THAN HOLLYWOOD COULD HAVE IMAGINED; AND THERE ARE THE CITIES—SALT LAKE CITY, PROVO, LOGAN, OGDEN, ST. GEORGE—EACH WITH ITS OWN CHARACTER, ITS OWN HISTORY, ITS OWN WAY OF BEING.

"HOMESICKNESS IS A GREAT TEACHER. IT TAUGHT ME . . . THAT I CAME FROM THE ARID LANDS, AND LIKED WHERE I CAME FROM. I WAS USED TO A DRY CLARITY AND SHARPNESS IN THE AIR. I WAS USED TO HORIZONS THAT EITHER LIFTED INTO JAGGED RANGES OR RIMMED THE GEOMETRICAL CIRCLE OF THE FLAT WORLD. I WAS USED TO SEEING A LONG WAY. I WAS USED TO EARTH COLORS—TAN, RUST RED, TONED WHITE . . . I WAS USED TO A SUN THAT CAME UP OVER MOUNTAINS AND WENT DOWN BEHIND OTHER MOUNTAINS. I MISSED THE COLOR AND SMELL OF SAGEBRUSH AND THE SIGHT OF BARE GROUND."

- Wallace Stegner -
"Finding the Place:
A Migrant Childhood"
from Where the Bluebird Sings
to the Lemonade Springs

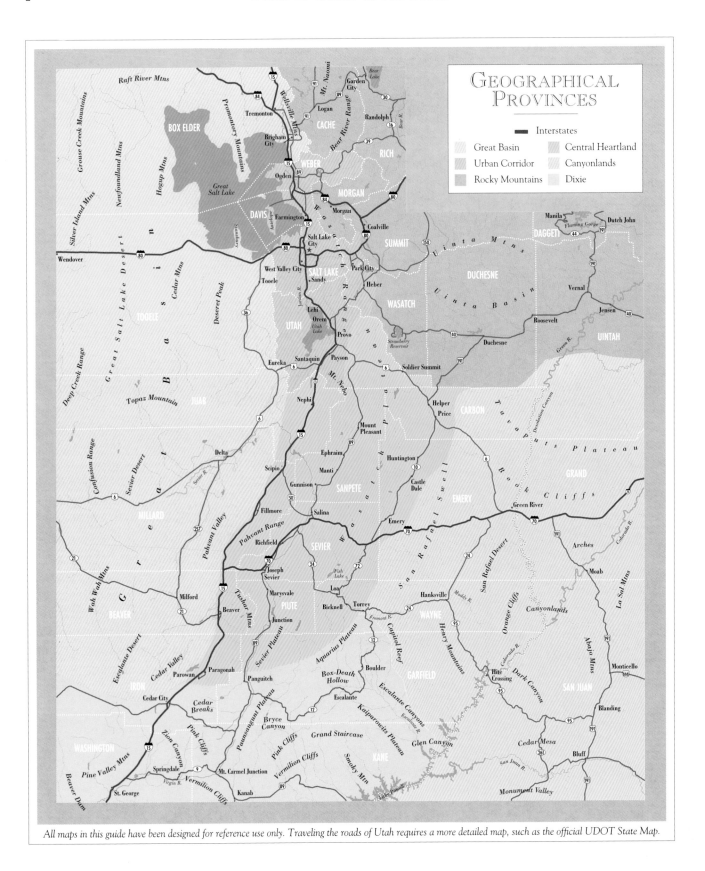

LANDSCAPE

South of the Uinta Range is the Uinta Basin, a rugged valley bordered by mesas that rise gradually southward to the 10,000 foot summits of the Tavaputs Plateau. South of the Uinta Basin are the Canyonlands of the Colorado Plateau, which cover nearly a fourth of Utah's surface. Here, streams have cut steep-walled gorges hundreds of feet deep, and the forces of wind, ice, and water have carved the land into startling and eerie formations. In the canyonlands the bare bones of the earth show through; the working of the forces that shape the landscape are open to the eye, innocent of the vegetation that softens reality in more tempered climates. South of Interstate 70, Route 191 will take you across the Colorado River to Moab, once the center of uranium mining in Utah, and, farther south, to the Navajo Reservation—Dinetah, the Land of the People.

West of the Wasatch Range, the Great Basin is enclosed by highlands on all sides; the water that falls here does not find its way to the sea but is absorbed by the land or evaporates. The rivers of the basin disappear in great sinks or feed shallow lakes, of which the Great Salt Lake is only the largest and most permanent. Much of the basin was once covered by a much larger body of water, prehistoric Lake Bonneville; the Great Salt Lake is what remains of that inland sea. Most of the basin is desert, devoid of drinkable water, a beautiful and desolate wasteland without shelter or forage. In the latter part of the 19th century it formed one of the great obstacles to American westward migration. Dominguez and Escalante stayed south of the worst areas in 1776 when they tried to find a route from Santa Fe to the Spanish settlements of California. Jedediah Smith crossed the heart of the west desert in 1826 on his return from California. Twenty years later the Donner party passed through on the way to their ordeal in the snow of the Sierras. Tourists now float through the same landscape in air-conditioned cars on Interstate 80, with little more to worry about than the availability of hotel rooms in the casinos of Wendover.

CULTURE

For at least 10,000 years before Europeans came, desert peoples hunted and gathered edible plants and seeds in this seemingly uninhabitable land. Invisible to our eyes, which recognize as the marks of civilization only those concrete and steel monuments with which we cover the land, they lived in a balanced relationship with their environment and created a

Contrasting the eroded canyons of Utah's red-rock desert are the fertile green valleys and snow-shrouded mountains of the higher elevations – Frank Jensen, UTC

Much of the Great Basin was once covered by prehistoric Lake Bonneville; the Great Salt Lake is what remains of that inland sea – François Camoin

complex and enduring culture.

At the foot of the western slopes of the Wasatch Range and High Plateaus, where the soil washed down from the mountains is fertile and there is water for irrigation from the streams entering the basin, Utah's European settlers established themselves. The majority of Utah's population still lives in the long shadow of the Wasatch and its southern extension, though the traditional distribution of people is being modified by tourism, the new geopolitics of retirement, and out-migration from California and the perceived troubles of life on the Pacific coast. Hitherto lightly populated areas of Utah are experiencing sudden and rapid growth. St. George has become a fashionable retirement community; Moab, gateway to both Arches and Canyonlands National Parks, remembers the booming times when uranium was king; Torrey, a few miles from the entrance to Capitol Reef, suddenly has art galleries, chain motels, gourmet restaurants, and fast-food places. California artists and telecommuters are finding a way to live in harmony with the descendants of the people who came here to build the outposts of Brigham Young's religious empire.

The Mormons

Like Massachusetts, Utah was settled by a religious group seeking a place where they could practice their beliefs in relative isolation, where they could establish a community without interference from established governments. In telling the story of the Mormons it is sometimes difficult to distinguish history from those narratives constructed by a people intent on creating a new way of life, stories told to hold a nation together in the face of hardship and doubt.

Led by Brigham Young, the Latter-day Saints arrived at the mouth of Emigration Canyon on July 24, 1847. Young, according to legend, stared down at the valley below and said, "This is the place." By the afternoon of their arrival the Mormons were breaking ground to plant the crops that would sustain them over the coming months and digging the first irrigation ditches to capture the water flowing out of the mountains. Within a few days parties were moving up the slopes to cut lumber for buildings and stockades, streets were laid out around the site where the temple would rise, and a new way of life—a new order—had come to the valley of the Great Salt Lake. That is the myth, the necessary legend; history tells

us that the decision about where the Mormons were to settle had of course been made long before, and that the main body of emigrants actually entered the promised land on July 23 while Brigham Young, delayed by a bout of mountain fever, waited one more day.

Nevertheless, give a day here, a day there, an interesting moment in history had begun, a moment not yet ended as we make this book. While the pioneers planted and ploughed, Brigham Young, well aware that new conditions call for new ways, pronounced the first civil laws in the valley with an eye to the immediate circumstances and his vision of the shape of the future. Land was neither to be bought nor sold; it was to be apportioned among the settlers and they must make good use of what they had been given if they were to keep it. Other laws governed the distribution of goods and services and the general behavior of the Saints in their new country.

The land reflects its spiritual heritage. Like that of the Massachusetts colonists, and certainly in response to similar fears and desires, the Mormon pattern of settlement took the form of clusters of closely huddled dwellings surrounded by tracts of cultivated land. Unlike the midwestern states, with their repeated pattern of individual houses set in the middle of a square of land, Utah is peppered with small towns at whose core are the buildings of commerce, government, and worship. Like the Massachusetts colony, Mormon Utah was founded as the physical manifestation of a particular idea. Both colonies were intended to be spiritual enterprises, examples to the rest of the world, living proofs of humankind's ability to lead happy and prosperous lives governed by strict adherence to certain codes of behavior, by a singular vision of the relationship between man and God.

In Utah, religion and its attendant politics rather than convenience or the hope of gain dictated where new towns were to be built and what enterprises were to take precedence. Mining, for example, was discouraged by Brigham Young as likely to lead to ungodly behavior fueled by the immoral desire to get rich quickly. Young also feared that the discovery of valuable minerals might attract large numbers of non-Mormons to the new land, and that they would bring with them the problems the Saints had come west to escape. New towns were founded not because of population pressure but as a strategy to hold ground as the outposts of a new country.

Brigham Young imagined a religious empire he called Deseret, an independent state that would extend not only through Utah but would also take in large parts of what are now the neighboring states of Idaho, Nevada, and California. The new state coined its own money, made its own laws, and at one time devised its own alphabet, though the new writing never really took hold. Governed by a powerful and intelligent leader with a united people behind him, Deseret might well have come to be all that Young had envisioned had it not been for the purchase of the western territories by the United States, which placed the Mormons once more (technically at least) under the jurisdiction of the federal government. The discovery of gold at Sutter's mill in 1848, which put Utah's new settlements square in the path of the gold rush, and the outbreak of the Civil War thirteen years later, changed Utah from a place no one else wanted, out beyond the reach of reasonable migration, into the highway to the West. Eventually the Pony Express, the continental telegraph that shortly made it obsolete, and the transcontinental railroad all passed through Utah. The federal government, anxious to preserve communications with the Pacific, sent out army detachments to keep an eye on the Mormons, began to take a lively interest in the affairs of the territory, and put an end to Brigham Young's dream of empire.

In 1896, after long and sometimes difficult negotiation with Washington, in the course of which the Mormons gave up the doctrine and practice of plural marriage and set up a system of government that, in theory at least, established a separation between church and state, Utah was admitted to the Union. A hundred years later Utah is still different in some ways from the other forty-nine states. The tensions between commerce and religion, between the spiritual and the political, are by no means unique to Utah, but they sometimes express themselves with more fervor here than they do in other places. The difference shows in the names of towns—Nephi, Moroni, Orderville, Moab—in the appearance of these settlements, laid out in neat squares, the houses hedged by Mormon poplars to temper the winds that can drive men mad. It shows in the state's newspapers, where the letters column is often the forum for intense and spirited theological debate. It crops up in the annual deliberations of the state legislature on liquor laws and in the ongoing battle over wilderness and development, which are often debated with the extensive help of quotations from the Bible and the Book of Mormon.

At the same time it's necessary to remember that Utah is not only an idea but also a place in the world, part of the American Southwest and also of the intermountain region—some of it desert, some of it alpine country, cut by high valleys, dominated by plateaus—a place where ancient cultures and new ways of life are in collision.

Traveling in Utah
Climate

The land imposes its own restrictions on how people may live in it. Rainfall in Utah averages 13 inches a year, which makes it the second driest state in the country; not enough water falls to grow much of anything without the help of irrigation. Travel, particularly in the southern portions of the state, was made nearly impossible by the extraordinary convolutions of the land, the deep canyons, the cliffs, the mountain ranges; it is still not an easy matter to get from one place to another in southern Utah. Radio reception is a sometime thing, and television in most places comes only from the satellites and their attendant paraphernalia, each house its own downlink from space. It's not unusual in the more remote sections of the state to drive a hundred miles to get a haircut, see a movie on the big screen, or buy a part for the washing machine.

Though the state lies in the temperate zone at about 40 degrees of north latitude, Utah's climate is determined by local as well as global influences. The altitude above sea-level of a particular spot and its orientation relative to nearby mountains and canyons often governs the weather more surely than the season or the latitude. Utah, in other words, has climates, plural. The West Desert, for example, is extremely hot in summer, can be bitterly cold in winter, and is dry, lying as it does in the rain shadow of the Sierras to the west. Prevailing winds are westerly, and the air drops much of its moisture before it reaches Utah. A few miles away is the Wasatch Front, where Salt Lake City was built—cooler in summer, colder yet in winter, and apt to receive surprising amounts of rain or snow as the air is further squeezed of water in its climb to clear the slopes of the Wasatch. The capital city itself has its microclimates; its weather can be unpredictable and interesting. Storms sometimes pick up moisture as they come across the lake and deposit it whimsically across town, with one neigh-

The scenic Moki Dugway was once an Indian trail – Frank Jensen, UTC

borhood buried by two or three feet of snow while another down the road gets barely enough white stuff to wet the streets. Occasional concentrations of high-pressure air on the east of the Wasatch have been know to drive sixty-mile-an-hour east winds out the mouths of the canyons while only the gentlest of breezes blow elsewhere in town. Some winters find the city buried in snow before Thanksgiving; other times Christmas comes while the capital still enjoys a kind of Indian autumn, with shirtsleeve temperatures in the afternoons, and the only snow to be seen is on the mountaintops to the east.

And so for the rest of this variable state. It is quite common in February or March to drive out of spring in Moab at an altitude of 3,000 feet and into the depth of winter in Monticello, fifty miles to the south but 4,000 feet higher. The canyon country of southeastern Utah is as hot and dry in summer as anyone could wish, but sudden rainstorms can drop several inches of water in a few minutes and turn dry washes into torrents that trap the unwary and innocent traveler.

Commercial travel in Utah is much like commercial travel anywhere else in the United States; touring on bicycle or on foot is a specialized enterprise better dealt with in other vol-

umes than this book, which offers itself only as a general guide to the state of Utah. Some notes on automobile travel, however, might be useful here.

Back Roads

Many places described in these pages can only be reached on unpaved roads. Dirt roads in Utah range from well-graded, regularly maintained throroughfares easily traveled in ordinary two-wheel-drive sedans, to some that are little more than trails across very difficult country, almost impassable even in specially equipped off-road vehicles. It's not always easy to judge the condition of a particular road from a map. It is also important to remember that even the best and most detailed maps are sometimes outdated and occasionally wrong. (This is also true, alas, of the best-intentioned guidebooks.) Make local and timely inquiries before setting out into the backcountry.

Many Utah dirt roads are carved through clay; easily traveled when dry, they may become completely impassable after a rain. Unwary travelers have become irretrievably stuck on innocent-looking stretches of road. Wet clay roads can be as slick as the best ice; a gentle camber of the road can take your vehicle into the ditch or into a ravine. River crossings are also unpredictable; firm-looking sandy bottoms can in fact be quicksand and leave your car sunk to the frame, at the mercy of a tow truck that could be a hundred miles from where you sit stranded and helpless.

If you intend to leave the pavement you should carry at least rudimentary emergency supplies: a minimum of one gallon of drinking water for each passenger, a blanket, some food, a first-aid kit. Comfortable shoes are also important; you may have to hike out to the nearest settlement to get help, and the nearest settlement may be a long walk away.

All this is not to discourage the adventurous traveler; there's a certain pleasure in leaving the asphalt and following your desires along a less-travelled road. There's more than one way from Goblin Valley to Hanksville, or from Bullfrog to Boulder. The backcountry of Utah is still in many ways a frontier; local people are for the most part helpful and friendly, but travelers are expected to exercise some foresight, and gas stations can be a hundred miles and more from each other. Check your vehicle before you set out; make sure you have a full tank and your emergency supplies. Read the maps. Ask questions. Ask more questions.

The Navajo, or Diné as they call themselves, migrating from western Canada, reached southwestern Utah by the 17th century – Utah State Historical Society

The Indians of Utah

by Gregory C. Thompson

Today, Utah's oldest residents, the Native Americans, don't receive much attention from the state's citizenry. Yet, this minority represents a presence in the state and region that dates back at least 10,000 years. In part, a general lack of awareness is due to the fact that Native Americans represent only a fraction of the state's current population base. Utah's Indians represent less than one percent of the state's total citizenry. The majority of these American Indians are located in the more remote areas of southeastern and eastern Utah, or are lost in the urban setting of the state capital, Salt Lake City.

The earliest native American residents, the Paleo-Indians and Deseret Archaic people, leave scant record of a presence dating back 10,000 years. They remain a challenge for archaeologists and anthropologists to interpret. The research to date, based on remaining artifacts and archaeological digs, indicates these peoples likely migrated over a very long period into the Utah region from Siberia. Sizeable populations lived along the shores of the Great Salt Lake and other Utah waterways for extended periods of time. The archaeological evidence also indicates long periods of time when few, if any, Native Americans populated the Utah and Great Basin region.

Beginning about 6500 B.C., a people identified as Desert Archaic first arrived in Utah and, through time, established themselves in the state. Caves that ring the edges of the Great Salt Lake provide significant archaeological evidence of their existence and suggested a settled lifestyle that supported sizeable populations. Danger Cave, near Wendover, along the Utah-Nevada border; and Hogup Cave, along the western edge of the Great Salt Lake, are two important sites where researchers uncovered valuable information.

Through the use of a weapon called an atlatl that boasted spear-like thrusting capabilities, these people hunted small game and antelope as an important part of their food and economic base. They fashioned holding pens from plant fibers and twisted lengths of rabbit hide into netting to capture animals as an additional food supply. Crafted duck decoys assisted in the hunting of fowl. But the staple of their diet appears to have been the cattail root and salt-tolerant plants, such as prickleweed, burrows weed, and sedge, all high in nutritional value and a main factor in supporting a large population base.

As the waters of the Great Salt Lake expanded and contracted, so too did the Desert Archaic population. From 6500 B.C. to 3500 B.C., these people appear to have maintained settled lives around the lake; however, about 1500 B.C., a dramatic rise in the lake level covered the important life-sustaining marsh and lake-edge areas. It appears the Desert

Archaic peoples failed to meet this radically changing environment and may have disappeared altogether, leaving the land uninhabited, or leaving so little evidence that their continued existence becomes impossible to detect.

Not until about 500 B.C. do archaeologists find evidence of a new and dramatically different people occupying the region of Utah. Like their predecessors, the Fremont culture group also inhabited the areas adjacent to Utah's waterways, but the Fremont employed an economy and cultural pattern that distinguished them from previous inhabitants. The use of the bow and arrow increased their hunting abilities. Pit houses built partially below ground using poles and dirt to form a roof improved on the cave homes of the Archaic peoples. These people could move the food and water supplies and better adapt to changing climate conditions. The addition of food storage structures and the adoption and adaptation of maize, beans, and squash into their economic base added important new diet staples. Coiled pottery allowed for previously unknown cooking techniques and enhanced the people's ability to store crops and prepare meat.

The Fremont people incorporated a rather distinctive pictograph form of drawing that helped to describe their presence and lifestyle. Clay figurines located at a number of Fremont archaeological sites appear complementary to the lifestyle depicted on the pictographs found on Utah rock walls. The Fremont apparently lived in extended family groups or clans with wide contact patterns and extended trading experiences. Their origin is speculative but the evidence of their existence on the Utah landscape is strong and shows a people who borrowed freely from other groups in distant regions while successfully meeting the challenges of living for hundreds of years in a harsh environment represented by both Utah's Basin and Range and Colorado Plateau.

Developing parallel to the Fremont people was another impressive and complex culture, the Anasazi. These people established themselves in the southern portion of Utah and the Four Corners region where today's state boundaries of Utah, Arizona, New Mexico, and Colorado meet. Dramatic and distinctive in their settlement patterns, the Anasazi's earliest appearance dates before the Fremont, and the Anasazi continued to occupy what would become southeastern Utah and the adjoining region for approximately 1,300 years before these people suddenly abandoned their highly stylized pueblo homes and sophisticated agricultural practices.

The early Anasazi, a word meaning "ancient ones," resembled the earlier described Archaic peoples. However, Anasazi culture soon changed, and by about 200 B.C. the Anasazi supplemented a hunting-and-food-gathering economy with a horticultural system based on maize.

The earliest of the developmental periods for the Anasazi are labeled Basketmaker I, II, and III, pre-1000 B.C. to A.D. 750, and the later stages are identified as Pueblo I through III stages, A.D. 750 to A.D. 1300.

By A.D. 750, the Anasazi evolved from the earlier wandering lifestyle patterns to that of permanent village-like settlement. This development led to several large settlements, including the Mesa Verde Anasazi of southwestern Colorado, the Anasazi of southeastern Utah, the people of the Chaco region of northwestern New Mexico, the western Anasazi of northeastern Arizona, and the Virgin Anasazi of southwestern Utah and northwestern Arizona.

Exquisite baskets and sandals, food storage pits, and hogan-styled houses define the Basketmaker periods of the Anasazi. Farming-village residential patterns, using pit and hogan-like structures, evolved into pit-house architecture, a distinctive Anasazi pattern. By A.D. 700, this development became very sophisticated and village-like in political, religious, and architectural aspects. In addition, two forms of pottery—a gray utility ware and a black-and-white painted work—appeared. The people replaced their earlier atlatl with the bow and arrow. To supplement their diet, beans were added to corn and squash. By A.D. 1200 this culture had become highly developed and productive before it began to decline.

Where the Anasazi went is an interesting question, but contemporary Southwest Pueblo people believe the Anasazi to be their ancestors, and most archaeologists agree. If this is true, then the Anasazi left Utah and Colorado and migrated into New Mexico and Arizona to establish the present Pueblo communities along the Rio Grande River and to the west at Zuni and Hopi pueblos.

Well before the disappearance of both the Anasazi and Fremont peoples, a third distinctive group arrived who, in time, expanded across the Great Basin, eventually becoming the ancestors of Utah's contemporary Indian tribes. Named the Numic people by archaeologists and anthropologists, this group has been identified by their common language trait, Shoshonean, a language that is defined as a subunit of the larger Uto-Aztecan language family.

The Numic, a term defined by these groups as "The People," appeared about A.D. 1100, coming from either the greater southwest Great Basin or west-central Great Basin regions. The population spread east and north across the Great Basin into the Colorado Plateau, northern Utah, southern Idaho, and western Wyoming. Changing environments with warmer temperatures and a drier climate meant that sedentary peoples relying on agriculture were unable to sustain their economic and cultural life patterns. The Numic people with their highly mobile lifestyle based on hunting and gathering were more adaptive and able to prosper.

In a rather short time, Northern and Western Shoshonie, Goshute, Southern Paiute, and Ute peoples—all Numic speaking—spread across present-day Nevada, Utah, Colorado, Idaho, and Wyoming. While little is known of how the Anasazi and Fremont peoples related to the Numic groups, archaeologists believe that there was interaction and use of the previous cultures' traits and customs. Yet to be determined is whether the Numic people's pressure on the older cultures helped lead to their demise or whether the harsher environment and required change in lifestyle meant the remnants of these cultures were absorbed into the Numic groups.

The ability to hunt small game effectively and to gather native plant seeds with more efficient tools and technology led to more intensive use of immediate lands and a more diverse economy. The southern Utah-dwelling Southern Paiute and Utes grew squash, corn, beans, and sunflowers as part of their subsistence bases—a limited agricultural practice perhaps inspired by the Anasazi and the Fremont.

At the time of contact with the European societies in the 18th century, beginning with the Spanish expedition of 1776 under the leadership of two Franciscans, Fray Francisco Dominguez and Fray Velez de Escalante, most of Utah was occupied by various Numic tribes. The Southern Paiutes were organized into approximately 18 loosely structured groups, which included several or more families known as bands. Larger bands in Utah include the Tonoquints in the St. George vicinity, the Kumoits in the Cedar City area, the Kwiumpats to the north in the Beaver region, the Paquits at Pogu Lake or east of the Kumoits, and the Kaibabits southeast of the Paquits.

The Utes occupied areas north and east of the Southern Paiutes. They also organized into bands that consisted of several or more families grouped together for economic and social purposes. Like the Southern Paiutes, these bands identified geographic regions as their home and over time incorporated the resources of the region into their economic base. Bands who lived around lakes and along rivers relied on fishing. Those who lived near grassy plains became big game hunters, while those people living in the valleys of southern Utah became traders and farmers. The Utah bands included the Weeminuche in southeastern Utah and southwestern Colorado; the Sheberetch to the north and in the area of the La Sal Mountains; the Pah Vants north of the Southern Paiutes and along the Sevier River; the San Pitch to the north and in the present-day Sanpete Valley; the Tumpanawach near Utah Lake; the Cumumba near the Great Salt Lake; and the Uinta Ats east of the Wasatch Mountains and near the Uinta Mountains in northeastern Utah. Four additional bands lived along the western slope of Colorado and in northern New Mexico. They included the Yamporihain, the Parianuche, the Taviwach, the Kapota, and the Moache.

To the west and north of the Utah Utes resided the Goshutes and the Western Shoshone people, whose tribes extended into present-day Nevada. The Northern Shoshone tribe occupied a region north of the Great Salt Lake in the Bear River Valley stretching into Idaho and western Wyoming.

Nomadic small and large game hunting, seed, root, nut, and wild berry gathering, and river and lake fishing sustained the basic economic system of the Numic people. Sophisticated knowledge of nature, plants, the use of seasonal patterns for both plants and animals, technology created and adopted to these uses, and the incorporation of large and varied land bases into their economic systems allowed the Numic to survive and prosper in a more severe climate and on a more harsh landscape than their predecessor groups. Hunting patterns, social gatherings, and religious practices brought families and bands of the larger groups together, which allowed and encouraged interband marriages. Extended trading patterns encouraged intertribal contacts while supporting a general knowledge of the Numic groups, their lifestyle, and the geographic areas they used to sustain their economic patterns.

At roughly the same time the Numic peoples were establishing themselves in Utah, another group, Athabascan speaking and linguistically related to the Apache of the Southwest, moved into New Mexico. The Navajo, or Diné as they called themselves, reached southwestern Utah by the 17th century, after long migration patterns from western Canada onto the Plains and through the Mountain West. The Navajo were very adaptive and their economic, social, and religious patterns included beliefs inspired by the Pueblo peoples, as well as other groups they had come into contact with. Originally quite small in number, the Navajo population expanded rapidly and their land base increased until they became one of the dominant tribal groups in Utah in the late 19th and 20th centuries. Their early and current presence in Utah centers around San Juan County in the southeast corner of the state.

Like other groups before them, the Navajo adapted to a harsh environment with a multifaceted economic system that included gathering, large- and small-game hunting, horticulture, and sheepherding, which was adopted from contact with the Spanish in the 17th and 18th centuries. The Navajo also adopted an architectural style conducive to their environment—the hogan. Made of poles and dirt, this round house was both protective and comfortable. Their social and cultural patterns are exhibited by complex clan and religious patterns and systems. The Navajo remain distinctive today and have so successfully adjusted to the challenges of the past 300

years, they are now the largest Indian tribe in the United States.

As mentioned earlier, Utah Indians first came into contact with European peoples when the Escalante and Dominguez exploration party was traveling from Santa Fe, New Mexico, seeking an overland route to the Los Angeles Basin in Southern California. The expedition was unsuccessful in reaching its goal, but this friendly 18th-century contact began a process that eventually turned into conflict and would prove catastrophic to Utah's Indians.

After several Spanish expeditions into Ute country, Mexican traders, operating now under the independent nation of Mexico, established the old Spanish Trail to California in the late 1820s. Annual trading caravans traversed this 1,200-mile-long route. Along the way, the traders brought goods to the Utes, most notably with a Ute leader by the name of Wakara, in exchange for horses and Southern Paiute slaves. Men, women, and children were captured by the Utes and traded to the Mexicans, who took them to New Mexico and even into Mexico where they were used as field hands and domestic servants. Some captured Paiute men were sent as far away as the mines of northern Mexico.

Later Mexican, English, French, and American fur trappers invaded the Great Basin and elsewhere in Utah, creating an exchange with the native people. By this time, the Utes had a long history with the horse, first introduced to them through Spanish contact. This new means of travel rendered the Utes a highly mobile people, offered them an advantage in hunting, and gave them valuable horses to trade to the trappers.

Until the 1840s all of the people traveling through this area, which would become Utah, came, conducted their business, and left with little permanent impact on the landscape. Even the early overland migration of Americans out of the East into Oregon and California in the early 1840s followed the same pattern.

The arrival in 1847 of the first members of The Church of Jesus Christ of Latter-day Saints, or Mormons, under the leadership of their prophet, Brigham Young, changed this pattern dramatically. When the Mormons arrived in the Great Salt Lake Valley, they were intent on establishing a new, permanent homeland, and did so over the top of Ute, Southern Paiute, Goshute, and Shoshone lands. The Utah Indians expected these early settlers to move on and leave their lands, but they didn't. In fact, they expanded their settlements to the south, north, and west.

Soon the Indians could see that these new arrivals were a major challenge to their lifestyle and even their existence. Conflicts broke out, skirmishes were fought, numerous raids on cattle and horse herds were conducted, and people on both sides were killed. The major conflicts included the

Wakara, or Walker War of 1853–54; the killing of Captain J. W. Gunnison's government survey party in 1853; the Mountain Meadows massacre of a large wagon train group in 1857, first thought to be the work of the Southern Paiute Indians but later found to be instigated by Mormons; the Bear River Massacre in 1863 by Fort Douglas military troops, killing 250 Shoshone peoples; the Black Hawk War of 1865–68; and later, in 1879, the Ute attack on soldiers sent onto their northern Colorado White River reservation, killing a number of soldiers and the Indian agent for the White River Agency, N. C. Meeker.

Reviewing this nearly 35-year period in the 19th century, one sees a determined effort by Utah's Indians to preserve their traditional lands and lifestyles. They failed and the result was the establishment of a reservation system that severely confined Utah's Indians to the state's least desirable lands.

The Southern Paiute lands were combined into reservations located at Shivwits, near St. George and later moved to a second location along the Santa Clara River in southern Utah; Indian Peaks, west of Milford; Koosharem, west of Fish Lake; Kanosh, south of Fillmore; and Cedar City, a group recognized later by the federal government.

The Goshutes were confined to a small reserve along the Utah-Nevada state border, some seventy miles south of Wendover, Utah. The majority of the Western Shoshone were located on a reservation north of Elko, Nevada, straddling the Nevada-Idaho border. The Utes, after several attempts and locations, were combined on lands in the Uinta Basin, where the northwestern Colorado tribes were relocated after the Meeker incident. Today, three major bands—the Uintahs, the White Rivers, and the Uncompahgres—live on a reservation stretching from the Uinta Mountains south to the Book Cliffs in central eastern Utah. Finally, the remaining Northern Shoshone peoples were driven from an area north of the Great Salt Lake and out of the Bear River region to a combined reservation located at Fort Hall, Idaho, just north of Pocatello.

During the 20th century these tribal groups have faced many challenges for survival, both individually and as identifiable tribal groups. The greatest of these were two federal programs designed to eliminate reservations as a legal concept and to reduce the number of Indian people recognized within the tribes. The first was known as the Dowes Severalty Act, passed by Congress in 1887. It attempted to give each adult Indian and his family a homestead to farm, while doing away with the reservation as a legal concept. The second attempt to terminate the federal status of reservation lands was through legislation by Congress, which made Indian lands subject to state laws and regulations. Passed in 1953, the termination act, coupled with the earlier allotment act, both reduced tribal lands and recognized American Indian populations in Utah.

As Utah's Indians complete the 20th century and begin the 21st century, their future is uncertain, their populations–except for the Navajo–are small, and their ability to attract economic resources severely limited. Against these overwhelming odds, these people continue to represent 10,000 years of existence as Native American tribal people.

BIBLIOGRAPHY

Alexander, Thomas G. *Utah: The Right Place*. Salt Lake City: Gibbs Smith, Publisher, 1995.

Benally, Clyde, et al. Diné Jí Nákéé´ Nááhane´: *A Utah Navajo History*. Monticello, Utah: San Juan School District, 1982.

Conetah, Fred A. Edited by Kathryn L. MacKay and Floyd A. O'Neil. *A History of the Northern Ute People*. Fort Duchesne, Utah: Uintah-Ouray Ute Tribe, 1982.

Holt, Ronald L. *Beneath These Red Cliffs: An Ethnohistory of the Utah Paiutes*. Albuquerque: University of New Mexico, 1992.

May, Dean L. *Utah: A People History*. Salt Lake City: University of Utah Press, 1987.

Madsen, David B. and David Rhode, eds. *Across the West: Human Population Movement and the Expansion of the Numa*. Salt Lake City: University of Utah Press, 1994.

McPherson, Robert S. *A History of San Juan County: In the Palm of Time*. Salt Lake City: Utah State Historical Society and San Juan County Commission, 1995.

Newe: A Western Shoshone History. Reno: Inter-Tribal Council of Nevada, 1976.

Nuwuni: A Southern Paiute History. Reno: Inter-Tribal Council of Nevada, 1976.

Poll, Richard D., general ed. *Utah's History*. Provo, Utah: Brigham Young University Press, 1978.

Powell, Allan Kent, ed. *San Juan County, Utah: Peoples, Resources, and History*. Salt Lake City: Utah State Historical Society, 1983.

Powell, Allan Kent, ed. *Utah History Encyclopedia*, Salt Lake City: University of Utah Press, 1994.

Utah Historical Quarterly, vol. 39, no. 2:90–195 (spring 1971).

Delicate Balance – Tom Olson

Utah's Treasures: Parks and Monuments

T HE STATE OF UTAH IS HOME TO A STUNNING ARRAY OF OUTDOOR WONDERS. FROM THE LARGEST CONCENTRATION OF NATURAL STONE SPANS IN THE WORLD AT ARCHES NATIONAL PARK TO ONE OF NORTH AMERICA'S LARGEST RESERVOIRS IN LAKE POWELL, THERE IS A GREAT DEAL TO EXPLORE AND MARVEL AT IN THE STATE'S OUTDOORS.

UTAH IS HOME TO FIVE NATIONAL PARKS, SIX NATIONAL MONUMENTS, TWO NATIONAL RE-CREATION AREAS, AND ONE NATIONAL HISTORIC SITE. IN ADDITION, THERE ARE 45 STATE PARKS, NINE MILLION ACRES OF NATIONAL FORESTS, AND MORE THAN 22 MILLION ACRES ADMINISTERED BY

Anasazi ruins await return of the ancient ones – Frank Jensen, UTC

THE BUREAU OF LAND MANAGEMENT. IT'S LITTLE WONDER, THEN, THAT OUTDOOR ATTRACTIONS RANK HIGH WITH THE STATE'S RESIDENTS AND VISITORS. AUTOMOBILE TOURISTS MAY VIEW LESSER-KNOWN ATTRACTIONS BY SEEKING OUT THE STATE'S OFFICIAL "BACKWAYS AND BYWAYS," WHILE THOSE SEEKING SOLITUDE MAY WANT TO SEEK OUT ONE OF THE STATE'S MANY DESIGNATED WILDERNESS AREAS.

"A WEIRD, LOVELY, FANTASTIC OBJECT OUT OF NATURE LIKE DELICATE ARCH HAS THE CURIOUS ABILITY TO REMIND US—LIKE ROCK AND SUNLIGHT AND WIND AND WILDERNESS—THAT OUT THERE IS A DIFFERENT WORLD, OLDER AND GREATER AND DEEPER BY FAR THAN OURS. . . . FOR A LITTLE WHILE WE ARE AGAIN ABLE TO SEE, AS THE CHILD SEES, A WORLD OF MARVELS. FOR A FEW MOMENTS WE DISCOVER THAT NOTHING CAN BE TAKEN FOR GRANTED, FOR IF THIS RING OF STONE IS MARVELOUS THEN ALL WHICH SHAPED IT IS MARVELOUS, AND OUR JOURNEY HERE ON EARTH . . . IS THE MOST STRANGE AND DARING OF ALL ADVENTURES."

- Edward Abbey -
"Cliffrose and Bayonets"
in Desert Solitaire: A Season in the Wilderness

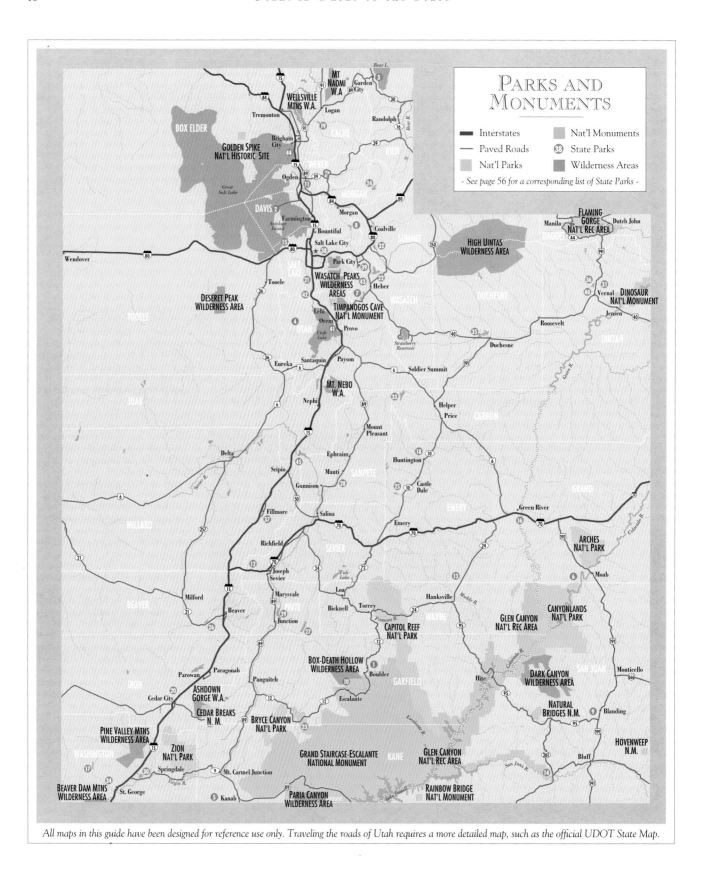

ARCHES NATIONAL PARK

Highway Approach: *Visitor Center and park entrance, 5 miles north of Moab via Route 191.*

Season: *Open all year.*

Administrative Office: *Superintendent, Arches National Park, PO Box 907, Moab, Utah 84532, (435) 259-8161.*

Information: *Visitor Center at park entrance, 5 miles north of Moab.*

Accommodations and Facilities: *Accommodations in Moab. Park campground at Devil's Garden, 18 miles from Visitor Center, has 54 sites. The campground is very popular and visitors are advised to show up early.*

Transportation: *Private car.*

Climate, Clothing, and Equipment: *Elevation of the park is 4,000–5,000 feet. Mostly arid with summer showers; winter snowfalls seldom exceed 4 inches or last more than a day. Daily temperature range, however, is diverse: hot days in summer, cool evenings; cold in winter. Warm clothing is advisable for evening wear year round. Except in winter, light rugged clothing is usually sufficient in daytime. Rubber-soled shoes are helpful for scrambling over slickrock.*

Recreation: *Photography, hiking, climbing, mountain biking on paved roads only. Nightly campfire talks at campground. Naturalist-led hikes.*

Medical and Dental Services: *Available in Moab.*

Warnings and Regulations: *Usual park regulations. Practice outdoor etiquette and common sense: do not destroy property, carve initials, or remove artifacts, plants, or other natural objects. Stay on trails. Carry drinking water. Backcountry hikers should inform rangers about plans.*

Admission: *Admission fees charged.*

Arches National Park is in the red-rock country north of Moab, between the Colorado River and Route 163. It is a region of desert sandstone, of deeply cut and often tortuous canyons, and its thin, multicolored topsoil supports grasses, shrubs, and occasional patches of pinyon pine and juniper. An eyewatering shade of blue, the La Sal Mountains extend to the south from the valley floor, and the high peaks often hold snow all year long. Northward are the Book Cliffs of the Tavaputs Plateau, but eastward and westward the desert stretches out for long distances.

Within the park itself, the wind has carved massive rock into forms that are remarkable, even in a region famous for spectacular erosion. Here are arches and windows through solid stone, from a size barely large enough to crawl through to immense spans that would accommodate a troop of cavalry; monoliths measured in hundreds of tons, balanced on fragile, decaying bases; chimneys, deep caves, and high, thin, sculptured walls or "fins" of rock. There are arches in all stages, from caves not yet cut through to towering spans that have fallen, their buttresses pointing skyward. There is a difference, incidentally, between arches and bridges. A bridge occurs as the effect of stream erosion and it spans a stream course. An arch (or window) occurs where there is no stream course, and is mainly the product of weathering. There are more than 100 arches and other openings measuring three feet or more in the park.

The rock in Arches National Park was laid down as sediment in ancient seas, streams, and lakes, or as windblown sand. All of the arches and windows in the park are composed of Entrada sandstone, a wind-formed rock that ranges in color from white to salmon, watermelon pink, and red. Because its cementing material is readily dissolved and because the quartz grains that constitute its main bulk are small and uniform, Entrada weathers easily into low configured domes, toadstool-shaped monuments, and hourglass forms that, wearing through at the waist, topple the upper half or leave it in precarious balance. Here, many of the rock layers have been fractured by a crisscross of cracks or joints. Rainwater, seeping through, has carried with it the cementing material and small grains of sand, enlarged the cracks and crevasses, and left immense upright slabs of pink and orange sandstone standing between. Wind-borne sand has found weak spots and pecked windows through, chiseled out pinnacles, and chipped the contours of a stubborn piece of stone into exotic life-forms and ragged battlements.

The whole Arches area is rich in desert flora, especially in the canyon bottoms. Pinyon pine, desert ash, and juniper are the only common trees, but brush, cacti, and grasses are everywhere. Coyote, gray fox, bobcat, skunk, Colorado cottontail, jackrabbit, chipmunk, gopher, pack rat, porcupine, and mule deer are present. Birds are numerous, with smaller species most visible, though golden eagles, ravens, and red-tailed hawks are present.

Historical Background

Fremont and Anasazi Indians occupied this area between A.D. 1 and A.D. 1300. Later, Ute Indians settled in the area and drove out the first group of European settlers. Enterprising cattlemen moved into the Moab area in the 1870s, and were ranging the whole countryside by 1885.

In the 1920s a number of individuals and agencies were involved with encouraging establishment of the first Arches National Monument. Alexander Ringhoffer, a prospector, urged officials of the Denver and Rio Grande Railroad to visit the area; they in turn recommended national monument status to the National Park Service.

Professor L. M. Gould, an eastern geologist, visited the area and also pushed for the creation of a monument. The National Park Service agreed, arranged for surveys, and succeeded in convincing President Herbert Hoover to proclaim two sections totaling 4,520 acres a national monument in 1929.

During the 1930s, the Moab Lions Club worked actively for enlargement of the monument and improvement of roads and facilities. Dr. J. W. Williams and L. L. "Bish" Taylor of the Moab *Times-Independent* were among a number of enthusiastic local boosters, Dr. Williams eventually becoming known as the "Father of the Arches." The efforts of these boosters, in addition to the work of others, encouraged President Franklin D. Roosevelt to expand the Monument in 1938 to a total area of 33,680 acres. The monument was again greatly enlarged in 1969 and became a national park in 1971, with an area of more than 70,000 acres. In addition, author Edward Abbey's natural history classic *Desert Solitaire*, based upon the several years he spent as a seasonal ranger here, encouraged a number of visits to the area. Annual visitation has grown from 2,500 in 1940 to 290,000 in 1980 to more than 800,000 in 1995.

Seeing the Park

Arches National Park has six fairly distinct sections, each different in geologic interest and scenery. They are, in the order seen from the main scenic drive, Courthouse Towers, The Windows, Delicate Arch, Fiery Furnace, Devil's Garden, and Klondike Bluffs.

The scenic drive is an excellent paved road that switchbacks up a steep cliff from the Visitor Center and affords spectacular high-level views of Moab Canyon, the Colorado River, Moab Valley, and the La Sal Mountains.

– Courthouse Towers –

The Courthouse Towers section lies in a system of broken cliffs, ledges, and freestanding monuments 2 miles from the Visitor Center. Its principal feature is Park Avenue, a rocky lane whose walls resemble a row of high-rise buildings. The relatively easy one-mile downhill trail through Park Avenue leads along the base of a continuous slab of Entrada and Navajo sandstone from 150 to 300 feet high, perfectly vertical and intricately eroded. Among the more spectacular forms are Egyptian Queen and Sausage Rock. Northward the trail works through wind-carved piles to Unjoined Rock, an undercut block of stone 20 feet thick, which overlooks the canyon from its wall 300 feet above, and to the Three Gossips, which take form at the top of a 400-foot-high fin that is no more than 50 feet thick at the base. Here also is The Organ, a V-shaped fin, knife-thin at the top and hundreds of feet high.

– The Windows –

The Windows section is an eroded crest of ruddy Entrada sandstone 9 miles from the Visitor Center. From the highway north of Moab, its contour—half mosque, half feudal castle—dominates the skyline, and patches of blue show clearly through its arches. Balanced Rock, eight miles from the Visitor Center, is a 200-foot pinnacle of hard stone that has survived erosion; balanced atop it is a 50-foot block of even harder stone, its edges extending precariously past its base.

Near Balanced Rock, a three-mile branch drive (right) leads past a vantage point from which Delicate Arch and Devil's Garden can be seen to the northeast, then on to the Garden of Eden. There are Adam and Eve, clearly sculptured down to the apple, with Adam holding the fruit to take the first bite. Nearby, on a 250-foot pinnacle, Eagle Rock surveys the scenery. The road continues past intricate cross-bedded slopes of Navajo sandstone and the Cove of Caves, an amphitheater whose wind-pocked walls return echoes that double back on themselves. It ends at several parking areas half surrounded by fantastic eroded forms. On the north is Double Arch, sometimes known as the jug handles. Here, two massive arcs of streaked salmon pink stone swing outward and downward from the common abutment of Windows Reef. The larger extends 165 feet from reef to base, and towers 156 feet above the debris below. The smaller is probably barely high enough to shelter a three- or four-story building. From

Double Arch, foot trails lead by a sculptured butte where Satan perches and a Parade of Elephants marches, trunk to rump.

A short distance south of Double Arch near the parking area is South Window, 66 feet high and 105 feet long, and its companion, North Window, of like size. Turret Arch, the last major formation in The Windows area, terminates in a great spearheaded tower. The arch itself is shaped like an immense keyhole and is accompanied by a smaller window.

– Delicate Arch –

Beyond Balanced Rock a branch of the main drive leads 2 miles east into Salt Wash to the Wolfe Ranch cabin. In the Delicate Arch section 14 miles from the Visitor Center, there is only one significant arch, yet it is probably the most popular section with return visitors, and has become a symbol of Utah, equally at home on beer-bottle labels and promotional literature. The Wolfe Ranch cabin is a specimen of the frontier log-and-mud-chink construction. From the cabin, the west buttress of Delicate Arch is visible against the skyline. A 1.5-mile foot trail (strenuous) begins in the canyon bottom, ascends from it after a quarter of a mile, and climbs across slick-rock to the top of the canyon wall. Below, in a shallow depression, its sides rising like those of an irregular saucer, is a platform almost as high as the walls, and atop it, alone and sharp against the sky, is Delicate Arch. The arch's opening (33 feet wide, 45 feet high) frames the La Sal Mountains and Colorado River country between. Delicate Arch also can be viewed across a deep gorge at a distance by hiking up a ridge from the end of the side road one mile beyond the cabin. Delicate Arch Viewpoint allows visitors, who don't have the ability or the inclination to hike, another perspective on this famous sight. Follow the access road to the viewpoint, which is .5 miles to the north of the parking area.

– Fiery Furnace –

This extremely broken terrain is viewed from a parking area 14 miles from the Visitor Center and about 2-1/2 miles along the scenic drive from the Delicate Arch turnoff. It is a labyrinth of great fins and pinnacles, separated by narrow slots. Guided hikes are conducted in summer. Visitors wishing to enter this maze should consult with park personnel in advance.

– Devil's Garden –

Located at the end of road 18 miles from the Visitor Center, Devil's Garden, which contains the majority of the park's arches and windows, extends along a continuous sandstone ridge (the east slope of Salt Valley Anticline), eroded into jungles of upright fins, huge amphitheaters with sinuous interconnecting passageways, and wind-gnarled monoliths. Small parks with sweet-water springs are tucked away here and there, surrounded by vertical slabs of sandstone and sometimes joined to natural slickrock corrals that were used by cattlemen at branding time. This is a perfect region for hikers, and it is hardly possible to get lost in it because you have to come out the way you go in.

Northward from the end-of-road parking area, the foot trail winds in a cliff-lined notch and across slickrock ledges for several miles, passing numerous arches on the way. Pine Tree Arch, half a mile beyond Arch-in-the-Making, has an opening 46 feet wide and 48 feet high, and takes its name from a hardy pine that grows immediately beneath it. Hole-in-the-Wall, another half mile northward, is a kind of gargantuan peephole located high in the cliff. Landscape Arch, at the end of the improved trail a mile from the parking area, is perhaps the most spectacular formation in Devil's Garden. Only a few feet thick, it has a length of 291 feet and rises 118 feet above the canyon floor. Landscape Arch is believed to be the longest natural span in the world. There are those who, upon seeing it, are content to turn back without further exploration. Others push on through scored corridors, past Wall, Navajo, and Partition Arches, to Double-O Arch, a pair of windows arranged in a double-deck position, 2.5 miles from the trailhead. In addition, there are numerous other arches in the broken country beyond.

– Klondike Bluffs –

Reached by the unpaved side road from the main scenic drive in Devil's Garden, the Klondike Bluffs section is the least-visited portion of the park. It is a jungle of salmon-hued sandstone, not very large in area but endless in variation. One butte resembles Joseph Smith, the Mormon prophet. The wind has carved beautifully symmetrical Tower Arch into another butte.

Additional information is available in two booklets that can be purchased at the visitors center. "Road Guide: Arches National Park" is an excellent companion for the 18-mile-long park scenic drive. The park's "Hiking Guide" includes summaries and maps for thirteen trails in the park.

Bryce Canyon National Park

Highway Approach: *Via State 12, turning east from U.S. 89 seven miles south of Panguitch.*

Season: *Open all year. Road south of Inspiration Point usually closed by snow November–April. Bryce Canyon Lodge open April–October. National park campgrounds are officially closed during the winter months. The 206 campsites in the park often fill up during the summer months. Visitors are advised to arrive by mid-morning. Commercial facilities adjacent to park are open all year.*

Administrative Office: *Superintendent, Bryce Canyon National Park, Bryce Canyon, Utah 84717, (435) 834-5322. Information available from rangers or museum-visitor center.*

Accommodations and Facilities within the park: *lodge, inn, restaurant, store, cabins, service station. Outside the park, near entrance station: motels, restaurants, stores, service stations. Services also at Panguitch, Hatch, Tropic, other nearby towns. Horseback Rides: Horseback tours are available within the park for a fee. Write or call Bryce-Zion-Grand Canyon Trail Rides, PO Box 128, Tropic, Utah 84776, (435) 679-8665.*

Climate, Clothing, and Equipment: *Cool to chilly evenings, days may be quite warm; dress accordingly. In winter, low temperatures and high winds; winter camping is for the very hardy. Shops in park or vicinity carry camera supplies, groceries, and souvenirs. Bring comfortable clothes and hiking shoes.*

Recreation: *Museum and visitor center provide exhibits, audio-visual program, publications, schedule of programs and hikes. Naturalist-conducted hikes are scheduled several times daily during warmer months; also, illustrated lectures, evening nature walks, star programs, animal and plant study, and other programs conducted by park personnel.*

Medical and Dental Service: *Registered nurse at lodge. Medical and dental facilities at Panguitch.*

Warnings and Regulations: *Snow tires recommended in winter. Parking permitted in designated areas only. Picnicking permitted only in picnic areas. Remember to practice trail etiquette and common sense.*

Admission: *Admission fees charged.*

BRYCE CANYON NATIONAL PARK is really not a canyon but a series of "breaks" in fourteen enormous amphitheaters extending down a thousand feet through the pink-and-white limestone of the Paunsaugunt Plateau. Perhaps no language is sensitive enough in distinctions of form and color to give more than a general characterization of this amazing area. Sixty tints have reportedly been recognized in the park; imaginative observers can identify almost every conceivable shape in the myriad fantastic figures. Bryce Canyon is popular with tourists, accommodating almost 1.5 million in 1995.

Although chiefly known for its scenic and geological interest, Bryce has fairly abundant wildlife. Deer are most commonly seen, while bobcat tracks and signs of mountain lion are occasionally observed after rain or snow. Small animals such as porcupine, yellowbellied marmot, chipmunk, and golden-mantled ground squirrel are abundant here. Bird life includes crossbills, Clark nutcrackers, jays, and many others.

Bryce is entered at the rim with trails leading to the floor. The Rim Road at Bryce leads to parking places, where a number of short hikes lead to the rim at the north and south ends of the park. All the trails are relatively short and moderately difficult, always picturesque.

Terms such as grotesque, bizarre, and beautiful are often used to describe the pinnacles, spires, and temples in this park. The amphitheaters were compared in the 1982 edition to great tubes of paint that have exuded from the canyon floors and solidified as the ruins of an ancient city.

Not least astonishing are the changes in coloring that come every time the light shifts. This phenomenon is especially apparent on a cloudy day, when the sun alternately appears and disappears. A group of monuments may in one moment be a dull orange and in the next a brilliant yellow. A sullen red statue becomes almost vermilion; golden dunes flash as if diamonds had been scattered upon them; and a shrouded wall stands forth in blinding glory. The colors not only shift in tints with morning, noon, or evening sun, or after dusk, but the shapes grow and diminish in size. By moonlight, deep shadows set brilliant white spires aglow with a light that is almost phosphorescent. When the morning sun lights up the canyon, it resembles a huge bowl of glowing embers.

Fifty-odd million years of geological history is covered in the rocks at Bryce, tracing the earth's history since the Cretaceous Period. The history continues today—older forms are crumbling, new ones appear. The rim of the canyon is receding at a rate that undermines trees, some of which cling precariously with their roots exposed. At times, Bryce was covered by the sea; at other times, broad rivers flowed across it; at still other times, it was swept by hot desert winds. A great block of the Pink Cliffs was raised from near sea level to a high altitude, steepening the pitch of the streams, causing them to flow and erode more rapidly. Running water, frost and rain, groundwater, and chemical agents carried billions of tons of ground-up rock to the Colorado River.

The Kanarra Cattle Company and several sheepmen used the plateau adjacent to Bryce for grazing in the early 1870s, but the first permanent settler was pioneer cattleman Ebenezer Bryce, who homesteaded here in the fall of 1875. When asked about these twisting canyons, he supposedly said, "Well, it's a hell of a place to lose a cow."

Ruben C. Syrett purchased 160 acres of land adjacent to Bryce in 1916, and made homestead entry on another 160 acres within the present park. In the spring of 1920, he built a small lodge and cabins near Sunset Point and began accommodating tourists. The same year, he was made the first postmaster of Bryce Canyon. Water was hauled for three miles to the camp. In the fall of 1923 the Utah Parks Company purchased his improvements, and the following year he opened Ruby's Inn.

Established in 1928, Bryce Canyon National Park was greatly enlarged in 1931 to its present size. The Rim Road was completed in 1934. Not until it was extensively advertised in the early 1930s by the Union Pacific Railroad, which built lodges and provided transportation, did Bryce become widely known, even within the state.

Roads, Trails, and Views

Route 12 branches eastward from U.S. 89 at a point 7 miles south of Panguitch. Fourteen miles east of this point, Route 12 makes a junction with Route 22. Turning south at this junction, the highway enters the park. Three miles from the junction is the entrance station.

All trails from rim to lower elevations are at least somewhat strenuous. The most popular conducted hike is the Navajo Loop Hike, which begins twice daily at Sunset Point, descends 520 feet, and follows the Navajo Loop trail for 1-1/2 miles from start to finish. Points of interest on this trip are Wall Street, the Temple of Osiris, Thor's Hammer, and The Pope. The climb into or out of Wall Street, over what has been called 34 zigs and 35 zags, is worth the trip by itself.

Fairyland, a huge amphitheater, is most beautiful in early morning light. In the foreground are walls and columns, rose-colored below and with cream-colored capitals; in the center is a huge crumbling monument that looks like a thousand tons of disintegrating copper; and beyond to the right and left are acres of ruins. They stand in eroded abutments and terraces, their gaunt and wind-beaten skeletons softened by the play of sunlight upon the rose, yellow, and gold of the stone.

Park headquarters has a public campground, restaurant, cabins, store, visitor center, and Bryce Canyon Lodge. The Rim Road leads south, but there are well-marked turnoffs to the principal views, parking spaces, and short trails to the rim.

From Sunrise Point on the trail east of the lodge, the eastern view reveals a gently rolling landscape that looks like fields of spun gold. Its structures are more massive than those of Fairyland; the great walls, saturated with red, are in sharp contrast with monuments that seem to be of white chalk. The sculpturing here is gigantic, though there are many lean shafts, emaciated bulkheads, and weirdly lacquered crags.

Sunset Point, half a mile south of Sunrise Point, offers a broader panorama. The immediate foreground of Sunrise Point is a series of massive welded structures, with great columns of yellow and orange rising to a garden of ragged spires on the left and to orchid and pale rose pediments on the right. The columns support capitals that look like solidified cream. Directly below Sunset Point is Thor's Hammer. On the right, the chasm is full of ruins. Down below is Wall Street, a long, corridor, and on the right of it are acres of brilliant upthrusts, like a field of stalagmites, known as Silent City.

Beyond, to left and right, the forms boast more severe lines, leaner columns, and more austere buttresses. The far view is deceptive; when brought close with binoculars, this area is a menagerie of statuary, idols of men and beasts standing on extravagant pyramids and escarpments. In the far-left center is Fairy Castle.

Inspiration Point, a mile south, offers a most comprehensive and overwhelming view. On the right is the Wall of Windows; below it is an area of old-rose battlements adorned with rows of pale mauve spires, and far beyond is the cavernous southern wall reaching from the floor to the rim. Most spectacular is the view toward Sunrise Point—here is Bryce in all its unmediated glory.

The Rim Road proceeds southward to other views, including Bryce Point, atop a thrilling sheer-walled peninsula that affords one of the park's best views of the great amphitheater. Beyond the turnoff to Bryce Point, the main road leads to Rainbow Point, Paria View, and Bryce Natural Bridge, a ragged arch in yellow and orange and gold.

CANYONLANDS NATIONAL PARK

Highway Approaches: *Island in the Sky (North District)—Routes 313 and 279 from Route 191 near Moab. The visitor center here has maps, literature, information. Needles (South District)—Route 211 from Route 191, 13 miles north of Monticello. Limited system of improved roads within park. Maze (West District)—Unnumbered dirt road from Route 24, 20 miles north of Hanksville (Temple Mountain Junction); or unnumbered dirt road from Route 95 near Dirty Devil Bridge at Lake Powell.*

Season: *Open all year.*

Administrative Office: *Superintendent, Canyonlands National Park, 2282 SW Resource Blvd., Moab, Utah 84532.*

Information: *Moab Information Center, corner of Main and Center, Moab (435) 259-8825; or ranger stations in each district.*

Accommodations and Facilities: *The massive increase of interest in this unique park has forced the National Park Service to tighten camping regulations. Policies on backcountry camping vary in each of the park's three districts; it's essential, therefore, for visitors to learn and adhere to current regulations. If in doubt, check with a ranger. Limited camping and picnicking facilities within park. Motels, restaurants, stores, vehicle rentals, supplies, and services at Moab, Monticello, Blanding, and Hanksville.*

Transportation: *Private car or raft. Aerial scenic flights, vehicle and boating tours may be arranged locally.*

Climate, Clothing, and Equipment: *Spring and fall are the most pleasant months for hiking and exploring. Park elevation ranges from 4,000 feet at river level to 5,000 feet at intermediate levels (White Rim, Maze, Needles) to 6,000–7,000 feet on the mesa tops (Island in the Sky, Cedar Mesa). Climate is mostly arid with light annual rain- and snowfall, except during summer months when short, sometimes intense thundershowers are common. Winter snowfall seldom exceeds a few inches, but during the coldest months snow may remain on the ground for several weeks. Daily temperature range is diverse with hot days, cool nights; cold in winter. Carry drinking water. Insect repellent is almost a necessity in summer. Backcountry travelers should take special precautions: make certain that vehicles are in good condition; carry tools, spare tire, shovel, extra gasoline, and water, food, first-aid kit, matches, cooking fuel (firewood cannot be collected in park).*

Medical and Dental Services: *Available in nearby towns.*

Recreation: *Photography, hiking, climbing, rafting, exploration, off-road vehicle travel, camping, study of nature-archaeology-geology, tours.*

Warnings and Regulations: *Follow common sense and practice backcountry etiquette. Do not damage, destroy, or remove antiquities or other property, carve initials, disturb plants or other natural objects. Stay on designated trails and roads. Carry drinking water. Backcountry hiking and boating permits required.*

Admission: *Admission fees charged.*

CANYONLANDS NATIONAL PARK was created in 1964, then enlarged in 1971. Its 337,000 acres (more than 500 square miles) incorporate the rugged Junction Country, a wilderness of rock where the Colorado and Green Rivers join in a chasm more than 1,000 feet deep. This terrain has always defied easy overland travel.

Bare rock is probably the single most overwhelming characteristic of Canyonlands National Park: naked rock exposed in the steep walls of countless washes, canyons and gorges; chalk-smooth rock in the faces of hundreds of miles of cliffs; sculpted slopes, only here and there concealed by sand and a sparse covering of vegetation; cream- or orange-tinted sandstone molded into a plethora of shapes, their sheer numbers and variety of forms straining the imagination.

One result of this extreme ruggedness is that the three districts of the park—though visible in overview from a high-flying plane or from several promontories—are so effectively cut off from each other by gorges and cliffs that many miles of travel outside the park are required for visiting them individually. For example, someone wishing to visit both the Needles and Maze districts (which are physically separated only by Cataract Canyon) must drive from 200 to 300 miles from one area before reaching the other. Similarly, Island in the Sky is separated from the Needles by more than 100 miles of road, though they are only ten miles apart by air.

Natural History

Canyonlands National Park is desert in the technical sense that annual precipitation places it in that category. Yet the park's higher reaches and its riverbanks are lush with vegetation. Pinyon pines and junipers and a variety of moisture-conserving shrubs and flowers are found at 6,000 feet or more. At an altitude of 4,000 feet, the riverbanks and floodplain harbor a great variety of plants, including cottonwoods and other broadleaf trees, numerous kinds of shrubs and bushes, willows and tamarisk.

Animals and insects are common. Flies and gnats (sometimes called no-see-ums in the local vernacular) are pests in warmer months. Lizards are common, as are jackrabbits. In addition, the park harbors populations of bighorn sheep, deer, cougars, and coyotes, as well as many bird species.

Seeing the Park

Because of the park's extreme ruggedness and the great travel distances involved, an individual is likely to tour only one or two of its districts during a single visit. This is the main rationale for describing the various districts separately.

North District
~ Island in the Sky ~

Island in the Sky is a high triangular peninsula contained between the Green and the Colorado Rivers. The summit of the island is a series of rolling flats at about 6,000 feet altitude, but these flats are gashed by deep gorges, and the island is bounded on the east and west by great red cliffs known as the Orange or Wingate Cliffs, which are almost uniformly perpendicular for 400 feet or so above their sloping talus base. The serpentine course of soaring red cliffs around Island in the Sky is at least 70 miles in length; elsewhere throughout the park they total several hundred more. The cliff-ringed Island is based on a broad intermediate terrace known as the White Rim, a thousand feet below the Island's crest and itself a thousand feet above the rivers, which are entrenched in gorges beneath the White Rim. The Island in the Sky district, then, is comprised of two principal divisions: Island in the Sky peninsula or mesa, and the White Rim terrace.

From its high rim, Island in the Sky provides some of the park's most stunning panoramic overviews, similar to those from Dead Horse Point State Park, Canyon Rims, and cliff-top vantage points to the west but differing in the details. Breathtaking views are almost commonplace all along the rim; Green River Overlook, Murphy's Point Overlook, and Grand View Point are the most popular. Green River and Murphy's Point Overlooks give high-level panoramas of the park's Maze district, the broad basin of the Green River, and the White Rim, with the river itself appearing here and there within its green-fringed inner gorge. From Grand View Point on the southernmost tip of the island, the heart of inner Canyonlands spreads away beneath your feet. The point offers an introduction to the park's surface personality, a visual, emotional, and geological banquet. The rivers cannot be seen—they are too deeply confined—but their general courses can be traced toward their confluence in a jumble of cliffs, canyons, ledges, and standing rocks. Great buttes rise in

every direction, and the weird sandstone forest of the Needles presents itself only a few miles away toward the south. Immediately below the point is Monument Basin, gouged out from the White Rim in multiple pockets, filled with dark brown pinnacles hundreds of feet high. A short foot trail leads east from the point to Grand View Overlook.

Grand View Point is reached by a paved road leading 22 miles from its junction with Route 313 (28 miles from Route 191). Several miles north of the point, a short side road forks west for 1.5 miles to Murphy's Point Overlook on the rim overlooking lower Green River Canyon and the Maze-Standing Rocks country beyond. About six miles south of the junction with Route 313, a side road forks east, in four miles dropping 1,000 feet down the cliff face in tight, steep switchbacks to the White Rim road. This corkscrew drive is known as the Shafer Trail, one of the most hair-raising stretches of road in Utah. Near the Shafer Trail turnoff is the Neck, a natural causeway joining Island in the Sky to the "mainland" on the north. The Neck is a narrow ridge between two rapidly deepening gorges: Taylor Canyon of Green River on the west and South Fork of Shafer Canyon of the Colorado River on the east. About six miles south of the Neck, a side road forks west to Green River Overlook and Upheaval Dome (5 miles from junction). Upheaval Dome is a circular, crater-like depression with a perpendicular inner wall of wingate sandstone; above this a concentric outer wall of light-colored navajo sandstone. It is apparently the eroded remnant of a salt-related uplift of ancient times.

The White Rim is a broad, incised but relatively level terrace midway in elevation between Island in the Sky and the rivers. Formed from the light-colored White Rim sandstone, the White Rim serves as a platform for the Orange (Wingate) Cliffs. Into it are sunk the inner gorges of the Green and Colorado Rivers as well as tributary channels and "hanging valleys" such as Monument Basin. The rim is traversed by a dirt road known as the White Rim Trail, suitable for off-road vehicles or mountain bikers with vehicle support. Approximately 100 miles long, the trail winds over slickrock, through sand, across packed sediments, into and out of washes, heading gorges, and surmounting jagged cliffs. Travelers should carry drinking water, stove fuel, gasoline, food, etc., scheduling two or three days for maximum enjoyment of the route. Be advised that visitor demand exceeds availability during the relatively temperate spring and fall seasons. Apply early for a backcountry camping permit by writing or phoning (435) 259-4351.

The Rivers

More than 90 miles of river are found within Canyonlands National Park: 46 miles of the lower Green, 30 miles of the upper Colorado and 15 miles of the main Colorado in Cataract Canyon below the confluence. With one exception (The Slide), the rivers upstream from Cataract Canyon are rapid-free, allowing leisurely floating with the current or powerboat travel at almost any desired speed, subject to the limitations of driftwood and seasonal low water.

Canyonlands boating parties embark at Green River, Moab, Potash, or the mouth of Mineral Canyon. The majority of rafting parties launch at a site near the Potash mine downriver from Moab. Most motorized boaters travel the 183 miles between Green River and Moab, a distance of 118 miles on the Green and 65 miles on the Colorado. Other power-boaters put in at Potash or Moab or Green River, and a few at Mineral Canyon. Powerboating is restricted in both season and locality by water level, which usually is adequate only during spring runoff (May–June). Floaters run the rivers on rubber rafts, or in kayaks or canoes, while commercial outfitters provide diversified tour offerings such as guides and pontoon rafts for the traverse of upper Cataract Canyon's 20-odd rapids.

During historic times the rivers have been the stage for much of the park area's human history. Vehicle roads were almost nonexistent before the 1940s, when the four-wheel-drive jeep came on the scene. Except for travel on foot or horseback, the rivers were the only convenient arteries of transportation until about 50 years ago. The Green has carried an impressive volume of small boats, apparently beginning with Denis Julien in 1836 and John W. Powell's first expedition in 1869. The Colorado below Moab was used less frequently than the Green as an entrance to Cataract Canyon and the lower Colorado, though it did witness oil-rig freighting and perhaps as much local boating traffic.

South District
The Needles

The Canyonlands region of the Colorado Plateau does not have a monopoly on magnificent canyons and cliffs, rivers, and red-rock overlooks, though this area is certainly among the most spectacular anywhere in the world. However, there is only one Needles, so geologically distinctive and scenically marvelous that the area can only be called unique. The name is appropriate—sharp-pointed spires are the best-known attribute of the Needles—yet there is much more to the district than those forms. The district was first described in print by Professor J. S. Newberry of the Macomb Expedition of 1859, and soon thereafter by Major Powell who applied the Indian name Toom'-pin wu-near' Tu-weap' (Land of Standing Rock) to the general area of the Junction Country.

The Needles includes a series of closely spaced, parallel, north-south-trending fault lines, where graben valleys have formed between some of them—that is, depressions caused by down-dropping of the valley floor, leaving steep-sided ridges between the valleys. These ridges of banded sandstone in turn are fractured at right angles to the valleys, resulting in a surface of close-knit, crisscross jointing. Subsequently, multiple erosional agents have taken advantage of crustal weakness to create the fantastic sculptures that we see today.

Whereas the Needles are remarkable for their complex small-form erosion, spires and pinnacles, linear fault-line lanes, and open parks ringed by sawtooth standing rocks, the adjoining Salt Creek-Horse Canyon area—not so influenced by faulting and jointing but composed of the same rocks—displays erosional artistry similar to that of the Needles. The forms and lines of the Needles are sharper, more abrupt, somewhat more angular, while those of Salt Creek-Horse Canyon are more softly contoured, with gentler angles and ridges that tend to roundness. Canyons of Salt Creek-Horse Canyon form a meandering, many-tentacled labyrinth, with delightful spacious parks in its higher southern reaches.

The Needles-Salt Creek district is terrain for discovery on foot or with four-wheel-drive. Its many recesses invite exploration. Before the area became a park, it was cowboy country—perhaps the wildest cattle range in America—and since then there has been a minimum of development on roads and trails. Elephant Hill, bulldozed by cattlemen in the 1940s, remains a challenge for off-road vehicles. Salt Creek and Horse Canyons still are entered along their streambeds, intermittently wet or impassable, depending on weather. And roads to Confluence Overlook, Chesler Park, and Beef Basin, or into Lavender and Davis Canyons, remain best-suited for four-wheel-drive vehicles. Only the main access road to the entrance station at Squaw Butte (Route 211) is paved, as are short spurs to Squaw Flat Campground and Big Spring Canyon. In other words, almost the entire district is close to being wilderness and is likely to remain so, accessible only by off-road vehicles or by foot.

Of special scenic interest are the area's many natural arches, several of which are among the most distinctive in Utah. Chief among these are Angel and Druid Arches. The district also displays some remarkable Indian antiquities (ruins and rock art). Cave Spring is an authentic cowboy camp.

- The Maze -

This district includes the Maze, Land of Standing Rocks, the Fins and Horseshoe Canyon. The Maze district consists of 60,000 acres of extremely rugged terrain west of the confluence of the rivers. From the time of Major Powell, this area was known generally as the Land of Standing Rocks. This term has been gradually replaced by more specific names such as the Maze, the Fins, the Standing Rocks, and the Doll House. Today the west district is called the Maze district by the National Park Service.

Except for Horseshoe Canyon, which is a detached unit, features of the Maze district are clustered together on an intermediate terrace between river gorges on the east and the Orange Cliffs rampart on the west. They can be seen in panorama from the upper edge of the Orange Cliffs. The overview points are approached from Route 24 or from Green River by 60 miles or more of rough, sandy road. The descent from cliff top to lower elevations via the steep switchbacks of the Flint Trail matches the thrills of Island in the Sky's hair-raising Shafer Trail.

Another main access road winds north from Route 95 just east of where the highway crosses Lake Powell at the Dirty Devil Bridge. It parallels Narrow and Cataract Canyons, which can be viewed from their rims by short crosscountry drives or hikes. Spur roads within the district are best suited for rugged vehicles or mountain bikes. One spur leads north from the bottom of Flint Trail through Elaterite Basin to the Millard Canyon Benches and the bottoms of the Green River. A branch of this spur leads to the Maze Overlook (17 miles from Flint Trail). The Maze Overlook and other rim overlooks provide views of the Junction Country's wilderness of rock as well as intimate glimpses downward into the bewildering Maze labyrinth of narrow, many-fingered box canyons—complexly

eroded tributaries of the Green, beautifully colored and containing little water except during stormy periods.

Another spur, even rougher than that leading to Maze Overlook, leads north from the junction near Sunset Pass (Water Hole Flat) to the Fins, Lizard Rock, Totem Pole, and the Doll House, where it dead-ends about 20 miles from the junction. This spur penetrates a compact tangle of varied erosional forms ranging from giant parallel fins and natural arches, to skyscraping pinnacles, to a fairyland of dainty sculptures. Foot trails lead to Pete's Mesa, overlooking the heart of the Maze canyons, down to the Maze itself; and to Spanish Bottom on the Colorado River. Other hiking and scrambling possibilities are limited only by time, desire, and expertise. Though traversed by Indians, outlaws, and stockmen, this area was not entered by wheeled vehicles until 1957, after construction of mineral exploration roads to its outskirts made vehicle access possible.

Horseshoe Canyon, though far from the park proper, was included as a unit of Canyonlands National Park because it contains some of the nation's best examples of prehistoric Indian rock art (pictographs and petroglyphs). Known also as Barrier Canyon, Horseshoe is a huge cliff-walled gorge, tributary to the Green, and so large that it may have been the channel of a major stream at some distant time in the past. Today it contains running water only intermittently.

Horseshoe Canyon contains a number of splendid examples of rock art. Today, many researchers believe that the ghostly, trapezoidal figures associated with this area were rendered by the Desert Archaic people, who predated the Fremont and Anasazi. The best-known panel, the Grand Gallery, extends along the cliff face for about 80 feet and contains more than 50 human figures, nearly half of which are life-size or larger.

Horseshoe Canyon may be entered from the west (by trail) or the east, from Hans Flat Ranger Station, by four-wheel-drive road and/or trail. The 20-mile fair-weather road from Hans Flat, which is very rough and sandy, descends in sharp switchbacks to the canyon bottom and thence a short distance to a camping area. From there the Grand Gallery requires an up-canyon hike of nearly two miles. Carry all supplies, including water, food, and cooking fuel.

More than 15 million years of earth building is shown in the layers of moenkopi, chinle, and wingate formations of Capitol Reef National Park – François Camoin

CAPITOL REEF NATIONAL PARK

Highway Approach: *State Highway 24.*

Season: *Park and highway open all year. Trails and unpaved side roads may be closed for short periods during rains or in midwinter.*

Administrative Offices: *Visitor Center and headquarters are at Fruita within the park. Address: Superintendent, Capitol Reef National Park, HC 70, PO Box 15, Torrey, Utah 84775.*

Accommodations and Facilities: *Nearest motels in Torrey vicinity, 10 miles west. Restaurants, stores, gasoline at Torrey. Motels and services also at Bicknell, Loa, Hanksville. No services or accommodations within park; camp and picnic areas only; film, souvenirs, and publications at Visitor Center.*

Transportation: *Private auto or charter bus. Commercial guide and tour service available in Torrey.*

Climate: *Four distinct seasons. Climate is influenced by altitude (5,000 to 7,000 feet within park; up to 11,000 feet in nearby highlands). The most moderate months are May, June, September, October. Temperature may reach 100° F. in summer with cool evenings. Winters are cold. Expect rain showers in spring and August–September. Insects may be a nuisance during hot season; bring repellent.*

Clothing and Equipment: *Carry food and supplies; none available in park. Wear suitable outdoor clothing, comfortable hiking shoes. Light jacket advisable for summer evening wear; warmer clothing for winter, spring, and fall.*

Medical and Dental Services: *Public medical clinic, dentist in Bicknell, nearest hospital in Richfield.*

Recreation: *Hiking, climbing, photography, sightseeing, camping, picnicking, wildlife observation. Naturalist tours and lectures. Exhibits and orientation film at Visitor Center. Wading in Fremont River. Fishing, hunting, camping, exploring in adjoining forests and red-rock wilderness.*

Warnings and Regulations: *In case of cloudburst or heavy rain, get out of dry washes immediately! This warning applies even if storm appears miles away in headwaters area. Always carry water on hikes. Register with park personnel for backcountry camping permits. Do not gather or cut native wood for a fire. Do not remove artifacts, plant life, petrified wood, or rock samples.*

Admission: *Admission fees are charged for the scenic drive.*

CAPITOL REEF NATIONAL PARK features splendid erosive forms—grand cliffs, goblin rocks, carved pinnacles, stone arches, great buttes, and deep gorges. It combines the fantasy of Bryce and the grandeur of Zion National Parks with more variety of color than either, and is larger than both combined (378 square miles). It also contains archaeological and historical resources.

The park's vivid colors run in streamers, bands, and layers, both vertically and horizontally. There are blues and greens in broad stripes, and purple, orchid, and lavender give remarkable softness to the rock walls. Every primary color is visible, but shades of red and white predominate.

Capitol Reef gives its name to the entire park, though it is only a segment of the area. The term refers to an upthrust ridge with a cliff face. A part of the Waterpocket Fold, the reef stands high above its surroundings and has long presented a barrier to travel. The park's name was derived from the fact that white domes of navajo sandstone resemble the domes of various capitol buildings. The Waterpocket Fold received its name from numerous natural pockets, or tanks, that collect and hold runoff water.

The 75-mile-long Capitol Reef National Park includes not only Capitol Reef itself but much of the remainder of the Waterpocket Fold, which stretches from Thousand Lake Mountain on the north almost to Lake Powell on the south— a total distance of approximately 100 miles. Despite its great length, the park is relatively narrow—only five to ten miles wide in most places.

The rocks of the fold were laid down, for the most part, during the Jurassic and Triassic periods, about 150 to 225 million years ago. To the east and west and in deep canyons within the park, older and younger rocks are present. Originally laid down in layers, the older rocks were uplifted and bent (flexed) along a north-south axis some 60 or 70 million years ago. At that time the rocks now exposed in today's park were overlain with thousands of feet of younger strata. Since then, most of the younger rocks have been removed by erosional processes, and the older rocks now exposed are being affected by the same processes.

Historical Background

Archaeologically, the park and its environs were rich; early settlers collected large quantities of baskets, pottery, weapons, sandals, and even skeletal remains. Prehistoric Fremont Indians carved petroglyphs and painted pictographs on cliff walls of the region.

During the 1870s, Mormon pioneers established settlements in upper valleys on the river that Major John W. Powell first called the Dirty Devil and later renamed the Fremont. The Fruita area was settled in 1878 by Franklin D. Young. Other settlers followed, homesteading every likely spot. E. P. Pectol of Torrey became interested in the "Wayne Wonderland" as a potential park area. Joseph H. Hickman, a local teacher and a member of the state legislature, convinced fellow legislators to set aside 160 acres at Fruita as a park. Dr. J. E. Broaddus of Salt Lake City did much to publicize the region, as did others. In 1933 Pectol memorialized Wayne Wonderland to Congress as a national park. In 1937 the Capitol Reef area was set apart as a national monument by presidential proclamation, largely as a result of efforts by Pectol, Dr. Broaddus, and Dr. A. L. Inglesby of Fruita. During the 1960s, the monument area was greatly expanded to include most of the southern and northern extensions of the Waterpocket Fold. In 1971 the boundaries were changed again and Capitol Reef was designated a national park.

Desert and semidesert plants are plentiful in the park. In late April, May, and June, several dozen varieties of desert wildflowers are in bloom. Varieties of cacti continue in flower through most of the summer. Among numerous other forms of plant life are juniper, desert primrose, Indian paintbrush, Spanish bayonet (yucca), desert geraniums, sagebrush, prickly pear, and cactus roses in red, yellow, and green. Areas that seem barren often have sagebrush, rabbitbrush, saltbush, greasewood, clumps of grass, and an occasional yucca.

Deer are frequently seen in the park's orchards, as are occasional foxes. Bull snakes and garter snakes are plentiful throughout the area. Small animal life includes field mice, cliff mice, pack rats, ground squirrels, chipmunks, coyotes, and various lizards. Pinyon jays, sage sparrows, rock wrens, and sage thrashers are some of the birds found in the area.

Seeing the Park Districts

The park can best be described by districts, each of which differs from the others:

Central District
- Capitol Reef -

Encompassing the original monument area, this district includes the cliff face of Capitol Reef, the Visitor Center-Park Headquarters, the site of old Fruita, fruit orchards, the former Sleeping Rainbow Ranch, and ancient Native American rock art. Here, too, are all the park's improved hiking trails, its most renowned canyons, its only paved highway, and the Capitol Reef Scenic Drive.

Between Torrey and Caineville, a distance of 30 miles, Route 24 parallels the face of Capitol Reef, winds beside the Fremont River where it has cut through the Reef in a splendid canyon, and penetrates Utah's Painted Desert east of the park. Most visitors view the park from this paved road. For scenic views, this 30-mile drive ranks among the best in Utah.

- Scenic Drive South -

South of the Visitor Center, the park's scenic drive winds southward along the multicolored face of Capitol Reef, allowing access to the site of old Fruita, the picnic area, campground, Grand Wash, Capitol Gorge, and Pleasant Creek. Improved trails are accessible from this drive. Also within the Central District are the deep gorges of Fremont River, Sulphur Creek, and Pleasant Creek where they cut through Miner's Mountain.

This road served for 80 years as the main highway through the Reef. It is only partially paved but well graded and maintained. For short periods when wet or snowpacked, it may be closed. Mileages are from the Visitor Center.

The Visitor Center-Park Headquarters is an attractive structure of native rock. It contains an information desk, publications, exhibits, orientation film, and restrooms.

Fruita community (0–1 mile), the park residential area, is the site of a former village dating from about 1880. Early residents planted hundreds of fruit trees here in the valley formed by Sulphur Creek and the Fremont River. The orchards are being preserved by the National Park Service, though nearly all the original buildings have been removed. Orchard fruits include apples, pears, peaches, apricots, cherries, and plums.

The main campground (1.4 miles) contains tables, fire stands, and rest rooms with running water. From this vicinity, trails lead to Fremont River Overlook (2.5 miles round-trip), a scenic viewpoint about 800 feet above the valley floor, and

Cohab Canyon. The trail to Cohab Canyon zigzags up a steep slope into a narrow, weirdly eroded gash in the rim of a cliff overlooking Fruita and the campground. The canyon's name is an abbreviation of "cohabitation," a reference to Mormon polygamists of the last century who reportedly used the canyon to avoid federal officers. The round-trip hike up the canyon and back totals about two miles.

Grand Wash (3.5 miles), left, is marked by an opening in the cliff. A dirt road (closed in wet weather) gives access to the first mile or so of this beautiful gorge. Visible to the left near the entrance of Grand Wash are excavations in the rocks at the base of the cliff, marking the Oyler Mine where small quantities of uranium ore were once removed. A mile down the wash, a red cliff rises perpendicularly hundreds of feet from the road, like the wall of a giant's house. Left of this cliff and about 400 feet above the floor of the wash is the second largest natural arch in the park, which is easy to overlook. This is Cassidy Arch, which can be reached by improved foot trail (3.5 miles round-trip) from the parking area in Grand Wash. Singing Rock (1 mile) is an arched grotto in the wall of the wash. The grotto, which has unusual acoustical properties, was used for dedication ceremonies at the opening of the monument in 1937. Shinob Canyon, a deep, narrow, dead-end gorge, forks south in this vicinity. Several interesting natural arches can be found in this canyon. At 1.2 miles is the end-of-road parking area from which trails lead to Cassidy Arch (above), Frying Pan Trail, and the Grand Wash Narrows. the Narrows trail leads to The Narrows (1.3 miles) and eventually (2-1/4 miles) to State Highway 24 in the Fremont River Canyon. The cliffs reach overhead for hundreds of feet; in one place they are 500 feet high and only 20 feet apart.

One enters Capitol Gorge (8 miles) between widely separated portals—castellated formations set high on sloping purple bases, their summits a thousand feet or so above the canyon floor. The gorge is walled by red-and-cream-colored cliffs, hundreds of feet high.

Until 1962, Route 24 passed through Capitol Gorge. Cloudbursts rushed off the landscape and raced through the gorge, tumbling boulders weighing tons. Highway maintenance here was always costly and troublesome. Today, the road ends at a parking area 2 miles from the main scenic drive; from there a trail leads a mile or so farther through the Narrows to Fremont Indian petroglyphs and the Pioneer

Register, where 19th- and early-20th-century travelers inscribed their names. At the east end of the Narrows are natural tanks, or depressions, in the rock.

Another trail from the Capitol Gorge parking area climbs the north wall to the base of Golden Throne, one of several huge sandstone monoliths on the crest of Capitol Reef. The trail is fairly strenuous (2 miles each way) but repays the effort required with a display of dramatic rock erosion.

South of the Capitol Gorge turnoff, the main road continues to Pleasant Creek Canyon, through which a trail passes east to meet the Waterpocket Fold road near Notom. A fair-weather road continues beyond Pleasant Creek to Tantalus Basin, Lower Bown's Reservoir, and the junction with the Grover-Boulder highway.

– Scenic Drive West –

Chimney Rock (3 miles) is a tall spire of layered moenkopi rock capped by a block of shinarump sandstone. From a parking area near the spire's base, a fairly strenuous improved trail (3.5 miles round-trip) climbs to the top of a ridge above Chimney Rock, giving nice panoramic views of Capitol Reef for 20 miles as it curves in a great semicircle from west to south. From this trail an unimproved route leads to the awesome lower reaches of Spring Canyon, the Park's longest, emerging at the Fremont River 4 miles east of the Visitor Center.

Goosenecks Overlook and Panorama Point (2.7 miles) can be accessed by a short side road leading 1 mile from the highway to the Goosenecks parking area. From there, a short trail climbs to the upper rim of Sulphur Creek Canyon where it winds around in curving goosenecks. The canyon is about 800 feet deep here and the view is practically indescribable.

Panorama Point, only a few hundred yards from the highway along the Goosenecks road, provides a full-circle panorama of Capitol Reef's face, Torrey Breaks, Thousand Lake Mountain, the swell of Miner's Mountain, Aquarius Plateau, and the peaks of the Henry Mountains.

East of the Visitor Center, the historic Fruita Schoolhouse (1 mile) is a restored wood structure built in 1896, with interpretive information.

Fruit orchards (1 to 2 miles) were planted by pioneer settlers and their descendants, and are now maintained by the Park Service. Mule deer are often seen here at dusk, grazing among the trees.

Prehistoric Indian rock art (1.1 miles) can be seen on the face of the cliff to the north. Nearly a thousand years ago this area was occupied by the Fremont Indians, who carved and chipped these petroglyphs into the rock face.

From the trailhead and parking turnoff (2 miles), Capitol Dome looms in a curve of the canyon to the east. The Cohab Canyon Trail is across the highway. From the parking area, an improved trail leads 1 mile to Hickman Natural Bridge, the largest natural span in the park, measuring 133 feet from rim to rim, 125 feet above the streambed. A spur trail leads 2 miles from the parking area along the steep slope of the Waterpocket Fold to the Rim Overlook, a cliff-edge viewpoint nearly a thousand feet above the Fremont River.

North District
– Cathedral Valley –

Generally referred to as Cathedral Valley for its most-visited natural features, this district includes or is adjacent to other points of interest that are less renowned but still remarkable in their own right.

Cathedral Valley is an extensive area located east of the Waterpocket Fold where it emerges from Thousand Lake Mountain. The valley consists of many miles of beautifully sculptured cliffs and several groups of sculpted buttes that bear a passing resemblance to cathedral spires.

In addition to buttes and cliffs, the Cathedral Valley area contains curious and impressive igneous features (dikes and sills), a pit known as the Gypsum Sinkhole, and a large mound of selenite crystals known as Glass Mountain.

Visible from higher points is the South Desert, an arid basin east of the Waterpocket Fold. The South Desert features sculptured cliffs and buttes. Westward, corrugated slopes of the fold unite with Thousand Lake Mountain. This is a wild area of deep canyons and impressive butte forms; one section is aptly called "Paradise." Explorers can access this area on dirt roads from Torrey or Fremont.

South Desert is a challenge for hikers. So, too, are Deep Creek and its tributary, Water Canyon, exceptionally deep and rugged gorges in the slopes of the fold. Anyone interested in hiking this country should confer and register in advance with park rangers, and carry plenty of water.

The Cathedral Valley area can be reached by high-clearance vehicles via dirt roads leading from several directions as follows: (1) From Route 24 at River Ford, 12 miles east of the Visitor Center (28 miles into Cathedral Junction); (2) from Route 24 at Caineville, 19 miles east of Visitor Center (21 miles to Cathedral Junction); (3) from Route 72 at Loa, about 25 miles to Cathedral Valley via Fremont, passing over a high shoulder of Thousand Lake Mountain; and (4) from Interstate 70.

South District
~ Waterpocket Fold ~

The Park's South District is comprised of the long narrow spine of the Waterpocket Fold south of Capitol Reef. The fold here is characterized by naked rock, painted in shades of red and white, rising as much as 2,000 feet above its eastern base. The convoluted rock is a confusion of erosional forms: cliffs and slopes, canyons and chasms, buttes and numberless forms.

As with the North District, wilderness and natural beauty are the appeals of this district. Cloistered canyons and slickrock slopes invite the hiker and scrambler. Remember to carry water and all other supplies.

The area is accessible by a road that parallels the eastern base of the fold between Route 24 on the north (9 miles east of the Visitor Center) and Bullfrog Marina on Lake Powell to the south. This road also gives access to the Henry Mountains and the Circle Cliffs. Short hikes from the road lead to canyon recesses and remote slickrock slopes.

Canyons of the fold range from one to more than ten miles long. The short canyons are perfect for day hikes. Some are extremely narrow, mere slots gouged out of stone. In this southern district, too, are the park's largest tanks or waterpockets; natural arches such as Peek-a-boo and Brimhall; and the Burr Trail road, a narrow switchback route clinging to the steep wall of the fold (not for the faint of heart).

Grand Gulch (Halls Creek Canyon), which parallels the fold south of the Burr Trail to Lake Powell, is about 30 miles long, a truly wild sanctuary for adventuresome backpackers. Lower Muley Twist Canyon, accessible from the top of the Burr Trail, is a favorite hiking route. An exceptionally scenic gorge, the canyon is 12 miles long, but those who hike its full length must walk another five miles to the nearest parking area plus another four miles back to the trailhead. Those desiring a shorter route may leave the canyon after four miles, hiking about two miles from that point to the Post parking area.

A northern extension of Lower Muley is Upper Muley Twist Canyon, which heads a mile west of the former. The first three miles of this narrow, rugged, exotic gorge may be traversed by high-clearance vehicles; the final six miles, however, are for hikers only. A number of natural arches appear along the way. From the end-of-the-road parking area, a primitive trail leads about half a mile through sand and over slickrock to Strike Valley Overlook on the crest of the fold. From this point, 1,000 feet above the floor of Halls Creek Valley, the eye sweeps in a half-circle overview across the upturned edges of rock layers formed over a hundred million years as oceans, swamps, rivers, lakes, tidal plains, deltas, and sandy deserts. Across the eastern horizon, the peaks of the Henrys loom high above a colorful landscape. The view is one of Utah's most remarkable spectacles.

Blazing reds, sultry yellows, molten gold sandstone with shadows of purple and blue caused the Indians to name Cedar Breaks "circle of painted cliffs" – Frank Jensen, UTC

CEDAR BREAKS NATIONAL MONUMENT

Highway Approaches: *20.4 miles east of Cedar City via Route 14 to junction with Route 148; 26.8 miles west of Long Valley Junction (on Route 89) via Route 14 to junction with Route 148; or approximately 20 miles south from Parowan on Route 143 to 148.*

Season: *Memorial Day to Nov. 1; viewpoints closed by snow, winter through late spring.*

Administrative Offices: *Superintendent, Cedar Breaks National Monument, Cedar City, Utah 84720. Information at Visitor Center, 82 North 100 East, Room 3, Cedar City, Utah 84720.*

Accommodations and Facilities: *Public campground with water, fireplaces, and rest rooms in monument and at Forest Service camps nearby. Accommodations and services at Cedar City and Parowan; limited selection at Brian Head Resort.*

Transportation: *Private vehicle.*

Climate, Clothing, and Equipment: *Nights cool, days may be warm; sudden temperature changes due to altitude (10,300 feet). Suitable hiking shoes and outdoor clothing should be worn.*

Recreation: *Hiking, fishing nearby. Photography, ranger-naturalist lectures, self-guided and naturalist-guided trails. Visitor Center with exhibits on plants, animals, geology, cross-country skiing in winter.*

Medical and Dental Services: *Cedar City and Parowan.*

Warnings and Regulations: *Usual regulations applying to National Parks and Monuments. Roads from Cedar City and Parowan to the monument climb more than 4,000 feet in 20 miles; steep switchbacks in places.*

Admission: *Admission fees charged.*

CEDAR BREAKS NATIONAL MONUMENT, set aside by presidential proclamation in 1933, covers 6,154 acres in the high Markagunt Plateau. It is a vast amphitheater, almost a half-mile deep and two miles from rim to rim, enclosing several semicircular basins. Its walls are furrowed, eroded, and broken into massive ridges radiating from the center (fitting the western definition of breaks: an abrupt, broken, and deeply eroded canyon or amphitheater), and painted like the wheel of a gigantic circus wagon.

Although Cedar Breaks is cut from the same geological formation as Bryce, it is 2,000 feet higher. The cliffs are white or orange at the top, breaking into deep rose and coral. The Pink Cliffs here have a thickness of nearly 2,000 feet, and a selection of warm red shades predominate. Color, which caused the Indians to name Cedar Breaks "circle of painted cliffs," is the chief feature of the monument. It blazes with reds, is sultry with yellows, blinds with sun-reflecting whites, is drenched with molten golds and, as the shadows lengthen toward evening, holds lustrous shades of purple and blue.

In the alpine country surrounding the breaks is an expansive forest, lush with mountain meadows and grassy parks, streams, and lakes where big trout wait. A road leads to the summit of volcanic Brian Head, 11,315 feet, highest mountain in Utah's southwestern corner. From its observation station, a sweeping view encompasses the country surrounding Zion and Bryce—country draining to the Colorado and Great Basin and reaching out to the seared Nevada desert. Brian Head Ski and Summer Resort is nearby. Large

Engelmann spruce predominate in the typical timberline forest cover on the rim, which includes fir, limber pine, and bristlecone pine. Farther down the mountain is the white-boled quaking aspen. One large bristlecone on the rim is estimated to be about 1,600 years old. From mid-July to mid-August alpine flowers decorate the mountain around the breaks: penstemon, lupine, bluebells, enormous white starlike columbines, and the vivid blues of fringed gentian and larkspur. Bird life is common and mule deer are often seen.

Roads and Views

The usual entry to Cedar Breaks is by way of Cedar City or Parowan, turning eastward from Interstate Highway 15. It may also be approached by turning west from Route 89 at Long Valley Junction and traveling across the high Markagunt Plateau on Route 14. Northward from Route 14 on Route 148 the road passes through mountain meadows dotted with fir trees and enters Cedar Breaks National Monument, 3 miles from the junction. One mile farther at Point Supreme is the Visitor Center. The public campground is 1/2 mile from the Visitor Center.

At Point Supreme, Cedar Breaks is suddenly and magnificently present. It is hard to tell whether the brilliant coloring of the breaks or its grotesque sculpting is more remarkable. Forty-seven tints have been identified by one artist, and the formations run the gamut from cathedrals to tombstones. The physical aspects of this enormous basin will bring to mind dozens of comparisons. As one gazes down upon the hundreds of columns and towers, balconies and pinnacles, arches, gateways, and standing walls, it is not difficult to imagine that an ancient civilization with an architectural taste for the Gothic was once crowded into this huge bowl.

From Point Supreme, the Wasatch Ramparts foot trail leads two miles along the rim toward the west, affording views into the great amphitheater. The trail passes through forests and open meadows, giving access to a stand of bristlecone pine on Spectra Point.

Two other points of vantage are worthy of note: Sunset View at 1.5 miles north of the Visitor Center (25-yard walk left to edge of break), and Chessmen Overlook (2 miles farther), which involves a half-mile hike to the rim. A short trail leads also to a stand of bristlecone and limber pine on the ridge.

For the fullest appreciation, the amphitheater should be viewed at sunset when the thousands of formations stand gloriously desolate in their ruins.

DINOSAUR NATIONAL MONUMENT

Highway Approaches: *Quarry Visitor Center is 7 miles north of Route 40 and Jensen, Utah, via paved Route 149. Monument Headquarters, Superintendent, and entrance to Harpers Corner Scenic Drive, 2 miles east of Dinosaur, Colorado.*

Season: *Quarry Visitor Center open daily all year (except Thanksgiving, Christmas, and New Year's Day). Backcountry roads are usually closed during winter months (October–November to April) and after heavy rains. Rafting is most enjoyable during warmer months from May to September (June–July are ideal). The Yampa River can seldom be run after August 1 and may be closed even sooner by low water.*

Administrative Offices: *Rangers and information, Quarry Visitor Center, Jensen, Utah 84035. Superintendent and Monument Headquarters, PO Box 210, Dinosaur, Colorado 81610.*

Accommodations and Facilities: *No lodging or commercial services in Monument. Vernal, Rangely, and Craig are nearest communities with comprehensive services, supplies, and lodging. Limited services and supplies are available at Jensen, Dinosaur, and smaller communities along Route 40. Two improved campgrounds are beside Green River near Quarry Visitor Center: Split Mountain (open all year) and Green River (most spacious and shady).*

Transportation: *Private car or boat.*

Guides: *Boating tour services (guides and boats) available in Vernal.*

Climate, Clothing, and Equipment: *Winters are cold, summers fairly hot, spring and fall are cool to warm. Wear appropriate sports or outdoor clothing, depending on season (see above). Coat or jacket desirable for evening or high-country wear, even in summer. Wear suitable shoes for hiking. Boaters are subject to strict requirements regarding equipment.*

Recreational Activities: *Sightseeing, study of nature and geology, boating, camping, fishing, photography, hiking, scenic touring. Interpretive displays and bookstore in Quarry Visitor's Center.*

Warnings and Regulations: *Observe all National Park Service regulations within monument. Permits and campground reservations must be obtained in advance for private boating, which is subject to strict regulations and requirements. Write or call for details.*

Medical and Dental Services: *Nearest services are at Vernal, 20 miles from Quarry Visitor Center. Also Rangely and Craig, Colorado.*

Admission to Quarry: *Admission fees charged.*

DINOSAUR NATIONAL MONUMENT is most noted for its rich deposits of fossilized dinosaur bones; the monument was originally established and named in recognition of these signs of ancient life. The fossils are a national treasure and attract many visitors every year to view the Quarry Visitor Center's fascinating exhibits.

First established in 1915, Dinosaur's size was increased in 1938 from the original 80 acres to more than 200,000 acres (326 square miles), to include a rugged wilderness to the north and east. Here at the east end of the Uinta Mountains, the Green and Yampa Rivers have carved splendid canyons. Those of the Green (Lodore, Whirlpool, and Split Mountain)

are among the deepest and most awesome along its 700-mile length, and they contain some of its most challenging rapids. The Yampa's canyon is remarkable for its serpentine layout, coloring, and geologic beauty. The entire monument is a geologic spectacle, where weathering, faulting, folding, and uplift have sculpted the earth's rainbow crust, creating an astonishing landscape in the process.

Seeing the Park
– Visitor Center and Quarry –

Overlooking the Green River where it emerges from the mouth of Split Mountain Gorge, built flush against the ledge where the dinosaur fossils are embedded, a striking glass structure encloses the face of the dinosaur quarry. An attached building contains offices and an information center. This is the Quarry Visitor Center of the monument, located 7 miles north of Jensen and Route 40 via Route 149.

The Visitor Center was opened in 1958. In recent years it has attracted so many visitors that mass transit is required during the summertime from a parking area some distance away. The quarry itself is a sandstone face, which was a sandy bar of a Jurassic river some 140 million years ago. This bar was the burial site for various creatures (mostly dinosaurs) whose carcasses apparently floated downstream and collected at this point. As their flesh disintegrated, skeletal material became buried and preserved in sand. During the intervening ages, the bar was covered with thousands of feet of younger sediments, the bones gradually being fossilized and the sand turning to rock. Earth movements uplifted and tilted the rock layers, and erosion exposed some of the ancient burial ground to the view of modern scientists. For some years after discovery of the deposit in 1909, excavation was carried on by various institutions (see below) and thousands of bones were removed. Today, however, the fossil bones are left in place in the ledge as they are uncovered by careful chiseling. Only enough matrix rock has been removed to outline each bone in distinct relief.

A number of interpretive displays complement the quarry, relating a story of ancient life and clarifying the monument's geology. Through a window, visitors can watch technicians at work in the laboratory. Attendants are on duty to answer questions, and educational materials are available at the bookstore.

From the time of the quarry's discovery in August 1909 until 1923, the Carnegie Museum removed from the quarry 350 tons of bones, including parts of 300 dinosaur specimens representing 10 different species. Various institutions, including the Smithsonian and the University of Utah, continued the work. By 1940, 22 complete skeletons and thousands of individual bones had been found in the monument, representing 10 species of dinosaurs, crocodiles, invertebrate forms, and plants. These fossils were sent to many important museums.

The American Museum of Natural History became actively interested in the fossil deposits about 1931, and in 1934 the museum's curator of fossil reptiles, Dr. Barnum Brown, became consulting paleontologist for the monument. Since 1933, the program of development at the quarry has been under the direction of the National Park Service. The new Visitor Center

was opened in 1958, and in the meantime technicians have exposed nearly 1,450 bones, using only small hammers and chisels to chip away the matrix stone. In addition to other important discoveries during this period, a new species of extinct turtle was found in the late 1960s, and a very young dog-size stegosaurus was found and mounted in the 1970s.

The fossil remains at Dinosaur represent 10 of the dinosaur species that lived during a part of the Jurassic period, about midway through the dinosaur age. The quarry has yielded a nearly complete skeleton of the gigantic apatosaurus, formerly known as the brontosaurus, a huge plant eater more than 70 feet long. Even more plentiful have been the bones of diplodocus, a less massive but even longer (84 feet) plant eater resembling the apatosaurus in general form. Most fascinating of all, perhaps, is the fearsome allosaurus, a large carnivore that walked on two legs and displayed a set of frightful teeth. Most numerous of all fossils have been those of stegosaurus, the armored dinosaur with upright plates along its spine. Among other species represented by the quarry's fossils are Dryosaurus, Camarasaurus, Barosaurus and Camptosaurus—altogether the skeletal material of more than 300 individual dinosaurs of 10 different species. Models of several of the quarry's dinosaur types are on display at the Dinosaur Museum in Vernal.

– The Rivers –

Leaving Flaming Gorge National Recreation Area, the Green River passes through Brown's Park. In Colorado, east of the Utah line, it enters Dinosaur National Monument. For the next 46 miles the river's course is within the monument, and for most of that distance the water is confined in deep narrow gorges. Traveling downstream within the monument, the first and largest of these gorges is the Canyon of Lodore.

Here are some of the most challenging rapids along the Green River, and the dark walls rise precipitously from the river to more than 3,000 feet. The canyon extends about 19 miles, from the Gates of Lodore on the north to the mouth of the Yampa on the south, and for most of this distance it passes through very ancient rocks dating from Precambrian era to Permian period, deposits representing a billion years or more. At Echo Park, marked by a sheer-walled sandstone monolith known as Steamboat Rock, the Green is joined by the Yampa, coming from the east.

The lower 46 miles of the Yampa River are within Dinosaur

National Monument. The Yampa's canyon is noted for the beauty and grandeur of its walls, which are colored in pleasing hues of red, tan, and white. Since the river's volume is similar to that of the Green, water is usually adequate for an early summer rafting season. Canyon walls immediately above the river are not as high as those in Lodore, but summits several miles away are two to three thousand feet higher than the river.

Downstream (west) from Echo Park where the Green and Yampa merge, the combined rivers enter Whirlpool Canyon. Though this canyon is only 14 miles long, it is very deep (3,000 feet) with steep walls and exceptional geological exposures in ancient Paleozoic rocks. The river then enters an open expanse of parks and islands known as Island Park and Rainbow Park. Here the Green meanders in a lazy loop before entering Split Mountain Canyon. In the 7.5-mile length of this spectacular gorge, the river drops 147 feet. At the mouth of the gorge the river slackens its pace and enters the Uinta Basin. Here, near the Quarry Visitor Center, a boat landing and campground have been developed on the west bank.

Both the Green and Yampa within the monument are extremely popular for boating. Trips of varying length, time, water conditions, and scenic surroundings are possible. For example, trips offered by one commercial operator within the monument range from one to six days.

Put-in points within the monument are located at (1) the Gates of Lodore, reached by circuitous improved roads from Utah, Colorado, or Wyoming; (2) Echo Park at the mouth of the Yampa, reached from the Harpers Corner road; (3) Deerlodge, reached by improved road from Route 40 in Colorado; and (4) Rainbow Park, reached by a dirt road from Vernal or the Quarry area.

Whether boating with commercial groups or in private parties, boaters within the monument must observe National Park Service regulations and requirements. Information, permits, and a list of commercial outfitters are available by writing or calling the monument.

- The Monument by Road -

A network of backcountry roads surrounds the monument. Several of these extend inside the monument. Only one is paved, however, the scenic drive leading from monument headquarters (2 miles east of Dinosaur, Colorado) to Harpers Corner Viewpoint (31 miles). Other roads lead from Vernal to Rainbow Park and Island Park; to Jones Hole Fish Hatchery, from which a trail leads down-canyon to Green River; and to Brown's Park upstream from Lodore Canyon. These roads, which may be closed in winter, provide splendid panoramic views and intimate close-ups of the colorful, corrugated Uinta-Dinosaur country. Still other roads in Colorado crisscross the heights of Blue Mountain and Douglas Mountain and along Yampa Bench, affording aerial glimpses across the haunting, surrealistic Dinosaur landscape. One of these, the Harpers Corner Scenic Drive, ranks among one of the most beautiful drives in western America. It is generally open from April to late October. The drive gradually climbs up more than 2,000 feet from the monument headquarters on Route 40 to the rolling summit of Blue Mountain (Yampa Plateau) at almost 8,000 feet altitude.

From the main scenic drive, 6 miles from Harpers Corner, an unpaved road forks east to Echo Park at the confluence of the rivers (13 miles). This steep 13-mile route descends 2,000 feet through Sand and Pool Creek Canyons, past Indian petroglyphs, and into Echo Park, which is dominated by towering Steamboat Rock. A primitive campground is located near the confluence of the Green and Yampa Rivers. Because of soil conditions, all backcountry roads are impassable when wet.

Plants and Animals

Typical vegetation away from the streams includes sagebrush, greasewood, grasses, shadscale, rabbitbrush, wildflowers, and other small plants. Pygmy evergreens (junipers and pinyon pine) are common at intermediate levels. Higher elevations support stands of aspen, ponderosa pine, Douglas fir, and mountain mahogany. Along stream channels, one can find cottonwood, box elder, willow, tamarisk, alder, and birch.

Deer, bobcats, and coyotes are found throughout the monument. Resident rodents include beavers, muskrats, porcupines, marmots, prairie dogs, and chipmunks. Other mammals of the monument include bighorn sheep, badgers, mountain lions, foxes, weasels, minks, and skunks.

Birds include robins, swallows, raptors, magpies, and ravens. Fish are limited in variety within the monument. Catfish are found in the Green and Yampa. Humpback chub and Colorado squawfish, both listed as endangered species, are rare. Trout may be found in Jones Creek. Many years ago, Colorado squawfish, locally known as Colorado white salmon, reached six feet in length and 80 pounds in weight, but such specimens are rarely if ever noted today.

Antiquities

The monument contains numerous archaeological sites, ranging from petroglyphs and pictographs on the cliffs to caves, open village sites, rock shelters, and chipping grounds. Many of these antiquities originated with the Fremont culture of 800 to 1,000 years ago, while others may date from 2,000 to 7,000 years ago, and still others are of uncertain age and origin. Particularly noteworthy are the McKee Springs petroglyphs, located near the Island Park road, 19 miles from Vernal. This famed panel extends in a series along the cliff face. Attributed to the Fremont culture, this ancient art is considered to be some of the finest of its type in Utah. All monument resources—whether natural or man-made—are protected by law. Laws against collecting are strictly enforced.

FLAMING GORGE NATIONAL RECREATION AREA

Highway Approaches: *From the south—Route 191 from Vernal to Dutch John and then Route 44. From the north—Roads connecting with Green River, Rock Springs, and Fort Bridger in Wyoming (Interstate 80).*

Season and Climate: *Dam, visitor center, lake open all year. Four distinct seasons. Most pleasant season for camping and water recreation is May–September. Fishing permitted on the lake all year; fishing on streams according to state regulations. Most forest campgrounds and some visitor services open only from April–May to September–October. Check with national recreation area offices or local chambers of commerce.*

Administrative Offices: *Flaming Gorge National Recreation Area is a joint project of National Park Service (Department of the Interior) and U.S. Forest Service (Department of Agriculture) but is managed by the U.S. Forest Service through Ashley National Forest. Address: Flaming Gorge Ranger District/Manila Headquarters, PO Box 279, Manila, Utah 84046, (435) 784-3445. Office is located at the junction of Route 44 and Route 43 in Manila. Rangers are on duty at visitor centers (dam and Red Canyon Overlook), marinas, and boating campgrounds.*

Naturalist Service and Information: *Rangers and information at visitor centers and marinas. Information centers at the dam and Red Canyon Overlook provide seasonal orientation programs, exhibits, guided walks and self-guided tours, interpretive literature. Information also available from offices below.*

Accommodations and Visitor Facilities: *Lodging and supplies available outside the recreation area, at Vernal (via Route 191) and Wyoming communities (I-80). Nearby, lodging is available at Manila, Flaming Gorge Lodge between the dam and Greendale Junction, Red Canyon Lodge near Red Canyon Visitor Center. Limited supplies and fuel available at Manila, Dutch John, lodges and marinas. Numerous public campgrounds within recreation area and in Ashley National Forest nearby.*

Transportation: *Boats, fishing equipment, and water skis may be rented at marinas (check in advance). Commercial Green River float trips available.*

Clothing and Equipment: *Wear outdoor and recreation clothing suitable for season and activity. Carry jacket or sweater for cool nights in summer, warmer clothing at other times. Boating regulations strictly enforced, including requirements for life preservers, spotters for waterskiing.*

Medical and Dental Services: *First-aid assistance at marinas or from rangers. Medical and dental service available only at Vernal and larger Wyoming communities. Remember: this is wild remote country, far from city services. Prepare in advance for health needs.*

Warnings and Regulations: *Be acquainted with and observe all applicable regulations, including those covering boating safety and camping. Flaming Gorge Lake has special hazards, including deep cold water, sudden strong winds, abrupt drop-offs, steep banks. Carry adequate fuel and supplies, including drinking water.*

Admission: *Expect to pay fees for camping, marina services, rentals, licenses.*

FLAMING GORGE NATIONAL RECREATION AREA is centered on Flaming Gorge Lake, a deep, cold, man-made lake formed by Flaming Gorge Dam. The lake fills the entrenched channels of the Green River for 91 miles, backing up behind the dam (in Utah) almost to the city of Green River in Wyoming. One of the largest lakes in western America, Flaming Gorge Reservoir has an area of more than 66 square miles and a shoreline of 375 miles.

The lake provides a base for boating, waterskiing, swimming, fishing, camping, and rafting. The surrounding terrain—ranging from high forested mountains to semiarid badlands—is the scene for even more varied activities. These include camping, hiking, hunting, stream fishing, and photography. Downstream from the dam, the Green River flows clear and cold through the depths of Red Canyon, an ideal setting for stream fishing and boating. The entire region is also a geological exhibit of erosional features painted in vivid colors.

The roaring waters of the Green River in Red Canyon below Flaming Gorge Dam were navigated by John Wesley Powell in 1860 – Frank Jensen, UTC

Historical Background

Until the 1950s this northeastern corner of Utah was relatively unknown, largely because it was isolated and accessible only by rough unpaved roads. Fur trappers were in the area by 1825, boating Green River in the spring, then later that same year, holding the first rendezvous of trappers, traders, and Indians west of the main Rockies on Henrys Fork. Major Powell and his two exploring expeditions traveled down the Green in 1869 and again in 1871, applying names to many of its natural features—names by which they are known today. Among these is Flaming Gorge itself.

Soon after leaving the gate of Flaming Gorge, the Powell explorers faced the first of the frightful rapids they were to encounter on the rivers. They named Horseshoe Canyon, Kingfisher Creek-Park Canyon, Beehive Point, Red Canyon, Ashley Falls, and Brown's Park (changing that name from Brown's Hole).

Shortly after Powell's voyages, the few resident old-timers were joined by other settlers in greater numbers who relied primarily on raising livestock for a living. Ranchers came to Brown's Park and to Lucerne Valley, the site of Manila and Linwood, Daggett County's only communities before the establishment of Dutch John in 1957.

Dutch John, the largest community in Daggett County, was born in 1957 and 1958, built by the U.S. Bureau of Reclamation to house officials and workers involved in construction and operation of Flaming Gorge Dam. For a time the new town was known informally as Flaming Gorge; the name Dutch John was not adopted until 1958 after a newspaper contest brought scores of suggestions. (Dutch John was the name of a low mountain to the north.) During the peak of dam construction, the town's residents numbered in the thousands.

Flaming Gorge Dam blocks Green River in Red Canyon.

The dam is a thin, gracefully tapering concrete structure, its crest rising 455 feet above the riverbed and 502 feet above the lowest point in its foundation. The dam's crest, which carries a two-lane road (Route 191), is 1,180 feet in length, many times the 150-foot width of its base. Within the dam are three huge generators, together producing more than 100,000 kilowatts of electricity. The dam and powerhouse may be seen by tours (self-guided from April to late September and guided from early May to late September), beginning from a visitor orientation center where information is available.

Water Recreation

Flaming Gorge Reservoir and the Green River downstream from the dam form the recreation base for the majority of visitors. Fishing, boating, waterskiing, and swimming are the most popular activities. Downstream from the dam, the Green River flows through Red Canyon to Little Hole and Brown's Park, a popular stretch for rafting and fly-fishing (no motors allowed).

Marinas and launching sites located within the Utah section of the recreation area (from north to south) include Lucerne Valley, accessible from Manila; Antelope Flat, accessible from Dutch John; Sheep Creek Bay; Cedar Springs, south shore near the dam; Mustang Ridge and Spillway Boat Ramp, north shore near the dam; Little Hole, downstream from the dam (boat launching). Campgrounds are attached to all of these boating sites except Sheep Creek Bay. Commercial services such as boat rentals, beaches, and picnic areas are provided at the larger marinas. In addition there are boating campgrounds at several sites where launching/take-out are not feasible.

Seeing the Park by Road

Within Utah, the national recreation area is almost surrounded by the Ashley National Forest. Summits reach 8,000 and 9,000 feet in altitude. Most parts of the forest are heavily wooded with pygmy evergreens at lower levels, larger conifers and aspen in the higher reaches. The federal government has developed more than a dozen non-boating campgrounds in forested areas away from the lake, including several sites along Route 191 between Greendale Junction and the dam. Still others are accessible from Route 44 and the Sheep Creek loop road. Visitors are advised to obtain detailed maps and information in advance.

Red Canyon Visitor Center and Overlook provides one of the more spectacular canyon vistas of Utah. This overlook is perched on the south rim of Red Canyon, which is 1,500 feet deep here, and the blue lake extends away in two directions. A nature trail includes interpretive signs about local ecology. Ranger and information services are also available. Forest Service campgrounds and commercial lodging are nearby. Overlook is 3 miles by paved road from Route 44.

Swett Ranch is 1 mile west of Greendale Junction. As described in its national historic register listing, "the Oscar Swett Homestead is a capsule of frontier life . . . operated by horse and man power for nearly sixty years. Most of life's necessities were produced on the ranch land and in the National Forest. The beautiful ranch provides an opportunity to preserve an example of homesteading life so important to America's frontier development and a vivid example of man learning to live in harmony with nature in order to survive." The Forest Service provides daily tours in the summer months of the ranch house, barns, sheds, and other buildings.

Sheep Creek-Hideout Canyon Overview is on Route 44, about 9 miles south of Manila. Sheep Creek Canyon Geological Area (U.S. Forest Service) is reached by loop road from Route 44 south of Manila. The area features dramatic palisades in which the strata have been twisted by forces that uplifted the Uintas and created "an immense earth fracture, the Uinta Crest Fault." According to an official description, "The earth's crust on the south side of [the fault] was once thrust up over 15,000 feet. Along its northern line, however, there was little vertical movement. Instead the strata [were] bent up like the ruffled pages of a book—pages filled with geologic history. Sheep Creek originates south of the geological area in quartzite uplifts estimated to be 2-1/2 billion years old. Among the canyon's interesting features are Sheep Creek Cave within its west wall, fossils of trilobites, marine crustaceans, gastropods, brachiopods, corals, sponges, and sea urchins—reminders that this land was once a part of the 'briny deep.' Tracks of crocodile-like reptiles are also found in the area, along with petrified wood." The present access road was the route of Utah 44 before the highway was rerouted at the time Flaming Gorge Dam was built.

Dispersed camping is allowed along the drive from May 15–October 15.

GLEN CANYON NATIONAL RECREATION AREA

Highway Approaches: *South End (Wahweap, Page, and Lee's Ferry)—Route 89. North End (Bullfrog, Hite, Halls Crossing)—Utah Highways 24, 95, 276, 261. Unpaved roads give overland access to Hole-in-the-Rock, Escalante canyons, the Orange Cliffs, and other benchland areas above the lake.*

Season and Climate: *Paved access roads, lodging, and boating facilities are open all year. Backcountry roads normally are open all year but may be snowpacked or muddy at times. Winter temperatures may fall below freezing at night but snowfall is rarely heavy and winter days may be sunny and relatively mild. Annual precipitation totals only 5 inches; wettest months are August and September. The lake's water temperature exceeds 60 degrees from May to November.*

Administration Office: *Superintendent, Glen Canyon National Recreation Area, Box 1507, Page, Arizona 86040. Rangers and information at marinas and resorts. Official information center at Carl Hayden Visitor Center, located on the western side of Glen Canyon Dam, (520) 608-6404. Campfire programs and interpretive activities at Wahweap.*

Accommodations and Facilities: *Lodging and supplies available at highway access points including Page, Kanab, Hanksville, Blanding, Green River, Mexican Hat, and at Lake Powell marinas and resorts described in text. For marina and resort information, write individual marinas or Lake Powell Resorts & Marinas, PO Box 56909, Phoenix, Arizona 85079-6909.*

Transportation: *Bus and scheduled air service to Page and several other towns in vicinity; consult Utah Travel Council or travel agent for details. Commercial air, boat, and vehicle tours are available from Page, some of the marinas and resorts, and other points in lake vicinity; also charters and rentals. Landing strips at all marinas and resorts, and nearby towns. Several firms offer river trips from Lee's Ferry, Green River, Moab, Bluff, Mexican Hat; inquire from area superintendent or Utah Travel Council.*

Clothing and Equipment: *As with all outdoor exploration, wear clothing suitable for season and activity. Hats advised. Carry jacket or sweater for cool nights in summer; dress warmly in winter.*

Recreation: *Lake Powell—Boating, waterskiing, swimming, fishing, nature study, sightseeing, and photography. Benchlands—Vehicle sightseeing, exploring, hiking and backpacking, camping, photography, nature study.*

Medical and Dental Services: *Medical assistance at marinas or from rangers. Limited medical and dental services at nearby towns. Remember: this is wild, remote country, far from city services. Be prepared.*

Warnings and Regulations: *Be acquainted with and observe all regulations, including those covering boating safety and camping. Lake Powell has special hazards, including sudden strong winds, submerged rocks, cold and very deep water, abrupt ledges and drop offs, rockfalls, sheer-walled banks, and relatively few campsites. Carry adequate fuel and supplies, keeping in mind that supply points are far apart.*

Admission: *Expect to pay fees for camping, services, tours, rentals, etc.*

GLEN CANYON NATIONAL RECREATION AREA, a unit of the National Park Service, constitutes about 1.2 million acres of extremely rugged terrain in southern Utah and northern Arizona. It is by far the largest national park area in Utah and one of the largest in the nation. Measuring about 150 airline miles from north to south, Glen Canyon National Recreation Area includes within its boundaries all of the main channel of the Colorado River from Canyonlands National Park on the north almost to Grand Canyon National Park on the south. Arms extend far up the San Juan and Escalante river channels. Its northern extremity flanks Canyonlands National Park on the west, incorporating spectacular sections of the Orange Cliffs-Robbers Roost-Green River Junction country. As a national recreation area Glen Canyon differs from national parks in that it is open to multiple use; that is, mining, grazing and other activities may be permitted. Recreation, however, is the primary use.

The area's central feature is Lake Powell, the great reservoir that backs up behind Glen Canyon Dam for nearly 200 miles. The lake is contained in the basin of the former Colorado River, extending northward from the dam into the lower reaches of Cataract Canyon. The lake's shoreline is ten times as long as the length of its main body, nearly 2,000 miles.

Glen Canyon, as the river's main channel was named by the Powell expeditions, was noted for 90 years as one of the loveliest of the Colorado's canyons. The river's flow here was relatively tranquil and uninterrupted by rapids. Every bend opened new vistas of bare red rock sculptured into infinitely varied contours. Scores of side canyons opened into the main channel, most of them narrow and winding, containing flowing water only during runoff but harboring oases of vegetation and wildlife. For 70 years or so after the Powell expeditions of 1869 and 1871, only a few hundred boaters and gold miners became familiar with Glen Canyon's remote stretches. Then World War II brought the versatile rubber raft and a desire for adventure, and Glen Canyon—among other segments of the Colorado River system—witnessed an explosion of

Boating on the Colorado River as it transforms into Lake Powell, Glen Canyon National Recreation Area – Frank Jensen, UTC

recreation boaters. This heyday of travel through Glen Canyon lasted for little more than a decade, but during that brief period some thousands of modern river travelers experienced the canyon's unique charms. In 1963 water began backing up behind Glen Canyon Dam, gradually changing the free-flowing river to a static reservoir, flooding the maze of side canyons and drowning the many riverside beaches.

Today's travelers are fascinated by the strange landscape, but most do not realize that they see only the upper levels. The sheerest cliffs and narrowest chasms, vegetation, Indian antiquities and historical sites, nearly all the secluded grottoes, natural arches and standing rocks, and much of the erosional artistry now lie mostly beneath the water.

Basically, Lake Powell was a trade-off in values. It is one unit of the Colorado River Storage Project, authorized in 1956, and the material results of this grandiose water and power engineering feat can be seen in the cities of southern California, Arizona, Nevada, Utah, Wyoming, and Colorado. The recreation area itself is a result, and the lake has become a playground for millions who enjoy what is still visible of the Glen Canyon landscape and do not miss what they never knew. What was lost by the flooding of Glen Canyon has been described by numerous writers. The best visual treatment of the canyon in its original state is *The Place No One Knew: Glen Canyon on the Colorado* (Sierra Club, 1963). Edward Abbey, writing in *Slickrock* (Sierra Club, 1971), compared the original canyon with the present lake on the basis of values.

Natural Setting

The immediate shoreline of Lake Powell for most of its length is formed by navajo sandstone of early Jurassic age. Navajo sandstone, for the most part, was laid down as dune sand in ancient deserts; its great thickness (hundreds, even thousands of feet) and the fact it is present throughout a vast region today indicate the widespread, long-lasting nature of the original desert.

Lake Powell's maximum surface level is 3,700 feet above sea level or some 500 feet above the original river channel at Glen Canyon Dam. The lake is shallowest in Cataract Canyon. Topographic relief in the recreation area and nearby is extreme, varying from an altitude of about 3,000 feet at Lee's Ferry to more than 10,000 feet at Navajo Mountain and the Henry Mountains. Changes in elevation are often very abrupt since cliff faces mark the boundaries of canyons, plateaus,

mesas, and buttes. In general, the benchlands immediately surrounding the lake range from 4,500 to 6,000 feet in altitude.

The region is temperate and semiarid with well-defined seasons. In the lake area, precipitation totals only 5 inches annually, a third of which falls in August and September as rain showers. The temperature range is great between seasons, and even between daytime and nighttime. Daytime temperatures may reach more than 100 degrees in midsummer (July and August), when the heat is stored and amplified by the rocks. Lake water ranges from about 45 degrees in January (coldest month) to 80 degrees in July and August, the hottest period.

Though Lake Powell is fairly rich in fish, its immediate shoreline is not a favorable habitat for vegetation or wildlife because of water fluctuations and lack of soil. Plants and animals are more likely to occur beyond the lake in the upper ends of canyons, on the benchlands and highlands. Pygmy evergreens (pinyon pine and juniper) are the most common trees of the region. Where sufficient water is present along streambeds, cottonwoods, willows, and tamarisk flourish. Cacti, wildflowers, grasses, and small shrubs are fairly abundant. Animals include mule deer, bighorn sheep, antelope, coyote, badger, beaver, rodents, snakes, frogs and toads, insects, and other creatures. Many of these are not likely to be seen or heard, but deerflies and gnats can be troublesome.

Historical Background

Before dam construction began in the late 1950s, the Glen Canyon area had very few permanent inhabitants. It was too remote, too rugged, and too limited in opportunities for agriculture to attract settlers. Therefore, the area's human background during historic times consists of relatively few episodes. However, some of these were of epic dimensions, romantic and significant chapters in the history of the West.

Europeans did not enter the region until 1776 (see below). Prior to that time it was the domain of Utes, Navajos, and Paiutes. And before that, until about A.D. 1300, it was the home of Anasazi and Fremont Indians. Archaeologists from the University of Utah and the Museum of Northern Arizona surveyed the Glen Canyon area over a period of years beginning in 1956, under the auspices of the National Park Service, studying and salvaging as many antiquities as possible before they were flooded by Lake Powell. They found that Native Americans had used the area for centuries, leaving hundreds of structures (most of them small storage granaries) in every likely location, and marking their passage with petroglyphs and pictographs on the rocks. Today most signs of ancient occupation are beneath the lake.

This is also the case with fabled Crossing of the Fathers, or *El Vado de los Padres*. This ford of the Colorado River apparently had already been used extensively by Utes, Paiutes, and Navajos—perhaps even by the Anasazi. Mormon settlers knew of it and called it the Old Ute Crossing. Jacob Hamblin, noted Mormon missionary to the Indians, crossed there in the 1850s and 1860s.

But the Mormons had been preceded across the ford by the Dominguez-Escalante party from New Mexico, the first Euro-Americans in Utah. Here at Glen Canyon in October and November 1776, this small group of explorers encountered the most formidable natural barrier on their journey. They had been informed of the ford by Indians but had difficulty locating it. After unsuccessful attempts to cross the river at the mouth of the Paria (Lee's Ferry), they spent anxious days exploring the broken country to the north. Finally, on November 7 they succeeded in crossing the river at the ford, which they called *La Purisima Concepcion de la Virgen Santisima*. Today it lies under more than 400 feet of water, marked by a series of landmark buttes.

The ford was used by New Mexicans in ensuing years until a new route (the Spanish Trail) was established to the north, and it was utilized by Jacob Hamblin and other Mormon missionaries before the first ferryboat was built at Lee's Ferry in 1869. Thereafter, it fell into disuse and Lee's Ferry became the only Colorado River crossing for hundreds of miles until Marble Canyon bridge was opened nearby in 1929.

It is doubtful whether Euro-Americans explored the entire length of Glen Canyon before 1869, when Major Powell's first expedition passed through. This was a reconnaissance survey, and not until the second, more scientific Powell expeditions of 1871–72 were formal maps drafted and numerous topographic names applied. It was the Powell survey that gave it the name Glen Canyon, as described in Powell's report of 1875 titled *The Exploration of the Colorado River*. The Powell survey also applied formal names to such area features as the Henry Mountains, Dirty Devil (Fremont) River, Orange Cliffs, Land of Standing Rocks, Cataract Canyon, Kaiparowits Plateau, and Escalante River.

More years elapsed before the canyon above Lee's Ferry witnessed the sound of human voices. In the winter of 1879–80 a party of Mormon pioneers made an epic crossing of the river at Hole-in-the-Rock, a slot in the cliff several miles south of the Escalante's mouth. This group established a settlement at Bluff in the state's southeastern corner, and for some years afterward there were fordings of the river at Hole-in-the-Rock and Halls Crossing farther upstream. Neither of these crossings was ideal, however, and they were largely superseded by Dandy Crossing (Hite). Dandy Crossing was founded by a prospector-gold miner named Cass Hite, whose findings of placer gold in Glen Canyon sparked a "rush" that involved some hundreds of miners between the mid-1880s and the turn of the century, not only in Glen Canyon but also in the Henry Mountains and along the San Juan River. Heavy machinery was set up in Glen Canyon and the San Juan River. Though great effort was expended and some gold was found, the region never became a major gold producer.

Major Powell's expeditions were followed by a legion of adventurers and visionaries: Frank M. Brown and Robert B. Stanton, the Kolb brothers, Nate Galloway, Billy Hay, Julius Stone, E. C. LaRue and government engineers and mappers, Bert Loper, Harry Aleson, Georgie White, Norman Nevills, Arthur Chaffin, and others. Glen Canyon was only one segment of the entire river system, a gentle and lovely interlude between rapids, but during the 15 years or so before Lake Powell came into being, it attracted many more boaters than other stretches of the river. Thousands passed through the canyon to experience its natural and historical treasures. After Lake Powell was established, river guides moved on to the rapids of the Green and upper Colorado, Cataract Canyon, Marble and Grand Canyons.

The uranium years of the 1940s and 1950s brought a network of dirt roads (many of them now washed out), which opened the region to vehicle access. Key highways have been improved. Lake Powell, helicopters, and small planes have made access much easier. Still, foot travel remains the only feasible means of becoming intimately familiar with much of the area. Despite the hordes of boat visitors and machine-borne sightseers, large parts of Glen Canyon National Recreation Area continue to be wild, a sanctuary for those willing and able to leave the beaten path.

LAKE POWELL

Lake Powell is one of the world's largest man-made reservoirs, with a seemingly endless shoreline and scores of intriguing side canyons that invite exploration. As a result, it is hugely popular with the vacationing public, who number between three and four million every year.

The National Park Service provides public campgrounds, ramps and docking facilities, ranger and information services. Concessionaires operate stores, rentals, tours, lodging and eating facilities, and marina services. For rates, reservations, and information, contact individual marinas or Lake Powell Resorts and Marinas, PO Box 56909, Phoenix, Arizona 85079-6909.

Marinas are located along the lake at approximately 50-mile intervals. All except Rainbow Bridge are land-based and accessible by paved highway; Rainbow Bridge is a floating facility of modest size.

Marina Descriptions

Hite Crossing Marina [Lake Powell, Utah 84533, (435) 684-2278]: reached via Route 95. East side of lake, several miles south of Route 95 and about 40 miles north of Bullfrog-Halls Crossing. Houseboat and powerboat rentals, boat docking and storage, equipment rentals, fishing charters, store, boat fuel and service, airstrip. Public campground and launch ramp. Hite Marina gives easiest access to lower Cataract and Narrows Canyons, Dirty Devil Canyon, White and Red Canyons, and others in the Henry Mountains area.

Halls Crossing Marina [Route 276, Lake Powell, Utah 84533, (435) 684-7000]: reached via Routes 95 and 261. East side of lake, 82 miles from Blanding, two miles from Bullfrog Marina across the lake. Boat and equipment rentals, boat tours and fishing charters, store and restaurant, boat fuel and service, docking and storage, airstrip. Public campground and launch ramp. Halls Crossing Marina is the east-side equivalent of Bullfrog Marina with respect to point-of-interest access. The marinas are only two miles apart by water, 160 miles or so by road. The John Atlantic Burr Ferry allows vehicle access between Halls Crossing and Bullfrog six times a day during the busy summer season, and four times a day during the rest of the year. However, ferry service is briefly suspended during the fall for maintenance.

Bullfrog Marina and Resort [Lake Powell, Utah 84533, (435) 684-3000]: 72 miles south of Hanksville via Routes 95 and 276. Bullfrog is on the west side of the lake and in size is next to Wahweap, about 100 miles to the south. This is the most extensive of the Lake Powell marinas on the Utah side, with a clinic, campground, accommodations and RV park.

Rainbow Bridge Marina is a modest floating facility near Rainbow Bridge, about 50 miles from either Wahweap or Bullfrog-Halls Crossing. Limited services and supplies including fuel, store, rest rooms.

Wahweap Marina [PO Box 1597, Page, Arizona 86040, (520) 645-2433]: overlooking Wahweap Bay, several miles from the dam. Accessible by Route 89; scheduled bus and air service to Page. Commercial lodge and motel, dining, camper and trailer village, golf and tennis courts, houseboat and powerboat rentals, boat docking and storage, equipment rentals, fishing guides, scenic boat-vehicle-air tours, boat charter service, landing strip. Public campground and boat, drinking water and toilets. Public campground at Wahweap fills early on summer and holiday weekends.

Wahweap Marina is about 100 miles from Bullfrog, 51 miles from Rainbow Bridge, 58 miles from San Juan River arm, and 67 miles from Escalante River arm.

Lee's Ferry, on the Colorado River below the dam site, is a put-in point for boating expeditions through Marble Canyon and the Grand Canyon. Boating facilities, ranger, campground; store and restaurant nearby. Write Superintendent of the Glen Canyon National Recreation Area for details.

Water Sports

Boating, of course, is the most popular activity on Lake Powell. Thousands of private boats—motorboats, sailboats, and houseboats—ply the lake. Houseboats, powerboats, and fishing boats may be rented at the larger marinas. Many visitors take advantage of commercial tours offered at several of the marinas. Fishing ranks next to boating and sightseeing in popularity. Lake Powell is renowned for its bass and catfish, as well as walleye, brown and rainbow trout, northern pike, and kokanee salmon.

Hiking and Vehicle Exploring

Lake Powell is the heart of the recreation area, so boating is by far the most popular activity. Nevertheless, parts of the area are suited only for land activities such as hiking, backpacking, and vehicle exploring.

For example, the Escalante River canyon system is one of the most popular wilderness hiking areas in Utah. In the lower system, flooded by the lake, boaters may disembark and hike the main Escalante and side canyons. Land-based visitors approach the canyons from the town of Escalante. This magnificent system of entrenched meanders somewhat resembles the original Glen Canyon in physical characteristics; the canyons are a labyrinth of narrow gorges with vertical or overhanging walls, hundreds of feet deep near the main canyon.

Not so well known is the recreation area's northern extension, which adjoins Canyonlands National Park on the west. Access to this remote region is by unpaved road either from Route 24 north of Hanksville, or south from Green River. This part of the recreation area embraces a great deal of the fabled Robbers Roost country of Butch Cassidy fame, and broken rimrock overlooking the Junction country. High points atop the vertical Orange Cliffs in this area provide some of western America's most beautiful panoramas. (See Canyonlands National Park.)

GOLDEN SPIKE NATIONAL HISTORIC SITE

Highway Approach: *Visitor Center at Promontory Summit is 32 miles west of Brigham City via Route 83 and paved side road.*

Season: *Visitor Center open daily all year.*

Administrative Office: *At Promontory Summit. Golden Spike National Historic Site, PO Box 897, Brigham City, Utah 84302, (435) 471-2209.*

Information: *Visitor Center at Promontory Summit. Exhibits, information and publications, audiovisual program.*

Accommodations and Facilities: *Accommodations and services at Brigham City or Tremonton. Rest rooms and water at Visitor Center.*

Transportation: *Private car.*

Climate: *Elevation of Promontory Summit is 4,900 feet. Climate is relatively arid with few rain showers in warmer months and sparse snowfall in winter. Warm days, cool nights between mid-May and mid-October; cool or cold days and nights generally prevail at other times. The historical site is noted for strong winds.*

Recreation: *Viewing historic exhibits and authentic locomotive replicas; touring historic railroad sites; witnessing commemorative ceremonies.*

Warnings and Regulations: *National Park Service regulations apply. Do not damage property, carve initials, or remove artifacts, plants, or other objects.*

Admission: *Admission fees charged.*

GOLDEN SPIKE NATIONAL HISTORIC SITE was authorized by Congress in 1965 to commemorate the spot where the nation's first transcontinental railroad was completed. Containing 2,200 acres, the historic site features a Visitor Center-Museum, working replicas of the two steam locomotives involved in the Golden Spike ceremony of 1869, and approximately 15 miles of the old railroad right-of-way. The locomotives travel 1.7 miles of track laid on the original rail bed between an engine house and the Visitor Center.

On May 10, 1869, the Union Pacific and Southern Pacific Railroads met at Promontory Point, Utah, to drive the Golden Spike and commemorate the linkage of a continent. It was a cold blustery day and a crowd of 500 onlookers waited hours for the delayed Union Pacific train. At last, the whistle was heard, and the Union Pacific special chugged into Promontory. Following a number of speeches and ceremony, California Governor Leland Stanford raised his hammer and delivered a mighty blow. According to legend, he missed the golden spike entirely, but a thoughtful telegraph operator, simulated the striking with his key and tumult broke out across the country.

Following the ceremony, the town of Promontory enjoyed a brief but colorful history as a home to brothels, saloons, and gambling establishments. In 1870, the terminus was relocated to Ogden, and the 1904 completion of the Lucin Cutoff across the Great Salt Lake deprived the town of its railroad importance. Finally, during World War II, the rails were torn up and relaid at military depots elsewhere. The Southern Pacific Railroad erected a monument at Promontory in 1919, the half-century anniversary of the original Golden Spike driving. This monument served as the principal reminder of the site's historical significance until the Visitor Center was completed in 1969, Promontory's centennial year.

The centennial observance was marked with a ceremonial reenactment at Promontory attended by at least 12,000 visitors. Since the original locomotives—Union Pacific's No. 119 and Central Pacific's Jupiter—no longer existed, locomotives of contemporary vintage were modified to resemble the originals, and transported to Promontory for the 1969 ceremonies. Authentic working replicas of No. 119 and Jupiter were completed in California during the late '70s. These replicas are on display and running at the Visitor Center from May through October.

Activities and Events

Events at the historic site include an annual reenactment of the driving of the last spike on May 10, and an annual Railroader's Day in August. In addition to interpretive signs, exhibits, films, and talks about the transcontinental railroad and steam locomotives, the historic site offers a self-guided tour along "The Promontory Trail." The trail is a 15-mile section of the original rail bed, along which can be seen impressive rock cuts, fills, grades, overlapping parallel grades of the two railroads, box culverts, and the area where Central Pacific workers laid ten miles of track in one day to set a record. The monument also hosts an annual steam demonstration and film festival the last weekend in December.

The Grand Staircase-Escalante National Monument

Highway Approaches: *Route 12 for northern end of monument (the Circle Cliffs, Escalante River Canyons); Route 89 for southern end of monument (Vermilion Cliffs and the Grand Staircase).*

Season: *Open all year, though dirt roads may be impassable at times.*

Administrative Office: *Grand Staircase-Escalante National Monument Planning Office, 337 South Main Street, Suite 010, Cedar City, Utah 84720, (435) 865-5100. For local information, contact the Bureau of Land Management Escalante Field Office, PO Box 225, Escalante, Utah 84726, (435) 826-4291; or the Kanab Office, 318 North 100 East, Kanab, Utah 84741, (435) 644-2672.*

Accommodations and Facilities: *From Route 12, motels, guides, etc., can be found in the town of Escalante. Kodachrome Basin State Park (30 miles south of Escalante) offers 24 camping sites. From Route 89, services are available at Kanab.*

Transportation: *Private car. Guided tours available in local communities.*

Climate, Clothing, and Equipment: *Weather at the monument may vary tremendously, depending upon which of the three regions (Vermilion Cliffs, Kaiparowits Plateau, canyons of the Escalante River) one is exploring. Be prepared. This is isolated, rugged country, and help may be a long way off.*

Recreation: *Hiking, biking, photography, hunting, fishing, climbing, horseback riding.*

Warnings and Regulations: *Usual park regulations. Practice outdoor etiquette and common sense. Do not destroy property, carve initials, or remove artifacts, plants, or natural objects. Stay on trails. Carry plenty of drinking water. Backcountry hikers should leave an itinerary.*

Admission: *No fees charged.*

THE GRAND STAIRCASE-ESCALANTE NATIONAL MONUMENT was created by presidential proclamation on September 18, 1996. Encompassing 1.7 million acres of desolate canyons, buttes and pinnacles, mixed pinyon-juniper forests, and whorled dun-colored expanses of navajo sandstone, our nation's newest monument offers a stunning variety of topography, character, and scenery. The monument is large—about four times the size of the Salt Lake Valley. It

Devils Garden is a picturesque spot, perfect for a picnic – Frank Jensen, UTC

is also isolated, with two paved roads (Routes 12 and 89) roughly skirting its northern and southern boundaries and two improved dirt roads (the Cottonwood Road and the Smokey Mountain Road) intersecting the monument. The rest is open space connected by intermittent corduroy tracks and steep-walled canyons. The monument contains some of the most remote country remaining in the lower 48 states.

The plan for an Escalante National Monument dates back more than half a century to the mid-1930s, when Harold Ickes, Secretary of the Interior under President Franklin D.

Roosevelt, began developing a proposal to create an immense national monument in southern Utah. Ickes' plan called for the protection of a 7,000-square-mile expanse—an area roughly the size of the combined land masses of Connecticut and Rhode Island, with the confluence of the Green and Colorado Rivers at its heart.

Ickes' proposal encountered resistance from a variety of sources: Stockmen and farmers were opposed, as were Utah's politicians. The U.S. Bureau of Reclamation had plans for the Colorado River and insisted that the National Park Service make allowances for dam-building within the proposed monument, further cutting the acreage. The proposal was finally abandoned after the bombing of Pearl Harbor, when the country turned its attention to the matters of war.

Today's monument contains 2,700 square miles, rather than the 7,000 proposed by Ickes. It is composed of three distinct regions: the Grand Staircase, the Escalante Canyons, and the Kaiparowits Plateau.

The Grand Staircase extends across the southwestern corner of the monument and occupies about 30 percent of the total acreage. The four cliff forms—the Vermilion, White, Gray, and Pink Cliffs—are a textbook example of biological diversity. The staircase spans five different life zones and harbors an array of plants, mammals, and birds.

Among the outstanding natural features here are Grosvenor Arch, a striking double arch; the Cockscomb, an erosion-formed hogsback, or narrow fin of rock; and the abandoned town of Paria and a nearby movie set from the 1960s.

The Kaiparowits Plateau occupies the central section of the monument. Historians speculate that "Kaiparowits" is a corruption of the Paiute Indian word for "one-armed"–a reference to Major John Wesley Powell, pioneering explorer and student of the Colorado River and its corridors, who had lost an arm in the Civil War. Bordered on the west by the Cockscomb and on the east by the Straight Cliffs, the Kaiparowits is the monument's most rugged region.

More than 1,000 ancient Fremont and Anasazi Indian cultural sites have been recorded on the Kaiparowits. There are also paleontological resources, including the fossil remains of dinosaurs, crocodiles, mammals, fish, and plants. A herd of reintroduced bighorn sheep roams the plateaus, and a 1,000-year-old community of Utah junipers may be found on Four Mile Bench.

Abutting the Waterpocket Fold to the east, the Escalante Canyons offer outstanding opportunities for hiking, viewing ancient Indian cultural sites, and exploring the backcountry via the Burr Trail and the Hole-in-the-Rock Road. Discovered and named by John Wesley Powell's second expedition in 1872, the Escalante River is the last major river to be mapped in the continental United States.

A few of the outstanding natural features here include the Wolverine Petrified Forest, Dance Hall Rock, and the Calf Creek Recreation Area. This area also provides access to popular hiking routes, including Spooky and Peek-A-Boo Canyons and the Devil's Garden.

Warning: Before entering any part of the Grand Staircase-Escalante National Monument, consult locally for information. Equip yourself with maps and watch the weather. Dirt roads may be impassable after a storm.

HOVENWEEP NATIONAL MONUMENT

Highway Approach: *From Utah: turn east from Route 191 at junction between Blanding and Bluff, drive 8 miles on paved Route 262, then 15 to 20 miles on fair-weather dirt road to ruins in monument. From Colorado: drive 40-odd miles west from Cortez on partly paved road. The Colorado approach road is better, but inquire at Mesa Verde National Park, (970) 529-4461, as to road conditions.*

Season: *All year. Best in spring or fall.*

Administrative Office: *Superintendent, Hovenweep National Monument, McElmo Rt., Cortez, Colorado 81321.*

Accommodations and Facilities: *Campground at monument. Rooms and meals at Cortez, Colorado, and at Bluff and Blanding, Utah.*

Transportation: *Private automobile.*

Climate, Clothing, and Equipment: *Altitude at Hovenweep is about 5,000 feet. Nights are usually cool and days are hot during summer months. Carry drinking water and equipment for camping and hiking.*

Warnings and Regulations: *Usual regulations applying to national parks and monuments. Practice common sense and outdoor etiquette. Stay on trails. Do not remove artifacts or vandalize dwellings. All trails are self-guided. To see all dwellings in Hovenweep requires at least a full day and a hike of about 12 miles.*

Admission: *No fees charged.*

HOVENWEEP NATIONAL MONUMENT, in the remote canyon country north of the San Juan River, straddling the Colorado-Utah line, was established in 1923 to extend Park Service protection to the ruins of a prehistoric civilization. The reserve, though small, contains six separate groups of buildings; among them are several towers that are of great interest to archaeologists. The monument includes four large and several tributary canyons in the mesa between Montezuma and McElmo Creeks; the principal ruins are in Ruin and Cajon Canyons in Utah, and Hackberry and Keeley Canyons in Colorado. Sage Plain, the mesa into which the canyons at Hovenweep are cut, stretches to the horizon in all directions, broken only by the blue Abajos and the distant La Sal Mountains to the north.

The ancient Anasazi ruins of Hovenweep Castle glow in the fading light of sunset – Tom Till, UTC

In the Ute language, Hovenweep means "deserted valley." By 1910 the dwellings in Ruin and Cajon Canyons were well-known landmarks, a few of them had been looted, and archaeologists were interesting themselves in the tower structures. J. Walter Fewkes, chief of the Bureau of American Ethnology, published a detailed study of the Hovenweep ruins for the Smithsonian Institution in 1923.

Ruin Canyon and its south fork, sometimes called Square Tower Canyon, contains the most numerous and important group of buildings in the monument. Along a ledge near the head of the canyon, in caves within the canyon wall, and along its base are the prehistoric ruins. Hovenweep House stands next to the cliff rim at the head of Square Tower Canyon. Atop a pinnacle that rises from the canyon is Square Tower, the remarkable ruin from which the canyon takes its name. Hovenweep Castle, a well preserved building, is located on the north rim of Square Tower Canyon.

On the rim of Ruin Canyon, a short walk from Hovenweep Castle, are dwellings including the Unit Type House, a circular kiva surrounded by rectangular rooms, and picturesque Stronghold House. On the south rim is Eroded Boulder House, perched atop a projecting rock much like Square Tower, and Twin Towers which occupy a platform at the cliff rim.

Cajon Canyon, a few miles southwest of Ruin Canyon, contains one major ruin called Cool Spring.

The towers of Hovenweep have been described as forts, storage bins, observatories, lookout towers, and as temples for religious rites. Perhaps they were put to all these uses: several are in canyon bottoms where they have no view at all, others are built directly over subterranean kivas, which are known to have been used in religious ceremonies, and others occupy strategic cliff-edge positions that seem to have been selected with an eye to defense.

NATURAL BRIDGES NATIONAL MONUMENT

Highway Approach: *38 miles west of Blanding on Routes 95 and 275.*

Season: *Open all year.*

Administrative Offices: *Natural Bridges, Box 1, Lake Powell, Utah 84533, (435) 692-1234.*

Accommodations and Facilities: *Motels at Fry Canyon, Blanding, Mexican Hat, Bluff, Monticello. Campground at Visitor Center.*

Transportation: *Private automobile.*

Climate, Clothing, and Equipment: *Summer temperatures may vary 50 degrees in a single day from hot days to cool nights. Low humidity; heat not oppressive. Cold nights in winter, though days may be pleasant. Snowfall in winter (November to March) seldom exceeds a few inches; however, roads may be snowpacked or slick for short periods. Wear outdoor clothing, including suitable hiking shoes.*

Recreation: *Hiking, climbing. Fishing, hunting in season in adjacent Manti-La Sal National Forest. Boating, fishing on Lake Powell.*

Medical Service and Dentist: *Doctor and dentist at Blanding. Nearest hospitals: Monticello (64 miles) and Monument Valley (66 miles).*

Naturalist Service: *Visitor Center open daily. Roving patrols six months of year.*

Warnings and Regulations: *Do not remove artifacts, wildflowers or other objects. Do not carve initials on rocks. Usual regulations applying to national monuments.*

Admission: *Admission fees charged.*

NATURAL BRIDGES NATIONAL MONUMENT is renowned for its 3 immense water-carved bridges and a number of prehistoric cliff-dweller villages. Eastward, the green-wooded diagonal rise of Elk Ridge leans against the sky; in all other directions the unending red-and-tan shades of the plateau roll toward the horizon; 40 miles westward the waters of Lake Powell lap the red walls of Glen Canyon.

Owachomo is the most fragile of the natural bridges – Mel Lewis, UTC

The entire region between Blanding and Lake Powell is, in a sense, a single plateau, overlain by smaller plateaus that ascend and descend step-wise, or rear up as isolated buttes, or reach from horizon to horizon as immense mesas. The forces that raised the plateaus tilted them gently, forming the essential features of the Colorado drainage system. In addition, rainwater, working oceanward through it, carved a meshwork of intricate cracks and cleavages, and enlarged the cracks to box-walled gorges and canyons sometimes as much as 2,500 feet deep. Where soft and hard beds of stone alternate in the canyon, the soft beds have been eroded out, leaving massive overhangs, caves, alcoves, fluted columns, and bridges. The meandering course of San Juan waterways often takes the form of great loops. The streams, throwing their force against the loop necks, in time cut through and leave islanded buttes beside the new course. Where the capstone is hard and the underlying beds soft, the water carves deep, overhung alcoves in the soft material, and eventually may punch completely through it in a narrow neck, leaving an island that is joined to the "mainland" by a bridge or capstone. Subsequent erosion of the new channel cuts it deeper without affecting the overspanning capstone, and a bridge such as the Sipapu is slowly formed over eons of time.

Wildlife and vegetation on the plateau are diverse. The igneous Abajo Mountains, 10 miles north of Blanding, have been driven up wedge-wise through the plateau face to altitudes of 10,000 feet, and they are heavily wooded, as is Elk Ridge, about halfway between Blanding and the monument. Desert shrubs, pinyon, and juniper are found in the coarse dry patches of soil on the plateau face, but in the well-watered canyons it is not uncommon to see pine, white fir, manzanita, and snowberry growing beside saltbush, chaparral, greasewood, and yucca. In the Dark Canyon Wilderness and Grand Gulch Primitive Area nearby, bighorn sheep, mule deer, mountain lion, bobcat, bear, and beaver have been sighted. Birds of the high mountains and those of the desert nest within a few miles of each other—magpies, mourning doves, pinyon jays, sage, canyon towhees, bluebirds, rock wrens, swallows, and chickadees are the most plentiful, though eagles, ravens, meadowlarks, cranes, and other birds are sometimes seen.

In prehistoric times the plateau was occupied by the Anasazi. White and Allen Canyons and Grand Gulch have large clusters of houses (built sometimes of fitted stone, sometimes of adobe) that yield fine examples of pottery, as well as stone and bone implements; smaller communities have been found elsewhere in the area. Herbert E. Gregory of the U.S. Geological Survey was so moved by the remarkable preservation of the dwellings that he felt "the families have merely gone on a long visit." The Anasazi of this region, however, abandoned their dwellings at least 600 years ago, to be followed by Ute and Paiute Indians, whose descendants now occupy Allen Canyon. The first white visitors are anonymous. A few trappers may have traversed the country, but they left no record. In the 1880s, Cass Hite, whose name still graces a marina on Lake Powell, worked his way through this country and, according to historical gossip of San Juan old-timers, brought back accounts of many wonders, including three large natural bridges. About 1885, cattlemen began filtering into the Grand Gulch and Dark Canyon country, and some of them stayed. In 1895, cattleman Emery Knowles saw the bridges in White Canyon, and later in the same year, James Scorup visited them. In 1903, Scorup guided Horace M. Long to his find, and in August 1904, W. W. Dyar published an account of their explorations in *Century Magazine*. By 1908, the bridges were sufficiently well known to be set aside as a national monument, and in 1928, a road was extended from Blanding over Elk Ridge (Bear's Ears Buttes). This rough mountain route was replaced later by a paved highway at a lower level.

Highway Access

ROUTE 95—This road connects Blanding on the east with Hanksville on the west. The 133-mile link affords vehicle access to Natural Bridges, Lake Powell and its northern marinas, and numerous other scenic and recreational points that formerly were among the most remote parts of the nation. The present route, bypassing Elk Ridge at a lower level, was made possible by a notable engineering feat, cutting a road through the 800-foot face of Comb Ridge.

ROUTE 261—The monument can be reached from the south by way of Route 261, a mostly paved link with Route 163

near Mexican Hat. This highly scenic route gives access to Grand Gulch Primitive Area, Muley Point Overlook, Moki Dugway Switchbacks, Valley of the Gods, and Grand Goosenecks of the San Juan River.

Seeing the Bridges

A paved access road leads 5 miles from Route 95 to the monument's Visitor Center and Museum, where visitors can pick up information. From the Visitor Center an 8-mile loop road (one-way) links parking areas at the head of trails leading to the three bridges.

The paved loop road passes within a few hundred yards of all three bridges, beginning with Sipapu. Trails are short but in some cases steep, because the bridges are in canyons below the parking areas.

SIPAPU BRIDGE, largest of the monument's stone spans and first along the scenic loop, measures 220 feet in height and has a span of 268 feet. Many visitors believe this is the most impressive of all the monument's bridges. The name Sipapu was taken from Hopi legend, and it refers to "the gateway through which the souls of men come from the underworld and finally return to it."

KACHINA BRIDGE, 5 miles from the Visitor Center, measures 210 feet in height with a span of 206 feet. The trail descends about 600 feet with hand rails in one section. He chose this one and called it Caroline. Government officials, in the proclamation establishing the monument, named the bridge Kachina because prehistoric art work on the bridge's abutment resembles the elaborate masks worn by Hopi kachina spirits.

OWACHOMO BRIDGE, smallest and most fragile of the bridges, measures 106 feet in height with a span of 180 feet. The access trail descends only 300 feet. This was named Little Bridge by Long and Scorup, and renamed Edwin for a time. The word Little is appropriate only in comparison with the other two bridges. Owachomo, a Hopi word meaning "flat-rock mound," was chosen for a nearby promontory. The stone of Owachomo Bridge is light, a pale salmon pink, shot through laterally with vermilion streaks and accented here and there by green-and-orange lichens.

RAINBOW BRIDGE NATIONAL MONUMENT

Access: *By boat on Lake Powell from Wahweap Marina, Arizona, 50 miles; or from marinas on the lake in Utah (Bullfrog, Halls Crossing, Hite), 45 to 85 miles.*

Season: *Weather permitting, the monument may be reached at any time of year. Midsummer is very hot, winter is cold.*

Administrative Office: *c/o Superintendent, Glen Canyon National Recreation Area, Box 1507, Page, Arizona 86040, (520) 608-6404.*

Accommodations and Facilities: *Page, Arizona; Wahweap Marina, Arizona.*

Transportation: *Private, rental, or charter boats; boat tours from marinas on Lake Powell; also scenic flights from Page.*

Climate, Clothing, and Equipment: *Occasional severe winters, hot in summer. Wear suitable outdoor clothing; very limited walking is required, so clothing and equipment should be more appropriate for boating than for hiking.*

Medical and Dental Services: *Nearest medical services are many miles away by boat, at marinas or Page. First-aid kits are advisable.*

Warnings and Regulations: *Observe National Park Service rules and regulations; both Rainbow Bridge and Lake Powell are federal park areas.*

RAINBOW BRIDGE NATIONAL MONUMENT is about 6 miles north of the Arizona line on an arm of Lake Powell. It includes 160 acres around the largest natural bridge yet discovered, and was set apart by President Taft as a monument in 1910. The bridge is not accessible by car.

The monument is in one of the most rugged areas of the United States. The Colorado River made it impractical for roads to reach the region; and before Lake Powell made it comparatively easy to reach the bridge by boat, seeing it by land required a two-day pack trip northeast from lodges at

Rainbow Bridge was a favorite of Teddy Roosevelt – Frank Jensen, UTC

the base of Navajo Mountain, or longer trips from Mexican Hat or Monument Valley. Riverboaters formerly visited the bridge by hiking up Forbidding and Bridge Canyons from the Colorado River.

Rainbow Bridge, which is sacred to Navajos, has been named one of the seven natural wonders of the world. It is 290 feet high and 32 feet thick at its narrowest point. The bridge was first seen by Euro-Americans when competing expeditions led by W. L. Douglass of the U.S. General Land Office and Byron S. Cummings of the University of Utah

joined forces and, with the assistance of John Wetherhill and two Paiute guides, Nasha Begay and Jim Mike, reached their goal on August 14, 1909.

Theodore Roosevelt, who was guided by John Wetherill, visited Rainbow Bridge in 1913, and described it for *The Outlook* of October 11 that year. The season was wet, for "T. R." found deep pools of water in the canyon under the bridge. The former president, hailing an opportunity for a bath after a hard, dry desert journey, floated luxuriantly on his back in the water with the great arch towering above him.

Since Lake Powell began to offer easy access by boat during the 1960s, Rainbow Bridge does not have the romance of days when it was remote and isolated, a difficult and magic goal to attain. Now it can be reached in several hours from the nearest marina, or seen from a fast-moving plane within minutes of takeoff. During the 50 years between its discovery and the advent of Glen Canyon Dam and Lake Powell, only a few thousand people had seen Rainbow bridge. Now it is visited by hundreds of thousands every year.

TIMPANOGOS CAVE NATIONAL MONUMENT

Highway Approaches: *12 miles east of I-15 at Alpine exit (Route 92); 8 miles north and east of American Fork on Route 74, State 92; 9.6 miles north and east of Pleasant Grove on Route 146 and Route 92; 17.6 miles northwest of Wildwood on Route 92.*

Season: *Cave open May through September with guide service available (required but included in fee). Visitor Center with exhibit room and free 12-minute slide program open all year.*

Administrative Offices: *Superintendent, Timpanogos National Monument, Route 3, Box 200, American Fork, Utah 84003, (801) 756-5238 summer, (801) 756-5239 winter.*

Accommodations: *Nearby communities.*

Facilities: *Picnic area with water, tables, and fuel; a snack and gift shop available at Visitor Center, foot of trail to Timpanogos Cave. Campgrounds in U.S. Forest Service areas nearby.*

Transportation: *Private car.*

Climate, Clothing, and Equipment: *Cold nights and cool days in summer; snow between November and April usually makes area too cold for winter camping or hiking. Hiking shoes for steep climb to cave, jacket to wear in cave where temperature is 42 degrees; hiking or climbing togs for ascent of Mount Timpanogos and glacier. Film available at Visitor Center gift shop.*

Medical and Dental Services: *Doctors and dentists in nearby communities. Directions to first-aid stations at Visitor Center.*

Warnings and Regulations: *Do not damage natural objects within monument. Do not touch formations in cave; acids from human body are deleterious to them. Do not appropriate, deface, remove, or destroy any features of the monument. Observe Forest Service regulations in surrounding areas.*

Admission: *Admission fees charged.*

Timpanogos Cave National Monument, a 250-acre area containing Utah's outstanding scenic cavern, is on the northern slope of Mount Timpanogos in the Wasatch Range, and is reached by a trail up the south wall of American Fork Canyon. The monument is in a small area, easily accessible from good roads and only a few miles from towns and accommodations. Crowded into a restricted section around it are scenic wonders and natural phenomena on a large scale. The road that swings in a rough circle around the larger area of Mount Timpanogos is known as the Alpine Scenic Drive. Along the drive are the limestone cave, a rugged canyon, a towering mountain, an outdoor summer school and theater, a tiny "glacier," and Sundance Resort.

The cave is approached from the Visitor Center on the canyon floor by a 1.5-mile-long zigzag trail that climbs 1,065 feet up a steep mountainside. Tickets are purchased at the monument Visitor Center. The well-equipped visitor to the cave wears low-heeled hiking shoes and carries a jacket to put on upon entering the cavern. A good, steady stride with occasional stops at benches to get the second, third, and fourth wind will take the climber to the cave in the average time of one hour. The ramp-like trail follows a naturally flower-bordered course up the slope. There is a pungent aroma of sun-warmed pine as the trail climbs higher.

Timpanogos Cave (6,730 feet altitude), half a mile long, is actually three caves connected by man-made tunnels. They are all part of the same geologic structure, a fissure along the lines of a fault that occurred probably 50 million years ago. It is thought that the fissure was washed out by the waters of a stream corresponding to American Fork Creek, which in the succeeding Miocene epoch began cutting American Fork Canyon. Deposits within the cavern—icicle-like stalactites, upthrust stalagmites, and the branched, oddly-angled helic-tites—are thought to have required the same time to grow as the cutting of American Fork Canyon. Once the streambed was cut below the cavern fissures, water was scarce, and dripped rather than flowed. As the calcium-saturated drops came slowly down, evaporating all the while, they began to deposit limy material on the ceiling of the cave, the beginning of stalactites. Falling to the floor, they deposited other infinitesimal particles, and began to build stalagmites upward. In the course of time some of the stalactites and stalagmites joined to form columns; others in the cave have not yet joined. The "macaroni-like filigree" of helictites apparently formed where less moisture was present; they branched off in every direction, forming complete circles, having left deposits where water was drawn out by capillary action and evaporating completely.

Hansen Cave, through which entrance is made, was discovered in 1887 by Martin Hansen, who then owned the land. The cave was almost completely stripped of formations, some of which were sold to curio hunters, some of which were taken by chance visitors. This, like the other caverns, is ingeniously lighted by a system of indirect electric lights. The guide, who knows where the light switches are concealed, turns off a circuit behind and turns on another ahead, sometimes leaving visitors in absolute darkness for a moment to give them a notion of the profound gloom. The way trends downward and eastward, the caverns passing through the mountain behind the stone rest station. An 85-foot arched tunnel, built by hand, leads to Middle Cave.

The stalactite heart of Timpanogos Cave – Frank Jensen, UTC

Middle Cave, discovered in 1922 in the course of penetrating Timpanogos Cave proper, is a narrow winding channel with a high vaulted ceiling, sometimes reaching a height of 125 feet. A series of winding passages, stairs, and grilled footways leads from one area in the cave to another. Here the formations are for the most part unspoiled, in colors that range from pure white through yellow, ivory, coral, brown, and mauve.

Timpanogos Cave proper, connected to Middle Cave by a 190-foot man-made tunnel, reaches an area abounding in coloration and odd forms. There is a hidden lake, and hundreds of formations, configuring to the imagination of each person a different set of resemblances—the Dove's Nest, the Reclining Camel, Father Time's Jewel Box, Mother Earth's Lace Curtains, the Chocolate Fountain (well named), a seal, a dressed chicken, and scores of others. The "Heart of Timpanogos," bearing a remarkable likeness to the human vital organ, is illuminated from behind; variations in opacity give it a lifelike appearance. There is more to see after the heart, more marvels of lighting, form, color, more likenesses pointed out by the guide, more of that vague loss of direction within a cave, more dripping water. Finally there appears ahead and below a faint shining of blue light, as if the electrician had prepared a new and different set of glows and indirects. It is the sunlight, shining in around the wooden exit door. The eyes, accustomed to half a mile of yellow or red artificial light, refuse temporarily to accept all the colors of sunlight, and translate only the blue.

Official discovery of the cave is credited to Vearl J. Manwill, who told the story in the *American Fork Citizen* for April 28, 1939. The Forest Service later took the cavern under its protection and a trail was built. Civic groups contributed to development of the cavern, and about 10,000 persons visited it the first year, 1922.

Zion National Park

Highway Approaches: *Main entrance: 1 mile north of Springdale on Route 9. East entrance: 12 miles west of Mount Carmel Junction on Route 9. Kolob Canyon: enter from 1-15 at turnoff 2 miles south of New Harmony junction. Kolob Section: turn north from town of Virgin on paved road.*

Season: *Visitor Center and roads within Zion Canyon as well as Mount Carmel Highway are open the entire year. Kolob Canyons road from I-15 is closed by snow during winter months, usually from early November to Easter weekend.*

Administrative Office: *Superintendent, Zion National Park, PO Box 1099, Springdale, Utah 84767, (435) 772-3256.*

Accommodations and Facilities: *Zion Lodge and park campgrounds are open all year. Accommodations and services in Springdale, nearby towns.*

Transportation: *Private automobile, commercial tours.*

Climate, Clothing, and Equipment: *Lightweight clothing is preferable during warm months. For hiking, serviceable shoes should be worn. Water should be carried on some hikes (inquire at Visitor Center). Jackets needed for evenings during spring and fall, heavier clothing for winter.*

Recreation: *Hiking, horseback riding, motor trips.*

Medical and Dental Services: *Cedar City, Hurricane, St. George, Kanab.*

Warnings and Regulations: *National Park Service regulations must be observed. Keep to posted trails except where off-trail hiking is permissible. Permit required for backcountry hiking. Permit not required for day hikes except for Virgin River Narrows. All overnight camping trips require a permit.*

Naturalist Service and Information: *Visitor Center and Museum at Park Headquarters. Naturalists conduct nature study walks and hikes daily; variable schedule posted at Visitor Center, Zion Lodge, campgrounds, and facilities in Springdale. Evening talks in summer at public campgrounds and Zion Lodge.*

Admission: *Admission fees charged.*

ZION NATIONAL PARK, an area of 147,000 acres in southwestern Utah, is the best known example of a deep, narrow, vertically-walled canyon readily accessible for observation. Through much of its course it is about as deep as wide, though in the Narrows it is 2,000 feet deep and less than 50 feet wide. The park area is one of towering walls and steep slopes, which here and there recede into alcoves and amphitheaters, every-

The Great White Throne, a huge cliff of navajo sandstone – Tom Till, UTC

where decorated by broad arches, pilasters, statues, balconies, and towers. In winter, when the upper reaches are blanketed with snow, the lower walls are all the more brilliant by contrast; in autumn, they are a gorgeous backdrop for the yellow and golden foliage of deciduous trees and shrubs on the canyon floor; and in the spring, innumerable cascades plunge down the vast escarpments, some of them dropping a sheer thousand feet, and are colored by their burden of sand, each waterfall a different hue from its neighbor.

This is a realm of temples and cathedrals. Some of the names were bestowed by persons who were not members of any church, but no other nomenclature would fit: mountains of stone are called temples, patriarchs, Angels Landing, cathedrals, and thrones.

Visitors enter the park on the floor of Zion Canyon, or descend to it from the east entrance (Mount Carmel). Most visitors are content with the grandeur that towers above them from the canyon floor. The relative few who climb to the east or west rim, or even to Angels Landing, get a vista of a far different kind. From the floor, the viewer is walled in by tremendous cliffs that rise half a mile in places. From the summits, he looks out over a breathtaking landscape of wondrous erosional forms and riotous colors.

The relatively high altitude of Zion provides the park with a cooler atmosphere in summer than the surrounding section of southern Utah. Compared with desert country round-about, the streams and cascades, the trailing ferns and flowering plants, the pines and firs make Zion a multi-colored oasis. Mule deer are sometimes seen in the evenings. Cougars, coyotes, and bobcats leave their tracks after rain or snow. Porcupines, marmots, chipmunks, and squirrels are present, as are several types of lizards. Bird life includes the forms typical of areas having heavier rainfall as well as those indigenous to arid and semiarid country. Bighorn sheep have been seen most frequently in the Zion-Mount Carmel switch-backs area and across the river from the Visitor Center.

The park's most impressive rock—the navajo sandstone that forms the sheer cliffs and great domes—was formed in ancient deserts as windblown sand. The original sediments were converted into solid rock by the weight of the layers above them and by the cementing of lime, silica, and iron.

Today, Zion is an area of gorges, cliffs, and mesas. From the hard surfaces, softer layers have been stripped away by water and wind. The principal gorge, Zion Canyon, was cut by the north fork of the Virgin River. The stream, carrying nine times the fall of the Colorado River, carries out of the park about 180 carloads of ground rock daily. Adding to the ero-sional process are rainfall, surface runoff spilling over the high rims, ground water emerging as springs, wind, frost, growing tree roots, and chemical agents that weaken the stone.

From about A.D. 300 to A.D. 1200, Zion was the home of the Anasazi Indians. Their habitation sites, rock art, and chippings have been discovered in the park. These ancient people farmed near the creeks and rivers, raising corn, squash, and melons. After the departure of the Anasazi, a band of nomadic southern Paiutes lived in this area seasonally, sub-sisting by gathering, hunting, and some farming.

Zion Canyon was explored in 1858 by Nephi Johnson, a Mormon pioneer who rode up the canyon as far as the present Zion Stadium. Three years later Joseph Black explored the region and led farmers and stock growers into the canyon, where their descendants tilled and grazed the land until it was proclaimed a national park. In 1872 Major John W. Powell vis-ited the canyon and applied the Indian names, Mukuntuweap to the north fork of the Virgin River (Zion Canyon), and Parunuweap to the east fork. Indians refused to live in the canyon and were fearful of being overtaken by darkness there. This happily provided a sanctuary for the Mormons, who called their small settlement Little Zion. When Brigham Young visited and discovered evidence of wine drinking and tobacco use, he told them it was not Zion at all, and they called it, for a while, Not Zion.

A portion of the area was set aside as Mukuntuweap National Monument by President William Taft in 1909. Nine years later the monument was enlarged by President Woodrow Wilson and the name changed to Zion. In 1919 the status was changed by act of Congress to that of a national park, and in 1931 the Park was enlarged. Zion National Monument, cre-ated in 1937, was made a part of the park in 1956.

Roads, Trails, and Views

Visitors enter Zion Canyon by way of Route 9, which con-nects I-15 on the west with Route 89 on the east. There are 35 miles of improved roads in the park, including the 11.5 miles of Zion-Mount Carmel Highway within the park boundaries. The main Zion Canyon scenic road, with several short branches, runs north from Park Headquarters-Visitor Center to the Temple of Sinawava. Car travelers will find it advantageous to make frequent stops, since the top of the car obscures the stunning overhead views. Approximately 26 miles of well-kept trails lead to sections of the park not reached by roads. They can be used at all seasons except those to the canyon rims, which are closed by snow in winter. A horseback trail leads to the west rim.

Roads, trails, and features covered in this log are listed in order of distance from Park Headquarters-Visitor Center, moving north to the Temple of Sinawava.

Park Headquarters-Visitor Center, located in a canyon of nearly perpendicular cliff walls, is surrounded on all sides by stupendous sandstone formations. Soaring skyward to the west is the highest point in the southern portion of the park, West Temple (7,795 feet). Across the canyon from it is the Watchman, with red dominating the orange and rust, green and rose; in design, it looks as if a dozen Gothic skyscrapers had been placed side by side, then heated and welded into one enormous cathedral. A 1-mile trail leads from South Campground to the edge of a cliff above the campground, giv-ing an exciting view of the Watchman, West Temple, and the village of Springdale.

Bridge Mountain, overlooking the Zion-Mount Carmel switchbacks from the south, is named for a natural bridge on its face—a slender arch of stone 156 feet in length. Even through powerful glasses, the bridge looks like a thread of rock that a person could shoulder and carry away; its insignificant size against the wall emphasizes the colossal proportions of these monuments. Beyond Bridge Mountain to the north of the switchbacks is East Temple, its great size and exquisite coloring closely resembling West Temple across the canyon.

Across the main canyon (west) from East Temple, the superlative Towers of the Virgin, the Beehives, and the Sentinel combine with West Temple and Mount Kinesava to form the great amphitheater in which the Visitor Center is set. This Great West Wall, three miles long and from 3,000 to nearly 4,000 feet high, is regarded by many as the single most impressive feature in the park. It is best viewed from the Zion-Mount Carmel switchbacks.

Zion Canyon becomes narrower beyond the gateway formed by East Temple and the Sentinel. Within a short distance the west wall is broken by the mouth of Birch Creek and the cool green Court of the Patriarchs, over which loom the Three Patriarchs themselves. Opposite is the Mountain of the Sun, catching the first golden rays of sunrise and the last brilliant colors of sunset. In an expansive wooded valley bottom in this vicinity, 3 miles from the Visitor Center, is Zion Lodge (lodging, meals, supplies, horseback trips, tram tours). The lodge is a focal point for several trails. Sand Bench Trail crosses the river from the lodge and follows the base of the west wall to Court of the Patriarchs and the foot of the Sentinel (3.5 miles round-trip). The Emerald Pools Trail begins at the lodge or Grotto Campground (below); from the lodge, it crosses the river on a footbridge and joins the West Rim Trail. Emerald Pools are small pockets of water formed by ribbon-like waterfalls that plunge hundreds of feet down the face of steep cliffs. Hikers may also walk from the lodge to Grotto Picnic Area, 3/4 mile, and connect there with trails leading to West Rim and Angels Landing (see below).

Leaving Zion Lodge, the road continues up the canyon past the Great White Throne, Angels Landing, and Weeping Rock to the Temple of Sinawava. This is an area for viewing the vividly colored waterfalls that appear immediately following a shower or during spring runoff.

Four miles from the Visitor Center (Grotto Picnic Area), signs point the way to West Rim Trail, Angels Landing, Emerald Pools, and Court of the Patriarchs. West Rim Trail, oil-surfaced for the first mile, is a strenuous foot or horse trail of 13 miles round-trip to West Rim Viewpoint. The trail leaves the canyon floor at the foot of Angels Landing and is benched along a ledge of the west wall for 600 feet into Refrigerator Canyon. Hewn into the face of the almost-vertical cliffs, it winds through cool narrow gorges and comes out on top of bare rock ledges. The trail zigzags up, nearly to the level of Angels Landing, and turns north, continuing over the colorful sandstone formation for two miles before making the final ascent to the rim. Coming out on top, 3,000 feet above the river, it extends along the rim to Potato Hollow on Horse Pasture Plateau and beyond to Lava Point. From the rim there is a view of Zion Canyon and into the broken wilderness of the right fork of North Creek. Carry water.

A sign at 5 miles points to the Weeping Rock Parking Area, departure point for trails to the East Rim and Weeping Rock. The East Rim Trail involves a fairly strenuous 7-mile round-trip for the full hike, leaving the canyon floor at the foot of Cable Mountain and ascending its north flank. There are wonderful views of Zion Canyon from various points on the trail, but the finest is reserved for the last—Observation Point, more than 2,000 feet above the canyon floor. From this point the Kaibab Forest can be seen on the North Rim of the Grand Canyon, far to the southeast; Cedar Mountain in the Cedar Breaks country stands on the northern horizon; and to the southwest is the Virgin River Valley and St. George. Carry water. An easy, self-guiding trail leads from the parking area to Weeping Rock. Also from the Weeping Rock Parking Area, a fairly strenuous trail leads 1 mile to the mouth of Hidden Canyon, a typical hanging valley.

Back on the main road, there is a good view of the Organ, and at 5.5 miles is a parking area with a choice view of the Great White Throne through the saddle between the Organ and Angels Landing. The Great White Throne (6,744 feet) is the best known monolith in the park. Directly opposite is Angels Landing (5,785 feet), its dull red color in contrast to the white of the throne. A trail from the Grotto picnic area leads to the summit of this peak, 2.5 miles from the trailhead and 1,500 feet above. The trail affords an excellent bird's-eye view of Zion Canyon, but the last half mile is strenuous and best avoided by those who fear heights.

Leaving this viewpoint, the road and river make a great bend around the colossal Organ, a red spur projecting from Angels

Landing. The road terminates at the Temple of Sinawava, 6.5 miles from the Visitor Center, a truly spectacular amphitheater almost surrounded by sheer cliffs. The parking area is shaded by trees. Here begins the hard-surfaced Gateway to the Narrows Trail, over which ranger-naturalists conduct parties daily. A trailside exhibit explains the geology and natural history of the area. Half a mile up is Zion Stadium, a walled-in alcove with wildflowers growing from crevices and clinging to the cliffs; on the canyon floor is a pool of cold lucid water. At the Narrows, a mile up the canyon from the parking area, the walls rise vertically for 2,000 feet but are only 50 feet apart at river level. At the end of the trail, those who would venture farther must wade along the river edge. A permit is required for Narrows hiking.

Automobile tourists view the Virgin River Narrows here as a gateway. For downstream hikers, however, the Narrows in this vicinity marks the end of a thrilling 12-mile hike for those descending from the high reaches of the Kolob Terrace. Details about this wilderness experience may be obtained from the park Visitor Center. The Narrows (full length) is typically open from late June through early October, with weather conditions closely monitored by the park; adverse conditions result in immediate closure. Upstream beyond the end of the trail, the Narrows is closed between early October and late June because high water may be dangerous and/or cold air and water might result in hypothermia.

Zion-Mount Carmel Highway (Route 9)

About half a mile north of the Visitor Center, the paved road forks: the Zion Canyon scenic drive (preceding section) continues up the canyon to the left, and Route 9 switchbacks up the steep slope of cliff-walled Pine Creek Canyon to the right. Pulloffs at intervals allow dizzy views down into the main canyon and across to the wall formed by West Temple, Towers of the Virgin, and the Sentinel. Beautifully colored East Temple looms above the road as it enters the Zion-Mount Carmel Tunnel, where the road has been cut through solid rock for a mile. Windows in the sheer cliff give tantalizing glimpses of giant forms, but parking within the tunnel is not permitted. From a parking area at the tunnel's upper (east) end, a self-guided trail leads to an overview of Zion Canyon, Pine Creek Canyon, and the Great West Wall. A half-mile round-trip, this Canyon Overlook Trail leads to a point directly above the Great Arch of Zion. The highway tunnel, a marvel of engineering, was built during the 1920s.

East of the tunnel, Route 9 winds for miles through a wondrous landscape of beautifully colored, gently contoured, slickrock slopes, domes, cones, plateaus and deep gorges. Forms are completely different from those seen in Zion Canyon. Gradually, near the park's east entrance, the terrain changes from bare rounded rock to more open woodlands, with vistas of mountains and cliffs.

Kolob Section

The Kolob Section, formerly Zion National Monument, northwest of Zion Canyon, can be entered by road from Interstate 15 near New Harmony (the Finger Canyons), or north from Route 9 at the town of Virgin.

The Kolob Finger Canyons are visible from the vicinity of New Harmony. They can be seen close-up from the paved Kolob park road that forks east from I-15 two miles south of the New Harmony turnoff. The road climbs in switchbacks, ascending 1,300 feet in 5 miles to a spectacular viewpoint-parking area overlooking the yawning mouths of half a dozen sheer-walled, red-rock gorges. These wild canyons offer delightful backcountry hiking.

The otherworldly beauty of the Kolob Terrace, into which the canyons of Zion National Park have been sunk, undoubtedly prompted Mormon pioneers to name the area for the star nearest the throne of God. Red cliffs rise abruptly from the canyon bottoms, breaking into a series of rugged canyons with walls 1,500 to 2,500 feet high. The most southerly canyon carries the waters of LaVerkin Creek. Sparkling streams from the Kolob Terrace flow through some of the eastern canyons, covering the floors with wildflowers and dense vegetation.

The second access road, from Route 9 at Virgin, climbs from less than 4,000 feet at Virgin to more than 9,000 feet on the Markagunt Plateau. En route, it traverses the broken Kolob Terrace, an intermediate platform into which the park's canyons have been cut. The road involves steep climbs and hairpin turns, but it affords a series of breathtaking views of Zion's temples, cliffs, mesas, buttes, knolls, lava formations, and tremendous gorges. Views of West Temple and the Guardian Angels are particularly impressive.

From this road, hiking trails and unimproved routes lead to remote canyons and rims such as Hop Valley, Timber Top, Kolob Arch, and the Finger Canyons, all in the Kolob Section. Great West Canyon, North Creek, Wildcat Canyon, and West Rim Trail lead to Zion Canyon.

STATE PARKS

The state of Utah has developed 45 heritage, scenic, recreation, and waterfront parks. Many of these are described in the tour section, and a complete listing follows. There are user fees at many of these areas, particularly where services such as campgrounds and boat marinas are provided. Additional details are available at the Utah Travel Council, Council Hall / Capitol Hill, Salt Lake City, Utah 84114, (801) 538-1030 or (800) 200-1160; the Utah Division of Parks and Recreation, 1636 West North Temple Street, Salt Lake City, Utah 84116, (801) 538-7221; or from numerous visitor information centers.

The undulating curves of Coral Pink Sand Dunes State Park – Frank Jensen, UTC

Note: Numbers represent State Park locations on the Parks and Monuments map, page 16, and Geographic Province chapters on pages 64, 104, 130, 156, 180, 212.

Map # and Name	Location	Phone	Map # and Name	Location	Phone
❶ ANASAZI	Boulder	(435) 335-7308	㉔ LOST CREEK	Morgan	(801) 829-6866
❷ ANTELOPE ISLAND	Syracuse	(801) 773-2941	㉕ MILLSITE	Ferron	(435) 687-2491
❸ BEAR LAKE	Garden City	(435) 946-3343	㉖ MINERSVILLE	Minersville	(435) 438-5472
❹ CAMP FLOYD	Fairfield	(801) 254-9036	㉗ OTTER CREEK	Antimony	(435) 624-3268
❺ CORAL PINK DUNES	Kanab	(435) 648-2800	㉘ PALISADE	Sterling	(435) 835-7275
❻ DEAD HORSE POINT	Moab	(435) 259-2614	㉙ PIUTE	Junction	(435) 624-3268
❼ DEER CREEK	Heber	(435) 654-0171	㉚ QUAIL CREEK	St. George	(435) 879-2378
❽ EAST CANYON	Morgan	(801) 829-6866	㉛ RED FLEET	Vernal	(435) 789-4432
❾ EDGE OF THE CEDARS	Blanding	(435) 678-2238	㉜ ROCKPORT	Wanship	(435) 336-2241
❿ ESCALANTE	Escalante	(435) 826-4466	㉝ SCOFIELD	Scofield	(435) 448-9449
⓫ FT. BUENAVENTURA	Ogden	(801) 621-4808	㉞ SNOW CANYON	St. George	(435) 628-2255
⓬ FREMONT INDIAN	Sevier	(435) 527-4631	㉟ STARVATION	Duchesne	(435) 738-2326
⓭ GOBLIN VALLEY	Hanksville	(435) 564-3633	㊱ STEINAKER	Vernal	(435) 789-4432
⓮ GOOSENECKS	Mexican Hat	(435) 678-2238	㊲ TERRITORIAL STATEHSE	Fillmore	(435) 743-5316
⓯ GREAT SALT LAKE	Salt Lake City	(801) 250-1898	㊳ THIS IS THE PLACE	Salt Lake City	(801) 584-8391
⓰ GREEN RIVER	Green River	(435) 564-3633	㊴ U.P. RAIL TRAIL	Park City	(435) 649-3602
⓱ GUNLOCK	St. George	(435) 628-2255	㊵ UT FIELD HSE/NAT. HIST.	Vernal	(435) 789-3799
⓲ HUNTINGTON	Huntington	(435) 687-2491	㊶ UTAH LAKE	Provo	(801) 375-0731
⓳ HYRUM	Hyrum City	(435) 245-6866	㊷ VETERANS' MEMORIAL	Bluffdale	(801) 254-9036
⓴ IRON MISSION	Cedar City	(435) 586-9290	㊸ WASATCH MOUNTAIN	Midway	(435) 654-1791
㉑ JORDAN RIVER	Salt Lake City	(801) 533-4496	㊹ WILLARD BAY	Brigham City	(435) 734-9494
㉒ JORDANELLE	Heber	(435) 645-9540	㊺ YUBA	Nephi	(435) 758-2611
㉓ KODACHROME	Cannonville	(435) 679-8562			

NATIONAL FORESTS

Utah's national forests encompass nearly all the highest mountains and total over nine million acres, or about a sixth of the state. This is an enormous area—it is larger than some eastern states—yet it is smaller than the national forest acreage in every western state except Nevada. The lands are used for a variety of purposes: watershed protection and management, timber harvesting, recreation, wildlife habitat, grazing, and mining. The state's national forests were originally created primarily for protection of watersheds, and that remains an important objective. During the summers the forests are heavily grazed by sheep and cattle; in addition, up to 74 million board feet of timber have been cut in the state's national forests some years.

By far the greatest share of the state's rain and snow falls in the high altitude national forests. Major streams originating in Utah have their sources in national forests, and hundreds of small lakes are located in national forests, as are a number of reservoirs. So, too, are most improved campgrounds, developed picnic areas, and ski resorts. The U.S. Forest Service has established several thousand individual camp and picnic units in several hundred different locations. A number of these are mentioned in the tour section.

National forests also provide habitat for much of the state's wildlife. Deer, elk, and moose prefer forests at least part of the time, as do bear, cougar, bobcat, pine martin, and many other animals and birds. Big game hunting, for the most part, takes place on national forests. Streams and lakes of the national forests are home for cool-water fish such as rainbow and brown trout. Utah's forest streams commonly are swift and rather small. Hundreds of plant species are found in Utah's national forests, ranging from wildflowers and small shrubs to brush, pygmy evergreens (pinyon pine and juniper), quaking aspen, and large evergreens such as Douglas fir, ponderosa pine, lodgepole pine, blue spruce, and Engelmann spruce.

Sawtooth National Forest

The Sawtooth National Forest, District Rangers Office, 2621 South Overland Avenue, Burley, Idaho 83318, (208) 678-0430, oversees 92,403 acres in northwestern Utah, including the Raft River Mountains. This forest area may be Utah's best kept secret, with trail systems reaching 9,500 feet in elevation, peaceful streams, excellent hunting and lakes in mountainous settings.

Wasatch-Cache National Forest

The Wasatch-Cache National Forest, Main Office, 8226 Federal Building, 125 South State, Room 8103, Salt Lake City 84138, (801) 524-5030, oversees 1,300,000 acres in northern Utah, including Utah's Wasatch Mountains. Ski resorts located in this forest provide world-renowned downhill skiing.

Ashley National Forest

The Ashley National Forest, Main Office, 355 North Vernal Avenue, Vernal 84078, (435) 789-1181, oversees 1,300,000 acres in northeastern Utah, including the Flaming Gorge National Recreation Area, famous for trophy trout fishing. The Ashley National Forest also provides outstanding backpacking in the pristine High Uintas Wilderness.

Uintah National Forest

The Uintah National Forest, Main Office, 88 West 100 North, PO Box 1428, Provo 84603, (801) 377-5780, oversees 949,848 acres in north-central Utah, including the Mt. Nebo Loop, a scenic byway. A photographer's dream, this route is a 32-mile paved drive full of rugged mountain beauty and many stunning overlooks of surrounding valleys. In another part of the forest, Strawberry Reservoir is Utah's top trout fishing destination.

Fishlake National Forest

The Fishlake National Forest, Main Office, 115 East 900 North, Richfield 84701, (435) 896-9233, oversees 1,434,604 acres in south-central Utah. The nationally recognized Paiute ATV Trail winds through 250 miles of the forest's most scenic terrain. In addition, the Fish Lake-Johnson Valley area, a 13,700-acre region, boasts spectacular mountain lake fishing in 3,000 acres of lakes and reservoirs, along with campgrounds, picnic areas, boating, and resorts.

Manti-La Sal National Forest

The Manti-La Sal National Forest, Main Office, 599 West Price River Drive, Price 84501, (435) 637-2817, oversees 1,400,000 acres in central and southeastern Utah, including three mountain blocks—the La Sal and Abajo Mountain Ranges provide excellent opportunities for cross-country skiing and hiking, and also serve as scenic backdrops to state and national parks in the desert lands of southeastern Utah. The Manti Division in central Utah is characterized by narrow canyons and broad rolling ridges covered with aspen and spruce. Excellent fishing is available throughout the forest.

Dixie National Forest

The Dixie National Forest, Main Office, 82 North 100 East, PO Box 0580, Cedar City 84721-0580, (435) 865-3700, oversees 1,900,000 acres in southern Utah. The largest national forest in the state, in a day's drive, visitors may choose to enjoy a hike in Pine Valley, see scenic Navajo Lake, fish at Panguitch Lake, tour the east fork of the Sevier River, or travel the scenic Boulder/Grover Road on Boulder Mountain.

Bureau of Land Management

Over 40 percent of Utah, or 22,000,0000 acres, is administered by the federal Bureau of Land Management (BLM). This includes mountains, rivers, canyons, and plains. There are 5 BLM district offices divided into 16 resource areas located throughout the state. For additional information, contact the Utah State BLM Office, 324 South State Street, Salt Lake City, Utah 84111, (801) 539-4001.

The **Cedar City District Office**, 176 East D.L. Sargent Drive, Cedar City 84720, (435) 586-2401, administers 6,034,741 acres in southern and southwestern Utah. This includes portions of almost all of the scenic byways and backways in the state, the Escalante River, and the Circle Cliffs.

The **Moab District Office**, 82 East Dogwood, Moab 84532, (435) 259-6111, administers 5,805,426 million acres in east-central and southeastern Utah, including the San Rafael Swell, part of the Book Cliff Mountains, the Grand Gulch Plateau, and the Kokopelli and Slickrock Mountain bike trails.

The **Richfield District Office**, 150 East 900 North, Richfield 84701, (435) 896-8221, oversees 6,126,225 acres spread across 7 counties. This includes reservoirs, the Little Sahara Recreation Area, and the Henry Mountains.

The **Salt Lake District Office**, 2370 South 2300 West, Salt Lake City 84119, (801) 977-4300, oversees 2,506,804 acres in northern Utah, including the Deep Creek Mountains and the Bonneville Salt Flats.

The **Vernal District Office**, 170 South 500 East, Vernal 84078, (435) 789-1362, oversees 1,607,602 acres in northeastern Utah, including the outstanding Native American rock art of Dry Fork Canyon and the rugged Book Cliffs.

Wilderness Areas

As defined by the Wilderness Act of 1964, a designated wilderness is a federally owned area that offers opportunities for outstanding solitude, remains essentially wild and undeveloped by mankind, and is large enough that continued use will not permanently alter or mar its wild characteristics. Except under special circumstances, motorized transportation and mountain bikes are not allowed in designated wilderness areas; visitors must rely on the power of nonmechanized transportation (i.e., paddles, packstock, and the power of two feet). Wilderness areas are widely used for hunting, fishing, horseback riding, backpacking, and camping. Mining is allowed on preexisting claims; grazing is allowed to continue where it has already been established.

For more information on Utah's wilderness areas and tips on backcountry etiquette, contact the U.S. Forest Service, Intermountain Region Office, 324 - 25th Street, Ogden, Utah 84401, (801) 625-5306; or the Bureau of Land Management, Utah State Office, PO Box 45155, 324 South State Street, Suite 301, Salt Lake City, Utah 84145-0155.

There are 13 designated wilderness areas in national forests within the state of Utah. These range from southwestern Utah's Beaver Dam Mountain Wilderness, which protects 2,600 acres, to the High Uintas Wilderness in northern Utah, which contains 456,705 acres.

Ashdown Gorge Wilderness, Southwestern Utah, 7,000 acres	Mt. Nebo Wilderness, Central Utah, 28,000 acres
Box-Death Hollow Wilderness, So-Central Utah, 25,814 acres	Mt. Olympus Wilderness, Northern Utah, 16,000 acres
Dark Canyon Wilderness, Southeastern Utah, 45,000 acres	Pine Valley Mtns, Wilderness, Southwestern Utah, 50,000 acres
Deseret Peak Wilderness, Western Utah, 25,500 acres	Timpanogos Wilderness, Northern Utah, 10,750 acres
High Uintas Wilderness, Northeastern Utah, 456,705 acres	Twin Peaks Wilderness, Northern Utah, 11,463 acres
Lone Peak Wilderness, Northern Utah, 30,088 acres	Wellsville Mtns. Wilderness, Northern Utah, 23,850 acres
Mt. Naomi Wilderness, Northern Utah, 44,350 acres	

The Bureau of Land Management administers two wilderness areas in Utah:

Paria Canyon Wilderness, South-Central Utah, 20,000 acres	Beaver Dam Mtns. Wilderness, Southwestern Utah, 2,600 acres

SCENIC BYWAYS AND BACKWAYS

The state of Utah's official Byways and Backways program includes a total of 85 scenic routes. There are currently 27 byways, which are paved roads accessible to passenger cars, and 58 backways, which in general are less conventional routes ranging from unmaintained dirt roads to paved but sometimes tortuous roads. A list of byways follows:

Joshua Tree Road in Utah's Dixie is a scenic backway that catches the northern edge of the great Sonoran desert of the Southwest – Frank Jensen, UTC

BEAVER CANYON SCENIC BYWAY, State Hwy. 153 from the town of Beaver to Elk Meadows Resort

BIG COTTONWOOD CANYON SCENIC BYWAY, State Hwy. 152 east of the Salt Lake Valley

BLUFF SCENIC BYWAY, State Hwy. 163 between the town of Bluff and Monument Valley Navajo Tribal Park

BRIAN HEAD–PANGUITCH LAKE SCENIC BYWAY, State Hwy. 143 from Parowan to Panguitch

CEDAR BREAKS SCENIC BYWAY, State Hwy. 148 between State Hwy. 14 and State Hwy. 143

COLORADO RIVER SCENIC BYWAY, State Hwy. 128

ECCLES CANYON SCENIC BYWAY, State Hwy. 264 west of Fairview

FISHLAKE SCENIC BYWAY, State Hwy. 25 between State Hwy. 24 and State Hwy. 72

FLAMING GORGE–UINTAS SCENIC BYWAY, U.S. 191 from Vernal to the Wyoming border; and from the Junction of U.S. 191/44 to Manila

HIGHWAY 12 SCENIC BYWAY, State Hwy. 12 from the junction of U.S. 89 to the town of Torrey

HUNTINGTON CANYON SCENIC BYWAY, State Hwy. 31 from Fairview to Huntington

INDIAN CANYON SCENIC BYWAY, U.S. 191 from Helper to Duchesne

KANAB SCENIC BYWAY, U.S. 89 from Kanab to its junction with State Hwy. 12

KOLOB FINGER CANYONS ROAD SCENIC BYWAY, Accessed from I-15 south of Cedar City, the byway enters the Kolob Section of Zion National Park

LAKETOWN SCENIC BYWAY, State Hwy. 30 from U.S. 89 to Laketown on the shores of Bear Lake

LITTLE COTTONWOOD CANYON SCENIC BYWAY, State Hwy. 210 east of the Salt Lake Valley

LOA–HANKSVILLE SCENIC BYWAY, State Hwy. 24 through Capitol Reef National Park and vicinity

LOGAN CANYON SCENIC BYWAY, U.S. 89 from Logan to the Utah/Idaho Border

MARKAGUNT SCENIC BYWAY, State Hwy. 14 from Cedar City to its junction with U.S. 89

MIRROR LAKE SCENIC BYWAY, State Hwy. 150 from Kamas to the Utah/Wyoming border

OGDEN RIVER SCENIC BYWAY, State Hwy. 39 from Ogden to the eastern boundary of the Wasatch-Cache National Forest

POTASH SCENIC BYWAY, State Hwy. 279 north of Moab

PROVO CANYON SCENIC BYWAY, U.S. 189 from Provo to Heber

SQUAW FLATS SCENIC BYWAY, State Hwy. 211 north of Monticello

TRAIL OF THE ANCIENTS SCENIC BYWAY, State Hwy. 95

ZION PARK SCENIC BYWAY, State Hwy. 9 from I-15 to Mt. Carmel Junction through Zion National Park

For more information on Utah's Byways and Backways, contact the Utah Travel Council at (801) 538-1030 or (800) 200-1160.

The ferry on the banks of the Colorado River at Hite Crossing is now silent below the depths of Lake Powell – William Barclay

THE LAST FRONTIER OF LONELINESS

BY BARRY SCHOLL

With old photographic images of Hite Crossing on the Colorado River imprinted on my mind, I stood high above the mineral-stained sandstone and watched water-skiers skim across the foamy surface of Lake Powell. It was August 1992, and the reservoir was nearing a record low after a series of very dry winters. From my vantage point, I saw skeletal cottonwood branches, discarded beer cans, and rotten tires scattered across the exposed mud banks. Somewhere to the west, still hundreds of feet underwater even in a drought year, lay the remains of my great-uncle's dreams—his former farm on the banks of the river at Hite Crossing.

The Hite we know today is very different from the Hite of 100 or even 50 years ago. On September 18, 1883, a prospector named Cass Hite followed old Indian trails down White Canyon and found a river ford he later dubbed Dandy Crossing. It was one of the few sites between Moab and Lee's Ferry—a distance of more than 200 miles—where livestock and wagons could safely navigate the often cantankerous Colorado River.

Dandy Crossing was soon called Hite in honor of the area's sole inhabitant. It became the site of a minor mining boom when Cass Hite discovered gold in the sandbars of the river. A quick study, Hite took a look at the underequipped miners and began work on a mercantile to outfit prospectors. I've often wondered what kinds of goods he carried and how much he charged without the moderating effects of competition. There was also a post office, which received mail by horseback more than 100 miles from Green River.

By some estimates, as many as 1,000 small-time miners struggled in the early years of the 20th century to extract the fine "flour" gold from the river's sands. But by the 'teens, most miners realized that their equipment was inadequate and gave up. Cass Hite himself died in 1914 and the place soon reverted back to its formerly quiet state.

Until the 1940s, Hite was one of the most isolated places in the United States—70 miles from the nearest community and 120 miles from the nearest railroad. The closest downstream neighbor was 162 miles away at Lee's Ferry.

In 1933 my Great-Uncle Arthur bought the property and began building a ranch. Gold prices were on the rise, the nation was stuck in the trough of the Great Depression, and Uncle Arthur, who had grown up in a family of freighters and spent most of his life in the canyons of the Colorado, was struck with what must have seemed a crazy notion: In addition to mining, he wanted to "open up" this end-of-the-road site on the Colorado River to tourism.

The few travelers who ventured to Arthur's ranch in those years described it as an "oasis in the desert." He grew wine grapes, peaches, watermelons, figs, pears, almonds, peanuts, pomegranates, and dates. Because it was located at a relatively low altitude (3,300 feet) and sheltered by cliffs, Hite enjoyed a nine-month growing season, something unheard of in that part of southern Utah.

When he wasn't busy tending his crops, Arthur Chaffin dreamed of devising a way of spanning the Colorado River. In the mid-1940s he managed to convince state officials that what Utah needed was a passable route down North Wash and across the Colorado, an area that had been closed off previously because of its ruggedness. Chaffin pointed out that a ferry across the river would allow access to the remote wonders of Natural Bridges National Monument, the fabled scenery of Monument Valley, and the isolated communities of far southeastern Utah. His chief ally, Ora Bundy of the Utah Department of Publicity and Industrial Development, allocated the initial $10,000 that would go toward constructing the route known today as Utah State Highway 95.

Still, skepticism abounded. (The 1941 edition of this book, for instance, devoted a single, somewhat dismissive paragraph to Hite and its lone inhabitant, Arthur Chaffin.) However, Uncle Arthur was undeterred. He operated the heavy machinery to build the road down North Wash, and, in his spare time, cobbled together a ferry boat from the engine and chassis of a 1928 Model A Ford, bits of old mining machinery, and a wooden platform. A steel cable bolted to the cliff walls served as a guideline and towed the contraption back and forth across the river.

On September 17, 1946, more than 400 people rattled over washboard roads to witness the official dedication of the Hite Ferry. For the next 10 years, it shuttled hundreds of people across the river, including, among others, author Edward Abbey, cartoonist Dick Sprang , and river runner Harry Aleson.

At the ferry's dedication, Arthur Crawford of the state Commission of Publicity and Industrial Development remarked, "Utah with its rich lore of pioneer background is at last emerging from what President Roosevelt called the 'horse and buggy days,' to claim its share of tourists and of world travelers who seek out the lands of legend and of story—the quiet beauty spots of the world—the last frontiers of loneliness."

Arthur Chaffin sold the ferry in 1956, ten years after those words were spoken. Two factors led to his decision. First, he was beginning to hunger for a new kind of adventure. Second, he was profoundly troubled by the Bureau of Reclamation's plans to construct a giant reservoir on "his" river, the place where he had grown up and watched some dreams wither and die and others reach fruition. Naysayers had warned him that tropical fruits would never grow at Hite; critics at the state capital had ridiculed his plans to attract tourists into the remote canyon country. Undeterred, Arthur Chaffin had proven them wrong both times. But in this instance, he was battling a growing postwar population and a government agency bent on "watering the West." The Hite Ferry made its last official run on June 5, 1964. Today, when the reservoir is at maximum level, the ferry site is 255 feet underwater.

Driving along Highway 95 en route to the Glen Canyon National Recreation Area, it's possible to stop at an overlook and gaze downward—as I did that day in 1992—at the luxurious houseboats and runabouts bobbing on the jeweled surface of the waters, at the kids struggling to stay upright on jet skis, at the people sprawled out on beach towels sunning themselves on the red sand beaches. Today, Lake Powell is one of the premier tourist sites in the Southwest, attracting more than three million visitors annually. It's hard to deny the beauty of the setting. I once spent an afternoon drinking ice tea in a restaurant at Bullfrog Marina while looking out over a sparkling blue bay circled by towering pumpkin- and salmon-colored cliffs. I could almost forget the old photos imprinted in my memory.

But not quite. Given my family history, I can't help but recall what was lost—a living place, now drowned and covered with a layer of Colorado River silt. Even a mention of the locations of the river—all of them now inundated—inspires an almost overwhelming sense of loss: Twilight Canyon, Wild Horse Bar, Last Chance Canyon, Cathedral in the Desert, Music Temple, Mystery Canyon, Chaffin Bar, Ticaboo, and Tracheyte Creek, among many others.

Only half a century ago, a state official speaking at the Hite Ferry dedication lauded the fact that the lands of "legend and story" were at last accessible to visitors. Today, a network of roads have opened up the "last frontier of loneliness" to an extent unimaginable in 1946. We have gained much in comfort and safety.

But I can't help wondering just what has been surrendered in the process.

City of Salt Lake – Tom Olson

Chapter
3

Bright Lights: Utah's Urban Corridor

– Davis, Salt Lake, Morgan, Summit, Wasatch, Weber, and Utah Counties –

Utah's urban corridor extends down the west side of the Wasatch Mountains from Ogden in the north to Payson at the south end. It was along this relatively narrow stretch of land that Utah's early pioneers first settled because of the fertile soil washed down from the mountains, the temperate climate, and the fresh water available for irrigating their crops. Interstate 15 roughly follows the trails of early explorers, from Dominguez and Father Escalante to Jedediah Smith and those Forty-niners who chose the alternate route to California instead of the harsher one over the Sierras. It is now the major north-south route from the intermountain region to Las Vegas and Los Angeles, and has encouraged the growth of commerce and industry along its path through Utah.

The Salt Lake Mormon temple was completed in 1892 – courtesy USHS

"It has such a comfortable, old-clothes feel that it is a shock to see again how beautiful this town really is . . . how it lies under a bright clarity of light and how its outlines are clean and spacious, how it lies protected behind its rampart mountains, insulated from the stormy physical and intellectual weather of both coasts. Serenely concerned with itself, it is probably open to criticism as an ostrich city; its serenity may be possible only in a fool's paradise of isolationism and provincialism and smugness. But what is a hometown if it is not a place you feel secure in."

- Wallace Stegner -
"At Home in the Fields of the Lord"
in Sound of Mountain Water

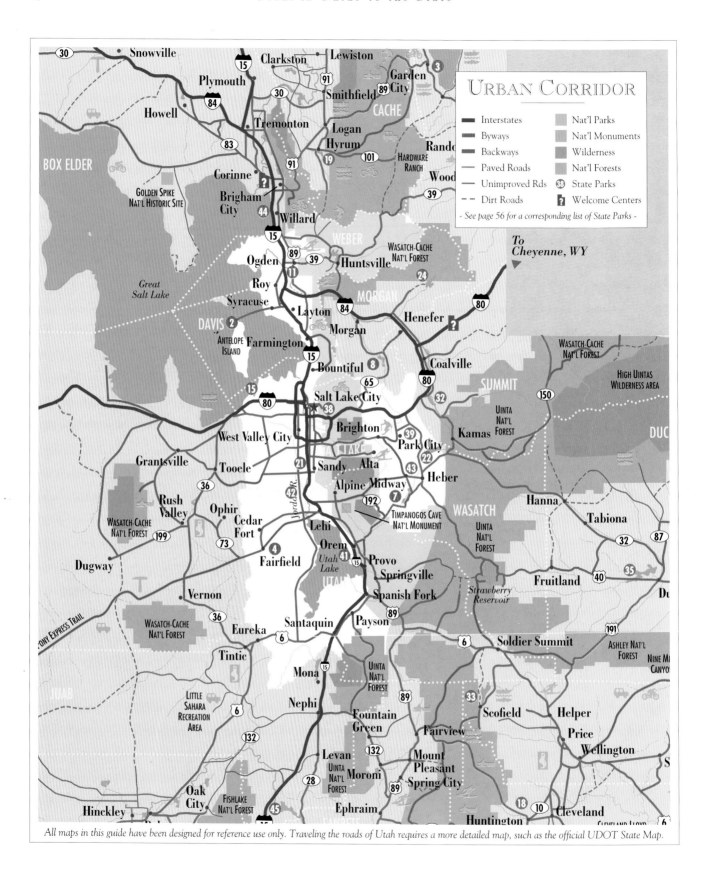

All maps in this guide have been designed for reference use only. Traveling the roads of Utah requires a more detailed map, such as the official UDOT State Map.

Central Corridor: Salt Lake Valley
Natural Setting

Salt Lake City, the capital of Utah, is a metropolis of broad streets. It was the first of many Utah towns laid out by early Mormon settlers foursquare with the compass. In 1940 the city's population was 150,000; in 1994 it was 171,849. These figures, however, reveal little of what has actually happened in the way of population growth in Salt Lake Valley during that period; Salt Lake City proper—a tight enclave with formal boundaries that have changed little in many years—is really only the core of a fast-growing metropolitan area that has more than tripled in population since 1940. Approximately 800,000 people now live in greater Salt Lake County.

When the term Salt Lake City is used today, it is meant as a reference to the metropolitan area in the same way that the names Los Angeles and New York City are used, in a general rather than specific sense. The Salt Lake City metropolitan area, as considered here, is more or less synonymous with the Salt Lake Valley and Salt Lake County. The county's population was 619,000 in 1980, while more than a million people resided within 50 miles of Salt Lake City's downtown center.

The capital of an arid state, Salt Lake City and its environs present the paradox of a well-watered metropolis. The valley's lawns are well-flowered and well-turfed. Another paradox for a city 700 miles inland is the sight of seagulls flying overhead or anxiously awaiting handouts in public parks.

Visitors are usually taken to the tops of high buildings or along the bench drives for a panoramic view of the valley. Sloping down from the foothills toward the lowest-lying center of the great valley where the Jordan River flows, the city and its suburbs spread across the benches and valley floor. To the north are the state capitol, the central business district, and the LDS Church complex. State Street divides the populated area in a nearly straight line from the capitol to Draper, nearly 20 miles away. Commercial and industrial clusters and scattered residential areas add an urban accent to the outlying semi-pastoral fringes, finally thinning at the southwestern and western outskirts. On the east stretches the majestic Wasatch Range, its heights rising to the 11,000-plus feet of the Cottonwood peaks, blocking the horizon 20 miles to the south. Westward, in a north-south tangent, the Oquirrh Range stabs the sky. To the west, across the valley's flat bottom, are mushrooming industrial centers, the runways of the International Airport, and the waters of the Great Salt Lake, hidden from full view by the obstructing slopes of Antelope Island.

Temple Square is the undisputed hub of tourist activities—it hosts several million visitors each year and the streets around it are lined with cars bearing out-of-state plates. Temple Square is the site of the city's oldest scheduled mass gatherings—the spring and fall conferences of the LDS, or Mormon, Church—when downtown accommodations are crowded. Downtown traffic jams are common then, as they are after a symphony performance or a popular event at the Delta Center.

Historical Background

The history of Salt Lake City is almost inseparable from that of Utah. The city was the capital, in turn, of the State of Deseret, Territory of Utah, and State of Utah, except for a period of several years during the 1850s. The major part of the city's story is that of the state. The following excerpts below are from the 1941 edition of this publication, with slight modification:

BRIGHAM YOUNG . . . WAS NOT LOOKING FOR A LAND FLOWING WITH MILK AND HONEY. WHEN SAM BRANNAN URGED HIM TO GO ON TO CALIFORNIA, THE CHURCH LEADER IS REPORTED TO HAVE SAID, "BRANNAN, IF THERE IS A PLACE ON THIS EARTH THAT NOBODY ELSE WANTS, THAT'S THE PLACE I AM HUNTING FOR." IN THE EYES OF SOME OF HIS FOLLOWERS, HE HAD FOUND IT. TO GEORGE WASHINGTON BRIMHALL AND TO GILBERT BELNAP, BOTH OF WHOM CAME IN 1850, THE VALLEY SEEMED . . . A VAST DESERT WHOSE DRY AND PARCHED SOIL SEEMED TO BID DEFIANCE TO THE HUSBANDMAN.

The day they arrived in the valley, on July 23, 1847, the vanguard of the pioneers began to plow, "and the same afternoon built a dam to irrigate the soil." The following day Brigham Young came behind the main body of the pioneers: 143 men, 3 women, 2 children, 70 wagons, 1 boat, 1 cannon, 93 horses, 52 mules, 66 oxen, and 19 cows.

Four days after their arrival, according to Wilford Woodruff's journal, Young called a council of the Quorum of the Twelve, and they "walked from the north camp to about the centre between the two creeks, when President Young waved his hand and said: 'Here is the forty acres for the Temple. The city can be laid out perfectly square . . .'" The quorum then decided that the blocks would contain 10 acres each, the streets would be 132 feet wide, and the sidewalks 20 feet across. The following Sunday the first bowery was built in Temple Square, and the next day Orson Pratt "commenced laying out the city, beginning with the Temple block."

By the time Captain Howard Stansbury came to the Great Basin to survey the Great Salt Lake in 1849, he found that "a city has been laid out upon a magnificent scale, being nearly four miles in length and three in breadth. . . . Through the city itself flows an unfailing stream of pure, sweet water, which by an ingenious mode of irrigation, is made to traverse each side of every street spreading life, verdure and beauty over what was heretofore a barren waste."

Brigham Young, with characteristic energy and leadership, authorized construction of a wall around the city and around the Temple. The temple foundation was started in 1853, and there was almost constant activity within Temple Square in succeeding years. Meanwhile, the California gold rush brought emigrants through Great Salt Lake City, and though the Mormons for the most part kept strictly to agriculture, trade with emigrants brought them a measure of prosperity.

During the so-called Utah War of 1857–58, when the United States government declared "a state of substantial rebellion" in Utah, the people of Great Salt Lake City joined a general movement southward. When the troops came through the city that summer day in 1858, as recorded by an army correspondent, "the utter silence of the streets was broken only by the music of the military bands, the monotonous tramp of the regiments, and the rattle of baggage wagons." George "Beefsteak" Harrison, a cook with Johnston's army, said that "Salt Lake was still as a cemetery when they marched in. He saw only two people, a man riding a sorrel mule and an old lady who peeped out of a window blind at the troops."

Great Salt Lake City became a Pony Express post in 1860 when the first riders came in from Sacramento and St. Joseph. Upon completion of the Pacific Telegraph line to Great Salt Lake City in 1861, Brigham Young sent the first eastbound message. The Nevada-California Volunteers, under the leadership of Colonel P. E. Connor, marched through the city in 1862, surprised to find women and children out to greet them; they had heard rumors of rebellion in Utah.

The 1870s and early 1880s were railroad years, in the course of which Salt Lake City (the "Great" was dropped in 1868) was connected by rail to cities in each of the four cardinal directions.

Meanwhile, the Salt Lake Theater was opened in 1862 and took its place as the leading theatrical center of the Inter-mountain West. The Salt Lake Tabernacle was sufficiently completed to house the annual conference of the Mormon Church in 1867. Musical history was made in 1875, when Handel's *Messiah* was presented in the Salt Lake Theater. At the same time, construction progressed on the Salt Lake Temple, its granite walls gradually rising in tier after tier, and Temple Square was a scene of constant industry.

The death of Brigham Young in 1877 was a shocking event that drew 25,000 people to view the body of the great church leader as it lay in state in the flower-decked Tabernacle. Music played on the Tabernacle organ included "Brigham Young's Funeral March," composed for the occasion by Joseph J. Daynes. The funeral address by Daniel H. Wells probably occupied less than a minute. "I have no desire or wish to multiply words," he said, "feeling that it is rather a time to mourn. Goodbye, Brother Brigham, until the morning of the resurrection day . . ."

Young's death occurred just as political battles, initiated in 1870 by the formation of a non-Mormon Liberal Party, took on greater heat. For all their strenuous efforts, however, the liberals could not carry the city until 1890, when the "manifesto" disavowing polygamy in the church ended the warfare in the city and territory over that issue.

Construction on the temple had been slow up to 1873, when a branch railroad line was run into Little Cottonwood Canyon to facilitate the moving of granite blocks. After that, the pace accelerated, and the capstone was placed at the time of the annual church conference in 1892. Andrew Jenson, assistant church historian, writing in the *Utah Magazine* for September 1936, relates that "over 40,000 people gathered within the confines of Temple Block, while other thousands, unable to find a place in the great square stood in the street or looked down from roofs or windows of adjoining buildings. This was the largest assembly of people ever known in Utah up to that time." Pending completion of the interior, work was delayed until the following year.

In the closing decades of the 19th century and the early decades of the 20th, Salt Lake City began to assume the familiar physical characteristics it was to retain, relatively unchanged, until the years following World War II. Streets were paved, electric trolleys were installed, the capitol was built, and many new business buildings were erected, including a number of high-rise structures. Until 1928 streetcars

Temple Square is the symbolic heart
of worldwide Mormonism
and is the most-visited site in Utah
— Tom Till, UTC

served the city's transportation needs; in that year the first trolleybus was installed. During the 1930s streetcars were gradually replaced by gasoline and trolleybuses, and the last streetcar line was put out of service in 1941.

The decades since 1940 have altered the face of Salt Lake City and its surrounding communities. Even the giant mountains that overlook the valley are hardly the same; they cannot be seen clearly on many days of the year because of inversions, and because of creeping development in the canyons and high on the mountain slopes. Although the population of the city proper has not changed considerably since 1940, that of the county has more than quadrupled; in 1994 the population of Salt Lake County was 806,000.

In 1940 Salt Lake City was a quiet, almost sleepy provincial capital, still in the throes of the Great Depression. Many of its landmark buildings have been remodeled or replaced since then. Evidence of the pioneer past is now visible in a few antique buildings, monuments, murals, and museum exhibits. Even the great Salt Lake Temple, once a dominant feature of the city's skyline, is overshadowed by taller structures. The state capitol—built high on a bench where it was meant to be an inspiration from every vantage point—has been surrounded by high-rise apartment buildings, office complexes, a residential subdivision, and restored historic structures moved from their original sites. Main, State, and other streets in the central business district have been redesigned with new sidewalks, planter boxes, trees, crosswalks, and lighting fixtures—not to mention the removal of overhead signs, the addition of many new buildings, the renovation of others, and the closing of several streets. Not of minor significance is the development of the interstate highway system. Residential areas have replaced farmlands in much of the valley, extending southward and west across the Jordan River as the eastern benchlands and foothills approach the saturation point of building. State Street, which formerly included numerous homes south of the central business district, has become an unbroken commercial strip extending for ten miles or more through Salt Lake City, South Salt Lake, and Murray, to Midvale and beyond. Main Street, while not as long, has undergone a similar metamorphosis. Whereas in the years before 1960, State Street was the principal north-south thoroughfare in the valley, I-15 and I-215 now carry a volume of north-south traffic that would have been inconceivable to most people in earlier days. Interstate 80 has replaced 2100 South and other east-west routes as the carrier of volume traffic in those directions.

Large industrial parks and square miles of commercial developments have sprouted across the valley, and automobile emissions combined with other pollutants and atmospheric inversions make the valley's air unfit for health at times. However, today's Salt Lake Valley, while it has lost much of the distinctive historic, cultural, and architectural flavor of 1940, is in many respects a richer and more exciting place to live. It has certainly become much more cosmopolitan. Recreational possibilities and cultural opportunities are much greater than they were in 1940. For years the economic climate has ranked as one of the best among metropolitan areas, and the valley's population growth is one of the nation's highest. Utah's young people have no reason to feel nostalgia for pioneer adobe and logs, Victorian architecture, or a slower pace of life. Even polluted air means less to them than to their elders because they have grown up with it.

For better or worse, the Salt Lake Valley has joined the urban American mainstream. What the valley will be in another 20 years is hard to imagine, but it is likely to be as different from the valley of today as today's valley is different from that of 1940.

Salt Lake City Proper

The incorporated area of Salt Lake City proper follows an irregular outline and totals about 50 square miles. The Salt Lake Valley is about 20 miles long (north to south) and slightly less from west to east. A system of freeways, boulevards, and other roads gives convenient access to all parts of the valley, though traffic congestion is a problem here as in other large urban areas.

Most visitors content themselves with touring Temple Square and nearby attractions, as well as the Utah state capitol less than half a mile away. But by limiting oneself in this way, one is missing out on literally hundreds of diverse attractions across the valley. In the following pages, these sites have been grouped in distinct areas or districts according to location, an organization that assures the least amount of travel required to visit them. Maps, brochures, and visitor information are available at motels, hotels, the airport, the Salt Palace Convention Center (Salt Lake Visitors Bureau), Utah

Travel Council (300 North and State, across the street from the state capitol), and in the lobby of the state capitol, as well as many other information centers.

LDS Church Complex

The Mormon Church complex includes Temple Square, the church administration block adjoining Temple Square on the east, and several points of interest nearby.

- Temple Square -

Temple Square is considered the symbolic heart of world-wide Mormonism and is the most-visited site in Utah, drawing nearly four million visitors a year. The square is a 10-acre city block dating from the 1850s, dominated by the six-spired temple of The Church of Jesus Christ of Latter-day Saints on the east side and the turtle-backed Tabernacle on the west. The Assembly Hall, two visitor centers, and several monuments present a cross section of LDS religious architecture, history, and beliefs. More than 1,000 employees and volunteers act as guides for those who annually visit the square. Tours and organ recitals are conducted frequently.

Visitor centers at the north and south gates are designed to interpret Mormon theological beliefs and church history for Temple Square's millions of visitors. Both centers are equipped with informational and interpretive displays as well as auditoriums in which films are shown.

Seagull Monument, east of the Assembly Hall and surrounded by a granite-rimmed pool, was erected in 1913 as a memorial to the gulls for saving crops of the pioneers during the cricket invasion of 1848.

Assembly Hall, a granite, semi-Gothic building located in the southwest corner of the square, dates from 1877–82, when it was built as a meeting place for the Salt Lake Stake. The hall, which seats about 2,000, serves a wide variety of functions from religious gatherings to musical concerts to funerals.

The Salt Lake Temple, open only to LDS Church members in good standing, is a six-spired gray-granite edifice representing more the inspiration and theological functionalism of its founders than any one architectural style. The building is 186-1/2 feet long and 118 feet wide, with walls 167-1/2 feet high. The east center tower rises 210 feet, capped by the shining, trumpet-bearing statue of the angel Moroni. The 12.5-foot-high statue of hammered copper covered with gold

leaf is anchored by a pendulous iron rod, extending into the spire beneath where it is heavily weighted, allowing movement of the figure in high winds.

The building is used exclusively by members of the church for such religious rites as baptisms for the dead, sealing ceremonies, and for marriages.

The plan for the Salt Lake Temple was conceived by Brigham Young, and the details were worked out by church architect Truman O. Angell. Ground was broken in 1853 and the first cornerstone was laid that year. Some of the great stones were hauled, one at a time, by four-yoke ox teams from Little Cottonwood Canyon, 20 miles south. After the arrival of the railroad, a spur was built into the canyon in 1873. The walls of the temple were 20 feet high when Brigham Young died in 1877. Construction was completed and the temple dedicated in 1893, 40 years to a day after it was begun.

For a short time following the dedication, the public was allowed inside, but the building was soon closed to all except church members. Several readily available books describe and illustrate the temple's interior and its religious functions. Inquire at Sam Weller's Zion's Bookstore, one of the area's best-stocked sources of literature on the area and its history.

The Salt Lake Tabernacle is open for public functions, organ recitals (daily from noon to 12:30 P.M. and from 2–2:30 P.M. on Sundays), or when accompanied by a guide. It is a mammoth (250 foot by 150 foot) oval auditorium seating about 8,000. Unique and severe in design, it is a pioneer among structures employing the self-supported, vaulted type of roof that was designed as an ellipsoid with a focal point at either end; this, together with the unbroken inner ceiling surface, accounts for the unusual acoustics of the building. When the building is quiet, a pin dropped at either focal point can be heard at the opposite end, more than 200 feet away. Forty-four gray-painted buttresses of red sandstone mark the circumference of the building. Upon them rest giant wooden arches, 10 feet thick, making a span of 150 feet, 80 feet high at the center.

The great pipe organ at the west end of the Tabernacle was first constructed in 1867 with 700 pipes; since then it has been modified and greatly enlarged. The 51 facade pipes are reputedly the only round wooden organ pipes in the world. They were made from specially selected white pine found in southern Utah. Today's organ includes 11,000 pipes of all sizes, shapes, and configurations, ranging from 3/8 inch to 32 feet in length. The organ may be heard at Mormon Tabernacle Choir rehearsals on Thursday at 8 P.M.; during the CBS radio/TV choir and organ broadcast on Sunday mornings; and during certain religious services and musical events. Spring and fall conferences of the LDS Church are held in this auditorium, and it has been the scene of many civic and patriotic gatherings, including the appearances of U.S. presidents and other dignitaries.

- Temple Square Environs -

The Museum of Church History and Art, 45 North West Temple, is devoted to "telling the history of the Latter-day Saint people." Featured are items relating to the martyrdom of Joseph and Hyrum Smith; the oldest house in Salt Lake City, built by Osmyn Deuel in 1847; an original handcart; church-related objects from other countries; arts, crafts, photos, paintings; Indian antiquities; and artifacts connected with prominent church leaders.

The Family History Library, more commonly known as the church genealogical library, is located just south of the Musuem of Church History and Art. Its vast collections of vital and biographical records from around the world are the most comprehensive to be found. For decades the church has been engaged in a systematic global program of microfilming documents, books, and records for genealogical research, resulting in some million rolls of microfilm—the equivalent of nearly five million printed volumes of 300 pages each. These microfilms, as well as more than 170,000 printed volumes, more than six million family record sheets, and tens of millions of individual index cards, are available for public use. To assist researchers, the library offers orientation classes, booklets, and classes. It is open to the public six days a week. However, beginners are often advised to start at the Joseph Smith Memorial Building in its Family Search program.

The phenomenal interest of Mormons in genealogical research is a result of church belief in continuing family relationships after mortal death. These relationships involve not only those of husband and wife, parents and children, but of ancestors, descendants, and relatives of every degree. Mormon doctrine teaches that individual salvation in the fullest sense requires an acceptance of the gospel of Jesus Christ, if not in mortality then in afterlife.

The Brigham Young Monument, located north of the inter-section of Main and South Temple Streets, is a heroic bronze figure of the church leader on a granite base. The 25-foot monument was unveiled during the Utah Jubilee in 1897.

- Church Administration Block -

The Joseph Smith Memorial Building, located on the northeast corner of Main and South Temple Streets, was known as the Hotel Utah until 1987, when it was closed for renovation. The original building, erected in 1911, was renowned for its high-quality accommodations. (Incidentally, the Hotel Utah figured prominently in Wallace Stegner's novel *Recapitulation*.) Today, the Joseph Smith Memorial Building houses meeting and reception rooms, a theater, a chapel, a visitor center, and Family Search genealogical computer programs that are geared toward those who are just beginning to research their ancestors. In addition, a rooftop garden restaurant affords a non-pareil view of Temple Square and the Salt Lake Valley.

The Church Administration Building, 47 East South Temple, was completed in 1917; this building houses the offices of LDS Church leaders. The lobby displays walls and stairway of polished marble.

The Lion House, 63 East South Temple, is a two-story, cement-covered adobe structure with small-paned windows, shutters, tall chimneys, and a tile roof. The Lion House was home to many of Brigham Young's 26 wives and most of his children. It is open for lunch weekdays from 11 A.M. to 2 P.M. and caters receptions by appointment.

Brigham Young's Office, 67 East South Temple, is a small adobe structure connecting the Lion and Beehive Houses, serving today as a visitor reception area for the Beehive House. Built in 1852, it has a one-story portico surmounted by iron grillwork and small-paned windows.

The Beehive House, located at the corner of South Temple and State Streets, is the restored residence of Brigham Young. Built in 1853–54, it is one of the oldest residences still standing in Utah, and is certainly the most elaborate building of its time in the state. Truman O. Angell, church architect and designer of the Mormon temple in Salt Lake City, was its architect. The Beehive House is open to the public for guided tours from 9:30–4:30 P.M. daily and from 10 A.M.–1 P.M. on Sundays.

There is much of interest in the house: Brigham Young's office and bedroom, a 19th-century kitchen, a store from which his families were supplied, a gracious sitting room, a grand parlor known as the Long Room, a formal dining room, many bedrooms, children's playroom, the family dining room, and a pantry.

The Eagle Gate, spanning North State Street at South Temple Street, marks the former entrance to the private property of Brigham Young. The present gate, bearing little resemblance to its predecessors, was dedicated in November 1963 as a more functional replacement for an older, narrower gate. Its copper eagle, patterned after the original model, is much larger, weighing two tons and boasting a wingspread of 20 feet.

The Church Office Building, 50 East North Temple, is among the valley's tallest buildings (28 floors above ground, 3 levels below). Built over a three-year period between 1969 and 1972, the massive white structure houses nearly all auxiliary and departmental organizations of the LDS Church. The central tower is flanked by two four-story wings. On the 26th floor is an observation deck, which offers a spectacular circle view of the city, valley, and mountains.

Capitol Hill District

Capitol Hill extends from North Temple on the south to Ensign Peak on the north, and from 2nd (200) West to City Creek Canyon (Memory Grove). The district incorporates not only the capitol complex of state buildings but architectural examples ranging from quaint pioneer-era houses in the Marmalade District—which clings to the steep slopes west of the capitol—through a spectrum of styles representing every period from Victorian to contemporary modern. In recent years, the character of the hill has been altered by the erection of high-rise apartments and the demolition of older buildings. The pace of change has been slowed by its classification as a Historic District and listing on the National Register of Historic Places.

North Main Street

The McCune Mansion, 200 North Main, is one of the stateliest of Utah's turn-of-the-century homes. Now occupied by private offices, the tile-roofed and towered mansion was built as a residence for Alfred W. and Elizabeth McCune.

The Pioneer Memorial Museum and Carriage House, 300 North Main immediately west of the State Capitol, is maintained by the Daughters of the Utah Pioneers (DUP). The museum's historical collections, numbering thousands of items on four floors, feature relics, artifacts, and craftwork from the early days of Utah, including displays of furnishings, furniture, clothing, and artifacts involving 19th-century transportation, industry, Native Americans, religious and military life, etc. Utah's largest doll exhibit is a special attraction. A two-story carriage house displays antique wagons, coaches, buggies, and a streetcar, among other vehicles.

The Marmalade District, so-called because of the names of some of its streets (Apricot, Quince, etc.), is an area of older homes huddled on the steep hillside west of the state capitol. Many homes in the district were built in the 19th century. A number of the area's older homes have been restored. The Thomas Quayle House, 355 Quince Street, is a wood-frame structure dating back to the 1880s that originally stood on West 400 South. The house was moved to its present location in 1975 and restored to serve as headquarters of the Utah Heritage Foundation. The John Platts House, 364 Quince Street, is a modified cobblestone structure dating from the late 1850s.

State Capitol South

The Council Hall, State and 300 North, across from the state capitol (free admission; travel information), is a reconstruction of the historic building that served for 30 years as the Salt Lake City Hall and an early meeting place for the territorial legislature. The present structure was moved from the original site at 120 East 100 South, where the Federal Building now stands. Today, the building serves as the office of the Utah Travel Council.

White Community Memorial Chapel, across 300 North from the state capitol, just east of Council Hall, is a replica-reconstruction of a distinctive 19th-century Mormon chapel. In general design it represents the old 18th Ward chapel, originally built in 1881 at 2nd Avenue and A Street and dismantled in 1973. The original chapel's steeple and window were utilized in the reconstruction, which began in 1979. The chapel is used for civic and religious purposes; it also houses the Honors Library of Living History.

State Capitol Grounds

The Utah State Capitol overlooks the valley from the north end of State Street. It is a classically styled four-story structure built on the lines of the U.S. Capitol, and occupies a bench of the Wasatch foothills at the northern rim of the city, its magisterial air emphasized by its elevation 300 feet above the valley floor. The capitol was designed by Salt Lake architect Richard K. A. Kletting. Following the structural precedent of two wings, one for each branch of a bicameral legislature, it departs from the precedent by placing the House of Representatives in the west wing, the senate in the north center, and the state supreme court in the east wing. Built of Utah granite, it is 404 feet long, 240 feet wide, and 285 feet high at the tip of the dome, which is covered with Utah copper. The south facade is broken only at the center by the customary monumental entrance leading up to a well-proportioned Corinthian portico.

Construction on the capitol began in 1912, when $1,500,000 had been collected from inheritance taxes. The cornerstone was laid by Governor William Spry in 1914, and the edifice was completed the following year at a cost of $2,739,528.54.

In the pendentives, or arched triangles, leading up to the dome are four murals depicting phases in Utah's early history—the trek of the Dominguez-Escalante expedition in l776; Peter Skene Ogden, Hudson's Bay Company trader; John C. Fremont at the Great Salt Lake; and Brigham Young with an ox-drawn covered wagon.

The Gold Room (opened for display by guide), located southwest of the main hall, is the state reception room in which presidents and royal visitors have been received. It is a long rectangular room with a vaulted ceiling, liberally decorated with yellow metal. The capitol also features a fine collection of historical memorabilia in the basement.

– Memory Grove –

Memory Grove is a secluded, beautifully landscaped park on both sides of Canyon Road in City Creek Canyon, below the state capitol. It is dedicated to Utah soldiers who lost their lives in America's wars, and contains a number of monuments. The tree-lined road up the canyon above Memory Grove is popular with bicyclists, joggers, and hikers. Enter from Canyon Road, which forks north from 2nd Avenue one-half block east of State and North Temple.

Central District

With a few exceptions, the important attractions in this district are concentrated within a mile of Temple Square; walking is the best way to tour this district, perhaps with occasional vehicle assistance. For tour purposes, the district extends from 400 West to 1300 East and from the north

foothills to 1700 South.

The Central District was the first part of the valley to be settled. It has long been the financial core of Utah, containing the tallest buildings, the largest concentration of retail stores, and the main offices of the largest banks. The district is the site of the Salt Lake Art Center, the Salt Palace, Gallivan Center, theaters, hotels and restaurants.

– Central District Downtown –

This area includes State, Main, West Temple, and South Temple Streets.

The Hansen Planetarium, 15 South State, features an auditorium or star chamber, Space Science Library, Space Museum, black-light mineral display, etc. For many years the building in which it is located was occupied by the city's main library. Currently, the planetarium offers star shows, laser shows, and live plays. The Hansen Planetarium began operating in 1965.

The Federal Office Building, corner of 100 South and State Street, an eight-story edifice with white facade, was completed in 1964.

The Promised Valley Playhouse, 132 South State, owned by the LDS Church, specialized in church-theme and popular stage entertainment. First opened in 1905 as a vaudeville theater, it passed from vaudeville through the golden age of cinema as a movie palace. At press time, the theater was no longer operating and its future was uncertain.

The Salt Lake City and County Building occupies a city block, known as Washington Square, between 400 and 500 South, State and 200 East. Modeled after the London City Hall and completed in 1894, the many-turreted castle displays ornate Romanesque Revival features. Exterior restoration during the late 1970s and early 1980s required a spectacular maze of high scaffolding.

Buildings on the block to the east of Washington Square are occupied by city/county courts and jail, city police, and the Salt Lake City Public Library.

The most imposing structures on Main Street are the massive ZCMI and Crossroads shopping malls on either side of Main Street between South Temple and 100 South. The 17-story Kennecott Building, dating from the mid-1960s, is one of the first of the city's modern skyscrapers. It occupies the corner across South Temple from the Joseph Smith Memorial Building. A walking tour along Main Street reveals a melange of architectural styles dating from the 1890s or earlier. Some

Architectural styles dating from the 1890s along Salt Lake City's Main Street are being replaced by contemporary glass-and-steel structures – Steve Greenwood, UTC

of the older buildings still display their original facades, others have since received face-lifts and bear little outside resemblance to their former incarnations as historical structures.

The ZCMI Center incorporates approximately 60 shops as well as the ZCMI department store. It is topped by a 27-story office building known as the Beneficial Life Tower, and includes a 2,000-car parking garage.

Crossroads Plaza, across Main Street from the ZCMI Center, is one of Utah's largest shopping malls and features a facade extending more than 400 feet. The center's retail area offers a food court, small retailers, and major department stores.

Exchange Place, between 300 and 400 South, separates the twin Boston and Newhouse buildings, built more than 80 years ago by mining magnate Samuel Newhouse. This is the center of an aging cluster of buildings dating from the first decades of the century. Although south downtown has seen an exodus of shoppers and a number of vacant stores in recent years, the recent completion of the recreational John W. Gallivan Utah Center (36 East 200 South), among other factors, seems to be fomenting new interest in this historically rich area.

The Salt Palace, located on the west side of West Temple Street between 100 and 200 South, is Utah's oldest integrated exhibit and convention complex. In the early 1990s, the Salt Palace underwent a massive renovation designed to help its convention facilities compete with newer centers across the country. Prior to the completion of the Delta Center, the Salt Palace was utilized for concerts, circuses, rodeos, basketball and hockey events, etc.

Abravanel Hall, overlooking an expansive plaza and fountain on the southwest corner of West Temple and South Temple, is renowned both for its remarkable quality of sound and its ornate interior. There are crystal chandeliers, oak ceilings, brass leaf, and gold trim. The illuminated fountain on the plaza was the gift of philanthropist Obert C. Tanner. The hall seats 2,800.

The Salt Lake Art Center, adjoining Abravanel Hall on the south, is a two-level gallery emphasizing the visual arts. Classrooms, an auditorium, studios, and galleries support the center's teaching and creative programs, including the educational efforts of the Utah Media Center.

The Capitol Theater, 46 West 200 South, is the restored edition of one of the city's most popular movie theaters. Originally opened as the Orpheum, it served as a cinema show-case for more than 60 years. After an extensive restoration, the new theater was feted with a grand opening in 1979. The seating is designed for comfort and unobstructed views of the large stage. Of special interest is the great Wurlitzer pipe organ, originally installed in 1927 and carefully restored for use today.

~ Central District West ~

This district extends west from Temple Square and the Salt Palace for about a mile, and south to Franklin Quest Field. For the most part, it is an area of older buildings, a mixture of residential, commercial, and industrial zoning. However, much of the district is in the process of redevelopment; within a few years the zone's character will be dramatically altered by new construction.

The Delta Center, 301 West South Temple, is a 20,600-seat auditorium completed in 1991. In addition to being the home of the Utah Jazz basketball franchise, the Delta Center also hosts other sporting events and concerts.

Pioneer Park, a tree-shaded block between 300 and 400 South, 300 and 400 West, is the site where Mormon settlers built their first fort and living quarters in 1847–48. Various proposals for "higher" use of the park have been offered through the years. Plagued by recurring bad publicity regarding drug trafficking, Pioneer Park will certainly benefit from ongoing redevelopment in the area.

The Denver & Rio Grande Railroad Depot, 300 Rio Grande Street (400 West), forms a massive barricade across the west end of 300 South. After its completion in 1910 the depot served for many years as one of Salt Lake City's principal railroad stations. In 1977 the depot was purchased by the state of Utah for $1.00. Since 1981, the site has housed the Utah State Historical Society.

Other than the building itself, which is listed on the National Register of Historic Places, visitors will find extensive research and archival materials, a state history museum, a bookstore, and the State Historic Preservation and State Antiquities Offices, which include the State Archaeologist and State Paleontologist.

The Union Pacific Depot, facing east, blocks the west end of South Temple at 400 West. The huge waiting room is adorned with painted murals and stained-glass windows depicting historic scenes. The depot is listed on the National Register of Historic Places and is a distinctive element in redevelopment plans for the district.

Mormon Welfare Square (751 West 700 South) offers tours that include the granaries, food processing facilities, and storehouses, along with an explanation of the remarkable church welfare program that has assisted needy members since the Great Depression of the 1930s. Visitors may join tour groups at Temple Square or phone Welfare Square for tour details.

The International Peace Garden in Jordan Park, 1060 South 900 West, might be described as a United Nations in landscaping. Beside the Jordan River, groups of different ethnic and national origin have created gardens representative of their original homelands.

Franklin Quest Field, 1301 South West Temple, is the outdoor playing field of the Salt Lake Buzz of the Pacific Coast League. The field also hosts outdoor festivals and concerts.

- Central District North -

This part of the city extends somewhat indefinitely to the north of Temple Square and west of Capitol Hill.

The Children's Museum of Utah, 840 North 300 West, is located in the former home of Wasatch Springs Municipal Baths. Exhibits allow young visitors to experience jet-piloting, excavating a saber-toothed tiger's bones, operating a bank, and broadcasting from their own television station.

The Avenues are made up of a large hillside district extending north of South Temple and east of State Street. The architecture here is very diverse, ranging from 19th century in the lower avenues to ultra-modern mansions on the higher foothills. This is largely a residential district, but the area also contains a few small businesses and several hospitals.

The Avenues Historic District, bounded by 1st and 7th Avenues south to north, Canyon Road-Memory Grove on the west, and Virginia Street to the east, contains more than 2,000 buildings that are at least 50 years old. The historic district is listed on both state and national historic registers.

- Central District East -

For our purposes, Central District (East) is located between State Street and 1300 East, and from South Temple to 1700 South. South Temple Street, forming the south boundary of Temple Square, extends from the Union Pacific Railroad Depot on the west (400 West) to about 1400 East, where it dissolves into the narrow curving streets of the Federal Heights

area. All north and south addresses in the valley are based on South Temple, which serves as the point of division, as Main Street divides east and west.

In many respects, South Temple is the most historic and prestigious street in Utah. It was the residence at one time or another of many of the state's distinguished citizens and businesses. Many of Utah's most impressive mansions of the turn-of-the-century era were located along South Temple or in its immediate vicinity. The majority no longer exist, though a few distinguished examples have been preserved, among them Brigham Young's Lion House and Beehive House, and the Executive (Kearns) Mansion. Other survivors of notable architectural and historical interest include the striking European villa built by Enos A. Wall, wealthy mining magnate, now the home of LDS Business College, 411 East South Temple; the majestic David Keith mansion, 529 East South Temple; and the Glendinning Home, 617 East South Temple, dating from the 1870s and now serving as offices of the Utah Arts Council.

The Cathedral of the Madeleine, 331 East South Temple (corner of South Temple and B Streets) was built in the early 1900s. This is a splendid building, and its ornate twin towers, decorated with gargoyles, are a landmark. Inside the cathedral, pipes of the organ outline a huge circular rose window comprised of individual sections that picture angels playing various musical instruments. This and other richly colored stained-glass windows in the cathedral were done by the House of Zetter, Royal Bavarian Institute, Munich, Germany.

The First Presbyterian Church, 347 East South Temple near the Cathedral of the Madeleine, was completed in 1906. Built of red stone, the distinguished religious edifice displays a striking English Gothic Revival style.

The Executive Mansion (Kearns Mansion), 603 East South Temple, is a palatial three-story building of cream-colored oolitic limestone. The mansion was completed in 1902 at a cost of a quarter of a million dollars. Designed by architect Carl M. Neuhausen, it was built as a family residence for Senator Thomas Kearns, wealthy mining magnate and an owner of the *Salt Lake Tribune*. The mansion originally contained 36 rooms, ten fireplaces, 4-1/2 bathrooms, a bowling alley, and a billiard room. Today, it is the official residence of Utah's governor. Tours are offered weekly.

St. Mark's Episcopal Cathedral, 231 East 100 South, is the

The Cathedral of the Madeleine was built in the early 1900s with stained-glass windows imported from Munich, Germany – François Camoin

oldest non-Mormon cathedral in Utah, dating from 1871. The venerable church resembles the cathedrals of Europe with its transepts, nave, vestibule, cloisters, bell gable, Gothic arches, and stained-glass windows. It is listed on the National Register of Historic Places.

Trolley Square occupies a city block between 600 and 700 East, 500 and 600 South, with the main entrance on 700 East. Trolley Square utilizes a group of rustic brick buildings that originally housed the trolley cars and motor buses of the city's early public transport system. Restoration was begun during the 1960s, and today the site is a popular shopping-entertainment center and a magnet for out-of-state visitors. The square features a variety of restaurants, theaters, and shops in a picturesque "antique" environment of old brick and stone, massive timbers, stained glass, wood and brick walkways.

Liberty Park occupies 110 acres, or the equivalent of eight city blocks and the 600 East right-of-way. It is bounded by 900 and 1300 South, 500 and 700 East. Originally a part of Brigham Young's estate, the grounds were acquired by the city in 1880 and developed over the years with lawns, trees, flower beds, lake, bandstands and picnic facilities, swimming pool, tennis courts, playground, concession area (refreshments, merry-go-round, ferris wheel), aviary, etc. The Tracy Aviary displays several hundred varieties of birds, including many water species. Most of these are on outdoor display in warmer months. The aviary originated as a gift to the city in 1938 by Mr. and Mrs. Russell L. Tracy.

The Isaac Chase Mill is a gable-roofed gray adobe building. According to the 1941 edition of this book, "Chase, who transported the millstones and irons across the plains by ox-team, built the mill in 1852. Free flour from this mill saved many lives in a famine winter of the fifties." Brigham Young became its owner by 1860. Some of the mill's original machinery remains. Under a canopy beside the mill is one of the first log cabins built in Utah, erected in 1847. To the north, adjoining the greenhouse, is the Chase Home Museum of Utah Folk Art, a two-story yellow adobe building erected in 1852.

Westminster College, 1840 South 1300 East, occupies a 27-acre campus organized around the distinctive four-story Converse Hall (1906), which houses administrative offices. The only private liberal arts college in the Intermountain West, Westminster is an "interdenominational, co-educational, four-year, fully accredited liberal arts college."

Westminster was founded in 1875 as the Salt Lake Collegiate Institute, an evangelical school established by the First Presbyterian Church. At the turn of the century the name was changed to Westminster. Westminster became a senior college in 1944.

East Bench

~ University of Utah ~

The University of Utah, the state's largest and oldest public institution of higher learning, sprawls across 1,500 acres of sloping benchland overlooking Salt Lake City and Salt Lake Valley. The University of Utah consists of 230 buildings located between North Campus Drive and 5th South, University Street on the west and the mountains on the east. Enrollment totals more than 27,000 students taught by 3,651 faculty members.

The university offers degrees in 68 undergraduate and 92 graduate subjects, including advanced degrees in medicine and law. A number of its programs are noted for excellence. In addition to its full-time educational program, the university provides adult and continuing education services to thousands of part-time students.

The University of Utah was first established as the University of Deseret by the Provisional State of Deseret in 1850, and the first classes were held that year. It was chartered the following year but classes were suspended from 1851 to 1867 for lack of funds. Reestablished as a commercial academy in 1867, it was reorganized by Dr. John R. Park two years later; classical and scientific curricula were introduced at that time. In 1884 the university was empowered to confer degrees. The name was changed to University of Utah in 1892, and the university settled on the present site in 1900.

The Utah Museum of Natural History, southeast corner of 200 South and University Street (1450 East), illustrates the anthropological, geological, and biological story of Utah and the intermountain region in more than 100 exhibits. Featured are dioramas of animals in their natural environment, illustrated displays on the history of humankind, reconstructions of prehistoric dwellings, and exhibits of fossilized plants and animals, including the mounted skeletons of dinosaurs and other strange creatures. Of special note is the collection of rocks, minerals, and gemstones in the Norton Hall of Minerals. Gift shop. Open seven days a week.

The State Arboretum of Utah consists of more than 8,000 trees dispersed around the campus, representing more than 300 different species and hybrids. The arboretum's largest and oldest cluster is located on the central lawn of the Presidents' Circle and in the vicinity of the Museum of Natural History, the Park Building, and the greenhouse east of the Park Building. A tour guide pamphlet is available at the Arboretum Office one block south of the Huntsman Center in Building 436. In addition, arboretum collections can be viewed at Red Butte Garden east of the university. Red Butte features a stream, waterfall, ponds, and plant collections with explanatory signs.

In addition to these two sites, the University of Utah also features a small but eclectic Museum of Fine Arts that hosts lectures, gallery talks, etc.; Kingsbury Hall, described as "[one of] the state's most versatile and best known culture center[s]"; the Pioneer Theatre Company; the J. Willard Marriott Library; the A. Ray Olpin University Union; the Huntsman Center, a 15,000-seat arena; and the U of U Health Sciences Center. For more information on the University of Utah and its facilities and programming, check at the information desk at the Olpin Union.

- East Bench Attractions -

A short distance from the main campus is the University Research Park, south of Fort Douglas and east of the Veterans Medical Center (accessible from Foothill Boulevard). Situated on 320 university-owned acres, Research Park has 56 tenants and 21 buildings at this time. Many tenants involve students and faculty as consultants or in research, and university-owned equipment for many projects.

Fort Douglas (east on 500 South and South Campus Drive) has been an independent community on the city's outskirts for more than a century. Once controlling an area of many thousands of acres of benchland, canyon, and mountain slopes, the fort has diminished to only a few hundred acres today. However, the historic core of the fort remains fairly intact, surrounded on three sides by the university campus, Research Park, and the Medical Center.

Fort Douglas was established as Camp Douglas in 1862 by California-Nevada volunteers under the command of Colonel Patrick E. Connor. The official purpose for its founding was protection of the overland mail during the Civil War, but federal officials, including Connor, were convinced that the Mormons required surveillance from a strategic post.

In 1991, after periods of use as a training base, a fixed post for regular army troops, a prisoner-of-war camp, and an induction and discharge center, among other uses, Fort Douglas was decommissioned and turned over to the University of Utah. Today's visitors may explore the quiet roads and circles on self-guided tours. Information and maps are available at the Military Museum on the south side of the parade ground. Of special interest is the old Post Cemetery containing the graves of hundreds of soldiers and prisoners of war, including those of the fort's founder, Colonel Connor, and soldiers killed at the Battle of Bear River in 1863.

This Is the Place State Park, 2600 East Sunnyside Avenue (850 South), at the mouth of Emigration Canyon across the road from Hogle Zoological Gardens, features the famed This is the Place Monument, Pioneer Mural, and Old Deseret Village. Occupying more than 500 acres of grassy foothill overlooking the valley, the park is situated in the general area where the first group of Mormon pioneers emerged from the Wasatch Mountains in July 1847 and their leader, Brigham Young, reputedly uttered the immortal words "This is the right place. Drive on."

This is the Place Monument was dedicated on July 24, 1947, to commemorate the arrival of Utah's first permanent settlers a hundred years earlier, as well as the explorers and trailblazers who preceded them. The monument features three bronze groupings. The largest figures, 12 feet high atop the central pylon, depict Mormon leaders Brigham Young, Heber C. Kimball, and Wilford Woodruff. The north pylon features a group of trappers and fur traders, the most noted of that intrepid band of adventurers who preceded the Mormon pioneers by several decades. The south pylon depicts Utah's first European explorers, the Catholic Dominguez-Escalante party who traversed much of Utah in 1776 on an exploring expedition from New Mexico.

Bronze figures and plaques on the monument's west and east fronts commemorate important events and personages of 1847 and prior years.

The Pioneer Mural, located in the visitor center to the monument's north, is a three-wall mural depicting major episodes in the migratory trek of the Mormons from Nauvoo, Illinois, to Salt Lake Valley in 1846 and 1847. Remarkable for color, detail, and craftsmanship, the mural was completed in 1959 by the late Lynn Fausett, a Utah native who gained renown as a muralist and landscape painter.

Old Deseret Village is a "living museum" designed to teach about life in an early Utah community between 1847 and 1869. The village features a number of authentic early-day homes of adobe, log, and frame construction brought from sites around the state. The village currently boasts a social hall, a black-smith shop, the Manti ZCMI Mercantile building, and several reconstructed houses. An ongoing project, Old Deseret Village will eventually represent every facet of pioneer life, with a school, church house, industrial and commercial establishments, etc.

The Hogle Zoo, 2600 Sunnyside Avenue (850 South), occupies about 50 acres at the mouth of Emigration Canyon where it emerges from the Wasatch Mountains, across Sunnyside Avenue from Pioneer Trail State Park. More than a thousand animals are on display, including gorillas, giraffes, bears, cats, elephants, reptiles, deer, rhinoceros, and other animals such as orangutans, monkeys, and chimpanzees. There is also a petting zoo and a miniature railroad for children. In addition, a new butterfly exhibit allows visitors to view specimens flying free in a climate-controlled glass building.

Perhaps the zoo's most famous inhabitant was Shasta the Liger, an unusual animal born in 1948 of a tigress mother and lion father. Shasta lived for 24 years, dying in 1972 at an age equivalent to that of a 120-year-old human.

Salt Lake Valley South

The Wheeler Historic Farm, 6351 South 900 East, is a "working" farm or museum of rural life operated by the Salt Lake County Recreation Department since 1976. The 75-acre farm was formerly a dairy operation in the rural outskirts; today it is surrounded by the city's residential suburbs. Wheeler Farm appeals especially to children, who may participate in or view butter churning, milking, hayrides and wagon rides, farm chores, etc.

The Jordan River Temple (LDS), 10200 South 1300 West in South Jordan, is devoted to the performance of sacred ordinances. Dedicated in 1981 and completed in 1982, the temple was the first to be built in the Salt Lake Valley since the completion of the Salt Lake Temple in 1893. It is one of the largest of all Mormon temples and was financed entirely

with donated funds.

The Utah State Prison, visible from I-15 as the highway ascends Point of the Mountain near Draper, is a complex of gray concrete buildings surrounded by a double row of wire fences. Four guard towers overlook the prison compound, which is brightly illuminated at night.

Camp W. G. Williams Military Reservation straddles the Salt Lake-Utah county line between Jordan Narrows and the foothills of the Oquirrh Mountains. Incorporating an area of more than 50 square miles, the reserve serves as a training base for units of the Utah National Guard.

Salt Lake Valley West

The Utah State Fairgrounds occupy a large expanse between 1000 West and the Jordan River, north of North Temple Street. A cluster of exhibition buildings, arena, stadium, lawns, and gardens, the fairgrounds host not only the annual Utah State Fair in September but special events as well. The first state fair was held at this location in 1902.

The Jordan River, about 1000–1500 West, flows from Utah Lake on the south to the Great Salt Lake on the north, dropping 300 feet from source to outlet in an airline distance of 35 miles. Along the river for six miles north of 2100 South Street, the State Park & Recreation Division has developed a recreational parkway with a picnic area, trails and pathways, canoe docks, etc. Long-range plans include a developed parkway along the entire length of the river.

Seven miles west of downtown is the Salt Lake City International Airport. Served by nine major airlines and three regional carriers, the airport offers more than 500 daily flights. A full range of services, including car rentals, cafeterias, hotel courtesy phones, visitor information, and ski rentals, are available on-site.

The Morton Salt Company operates a large salt-processing complex located south of I-80 (Route 40/North Temple), about five miles west of the International Airport. Morton extracts salt by pumping brine from the lake into a vast series of ponds, where various minerals are precipitated through solar evaporation. Salt is harvested with special machines and trucks, then dried, crushed, screened, and otherwise processed for culinary, industrial, and agricultural use. Salt bearing the Royal Crystal name has been produced here since the 1920s.

Beyond the salt plant, the highway soon curves southwest

along the shore of the Great Salt Lake, America's famed inland sea, one of the world's remarkable inland bodies of water. Along this shore have been located, over a period of 130 years, a number of resorts and marinas, nearly all of them transitory and ill-fated. Only in recent years has the government entered the lake's recreational scene with adequate funds for the provision of fresh water, sewage disposal, insect control, beach development, etc.

West of the South Shore beaches, I-80 continues on to Wendover, Nevada, and California (see Chapter 4).

At the north tip of the Oquirrh Mountains, where that range abuts the lake, Route 201 forks east from I-80. This important highway connects Salt Lake City with the huge concentrators, smelter, and refinery of Utah Copper Division, Kennecott Minerals Company. Looming skyward near the junction is the 1,200-foot stack of the smelter, the tallest man-made structure in Utah. Two miles east of the smelter, on a foothill terrace overlooking the lake, is Utah Copper Division's electrolytic refinery, which was completed in 1950.

In the cove between the refinery and the highway once existed the community of Garfield, which flourished from the early years of the century until the mid-1950s, when its buildings were sold and removed or demolished.

Near the refinery on the east is the great Magna industrial complex, a maze of railroads, enormous buildings, and dikes. Located here are Utah Copper Division's power plant and three huge mills for crushing, grinding, and concentrating the more than 120,000 tons of material removed every day at the Bingham mine, including 60,000 tons of copper ore and 60,000 tons of waste. The Magna and Arthur concentrators date from the first decade of this century; they have been modified and expanded numerous times since then. The Bonneville plant (crushing and grinding) was built during the 1960s.

Magna was founded in the early years of the century during construction of the copper mills. Many of its residents are employees or former employees of Kennecott and their families, though the majority no longer belong in that category. In 1940 the town's population was only 1,604; its most rapid growth occurred during the 1970s.

Turn east from Magna to West Valley City, Kearns, and other sprawling suburban communities that are rapidly occupying this part of the valley.

Kearns is a western suburb with distinct boundaries that are somewhat blurred in the public mind. Its staid residential and commercial personality gives no indication of its origins in 1942 as a military base. The area flourished during World War II years as Kearns Air Base, which briefly became one of the state's largest communities. At an estimated cost of $17 million, the government built a complete utility system (water, electricity, paved streets, sewage treatment, railroad) and about a thousand buildings, including warehouses, barracks, theaters, recreational facilities, mess halls, railroad station, library, chapels, and a large hospital. After the war, in 1948, the 1,200-acre townsite—complete with utilities and a few of the buildings—was sold to a New York firm for less than $300,000. Home building on a mass scale soon followed.

South of Magna, Route 111 clings to the foothill base of the Oquirrh Mountains, overlooking the valley. Bacchus was created in 1913 by the Hercules Powder Company. The name Bacchus today refers more specifically to the Bacchus Works of Hercules Inc., a large industrial enterprise occupying 3,000 acres of land south of Magna.

Six miles south of Bacchus Junction, Route 111 intersects Route 48, the east-west highway connecting Bingham Canyon with Midvale. Turn west from this junction to Copperton, Bingham Canyon, and Bingham Copper Mine.

Copperton, at the mouth of Bingham Canyon, is a quiet, largely residential town southwest of Salt Lake County. Copperton was built by the operators of the Bingham mine, and at one point was one of Utah's largest communities. It boasts a large city park and picnic facilities. The town is also home to the Kennecott Bingham Copper Mine Visitors Center, which offers incredible views of the mine.

The Bingham Copper Mine has nearly engulfed Bingham Canyon and the site of the former community of that name. The mine is one unit in Utah's largest industrial enterprise, Kennecott Minerals Company's Utah Copper Division, which operates the mine as well as concentrating mills, a smelter, and a refinery at the north end of the Oquirrh Range (see above).

The Bingham mine is the world's oldest and largest open-pit copper mine, the largest single mining operation ever undertaken, and the largest man-made excavation. Since open-pit mining began in the early 1900s, more than 4.5 billion tons of earth have been removed; from this, more than 11.5 million tons of refined copper have been produced.

Salt Lake Valley Wasatch Front

The Wasatch Range, with the southern High Plateaus, forms the eastern edge of the Basin and Range Province (Great Basin) in Utah. These mountains surely rank among the most rugged and precipitous ranges in the 48 contiguous states, and also among those with the greatest absolute elevation, rising steeply in places from 6,000 to 7,000 feet from base to crest. The range is approximately 150 miles in length, extending from the Bear River in the north to Mount Nebo in the south. Contrasted with its length, it is rather narrow, not exceeding 20 miles at most and measuring somewhat less than that over most of the range's length. With the Uintas, the Wasatch Range represents the Middle Rocky Mountains topographic province in Utah. It is an important playground for the million-plus people who live along its western front, and a critical watershed.

It is believed that the Wasatch Range we see today is essentially a product of the past 10 to 20 million years, the classic result of block faulting on a gigantic scale. Crustal compression in the past is credited with some of this work, but there is evidence that release from compression, or stretching of the crust, may be significant in recent ages. There is no doubt, however, that movement continues along the great Wasatch fault at the western base of the range, such movement being accompanied by earthquakes.

Glaciation has affected the Wasatch in three distinct stages during the past half million years or so. The latest stage, contemporaneous with the highest levels of Lake Bonneville, lasted from about 25,000 to 11,000 years ago. Glaciers formed along the higher reaches of the Wasatch from Mill Creek Canyon southward into Utah Valley (Mount Timpanogos and Provo Peak), and of course in the Uintas and on some of the high plateaus. Geologists believe that 33 glaciers once occupied that part of the range within Salt Lake County, none of which remain.

Little Cottonwood Canyon and its south-wall tributaries contained the longest and largest of the ancient glaciers in the entire range, according to many researchers. At one time the main Little Cottonwood glacier was more than 14 miles long and 650 feet thick near its terminus. Glaciers also affected upper reaches of Big Cottonwood Canyon and several of its tributary canyons, as well as Mill Creek Canyon and short canyons along the mountain front. Moraines left by these glaciers

are evident today.

Seven major canyons break the face of the Wasatch Range in the Salt Lake Valley. These canyons drain a complex watershed that provides a large portion of the valley's culinary water. The greater part of the watershed is included in the Wasatch-Cache National Forest. The national forest areas in the mountains east of the Salt Lake Valley are the most heavily utilized by visitors of any national forest in the nation. "People pressure" is intense not only in summer but in winter as well, creating problems of land use, water purity, waste disposal, and abuse.

Emigration Canyon is the route that climbs out of the canyon over Little Mountain (a popular area for tubing and sledding in winter); and, as the Pioneer Memorial Highway, it follows the route of the Mormon-Donner pioneer trail over Big Mountain, past East Canyon Reservoir, to junction with I-80N at Henefer or, alternately, to Morgan. East Canyon Reservoir is the site of East Canyon State Park, an important developed area for boating, waterskiing, fishing, camping, and picnicking. On either side of the road at the mouth of Emigration Canyon are This Is the Place State Park and Hogle Zoo.

Parley's Canyon was named for Parley P. Pratt, a pioneer Mormon leader who developed a road through the canyon in 1849–50, connecting with the original trail in Mountain Dell, as an alternate to the difficult Emigration Canyon route. In its upper reaches the canyon is expansive and verdant, allowing for far-spreading vistas of the Wasatch heartland; it narrows toward its mouth, emerging into the Salt Lake Valley between steep cliffs and slopes. Because I-80 traverses the canyon, highway travelers from the east first view the great valley and the distant lake from the mouth of Parley's Canyon.

Big Cottonwood Canyon enters the valley through a gateway formed by steep walls that soar thousands of feet on either side. Between the canyon's mouth and road's end in Brighton Basin, about 13 miles away, Route 190 traverses a region of alpine beauty. In places the canyon becomes the epitome of a gorge, hemmed in by giant cliffs and peaks. In other places, the road climbs steeply in sharp bends, and in its upper reaches the canyon becomes a great basin enclosed by majestic peaks and ridges.

Big Cottonwood Canyon is one of the most popular recreation areas for valley residents, resulting in traffic congestion that may be frustrating at times. The Wasatch-Cache National

Forest has developed a number of sites for camping and picnicking; a series of hiking trails gives access to mountain locales, and facilities at Solitude and Brighton serve a multitude of skiers in winter. The canyon also contains numerous homes, the majority of which are utilized part-time.

Located in a basin at the upper end of the canyon, 25 miles from downtown Salt Lake City, Brighton is a resort at 8,700 feet altitude. Brighton offers two quads, two triple chairs, and three double chairs. Approximately 39 percent of its runs are rated for experts, 20 percent are beginner, and 40 percent intermediate. There are more than 60 runs and trails; in addition, a day pass is available that allows skiers to ride the lifts at the resort's down-canyon neighbor, Solitude.

Brighton is one of the state's oldest winter sports resorts. Because of its abundance of relatively gentle terrain and reasonable lift rates, the resort has remained popular through the years, particularly with local people. Facilities at Brighton include a ski school, chalets, a lodge, and restaurants.

In snow-free months, drivers may travel the road over Guardsman's Pass (9,800 alt.) to Park City or Midway. Providing gorgeous panoramic views, this road was built by National Guard engineers and officially opened in 1958.

Solitude Resort, 2 miles down-canyon from Brighton, is developed with one quad, two triple-chair and four double-chair lifts, and boasts 63 different runs. Honeycomb Canyon, one of the resort's most celebrated attributes, features 400 acres of powder skiing, but the resort also has beginner and intermediate slopes. Altitude varies from 8,000 to 10,035 feet. The resort first opened to the public in 1959 under owner Bob Barrett.

Today, Solitude offers a ski school, restaurants, nordic skiing, and rentals. In 1995, the resort opened a one-, two-, and three-bedroom condominium complex.

Little Cottonwood Canyon is confined between tremendous walls formed by rows of high peaks on either side. The canyon is open and almost straight, a U-shaped gorge about 10 miles long. Its floor is steep, rising from 5,000 feet at its mouth to 8,100 at Snowbird, 8,500 at Alta, and even higher at Albion Basin. A number of peaks in the area exceed 11,000 feet. Lifts at Alta take skiers to 10,550 feet, at Snowbird to 11,000 feet, for vertical rises of 730 to 3,000 feet. Hiking trails give access to the high country, as do the resort lifts.

A short distance inside the canyon's mouth, markers indicate the location of the Granite Mountain Record Vaults and temple granite quarry. The vaults have been excavated from the steep north face of the canyon and are utilized to preserve genealogical and other records of the church. They are not open for public touring.

Broken granite in the vicinity of the vaults was used as a source of quarry stone for the LDS Temple in Salt Lake City, with operations continuing for some 30 years between the 1860s and 1890s.

Snowbird is a technologically advanced, all-season resort consisting of multistory lodges, a resort center, eight chairlifts, and a tram running from Snowbird Center to the top of 11,000-foot Hidden Peak. It is a popular destination for out-of-state vacationers, and appeals especially to advanced and intermediate skiers because of its challenging slopes and deep powder. Fifty percent of its runs are classified advanced, 30% intermediate, and 20 percent beginner.

Services include a number of restaurants, shops, bank, grocery store, helicopter excursions, ice skating, tennis courts, pharmacy, swimming pools, ski school, full-service spa, and a post office. Gourmet dining and cultural events (festivals, institutes, concerts, etc.) attract visitors throughout the year.

Alta is one of the oldest and best known ski resorts in Utah. It is situated at the upper end of Little Cottonwood Canyon, about 28 miles from downtown Salt Lake City and two miles from Snowbird. Alta's many adherents claim that its dry powder is unsurpassed for skiing. The terrain here resembles that of nearby Snowbird in challenging the expertise of intermediate and advanced skiers: 25 percent of its runs are classed as suitable for beginners, with 40 percent intermediate and 35 percent advanced. The area's 39 named runs are served by two triple and six double chairlifts.

Historically, Alta was described as a "a rip-roarin', rootin', shootin' mining camp" at one time, according to the 1941 edition of this book. The town came to life as a ski resort in 1937 following a colorful incarnation as a silver boomtown. In 1872, for example, more than 100 buildings were scattered over the flat, including 6 breweries and 26 saloons. The town's population was estimated at 5,000.

Today, Alta offers accommodations at several lodges and condominiums. There is also a ski school.

SOUTHERN CORRIDOR: UTAH VALLEY

This region encompasses parts of Utah's two highest mountain ranges—the southern Wasatch and western Uinta—as well as Utah Valley, Heber Valley, and valleys of the Provo and Weber Rivers. The main north-south artery through Utah Valley is I-15. Mountain valleys to the east are accessible via I-80, Routes 189 and 150, and several other roads.

Point of the Mountain is the popular name for the natural divide between Salt Lake and Utah Valleys. This divide is bisected by the Jordan River, which flows northward from Utah Valley through a channel known as the Jordan Narrows. No road follows the Jordan through the Narrows, but I-15 and Route 68 flank the river on either side at higher elevations.

Said the 1941 edition of this book: "The obvious parallel between the Utah river, which flows from fresh-water Utah Lake to salt-water Great Salt Lake, and the Jordan River of the Holy Land, which flows from fresh Galilee to the Dead Sea, impressed itself on Mormon explorers, who called the Utah river the 'Western Jordan.' "

From Point of the Mountain, 500 feet above Utah Lake, highway travelers can view Utah Valley in its mountain-girt entirety. It is an enclosed basin of irregular shape, 40 miles from north to south and 15 miles from east to west, containing in its bottom the largest natural freshwater lake in Utah. On a clear and sparkling day it is easy to agree with Miera's

Sundance view of Timpanogos from the Alpine Loop – Frank Jensen, UTC

appraisal of the valley in his 1777 report to the King of Spain, where he termed it "the most pleasing, beautiful, and fertile site in all New Spain." Mount Timpanogos dominates the eastern skyline with its immense bulk, flanked by sister peaks that are hardly subordinate in alpine beauty. Mount Nebo, highest of all, looms apart on the southern horizon.

In 1941, when this volume's first edition appeared, Utah Valley was a tranquil vale with a population of some 60,000. Communities were separate and distinct, the majority of them strung out along Routes 91 and 89. Agriculture was the most important industry. Brigham Young University enrolled about 2,800 students, and Geneva Steel Works were only barely under consideration. The snowy summits of the giant peaks could be seen with crisp clarity most days of the year.

Since those times the valley has been transformed. Its population has soared to more than 310,538, with no limit yet in sight. Some communities are distinguishable only by name, their formal boundaries absorbed by urban sprawl. Main Street no longer is the principal through-highway, and agriculture has become a secondary industry. The student enrollment of Brigham Young University is now over 27,000, or ten times that of 40 years ago. Utah County possesses one of the densest concentrations of active and dedicated Mormons in the world. About 80 percent of the county's population is listed on LDS Church membership rolls, compared with a state average of 70 percent. In significant ways the county is a living model of Mormon ideals and worldly achievement. Here, perhaps to a greater extent than elsewhere, Mormonism has found it possible to practice what it teaches with little impact from outside influences.

Mormons were the first Europeans to settle Utah Valley in 1849, two years after their arrival in Salt Lake Valley. Long before that, however, the valley was visited by the Dominguez-Escalante expedition in 1776. The New Mexican party entered the valley on September 23, departing several days later after a peaceful visit with the Indians. "The Timpanogotzis," wrote Escalante in his journal, "were so-called from the lake on which they live, which they call Timpanogo, and this is the special name of this lake . . ." Many of the Indians displayed heavy beards. Escalante wrote enthusiastically of the valley's advantages for settlement: its spacious land, the lake that abounded in fish, geese, beaver, and other animals, "plentiful firewood and timber, sheltered places, water and pasturage

for raising cattle and horses." Travelers from New Mexico returned to the valley or its vicinity in subsequent years, as traders, trappers, and slavers, if not as missionaries and settlers. Among these was Etienne Provost (Provot), a French-Canadian trapper based at Taos, New Mexico. In 1824 Provost and a dozen or so other mountain men explored the Uinta Basin, followed the Provo River to Utah Lake, and were attacked somewhere in the Wasatch region by Snake Indians. Seven of the party were killed. Provost returned to Utah with a larger party in 1825. Anglicized phonetically, his name eventually was applied to the Provo River and Provo City, though the river was commonly known as the Timpanogos for years after Mormon settlement.

Provo was settled in 1849 as the first Mormon community in Utah Valley, and before 1850 had ended, settlers were living on the sites of Lehi, Pleasant Grove, American Fork, Springville, and Payson. During the years since, it has continued to rank as the state's second most populous valley.

Before the establishment of the Geneva Steel Works during the early 1940s, Utah Valley was one of the state's most productive breadbaskets. In this respect it still occupies an important position but not to the same extent. As population has grown, land formerly devoted to crops, orchards, and livestock has been converted to residential, industrial, and commercial uses. Today, as an industry, agriculture in Utah County ranks far below manufacturing, trade, services (including private education), and government in the amount of money involved. The valley has increasingly drawn high-tech industries and is known in some quarters as the Silicone Valley of the Intermountain West.

Brigham Young University, with its enormous student body and staff, is of inestimable worth to the county's economy. Not only does the university contribute millions of dollars in salary income to county residents, but its operations affect such other economic activities as trade construction, finance, transportation, communications, services, and government.

Utah Valley North

Alpine, American Fork, and Sundance

At a junction two miles south of Point of the Mountain, turn east from I-15 on Route 80 to Alpine, American Fork Canyon, Timpanogos Cave National Monument, and Alpine Scenic Drive.

Alpine, settled in 1850, is a residential and farming community nestled in a coved corner of Utah Valley. Soaring 6,000 precipitous feet above the town on two sides are giant massifs of the Wasatch Range, supplying to Alpine an environment that resembles parts of Switzerland. American Fork Canyon opens a mile away to the southeast. The town's inspirational setting is a beacon for artists. Contemporary structures built by a growing populace overshadow in sheer quantity Alpine's 19th-century architecture, but some interesting early examples can still be seen. Among these are a number of antique homes. The Relic Hall of the Daughters of Utah Pioneers dates from 1857–63, and has served as a chapel, school, recreation and civic center, city hall, and museum. Also listed on a historic register is the Moyle Home and Tower at 800 North and 600 East on Grove Drive. The home was built of stone about 1858. Nearby is a ruined stone tower, built by the Moyle family in early days as a defense against Indians but never utilized.

Trails lead from Alpine to Lone Peak and other summits at 11,000 feet and more, as well as over a shoulder of Box Elder Peak (11,101 alt.) into American Fork Canyon. These trails provide stirring views. Most summits are attainable by persons in good health, in a single day or two at most, and well-worn trails lead to the better-known heights. There are many trail possibilities and combinations. Hikers are advised to make use of detailed forest maps or trail guidebooks such as the trail series issued by Wasatch Publishers of Salt Lake City.

American Fork Canyon separates Mount Timpanogos from Box Elder Peak. A true chasm, it ranks with Big and Little Cottonwood Canyons in grandeur and depth. For several miles, walls rise steeply on either side for thousands of feet. The Visitor Center of Timpanogos Cave National Monument is located beside Route 92 in the depths of the canyon, 3 miles east of its mouth (4 miles from Alpine Junction). The cave itself requires a steep 1.5-mile climb to the cave entrance. (See Timpanogos Cave National Monument.) Refreshments are available at the lower parking area during summer months, and a number of sites for camping and picnicking have been developed along the road by the U.S. Forest Service.

The road forks 7 miles east of Alpine Junction, about 3 miles from the monument Visitor Center. Turn left (north) along the main canyon to Tibble Fork Reservoir and summer-home area. At the reservoir the road forks again. One paved spur (left) leads to Granite Flat Campground. An unpaved spur of this side road winds to the Silver Flat Reservoir and summer-home area, from which foot trails lead to Silver Lake and high peaks behind Alta. The main canyon road continues from Tibble Fork Reservoir along the bottom of American Fork Canyon, becoming rougher as it proceeds. About 5 miles from the reservoir is Dutchman Flat. A fork of this road to Dutchman climbs eastward over a high ridge to Snake Creek Canyon, Wasatch Mountain State Park, Cascade Springs, Midway, and Heber City.

The main Alpine Scenic Drive (Route 92) bears right (south) from the canyon junction several miles east of the Timpanogos Cave Visitor Center. This paved but narrow road is normally open from May to late October. It climbs, dips, and winds in sharp curves as it circles the east shoulder of Mount Timpanogos. Here glaciation has gouged out huge cirques or basins rimmed by grand precipices several thousand feet high. The scene is one of alpine majesty, reminiscent of the Canadian Rockies.

Several developed camping and picnicking sites are situated beside the road between American Fork Canyon and Provo Canyon, a distance of about 12 miles. From Timpooneke Campground a foot trail leads to the summit of Mount Timpanogos, connecting with the trail from Aspen Grove. Also from Timpooneke a dirt road winds around the north end of the peak to spectacular overlook points above Utah Valley. The Ridge Trail, a popular hiking route, forks from Route 92 about a mile south of Timpooneke and follows a high ridge northward to connect with a network of other trails. From a junction in this vicinity, Cascade Scenic Drive forks east to Cascade Springs, which offers hiking trails. From Cascade Springs the road continues through Wasatch Mountain State Park to a junction with the Snake Creek Canyon road between Midway and American Fork Canyon.

From Aspen Grove a well-worn foot trail leads 6 miles to the 11,750-foot summit of Mount Timpanogos. The trail passes through the 11,000-acre Mount Timpanogos Scenic Area, retained by Uintah National Forest in "a nearly-pristine condition for the aesthetic and spiritual satisfaction of all of us, and of generations unborn." The scenic area embraces the mountain's famed "glacier" (a perpetual snowfield) as well as waterfalls, lakes, vegetation, and wildlife.

The Sundance Resort and residential area is on a spur beside Route 92 about 2 miles south of Aspen Grove. Before 1968

Sundance was known as Timp Haven Resort. In that year it was purchased by actor-director Robert Redford and associates, who since have made improvements in ski runs and facilities. Redford and others have homes in the area, making ecological balance a prime concern in development. The resort features restaurants, chair lifts, a ski school, rentals and sales, snack bar, and general store. More than 41 ski runs have been developed, with 40 percent advanced, 40 percent intermediate, and 20 percent beginner. Sundance is also known for its summer playwright's conference, summer theater, and of course the renowned independent film festival that bears its name, which is held each January in Park City.

Alpine Scenic Drive joins Route 189 in Provo Canyon, 3 miles from the Sundance Resort, 12 miles from Provo, and 8 miles from Orem.

Lehi and Pleasant Grove

From junction with Route 92 (above), continue south 1 mile on I-15 to the Lehi exit.

Lehi is an attractive residential community based largely on farming, manufacturing, and trade. Many of its people also commute to work in other places. According to the 1941 edition of this book: "Here, in [1891], the first successful sugar beet factory in the intermountain region was put in operation, and Isaac Goodwin planted the first alfalfa seed in Utah. Beets and alfalfa have become major crops in the state."

Of architectural note in Lehi is the Thomas Cutler Mansion, 150 East State, an elaborate residence built in 1875. The house's builder was Thomas R. Cutler, manager of the big sugar factory in Lehi. Later its second floor served as Lehi's first hospital. The Winn Home, 192 North 200 West, is a two-story adobe house with stucco exterior, built in 1859–60 by William H. Winn, who was mayor of Lehi, a state legislator, businessman, and church leader. Both buildings are listed on historic registers.

The John Hutchings Museum of Natural History, 685 North Center, was built in the 1960s as a community project to house the collections of the late John and Eunice Hutchings and their family. Its many outstanding exhibits include pioneer relics and Indian artifacts. The museum also features an excellent collection of mineral specimens.

Turn west from Lehi via State 73 to Fairfield, site of the Stagecoach Inn and Camp Floyd State Park (see Chapter 4.)

American Fork had less than a fourth of its present population in 1941, when it was described as "a community of small farms and modest homes . . . chiefly known as a poultry and egg producing center." Poultry Days of yesteryear long since gave way to an annual Steel Days celebration, recognizing the city's economic relationship with nearby Geneva Steel Works and offshoot metal industries. The Smith Home, 589 East Main, is listed on the National Register of Historic Places. Warren B. Smith, was an early civic and business leader.

Turn north from American Fork on Route 74 to Alpine, American Fork Canyon, Timpanogos Cave National Monument, and the Alpine Scenic Drive.

Turn south from American Fork to Utah Lake and the American Fork Boat Harbor, a popular launching site.

Pleasant Grove has a backdrop hardly surpassed for grandeur in the state, the stupendous western face and buttressed foothills of Mount Timpanogos rising like an immense wall for 7,000 feet. Utahns have a deep affection for "Timp," but not all of them appreciate the true magnitude of the great massif, which must be ranked among the nation's grandest peaks on the basis of bulk and absolute elevation. The peak's crest above 10,000 feet measures four miles in length, and its base covers more than 50 square miles. For the most part the peak consists of limestone laid down about 300 million years ago in Mississippian-Pennsylvanian times. People blessed with imagination have no difficulty seeing the profile of a sleeping princess formed by the mountain's summit ridge.

According to the 1941 edition of this book, Pleasant Grove was "named for the thick stands of cottonwood trees, which almost obscure the buildings. The benchlands about Pleasant Grove produce fruits and berries of excellent flavor, which are canned locally or shipped fresh, mainly to Pacific Coast markets, by refrigerator truck." The city's population has multiplied more than six times since 1941 and its boundaries are not as distinct as they were then, as the community becomes increasingly a part of the Utah Valley megalopolis. Pleasant Grove was settled in 1850; nostalgic reminders of its long past are evident to those who look for them.

Worthy of listing on the National Register of Historic Places is the Old Bell School in Memorial Park, a quaint building dating originally from 1861, with additions in 1880 and 1887. Now a museum operated by the Daughters of the Utah Pioneers, the venerable structure is reputed to be one of the oldest remaining pioneer schools in the state. Another registered site is the Benjamin W. Driggs Home, 119 East Battle Creek Drive, a two-story house built of stone in Greek Revival style. Dating from the 1880s, the house has been restored. Other noteworthy structures include the Fugal Blacksmith Shop, 436 East 700 North, dating from 1896, "a rare example of early blacksmith shops with much of the original equipment," according to the 1941 edition of this book; the Town Hall, 107 South 100 East, built of stone in 1886; the Olpin Home, 10 South Locust, built of rock about 1875, with brick addition about 1895. The home of the family of the musical King Sisters, 100 East 200 South, has been restored.

Orem

South of Pleasant Grove is Orem. Orem had a population of 1,915 in 1940 and was described in a single sentence in the 1941 edition of this book: "Orem . . . incorporated in [1919], produces garden stuff, much of which is canned at the Pleasant Grove Canning Plant in Orem, one of the largest tomato canneries in the Intermountain West." Today most of the truck gardens and many of the orchards have given way to residential areas, commercial developments, parks, schools, and industrial sites. Orem, in fact, is the largest and one of the youngest of Utah's "new cities," a product almost entirely of the second half of this century. It reflects the physical and cultural values of its time and locale, in particular those peculiar to Utah Valley and the state of Utah. While there is little of early historical interest in Orem, the city merits serious touring for no reason other than its status as a truly contemporary Utah community. Orem, Provo, and the surrounding county environs form a metropolitan area that ranks among the fastest-growing areas in the nation. Orem is notable for the length of its main street, Route 89 (State Street), which extends for five miles through the center of the city.

Orem's economy has a diversified base of manufacturing, trade, education, etc. Numerous industrial firms have located in the city. The Geneva Works of U.S. Steel Corporation has been the foundation manufacturing industry for almost 40 years, providing direct employment for approximately 2,400 workers and supporting a host of satellite industrial and commercial activities. Brigham Young University also is essential to Orem's economic stability, as it is to that of Provo.

Turn west from Orem to the Geneva Works of United States

Steel Corporation, a behemoth industrial plant on the shore of Utah Lake. The company's annual payroll is approximately $150 million. Geneva Works is a fully integrated steel plant that processes iron ore, scrap metal, coal, and limestone through complex steps resulting in products such as pig iron, steel plates, sheets, and coils; structural shapes; pipe; coal chemicals; and nitrogen products. Coal is shipped to the plant from mines in Colorado and Utah. Most of the iron ore comes from company operations near Lander, Wyoming, with smaller quantities from open-pit mines near Cedar City. Limestone and dolomite are mined at the Keigley Quarry near Payson for use in the blast furnace and open-hearth operations. During the steel-making process at Geneva, coal is converted to coke and gases by baking in ovens at 2150° F. for about 16 hours. Some of the resulting coke is sold to the chemical industry, while by-products of the coking process are separated and refined into coal-tar chemicals and nitrogen products. The remaining coke and by-product gas are utilized to fire the furnaces. In the blast furnaces, iron is separated from slag impurities in the open-hearth furnaces; many kinds of steel are produced from pig iron. Steel is then processed at Geneva's rolling and structural mills into a wide range of specialized products, or some of the plant's iron and steel may be shipped to U.S. Steel plants in California for processing, or sold commercially.

Geneva Works was constructed by the federal government between the years 1942 and 1944, a result of World War II's industrial demands. Total cost approached $200 million. After the war the plant was sold to United States Steel, its designer.

Drive southeast from Orem on 1200 South Street to Brigham Young University (see Provo). Near the 1200 South (BYU) offramp of I-15 is the Orem Campus of Utah Valley State College.

Utah Valley State College is a state-supported institution of higher learning with an enrollment of about 12,000 students. The college emphasizes vocational, technical, business, health, and paraprofessional training, and also offers programs in general education. Credits may be transferred to other schools in the state's higher education system.

Provo

Provo became Utah's second-largest city during the 1970s, when its population surpassed that of Ogden. It is the seat of

Utah County and the site of Brigham Young University, the largest church-related college in the world. Provo's setting was described as follows in the 1941 edition of this book:

THE CITY HUDDLES AT THE BASE OF THE PRECIPITOUS WASATCH RANGE, THE WESTERN FACE OF WHICH IS AN ALMOST PERPENDICULAR FAULT SCARP. PROVO PEAK, RISING TO AN ALTITUDE OF [11,068] FEET DUE EAST OF THE CITY, EXTENDS SHARPLY ABOVE THE JAGGED RIDGE OF THE WASATCH RANGE. ON THE BASE OF THE PEAK, ABOUT 2,000 FEET ABOVE THE UPPER LEVEL OF THE CITY, IS THE WHITE-BLOCK LETTER 'Y,' 300 FEET TALL, WHICH IS NEWLY WHITE-WASHED EACH YEAR BY FRESHMEN OF BRIGHAM YOUNG UNIVERSITY. NORTHWARD THERE RISES THE LONG BULK OF MOUNT TIMPANOGOS, [11,750] FEET HIGH. THE PROVO AREA SLOPES GENTLY WESTWARD, AND BEYOND THE CITY LIMITS ARE FARMLANDS AND PASTURES, AND BROAD, FRESH-WATER UTAH LAKE, WHICH CAN BE SEEN ONLY FROM THE UPPER STREETS OF THE CITY. ACROSS THE LAKE RISES THE LOW RANGE OF THE LAKE MOUNTAINS, AND OTHER MOUNTAINS ARE VISIBLE IN EVERY DIRECTION.

As the largest city in the state south of Salt Lake City, Provo is a commercial magnet for a vast area, and the presence of Brigham Young University has made it an important cultural center as well. The university is the city's largest industry. Students, faculty, staff, and their families constitute a significant part of the city's population. The diverse local economy is based on trade, manufacturing, and services.

"The town centers about the intersection of University Avenue and Center Street," said the 1941 edition. At that time its population was 18,000. "Within a four-block radius are the principal stores and most of the public buildings, mainly two- and three-story structures of the architectural style popular soon after the turn of the century." This downtown core has not changed dramatically since that time, though new malls and commercial developments have sprung up all around. "Like other Mormon-built towns, Provo has wide streets laid out in the four cardinal compass directions. There is a profusion of shade trees, mostly Lombardy and Carolina poplars, Norway maple, elm, and walnut. In the [older] residential sections the houses are set well back in spacious green lawns, which must be watered every day; and in the backyards there are usually vegetable and flower gardens." As far as the veteran central part of the city is concerned, this 1941 description of Provo is almost as true today.

Provo's historical background was nicely summarized in the 1941 edition:

IN MARCH, 1849, JOHN S. HIGBEE, AT THE HEAD OF THIRTY FAMILIES, TOOK WAGONS, HORSES, CATTLE, FARMING IMPLEMENTS, AND HOUSEHOLD EQUIPMENT, AND LEFT GREAT SALT LAKE CITY TO ESTABLISH A MORMON COLONY ON THE PROVO RIVER. THE PLACE CHOSEN WAS A FAVORITE INDIAN FISHING GROUND, WHERE THE UTES HELD A FISH CARNIVAL AT THE TIME OF THE SPRING SPAWNING. WITHIN A FEW MILES OF THEIR GOAL THE SETTLERS WERE CONFRONTED BY A BAND OF UTE INDIANS. AFTER SOLEMNLY PROMISING NOT TO DRIVE THE INDIANS FROM THEIR LANDS, THEY WERE ALLOWED TO CONTINUE. FORDING THE PROVO RIVER, THE SETTLERS ESTABLISHED THEMSELVES ON THE SOUTH BANK. FARMING AND BUILDING WERE BEGUN AND WITHIN A FEW WEEKS THEY HAD CONSTRUCTED A FORT, PLOWED 225 ACRES OF LAND, AND PLANTED RYE, WHEAT, AND CORN.

IN 1858 THE POPULATION OF PROVO WAS TEMPORARILY INCREASED BY THE ARRIVAL OF 30,000 MORMONS FROM GREAT SALT LAKE CITY AND OTHER NORTHERN UTAH SETTLEMENTS WHO FEARED THE ADVANCE OF COLONEL ALBERT SIDNEY JOHNSTON'S ARMY. WHEN THE FEDERAL FORCE MOLESTED NO PROPERTY, BRIGHAM YOUNG ANNOUNCED THAT HE WAS PREPARING TO RETURN TO GREAT SALT LAKE CITY. WITHIN A FEW HOURS, ALL OF THE SETTLERS HAD BEGUN THEIR HOMEWARD JOURNEY. THE UTAH SOUTHERN RAILROAD, NOW A PART OF THE UNION PACIFIC SYSTEM, WAS COMPLETED FROM SALT LAKE CITY TO PROVO IN 1873.

THE UTAH AND PLEASANT VALLEY RAILROAD, BUILT BY MILAN PACKARD TO TRANSPORT COAL FROM THE MINES NEAR SCOFIELD, WAS EXTENDED NORTH FROM SPRINGVILLE TO PROVO IN 1878. IT WAS KNOWN AS THE "CALICO ROAD" BECAUSE THE WORKMEN WHO GRADED THE ROADBED WERE PAID MAINLY IN GENERAL MERCHANDISE FROM PACKARD'S STORE IN SPRINGVILLE. IN 1881 THE CALICO ROAD WAS SOLD TO THE PREDECESSOR OF THE DENVER & RIO GRANDE WESTERN RAILROAD, AND PROVO OBTAINED ITS FIRST TRUNK LINE SERVICE. COMPLETION OF THE RAILROAD GAVE NEW IMPETUS TO THE CITY'S INDUSTRIAL GROWTH, AND WAS FOLLOWED BY INSTALLATION OF THE CITY'S ELECTRIC SERVICE (1890) AND A WATERWORKS SYSTEM (1892). CULTURALLY AND COMMERCIALLY, THE TOWN FORGED STEADILY AHEAD . . .

- Provo Attractions -

The construction of the Geneva Steel Works in World War II was a catalyst for industrial and population growth, contributing to a 60-percent jump in population during the 1940s. The phenomenal expansion of Brigham Young University—from a student body of 2,800 in 1940 to 27,000 in the mid-1990s—has been a crucial factor in the city's growth.

Because Provo is one of Utah's venerable and relatively conservative communities, not prone to discard or replace the old merely for the sake of change, the city still exhibits many interesting structures from its 19th-century and turn-of-the-century past. As stated above, the central business center displays the architectural styles of the early years of this century and before. Side-street cruising is rewarded by fascinating discoveries of quaint or unusual architecture. In Provo, as a rule, functional older buildings are cherished and maintained. Dilapidated or derelict structures are the exception.

Among Provo's many distinctive buildings listed on historic

registers are the following: the Knight Block, 20–24 North University, a three-story brick-and-stone commercial building erected about 1900 for Jesse Knight, prominent mining figure and philanthropist of that period; the Provo Third Ward Chapel, 200 North 500 West, an English parish Gothic style, dedicated in 1903; the Lower BYU Campus, 500 North and University, an imposing cluster of six distinctive buildings comprising the first campus, built between 1884 and 1912, and now being adapted to commercial use as Academy Square; the Provo LDS Tabernacle, 50 South University, a formidable steepled building of red brick, dating from 1885 and still used for church meetings; the Hotel Roberts, 192 South University, originally built in 1882 and remodeled in 1926, the oldest operating hotel in Provo. Numerous private homes are listed on historic registers. Among these are the following: the Beebe House, 489 West 100 South, with a Queen Anne tower, built around the turn of the century by a Provo businessman; the Talmage Home, 345 East 400 North, built in 1874 and associated with brothers James E. and Albert Talmage, prominent Utah educators; the Smith Home, 315 East Center, built for a wife of George Albert Smith, an early Mormon apostle; the Eggertsen Home, 390 South 500 West, dating from 1876 when it was built by S. P. Eggertsen, founder of an influential local family; the Beesley Home, 210 South 500 West, an adobe structure built in the 1860s.

Other homes of interest include the Allen Home and Carriage House, 135 East 200 North, a large brick Victorian house dating from the 1890s when it was built by Dr. Samuel H. Allen, a physician, and subsequently the home of other prominent residents. The Clark-Taylor Home, 306 North 500 West, an adobe house of very early vintage, "one of the first homes erected after pioneers of Provo moved out of the fort in 1852–53"; a consecration deed to Brigham Young in 1855 indicated that the home was already built by that year . . . one of the oldest and best preserved pioneer homes in Utah. The Reed Smoot Home, 183 East 100 South, the Utah residence of Senator Reed Smoot, advisor to five Mormon Church presidents and apostle in the church; "His house, built in 1892, reeks with the history of presidential visits, senatorial conferences, political intrigue, and religious persecution." The Brereton Home, 112 East 300 South, a two-story adobe structure built about 1860, is now adapted to office use. There are many other notable buildings in Provo, too numerous for list-

ing here. Visitors may obtain a historic tour guide from the Utah Valley Convention and Visitors Bureau, 51 South University Avenue.

The Utah County Building, Center and University, is "a classic structure of white oolite stone on a base of Utah granite." The Sowiette Park and Pioneer Museum, 500 West 600 North, occupies the site of the second fort built at Provo. According to the 1941 edition of this book, the park "was named for the principal war chief of the Utes who tried to protect the settlers from the warlike followers of Chief Walker. The latter, in the 1850's, camped near the fort planning to attack the small group of pioneers. Chief Sowiette moved his warriors into the fort and prepared to defend his white friends. Walker and his braves whooped around the stockade all night, but finally withdrew." The walls and clearing of the old fort have been replaced by trees, tennis courts, a swimming pool, a baseball field, and tourist grounds. The Pioneer Memorial Building (open during summer months) contains a collection of pioneer relics and Indian artifacts. The Pioneer Cabin, north of the Memorial Building, is a replica of an early Utah cabin, furnished with authentic pioneer furniture. The McCurdy Historical Doll Museum, 246 North 100 East, displays hundreds of dolls of varying vintage and origin. They illustrate fashions in dress, including folk and Spanish provincial dress, episodes of history and historical personages, Indian culture, etc. Categories include boy dolls, wax dolls, antique dolls, and First Ladies of America. Old Fort Utah, in the Lion's Club Park at 200 North 2050 West, is a log replica of the pioneer fort of 1849 that housed the first residents of Provo. The LDS Temple, on a hillside above Brigham Young University, is an architecturally striking building faced with white cast stone and surmounted by a central segmented spire. The temple was completed in 1972. Visitors are welcome to tour the landscaped grounds, but the building itself is closed to the public.

The Utah Lake State Park/Provo Boat Harbor is a developed marina and recreation site on the shore of Utah Lake, 3 miles west of Provo by way of Center Street. The 300-acre park has been developed with launching ramps, rest rooms, drinking water, lawns, and extensive facilities for camping and picnicking. Utah Lake is the state's largest natural body of fresh water, with a surface area of approximately 150 square miles. The lake drains into Great Salt Lake through the

Jordan River. It is fed by Provo, Spanish Fork, and American Fork Rivers, Hobble Creek, and lesser streams. The lake is extremely popular for pleasure boating, waterskiing, and fishing (carp, catfish, bass, walleye pike, yellow perch); however, it can be dangerous in high winds, while submerged rocks and sandbars are other hazards that warrant caution.

– Brigham Young University –

Known variously as BYU, the Y, and the Mormon University, Brigham Young University occupies a compact, ultramodern campus of some 650 acres in northeast Provo. Owned and financially supported by The Church of Jesus Christ of Latter-day Saints (the Mormons), BYU is recognized as the largest church-related university in the world and the largest school in Utah. In 1996, it also ranked as the nation's largest private university. Daytime and evening campus enrollment in 1995–96 totaled more than 27,000, while an additional 100,000 students were receiving instruction through the continuing education program.

The majority of students at BYU are members of the LDS Church. Though church membership is not a condition of admission, all students must observe strict standards of personal conduct, including a dress code. Students also are expected to observe the Word of Wisdom, which discourages smoking, the use of illegal drugs, and the drinking of alcoholic beverages, tea, and coffee. Offsetting the image of staidness engendered by its codes of personal conduct, BYU encourages student participation in a wide range of social, cultural, and athletic activities, which the school makes extraordinary efforts to support. Students come from every state and more than 70 foreign countries. Among them are thousands of former missionaries, recently returned from proselyting in 100 countries, thus adding special meaning to BYU's claim that "the world is our campus."

Brigham Young University offers a broad range of scholastic offerings in its colleges, which include biological and agricultural sciences; business, engineering sciences and technology, family, home, and social sciences; fine arts and communications; general studies, humanities, nursing, physical education; physical and mathematical sciences. Undergraduates may choose from a variety of religion courses, and an honors program has been designed to enrich the curriculum of superior students. As a church school, an active

pursuit of BYU is "the synthesis of spirituality and intellectual pursuit, culminating in a refinement of character." The school's motto is a teaching of the Mormon prophet, Joseph Smith: "The glory of God is intelligence."

While the educational accomplishments of BYU are hardly apparent to the casual eye, the remarkable campus is most dramatically evident. In 1941 the school's enrollment numbered less than 3,000 students, and the campus consisted of half a dozen buildings. During the 50-plus years since then, the enrollment has multiplied almost ten times, requiring an extraordinary building program. Construction of new facilities began accelerating in the 1950s during the 20-year administration of President Ernest L. Wilkinson. Much of the cost was borne by the church, with the remainder—totaling many millions of dollars—coming from contributions. On-campus housing for thousands of students was built as well as a new library, student commons building, administration building, field house, science center and laboratories, Fine Arts center, and numerous instructional buildings. The result is a most attractive community of strikingly diversified contemporary architecture, every building distinctive in style, separated by landscaped open spaces that allow the eye to roam—in particular to the east, where great peaks form the skyline.

Campus tours are available on regular or arranged schedules from the Thomas House Hosting Center. Among noteworthy points of interest on the campus are the following: the Franklin S. Harris Fine Arts Center, which houses the departments of art, communications, speech and dramatic arts, music, and communicative disorders. The center features two art galleries, including a grand gallery, five theaters, radio and television complex, classrooms, and offices. It was described by architect William L. Pereira as "the most comprehensive center of its kind ever commissioned by an American university." The Harold B. Lee Library (named for the eleventh president of the LDS Church), a massive mural-faced structure, contains nearly two million volumes. Outstanding special collections include Mormon Books and Chronicles, a Victorian collection of first editions, and volumes from presses of the 15th and 16th centuries. The Marriott Center, a 23,000-seat arena, is used for sporting events, devotionals, concerts and other large-group events. Ten stories high, the center was named for philanthropist J. Willard Marriott. The Wilkinson Student Center is one of the largest union buildings on any campus, with seven levels and about 290,000 square feet of floor space. The Eyring Physical Science Center features the Summerhays Planetarium; the Monte L. Bean Life Science Museum offers numerous public exhibits. The museum provides a variety of educational services for the public as well as faculty and students, and houses extensive collections such as the largest herbarium in Utah (200,000 mounted plants), more than a million pinned and preserved insects, 45,000 amphibians and reptiles, 6,000 birds, 10,000 fish, and more than 6,000 mammals. The BYU Museum of Art offers a family interactive center, a print study room, a 75-seat restaurant, a bookstore, and gallery talks.

Utah Valley South
Springville to Santaquin

South of Provo, I-15 passes through the open valley between the lake and the Wasatch Range, bypassing all communities. While the interstate does provide a magnificent mountain panorama as well as close-up views of intensively cultivated fields and picturesque farms, tourists who are more interested in architecture and other manifestations of longtime human occupancy are advised to travel Routes 91 and 89, the old highways. These roads, combined for much of the distance, generally parallel the foothills and serve as the main streets for Springville, Spanish Fork, Salem, and Payson—established communities that were founded 145 years ago as some of the earliest Euro-American settlements in the West. Those travelers with time and inclination for leisurely exploring will be richly rewarded by probing the area's side streets.

Springville is a clean and pleasant residential community, known as the Art City because of its celebrated Springville Art Museum. The city resembles other Utah Valley communities in having a long history (settled 1850). Growth during the intervening years has been orderly. Most inhabitants are long-time residents and have developed a pride in home and community that is evident.

Visitor attractions include Civic Center Park, featuring a contemporary city building. A Pioneer Mother Monument and Memorial Fountain in the park are the work of noted sculptor Cyrus E. Dallin, a Springville native. During a long and productive life, Dallin received widespread recognition for works such as *Paul Revere*, *Massasoit*, *Angel Moroni* (atop the Mormon

Temple in Salt Lake City), *Brigham Young* (Brigham Young Monument in Salt Lake City), *Signal of Peace*, *Medicine Man*, and other sculptures. A number of his works are in the Springville Art Museum. The Daughters of the Utah Pioneers Museum, 175 South Main, is open by arrangement. The Old Presbyterian Church, 251 South 200 East, dates from 1886 when it was built as part of the Hungerford Academy (National Historic Register). The Kelsey Home, 366 West 300 South, was built in 1889 with ornate Eastlake-style wood trim. The Bringhurst Home, 306 South 200 West, constructed of adobe, rock, and pine about 1860, was built for William Bringhurst, prominent in early church, civic, and business affairs.

Many other older architecturally distinct buildings are preserved in Springville, including a number of aged commercial buildings in the central business district.

The Springville Museum of Art is housed in an attractive Spanish-style building at 126 East 400 South. Dedicated in 1937, the museum was built by the Works Progress Administration to house the extensive collections of the local high school. Since then, the museum's collections have been expanded greatly through gifts and a systematic purchasing program. Many well-known artists (painters and sculptors) are represented, including Rockwell Kent, Frederick Waugh, Maynard Dixon. Also exhibited are Utah natives Cyrus E. Dallin, John Hafen, and Mahonri Young, among others. The museum is especially noted for its annual month-long National Art Exhibit in April, when works from far and near are exhibited. Open to the public.

Beside the old highway between Springville and Provo once stood an imposing iron-reduction plant known as Ironton, the predecessor of the Geneva Works. Operated by Columbia Steel, the Ironton Works were built in 1924 and dismantled after World War II. The plant included 56 coke ovens, a blast furnace, and by-product facilities. Neither the plant nor the adjoining village of Ironton remains today.

Turn east from Springville to Hobble Creek Canyon, the Uintah National Forest, and connecting roads leading to Strawberry Reservoir, Squaw Peak Trail, and Diamond Fork. Winding through gentle, wooded mountain country, the main drive and its forks offer access to a popular golf course in the canyon, excellent fishing streams, and numerous developed camping and picnic sites. The main drive and spurs are especially beautiful in late September and early October, when autumn colors are at their most glorious.

Spanish Fork, a solid commercial and residential community, lies in a productive agricultural region at the junction of I-15 and Route 6-89. Traditionally, its economy has been based largely on trade and the raising of crops and livestock in the vicinity, as well as dairy and orchard production. Livestock auctions and ram sales are important economic events. Spanish Fork is noted as the home of the Utah State Junior Livestock Show held in May, advertised as the oldest show of its kind west of the Mississippi River. Popular activities at this show include stock judging, horse pulling contests, parades, rodeo, sales, and a horse show. Recent years have seen the arrival of light manufacturing industries, including three large apparel firms. The community rates itself as the "No. 1 city in the country for the variety of recreational programs and number of participants." The Daughters of Utah Pioneers Historical Museum, 40 South Main, is open by arrangement.

Turn east from Spanish Fork on Route 6-89 to Spanish Fork Canyon, Price, and the valleys of central Utah.

Salem is a residential community at the base of Loafer Mountain and Santaquin Peak, twin summits of almost identical altitude (10,687 and 10,685 respectively), only a mile apart. Salem was settled in 1851 and was "first named Pond Town for the small spring-fed lake about which the town grew up." The lake remains the center of town; around it many fine new homes have been built, and on its shore is a lovely community park with picnic facilities and playground.

Between Salem and Spanish Fork can be seen a zigzag road high on the mountain to the southeast. This road gave access to the famed Koyle Dream Mine and, several miles beyond, to what the map refers to as "Old Spanish Mine (inactive)." The road continues to a microwave station.

In 1894, John Koyle of Spanish Fork announced that a heavenly being had appeared to him in a dream and had shown him the location of an ancient Nephite mine. (Nephites, according to the Book of Mormon, were among the ancient inhabitants of the Americas.) He was shown the spot where he should begin excavation that would connect with the Nephite tunnel and lead to nine large rooms filled with Nephite gold. Later a Mormon bishop (1908–13), Koyle was able to attract hundreds of believers, who invested both labor and money in his mining venture over a 50-year period

despite the fact that the Nephite rooms were never found and the mine failed to yield a discernible amount of precious metal. Koyle's claim that he received periodic instructions from the "Three Nephites" of Mormon legend gave hope to investors that the mine ultimately would be a success.

Santaquin is an appealing rural community in the south end of Utah Valley, surrounded by farms and fruit orchards that produce peaches, pears, apricots, apples, and cherries. The Santaquin area was settled in 1851 and first named Summit Creek, later changed to Santaquin for a local Sanpitch Indian chief who subsequently became a cattleman and farmer. Black Hawk, leader of the Utes during the Black Hawk War of the 1860s, died at Spring Lake near Santaquin in 1870 and was buried in the foothills near Santaquin. The Keigley Quarry, a large open-pit mining operation on the mountainside several miles north of Santaquin, furnishes limestone and dolomite for the furnaces of Geneva Works.

West of Santaquin, Route 6 leads to Goshen, Elberta, Eureka, and the Tintic Mining District. Goshen, in the words of the 1941 edition of this book, "is a tree-shaded livestock and farming community, settled in [1867], with a typical small-town business district, a residential section where old houses rub elbows with new, and outlying farms that crowd the city limits." In 1994 the town's population was smaller than it was in 1940. According to the 1941 edition:

PIONEERS IN THE VALLEY MOVED FROM PLACE TO PLACE TO FIND SUITABLE HOMESITES. ACCORDING TO SOLOMON HALE, BRIGHAM YOUNG, WHO MADE A SPECIAL TRIP FROM GREAT SALT LAKE CITY TO SELECT THIS SITE, CHIDED THE PEOPLE FOR THEIR CONSTANT MOVING: "YOUR CHICKENS HAVE BEEN MOVED SO MANY TIMES THAT EVERY TIME THEY SEE A WAGON THEY JUST TURN OVER AND STICK THEIR FEET IN THE AIR TO BE TIED FOR ANOTHER MOVING.

Archaeologists from Brigham Young University excavated a mound near Goshen in 1966, finding artifacts representing the Desert culture of 7,000 to 9,000 years ago and the Fremont culture of 800 years ago, as well as items from the historic era of the late 1800s.

NORTHERN CORRIDOR: WEBER, MORGAN, AND DAVIS COUNTIES
Weber County
Ogden

Located north of Salt Lake, Weber County is a sprawling mixture of rural and urban, agricultural and industrial, commercial and residential, private enterprise and government.

Weber is an industrialized county, with manufacturing plants, industrial parks, shopping malls, and a bustling downtown commercial district. Agriculture also is important to the local economy; local farms produce sizeable quantities of grain, hay, vegetables, and fruits, as well as livestock. Ogden is a major importer and processor of livestock and farm produce. Grain elevators are local landmarks.

Ogden became the railroad Junction City in the 1870s, gaining a financial base that has been of great economic worth in the century since. Hundreds of local residents are employed by the Union Pacific-Southern Pacific, and Denver & Rio Grande Western. Also, Ogden is an important crossroads for national highways (I-15, I-84, Route 30-89), and it is equally distant or nearly so from major cities west of Denver. These strategic advantages were instrumental in the selection of the Ogden-North Davis area for siting of the federal defense installations that have become keystones for the region's economy.

Ogden (68,000 pop.) is the third largest city in Utah and the principal railway center of the intermountain region. The city is built on the deltas of the Ogden and Weber Rivers, where these two streams once emptied into prehistoric Lake Bonneville. East and north of the city, the massive bulk of the Wasatch Range looms, topped with snow from November to June or July. Areas of prosperous farmland merge with the city's sprawling suburbs.

The most marked feature of Ogden is the broad, straight vista of Washington Boulevard, the city's main commercial thoroughfare running north and south. The city's wide streets, planned in true Mormon geometrical style on the four cardinal directions, are bordered by trees. Vestiges of a bygone era may still be seen, particularly along 25th Street, which is becoming a fashionable shopping and dining area; but central Ogden has been in the process of transformation for many years, with individual buildings and even entire blocks being razed and replaced with malls, a large hotel, and other developments. As in Salt Lake City, most of Ogden's historical heritage—as evidenced by architecture—is no longer concentrated in a relatively tight core; what remains is dispersed and requires seeking out. Such effort is rewarding, for Ogden possesses notable vintage and modern attractions.

Ogden's historical background was described in the 1941 edition of this book, which gave considerable attention to the trapper era. Excerpts are included below:

AFTER THE COMING OF [EUROPEANS], THE SITE OF OGDEN AND ITS VICINITY WAS AN IMPORTANT RENDEZVOUS AND WINTERING PLACE FOR FUR TRADERS AND TRAPPERS OVER A PERIOD OF SIX OR SEVEN YEARS. AS SUCH IT WAS A FOCAL POINT FOR EXPLORATIONS, AND FOR TRADE RIVALRY BETWEEN AMERICAN FUR COMPANIES AND THE BRITISH HUDSON'S BAY COMPANY. . . . THE [AMERICAN] TRAPPERS SPENT THE WINTER OF 1825–26 AT THE PRESENT SITE OF OGDEN, LIVING IN SKIN TENTS. MANY OF THEM HAD TAKEN INDIAN WIVES, AND THEY SETTLED DOWN, "HEALTHY AS BEARS," TO A WINTER OF EATING, SLEEPING, YARN-SPINNING, AND CONTESTS OF STRENGTH. MORE THAN A THOUSAND SHOSHONE INDIANS CAME DOWN AND CAMPED AROUND THEM. . . . EARLY IN THE SPRING FOUR MEN, ONE OF WHOM WAS JAMES CLYMAN, SET OUT IN BULLBOATS TO "CIRCUMAMBULATE" GREAT SALT LAKE, TO FIND BEAVER STREAMS, AND TO DETERMINE WHETHER IT WAS AN ARM OF THE PACIFIC. . . . THE SUMMER RENDEZVOUS OF 1826 ON THE SITE OF OGDEN WAS A GALA AFFAIR, AFTER THE ARRIVAL OF GENERAL ASHLEY FROM ST. LOUIS WITH 100 WELL-LADEN PACK ANIMALS. . . . AT THAT RENDEZVOUS GENERAL ASHLEY SOLD OUT HIS INTERESTS TO JEDEDIAH S. SMITH, DAVID E. JACKSON (FOR WHOM JACKSON'S HOLE, WYOMING, WAS NAMED), AND WILLIAM L. SUBLETTE. . . . THE FOLLOWING WINTER THE TRAPPERS SPENT ON THE SITE OF OGDEN, AND THE SUMMER, OR TRADE, RENDEZVOUS OF 1827 WAS HELD ON BEAR LAKE, NEAR PRESENT LAKETOWN.

AS THE FUR TRADE DECLINED AND THE TRAPPERS SHOWED A DISPOSITION TO SETTLE DOWN, THE SITE OF OGDEN CONTINUED TO BE AN OCCASIONAL CAMPING PLACE FOR INDIANS AND TRAPPERS, UNTIL THE ARRIVAL OF MILES GOODYEAR (1817–49), A NATIVE OF CONNECTICUT, WHO BUILT A CABIN HERE IN 1846. [GOODYEAR] WAS THE EARLIEST WHITE SETTLER IN OGDEN, AND PROBABLY THE FIRST IN UTAH TO PLANT A GARDEN. COMING WEST FROM PRESENT KANSAS WITH THE WHITMAN PARTY IN 1836, HE ASSISTED IN PIONEERING AN UNTRIED WAGON ROAD AS FAR AS FORT HALL, IDAHO, OUT OF WHICH HE WORKED AS HUNTER, TRAPPER, AND TRADER UNTIL HE HAD GAINED SUFFICIENT EXPERIENCE TO OPEN A TRADING POST OF HIS OWN. TO THE ORIGINAL CABIN, INTENDED FOR THE USE OF GOODYEAR, HIS INDIAN WIFE, AND THEIR TWO CHILDREN, WAS ADDED A STOCKADE FOR LIVESTOCK AND OTHER CABINS FOR HIS PARTNERS, ONE OF WHOM WAS JIM BAKER, NOTED MOUNTAIN MAN. THE ARRIVAL OF THE MORMONS IN 1847 INDUCED HIM TO SELL OUT, CLAIMING THAT HE HELD A MEXICAN GRANT; EXISTENCE OF SUCH A GRANT HAS NOT BEEN FOUND, BUT THE MORMONS PROBABLY CONSIDERED IT WORTH ABOUT $2,000 TO ESTABLISH A CLEAR TITLE TO ALL OF THE UTAH REGION. AS FOR GOODYEAR, NEIGHBORS FORTY MILES AWAY AT GREAT SALT LAKE CITY MADE THINGS TOO CROWDED, AND HE WAS GLAD TO DISPOSE OF HIS "PROPERTY." THE PURCHASE WAS MADE UNDER THE DIRECTION OF THE MORMON CHURCH BY CAPTAIN JAMES BROWN OF THE MORMON BATTALION, WHO MOVED HIS FAMILY INTO THE FORT AND WITH THE AID OF HIS SONS PLANTED FIVE BUSHELS OF SEED WHEAT AND HALF A BUSHEL OF SEED CORN, BROUGHT FROM CALIFORNIA. BUTTER AND CHEESE MADE FROM THE MILK OF COWS AND GOATS PURCHASED FROM GOODYEAR GAVE RISE TO OGDEN'S FIRST INDUSTRY.

BRIGHAM YOUNG CAME TO THE SETTLEMENT OF BROWNSVILLE, SO NAMED FROM CAPTAIN BROWN'S OCCUPANCY, LATE IN 1849, AND CLIMBED A NEAR-BY HILL "TO VIEW OUT A LOCATION FOR A TOWN." THE FOLLOWING YEAR THE TOWNSITE WAS SURVEYED AND 100 FAMILIES WERE SENT BY THE CHURCH LEADER TO SETTLE HERE.

THE MOST SIGNIFICANT EVENT IN THE HISTORY OF OGDEN WAS THE COMING OF THE RAILROAD. IN MARCH, 1869, THE FIRST TRAIN STEAMED INTO THE CITY. . . . IN 1870, THE YEAR THE UTAH CENTRAL RAILROAD WAS COMPLETED TO SALT LAKE CITY, CENSUS RETURNS SHOWED THAT OGDEN HAD DOUBLED ITS PREVIOUS DECENNIAL POPULATION OF 1,463. MOST OF THE NEWCOMERS WERE NON-MORMONS, AND THERE QUICKLY DEVELOPED, IN THE EARLY NEWSPAPERS, AND IN THE BATTLE FOR POLITICAL CONTROL OF THE CITY, A MARKED BITTERNESS BETWEEN MORMONS AND "GENTILES." THE MORMON CHURCH, WHICH HAD ACQUIRED THE SITE OF OGDEN FROM MILES GOODYEAR, RESENTED POSSIBLE CONTROL BY ROUGH PEOPLE BROUGHT IN BY THE RAILROAD.

BRANCH RAILROAD LINES WERE BUILT IN THE SEVENTIES AND EIGHTIES, CONNECTING THE TRANSCONTINENTAL SYSTEM WITH OTHER SETTLEMENTS IN UTAH, IDAHO, AND MONTANA. . . . BY 1880 THE POPULATION HAD DOUBLED AGAIN, BRINGING MORE NON-MORMON SETTLERS, AND THE ACRIMONIOUS FEELING BETWEEN CHURCH MEMBERS AND GENTILES WAS REFLECTED IN THE PLAIN-SPOKEN PRESS OF THE PERIOD. . . . BETWEEN 1880 AND 1900, OGDEN BOOMED. ELECTRICAL SERVICE WAS EXTENDED TO HOMES AND FACTORIES; THE TELEPHONE SYSTEM, ONE OF THE FIRST IN THE WEST, WAS ESTABLISHED; THE CANNING INDUSTRY BEGAN; AND A CLOTHING FACTORY WAS OPENED. AN ELECTRIC STREET RAILWAY SYSTEM WAS INSTALLED, REPLACING HORSE-DRAWN CARS. . . . THE CENSUS OF 1900 GAVE OGDEN A POPULATION OF 16,313.

IN THE EARLY YEARS OF THE TWENTIETH CENTURY CIVIC IMPROVEMENTS WERE NUMEROUS AND THE FEELING BETWEEN MORMONS AND NON-MORMONS GRADUALLY IMPROVED. . . . OGDEN IS ONE OF THE LARGEST DISTRIBUTION POINTS FOR MANUFACTURING, MILLING, CANNING, LIVESTOCK, AND AGRICULTURE IN THE INTERMOUNTAIN WEST; IT RANKS THIRD IN THE NATION IN THE NUMBER OF SHEEP RECEIVED IN ITS YARDS, AND ELEVENTH IN CATTLE. THE UNION STOCKYARDS IS THE LARGEST SHIPPING POINT FOR SHEEP AND CATTLE WEST OF DENVER . . .

- Ogden Attractions -

The Municipal Building and Municipal Gardens, on Washington Boulevard between 25th and 26th Streets, occupy ten acres in the heart of the city. The old City Hall, built in 1888, was replaced in 1938 by the present 10-story City and County Building, erected with WPA funds and a fine example of Art Deco architecture. The surrounding gardens are noted for their variety and beauty of landscaping.

The Lower 25th Street Historic District, which includes several blocks in the vicinity of the Union Depot (a part of the district), was formed to encourage the restoration of a number of deteriorating vintage structures dating from the years 1875 to 1920. An area rich with history and tradition, this was once the economic, social, and cultural center of Ogden. But as the age of railroad passenger travel declined after World War II, so did 25th Street. Restoration of the depot and redevelopment of the immediate area prompted civic action to save 25th Street. Today, this is a popular shopping and dining

area. An informative brochure is available from the Golden Spike Empire tourist office in Union Station.

The Union Station, 25th Street and Wall Avenue, "was designed on a grand scale by John and Donald B. Parkinson of Los Angeles," states the National Register of Historic Places. "The classic Spanish architecture of the building is seen in the vivid tile roof and rounded windows on the end gables. Inlaid brick designs, bright blue decorative mosaic tile, wood trusses with handhewn edges, and huge wrought iron chandeliers add to the beauty of this impressive monument to Ogden's role in the history of railroading. During World War II, more than 120 trains were served out of the depot daily."

The station was acquired by the city in 1977 and dedicated the following year as a civic center and museum. It houses the Ogden-Weber Convention and Visitors Bureau Information Center (open seven days a week during the summer, five days a week the remainder of the year); the Forest Service Information Center, with recreation information on the Wasatch forests; the Utah State Railroad Museum; the John M. Browning Firearms Museum, where models of guns invented by the Browning family, and the Browning workshop are displayed; the Browning-Kimball Automobile Museum, with a collection of antique automobiles; and the Myra Powell Art Gallery, with rotating exhibits. Special performances are held in the lobby of the Browning Theatre.

Fort Buenaventura State Park, between the depot and Weber River to the west across the railroad tracks, is a landscaped park containing a reconstruction of a log stockade (Fort Buenaventura) built in 1846 by trader Miles Goodyear, who sold it to Mormon pioneers in 1848. The park was reconstructed by the State Division of Parks and Recreation using authentic materials and construction methods for the stockade and three buildings. Guides, often dressed in mountain-man garb, offer interpretive information about the trappers and Native Americans of the area. Twice a year, on Easter and Labor Day weekends, mountain-man-rendezvous reenactments are held. Other programs are conducted throughout the year. It's open daily except during winter holidays; enter from 24th Street, turning south from the west end of the viaduct, then east to 2450 A Avenue (follow the signs).

The Ogden City Mall is west of Washington between 22nd and 24th. Built between 1979 and 1981 as a private-public redevelopment project, the mall houses more than 120 stores, shops, and restaurants in 772,000 square feet of retail space. The Newgate Mall, a few blocks south, is another large construction project of the same period.

The Mormon Temple-Tabernacle-Goodyear Cabin occupy a block between 21st and 22nd, fronting Washington Boulevard. A distinctive temple of white cast stone, gold-anodized aluminum grillwork, and segmented central spire (180 feet high), the temple was dedicated in January 1972. It is identical in plan to the Provo Temple, dedicated one month later. Used for sacred ordinances, the temple is not open to the public, but the grounds and white-steepled tabernacle to the south are open to visitors. A visitor center is located at the tabernacle. On the same block to the west is the Daughters of Utah Pioneers Museum-Relief Society Stake Meeting Hall. This quaint brick-walled building dates from 1902 when it was dedicated as the first and only Relief Society Stake Hall in the Mormon Church. It was presented to the DUP in 1926. Adjoining the museum, under a canopy, is the quaint Miles Goodyear Cabin, built in 1846 of cottonwood logs and moved to its present site by the DUP in 1928.

The Episcopal Church of the Good Shepherd, 2374 Grant Avenue, is a Gothic stone edifice with pitched roof, buttresses, Tudor stained-glass windows, and exposed wood rafters. Nostalgically reminiscent of aged Gothic churches of Europe, it is reportedly the oldest church in Ogden in continuous use and is listed on the National Register of Historic Places. The church was consecrated in 1875.

The Eccles Community Art Center, 2580 Jefferson Avenue, is a 2-1/2-story house of brick and red sandstone. It is decorated by round arch windows, dormers, and cylindrical towers with conical roofs. Built in 1893 for James C. Armstrong, it was sold to financier David Eccles in 1896. Since then it has been a private and public, social and cultural center, eventually becoming a civic center. It is now used for fine arts exhibitions, lectures, programs, and instruction.

The Ogden Nature Center, 966 West 12th Street, is a 127-acre wildlife sanctuary northwest of downtown with trails leading through woods, fields, and marshlands. Ecology exhibits offer interpretive information. The center is home to herons, egrets, ducks, geese, and blackbirds. Mammals include red foxes, porcupines, muskrats, and deer. The center also offers summer camps for children, and other special programs.

The visitor center here was built with timbers from the old Lucin Cutoff on the Great Salt Lake.

The Eccles Dinosaur Park, 1544 East Park Blvd., near the mouth of Ogden Canyon, is host to more than 40 life-size dinosaur replicas. Casts of fossils found in the children's area grant aspiring paleontologists the chance to uncover the fossilized remains of ancient creatures.

~ Weber State University ~

Weber State University is situated on a spacious 375-acre campus on the foothills of the Wasatch Mountains, overlooking Ogden and Weber Valley from the city's southeastern heights. Accessible from Harrison Boulevard, the campus is a modern complex of landscaped grounds and attractive buildings of harmonizing architectural styles and coordinated colors. A map and free parking pass is available at the information booth along the main road at 3750 Harrison Blvd.

The college has been a four-year institution since 1959; its first senior class was graduated in 1964. Its origins date to 1889, when it was founded by the Mormon Church as a church academy. In 1933 the academy was transferred to the state, becoming Weber Junior College. In 1991, by proclamation of the state legislature, Weber State College was renamed Weber State University. Today, approximately 15,000 students are enrolled in 50 departments and programs, including undergraduate degrees in the arts, humanities, natural and social sciences, business, education, and applied sciences and technology. Master's degrees are offered in accounting and education.

Weber State's attractions include the 12,000-seat Dee Events Center, which is used for college and community sports-cultural events. The theaters and auditorium of the Val A. Browning Center for the Performing Arts host cultural events such as ballet, symphony, concerts, lectures, and theater performances.

Also of interest to visitors are the Stewart Library, Collett Art Gallery, Shepherd Union Building, Ott Planetarium, Natural History Museum, and Stewart Carillon Tower, which contains a clock on each of four faces; in its base is an electronic carillon of 183 bells.

Huntsville via Ogden Canyon

Turn east from Ogden via 12th Street and Route 39 to Ogden Canyon and the Ogden Valley, a pastoral basin in the heart of the Wasatch. The road gives access to three ski resorts, Pineview Reservoir, numerous forest campsites, and continues across Monte Cristo Summit to Woodruff in Bear River Valley.

Ogden Canyon is a deep narrow gash, just wide enough for the highway and the Ogden River. Before construction of a toll road in the 1860s the canyon was nearly impassable except for a precarious Native American trail high on the south wall. It is the site of numerous vacation retreats.

Turn north across Pineview Dam via Route 158 to Eden and Liberty, villages on the North Fork of Ogden River. Between Eden and Liberty, on the slopes of the high Wasatch, is the Nordic Valley Ski Area, a resort which is especially popular with locals. Nordic Valley boasts two double chairlifts and 16 named runs. Thirty percent of these runs are suitable for beginners, 50 percent are rated intermediate, and 20 percent expert. Night skiing is offered on lighted runs. Facilities include a day lodge, snack bar, ski shop, and ski school.

North from Liberty, an improved road (closed in winter) winds through low, rolling mountain country to Avon and Paradise in Cache Valley.

Turn north from Eden to the Wolf Creek resort and golf course, 2 miles. The road continues up the canyon to the Powder Mountain Ski Resort, 8 miles from Eden on the highest slopes of a 9,000-foot ridge marking the Cache-Weber county line. Powder Mountain features seven chairlifts (two doubles, one triple, and four surface) serving more than 30 interconnected runs. As its name suggests, this resort is renowned for its plentiful soft powder. A Snow Cat provides access to the backcountry. Facilities include day lodges and overnight accommodations, ski shop, ski school, and restaurant. The main lodge is located at the top of the resort.

The Pineview Dam almost blocks the gateway to Ogden Valley, and Pineview Reservoir behind the dam occupies a large part of the valley floor. The many-fingered lake extends behind the dam 3 or 4 miles in several directions. The U.S. Forest Service has developed half a dozen picnic and camping areas containing several hundred units, as well as ramps and docks. The Pineview Dam was built in the l930s and enlarged in 1957 by the Bureau of Reclamation to its current water-retention capacity of 110,000 acre-feet. The lake is very popular for boating, fishing and waterskiing. In recent years the Forest Service has been forced to restrict the number of boats on the water during popular weekends.

Turn south from Route 39, 3 miles west of Huntsville, to Snowbasin Ski Resort, largest and oldest in the Ogden area. Founded in 1939, the resort currently offers four triple and one double chairlift accessing more than 40 runs. Terrain is varied with 20 percent of runs suitable for beginners, 50 percent intermediate, and 30percent expert. There are no overnight accommodations, but the resort contains a day lodge, cafeteria, ski school, and ski shop. Snowbasin will be the site of the downhill races at the 2002 Winter Olympic Games.

Huntsville, 3 miles from Ogden, is a rustic older village with a population of approximately 600. It was founded in 1860 by Captain Jefferson Hunt, former member of the Mormon Battalion. The Angus McKay Home, 141 South 7600 East, is a 2-story red sandstone house built in 1871–73 by Hugh McKay. The David O. McKay Summer Home, 155 South 7600 East, was built in 1870 for the grandfather of Mormon apostle and church president David O. McKay.

Route 39 continues east and north of Huntsville, traversing the canyon of the Ogden River's South Fork, along which the U.S. Forest Service has developed seven camping and picnicking areas. The road forks 8 miles east of Huntsville. Turn right 2 miles to the Weber County Memorial Park, Causey Dam and Causey Reservoir, and Skull Crack Forest Campground.

Route 39 continues up Beaver Creek from Causey Junction, gaining elevation gradually. (Higher reaches are closed in winter.) About 9 miles from Causey Junction, a fair-weather road forks north to the Hardware Ranch (16 miles), passing through gently contoured, sparsely forested plateau country at about 7,000 feet. This area is popular for snowmobiling in winter. Route 39 winds through groves of trembling aspen and sharp-pointed fir as it passes Monte Cristo Peak on the right (9,148 feet) and crosses the summit (9,008 alt.).

The Monte Cristo campground (8,400 feet) is a large developed area with tables, water, rest rooms, playground, amphitheater, and natural arboretum. Beyond the campground Route 39 descends the east slopes of the Bear River Range through Walton Canyon to Woodruff, 60 miles from Ogden.

Morgan County
via Weber River Canyon

Interstate 80 breaks to Interstate 84 at Echo. This route parallels the Weber River and the Union Pacific railroad through Weber Canyon, slicing through the Wasatch Range.

Mountain Green, north of the highway, is a tranquil town nestled in the midst of mountains and hills. Many newer homes have been built in the area in recent years. In 1964 the Browning Arms Company established a headquarters complex here with facilities for research and development. Mountain Green was the site of a confrontation between Hudson's Bay fur brigade leader Peter Skene Ogden and a group of American trappers in 1825, during which 23 of Ogden's men deserted.

Morgan is the seat of Morgan County, a commercial and residential center for the surrounding farming area. The grand 9,000-foot ridge of the main Wasatch forms the western horizon, with lower ranges and hills in all directions. Patchwork fields cover the valley floor and extend onto the foothills. Morgan County is a dairy and livestock area, with barley, wheat, and alfalfa the main crops. Many residents commute to the Wasatch Front for work.

Turn south from Morgan to East Canyon Reservoir, a 600-acre reservoir that is popular with Wasatch Front recreationists for boating and other water sports. Trout fishing in the reservoir and East Creek Lake is often good. The lake's shores have a state recreation area with ramps, picnic and camping sites, and concessions. Nearby, the private East Canyon resort has a restaurant that is open to the public.

The Devil's Slide, on the south side of the highway, 7 miles east of Morgan, is a natural rock formation resembling a playground chute consisting of two parallel limestone ridges 20 feet apart, standing about 40 feet above the canyonside.

Across the highway to the north is the cement plant of Holnan/Ideal Basic Industries. Cement has been taken from this area since early in the century. Several million barrels are produced annually, utilizing limestone as the primary raw material. Continue on this road to Croyden, a hamlet in the mouth of Lost Creek Canyon. From here, an improved road leads up Lost Creek Canyon to Lost Creek Reservoir. A state park features picnic and camping facilities and a boat ramp. The area is popular for fishing.

Henefer is a farming and livestock community. The road south of Henefer to East Canyon Reservoir and Salt Lake City marks the route of the Donner-Reed and Mormon pioneers of 1846 and 1847 respectively, and was used as a migration route for years afterward. Historic site markers are placed beside the road at intervals. The trail was first broken by the Donner-Reed party and followed by the Mormons a year

later. Johnston's army came this way in 1858, and the route was used by the Overland Stage and Pony Express.

At Echo is the junction of I-84 and I-80, leading to Salt Lake City. Interstate 80 traverses Echo Canyon enroute to and from Wyoming and the east.

Davis County

Davis County has one of the smallest land areas of any county in the state but ranks third in total population. Davis is also the second most densely settled county after Salt Lake County. Its population is confined to an area little more than 20 miles long and hardly 10 miles wide. Near the Lagoon Amusement Park, the county's waist is pinched to only three miles by Farmington Bay and the mountains.

Formerly a series of semirural, agrarian communities, the towns of Davis County, including Clearfield, Layton, Kaysville, Centerville, and Bountiful, combine diminishing agricultural lands with expanding residential, commercial, and industrial areas. Between 1970 and 1995 its population increased from 99,028 to 216,000, with the greatest growth occurring in the northern half of the county. During the 55-year period between 1940 and 1995, its population multiplied more than ten times.

- Davis County Attractions -

Sightseers interested in the contrast between old and new are advised to drive the original main highway along the foothills between Ogden and Bountiful. Those who choose to explore the side streets will be rewarded by glimpses of older houses, farms, and orchards.

Hill Air Force Base (HAFB) ranks only behind Utah state government as an economic enterprise. About 20,000 civilian and military personnel are employed on the base, and expenditures exceed $1 billion annually. The base's payroll contributes immeasurably to the economy of Weber County and northern Davis County.

HAFB is a unit of the United States Air Force located at the mouth of Weber Canyon. The base occupies an area of 6,600 acres between I-15 on the west and Route 89 on the east. Its facilities include more than 1,600 buildings, 112 miles of roads and 36 miles of railroad, more than 1,000 vehicles, and an extensive system of runways and aprons. Its longest runway, 13,500 feet (more than two miles), can accommodate any military aircraft. The largest of its many huge warehouses and

A Utah family enjoying the beaches of Antelope Island
as the sun sets west over the Great Salt Lake
– Steve Greenwood, UTC

hangars occupies 12.5 acres under a single roof.

In addition to the main base, HAFB also has accountability and responsibility for nearly a million acres of federal land in the remote Great Salt Lake Desert of western Utah, as well as a testing site at Little Mountain.

The principal unit at HAFB is the Ogden Air Logistics Center (Ogden ALC), one of five support centers of the Air Force Logistics Command in the United States. Its responsibilities include serving as a maintenance facility for strategic intercontinental ballistic missiles. Technicians also maintain the F-26 Flying Falcon, the F-4 Phantom II, and the C-130 Hercules. The 388th Tactical Fighter Wing arrived in 1976 and is among the units stationed here.

Hill Air Force Base was established in the late 1930s as the Ogden Air Depot. It was redesignated Hill Air Force Base in 1948 in honor of Major Ployer Hill, who died piloting the original B-17 bomber at Wright Field, Ohio. The first shovel of dirt was turned on January 12, 1940, followed by a period of construction that has hardly ceased. Many types of aircraft have been either repaired, modified, serviced, or stored at HAFB during its half century of existence. In 1977, Hill became the logistics manager for the Air Force's new F-16 fighter, which remains one of its most prestigious management responsibilities.

Visitors may tour the Hill Aerospace Museum, 7961 Wardleigh Road, which includes a theater, an indoor gallery, classrooms, and displays. The museum boasts one of the largest collections of vintage aircraft and ordinance in the United States, including a stealth bomber. The museum is open every day except Mondays and is also closed on major holidays. Admission is free.

Antelope Island State Park occupies all of Antelope Island. It is located 13 miles west of Clearfield via Route 127 and a causeway. Developed by the State Division of Parks and Recreation beginning in the 1960s, the park features picnic shelters, campground, a boat marina, nature trails, beach, and showers. Observation overlooks provide views across the lake to the north and west, and a visual sweep of the Wasatch Range for a hundred miles or more. After being closed by high waters for most of the '80s, the 28,022-acre park is once again poised to become a major tourist attraction, as it was during the 1970s. Antelope Island harbors populations of antelope, bobcats, badgers, and a free-ranging buffalo herd. Over 350 different species of birds have been identified in the area.

The Bountiful Peak Drive connects Farmington and Bountiful, climbing in switchbacks up the face of the Wasatch Range, overlooking the Davis urban strip, lake marshes, and the vast expanse of the Great Salt Lake itself. The Morgan Valley can be seen far below to the east. The Forest Service maintains two camping-picnic areas along the route. The distance between Farmington and Bountiful is about 16 miles. On the Farmington end the road passes through the narrow gorge of Farmington Canyon. In Bountiful the drive is approached from 400 North and 1300 East. Be aware that this is a steep winding route.

Bountiful-Davis Art Center, 2175 South Main, offers a variety of classes and exhibits throughout the year, and includes a gift shop. Open six days a week.

Lagoon Amusement Park and Pioneer Village, beside I-15 and Route 89 in Farmington, is an attractively landscaped entertainment resort. The resort dates back to 1886, and is reportedly the second-oldest amusement park in the country. In addition to dozens of midway rides, games, and refreshment stands, the park features a $7 million water-slide complex, lush landscaping, picnic facilities, miniature golf, and a stadium. Pioneer Village at Lagoon is a museum of old-time transportation equipment and authentic 19th-century buildings that house shops and extensive collections of guns, Indian relics, and pioneer artifacts. Among its vintage buildings are a rock church, an early schoolhouse, and original houses furnished in period style. The Lagoon Opera House, a Victorian structure, features popular musicals. Adjoining the resort is a large campground.

Davis County boasts a number of vintage buildings dating from as far back as 1849. Many are listed on state and national historic registers. Driving the foothill highway and side streets in Bountiful, Centerville, Farmington, and Kaysville will reward viewers with discoveries of appealing adobe, rock, and frame structures that have survived from pioneer days. Of special note are the following: the Mormon Tabernacle, Main and Center, Bountiful, completed in 1862 and revered as one of the state's outstanding early church buildings, and the Mormon Rock Chapel, 272 North Main in Farmington, built of rock in 1861–63 and still in use.

The Right Place

BY KATHARINE COLES

My favorite monument in Salt Lake City is an urban one—a concrete shrine under a small gazebo on Sixth East. As I approach it for the first time since I lived nearby fourteen years ago, I notice the junipers around the little shrine are now overgrown. The gazebo's paint is peeling, and the bit of petrified stump it shelters has shrunk considerably, whether from weather or the greed of pilgrims who want to possess a fragment of history, I don't know.

I like this monument not only for what it enshrines but also for the rhetoric on the two plaques near it. The first, erected on Pioneer Day in 1939, extols the "Lone Cedar" that still stood then at what had been Emigration Road, once the only eastern approach to the city. It talks of the pioneers, loggers, and lovers who sheltered under its branches.

The plaque under the stump tells another story. Also erected on Pioneer Day but in 1960, the plaque explains that this tree, "Utah's first famous landmark," was cut down by "someone in a moment of thoughtlessness." This last phrase is deceptively simple. If the "someone" is known, the Daughters of the Utah Pioneers had the grace, or political wisdom, not to tattle in the permanence of bronze. If the "someone" is unknown, these same daughters have attributed to the miscreant the mildest of crimes, simple "thoughtlessness."

Something else has changed since I was last here in my own thoughtless youth. A group of schoolchildren have planted another cedar, just a few feet away. It appears to be thriving.

On my way to my second favorite monument in Salt Lake City, I unexpectedly find myself stomping through heavy brush in my skirt and sandals, watching for rattlesnakes. I am a poet with a deadline. There is construction at the This Is the Place State Park's main entrance, and the ranger said that going overland would be quicker and easier than walking the back road in. The back road was almost a mile long, he said, and I was in a hurry. He also told me the brush would be calf-high. He didn't look that much taller than I am, but apparently his height is mostly below the knee. Or maybe he meant the bovine kind of calf. On me, the brush is waist-high.

I don't see any rattlesnakes, but Mormon crickets, also in season, are leaping everywhere. This seems appropriate since the park celebrates the valley's early explorers and, especially, the arrival of Brigham Young's party of Mormon pioneers. Nestled into the foothills overlooking the city, the park has a rural feel. Its centerpiece is a large stone monument, my destination. Atop its highest pillar, Brigham Young holds out his hand; chiseled beneath him are the words This Is the Place, which is not what he said, but which has a nice ring to it. What he actually said was, "This is the right place."

I like that little inaccuracy, but the reason I'm here, in the rumble and dust of construction, after pulling my skirts up two brushy hills, is to reread what the plaque on the monument's east side says about Lansford W. Hastings, the explorer whose note, left in a hollow tree, directed the Donner Party to the route through Emigration Canyon that would fatally delay their expedition. The party would be trapped by snow in the Sierras; 36 would die of starvation, and the rest would survive only by cannibalizing their fellow-travelers. According to the again tactful text, the "adventurous but erratic" Hastings "seemed to be unaware of the difficulties" of the route. Again, there may be a practical explanation for this forgiving tone. The text explains that the trail through Emigration Canyon, cut at such cost by the Donner Party, later saved Brigham Young's party two weeks of travel and was the reason they arrived in time to get crops planted for the winter harvest.

I decide to take the road back. On my way, I run across another, much smaller monument. Wooden steps lead to the site. In spite of more weeds and possible snakes, I climb to the marker—a simple, whitewashed pillar, with the worn relief of what appears to be an ox skull carved into it. The inscription reads, This Is the Place, July 24, 1847. It's quiet; the wind blows and a jay flutters by. There is no construction here; there are no detailed historical plaques, no tourists.

The walk back along the road takes six minutes, including my stop at the little monument—half as long as my shortcut in. I arrive at the car and begin to pull burrs out of my hem, wondering, Which is the right place? Does it matter?

I once judged the anonymous plaque writers with youthful harshness. Their tact seemed born of an unwillingness to speak truth, of an essential falseness. At twenty-two, I thought whoever cut down that tree was probably a monumental jerk. And Hastings was no less a felon than any drunk driver, anyone whose reckless disregard causes another's death. "Thoughtless" and "erratic" didn't cover their sins. I still feel this way, but the feelings are complicated by time.

History. Dislocation. Misdirection. We map the past, and the present, into landscapes we can live in. Mythology becomes as accurate as events, at least emotionally, and is different for each of us. Finally, I love these places, love the history and the plaques and all the spectrum of error they represent. After all, if the work of these two, the miscreant and the felon, can be chalked up to single moments of bad judgment from which redemption is not only offered but assumed, perhaps there is hope for us all.

Brigham Young was looking for "a place on this earth that nobody else wants." When he saw the valley he exclaimed, "This is the right place" – François Camoin

Dancing Clouds – Tom Olson

Chapter
4

Utah's Great Basin and Range

— Box Elder, Morgan, Weber, Tooele, Juab, Millard, Beaver, and Iron Counties —

WEST OF UTAH'S URBAN CORRIDOR LIES THE GREAT BASIN AND RANGE PROVINCE. HERE ARE FARMLANDS, A GREAT DESERT, MOUNTAINS IN ENDLESS VARIETY, AND A FEW RIVERS WHOSE WATERS NEVER REACH THE SEA BUT EITHER SINK INTO THE SOIL OR EVAPORATE IN THE DRY AIR OF THE REGION.

THE EUROPEAN HISTORY OF THIS PART OF UTAH IS MOSTLY A TALE OF DESPERATE AND TEDIOUS CROSSINGS, ATTEMPTS TO REACH A GOLDEN LAND BEYOND THE FAR SIDE OF THE DESERTS. THE DONNER PARTY CROSSED HERE; THE PONY EXPRESS RIDERS RELAYED EACH

View of the Wastach from Promontory Point – Scott Smith

OTHER ACROSS THE EMPTY LAND; NORTH OF THE GREAT SALT LAKE THE RAILROAD BUILDERS FINALLY LINKED THEIR RAILS ACROSS THE CONTINENT. MARK TWAIN AND HORACE GREELEY CROSSED THE GREAT BASIN BY STAGECOACH.

EVEN NOW, MUCH OF THE LAND WEST OF SALT LAKE CITY IS SEEN AS A PLACE TO BE ENDURED, CROSSED AS QUICKLY AS POSSIBLE ON THE WAY TO THE GAMBLING CASINOS AND OTHER PLEASURES OF WENDOVER, NEVADA. OTHERS SEE IT AS A REPOSITORY FOR THOSE ENTERPRISES WE

"ONE NIGHT, A FULL MOON WATCHED OVER ME LIKE A MOTHER. IN THE BLUE LIGHT OF THE BASIN, I SAW A PETROGLYPH ON A LARGE BOULDER. IT WAS A SPIRAL. I PLACED THE TIP OF MY FINGER ON THE CENTER AND BEGAN TRACING THE COIL AROUND AND AROUND. IT SPUN OFF THE ROCK. MY FINGER KEPT CIRCLING THE LAND, THE LAKE, THE SKY. THE SPIRAL BECAME LARGER AND LARGER UNTIL IT BECAME A HALO OF STARS IN THE NIGHT SKY ABOVE STANSBURY ISLAND. THE WAVES CONTINUED TO HISS AND RETREAT, HISS AND RETREAT. IN THE WEST DESERT OF THE GREAT BASIN, I WAS NOT ALONE."

- Terry Tempest Williams -
"Greater Yellowlegs"
in Refuge: An Unnatural History
of Family and Place

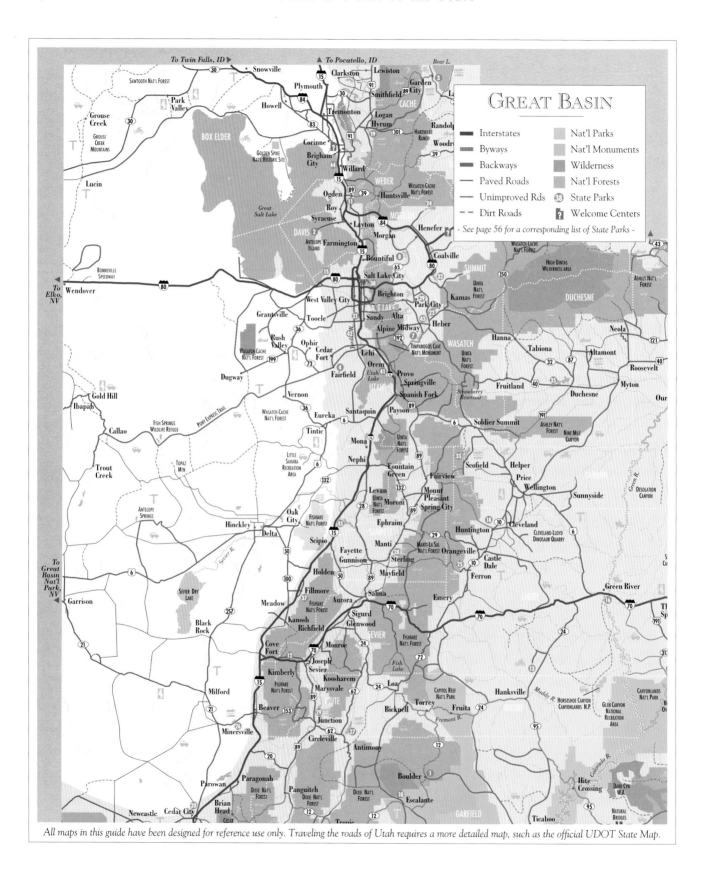

All maps in this guide have been designed for reference use only. Traveling the roads of Utah requires a more detailed map, such as the official UDOT State Map.

would rather not have next door; here are hazardous waste incinerators, landfills, bombing and rocketry ranges for the Air Force and the National Guard.

And yet there is a certain beauty to this part of Utah. Drive the Eisenhower Highway (I-80) through the endless white salt of the desert and you will see strange things—mirages, illusions, and also, if you pay attention, a perspective on the world you will not find elsewhere.

GREAT SALT LAKE DESERT
NORTH

The northwest corner of Utah, west of I-15 and north of I-80, is dominated by the presence of the Great Salt Lake. Sometimes called the Golden Spike Empire, after the ceremony marking the completion of the transcontinental railroad, this area encompasses more than 8,000 square miles, from the west side of the Wasatch Range to the Nevada border, extending south as far as the lower shore of Utah's dead sea.

Only the fertile Wasatch belt and Bear River Valley support more than a meager population. Elsewhere, people live on scattered ranches or in small towns, and thousands of square miles are virtually empty of human residents. The Great Salt Lake itself occupies a fluctuating area of more than a thousand square miles. The region's economy is broadly diversified, including large-scale and small-scale farming and ranching, transportation, trade, tourism, recreation, manufacturing, and defense industries.

Brigham City to Points West and North

- Bear River Migratory Bird Refuge -

Turn west from Brigham City on a hard-surfaced road that crosses a region of flats and salt marshes rimming the Great Salt Lake to the 73,000-acre Bear River Migratory Bird Refuge, 15 miles away, at the crossroads of two of the continent's major migratory waterfowl flyways. Visitors may gain a closeup view of the refuge from a 12-mile auto-tour route.

The Bear River's delta and its marshes have long been a natural feeding ground for millions of birds that pause here on their flights from Alaska to South America or to and from the Mississippi Valley. In pioneer days waterfowl were so thick they blackened the sky. Commercial hunters of the 1890s sold teal for $1 a dozen, mallard for $1.50 a dozen. About 60 species nest here. Among those that visit are the white-faced ibis, whistling swan, snowy egrets, the great blue heron and

black-crowned night heron, and the marbled godwit. Other birds seen at the refuge include pelicans, snow geese, bald and golden eagles, marsh hawks, prairie falcons, long-billed curlew, and several species of ducks.

Corinne and Environs

North of Brigham City, I-15 continues through Elwood, Riverside, and Plymouth into Idaho. Interstate 84 turns west just north of Elwood and traverses a region of low hills and increasingly high mountains where expansive grain fields follow the contours of the land. The fields gradually give way to the sparse ground cover typical of arid western Utah wherever the earth is not cultivated. Interstate 84 crosses into Idaho near Snowville, Utah.

A few miles north of Brigham City, Route 83 leaves I-15 and heads west to Corinne, Promontory Point, and the Golden Spike National Historical Site. Corinne "dreams in the sun, like an old man remembering his youth. The once roaring, fighting, hilarious rakehell town has little to show for its riotous past. A handful of houses, a few weather-stained business buildings, a church, and a school, are all that remain of a city of more than 20,000 people." So wrote the authors of the 1941 edition of this book. Since then the Railroad Village Museum, its locomotives, and old railroad depot have been moved to Heber City. Still remaining is the Bank of Corinne on Montana Street, a simple one-story frame-and-brick structure built in 1871. Serving as a bank until about 1875, the building was then used as City Hall from about 1890 to 1961. The Methodist Church, corner of Colorado and South 6th Street, was a quaint brick structure built in 1870 as one of the first (perhaps the first) non-Mormon church houses in Utah.

Corinne's founders hoped it would grow into a non-Mormon commercial center that would eventually rival and surpass Salt Lake City. A large three-decker paddle-wheel steamboat, *The City of Corinne*, was built in the hopes of making the town a major port. Soon after it was launched, however, the water level in the Great Salt Lake fell, the lower reaches of the Bear River silted up, and the enterprise failed. Further setbacks followed, and Corinne is now a small sleepy town, notable only for what it might have been.

West of Corinne, Route 83 passes across flat, marshy, former lake beds north of Bear River Bay. Terraces of prehistoric Lake Bonneville are prominent on the slopes of the hills near the highway and to the east along the base of the Wasatch.

Large Photo: The Tree of Life
along I-80 near Wendover
– *François Camoin*

Inset Photo: Ophir City Hall
is a nostalgic reminder of glory days past
– John George, UTC

At a junction 19 miles west of Corinne, Route 83 swings north towards Howell and I-84. A paved side road forks west from this junction to the Golden Spike National Historic Site (see National Parks and Monuments) and continues west beyond the historic site to Kelton and eventual junction with Route 30. Two miles west of the junction with Route 83, an improved road forks south from the historic site road, traversing a narrow strip between Bear River Bay and the Promontory Mountains to Promontory Point, the Southern Pacific Railroad, and the site of the former construction camp at Little Valley, active during the building of the rock-filled causeway across the Great Salt Lake. Visible to the east in Bear River Bay is the far-spreading expanse of dikes and ponds built by Great Salt Lake Minerals. The distance from Route 83 to Little Valley is 42 miles.

Snowville and the Northwest Corner

Snowville (4,550 alt.) is the center of Curlew Valley farming and dairying activities. It was settled by Idahoans and named for Lorenzo Snow, Mormon apostle and president.

Turn south on an unpaved road, passing through Curlew Valley to Locomotive Springs State Waterfowl Management Area, 20 miles away. This is an extensive marshland formed by Locomotive Springs at the north tip of the Great Salt Lake, popular for waterfowl shooting in season. An east-west road here follows the abandoned route of the transcontinental railroad, connecting Golden Spike National Historic Site on the east with Kelton and Lucin on the west.

Turn west on Route 30-42 from the junction with Interstate 84, 3 miles west of Snowville, 15 miles to Curlew Junction. Turn south on Route 30 to Park Valley, Rosette, and eventually Nevada. This paved highway—76 miles from Curlew Junction to the Nevada line—is an adventure road through the vast expanse of scrub-covered desert that marks the bed of vanished Lake Bonneville. The highway skirts the foothills of the impressively high and rugged Raft River Mountains (9,900 alt.) and Grouse Creek Mountains (9,000 alt.). For more than 30 years beginning in the 1840s, this now empty land was the route of travelers on their way to and from California. The first wagons to cross northern Utah were those of the Bartleson-Bidwell emigrant train, which came through in 1841. Though the majority of overland travellers passed to the west and north of the mountains on the main Salt Lake Cutoff, these early travellers pioneered what was to

become the route of the transcontinental railroad.

A web of fair-weather roads gives access to recesses of the mountain country of Utah's northwest corner; the land is forested in places and is utilized for stock grazing and sporadic mining. High points provide views of the desert west of the Great Salt Lake, its surface almost completely flat and devoid of vegetation to the south, higher and broken and less barren to the north, with scattered ranges here and there like islands in a sea. The area was described in the 1941 edition:

. . . IN SUMMER, THE HEAT WAVES OBSCURE THE LAND LIKE RIPPLING WATER AS THE SUN BEATS DOWN ON THE BAKED, WHITE CLAY FLATS. . . . PARK VALLEY WAS SETTLED BY RANCHERS IN 1869, THE RICH GRASS IN THE VALLEYS SUPPORTING LARGE HERDS OF CATTLE, THOUGH SCARCITY OF WATER ALWAYS COUNTERBALANCED FERTILITY OF THE SOIL. MORE LIVELY DAYS CAME WITH MINING EXCITEMENT IN THE LATE YEARS OF THE CENTURY. A VEIN OF GOLD WAS STRUCK, AND, AS RECALLED BY C.W. GOODLIFFE, EARLY SETTLER, FOR SOME TIME "EVERYTHING WAS HUSTLE AND BUSTLE." A SMALL FIVE-STAMP MILL WAS ERECTED AND MONEY WAS TURNED OUT AT THE RATE OF $500 PER DAY.

GREAT SALT LAKE DESERT
SOUTH
Salt Lake City to Points West and South

South of Interstate 80, seemingly endless valleys and mountain ranges—alternating in monotonous succession—march across western Utah and Nevada to the Sierra Nevada Range of California, 500 miles away. This arid and semiarid region in the rain shadow of the Sierra Nevada is known as the Great Basin or, more technically, the Basin and Range topographic province. In Utah it occupies a third of the state, extending westward from the mountainous spine of the Wasatch Range and the High Plateaus. No stream from this region reaches the sea.

Interstate 80, the Dwight D. Eisenhower Highway, stretches west for 120 miles from Salt Lake City to Wendover on the Nevada border. There are fewer curves and grades on this stretch of road than on any other in Utah; one 50-mile segment east of Wendover is arrow-straight. For many motorists the highway provides two hours of unrelieved monotony. This is regrettable, for few places in Utah have been the stage for more dramatic human exploits or boast a more interesting geological background—all within view of the highway. Those having an affection for unique landscapes will find this a weird and eerie world of peculiar charm. Along most of its route through Tooele County, I-80 passes across the exposed bed of ancient Lake Bonneville, predecessor of the Great Salt Lake, hardly deviating more than a few feet—for 70 miles—from a sustained altitude of 4,230 feet above sea level.

Lake Point Junction West to Wendover

At Lake Point the highway is confined to a narrow strip between the lake and the steep slopes of the Oquirrh Mountains. The Great Salt Lake State Park is here, and a marina down the road is the base for Salt Lake sailors. Across the interstate from the lake is the Kennecott smelter. The smelter's exhaust stack, completed in 1978, is 1,215 feet tall, the most conspicuous man-made object in the Salt Lake Valley.

At Lake Point Junction, I-80 diverges from state routes leading to Tooele and Grantsville. Tooele Valley borders the highway on the south, blue lake and barren flats on the north. For the entire distance to Wendover, highway and railroad run side by side.

Fifteen miles west of Lake Point Junction, Route 138 (old Route 40) forks south to Grantsville and the Stansbury Mountains. One mile west of this point, turn north on an unpaved road to Stansbury Island. This rocky range is about 11 miles in length, more than 2,000 feet high. Once used primarily for grazing, the island has seen a recent increase in mineral development. In actuality the island is a peninsula and has not been a true island for a hundred years, since the lake reached its historic high level of 4,211 feet in 1873. At that time, for a short period, Stansbury Island was cut off from the mainland by shallow salt water. It was named, as were the Stansbury Mountains to the south, for Captain Howard Stansbury, an Army engineer who headed the first scientific survey of the lake in 1850.

At Rowley Junction, 7 miles west of the Stansbury Island turnoff, side roads fork in several directions:

Turn north to the imposing brine-processing complex at Rowley, 12 miles away. Developed by NL Industries in the l970s at a cost of more than $150 million, the installation failed to return a profit and was sold in 1980 to AMAX Inc., now called MagCorp, for less than half that amount. Magnesium and other minerals are extracted from the lake's brine through a multistage process, beginning with solar evaporation, then continuing with heating and evaporation with gas, chemical refinement, drying and purifying, and finally separation in electrolytic cells.

West of Rowley Junction, side roads fork north at Delle (6 miles) and Low Pass (16 miles). These roads lead into and between the Lakeside and Grassy Mountains, an area that provides browse for surprising numbers of sheep. The unpaved main road from Low Junction ends at Lakeside (30 miles), a siding at the west end of the Southern Pacific causeway across the Great Salt Lake. En route, it passes through a portion of Hill Air Force Range, a military testing facility occupying more than 600 square miles of the Great Salt Lake Desert. The range is one unit of the vast Hill/Wendover/Dugway Range Complex, utilized by Department of Defense agencies for various military programs. These programs include practice in aerial bombing, gunnery, and rocketry; testing of explosives, munitions, and rocket motors; ordnance disposal; and testing of aircraft flight proficiency. (See also Dugway Proving Ground and Wendover Air Force Base.)

West of Low Pass the highway descends several hundred feet into the Great Salt Lake Desert. Even on maps the desert appears white. This is an appropriate color, for much of the desert is composed of salt or light-colored sand or clay. The desert is the bed of prehistoric Lake Bonneville, the ancestor of the Great Salt Lake—or, more accurately, a bay of that inland sea that became separated from Great Salt Lake by a low divide as the lake level declined. It is probable that the basin contained water in fairly recent times. Cut off from major streams, this portion of Lake Bonneville evaporated completely, whereas the Great Salt Lake has avoided the same fate because streams replenish what is lost by evaporation.

The Great Salt Lake Desert covers an area of more than 4,000 square miles and is one of the most desolate areas in the continental United States. Hundreds of square miles support little or no life. It is also one of the flattest land areas on the planet; most of its surface varies no more than 50 feet in elevation, and much of it is almost completely level. "On the edge of the desert, brush and grass supply winter forage for thousands of sheep; in the heart of the desert nothing grows," said the 1941 edition of this book. "With hardly a curve in more than 50 miles, the highway forms a black ribbon across the salt and alkali. Mirages are numerous. Small mountains seem like floating islands. In places the mountains appear to be upside down, with gigantic tunnels through them. Realistic water mirages are everywhere, and distances are tremendously deceptive." Even the curvature of the earth can be detected, it is said, from the Bonneville Salt Flats. Interstate 80 was completed across the desert in the 1970s, paralleling the Western Pacific Railroad and occupying in places the path of Route 40, its predecessor. Since World War II the greater part of the desert has been reserved for military purposes and is closed to public access.

Before the coming of the railroad and highway in this century, this central part of the desert was a forbidding barrier to travel. Several of the more dramatic incidents of the 19th century were recounted in the 1941 edition:

"The first recorded crossing of the Salt Desert was made from west to east by Jedediah Strong Smith and two other fur trappers on their return from California in 1827. Their course was over the southern edge of the desert, but Smith's uncomplaining 137-word description of the trip indicates some of the difficulties:

AFTER TRAVELING TWENTY DAYS FROM THE EAST SIDE OF MOUNT JOSEPH, I STRUCK THE SOUTHWEST CORNER OF GREAT SALT LAKE, TRAVELING OVER A COUNTRY COMPLETELY BARREN AND DESTITUTE OF GAME. WE FREQUENTLY TRAVELED WITHOUT WATER, SOMETIMES FOR TWO DAYS OVER SANDY DESERTS WHERE THERE WAS NO SIGN OF VEGETATION, AND WHEN WE FOUND WATER IN SOME OF THE ROCKY HILLS, WE MOST GENERALLY FOUND SOME INDIANS WHO APPEARED THE MOST MISERABLE OF THE HUMAN RACE, HAVING NOTHING TO SUBSIST ON (NOR ANY CLOTHING) EXCEPT GRASS-SEED, GRASSHOPPERS, ETC. WHEN WE ARRIVED AT THE SALT LAKE, WE HAD BUT ONE HORSE AND ONE MULE REMAINING, WHICH WERE SO FEEBLE AND POOR THAT THEY COULD SCARCE CARRY THE LITTLE CAMP EQUIPAGE WHICH I HAD ALONG; THE BALANCE OF MY HORSES I WAS COMPELLED TO EAT AS THEY GAVE OUT.

"In 1833 Joseph Walker's detachment of Captain Benjamin L. E. Bonneville's party circled the northern edge of the desert en route from Wyoming to California. No other crossing was attempted until 1841, when the California-bound Bartleson wagon train skirted the north end of Great Salt Lake and cut over the northern part of the desert . . ."

Captain John Charles Fremont, exploring the West for the United States government in 1845 with Kit Carson as guide, charted a route over the desert from Skull Valley to Pilot Peak, 20 miles north of Wendover. Mounted on horseback Fremont's party completed the trip with comparatively little difficulty. Fremont reported that the route was feasible, but he failed to take into account the difficulty of pulling heavy wagons through the desert.

Lansford Warren Hastings, empire dreamer, occupies an important if infamous place in the history of the Salt Desert.

Having led emigrant trains to Oregon and California in 1842 and 1843, Hastings apparently had an idea of conquering Pacific Coast territory and setting himself up as president. He returned east in 1844 and prepared his *Emigrant's Guide to Oregon and California*, then organized a party to return with him to the west coast. They followed the Oregon Trail to Fort Hall, Idaho, and then branched southwest to California. Seeking a shorter route, Hastings and a small party started eastward in 1846 with James Clyman, trapper, as a guide. Mounted on good horses, they took the route surveyed by Fremont and Carson, and completed the trip with no serious trouble, though Clyman wrote in his diary, "This is the most desolate country on the whole globe, there being not one spear of vegetation, and of course no kind of animal can subsist." Continuing to Fort Bridger, Wyoming, Hastings recommended the route to everyone he met.

At Fort Bridger, Hastings found four groups, totaling eighty wagons and including the parties of Samuel C. Young and George Harlan, who accepted his offer to guide them over the shorter desert trail. Hastings, however, had a penchant for trying new and uncharted routes. Deviating from the trail with which he was familiar, he attempted a new course between Fort Bridger and the Great Salt Lake, and his party had great difficulties in crossing the Wasatch Mountains. Eventually, however, they emerged through Weber Canyon and eventually brought the first wagon to come into the Salt Lake Valley by any route. Skirting the south end of the Great Salt Lake and traversing Skull Valley, the company began the first crossing ever attempted by wagon over the center of the desert. The distance was greater than they had anticipated, and they found no water. Oxen dropped from exhaustion and wagons were left strewn along the trail. When the emigrants finally reached Pilot Peak, they hauled water and grass over the back trail to save stock and to bring in abandoned wagons. Many days were required to collect their possessions before they could continue to California.

A week or ten days behind the Hastings party came the Donner-Reed wagon train. The caravan spent two weeks trying to get through a canyon, then found the route impassable. Eventually they worked their way down Emigration Canyon into Salt Lake Valley. It was early September when the Donner-Reed party began its tragic trek over the Salt Desert. After two and a half days of travel without water, Reed volunteered to ride in search of a spring. He found no trace of water until he reached Pilot Peak, 30 miles ahead. Returning, he met the first of his party still 20 miles out. The oxen were falling one by one and being left on the desert. Wearied by five days and nights without sleep, Reed found his wagon mired down. Carrying their small children, he and his wife began the long walk across the wasteland. Meantime Jacob Donner reached Pilot Peak, watered his oxen, and started back for the Reed family. He found them exhausted, resigned to death on the desert. Several wagons were abandoned and many cattle died, but the entire company survived. The delay, however, was costly. They reached the Sierra Nevadas too late to cross before winter, and became snowbound a hundred miles from Sutter's Fort. Many perished of starvation and exposure. Others survived by cooking and eating their boots, harness, and the flesh of dead members of the party. Of the eighty-seven emigrants who began the journey, only forty-four reached their destination.

Evidence of the Donner-Reed crossing is still preserved in the surface of the desert. Tracks made nearly a hundred years ago by wagons too heavy for the thin salt crust are still visible. The route of the Hastings Cutoff has been retraced and many articles left along the trail have been gathered.

In 1896 William Randolph Hearst, chain newspaper publisher, decided to send a message by bicycle from his *San Francisco Examiner* to his *New York Journal* as a publicity stunt. William D. Rishel of Salt Lake City was delegated to map out a portion of the course. Rishel and C. A. Emise took a train to Lucin, Utah, where they unloaded their bicycles and started back to Salt Lake City, laying their trail over the desert around the south end of the lake.

In 1903 the Southern Pacific Railroad built the Lucin Cutoff (see Great Salt Lake) across the Great Salt Lake and the Salt Desert. In 1907 the Western Pacific Railroad laid rails across the desert, closely following the Hastings Cutoff. Early attempts to build a highway over the desert were unsuccessful.

About 25 miles east of Wendover stands the *Tree of Utah*, an 87-foot-tall sculpture of reinforced concrete covered with ceramic tiles, put up in 1981 by sculptor Karl Momen.

Several miles east of Wendover, a road forks north to the Bonneville Salt Flats, site of the famed Bonneville Speedway.

The Bonneville Salt Flats are composed of rock-hard salt, laid down as Lake Bonneville evaporated. The area most suit-able for racing measures about 10 by 15 miles and consists of hard salt of sufficient thickness to support heavy vehicles. During most of the year the salt is either under water or too moist for racing, but the summer sun evaporates the surface moisture, and usually the flats are in ideal condition by August and September. Said the 1941 edition of this book, they look "very much like an immense lake of snow-covered ice. . . . The remarkable qualities of this natural course [were] first shown in 1914, when Teddy Tetzleff, nationally-known race driver, set an unofficial world record of 141 miles an hour for a measured mile. In 1926 Utah's Ab Jenkins drove for 24 hours without relief, and broke almost every world speed record by traveling 2,710 miles at an average speed of 112 miles an hour." Jenkins returned in the 1930s to establish new records. Sir Malcolm Campbell exceeded 300 miles per hour (mph) in 1935, the first person to reach that speed in an automobile. His record was broken in 1937 by Captain George Eyston's 311 mph. John Cobb set new world records in 1938, 1939, and 1947. Athol Graham, a Utahn, died in the crash of his City of Salt Lake in 1960 at 300 mph. That same year Donald Campbell of England survived a crash of his Bluebird at 365 mph. Cobb's record of 394 mph, set in 1947, was not officially surpassed until 1963, when Craig Breedlove—driving a three-wheeled jet racer—reached 428 mph in the one-way mile. Breedlove and Art Arfons competed in October 1964, "the greatest racing month in the speedway's history," when Breedlove attained a speed of 526 mph and Arfons 536 mph. The following year in November 1965, Arfons and Breedlove competed once again. This time Arfons reached a top speed of 576 and Breedlove 601 mph, giving Breedlove the honor of being the first person to surpass 500 and 600 mph in an automobile. His 1965 record held until 1970, when Gary Gabelich reached 631 mph in the one-way mile, driving a rocket-powered racer. In 1979 Stan Barrett's rocket vehicle attained the speed of 639 mph. In the fall of 1981 a British team attempted to set official records exceeding this speed but were defeated by bad weather.

In recent years the racing surface has deteriorated; events have occasionally had to be canceled, the course relocated, and the future of racing at the Bonneville Salt Flats is in doubt. The causes of the deterioration are not known, though the increased extraction of minerals by industry is suspected to have played a part.

Potash and sodium chloride (salt) have been recovered from the brines of Bonneville Salt Flats since 1917. The Salt Flats proper, including the speedway area to the north, is a rather limited area that fluctuates in size from 110 to 160 square miles, depending on precipitation. In effect it is a drainage sump for the much larger Great Salt Lake Desert. As such, its subsurface brines are extremely concentrated, and in places a hard salt pan has formed (at the speedway in particular).

Wendover (4,232 alt.) utilizes the Utah-Nevada state line as its western boundary of incorporation. Only the Utah side of town is incorporated. In 1941 Wendover was "a railroad town. . . . The railroad roundhouse and the large yellow frame depot are conspicuous among the unpainted frame houses." Long ago these ceded prominence to motels, casinos, new houses, and the huge military structures of Wendover Air Force Base. The first transcontinental telephone line was joined at Wendover in 1914. Wendover was founded in 1907 as a railroad watering point during construction of the Western Pacific Railroad, serving as a terminal for a pipeline carrying water from Pilot Peak, 20 miles to the north. Not until after the highway was completed in 1925 did it become a travelers' oasis with service stations and lodging. A casino was added on the Nevada side in the 1930s. This evolved into today's elaborate Stateline Hotel and Casino, joined in recent years by other such enterprises.

Danger Cave, about 2 miles northeast of Wendover in the Silver Island Range, is an undeveloped state park and is listed on the National Register of Historic Places. Utilized as a shelter by some of the most ancient peoples known to have lived in Utah, the cave was excavated during the 1950s by archaeologists from the University of Utah under the direction of Professor Jesse D. Jennings. Danger Cave is about 60 feet wide by 120 feet long and originally contained a layer of refuse as much as 13 feet deep. According to its National Register description, Danger Cave "has been one of the key sites for understanding the prehistoric cultures of the desert West." Five strata of cultural occupation were present, beginning with Archaic material (estimated to be at least 10,000 years old.) The thousands of artifacts of chipped and ground stone, bone, horn, antler, wood, leather, cordage, basketry, and shell recovered from the Archaic levels were the basis for defining the Desert Archaic lifeway, a model of prehistory that has since influenced all scientific work done in the west-

ern United States. After approximately A.D. 400 the site was used by Sevier culture peoples, who hunted buffalo and the abundant waterfowl found near the cave. While Danger Cave is listed as a state park, there is little provision for visitation and the site is fragile. Interested visitors should contact the Division of State Parks for information.

Wendover Air Force Base (Auxiliary Field), now but a skeletal remnant of the huge military base that flourished here during World War II, sprawls south of the highway on the eastern outskirts of Wendover. During the early 1940s the base contained more than 600 buildings: barracks, houses, hospital, warehouses, hangars, shops, and everything else required for a self-contained community where nearly 20,000 civilian workers and military personnel lived.

The facility was built in 1940. During World War II it served as a base for the training of heavy bomber crews. A city was built of salt for bombing practice. Lifelike battleship targets and a mobile machine-gun range were constructed. One program to train fighter pilots to fly bombers is said to have cost the lives of 121 men as a result of crashes. By late 1943 the base had a population of 17,500 military personnel and 2,000 civilian workers.

After the end of the war the miltary revealed Wendover Air Force Base had been the training site for the air crews who dropped atomic bombs on Hiroshima and Nagasaki.

The base continued to be used sporadically as a site for bombing, rocketry, gunnery, missile recovery, and other training purposes. It was deactivated and declared surplus in 1948; reactivated; deactivated again in 1957; reactivated on a minor scale in 1961; and declared surplus again in 1962. In that year only 128 buildings remained of the original 668. For several years in the late 1960s and early 1970s, Wendover Base and the Salt Desert were considered a potential site for a NASA spaceport. The base's facilities no longer are used by the military except in emergencies, though much of the former training range is a part of the Hill/Wendover/Dugway Range Complex of the Department of Defense.

Tooele County is the second-largest county in Utah—nearly 7,000 square miles of arid valleys, skeletal mountains, the bitter waters of Great Salt Lake, and the desolation of the Great Salt Lake Desert. Here and there—in the valleys, the canyons, or the deserts—the forbidding land gives way to human oases. They seem out of place, startling in their unexpectedness.

Some are but ghostly relics of bygone years, nostalgic reminders of the flow of time and change.

Lake Point Junction South to Tooele and Rush Valleys

In the vicinity of Lake Point Junction, a village flourished for 60 years or more. Settled in the mid-1850s by Peter Maughan and others (Maughan later was a prominent settler of Cache Valley), the community was long known as E. T. City in honor of Ezra Taft Benson, Mormon Church apostle and ancestor of the modern-day church president, who was a leader in the colonization of Tooele Valley.

At Mills Junction, 4 miles south of Lake Point Junction, Route 138 (old Route 40) forks west to Grantsville. Adobe Rock marks the junction. A historic landmark, Adobe Rock stands beside a route used since the days of the fur trappers and Salt Desert pioneers. A spring nearby provided fresh water for campers. West of Mills Junction a short distance, beside the highway, is the Benson Grist Mill. Dating from 1854, the antique gristmill was still in use as a flour mill in 1941 when the first edition of this guidebook appeared. It was referred to therein as Brigham Young's Gristmill. The Benson Mill is "one of the oldest buildings still standing in western Utah," according to its National Register description. "It was still in use in 1960 to grind feed for turkeys and cattle." The mill has been restored and is open to the public during the summer. Nearby, in 1941, stood the Utah Wool Pullery, "a group of buildings in which nearly a million pounds of wool are pulled from pelts annually."

Grantsville (4,300 alt.) is a residential community that stretches along the highway for several miles. In 1941 it was "a typical rural Mormon community, deriving its livelihood from alfalfa, grain, sheep, and turkeys. Squat adobe houses built by the first settlers rub shoulders with later brick dwellings. Water is obtained from artesian wells." Since 1941 the population has multiplied several times, and the economy depends to a lesser degree on agriculture. Many local people commute to work at Tooele Army Depot, Dugway Proving Ground, and MagCorp's magnesium plant at Rowley. But the pioneer heritage of Grantsville (settled in 1851) can be seen in older buildings and lanes bordered by tall lombardy poplars.

The Donner-Reed Memorial Museum, 90 North Cooley Street, displays artifacts left by the Donner-Reed pioneers of 1846 along the route of their memorable trek through west-ern Utah, in addition to other valuable historic relics and Indian artifacts. Open by arrangement.

Turn south from Grantsville 5 miles to South Willow Canyon in the Stansbury Mountains. A partially paved road climbs steeply through the Wasatch National Forest to a parking and camping area at 7,800 feet (12 miles from Grantsville), from which a foot trail leads about 4 miles through pleasant glades and over rocky ledges to the top of Deseret Peak (11,031 alt.), highest point in the range. This lofty perch affords a circular panorama across the western desert, Great Salt Lake, and seemingly boundless valleys and mountain ranges in every direction. A small stream provides a modest fishing experience. The road now ends at the boundary of the Deseret Peak Wilderness Area.

Route 36 continues south from Mills Junction to Tooele, passing through a wide-open expanse of dry farms and irrigated fields. The lofty Oquirrhs loom to the east, the even higher Stansbury Range to the west. A keen eye may detect the route of an aerial tramway rising from the valley floor near Mills Junction to the top of Coon Peak, 5,000 feet higher, where a television transmission station is located. The hamlet of Erda dates from pioneer days of the 1850s. Built around Tule (Tuilia) Springs, it was known first as Rose Springs Fort, then Bates and Batesville.

Tooele (5,100 alt.) is the seat of Tooele County, situated in the high southern end of Tooele Valley, only 12 miles from the Great Salt Lake but 700 feet higher. In Tooele reside more than half the population of the county, which is Utah's second largest with 6,923 square miles of area. The name is pronounced variously as Too-IL-uh or Too-EL-uh. Derivation of the name is uncertain and controversial. It may have originated from the Spanish *tule* (pronounced too-leh) for bulrushes in the valley's marshes, or from the name of Gosiute chief Tuilla.

Tooele was settled by Mormon pioneers in 1849 and is a clean, attractive city today with a busy main street and mod-ern residential developments. The city's population is a cosmopolitan mix, due in part to its mining and smelting background and the proximity of large military installations. Because of rapid growth, Tooele's early origins are not as apparent as they were a few years ago. However, early struc-tures do remain, as side-street driving will attest. The old Tooele County Courthouse, built in 1867, is a registered historic site. Parks in the downtown area contain a pioneer log cabin and a steam locomotive of former days.

Turn northeast from Tooele to the former site of the great lead concentrator and smelter of International Smelting & Refining Company. This landmark was closed and dismantled in the early 1970s after nearly 60 years of production. Built in 1910, the huge smelter was still processing a million tons of ore annually in 1940. Ore was brought over the mountain from the Bingham mine by aerial tramway. In this connection, the 1941 edition of this book described one of Utah mining's most ambitious and visionary projects, the Elton Tunnel. The tunnel was never completed, and the water flow has been cut off by a cave-in, but excavation did result in discovery of ore bodies now being mined by Kennecott.

Turn east from Tooele to Middle Canyon, a narrow, steep-walled gash in the Oquirrh Range. Paved for much of the distance, the road passes through wooded bottoms for a few miles, then rises swiftly in tight curves to Butterfield Pass (8,400 alt.), marking the divide between the Tooele and Salt Lake Valleys. (Trailers not permitted beyond Bingham Metals, 9 miles from Tooele.) The road forks at Butterfield Pass, the east spur descending Butterfield Canyon to Lark and Herriman. The north spur continues a steep and winding climb for another mile or two to Sunset Peak (West Mountain) Overlook, a parking area atop the Oquirrh summit ridge. From this 9,400-foot eyrie the view encompasses several thousand square miles of northern and western Utah—a breathtaking jumble of mountains, basins, valleys, and lakes. Tooele Valley can be glimpsed to the west, with Salt Lake Valley and Salt Lake City sprawling in their entirety to the east, 5,000 feet below. On a clear day the whole magnificent front of the Wasatch Range can be traced for 150 miles from one end to the other, from Mt. Nebo on the south to the range's northern terminus beyond Brigham City. Rivaling the natural scene in visual impact is the giant crater of Kennecott's Bingham Copper Mine.

The best view of the open-pit mine is reached by taking the 7800 South exit off Interstate 15 in Salt Lake City, and driving west on the Bingham Highway (Route 48) to Copperton.

Turn southeast from Tooele to Settlement Canyon, a popular scenic drive and the site of Legion Park, a community recreation area.

West of Route 36, 3 miles south of Tooele, is the entrance to Tooele Army Depot, a military installation and headquarters of a far-flung depot complex known as TEAD (Tooele Army Depot). The Tooele Valley installation occupies 25,000 acres, and all of this can be seen from the highway in panoramic overview: orderly rows of soil-covered igloos and magazines, warehouses, shops, rail yards, administrative and housing complex, and hundreds of acres of open-air storage aprons. An additional 19,000 acres are in the nearby Rush Valley (Depot South Area). As is the case for most defense installations in 1996, TEAD's Utah operations are in a state of reorganization, with some being shut down, others unused, and yet others seeking privatization.

A short distance south of the entrance to TEAD, another side road forks west to Bauer, where Combined Metal Reduction Company operated two mines (metallic ores) and a concentrating mill between 1923 and 1959. About 15,000 fruit trees were planted nearby to utilize water pumped from the mine workings. After closing of the mines, Combined Metals processed perlite from Nevada and fossil resins shipped from Carbon County. These resins were used in making paints and varnishes, inks, adhesives, fabrics, and chewing gum. The Bauer plant was destroyed by fire in 1980.

South of the TEAD and Bauer turnoffs, Route 36 passes over a low divide between Tooele and Rush Valley. A flat-topped ridge to the west of the highway, known as Stockton Bar or the Great Bar, is an interesting geological curiosity. The sand and gravel bar was created by the waves of prehistoric Lake Bonneville during its highest stages. As the lake fell, the bar became a dike separating shallow Rush Valley Bay from the main lake to the north. Stockton Bar and prominent benches formed by waves on the mountain slopes of this vicinity are among the most vivid reminders of the great lake's existence. Rush Lake—marked today by marshes in the valley bottom west of Stockton—is a remnant of a much larger body of water that once occupied Rush Valley. Rush Lake contained water and fish for years after white settlers arrived; for that reason it was selected as the site of military camps by Lt. Colonel Steptoe in 1854 and Colonel Connor a few years later.

Stockton (5,280 alt.) is a rather nondescript residential village dating from the 1860s and l870s, when several smelters were built to process ore from the area's mines. The first of these was constructed in 1864 by Colonel Patrick E. Connor, the "father of Utah mining," whose Fort Douglas soldiers discovered valuable ore deposits in the vicinity.

St. John Junction, 5 miles south of Stockton, is a major fork. Route 36 continues south from here to Route 6 near Eureka, while Route 73 turns southeast to Fairfield and Utah Valley, giving access to Ophir and Mercur (see Route 73 below).

Route 199 forks west from Route 36 at a point 4 miles south of St. John Junction. This paved highway is the main route to Dugway Proving Ground, running from Rush Valley to Skull Valley by way of Johnson's Pass, a natural divide between the Onaqui and Stansbury ranges. Clover and St. John are rustic farming hamlets in RushValley; they have now merged to become Rush Valley City. Clover was settled in the mid-1850s by Luke Johnson and others, and St. John in 1867 by former residents of Clover. These rural villages, isolated from big cities, still display poignant reminders of Utah's early years in the form of aging 19th-century structures. A log house in St. John, for example—owned by the Arthur family—dates from 1869 and is listed on a historic register.

Sprawling across the valley slope to the east of Route 36 is Depot South (see Route 73 below). The main line of the Union Pacific Railroad, connecting Salt Lake City with Los Angeles, parallels the highway through Rush Valley. East of the highway, 9 miles south of St. John Junction and near the south boundary of Deseret Depot, a farming settlement known as Centre and a remarkable establishment called the Ajax Underground Store once existed. The town disappeared long ago, and only an excavation in the ground marks the store's former location. What made the store unique was its underground location—11,000 square feet of floor space, excavated by hand, the soil-covered roof supported by cedar poles and the interior lighted by high south-facing windows. Lodging and food were available for both people and livestock, as well as a department-store selection of goods. By 1914 changing conditions forced the store to close, and within a few years it caught fire and collapsed.

Near Faust Station, 12 miles south of the junction with Route 199, an unpaved but graded and maintained side road forks west toward the mountains. This is the famous Old Pony Express and Stage Trail.

Vernon (5,500 alt.) is a farming village settled in the early 1860s. In 1900, it is estimated, 100,000 horses, cows, and sheep ranged the area's mountains and valleys. As a consequence of overgrazing, much of the area became unproductive as grass-lands and reverted to sagebrush. Dry land wheat farming was successful for a time, but eventually this was given up. Beginning in the 1940s, experiments at the Benmore Soil Conservation Project south of Vernon were successful in demonstrating how such overgrazed and marginal lands could be reclaimed for livestock by clearing unwanted vegetation, then reseeding with crested wheat grass and controlling subsequent grazing.

From its junction with Route 36 south of Stockton, Route 73 runs generally southeast and climbs Rush Valley's rising slope, passing near Deseret Depot (Depot South Area) below the highway to the west.

Occupying 19,000 acres, an area measuring 5 by 6 miles in extent, Deseret Depot was constructed in 1942–43 by the U.S. Army and given the name Deseret Chemical Depot. Thousands of workers quit their jobs during construction because of fierce dust and sandstorms. A new town was built with housing and support facilities for a thousand people, and during World War II as many as a thousand workers were employed at the depot. The depot's mission then was the storage and shipment of chemical warfare materials, including poison gases, chemicals, and chemical ammunition. After that war it was deactivated. The Korean War in the 1950s brought reactivation and new construction. In 1955 the depot was assigned to the Tooele Army Depot and is now known as the Depot South Area.

Ophir (6,500 alt.) is nestled among lush creekside trees and shrubs in the bottom of Ophir Canyon, 3 miles from Route 73. The pleasant little community of today gives only the slightest indication that it was a mining boomtown a hundred years ago. The last mine closed in 1972 and a small store is the only business today. Several venerable rock buildings, a few frame shacks, and the restored Old City Hall and Fire Station (1870) are nostalgic reminders of Ophir's glory days, which were described in the 1941 edition as follows:

INDIANS MINED SILVER AND GOLD FOR TRINKETS, AND LEAD FOR BULLETS, IN THIS LITTLE CANYON. CONNOR'S MEN, HEARING OF THE INDIAN MINE, STAKED THE ST. LOUIS LODE IN THE LATE 1860S. THE STRIKE TOUCHED OFF A BOOM. MINERS AND PROSPECTORS DASHED INTO CAMP FROM NEVADA AND CALIFORNIA, AND SOON THE POCATELLO, VELOCIPEDE, WILD DELIRIUM, AND MINER'S DELIGHT WERE LOCATED. MACK GISBORN, WHO MADE HIS STAKE AT MERCUR, BUILT A TOLL ROAD FROM OPHIR TO STOCKTON. WAGONS HAULED ORE OVER THIS ROAD AND NORTH TO LAKE POINT, ON GREAT SALT LAKE, WHERE IT WAS BOATED TO CORINNE AND THE RAILROAD. THE USUAL "BOOMERS"

HURRIED INTO CAMP AND THREW UP SHACKS. SALOONS LINED THE STREET, INTERSPERSED WITH BROTHELS AND GAMBLING DENS.

Ophir's ore contained relatively little gold but was rich in silver, lead, and zinc. It is estimated that production value of these minerals between 1870 and 1970 totaled more than 40 million dollars.

Ruined foundations, marking long-abandoned mining works, can be seen along the highway between Ophir Junction and the west-access side road leading to Mercur. This unpaved fair-weather road to Mercur passes through the shallow canyon of Mercur Creek and emerges finally into a mountain-girt pocket where one of Utah's largest and most famous mining communities once existed. The main highway, Route 73, continues to Fairfield and Utah Valley.

The site of Mercur is marked primarily by mine shafts, dumps, a few tumbledown shacks, collapsing walls, and empty foundations. Above all, the imposing ruins of the great smelter complex known as the Golden Gate mill occupies a hilltop like an ancient temple. It would be impossible, from what remains, to visualize the city of 6,000 or more that flourished here about the turn of the century.

Fairfield (4,900 alt.) is a farming village in the wide expanse of Cedar Valley, marked by aged cottonwood and poplar trees. The town's principal attractions, other than a picturesque old school building, are Camp Floyd Military Cemetery, Old Stagecoach Inn, and a reconstructed Army Commissary Building. These latter are state historical sites, open to the public, administered and maintained by the State Division of Parks and Recreation. The cemetery, a half mile south of town, marks the former site of old Camp Floyd/Fort Crittenden. Markers memorialize the graves of 84 soldiers known to have been buried there; the markers were placed in 1960. Old Stagecoach Inn is a quaint two-story structure, built of frame and adobe, with upper and lower porches across the front. Built about 1857 by the John Carson family as a dwelling, it was soon converted to an inn known thereafter as the Carson Inn and Fairfield Hotel. The building functioned in that capacity until 1947. It was restored by the state in 1959. The old inn also served as a Pony Express station in 1860–61 and as a stagecoach stop for years after that. Insofar as possible the inn has been restored to its original condition.

Camp Floyd was established by the army detachment of Colonel Albert Sydney Johnston immediately after its arrival in Utah in June 1858.

Overnight, Fairfield became one of those typical hell-roaring, wild places of the West and, with Camp Floyd, soon had a population of some 7,000 or more people. The population of Salt Lake City was then only 15,000. Along with tradespeople, artisans, and mechanics came a civilian riffraff of saloon-keepers (there were 17 saloons in the town), gamblers, women, thieves, and robbers, all attracted there by the Army payroll, which was about the only actual money in the Rocky Mountain West. A theater was built and a military Dramatic Association was organized. Plays were given weekly and later daily. Dances were frequent. And, of course, Frogtown, or "Dobieville," as Fairfield was called, just over the creek, furnished other outlets for those who could obtain off-bounds passes. By the 1860s, the storm clouds of the Civil War were gathering. Many of the troops were ordered away from Camp Floyd in that year, and by fall only 10 companies of troops remained. *(Material courtesy Utah Division of Parks & Recreation.)*

Rowley Junction South to Skull Valley and Dugway

Timpie Springs State Waterfowl Management Area is accessible from Timpie Junction. Turn south from Timpie (Rowley) Junction to Skull Valley, Iosepa, and Dugway Proving Ground. Skull Valley is a broad basin cupped between the Stansbury Range on the east and Cedar Mountains on the west. Despite its forbidding aspect, the valley has long been a favored winter range for sheep. Perennial springs furnish water for ranching operations as well as meadows and marshes.

Skull Valley is a most unlikely site for a settlement of Polynesian natives—a successful farming and stock-raising community that existed in the valley for nearly 30 years. The town of Iosepa was situated on the Stansbury foothills 15 miles south of Timpie Junction. (Its name is the Hawaiian version of the name Joseph, pronounced variously as Yo-seh-puh or Yo-say-puh, applied in honor of Mormon Church president Joseph F. Smith, who had been a missionary in Hawaii as a young man.) According to Dennis Atkins in his manuscript entitled *A History of the Polynesian Colony at Iosepa*, Iosepa was founded in 1889 by the Iosepa Agriculture and Stock Company, a Utah corporation formed by the Mormon Church to purchase a ranch and livestock owned by John T. Rich, for the express purpose of Hawaiian settlement. Most of the company's stock was owned by the church and directors representing the church. Numbering about 50, the first body of settlers arrived on August 28, 1889, a day observed thereafter as Iosepa's Pioneer Day. A sawmill was soon purchased and lots surveyed; construction of homes began in September. In the center of town was a public square of 11 acres, and every lot was a corner lot having sufficient room for a home, garden, barn, and corral.

The colony was disbanded between 1915 and 1917, following the building of a Mormon temple in Hawaii; many of the town's residents returned to their former island homes. Iosepa's cemetery is listed on the National Register of Historic Places. Privately owned; request permission locally before visiting.

About 10 miles south of the Iosepa turnoff, the Skull Valley Indian Reservation straddles the highway. As described in the 1941 edition of this book, the reservation "consists of 18,640 acres of desert land set aside for the Gosiute Indians, who herd a few sheep, gather pine nuts, till small poverty-stricken farms, and rent part of their grazing land to ranchers." This area has been occupied by the Goshutes (Gosiutes) since prehistoric times as a source of wild food before whites arrived and of cultivated crops since the 1860s. (See Goshute Reservation.)

In this vicinity in 1968, about 6,500 sheep died of unknown causes. Suspicion was directed at the nearby Dugway Proving Ground where open-air testing of chemical warfare agents was alleged to have been underway at the time. Though it never admitted direct responsibility, the federal government eventually compensated the owners of the sheep.

Skull Valley pinches to a narrow waist near the entrance to the Dugway Proving Ground. Here the highway rises to 5,000 feet, permitting sweeping views across the desolate heart of Great Salt Lake Desert. At Dugway the Skull Valley road is joined by Route 199, which connects with Route 36 in Rush Valley south of Tooele. Route 199 is usually preferred as the main access route to Dugway. Sixty years ago, this road— then known as the Lincoln Highway—continued west from Dugway to Granite Mountain, then south to the Old Pony Express and Stage Trail near Black Rock. South of Dugway, the Skull Valley road (unpaved beyond the Dugway gate) leads 11 miles to the Old Pony Express and Stage Trail.

Dugway Proving Ground (military reserve; access restricted) occupies about 841,000 acres (1,300 square miles) of Tooele County. Much of the reservation consists of near-barren, low-lying desert—the bed of Lake Bonneville—but low mountains on the east and north, undisturbed for years by livestock grazing, are the habitat of pygmy evergreens, lush desert ground cover, and relatively abundant wildlife. Dugway's general mission is a matter of public knowledge. Yet remoteness, limited access, the secrecy attached to some of its works, and the fearsome nature of certain projects have surrounded the proving ground with an aura of mystery.

Since its establishment in 1942, Dugway's projects have included the development and testing of chemical mortars, incendiary and flame-throwing weapons, and chemical and biological warfare agents (including toxic gases such as nerve gas). Other projects have included the development of protective clothing and equipment, and measures for defense, decontamination, neutralization, and detection. Dugway's work has not been limited to military weapons. It is involved as well in environmental and ecological research and development—for example, the study of animal and insect diseases, pollution abatement, and waste disposal. Sections of the proving ground also are utilized by the U.S. Air Force in its flight testing program.

Nevada via the Pony Express Trail

The Old Pony Express and Stagecoach Trail between Fairfield and the Utah-Nevada state line—a distance of about 154 miles—is an unpaved but maintained route, passable with automobiles when dry. (Several stretches in the Fish Springs-Callao area may be impassable when wet.) Travelers on this route find it easy to visualize pioneer travel of the 19th century, because the land remains much the same as it was 120 years ago when the route was surveyed by army troops.

Warning: Travelers should not expect to obtain food, gasoline, or other services between Rush Valley and Wendover, a distance of 150 miles. Carry tools, food, water, spare tire, etc. Extra gas may be advisable. Stay on traveled roads for safety, as sand and mud are real hazards. Remember that historic sites are protected under federal and state law. Leave the land as undisturbed as you find it.

For most of its length, this route was one of the earliest to cross western Utah, having been used—in part—as early as the 1840s. The trail was used by Chorpenning's Jackass Mail in the 1850s, and by hordes of other travelers during that decade. It was formally surveyed in 1859 between Camp

Floyd and Genoa, Nevada, by an Army detachment under the command of Captain J. H. Simpson. Thereafter the route was followed by the Pony Express in 1860–61, by stage-coaches and other horse-drawn vehicles from the1860s into the 20th century, and by uncounted thousands of other travelers to the present day. It was also the route of the first transcontinental telegraph line between 1861 and 1869.

The sites of original Pony Express and stagecoach stations— or the majority of them—are marked today by stone monuments and plaques. Some have been vandalized. The U.S. Bureau of Land Management (BLM) has restored several ruins, recreated a station at Simpson Springs, and provided interpretive exhibits at several sites. The mileage shown is the distance from the preceding station.

West of Fairfield, the Old Trail forks from Route 73 at Fivemile Pass (5 miles from Fairfield) and drops into Rush Valley, through which it passes for nearly 20 miles. East Rush Valley Station, 10 miles from Fairfield, is marked by a stone monument and plaque. Faust Station (9 miles), an important trail stop, is marked by a monument and BLM interpretive site at the trail's junction with Route 36. These mark the general vicinity of Faust Ranch, named for Henry "Doc" Faust, who operated the ranch and station during the 1860s. As a young man, Faust carried mail between Utah and California along this route, operated the Pony Express station at Faust, and served as a substitute rider. Lookout Pass or Point Lookout (8 miles) is marked by a monument and a small cemetery containing the remains of pet dogs owned by Horace and Libby Rockwell, who lived here for a time after 1870 or thereabouts. Government Creek Station (8 miles), marked by foundation ruins, was a telegraph station and is believed to have served as a Pony Express station.

Simpson Springs was named for Captain J. H. Simpson, army engineer who surveyed the route in 1859. It has been an important rest stop since 1851 or before because of its plentiful water. Simpson Springs was the site of a Civilian Conservation Corps camp during the 1930s; remains of this camp can still be seen. Located on the side of a hill, this area affords a sweeping panoramic view of Dugway Proving Ground, the western desert, and rugged island ranges.

Old River Bed Station (8 miles) was in the sandy channel of a prehistoric stream connecting the main body of Lake Bonneville to the north with Sevier Bay to the south. The main

THE GREAT SALT LAKE

Kennecott stack near Lake Point on the west shore – François Camoin

The Great Salt Lake dominates the north end of the Great Basin, that stretch of land that lies between the Rockies and the east slopes of the Sierras. It is the largest inland body of water in the continental United States after the Great Lakes. Seventy-five miles long and fifty miles wide, it is a tourist attraction, a barrier to travel, a haven for migrating waterbirds, and a source of minerals extracted by evaporation from its briny waters.

The size of the lake varies greatly with any increase or decrease in the waters that feed it. In 1983, after a season of heavy snows in the mountains, the waters rose high enough to flood Interstate 80, a good deal of farmland on the lake's eastern shore, and some of the industries on the south and west. The lake's rise was considered so threatening that the state legislature installed a series of huge pumps to move the excess water to evaporation ponds in the west desert. By the next year the waters had receded, the pumps were idle, and the lake had shrunk by several thousands of acres.

A major reason for the wild fluctuations in the lake's area is the gentle slope of the land in which it lies. A slight increase or decrease in the depth of the lake can flood or lay bare several dozen square miles. The Great Salt Lake's average depth is only about thirteen feet, the greatest depth in normal years less than thirty feet. Tourists can walk out into the lake until they are almost out of earshot of their friends, and still only be up to their knees in the salty water.

The Great Salt Lake is the impoverished remnant of a much larger body of water called Lake Bonneville, which in prehistoric times washed over much of the now-settled Salt lake—covering a much larger area than Sevier Bay—evaporated more rapidly and its level dropped faster than that of Sevier Bay, which therefore drained northward through the Old River Bed.

Dugway Station (10 miles), marked by a monument, was a dugout substation without water. Black Rock Station (14 miles), located beside a dark volcanic outcrop, was known also as Butte or Desert Station. The site provides a spectacular view of Great Salt Lake Desert, high ranges to the west, and the skeletal Granite Mountain in Dugway Proving Ground to the north. Jedediah Smith crossed the salt basin to Granite Mountain in 1827, en route from California to Great Salt Lake. Beckwith also crossed that desolate terrain in 1854. Between 1913 and 1927, the old trail west of Black Rock served for some

distance as the Lincoln Highway, which came in from the direction of Dugway and Johnson's Pass.

Fish Springs Station (10 miles) exists as a rock foundation in Fish Springs National Wildlife Refuge. The refuge is a remarkable oasis in a fearsome desert and was established in 1959 to administer and improve some 18,000 acres of marshland surrounding about 75 freshwater springs. The marshes invite migrating waterbirds such as ducks, cranes, herons, avocets, curlews, and egrets, as well as myriad shorebirds. A permanent government complex is located at the refuge. Visitors are welcome.

An area of hot springs, known as Little Yellowstone or Wilson's Health Resort, is near the road at the north end of Fish Springs Range. The springs are the result of hot mineral

Rider reenactment along the Pony Express Trail, which is well-maintained as a Utah backway and a pleasant drive in good weather – Steve Greenwood, UTC

water flowing out from an underground fissure. "Salt flowers"—globular incrustations of salt caused by the evaporation of upwelling saline groundwater—surround the springs. They are said to be especially colorful in June and July. These are not constructed pools but natural springs. *Warning: It is dangerous to leave the path in a hot springs area because of thin surface crust.*

Boyd Station (14 miles from Fish Springs) is marked by the crumbling rock walls of the original Pony Express station, guarded by a protective fence. The site of Willow Springs Station (8 miles) is in Callao. Its exact location is uncertain. Callao, known as Willow Springs in pioneer days, lies between the 12,000-foot Deep Creek Mountains and the Great Salt Lake Desert. One of the most isolated communities in the state, Callao also was one of the least changed until recent decades. A maintained county road forks south from Callao to Trout Creek, Candy, Eskdale, and Route 6.

North of Callao, the old trail passed through Overland Canyon, veering west from the present road at Sixmile Ranch, 4 miles from Callao. Three stations (Willow, Round, and Burnt) were located along this rough stretch of road between Callao and Ibapah (Deep Creek), but only the site of Round Station is definitely known and properly marked.

The present road skirts Montezuma Peak (7,368 alt.) along benches overlooking the salt desert before entering Gold Hill, 23 miles from Callao. According to a state travel publication, Gold Hill was born in 1869 and "saw a number of dramatic declines and revivals."

Some old buildings remain, and a few residents still live in Gold Hill. Travelers may continue northwest from Gold Hill to Route 93A and Wendover, or turn south to Clifton and Ibapah.

Clifton, a short distance south of Gold Hill, dates from the 1860s. It has experienced deaths and some rebirths but none to match the heydays of Gold Hill. Few evidences of its existence remain except for crumbled ruins and abandoned mine workings. Stephen L. Carr's *Historical Guide to Utah Ghost Towns* summarizes the history of these two ghost towns.

The old Pony Express Trail passed near Clifton to Ibapah, formerly known as Deep Creek, and thence into Nevada. Located in Deep Creek Valley, flanked by lofty peaks of the Deep Creek Range (Haystack Peak 12,101 alt.), Ibapah today is a picturesque farming and ranching village, one of the most isolated in the state. Here was the westernmost Pony Express and stage station within Utah's present boundaries, serving as a division headquarters. The station site is on private property.

Lake Valley. Eighteen thousand years ago Bonneville's waters covered not only what is now western Utah but a vast area of Nevada and Idaho. The marks of its former beaches can still be seen partway up the slopes of the Wasatch Mountains as a series of regular horizontal benches cut into the land. Some of Salt Lake City's more expensive neighborhoods perch on these ancient shorelines, now far above the valley floor.

Early explorers who came upon the Great Salt Lake searched hard for its outlet, hoping to find a river that would provide an easy route to the Pacific Ocean. Their search was in vain; three rivers enter the lake, but no water leaves it except by evaporation. Despite early tales about underground streams that carried its runoff to the Pacific, or dreadful whirlpools that sucked waters (and incautious mariners) down to the center of the earth, we now know that the Great Salt Lake has no outlet. Scientists once thought the lake was on its way to extinction and would gradually shrink until nothing was left to mark its former existence except a great stain of white alkali on the desert. Recent studies, however, indicate that runoff from the surrounding mountains tends to balance evaporative losses, and though the lake's area can fluctuate considerably, it will probably remain the dominant feature of the northern Utah landscape for the foreseeable future.

The question of who first saw the lake is of course impossible to answer; in fact, the question itself is largely meaningless, a manifestation of our desire to get back to origins, to find a starting point. Mountain man Jim Bridger may have been the first European to see the lake, in 1824 or 1825, but the Escalante-Dominguez expedition of 1776 was informed of its existence just a short distance north of where they were camping on the shore of Utah Lake: "The other lake that joins this one, occupies, as we are told, many leagues, and its waters are very harmful and very salty; the Timpanois assured us that anyone who moistened any part of the body with it would at once feel the part bathed greatly inflamed." As is the case with any exploration, someone had always already been there, walked this trail, seen the land long before.

In 1843 Captain John C. Fremont visited the island now named after him, located just north of Antelope Island, using a primitive inflatable boat. He performed experiments to determine the mineral content of the water. He also left behind a brass lens cover for his telescope, and a cross carved in the rock at the highest point of the island by an unknown member of the party, possibly Kit Carson. The first systematic survey of the lake was conducted by Captain Stansbury in 1849, two years after the arrival of the first Mormon settlers. His vision of the lake was not a happy one: "The stillness of the grave seemed to pervade the air and water;

The main road continues west into Nevada, where it joins the Wendover-Ely highway.

A side road forks south from Ibapah to Goshute, 12 miles, a cluster of modest homes in the Goshute (Gosiute) Indian Reservation. Public travel on the reservation is restricted. Forage and water limitations prevent more than marginal operations in farming and livestock raising.

Related to the Shoshoni of Nevada and Idaho, the Goshutes of Deep Creek are descendants of Native Americans who roamed the arid valleys and mountains of western Utah for ages before Europeans arrived. Known as "diggers" in early literature, the Goshutes (more technically, Gosiutes) were marvels of ecological adaptation, managing to survive in one of the West's least hospitable environments. When Europeans arrived, the Goshutes were utilizing about a hundred varieties of plants, including roots, seeds, and nuts of the pinyon pine. Insects, reptiles, fish, rabbits, birds, and rodents were used as food, supplemented by larger game when available. White settlement reduced the Goshutes to extreme levels of deprivation before farming and stock raising—radical departures from traditional customs—could be developed. Though the intervening years have gradually brought improved living conditions, the lot of the Goshutes has never been an enviable one. In 1962 the Indian Claims Commission ruled that the Goshutes, as well as other Shoshone and Bannock tribes, were entitled to compensation for loss of lands by white encroachment.

Great Salt Lake Desert West

Nevada via Route 6 West

This tour features the Great Basin in Juab and Millard Counties, from Utah Valley south to Cove Fort (via Interstate Highway 15), and from Santaquin west to Eureka, Delta, the Sevier Desert, and the Utah-Nevada state line (via Route 6). A land of far-spreading horizons, this is a region of exciting history, strange geology, and planned developments completely unforeseen only a few years ago. Historically, the greater part of its people have lived in towns strung like links of a chain along the general route of I-15, which follows the mountain front and its life-giving streams. Exceptions to this rule have been Delta and nearby population centers dependent on the western Sevier River, as well as Eureka and a few other communities based less on irrigated agriculture and mainline

highways than on mining, railroading, or dry farming.

From Santaquin, Route 6 crosses the fertile lowlands of the Goshen Valley, a southern offshoot of Utah Valley, through a pastoral scene of fruit orchards, farms, and the modest but prosperous-looking towns of Goshen and Elberta. Soon, however, the highway leaves the valley and climbs into the East Tintic Mountains, a stark landscape of rugged igneous highlands known familiarly as Tintic, more formally as the East Tintic Mining District. Evidences of extensive mining activity soon appear in the form of some modern, well-kept structures but more commonly as "old shafts, trenches, abandoned dumps, weather-beaten camps, and prospecting holes." Mount Nebo looms majestic in the near distance.

Eureka (6,400 alt.) remains one of Utah's most picturesque mining communities, though evidencing neglect, fluctuating fortunes, and an abundance of dilapidation. The description of Eureka in the 1941 edition of this book applies as well today:

. . . WOODEN HOUSES PAINTED LONG AGO, AND SQUAT BRICK BUILDINGS HUG THE NARROW STREETS. IN SOME SECTIONS OF THE TOWN BRICK BUNGALOWS STAND BESIDE TUMBLEDOWN, WEATHER-BEATEN BUILDINGS. THE DUMP OF THE GEMINI MINE—SYMBOL OF TWOFOLD PROSPERITY IN THE PAST—ALMOST PUSHES INTO THE LOBBY OF THE LEADING HOTEL, AND NEWER STORES STAND SCORNFULLY BESIDE FALSE-FRONT STRUCTURES OF ANOTHER DAY. THERE IS AN OCCASIONAL TREE, VIVIDLY GREEN.

Since 1941, Kennecott as well as other firms have spent millions of dollars trying to revitalize Tintic's mining industry by probing for richer ores and by applying new techniques of extraction and processing. Depressed market prices, rising costs of operation, poor grades of ore, processing and transportation costs, all have been obstacles to success. The following excerpts are from the 1941 edition of this book, which devotes considerable space to a recitation of anecdotes about Eureka's mining heydays. Interested readers are referred also to specialized publications such as Stephen L. Carr's *Historical Guide to Utah Ghost Towns* for detailed summaries of the history of such Tintic towns as Eureka, Mammoth, Silver City, Knightsville, Dividend, and others. The entire Tintic Mining District is listed on the National Historical Register.

With the discovery in 1869 of a "funny looking" piece of rock by George Rust, a cowboy, the valley arrived at its destiny. For several years, however, the shouts of rich strikes at Park City, Alta, and in the Cottonwood Canyons drowned out the news of more quiet prospecting in the Tintic

Mountains. Five men fought their way through a blizzard to locate the "Sun Beam" in December 1870, the first registered claim in the valley. In January 1871, another group of men located the "Black Dragon," and in the same month the "Corresser lode" now known as the "Carisa" was discovered. By April, Sunbeam ore was worth $500 a ton, Montana and Eureka ore $1,000 a ton, Mammoth ore $l,000 a ton, and the remaining thirteen mines ran down the scale to the Bull's Eye, which mined ore worth $86 a ton.

West of Eureka, Route 6 abruptly drops into Tintic Valley between the West and East Tintic mountain ranges where it is joined by Route 36, which forks north to Rush Valley, Stockton, and Tooele. Near this junction a paved road leads 1 mile east to Mammoth (6,000 alt.), high on a steep mountain slope. Today's town remnant bears scant resemblance to the large community of the glory days that prevailed between the l870s and l920s or thereabouts. Those years saw hundreds of residents, stores, hotels, saloons, serving a number of mines and mills. In 1941 Mammoth's main street consisted "of a few bleached, false-fronted buildings."

Silver City (6,100 alt.) in 1941 was "a trading center for numerous small silver, gold, and lead mines in the district" but today is not even a respectable ghost town. Nothing but dumps and foundations remind today's visitor that here was a community numbering 800 residents in 1899 and 1,500 in 1908, a peak from which decline soon began.

About 14 miles south of Eureka, an unpaved road forks east and south into Riley Canyon of the East Tintic Mountains. A 3-mile drive along this road and a half-mile hike up a dry streambed bring one within view of Paul Bunyan's Woodpile, overhead on a mountain slope. A geological curiosity, the woodpile is a cluster of lava logs—lengths of igneous rock that in ages past crystallized into orderly columns having three to six sides. The columns measure about a foot in diameter and up to 15 feet in length.

At Jericho Junction, 19 miles south of Eureka, a marked side road leads west to White Sand Dunes and Little Sahara Recreation Area, a development of the U.S. Bureau of Land Management. Jericho, at the junction of Route 6 and the main dunes access road, was a major sheep-shearing center for many years.

East from Jericho Junction a paved side road leads to Route 132 and Nephi. Route 6 continues south into the Sevier Desert

and, excepting here and there a solitary wild-duck floating motionless over the bosom of the lake, not a living thing was to be seen. . . . The bleak and naked shores [were] without a single tree to relieve the eye."

But of course all this story of the last 150 years or so is only the latest and not necessarily the most important narrative of human experience on the Great Salt Lake. Evidence found in Danger Cave near Wendover indicates that prehistoric peoples may have inhabited the Great Basin as early as ten or fifteen thousand years ago. When that much time has passed again, we ourselves may be thought of as a not particularly advanced civilization that flourished here for a brief moment. The western landscape, if it does nothing else, tends to force on the traveler some perspective in both space and time.

No fish live in the Great Salt Lake; the largest form of aquatic life that inhabits it is the quarter-inch-long brine shrimp. Brine flies are also abundant on the shores, particularly in certain seasons when they rise in seemingly impenetrable brown clouds to bedevil the visitor. The shrimp are commercially harvested for fish food; no one has yet found a use for the flies, except perhaps as an occasion to exercise self-restraint and a measure of humility. Everywhere are the famous seagulls, which are said to have miraculously saved the crops of the first settlers from an invasion of crickets, or locusts.

In a number of places the shores of the Great Salt Lake and its wetlands are home to great numbers of migratory birds. On Antelope Island a buffalo herd (these are imported animals, not native to the island) grazes more or less peacefully and generally ignores visitors. (Great care is in order, however, since these are not tame animals; they can attack with great speed and inflict serious if not fatal damage).

Other islands in the lake include Gunnison's Island, named for Lt. John W. Gunnison, assistant to Captain Stansbury. Bird Island is little more than a large rocky outcropping inhabited primarily by seagulls. Carrington Island, about 1,700 acres in area, was briefly homesteaded in the 1930s, and was used as a target by military aircraft during World War II. Stansbury Island is not really an island at all but a peninsula accessible from a road on the south shore of the lake. It is roughly 11 miles long by 5 miles wide, and was of course named after Captain Stansbury. It takes the form of a mountainous ridge extending into the lake; its highest point is about 2,400 feet. Parts of it are open to public travel, but the privilege should be exercised with caution, especially in wet weather when Utah's dirt roads can quickly become impassable.

The lake is also divided by the Southern Pacific causeway. The transcontinental railroad was first completed when

(Pahvant Valley), the vast sink of the Sevier River and the flat bed of vanished Lake Bonneville. White sand dunes occupy a large area west of the highway.

Lynndyl (4,800 alt.) is a rather nondescript farming center on the Sevier River. The mud-banked lazy river in this vicinity is but a sorry reminder of the noble Sevier at its headwaters. Yet even here, near the end of its long journey from the High Plateaus, enough water remains to irrigate some thousands of acres of farms in Pahvant Valley. Little if any is allowed to enter the river's age-old destination, Sevier Lake, now but a near-dry playa. From Lynndyl, Route 132 forks east to Leamington, a farming community, and Nephi.

Beside Route 132, 2 miles east of Leamington, are historic charcoal ovens, built in 1885. Wood was cut in the mountains nearby and hauled by mule to the ovens; the charcoal was then freighted to Salt Lake City. South of Leamington, Route 125 leads to Oak City and Delta. Oak City is an old-fashioned country town at the base of the rugged Canyon Range. East of town a forest road climbs along the canyon of Oak Creek into the heart of the Canyon Range to a campground (Fishlake National Forest). The Canyon Range is recognized by geologists as a vivid example of folding and overthrusting, an illustration of the results of the dramatic crustal deformation so apparent in the Basin and Range Province.

From Route 6, 5 miles south of Lynndyl, Route 174 forks west. Known as the Brush Wellman road, this route connects the large Brush Wellman beryllium mill in the vicinity of the junction with the firm's beryllium mines some 50 miles west. Also beside this road, 12 miles west of Route 6, is the site of the huge Intermountain Power Project (see below). The Brush Wellman mill began operations in 1969, when it began processing bertrandite ore, rich in beryllium, from deposits in the Topaz Mountain area 50 miles away. Concentrates are shipped to Ohio for further processing and manufacture into a variety of industrial products. The mill also processes imported beryl ores and uranium by-products. The Lynndyl mill was the first large-scale beryllium facility in the nation. By 1981 Brush Wellman had invested more than $30 million in the local mill and mines.

The giant Intermountain Power Project, one of the largest coal-fired power plants in the country if not the world, is 8 miles west of Route 6 via the Brush Wellman road. The huge installation was first proposed for siting in Wayne County near Hanksville, but proximity of that site to Capitol Reef National Park forced relocation to Millard County in the late 1970s. The plant is the largest and most costly industrial complex ever proposed for Utah, designed to produce more than 2,000 megawatts of electric power from four 820-megawatt turbine generators. Coal is hauled from mines up to 100 miles away, and as many as ten million tons are required every year. About 45,000 acre-feet of water are used each year, obtained from wells and Sevier River impoundment; rights to this water were purchased from more than 600 rights holders at a cost of some $4 million.

The plant's sponsor, Intermountain Power Agency, is a cooperative with more than 30 members, including six California municipalities (Los Angeles and vicinity), who together purchase 58 percent of the power; Utah Power and Light Company; and 20-odd Utah municipalities. Opponents of the project lodged suits in court to stop the project on grounds that it is illegal to divert Utah's agricultural water for California industrial use.

Delta (4,600 alt.) is the commercial center of the western Pahvant Valley, long a staid community of wide streets and modest homes. From its founding in 1907 until 1978 or so, life proceeded at an unhurried rural pace with hardly a hint of the transformation that was to come. Irrigated agriculture, stock raising, trade, and mineral production furnished a fairly stable economic base. Then in the late 1970s, with little warning, the Delta-Lynndyl area was selected as the site for the great Intermountain Power Project after its sponsor's first site choice near Hanksville was rejected by the Secretary of the Interior (see above). The result has been profound change, as indicated by a growing population, a local building boom, soaring real estate prices, and the sale of agricultural water rights to nonagricultural users (notably Intermountain Power Project).

Turn north from Delta and Hinckley to the farming clusters of Sutherland, Woodrow, Sugarville, and Abraham. Known as the North Tract, this area is a flat, sparsely settled expanse of irrigated fields bordered by forbidding desert. The scattered dwellings and farm buildings hardly suggest that many years ago the district was teeming with hundreds of homesteaders enticed by low-cost land, plentiful canal water, and the dream of prosperity. Between about 1909 and 1930 several small communities grew, thrived, and declined as new landholders arrived, developed sugar beet fields, built homes, became discouraged, and moved away.

Eight miles west of the paved highway leading to Sutherland and Sugarville, from a junction several miles north of the Mormon chapel in Sutherland, the Topaz War Relocation Center was constructed as an internment camp for persons of Japanese descent evacuated from the West Coast. Between 1942 and 1945, when it was closed, the camp housed about 9,000 evacuees. Topaz was one of ten camps in the nation devoted to this purpose during World War II. According to its National Register description, Topaz symbolizes "the extreme prejudice and war hysteria following the attack on Pearl Harbor." Its residents "lived in the barracks-type structures which were furnished from army stores. Residents made most of their own furniture. Dining, recreational, and sanitary facilities were shared." Stephen L. Carr, in his *Historical Guide to Utah Ghost Towns*, summarized the camp's history in more detail: culinary water came from wells; the townsite was laid out in 42 blocks with wide streets; three to four families lived in a building; and the town's 600 or so buildings included a hospital, fire station, post office, library, theater, churches, schools, stores, and recreation halls. A fence with guard towers enclosed the camp's 20,000 acres. After the camp was closed, its facilities were sold and removed, and the land was sold. Physical evidence of its existence remains in the form of some concrete foundation slabs, rubble, and a faint network of streets. Topaz is a registered historic site, marked by a monument of stone and concrete.

North and west from the area of irrigated lands, a web of roads—most of them unpaved—lead to mines, grazing ranges, and rock-hound areas. The Sevier Desert (Pahvant Valley) is one of the largest of Utah's Great Basin valleys, occupying about 3,000 square miles. In fairly recent ages—geologically speaking, the latest only 15,000 or 20,000 years ago perhaps—the valley was one of glacier-fed Lake Bonneville's largest bays. As the climate changed and the lake shrank, the bay's water retreated southward into Sevier Lake, but at a higher stage it had drained north through the channel of the Old River Bed into Lake Bonneville's main body (now the Great Salt Lake Desert). The main access road, Route 272, commonly known as the Brush Wellman road (see above), is paved; this route connects Brush Wellman's beryllium plant south of Lynndyl with the firm's mines in the Topaz Mountain area. An unpaved extension of that route proceeds north to the old Pony Express Trail and

the Central Pacific and Union Pacific railroads met at Promontory Summit near the north shore of the Great Salt Lake in 1869. In 1902 the Southern Pacific built a new right-of-way across the Great Salt Lake; the Lucin Cutoff replaced the longer route around the north end of the lake, shortening the distance traveled by 44 miles and eliminating the numerous curves and grades necessary to cross the Promontory Range. The roadbed was built partly on rock fill and partly on wooden trestles, but the trestles were replaced in 1956 by a new rock-fill rail bed paralleling the original right-of-way. The lake was thus divided in two; the northern section, which does not receive water from the rivers entering the lake, is now lower and significantly more salty than the southern section.

The lake has seen its share of industrial exploitation. A number of companies extract salts from the lake's waters by evaporation, among them the Magnesium Corporation of America, which also refines the extracted minerals and has been a center of controversy over air-quality standards because of the plant's emission of chlorine gas. The water quality in the lake is also the subject of debate; scientists point out that since the lake has no outlet, whatever pollutants enter it simply accumulate in the water or are deposited as sediments; what remains dissolved is further concentrated by evaporation. The 1,200-foot-high stack of the Kennecott Copper Refinery, almost directly across the highway from the Great Salt Lake State Park, is a constant reminder of the pressures and priorities of industrialization. Farther west, in the Great Salt Lake Desert, a number of waste-disposal sites and hazardous-material incinerators seem to have found homes in a land nobody else cares to inhabit.

A large body of water should have provided an easy route for the transport of goods between Salt Lake City and points north, and several attempts were made to establish a system of navigation on the Great Salt Lake. But boats ride high on the dense waters of the lake, and the shallowness of the water can multiply the power of sudden storms. The *Timely Gull*, launched by Brigham Young in 1854, was destroyed in a gale four years later. A three-decked stern-wheeler, the *City of Corinne*, was launched in 1872 to haul ores from Lake Point to Corinne, 20 miles up the Bear River, but in 1874 the level of the lake began to fall and the river became unnavigable.

The lake has been a popular place for bathing since the first months of the Mormon settlement in 1847. The high salt content keeps bathers afloat, and floating can be a relaxing exercise. During the past hundred years or so a number of resorts flourished for a while on the south shore: Black Rock, Saltair, Garfield Beach, Lake Shore, Sunset Beach, Sand Pebble Beach, and Silver Sand Beach. Various physical and economic disasters—fires, floods, lack of

Fish Springs. Other unpaved roads north and west from Delta lead to Hot Plug, Old River Bed, Dugway Pass, Drum Mountains, Fish Springs, Antelope Springs, and other points of special interest for rock hounds, geology students, and sightseers. Hot Plug, called by Frank Beckwith "a red mountain that smokes" and "the most beautiful object in Pahvant Valley," is a red-and-gray volcanic mass nearly 200 feet high and approximately the same diameter. The vent of an ancient volcano, Hot Plug still conducts heat from the depths of the earth, creating a visible vapor when the air is cool. Nearby is a group of hot springs, containing water at a very high temperature, the basis for a local spa known as Crater Springs Health Resort.

Topaz Mountain, a part of the Thomas Range, is well known to rock collectors as a fruitful source of topaz crystals. Though the surface has been exhaustively combed, weathering and excavating continually expose more crystals. The Drum Mountains, a low-desert range, received its name because of weird subterranean noises sounding like blows on a drum; other sounds are heard, such as rumblings thumps and grindings. Since the 1870s the Detroit Mining District in the Drum Mountains produced gold, silver, copper, manganese, and other minerals, though on a sporadic basis. Today's ghost town of Joy was for many years a center for miners and ranchers.

Route 50 joins Route 6 at Delta and continues into Nevada. At Hinckley, 5 miles west of Delta, paved Route 257 forks south to Deseret, Clear Lake, Black Rock, and Milford. Route 257 passes through a wide-open expanse of flat desert. Pahvant Butte and other volcanic remnants can be seen to the east. The village of Deseret is the site of Old Fort Deseret, just south of town, marked by the crumbling ruins of a defensive structure hastily built in 1865 by Mormon settlers (state historical monument, registered historic site).

The Gunnison Massacre Monument, about 5 miles west of Deseret and Hinckley, near what remains of the Sevier River, marks the site of the massacre in October 1853 of Captain John W. Gunnison and seven members of his government exploring expedition. Inquire locally for directions; the monument is not easy to find. While engaged in a federal railroad survey, the Gunnison party was attacked at dawn by Pahvant Indians intent on avenging the death of one of their tribe who had been killed by non-Mormon emigrants (it is said) a short time before. The site is listed on the National Register of Historic Places. Pahvant Butte, 850 feet high, juts dramatically

from the flat valley floor about 15 miles to the southeast of Deseret. An inactive volcano, Pahvant Butte (also known as Sugar Loaf Mountain) is the largest and most prominent crater of the Millard Volcanic Field. Evidence points to its having been formed during the time of Lake Bonneville, with eruptions occurring deep under water and building a crater high enough to project above the lake's surface.

A few miles south of Deseret, west of the highway, Dunderberg Butte is a striking reminder of the deep lake that once inundated the valley and planed off the butte's summit. Not far away, Clear Lake is a state waterfowl management area. Black Rock, a junction point on Route 257, is the locale of commercial obsidian deposits, which also attract collectors.

The Dominguez-Escalante exploring party traversed this region in October 1776, generally following the route of today's Route 257 from Clear Lake on the north to Milford, and from there to Cedar City. This segment of trail, about 70 miles in length, took the expedition 12 days to traverse because of marshy ground, snow, cold, loss of an Indian guide, and indecision about which route to take. Though Monterey lay to the west, terrain forced a detour to the south.

West of the Delta-Hinckley oasis, Route 6-50 penetrates one of Utah's most forbidding deserts, a stark and thirsty land of distant horizons. The unearthly white sink of Sevier Dry Lake looks like a mirage to the south. The dry lake bed superficially resembles the salt flats of the Great Salt Lake Desert, from which it differs in having a less substantial crust of salt over a deep layer of mud. When first mapped in 1872, Sevier Lake had a water surface of 188 square miles, was about 28 miles in length, and had a saline content of 9 percent. Less than ten years later, due to diversion of Sevier River for irrigation, the lake was almost dry. Since then, though maps continue to indicate the 1872 shoreline, the "lake" has actually been little more than a dry lake bottom or salt flat; however, water does stand in part of the area at certain times.

From junctions 27 and 37 miles west of Hinckley, unpaved side roads fork north from Route 6-50 to Whirlwind Valley and to the Drum and House ranges.

Notch Peak in the House Range, looming above the highway at Skull Rock Pass, is a western landmark all the way from Delta, its notched silhouette dominating the skyline. Reputed to be the largest limestone monolith in Utah, the huge massif towers 5,000 feet above its base in White Valley to the west, reaching an altitude of 9,700 feet and presenting a series of great precipices on the west. The House Range, particularly its steep western face, displays a magnificent exposure of layered sedimentary rocks of very ancient Cambrian age, into which igneous material has intruded. Like the nearby Drum Mountains, Notch Peak is noted for strange underground noises. To the north of Notch Peak, the grand dome of Swazey Peak (9,700 alt.) marks an area famed as a source of fossil trilobites. The 1941 edition of this book pronounced, "a surveying party found well-preserved fossil trilobites around the peak in 1870."

Remains of the extinct beetlelike marine creatures of the middle Cambrian period, more than 430 million years old, were thickly strewn in tiny reefs of rocks. Antelope Springs issues from the hillside above a Civilian Conservation Corps camp, at 23 miles on the main side road. Near here early-day bad man Arm Nay occupied a cave known as Robber's Roost. The old corral where stolen livestock was kept is standing.

The Confusion and Conger Ranges—relatively barren jumbles of warped strata and other geological curiosities—are the westernmost of Utah's mountains in this region. Along the Utah-Nevada border, the grand expanse of Snake Valley stretches for a hundred miles or so, its northern end emptying into the Great Salt Lake Desert at Callao.

Despite its desolate appearance, Snake Valley supports scattered ranches and small agricultural settlements such as Gandy, Trout Creek, and Eskdale. Because of its isolation, the valley is home for unorthodox religious groups who observe their tenets here in relative peace and obscurity.

Near Gandy is Crystal Cave, also known as Crystal Ball Cave, which features an underground display said to rival or excel that of nearby Lehman Caves National Monument in Nevada. The cave is on private land but may be available for tours by local arrangement.

Route 6-50 crosses the Utah-Nevada line near Baker and Great Basin National Park in Nevada, 67 miles east of Ely. Southward, Route 21 wends its way south and east through broad valleys and low mountain passes to Milford.

customers—killed off each one in turn. The present resort, once more named Saltair, was nearly wiped out by the floods of 1983 but has now been repaired. Occasional concerts are held in the ballroom, and some of the old railroad cars that once carried tourists out there have been restored as gift shops. Down the road, a large marina caters to local yachtsmen. Aside from the boaters, however, the passion for spending weekends at the lake seems to have passed, and the beaches are generally populated only by a few tourists from faraway places, eager to test the lake's legendary powers of flotation and willing to brave the brine flies.

Interstate 15 follows, more or less, the east shore of the lake on its way to northern Utah and the towns of Bountiful, Ogden, and Brigham City. At Syracuse, a causeway recently rebuilt after the 1983 floods leads to Antelope Island State Park; just south of Brigham City another road leads west into the Bear River Migratory Bird Refuge.

Interstate 80 heads west along the lake's south shore to the Great Salt Lake Desert, the Bonneville Salt Flats, and the gambling town of Wendover, which straddles the Utah-Nevada state line (gambling is illegal in Utah).

Access to the north shore is by dirt road to Promontory Point and by another dirt road that eventually arrives in Kelton. From Kelton an unimproved road leads south toward the Hogup Mountains and the west shore.

The Great Salt Lake is, except in a few places, difficult to approach directly, holding itself aloof from casual exploration. It is most easily appreciated from the air, on approach to the Salt Lake International Airport. From the vantage point of an altitude of a thousand feet or so, especially near sunrise or sunset, the Great Salt Lake, idealized by distance, is a remarkable sight. It's harder to love from up close when travelers are apt to find themselves blasted by the sun or cut by the icy winds of a northern Utah winter.

Probably the best place to get to know the lake is from the beaches and heights of Antelope Island, particularly in the early morning or evening when the island is relatively deserted. From Antelope Island, the lake can be seen as a magical place, a freak of nature enduring in a delicate and complex interaction between runoff and evaporation, a place of shifting light, shadows passing across the water and changing its color, a place gifted with a severe and subtle beauty.

Panoramic view into Utah's Basin and Range east from Great Basin National Park, Nevada – Scott Smith

CAPTAIN BONNEVILLE'S DESERT

BY STEPHEN TRIMBLE

Fifteen thousand years ago, an inland sea the size of Lake Michigan filled Utah's Great Basin. It covered nearly 20,000 square miles, stood a thousand feet deep, and teemed with fish. By eleven thousand years ago, this body of water had fallen to about the same level as its modern remnant, the Great Salt Lake. Great Basin ecological communities have been adapting to these changes ever since.

One hundred and sixty years ago, in 1835, Captain

Benjamin Louis Eulalie de Bonneville, Seventh Cavalry, sketched the most accurate map yet drawn of the American West. On leave from the U.S. Army, he had for four years bankrolled a company of trappers and seen much of the Rocky Mountains. The great mountain man, Joseph Reddeford Walker, was his field partisan. Bonneville sent Joe Walker to California, presumably to make the company fortune in fur but more likely to explore deep into Mexican territory. Walker discovered Yosemite, pioneered the California Trail, found no beaver country, and bankrupted Bonneville's trapping operation.

By the time the captain passed on his maps and notes to writer Washington Irving, he had returned to more typical Army duties. Irving's 1837 book, *The Adventures of Captain Bonneville*, became a best-seller. To explain Bonneville's lack of success in the West, Irving made Joe Walker the villain. The book claimed that Walker had been detailed westward to fulfill Bonneville's passion to explore the Great Salt Lake, not to wander off to California with sixty men, burning through the captain's resources.

In reality, the mountain men—Jim Clyman, Jim Bridger, and their companions—had explored the "sheet of brine" in their bull boats a decade earlier. Captain Bonneville certainly knew fully of Walker's distant destination, but the captain had never bothered to visit Great Salt Lake, though he had been close.

Nevertheless, Benjamin Bonneville inked a new name onto his map for this lake he had never seen: Lake Bonneville. No one but Bonneville and Irving ever used the term. To everyone else, it remained the Great Salt Lake.

In 1874, pioneer geologist Grove Karl Gilbert needed a name for that huge precursor to the Great Salt Lake. Evidently a fan of Irving's book, he decided on "Lake Bonneville" for the continent's greatest Pleistocene inland ocean. The captain had his lake after all.

Historian Dale Morgan summed up all this self-glorification in his classic 1947 book about the Great Salt Lake: "There was no ironic gleam in Gilbert's eye, but certainly there is an ironic aspect to the thought that Bonneville, who vainly endeavored to perpetuate his name by applying it to Great Salt Lake without ever having laid eyes on that lake, should find his immortality at last in a lake which no living man had ever seen."

The irony abides. The 1995 Salt Lake City phone book lists Bonneville Golf Course, Bonneville Gardens Mobile Home Park, Bonneville Car Wash Equipment, and fifty other businesses beginning with the captain's name.

The Great Basin Desert itself contains similar ironies. Comparable in weight to the Rocky Mountains or Great Plains, this is a major North American landscape but a forgotten one. The simplicity of sagebrush and shadscale rolling on for mile after mile belies this land's hidden diversity. An archipelago of mountains rises from basins once filled by the long arms of the Pleistocene lake. The higher ranges cradle alpine plants, Rocky Mountain evergreen forests, and ancient bristlecone pines. To describe where we are here, we sweep around our open palms expansively, taking in basins and ranges at the far horizons and playas sufficiently big and flat to reveal the curvature of the earth. We try to make sense out of both the glittering emptiness of the Bonneville Salt Flats and the energy of a million migrating Wilson's phalaropes feasting on Great Salt Lake invertebrates.

This desert is easily dismissed by those who do not know it. Nowhere else in the West is there such a continuous sweep of undeveloped country filled with such silence—a soothing bowl of wild basins and ranges that help put lives in perspective. Sleep here under a velvet sky pricked with stars and washed with the Milky Way. Crush sagebrush leaves between your fingertips and breathe deep. Look far. See close. Lose yourself. Find yourself. The contrast between our fragile selves and the emptiness of this spare land is a Zen riddle.

The urban residents along the Wasatch Front think of themselves as living at the foot of the Rockies. They orient to the east, toward the mountains—the source of their water, the place for recreation—but they do not live in the Rockies.

When we arrive in Salt Lake City from the west, the true character of the valley reveals itself. The approach can be either the roller coaster across Nevada's 300-mile barricade of north-south mountains on Highway 50 or the high-speed traverse along the more gentle ups and downs of Interstate 80. Either way, the rhythm of basin and range takes over—and continues into Utah. Deep Creek Range, Great Salt Lake Desert. Cedar Range, Skull Valley. Stansbury Range, Tooele Valley. Oquirrh Range, Salt Lake Valley.

From the west, the Salt Lake Valley takes its place in this Basin and Range chant—just another basin in the series of alternating mountain islands and basins draining inward. The Great Basin sends its messengers into town. Westerly winds bring the stink of the lake's rotting brine fly pupae. Gulls fly over the cities of the Wasatch Front. The sun rises over the Rockies but sets in an orange ball behind the peaks of Stansbury and Antelope Islands, the straight edge of the Great Salt Lake creating a double horizon in the west, the mineral surface of the water mirroring the colors of dusk: crimson, violet, silver, black.

The "place" in "this is the place" is the stunning, humbling Bonneville Basin of the Great Basin Desert.

Twilight Rise – Tom Olson

O Ye Mountains High: Utah's Mountain Province

– Cache, Summit, Wasatch, Duchesne, Uintah, Rich, and Daggett Counties –

THE ROCKY MOUNTAIN PROVINCE OF UTAH FORMS THE NORTHEAST CORNER OF THE STATE AND INCLUDES THE UINTA MOUNTAINS AND THE WASATCH RANGE. IT IS A REGION OF HIGH RUGGED MOUNTAINS, LAKES, AND RIVERS, OF WHICH ONE, THE GREEN, IS A MAJOR TRIBUTARY OF THE COLORADO TO THE SOUTH. IT INCLUDES THE CACHE VALLEY, ONE OF UTAH'S MOST FERTILE AREAS, AND THE HIGH UINTAS WILDERNESS, WHICH IS THE LARGEST WILDERNESS AREA IN THE STATE. THE BEAVER TRADE BROUGHT THE FIRST SETTLERS TO THE AREA, AND SEVERAL RENDEZVOUS WERE HELD HERE BEFORE THE TRADE DIED OUT. IT WAS ON THE GREEN RIVER THAT MAJOR JOHN WESLEY POWELL LAUNCHED HIS BOATS FOR THE FIRST EUROPEAN EXPLORATION OF THE COLORADO RIVER AND ITS CANYONS. BROWN'S PARK, NEAR THE COLORADO BORDER, WAS A NOTORIOUS HIDEOUT FOR OUTLAWS, INCLUDING BUTCH CASSIDY'S WILD BUNCH. OTHER POINTS OF INTEREST INCLUDE FLAMING GORGE RESERVOIR AND DINOSAUR NATIONAL MONUMENT.

Moosehorn Lake sparkles in the High Uinta Wilderness – Tom Till, UTC

"WE PASSED UP THE RIVER A FEW MILES, CROSSED, AND FOLLOWED A RIVULET WESTWARD TO ITS SOURCE IN THE MOUNTAIN, WHICH WE THEN ASCENDED TO ITS SUMMIT. FROM THIS ELEVATION BLEAK SNOW-CLAD PYRAMIDIC PEAKS OF GRANITE WERE BEHELD IN ALL DIRECTIONS JUTTING INTO THE CLOUDS. STERN, SOLEMN, MAJESTIC, ROSE ON EVERY SIDE THESE GIANT FORMS OVERLOOKING AND GUARDING THE ARMY OF LESSER HILLS AND MOUNTAINS THAT LAY ENCAMPED BELOW, AND POINTING PROUDLY UP THEIR SNOW-SHEETED CRESTS, ON WHICH THE STARS AT EVENING LIGHT THE SENTINEL FIRES OF AGES."

- Warren Angus Ferris -
"Greater Yellowlegs"
in Life in the Rockies,
A Diary of Wanderings, 1830–1835

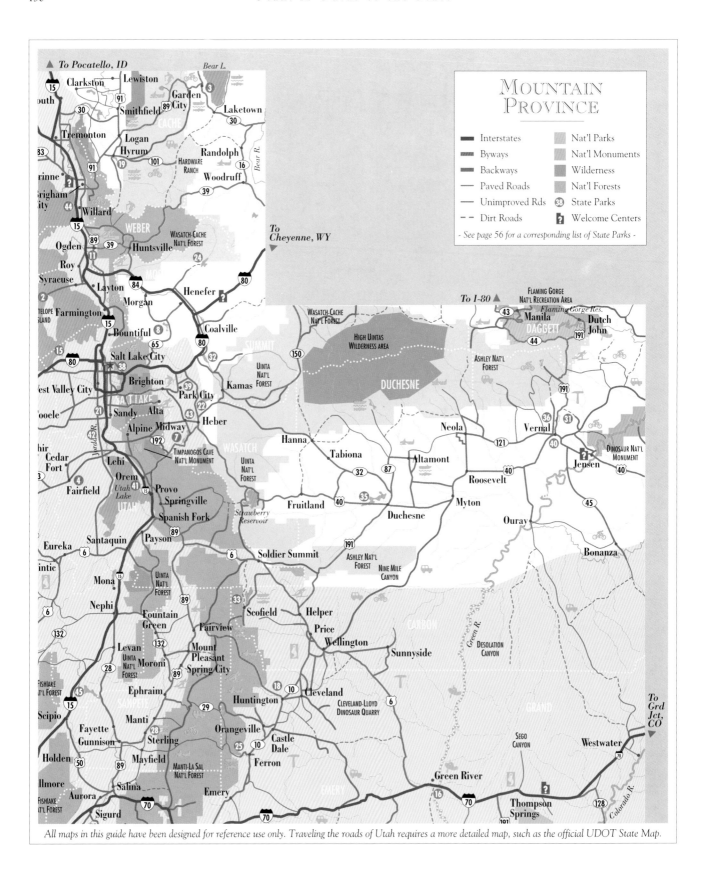

CACHE VALLEY

Michel Bourdon of the British North West Company (traders and fur trappers) visited the Cache Valley in 1819, but it was American fur trappers, arriving in force in the fall of 1824, who remained in the area for several years and harvested the greater part of its rich crop of beaver pelts. Their number included some of the most renowned of all mountain men, among them James Bridger, who followed the Bear River to its mouth and is considered the discoverer of the Great Salt Lake. The following year a large party of British trappers led by Peter Skene Ogden came south from Montana, passing through Cache Valley into present-day Ogden Valley and over the divide into the Weber River Valley. After an encounter there with American trappers he returned to the Snake River country. The Americans remained in the Cache Valley-Bear Lake region for several more years; they held a rendezvous in Cache Valley and two at Bear Lake.

Permanent settlement did not come for more than 30 years after the trappers arrived. Because of its frigid winters, even the Mormons avoided the Cache Valley as a colonizing site for the first few years after they arrived in the Salt Lake Valley. Finally, however, tentative beginnings were made at Wellsville (1856) and soon thereafter at other places in the valley. By the 1860s, settlements had been established at Logan, Hyrum, Smithfield, Richmond, Mendon, Hyde Park, Providence, and Paradise; still others were added in subsequent years. The Bear River Valley and the Bear Lake Valley also were settled in the 1860s.

The Cache Valley is a pastoral basin, trending north-south, bordered by high ranges on its long sides and by low divides on either end. The valley is about 50 miles long and up to 15 miles wide. It is watered by the Bear River and by tributary streams flowing primarily from the forested Bear River Range on the east. An extensive system of reservoirs, canals, and wells has been developed for irrigation, and some thousands of acres are devoted to dry-land farming of alfalfa, hay, and grain. Cache Valley farms are among the most productive in either Utah or Idaho. Though these farms tend to be modest in size, they are fertile, efficiently managed, and produce a wide variety of livestock, grains, garden crops, and other products. Dairy cattle provide the milk for Utah's largest concentration of cheese factories.

Entering the Cache Valley from the south, Route 89-91 climbs over a low divide (5,800 alt.) from Brigham City, passing through a picturesque highland park overlooked by rocky peaks of the northern Wasatch. The highway enters Cache Valley through Wellsville Canyon, near the mouth of which roads fork east and west.

Turn east from Route 89-91 to Hyrum, Hyrum State Park, Paradise, and Avon. Hyrum (4,700 alt.) is the largest community in the south end of the valley, about six miles from Logan. A clean and pleasant city, it was settled in the 1860s and named for Hyrum Smith, brother of the Mormon prophet Joseph Smith.

Hyrum Reservoir, formed by Hyrum Dam, impounds the water of the Little Bear River flowing down from the Monte Cristo area. On the shore of the 450-acre reservoir is Hyrum State Park, with developed camping, beach, and boating facilities. A historical marker near the dam marks its location as the site of a fur trapper cache.

Continue east from Hyrum on Route 101 to Blacksmith Fork Canyon, Bear River Range, and Hardware Ranch. Blacksmith Fork Canyon is an impressive gash in the mountains with steep walls that loom several thousand feet on either side. Its stream is popular for fishing, and there are four developed camping and picnic areas (Wasatch-Cache National Forest) in the main canyon and its left-hand fork. Hardware Ranch, 16 miles east of Hyrum, is a working ranch operated by the State Division of Wildlife Resources as a hay-growing and feeding station for elk. Sleigh rides are available in winter, Dutch-oven meals in summer. Check at the Visitors' Center.

Turn south from Hyrum on Route 165 to Paradise, 4 miles, and Avon, 6 miles, small towns at the south end of Cache Valley. Avon, the original site of Paradise, was settled in the 1860s; a few years later, worried by the threat of Indian attack, residents were advised to move to a more strategic location. Paradise Tithing Office, 28 North Main, dates from the mid-1870s.

North of Hyrum, Providence (4,600 alt.), a farming and residential community on the outskirts of Logan, was settled chiefly by Mormons of German and Swiss origin. Berries and fruits are important local crops and dry-farm wheat is grown on the slopes. From the west side of Route 89-91, roads fork to Wellsville, Mendon, Newton, and other communities on the west side of the Cache Valley.

Wellsville (4,500 alt.) is a dairying, farming, and residential community at the base of the Wellsville Mountains. Wellsville

Bear Lake is estimated by geologists to be at least 28,000 years old and is home to a unique species of native cutthroat trout
– Fast Focus, UTC

was the first Mormon settlement in Cache Valley, colonized in September 1856 by Peter Maughan, his family, and a few others from Tooele Valley.

The Wellsville Mountains loom above Wellsville and Mendon to summits of 9,356 feet in Wellsville Cone and 9,372 feet in Box Elder Peak. The mountains form the northern-most extension of the Wasatch Range, which terminates about ten miles north of Wellsville at the Bear River Canyon. The range is a topographic curiosity because of its narrow base combined with unusual height. Foot trails lead to its ridge from Mendon and Wellsville Canyon, affording dramatic views across parts of three states.

Route 89-91 continues across the nearly level floor of the Cache Valley to Logan, largest city in the state north of Ogden. Beside the highway, 6 miles south of Logan, is the Ronald V. Jensen Historical Farm. An outdoor museum displays thousands of farming artifacts of bygone years, including vintage tractors, threshing machines, wagons, plows, and household items. The farm is operated as a turn-of-the-century farm; special events are held year-round.

In Logan, Route 89 turns east to Logan Canyon, Bear Lake, Idaho, and Wyoming, while Route 91 continues north to Preston, Pocatello, and other northern points.

North of Logan, Route 91 passes through the open expanse of the Cache Valley, paralleling the foothills of the Bear River Range. The valley is well filled with farms, towns, and residential suburbs for a mile or so on either side of the highway.

Smithfield (4,200 alt.) is a commercial and agricultural center, and also a bedroom community for Logan, only a ten-minute drive away.

Turn east from Smithfield to Smithfield Canyon and Smithfield Canyon Forest Campground (Wasatch-Cache National Forest), 4 miles from town.

Turn west from Smithfield to Amalga, 3 miles, site of the Cache Valley Cheese Factory, which is reputed to be the largest maker of Swiss cheese in the world. Cheese-making is one of the valley's most important industries. Amalga received its name from the Amalgamated Sugar Company, which operated a number of sugar factories in Utah and other western states for many years.

Continue west from Amalga on Route 218 to Newton (4,500 alt.), an agricultural town 10 miles from Smithfield, situated near the canyon pass through which Bear River leaves

Cache Valley. It was settled as a "new town" in 1869–70 by residents of Clarkston to the north.

Turn north from Newton to Newton Reservoir, an irrigation impoundment on Clarkston Creek that covers an area of 200 to 300 acres and irrigates some 2,000 acres of farmland in the vicinity. The original Newton Dam, described in the 1941 edition of this book, was built of dirt and rocks; it was completed in 1886 after years of hard work and several failures. This dam may have been the first reservoir of substantial size in the nation to store water for irrigation. It was replaced during the 1940s by the present earth-fill structure, 101 feet high and more than a thousand feet long.

Turn south from Newton via Route 23 to junction with Route 30, which connects Logan with Garland-Tremonton and I-15. Near Newton, Route 23 crosses the Bear River not far upstream from Cutler Dam, which impounds the Bear River and its Cache Valley tributaries in a large lake known as Cutler Reservoir.

Turn northwest from Newton via Route 142 to Clarkston (4,900 alt.) at the foot of the steep, narrow ridge known as Clarkston Mountain. The area produces dry-land alfalfa and grain crops for the most part. Settled in 1864, Clarkston received its name from Israel Clark, one of the original colonizers. In the local cemetery, an 18-foot granite shaft marks the grave of Martin Harris, one of the three witnesses to the authenticity of the Book of Mormon, who was buried in 1875.

Richmond (4,600 alt.) almost doubled its population between 1970 and 1980. According to the 1941 edition, "Older houses stand in a close-knit group around the parked city square with its red-painted brick tabernacle. Farms lay on the slopes and valley floor, and, behind tree-shaded dwellings, are barns, corrals, and farm machinery." Visitors may judge for themselves how the Richmond of today resembles that of 50 years ago. The 1941 edition's description of the town's early history might be applied substantially to other Cache Valley communities:

PLEASED WITH THE LUSH GRASSES AND ADEQUATE WATER, SETTLERS BUILT SCATTERED LOG CABINS, DUGOUTS, AND A LOG FORT IN 1859. A DITCH WAS DUG FROM A NEARBY STREAM AND A DAM PLACED IN ANOTHER TO PROVIDE IRRIGATION FOR THE FIRST YEAR. THE SETTLERS BUILT SHINGLE, GRIST, CARDING, AND MOLASSES MILLS, AND A HORSEPOWER SAWMILL WAS ERECTED IN THE 1860s. A THRESHING MACHINE WITH MAPLE WOOD COGS AND CYLINDER WAS ASSEMBLED, AND THOMAS GRIFFIN, PIONEER MECHANIC, CONSTRUCTED THE FIRST MINIATURE STEAM ENGINE IN THE STATE.

Turn west at Webster Junction, 4 miles north of Richmond, to Lewiston (4,500 alt.), 2 miles, a prosperous farm and dairy community. The last major Indian battle in northern Utah took place near here in 1863 between a band of Shoshone-Bannock Indians and 300 Federal troops. Criticized later as a massacre and a dark stain on the history of the West, the battle was described in the 1941 edition:

IT WAS SUB-ZERO WEATHER, DEEP SNOWS SUBMERGED THE TRAILS, AND SEVENTY SOLDIERS WERE DISABLED BY FROZEN FEET. THE INDIAN CAMP WAS IN A GORGE TWENTY FEET DEEP AND FORTY FEET WIDE. "I ORDERED THE FLANKING PARTY," COLONEL CONNOR REPORTED, "TO ADVANCE DOWN THE RAVINE UPON EITHER SIDE, WHICH GAVE US THE ADVANTAGE OF AN ENFILADING FIRE AND CAUSED SOME OF THE INDIANS TO GIVE WAY AND RUN TOWARD THE NORTH END OF THE RAVINE. AT THIS POINT I HAD A COMPANY STATIONED WHO SHOT THEM AS THEY RAN OUT. . . . FEW TRIED TO ESCAPE, HOWEVER, BUT CONTINUED FIGHTING WITH UNYIELDING OBSTINACY. . . . THE MOST OF THOSE WHO DID ESCAPE FROM THE RAVINE WERE AFTERWARDS SHOT IN ATTEMPTING TO SWIM THE RIVER." FIRING CEASED IN FOUR HOURS. FEDERAL LOSSES WERE 14 KILLED, 49 WOUNDED. (EIGHT OF THE WOUNDED LATER DIED.)

Accounts of native casualties vary. "We found 224 bodies on the field," Colonel Connor officially reported. A Cache Valley settler, William G. Smith, later said: "Instead of offering the Indians a chance to surrender, and be taken peaceably, General Connor issued a very cruel order to his men—'Take no prisoners, fight to the death; nits breed lice'." Colonel Connor paid handsome tribute to his troops for their intrepidity and fortitude. Two months later he was brevetted a brigadier-general.

Route 91 crosses the state line 8 miles south of Preston, Idaho. The Cache Valley ends a few miles north of Preston at a low divide known as Red Rock Pass. Some 18,000 years ago this area formed the rim of the Cache Valley Bay of glacial Lake Bonneville at its highest level. As the lake rose, geologists say its waters spilled over the rim into the Snake River drainage, carving a deepening channel (Red Rock Pass) and draining the immense lake to a much lower level before hard rock stopped the draining process. Geological evidence in Idaho indicates that the resultant flood was catastrophic.

The Bear River begins in the Uinta Mountains and empties into the Great Salt Lake. It is said to be the largest stream in the western hemisphere that does not reach the ocean. The Bear takes a 500-mile circuitous route through three states before terminating only 90 airline miles from its source. Some geologists believe that the Bear originally emptied into the Snake River but was diverted southward by lava flows into

Lake Bonneville, causing that great body of water to rise to its highest level and eventually overflow at Red Rock Pass.

Logan

Logan (4,500 alt., 36,078 pop.), Cache County seat and the largest city in that part of the state, is built on the lowlands and terraces of a north-reaching arm of prehistoric Lake Bonneville. Sheltering it on the east is the lofty Bear River Range, with peaks as high as 9,000 feet and more within a few miles of the range's base. The imposing mouth of Logan Canyon opens into the eastern outskirts of the city, immediately behind the campus of Utah State University.

Logan has retained much of its original charm. Many of its older buildings have been preserved, and Center Street is listed in the National Register of Historic Places as a Historic District. Descriptions in the 1941 edition are still applicable: "The city is a pleasant residential community, its streets lined with trees. Lawns are numerous, and are kept green in summer. . . . Visible for miles from any approach in the valley, the Mormon Temple, with its twin gray towers, stands on an eastern terrace overlooking the tree-grown city. The square gray belfry of the Mormon Tabernacle rises above the trees in the downtown area; and to the northeast . . . is the bell tower of [Old Main]" on the campus of the university.

Utah State University is Logan's most important economic activity, as Brigham Young University is Provo's. The school's twenty thousand students and large staff contribute millions of dollars to the local economy. Logan also is a regional commercial center, not only for the Cache Valley but also for Box Elder County, southern Idaho, and western Wyoming as well. Though Wellsville was settled as Maughan's Fort in 1856, the Utah War discouraged further colonization until 1859, when Logan and other settlements were established.

- Logan Attractions -

The Mormon temple, 1st North and 2nd East, is maintained by the LDS Church for the administration of sacred ordinances, and is not open to the general public. The building, a castellated structure with octagonal corner towers surmounted by cupolas and massive buttresses, commands the city from the crest of an abrupt promontory two blocks east of Main Street. The walls of roughhewn limestone are unrelieved by ornamentation, except for moldings of light sandstone at the story levels and on the cornices. Fenestration is simple, and the end towers, 170 and 165 feet high, are capped with unornamented cupolas.

The Mormon tabernacle, Main and Center Streets, a cupola-crowned structure of gray stone, is an excellent example of early Mormon architecture. It seats about 1,500 and is open to the public.

The Cache County Relic Hall (Daughters of Utah Pioneers) occupies the lower level of the Chamber of Commerce offices at 160 North Main Street. The museum displays pioneer relics and artifacts such as pioneer tools, clothing, furniture and furnishings, and art. Open year round.

The Lyric Theater, 28 West Center, was built in 1913 and later restored by Utah State University for theatrical and musical productions.

The David Eccles Home, 250 West Center, a stately edifice of brick and white stone, was built in 1907 for financier David Eccles; since the 1940s it has been used as a dormitory as well as a sorority and fraternity house for USU students.

The Union Pacific Railroad Station, 6th West and Center, was built at the turn of the century, and is one of the finest remaining examples of its type in the state.

The Old Cache County Courthouse, 179 North Main, was built in 1882–83 by the local United Order.

St. John's Episcopal Church, 83 East 1st North, was built in 1906 by the Episcopal Church, which had established a school and mission in Cache Valley in the 1870s.

The Joseph Thatcher Home, 164 South 3rd West, was built about 1862 and is an example of pioneer rock construction.

– Utah State University –

Utah State University overlooks Logan and the Cache Valley from a bench at the mouth of Logan Canyon. Founded in 1888 by the territorial legislature to take advantage of a succession of federal land-grant acts that provided for support of agricultural colleges and experiment stations throughout the nation, it was known as the Agricultural College of Utah (AC) until 1929, then as Utah State Agricultural College (USAC) until the name was changed to Utah State University (USU) in 1957. The university embraces eight colleges, 44 departments of instruction, and some 600 courses of study. Enrollment totals more than 20,000. Students attend from all states and over 80 foreign countries; the majority are from Utah, but Idaho, California, Wyoming, Montana, and other western states are well represented.

Each year in late July and early August, thousands of visitors come to USU's campus to participate in varied activities scheduled by the Festival of the American West. Among the festival's diversified offerings is a spectacular historical pageant entitled "The West: America's Odyssey," held in the Spectrum arena, which combines dance, song, and multimedia sight-and-sound effects. The Great West Fair features pioneer and Indian craft exhibits and food booths, a quilt show, western cookout, photo and art exhibit, and Frontier Street, a reconstruction of an early western commercial street.

Bear Lake and Vicinity via Logan Canyon

Route 89 forks east from Route 91 in the center of Logan, entering the mouth of Logan Canyon. Logan Canyon is one of the longest mountain canyons in the state, extending for about 30 miles from its mouth to a summit pass on the Bear River Range at 7,800 feet. It is a delightful alpine drive, especially dramatic in late September when the reds and golds of autumn are at their height. The Wasatch-Cache National Forest maintains nearly a score of improved camping-picnicking sites in the canyon—one of the greatest concentrations of such facilities in the state. A maze of hiking trails and unpaved roads crisscrosses the mountains on either side of the highway.

The Bear River Range has been more thoroughly utilized for recreation, grazing, and timbering than any other mountain region in the state, with the possible exception of the Wasatch near Salt Lake City. For the most part the range is a gentle highland. It is commonly considered a northeastern segment of the Wasatch. The greater part of the range north and east of Blacksmith Fork Canyon is included within the Cache National Forest, with the exception of considerable private land in the headwaters of Logan River. Hikers are referred to forest maps or guidebooks such as *Cache Trails* (Mel Davis and Ann Schimpf) for trail and recreation details.

The Wind Caves (also known as Witches Castle, DeWitt's Cave, Sun Dance Cave, or Devils Cave) are a series of eroded arches and rooms more than a thousand feet above the highway. They are reached by a one-mile trail from DeWitt Campground, 5 miles from Logan.

Logan Cave is a two-story cavern about 2,000 feet in length, inhabited by bats. The cave is not recommended for casual exploration. It can be reached from Cottonwood Campground, about 15 miles from Logan.

The Old Jardine Juniper, the largest known Rocky Mountain red cedar, is perched on a limestone ridge about

1,500 feet above the highway. Its age estimated as 1,500 years, the tree now supports only a few green branches on its warped and twisted, mostly hollow trunk. Old Ephraim's Grave is marked by an 11-foot shaft denoting the height of a giant grizzly bear killed at the site in 1923. It can be reached on unpaved forest road or foot trail via Temple Fork (junction about 16 miles from Logan) and is about 6 miles from the highway.

Tony Grove Lake is a secluded scenic gem at 8,100 feet with forest campground, popular for fishing—about 5 miles from Route 89 (junction 20 miles from Logan).

The Beaver Mountain Ski Resort is a developed area on the summit of the mountains, about a mile north of Route 89 from junction 26 miles east of Logan. Launched in 1939 by the Seeholzer family, which still operates it, Beaver Mountain is advertised as "one winter ski resort that's big enough to chal-

lenge the really good skier, and small enough to include people who've never skied at all." Skiers come from the accomodations near Bear Lake; Beaver Creek Lodge is 1 mile from the resort; others come from Logan and more distant points. The resort features three double-chair lifts ranging from 1,300 to 4,600 feet in length and 350 to 1,600 feet vertical; 16 maintained runs, a day lodge with cafeteria, ski shop and rentals, night skiing, ski school, ski patrol. Altitude 7,200 to 8,832 feet.

Travelers from the west can see Bear Lake from a lookout point beside the highway, 30 miles from Logan and 10 miles from Garden City. A scenic spectacle because of its distinctive blue-green coloring and mountain setting, the lake is at an altitude of 5,900 feet. It lies equally in Utah and Idaho and is about 21 miles long by 7 miles wide. Bear Lake is fed

Logan Canyon is one of the longest mountain canyons, and has some of the finest fall scenery in the state – Scott Smith, UTC

indirectly by the Bear River and directly by numerous smaller streams and springs. Resorts, marinas, and houses are scattered along its shore and on the western mountain slopes, overlooking the fields of Garden City.

Bear Lake is estimated by geologists to be at least 28,000 years old. Until recent years its water was exceptionally clean. Between 1909 and 1918 canals and pumping stations were constructed at the north end of the lake by power companies to divert the Bear River water into the lake during times of high runoff and to pump water from the lake back into the river in periods of reduced flow. This converted the lake into a storage reservoir for water control, which was beneficial to downstream farmers and assured ample year-round water for power generation. However, the diversion has gradually altered the ecology of the lake, since the river contributes chemicals not originally found in the lake in such large quantities. Increased population and recreational use are adding pollutants as well. Bear Lake, as a result, is changing from cold-water to warm-water status and is showing signs of premature aging, or eutrophication. Government and private interests are cooperating in studies and corrective measures in an attempt to slow or halt this deterioration.

Garden City (5,890 alt.) has multiple personalities, changing with the seasons. It is a quiet hamlet in colder months. In warmer months it swarms with part-time residents and transient pleasure-seekers who come to boat, swim, water ski, fish, dive, or just relax.

Bear Lake State Park has three sites: Bear Lake State Park Marina, 1 mile north of Garden City, is a large breakwater marina developed by the State Division of Parks and Recreation. Its features include a visitor center, nearly 200 boat slips, a dry-storage area, camping and picnicking facilities, rest rooms and showers, launching and docking facilities. Open May–September.

Rendezvous Beach, at the south end of the lake near Laketown, was developed in the late 1970s and early 1980s with water, utilities, and numerous units for camping and picnicking. Covering a 65-acre area, the park area also includes a mile-long beach, boat-launching ramp, a boat-parking area, and boat rentals. The third site, Eastside, is on the east shore of the lake between North Eden and South Eden Canyons.

Laketown (6,000 alt.) is an agricultural community at the south end of Bear Lake, neighbor to Rendezvous State Beach

and some condominium developments. Laketown was settled during the 1860s, having been a rendezvous site for fur trappers many years prior to that in the late 1820s. In the 1870s, it is recorded, about 3,000 Indians camped in the vicinity, causing consternation among the settlers but departing peacefully for Wyoming.

Randolph (6,300 alt.) is the seat of Rich County, a trading center, and one of the most markedly rural towns in the state. "Randolph H. Stewart led the first group of settlers from St. Charles (now in Idaho) to the present site in 1870s," said the 1941 edition. "The town was surveyed with a rope in the absence of a surveyor's chain, and Brigham Young personally organized the town in 1871, when he made a treaty with the Bannock Indians."

Woodruff (6,340 alt.), 10 miles south of Randolph, is a center for farms and ranches, and is the eastern terminus of Route 39, which crosses the Bear River Range at Monte Cristo summit between Woodruff and Huntsville. Woodruff's winter climate is one of the coldest in Utah, and even in summer it is relatively cool.

South and east from Woodruff, Route 16 leads to Evanston, Wyoming, and Route 150, which in turn leads into the Uinta Mountains.

The Wasatch Range
Salt Lake City to Points East via I-80

Interstate 80 leaves the Salt Lake Valley through Parley's Canyon, a steep and tortuous gorge named for Parley P. Pratt, Mormon pioneer and apostle who opened a toll road through the canyon in 1850.

At a junction immediately east of Mountain Dell Reservoir, Route 65 forks north through Mountain Dell to a junction with a paved road from Emigration Canyon (see Salt Lake City). North of this latter junction, Route 65 is the Pioneer Memorial Highway, passing through Mountain Dell Canyon and surmounting Big Mountain, a formidable obstacle for the Donner-Reed pioneers in 1846 and the Mormon pioneers who followed a year later. Beyond Big Mountain it drops into East Canyon, skirts East Canyon Reservoir, and joins I-84 at the town of Henefer.

The mountains and slopes at Parley's Summit and for several miles to the east are witnessing an extensive residential construction boom, most home owners commuting the 15 or

20 miles to Salt Lake City. One of the most ambitious developments of recent years is at the Jeremy Ranch near the junction of I-80 and East Canyon Road.

At Kimball Junction, Route 224 forks south to Snyderville, The Canyons, and Park City.

Parley's Park has expanded here into a wide open, fairly level intermontane valley at 6,000 to 7,000 feet in elevation; it drains into the Weber River by way of East Canyon Creek. Since pioneer days the park has been utilized for grazing and high-altitude farming. Today, new housing developments are scattered across the floor of the park.

Park City and Vicinity

Turn south from I-80 at Kimball Junction, following Route 224 through Snyderville, past The Canyons to Park City, 27 miles from Salt Lake City. The Canyons, 4 miles from Park City, is a self-contained resort with townhouse condominiums, seven double-chair lifts, and 62 miles of runs, suited for all levels of expertise. Condominiums are available for rental. Lodge with restaurant and lounge, ski school, sports center (rentals, sales, repairs), night skiing. Helicopter ski flights may be arranged to remote areas in the Wasatch Range. Shuttle bus service to Park City. During the summer, The Canyons offers tennis, swimming, and a summer concert series featuring well-known artists.

Park City (7,000 alt., 6,188 pop.) is one of Utah's contemporary boomtowns. While the Old Town has been preserved more or less intact since recreational development began, its surroundings have been completely transformed. Old Town itself, with its authentic mining background, distinctive early western architecture, and old-time romance, has become a popular shopping district and entertainment center for visitors.

In 1960 Park City was a dilapidated, deteriorating town of 1,366 people, many of them unemployed, elderly or retired. Mining had long since seen its heyday, and the operations of scores of mines that once operated in the vicinity were consolidated into one firm, the United Park City Mines Company, which was finding survival difficult. Contrast that scene with 1996: The old section of town has become an important tourist attraction. Most of its aged buildings have been, or are being, restored and put to commercial or residential use. Ultramodern houses and lodges perch on the steep hillsides above the Old Town. Nearby, Park City Ski Area—

which includes an imposing Resort Center complex—houses an assortment of recreation-oriented businesses. To the east of that is a large residential and commercial district, including Prospector Square Convention Center. On the northwest is a municipal golf course. Condominium clusters sprawl across hundreds of acres of valley floor and climb the hillsides, and new construction meets the eye seemingly in every direction.

Over the mountain to the east is Deer Valley. Situated on three mountains—Flagstaff Mountain, Bald Mountain, and Bald Eagle Mountain—Deer Valley has 13 lifts, giving access to 67 runs and three bowls. The vertical drop is 2,200 feet. Skiers may stay in Deer Valley or Park City, or commute from Salt Lake City, about half an hour away.

While winter sports (November–December to April–May) provide the basic bread and butter to many Park City businesses, the area is promoted as an all-year, four-season resort. For example, the Park City Arts Festival, held every August, draws more than 200,000 visitors on a two-day weekend to historic Main Street, attracted by hundreds of exhibitors of arts and crafts, supplemented by performing arts and food booths. The city's 18-hole golf course is a summer attraction, as is the Jack Nicklaus golf course in Park Meadows. Writers at Work, founded in 1985, is held in July; it has become one of the major writers' conferences in the country, and brings agents, editors, and writers to Park City every summer. Local night life features several dozen restaurants, bars, and nightclubs. The Egyptian Theatre, constructed in 1926, is Park City's community theater, the locale for musicals, dramas, and comedies. The Kimball Art Center features a Main Gallery, gift shop, facilities for arts and crafts work, and an auditorium for musical and dramatic presentations. Numerous shops and stores offer a wide selection of goods throughout the year, and other businesses provide a full complement of services.

Historic Main Street District (Old Town) consists of a narrow commercial thoroughfare in the mouth of a canyon, flanked by several parallel streets at staggered elevations. Most of the buildings date from the turn of the century or before, the majority built following the great fire of 1898. Displaying a picturesque medley of styles and building materials from the past, the Main Street District is listed on the National Register of Historic Places as a Historic Commercial District: "the best remaining metal mining town business district in Utah." More than 60 edifices are considered of historic and architectural interest. Many are listed on national and state historic registers.

The Resort Center, a monumental group of multistoried brick buildings, serves as the lower terminal for Park City's complex of gondola and chairlifts, and the Alpine Slide. In the Center are shops for sales and rentals, Kinderhaus (child-care center), restaurants, state liquor store, food shops, Ski Patrol, Ski School, lounges, and other facilities. Lodging referrals are available through the Park City Chamber of Commerce, phone (435) 649-6100, or (800) 453-1360.

The gondola lift features four-passenger cars and extends from the Resort Center at 7,000 feet to the Summit House at 9,400 feet, a distance of 2-1/2 miles. Ski runs descend from there. The Summit House affords a spectacular view in addition to dining service. Mid-Mountain Restaurant, at the midway Angle Station, provides lodging and food service. The Snowhut at the base of the Prospector lifts is a popular lunch spot. In addition to the gondola, three quads, six triple, and four double chairlifts provide access to terrain of varying difficulty, crisscrossed by more than 68 designated ski runs, plus the wide-open Jupiter and Scotts Bowls (650 acres) serviced by the Jupiter chairlift. The Alpine Slide is comprised of shallow chutes on the mountainside in which riders descend on wheeled sleds. The top is reached by chairlift.

Park City's hotels, lodges, apartments, chalets and condominium units are estimated to have a capacity of 3,500 rooms. A wide range of lodging and package choices is available. Write Chamber of Commerce P.O. Box 1630, Park City, Utah 84060, for details. Limousine, helicopter, taxi, and rental car services also are available from Salt Lake City. Continuous shuttle bus service connects all points within Park City. Taxi service also is available within the area.

Like several other mountain towns in the West, Park City has undergone a transformation during the past thirty years. Once a hustling mining town, it is now a ski resort and a home for the rich and super-rich. The following summary of mining days is excerpted from the 1941 edition of this book:

IN 1853 CATTLE WERE GRAZING IN THE HIGH, COOL MEADOWS DURING THE SHORT SUMMERS, AND THE WINTERS WERE LOCKED IN LONG, SNOWY SILENCES. THEN, IN THE WINTER OF 1869, ORE WAS DISCOVERED. THE SOLITUDE WAS SHATTERED BY THE TRAMP OF PROSPECTORS' FEET, BY THE RING OF PICKS ON HARD ROCK, BY THE RUMBLE OF BLASTED EARTH, AND BY THE LAUGHTER OF HARD-FIGHTING, FAST-LIVING MEN.

ACCORDING TO GENERAL WILLIAM HENRY KIMBALL, KEEPER OF THE STAGE STATION (SEE BELOW) A FEW MILES FROM PARK CITY, THREE SOLDIERS FROM COLONEL PATRICK E. CONNOR'S COMPANY RAN ACROSS A BOLD OUTCROP OF QUARTZ ABOUT TWO MILES SOUTH OF PARK CITY. THEY BROKE OFF A CHUNK, MARKED THE SPOT WITH A RED HANDKERCHIEF, AND HURRIED DOWN THE CANYON. THE ASSAY DISCLOSED 96 OUNCES OF SILVER, 54 PER CENT LEAD, AND ONE-TENTH OUNCE OF GOLD. IT WAS NOT UNTIL 1870S, HOWEVER, THAT THEY BEGAN OPERATION, NAMING THE CLAIM THE FLAGSTAFF.

THE OPENING OF THE FLAGSTAFF STARTED A STAMPEDE. TENTS AND BRUSH SHANTIES SPRANG UP ALONG THE CANYON, FOLLOWED BY A BOARDING HOUSE, A GENERAL STORE, A BLACKSMITH SHOP, A LIVERY STABLE, A MEAT MARKET, AND SALOONS.

BY 1880 PARK CITY WAS A GOOD-SIZED TOWN. THE PARK MINING RECORD, LATER CALLED THE PARK RECORD, WAS ESTABLISHED BY THE RADDON FAMILY, AND HAS CONTINUED UNDER THEIR MANAGEMENT. THE FIRST TELEGRAPH LINE WAS COMPLETED FROM PARK CITY TO ECHO; A CATHOLIC CHURCH WAS ERECTED; AND A WATER SYSTEM, CONSISTING OF A SMALL RESERVOIR AND A PIPE DOWN ONE STREET, WAS INSTALLED. AMUSEMENTS WERE SIMPLE, AND, AS BEFITTED THE MEN OF THE DISTRICT, GENERALLY MUSCULAR—BOXING MATCHES, WRESTLING MATCHES, AND FOOT OR SNOWSHOE RACES.

BAD LUCK STALKED THE CAMP IN THE 1890S. THE PANIC OF 1893 DEALT PARK CITY A HARD BLOW, AND A SERIES OF FIRES NEARLY WIPED IT OFF THE MAP. THE FIRST FIRE BROKE OUT IN A FURNITURE STORE. NEXT TO GO WAS THE SAMPLING WORKS, FOLLOWED BY THE MOST DISASTROUS CONFLAGRATION OF ALL, THE HOTEL FIRE OF 1898. IT STARTED IN THE KITCHEN, AND, FANNED BY A CANYON BREEZE, SPREAD SO RAPIDLY THAT FIREMEN WERE UNABLE TO CONTROL IT. WHEN THE SMOKE CLEARED AWAY, PARK CITY COUNTED A MILLION-DOLLAR LOSS. THE TOWN DUG IN, AND WITHIN NINETY DAYS A NEW BUSINESS DISTRICT AROSE. THERE WERE RUMORS OF A "FIRE BUG." THE PARK RECORD, ALWAYS A BAROMETER OF PUBLIC OPINION, WROTE: ". . . SHOULD ANYONE BE CAUGHT IN THE ACT OF SETTING FIRE TO A BUILDING HIS LIFE WOULD NOT BE WORTH A STRAW. . . MURDER MAY BE COMMITTED AND THE LAW ALLOWED TO TAKE ITS COURSE, BUT THE LINE IS DRAWN ON THE FIRE BUG AND GOD HELP THE MAN . . . A LONG ROPE AND A SHORT-SHIFT WILL BE HIS PORTION AS SURE AS FATE."

THE COMING OF PROHIBITION, THE WORLD WAR, THE SLUMP IN SILVER PRICES, THE DEPRESSION, LABOR TROUBLES, AND THE DEATH OF MANY OF THE OLD-TIMERS, COMBINED TO PARTIALLY TAME THIS ONCE WIDE OPEN TOWN. ALTHOUGH STILLS COULD BE HEARD BLOWING UP IN THE MOUNTAINS, AND THE RESIDENTS WERE ABLE TO FIND A SPECIES OF ALCOHOL WHEN THEY WANTED TO, THE TOWN NEVER REALLY RECOVERED FROM THE SHOCK OF PROHIBITION. BEER PARLORS AND STATE LIQUOR STORES REPLACED THE PALACES OF DRINK; FIGHTING ON THE STREETS BECAME MORE SCIENTIFIC AND LESS SPECTACULAR; AND AUTOMOBILES TOOK THE MINERS INTO OTHER TOWNS ON PAY DAY. GAMBLING WAS CARRIED ON FURTIVELY BEHIND CLOSED DOORS, AND CHARACTERS LIKE "FIRST CLASS" SICKLER, WHO THOUGHT ALL ORE LOOKED FIRST CLASS, GREW SCARCE.

Kimball Junction East to Evanston

Interstate 80 crosses Parley's Park to join Route 40 at Silver Creek Junction (3 miles from Kimball Junction), then descends Silver Creek Canyon to the Weber River Valley at

Wanship. Between Kimball Junction and Silver Creek Junction, to the north of the highway, is the historic Kimball Stage Stop.

Travelers with time for leisurely sightseeing will be repaid by leaving I-80 at Wanship and driving the old highway to Hoytsville and Coalville. Settlement of this area began in the 1850s; much of nostalgic interest remains.

Hoytsville (5,700 alt.) is a farming village that dates from 1859; first named Unionville, it was renamed for Samuel P. Hoyt, a prominent pioneer. During the 1860s Hoyt built a gristmill with machinery transported laboriously from the East before completion of the railroad. The mill operated only a few years because the river changed its course. Its walls still stand after more than a hundred years.

Coalville (5,600 alt.) is the Summit County seat, "situated on a bench of land sloping from the narrow mouth of Chalk Creek Canyon to the Weber River." Traditionally the city has been a supply center for farmers and ranchers.

Summit County, with 1,849 square miles of land area, is not large as Utah's counties go. Farming, livestock raising, and logging have always been the economic mainstays in the river valleys, and metal mining in the Park City area until recent years, when recreation, leisure, and attendant economic activities have become dominant.

Echo Dam and Reservoir, part of the Weber Basin Project, date from 1927–30 when the dam was built by the U.S. Bureau of Reclamation. The reservoir has a surface area of 1,500 acres and a capacity of 74,000 acre-feet. Its water provides supplemental irrigation water for more than 100,000 acres of land in Weber and Davis Counties. The lake is popular for boating and waterskiing.

Echo (5,460 alt.) marks the junction of I-80 and I-84. The Union Pacific Railroad parallels the freeway east and west. At the junction are travel service facilities. Little remains to indicate that the population was larger in former days. In 1941 Echo was "a straggling railroad town" with "a more colorful past than present." Its past was described in the 1941 edition:

THE TOWN LIES A HALF MILE NORTHWEST OF THE SITE OF THE ORIGINAL WEBER RIVER STAGECOACH STATION, ERECTED IN 1853. THE STATION WAS EAGERLY HAILED BY TRAVELERS, WHO OFTEN MET WITH A RIOTOUS RECEPTION. A GROUP OF SHOSHONI WHO LIVED NEAR BY MADE IT A HABIT TO DESCEND HAIR-RAISINGLY ON THE STATION AS THE STAGECOACHES DREW UP.

During railroad construction in 1868, tent saloons, gambling houses, and brothels sprang up to fleece the Irish. Men often disappeared overnight. Seven unidentified bodies were removed from one hole under a saloon and gambling hall; it was thought that the tent covered a trapdoor, through which dead men and refuse were dumped.

Listed on the State Historical Register is the Echo Church-School at the head of Temple Lane. This small brick structure was built in 1876 as a Presbyterian chapel and school, served as a public school from 1880 to 1913, and as a Mormon chapel from 1913 until 1963. The Echo cemetery is nearby to the north.

Echo Canyon, "a cavernous ravine in which sounds reverberate weirdly from towering walls," is perhaps the most historic route of travel in Utah. Describing the path of Route 30S, predecessor of I-80/I-84, through Echo and Weber Canyons, the 1941 edition said:

THE CANYONS HAVE REECHOED TO THE PASSAGE OF INDIANS, TRAPPERS AND EXPLORERS, PACIFIC EMIGRANTS, MORMON PIONEERS, WAGON FREIGHTERS, CALIFORNIA GOLD-SEEKERS, PONY EXPRESS RIDERS, OVERLAND STAGE DRIVERS, AND TRAVELERS OF EVERY DESCRIPTION. THE FIRST TRANSCONTINENTAL RAILROAD FOLLOWED THE BEATEN PATH THROUGH ECHO AND WEBER CANYONS. LIKE DRAGON'S TEETH, RAILROAD SPIKES SPROUTED RAILROAD TOWNS, WHICH STAGNATED AS THE RAILS MOVED WESTWARD.

Among Echo Canyon's special points of interest is Cache Cave, about 20 miles from Echo and about a mile east of the highway via ranch road (private property; inquire locally). The cave was a prominent landmark on the old Mormon Trail, and was known as a "register of the desert, because many early emigrants and Mormon soldiers carved their names on its walls," according to the 1941 edition.

From Echo, I-80 continues north and west to Emory, Castle Rock, Wahsatch, and Evanston, Wyoming.

Heber Valley and Kamas
via Routes 40 and 150

From 3 miles east of the Park City exit, Route 40 heads south toward Heber City, then curves east toward Duchesne, Vernal, and the eastern part of Utah.

About 14 miles from the junction is Jordanelle Reservoir, completed in 1994. Jordanelle State Park was designed with wheelchair-bound visitors in mind. It has 280 developed campsites and accomodates boating, sailing, swimming, and fishing. The Jordanelle Dam rises 300 feet above the valley floor.

At Heber City, Route 189 forks southwest toward American Fork and Orem (see Chapter 3). Some 4 miles south of Heber City is Deer Creek Reservoir. Constructed between 1938 and 1941 by the U.S. Bureau of Reclamation, the dam is a massive earth-fill structure 235 feet high and 1,304 feet wide, connecting the lower walls of Provo Canyon. Among its major industrial users is Geneva Steel Works at Orem. Beside Route 189 on the lake's east shore is Deer Creek State Park, a boating and fishing development of the Utah State Division of Parks and Recreation.

Facilities include a concrete launching ramp, docks, and a large campground with rest rooms, showers, drinking water, sewage disposal. Fee area. Also on the lake's shore are some commercial boat camps.

There are few scenes more delightful than the Heber Valley in the late afternoon near dusk, looking westward across a green expanse of scattered trees and fields with grazing sheep and cows to the shadowy ramparts of Timpanogos and Cascade Mountain. Many of its people still rely on farming, livestock, and dairying for their livelihoods, as they have since pioneer days. Trade and recreation have become more important in recent decades.

Beside Route 189 near its junction with Route 40 is the Heber Valley Airport, a base for non-powered gliders or sailplanes, which may be seen on the apron or overhead in the air. Heber Valley's air currents are considered ideal for soaring. Route 189 joins Route 40 in Heber City, the two becoming one for ten miles to Hailstone Junction. South and east from Heber City, Route 40 traverses Daniels Canyon and the high Strawberry Reservoir country to Uinta Basin.

Heber City (5,600 alt.) is the seat of Wasatch County and contains more than half the county's population. The charm of new blended with old is its most notable attribute—this in addition to beauty of physical setting.

Heber City's most distinctive edifice is the old Wasatch Stake Tabernacle (Mormon) in a central park setting, built during the 1880s and converted to secular use in the 1960s. Also listed on historical registers are a number of picturesque 19th-century homes; St. Lawrence Catholic Church (1915), 100 West and Center; and several commercial buildings.

Heber Pioneer Village, Railroad Museum, and Heber Valley Railroad Depot are located on the west side of Heber City beside the road to Midway (Route 113). Here is Utah's largest collection of vintage steam locomotives and rolling stock . . . a museum building featuring railroad memorabilia . . . a village of original and replica structures from the turn of the century or before . . . and the Heber City Depot, from which the Heber Creeper tour train departs on scheduled excursions through Heber Valley and Provo Canyon.

Pioneer Village is a cluster of quaint wood-frame buildings of western style, some originals and some replicas, of varying age and design. They have been arranged along both sides of a street to resemble a western business district of the turn-of-the-century era. During visitor season, the buildings are occupied, serving as shops and stores, livery stable, jail, Chinese laundry, hotel, restaurant, etc. Many of the buildings were moved from Corinne, where they were maintained by the Sons of Utah Pioneers.

The Heber Valley Railroad is a recreational railroad, transporting passengers from the old Heber City Depot to Bridal Veil Falls and return, a distance of 18 miles each way. The route passes through the rural countryside of Heber Valley, follows the west shore of Deer Creek Reservoir, and parallels Provo River through Provo Canyon. Diesel and steam locomotives are featured, as are enclosed coaches as well as open-air lounge, concession, and dining cars. Passengers are entertained with activities and events such as murder-on-the-train scenarios. For details, write or phone Heber Valley Railroad, 450 South 600 West, Heber City, UT 84032, (435) 654-5601.

Turn west from Heber City on Route 113 to Midway and Wasatch Mountain State Park.

Midway (5,500 alt.) has a delightful rural setting of expansive fields, dairy farms, and grazing livestock on the west edge of the Heber Valley against the foothills of the Wasatch Range. Many of its native residents are descended from Mormon settlers of Swiss origin; Swiss influence can be detected in the town's architecture and neat agricultural order. Swiss Days is an annual celebration in September. Newcomers, many of them, are part-time residents, who choose the locale for weekend homes. In Midway are numerous "limestone craters [pots] . . . averaging about 20 feet in diameter, formed by deposition from springs or geysers." Limestone "pot rock" was used for buildings and fences. Water from these "hot pots" has been popular since early days for recreation and therapeutic hot springs bathing.

The Old Midway School (National Register), 100 North and 100 West, was built in 1901 of local limestone and pot rock. The Watkins-Coleman Home, 5 East Main, was built in 1869 by Mormon bishop John Watkins, an English architect-builder and polygamist, for his two wives.

Turn south from Midway to Charleston, a rural hamlet; to Deer Creek Reservoir; and to the junction with Route 189.

Turn north from Midway to Wasatch Mountain State Park and roads leading through the park to American Fork Canyon, Big Cottonwood Canyon (Brighton), and Park City.

Wasatch Mountain State Park, encompassing 22,000 acres of wooded mountain slopes, is Utah's largest state park. The park features an outstanding golf course, improved camping and picnic areas, and a network of scenic mountain-canyon roads. The entrance to the park features a Visitor Center located 2 miles north of Midway on Route 224. The beautifully landscaped championship golf course of 27 holes is set in a mountain alcove and is a complete golfing facility with cart and club rentals, clubhouse, and restaurant. A campground north of the golf course and adjacent to Route 224 has more than 125 units, improved with modern rest rooms, showers, electricity, water, and sewer hookups, and facilities for groups, campers, trailers, and tents. Fee area; reservations advised. Other camping and picnic areas are located throughout the park. Snake Creek Canyon is an impressive defile—particularly scenic when autumn colors are rampant—through which a forest road climbs to Pole Line Pass, then down into American Fork Canyon. For information and reservations, contact Wasatch Mountain State Park, P.O. Box 10, Midway, Utah 84049, or call (435) 654-1791 (Visitors' Center) or (435) 654-0532 (Golf Course).

North of the golf course, Route 224 ascends Pine Creek Canyon to overlook the Heber Valley. At a junction about 6 miles from the Visitor Center, the road forks. Continue north to Park City or turn west over Guardsman Pass (10,000 alt.) to Brighton and Big Cottonwood Canyon.

North of Heber City, Route 189-40 passes across the valley floor, affording views of the Wasatch Range to the west. Within a few miles it enters the narrowing channel of the Provo River, and at Hailstone Junction, 8 miles from Heber City, the road forks once more—Route 40 continuing north to I-80 near Park City, and Route 32 following the Provo River eastward to Francis. In 1941 Hailstone was "a lumber camp where 300,000 feet of lumber, 15,000 railroad ties, and 400,000 feet of mine props are cut annually."

Jordanelle State Park includes Hailstone and Rock Cliff recreation areas. Hailstone, on Route 40, has a breathtaking view of Jordanelle Reservoir and the Wasatch Mountains. Rock Cliff, on the east side of the reservoir, offers an elevated boardwalk system that meanders through the aspens and overlooks the Provo River.

Francis (6,500 alt.) is a farming and livestock hamlet beside the Provo River, in the south end of the Rhodes Valley. At Francis Route 32 turns north to Kamas.

Route 35 forks eastward from Francis following the river for a way, climbing gradually to Wolf Creek Pass (9,900 alt.), then dropping to Hanna and Duchesne in the Uinta Basin. The country through which the road passes is a vast, rugged region with few all-year residents. Streams drain to the Provo and Duchesne Rivers, and forest growth alternates with far-spreading expanses of open space. Hundreds of miles of fair-weather roads crisscross the area, providing access for fishermen, hunters, loggers, rangers, stockmen, backpackers, and summer home residents.

Kamas (6,500 alt.) is an incorporated town in Rhodes Valley at the mouth of Beaver Creek Canyon. Beaver Creek is a tributary of the Weber River. The town's economy is based on agriculture, logging, travel and recreation. Recent decades have seen the influx of more and more part-time summer residents in the area.

North of Kamas, Route 32 passes through mountainous terrain in a wide valley filled with productive fields, between foothills of the Wasatch Range on the west and the Uinta Range on the east. At Oakley (6,400 alt.), a farming village, paved Route 213 forks east into Weber River Canyon.

East of Oakley, Route 213 traverses the flat bottom of the Upper Weber River Canyon to Holiday Park, about 20 miles, the site of summer homes in the river's upper reaches. From Holiday Park, trails branch southward into a region of 11,000-foot peaks and many lakes and streams, a favorite locale for fishing and hiking. The Smith and Morehouse Reservoir is reached by a short side road from Route 213 at a junction about 12 miles east of Oakley. This large man-made lake—popular for fishing—is in an exceptionally scenic setting of steep slopes and bald-topped peaks. Two forest campgrounds are near the lake.

Rockport Lake, formed by Wanship Dam, is an important water-control unit of the Weber Basin Project, occupying the site of the former village of Rockport. On the east shore of the thousand-acre reservoir is Rockport State Park (6,000 alt.), an elaborate public resort with boat ramp, numerous camping and picnic units, rest rooms, showers, drinking water, and a commercial marina.

Wanship (5,900 alt.) is a roadside village at the junction of Route 189 and I-80. According to the 1941 edition, Wanship was "settled in 1859 and named for a Ute chief." In 1872 Wanship was an important stage station on the overland route.

THE UINTA MOUNTAINS

Turn east from Kamas on paved Route 150 to Mirror Lake (31 miles), the Uinta Mountains, and Evanston, Wyoming (79 miles). This drive is one of the most popular mountain routes in Utah, in particular that segment from Kamas to Mirror Lake. Route 150 winds and climbs through wooded terrain, gradually gaining in elevation as it penetrates the region of lofty glaciated peaks. For much of the distance to Mirror Lake, the road parallels the Provo River; beyond Mirror Lake to Evanston, the road follows the route of the Bear River. The

There are few scenes more delightful than the Heber Valley in the late afternoon near dusk, even in the winter months – Steve Midgley

region is hardly excelled in Utah for stream and lake fishing (trout), and the Wasatch National Forest has provided numerous developed picnic and camping sites in secluded locations beside the road. Of special interest between Kamas and Mirror Lake are the Upper Provo River Falls, a series of terraced cascades, and numerous lakes near the road.

Bald Mountain Pass (10,678 alt.) provides the first stunning view of the western end of the High Uintas Wilderness—here a great forested basin drained by the Duchesne River—containing Mirror Lake and a multitude of other glacial lakes. Looming above the basin are rocky peaks and ridges, in particular Bald Mountain (11,947), Hayden Peak (12,473), and Mount Agassiz (12,429). A foot trail known as the Bald Mountain National Scenic Trail leads from the pass to the top of Bald Mountain. Mirror Lake is the site of a large forest campground maintained by the Wasatch National Forest. Trails lead from Mirror Lake and the highway to other lakes in the basin as well as to other parts of the Uinta Range. Information and maps may be obtained from Wasatch-Cache National Forest offices, 125 South State, 8th floor, Salt Lake City, Utah 84138. Route 150 is often closed by snow between October and May or June, the dates varying slightly from year to year, and with altitude or location.

The Uinta Mountains, Utah's highest, are the largest individual mountain range in the contiguous 48 states having a distinct east-west axis. Together with the Wasatch Range, they represent the Rocky Mountains province in Utah. Nearly a dozen peaks exceed 13,000 feet in altitude, the highest being Kings Peak at 13,528 feet. As described in *The Geologic Story of the Uinta Mountains* (U.S. Geological Survey Bulletin 1291), the Uintas "have an overall length of about 150 miles and a mean width of about 35 miles. At their widest, toward the west, they are more than 45 miles across, and at their narrowest, near the center of the range, they are less than 30 miles across. The boundaries are somewhat indefinite, inasmuch as the flanks pass into bordering hogback ridges and broad sloping mesas that merge gradually with the high arid tablelands of the adjacent basins." The Uintas were further described on page 490 of the 1941 edition:

THE UINTA RANGE, PART OF WHICH IS INCLUDED IN THE PRIMITIVE AREA, IN GENERAL FORM IS A BROAD, ELONGATED, FLAT-TOPPED ARCH. THE CULMINATING PEAKS AND RIDGES LIE FOR THE MOST PART ALONG THE NORTH SIDE OF THE ARCH. THE PLATEAU-LIKE SUMMIT IN MANY PLACES IS DEEPLY DISECTED AND ERODED INTO JAGGED PEAKS AND RIDGES; AT THEIR BASES ARE IMMENSE AMPHITHEATERS, AND BELOW ARE DEEP CANYONS. THE CENTRAL PART OF THE RANGE, ALONG THE ANTICLINAL CREST, IS FORMED OF NEARLY HORIZONTAL ROCK STRATA, BURIED AT MANY PLACES BENEATH GLACIAL MATERIAL, WHICH IMPOUNDS NUMEROUS SMALL LAKES AND PONDS. A GREAT PORTION OF THIS REGION IS OCCUPIED BY GRASSY PARKS, OPEN MEADOWS, AND HEAVILY FORESTED SLOPES, ABOVE WHICH THE BARREN PEAKS RISE BOLDLY. THE NORTHERN FLANK OF THE RANGE SLOPES OFF STEEPLY TO THE UNDULATING GREEN RIVER BASIN OF WYOMING. THE SOUTHERN SLOPES DROP MORE GENTLY TO AN EXTENSIVE PLATEAU REGION AND THEN INTO THE UINTA BASIN. THESE SLOPES ARE DEEPLY INCISED BY STREAMS, MANY OF THEM WITH CANYON CHANNELS FROM 1,000 TO 2,000 FEET DEEP. IN THIS MOST HEAVILY TIMBERED REGION IN THE STATE THE ROCK COLORING IS DELICATE, RANGING THROUGH THE RICH WARM COLORS OF THE SPECTRUM TO MELLOW BLENDS OF GREEN, BLUE, LILAC, PEARL, AMETHYST AND PURPLE.

The High Uintas Wilderness Area

The High Uintas Wilderness represents the remote heart of the Uinta Range. A 237,000-acre federal preserve occupying parts of the Ashley and Wasatch National Forests, the Wilderness Area extends along both sides of the Uinta crest from Mirror Lake on the west to Kings Peak on the east, including within its boundaries many of the highest summits in Utah as well as hundreds of lakes. The following appears in the 1941 edition:

FIVE PLANT ZONES ARE REPRESENTED IN THE PRIMITIVE AREA: THE ARCTIC, ON THE GRASSY MOSS AND LICHEN COVERED BUT TREELESS PEAKS ABOVE 11,000 FEET; THE HUDSONIAN, MARKED BY ENGELMANN SPRUCE AND ALPINE FIR, USUALLY FROM 9,000 TO 11,000 FEET; THE CANADIAN, WITH WHITE BALSAM, BLUE SPRUCE, AND ASPEN AS LOW AS 7,000 FEET; THE TRANSITION BETWEEN 6,000 AND 7,000 FEET, REPRESENTED BY SCRUB OAK AND YELLOW PINE; AND THE UPPER SONORAN, WITH ITS JUNIPER AND SAGE BELOW 6,000 FEET. INDIGENOUS FLORA INCLUDES TWENTY-FIVE GENERA OF GRASSES, THIRTY DIFFERENT SHRUBS, AND MORE THAN ONE HUNDRED TYPES OF HERBS AND WEEDS. THE PINE, SPRUCE AND FIR ARE VARIED WITH QUAKING ASPEN, PIÑON PINE, MOUNTAIN ASH, HICKORY, JUNIPER, AND SCRUB OAK. BIRD LIFE COMPRISES ALL SPECIES INDIGENOUS TO THE WESTERN ROCKIES, AUGMENTED BY MANY MIGRANTS.

ANIMALS ARE ABUNDANT. BIGHORN SHEEP ROAM THE CRAGS, ELK BROWSE IN THE VALLEYS, BEAR PUT ON FAT BEFORE THEIR LONG WINTER SLEEP. THE MOST PLENTIFUL BIG GAME ANIMAL IS THE MULE DEER. BADGER, PORCUPINE, CANADIAN LYNX, MOUNTAIN LION, AND COYOTE ARE NUMEROUS, AND THERE IS A GREAT VARIETY OF SMALLER ANIMALS.

The most convenient paved access route leading to the edge of the Wilderness Area is Route 150 between Kamas, Utah, and Evanston, Wyoming. Near Mirror Lake, the Highline Trail begins and, according to the 1941 edition,

. . . RUNS IN A GENERAL EAST-WEST DIRECTION ALONG THE CREST OF THE UINTA MOUNTAINS; IT IS THE ONLY FEASIBLE PATH THROUGH THE LOFTY PASSES. THERE IS A NETWORK OF TRAILS ACROSS THE AREA, WITH THE

HIGHLINE TRAIL THE TRUNK OR MAIN ARTERY. WELL-MARKED CONNECTING TRAILS LEAD TO HIGHWAY POINTS OF ENTRY. . . . A ROUND TRIP, MADE AS DESCRIBED [FROM MIRROR LAKE TO HENRY'S FORK PARK, EASTERN TERMINUS OF THE TRAIL, A DISTANCE OF 56 MILES ONE-WAY] REQUIRES SEVERAL DAYS ON HORSEBACK [OR FOOT], STOPPING ONLY FOR MEALS AND SLEEP. FOOD, FIRST AID SUPPLIES, FISHING EQUIPMENT, WARM BEDDING OR A MEDIUM-WEIGHT SLEEPING BAG, AND WARM CLOTHING MUST BE CARRIED THE ENTIRE TRIP.

A number of roads lead from Route 40 in the Uinta Basin to trail heads in canyons of south-flowing streams such as the Duchesne, Rock Creek, Lake Fork, Yellowstone, and Uinta. In addition, numerous trails enter the area from roads to the west, north, and east.

Vernal via Route 40 East

Route 40 leads east to Vernal and eventually to the border of Colorado. From Vernal the traveler can turn north to Flaming Gorge Reservoir, continue east to Dinosaur National Monument, or turn south along any of several roads into the Uinta Basin.

This is a harsh land, having on average the lowest mean temperatures and moisture totals of any climatic region of the state. It is forbiddingly rugged, ringed by highlands, and even the relatively level Uinta Basin displays a surface of shallow pocket valleys, broad stream channels, and flat-topped ridges or benches. Traditionally, until recent years, the bulk of its population subsisted marginally on agriculture and recreational travel. Today, mineral production provides the region's most important economic cornerstone, and this industry is likely to expand even more dramatically in the years to come. *(The name is spelled Uinta or Uintah, depending on whether the reference is to a geographic or a political division respectively.)*

East of Heber City and the Provo River Valley, Route 40 enters the Uinta country through Daniels Canyon, a long defile with a gradual incline, a natural route of travel since time immemorial. Strawberry Reservoir, at about 7,600 feet altitude, is cupped between rolling summits in a transitional montane zone between the Uinta Range and the Tavaputs/Wasatch plateaus.

The reservoir has been a favorite fishing resort since the original impound more than 90 years ago as the state's first important federal reclamation project, and the first large-scale diversion of water from the Colorado River Basin into the Great Basin. The original Strawberry Valley Project involved construction of roads, dam, power plant, canals, dikes,

and a 20,000-foot-long concrete-lined diversion tunnel. Construction required many years, extending from 1905 to 1922. The first storage water was delivered to the Utah Valley in 1915. As a crucial element in the Bonneville Unit of the Central Utah Project, the reservoir was enlarged by construction of Soldier Creek Dam on the Strawberry River from a capacity of 270,000 acre-feet to a capacity of more than a million acre-feet. Additional water is brought from headwaters of the Duchesne River via 38 miles of tunnels and aqueducts. The reservoir's water flows in two directions: west via tunnels into the Great Basin, generating electricity en route, and east to Starvation Reservoir near Duchesne.

The U.S. Forest Service maintains four campgrounds on the lake; all are open from May to late October. Marinas, paved boat ramps, boat rental, and boat storage are available.

Between Strawberry Reservoir and Fruitland, the highway passes through rolling mountain country, sparsely vegetated with brush and pygmy evergreens. Near Fruitland it emerges into the vastness of Uinta Basin, and the massive bulk of the Uinta Range comes to dominate the northern horizon.

Fruitland (6,600 alt.) is a cluster of ranches, "settled in 1907 and named by land promoters who hoped to attract settlers." At a junction 7 miles east of Fruitland, Route 208 forks north to a junction with Route 35 (10 miles), which leads in one direction to Duchesne, in the other to Hanna, Wolf Creek Pass, and the Provo River Valley (see Duchesne below).

East of the junction with Route 208, Route 40 passes through a dense growth of pinyon pines and junipers, claimed by local enthusiasts to be "the world's largest pinyon cedar forest"—perhaps a dubious claim. In this vicinity is Pinyon Ridge, a rural land subdivision. Starvation Reservoir, a major impound in the valley formed by the confluence of Strawberry and Duchesne Rivers, is a 3,000-acre water-control unit of the Central Utah Project. On its shore is Starvation Lake State Beach, a recreational development with boating and camping facilities.

Here the highway has descended into the Uinta Basin, which is, in the words of the Utah Travel Council, "a vast bowl rimmed by mountains, a peaceful valley carpeted with irrigated fields, sagebrush flats, and undulating forests of juniper and pinyon pine. Along the streams flowing down from the mountains, farmers have literally turned the valley into a land of milk and honey, for dairying is an important local

*Llama packing in the High Uintas
Wilderness Area
– Mel Lewis. UTC*

industry and Basin honey is famous for its quality and flavor. In summer, thousands of sheep and cattle graze the hills and fields; in winter they feed on produce grown in the valley or graze the lower elevations . . ." About a third of the Basin's people live in three cities on U.S. Highway 40: Duchesne, Roosevelt, and Vernal. The other two-thirds are scattered across the valley in smaller towns, villages, and ranches. Many Utes reside at Whiterocks, Fort Duchesne, Myton, and Ouray, though some have homes elsewhere.

Duchesne (5,500 alt.) is the seat of Duchesne County, a vast domain of more than 3,000 square miles, thinly populated and bounded on three sides by high mountains. The county's population increased by 70 percent between 1970 and 1980, one of the highest growth rates among Utah's counties, with the majority of newcomers settling outside the limits of incorporated communities. Much of this growth was due to expansion of the petroleum industry, particularly in the rural basin area to the north and east of Duchesne.

Turn north from Duchesne via Route 87 and paved side roads to Mountain Home, Boneta, Bluebell, and other farming villages at the base of the Uinta Mountains. These hamlets are largely dependent on livestock and the growing of grain and feed crops. Unpaved roads lead north from Mountain Home, passing through the Indian reservation to Ashley National Forest, giving access to Rock Creek Canyon, Moon Lake (Lake Fork Canyon), and Yellowstone Canyon. Each of these is the site of forest campgrounds (Ashley National Forest) at the head of trails leading into the region of high peaks and the High Uintas Wilderness Area.

Route 87 curves eastward through Altamont, Upalco, and Ioka to a junction with Route 40, 5 miles west of Roosevelt.

From Route 87 at a junction 7 miles north of Duchesne, Route 35 forks west to Tabiona, Hanna, Wolf Creek Pass, Woodland, and junction with Route 32 at Francis. For 30 miles, Route 35 parallels the Duchesne River in the pleasant valley it has carved in its journey from the High Uintas. Unpaved side roads and trails penetrate the wild country, extending in all directions.

Turn south from Duchesne via Route 191 to Indian Canyon and junction with Route 6 at Castle Gate. This scenic 40-mile route passes through a gorge of gentle contours and soft colors, gradually ascending to a 9,100-foot pass on the summit of West Tavaputs Plateau, then dropping through Willow Creek Canyon to Castlegate. The Indian Canyon route was an important link between the Uinta Basin and the railroad at Helper and Colton, particularly during early decades of this century, between the freighting heydays of Nine Mile Canyon and improvement of the route now followed by Route 40.

East of Duchesne, Route 40 traverses the broad valley of the Duchesne River to Myton. The great Uinta Mountain uplift looms to the north, and though several high peaks can be glimpsed, the range's glaciated ridge of barren 13,000-foot summits is hidden from view.

Myton (5,280 alt.) is a quiet village in the valley of the Duchesne River, surrounded by thinly vegetated badlands. Though it has grown in the past few years, Myton has a history of still livelier days when it was a bustling trade center for prosperous farms and a stop along the Nine Mile freighting route. Before white settlers arrived in 1905 it was the site of an Indian trading post called "The Bridge."

Turn south from a junction 2 miles west of Myton to Nine Mile Canyon, Wellington, and Price (80 miles) This scenic route provides close-up viewing of numerous panels of curious petroglyphs (rock etchings), the work of prehistoric Indians, and romantic traces of turn-of-the-century years when the road was utilized for freight and traffic between Uinta Basin communities and the railroad at Price.

Also turn south from this junction (fork from Nine Mile road 2 miles from Route 40) to Sand Wash Launching Site on the Green River, 34 miles from Route 40 via mostly unpaved road. At the north end of Desolation Canyon, this site is preferred for launching by many river runners because it shortens downstream floating distance by more than 30 miles through rather uninteresting terrain below Ouray. At the site is a monument denoting the head of Desolation Canyon as a National Historic Landmark. Boaters travel from this point downstream to take-out points near Green River, a distance of 75 to 95 miles, passing through a magnificent gorge thousands of feet deep.

Roosevelt (5,200 alt.) is the commercial capital of Duchesne County, midway between Duchesne and Vernal. It also serves as the main commercial center for members of the Ute tribe. The city lies in a valley surrounded by flat-topped benches.

Roosevelt was founded in 1905 at the time much of the Ute reservation was opened to homesteading, and was named after Theodore Roosevelt by its first settlers, the Harmston family. In a history written for the Roosevelt Area Chamber of Commerce, George E. Stewart described the Basin's land-rush days:

FINALLY, IN 1905 AND 1906 THE UTE RESERVATION WAS OPENED TO HOMESTEADERS. THE BIG LAND RUSH WAS ON! IT WAS NOT LIKE THE LAND RACE ALONG THE CIMARRON IN OKLAHOMA, THE GOVERNMENT HAD LEARNED ITS LESSON THERE, SO IN THE BIG "U" COUNTRY THE RED TAPE MADE THE RUSH MUCH MORE ORDERLY. BUT THE HOMESTEADERS CAME BY THE HUNDREDS.

AN OLD UTE SAID, "WHEN THE AMERICANS CAME, THEY CAME BY THE MANY MANYS, THEY CAME NOSE TO TAIL LIKE A STRING OF BLACK ANTS CROSSING THE SAND." SOME CAME FROM COLORADO THROUGH VERNAL, SOME THROUGH STRAWBERRY VALLEY, BUT MOST CAME ALONG THE STAGE ROAD FROM PRICE THROUGH NINE MILE CANYON.

AN OLD TIMER WHO LIVED AT THE STRIP BEFORE AND DURING "THE OPENING" SAID IT WAS LIKE THE TOUCH OF A FAIRY'S WAND, YESTERDAY THERE WAS NOTHING BUT WILDERNESS AND DESERT, TODAY THERE ARE FENCES, DITCHES, PLOWING, PLANTINGS, HOUSES AND TOWNS; SETTLERS WERE EVERYWHERE . . . IT WAS ALMOST MAGICAL. IN THE "EARLY DAYS" ROOSEVELT WAS A TENT AND SHANTY TOWN. EVEN SOME OF THE BUSINESSES BEGAN IN TENTS. BUT, OF COURSE, THESE WERE ONLY TEMPORARY, LASTING ONLY UNTIL SOMETHING MORE SUBSTANTIAL COULD BE BUILT . . . THERE IT WAS, IT SPRANG UP ALMOST OVERNIGHT, A TOWN, ROCKY, DUSTY, ROUGH AND RAW WITH A PURELY FRONTIER FLAVOR.

Roads lead in all directions from Roosevelt and from Route 40 in the vicinity, giving access to rural towns, farms and ranches, oil fields, forests and canyons. Spread across the stream bottoms and benchlands, watered from flowing canals, are well-kept fields of alfalfa and grain, interspersed with drilling rigs, oil pumps, and storage tanks. Cattle, sheep, and horses graze serenely, and modern dwellings alternate here and there with forlorn log cabins or vacant-eyed frame homes. Many of the basin's humble old buildings—dating in some cases from the late l800s, in most cases from the homestead days of the early l900s—speak eloquently of hardship of many years when crops were poor and money scarce.

Fort Duchesne, 1 mile south of Bottle Hollow Junction, is the site of the Ute tribal offices and those of the Bureau of Indian Affairs. Little of a historic or nostalgic nature strikes the eye to denote that Fort Duchesne has been at this locale since 1886 when it was established as an army post, or that it was occupied by infantry and cavalry troops from that time until 1912 when it was abandoned as a military post. Several historic buildings remain, including a powder house, guardhouse, and post hospital, now occupied by the Bureau of Indian Affairs. Two companies of black cavalrymen, named "buffalo

soldiers" by the Utes and other western Indians, served at the fort between its founding and 1901.

Whiterocks, 13 miles north of Route 40, is an unassuming Ute residential community, more interesting for its history than its present-day status. Meager evidence indicates that the Reed Trading Post, established perhaps as early as 1828, was located near here. If that were the case, it was the first fixed trading post in Utah. Apparently this post was transferred to Antoine Robidoux in the 1830s. Thereafter known as Fort Robidoux or Fort Winty, the location served as a rendezvous, trading post, fort, and travelers' stop until 1844, when the post was burned to the ground and white males were killed by enraged Utes. Only Robidoux's absence at the time saved him from the same fate.

In June and early July of 1869, during their epic first journey down the Green and Colorado, Major Powell and his party stopped at the mouth of the Duchesne (then called the Uinta) for a few days.

Powell described pottery fragments, foundations of "ancient houses," and "mealing-stones that were not used by nomadic people." The Utes, seeing his interest, took pains "to show me several other places where these evidences remain, and tell me that they know nothing about the people who formerly dwelt here. They further tell me that up in the canyon the rocks are covered with pictures." One of the places shown Powell by the Utes may have been Whiterocks Village, a prehistoric settlement excavated by the University of Utah in 1966. A number of structures were unearthed, as well as a large quantity of cultural debris. Evidence indicates occupation by Fremont Indians about A.D. 850. Historic register listing.

The drive from Route 40 to Whiterocks passes through near-virgin terrain along the Uinta River—a wild streamside landscape of willows, brush, and deciduous trees, undisturbed by tilling, much the same as it might have appeared when Utes were the only inhabitants of the basin.

The road north from Whiterocks leads to Uinta Canyon where there are campgrounds (Ashley National Forest) and the beginnings of trails to Uinta streams, lakes, and high peaks. U-Bar Ranch, one of several working guest ranches in the Uinta Basin, features cabins, meals, horses, and guides for pack trips, fishing and hunting excursions. Uinta Canyon is also accessible by road from Neola.

From Route 40 at a junction 16 miles east of Roosevelt (14 miles west of Vernal), Route 88 forks south to Pelican

Lake, Ouray National Wildlife Refuge, and the Ute Indian settlement of Ouray.

Pelican Lake, 10 miles from Route 40 near Leota, is an impoundment of more than a thousand acres, popular for fishing (bass and bluegill) and waterfowl hunting.

The Ouray National Wildlife Refuge extends along the Green River for about eight miles, embracing some 13,000 acres of river, sandbars, islands, bottomlands, and riverbank. Beginning in 1961, the refuge has developed a system of dikes, canals, roads, and marsh habitat. More than 130 species of birds have been observed at the refuge, including Canada geese, numerous ducks and other waterfowl, hawks and eagles, owls, swallows, songbirds, pheasants, and woodpeckers. Wildlife is abundant, with animals such as mule deer, coyotes, bobcats, rabbits, and an occasional mountain lion and black bear. Though the refuge lies in a desert environment with scant rainfall, the river encourages a luxuriant growth of plants that, in combination with plentiful water, invite birds from both Pacific and Central flyways. Visitors are welcome. Migration seasons provide the most interesting times for bird watching: April–May in the spring, August–November in the fall. October through November are recommended as "the best months of the year to visit the refuge if you are interested in waterfowl."

Ouray is a small settlement near the confluence of the Duchesne and Green Rivers, an important Ute center since the early days of the reservation, named for Chief Ouray of the Uncompahgre Utes. A number of its rustic buildings date from the 1880s. Non-Indian farmers and ranchers also live in the Ouray area and nearby at Leota and Randlett. Some of the Basin's first Mormon settlers planted their roots in this area in 1879 and across the Green River near the mouth of the White River. At this latter site, Fort Thornburgh (predecessor of Fort Duchesne) was established in 1881; it was removed within a short time to Maeser. As early as 1833 this area apparently was the site of a trading post operated by Kit Carson. A bridge across the Green at Ouray gives access to the White River country and the East Tavaputs region. Ouray is a launching and take-out site for river runners.

Vernal

Vernal (5,300 alt.), Uintah County seat, is the largest and oldest city in northeastern Utah, for which it serves as a regional capital. The bustling Vernal of today hardly resembles the slow-paced community of 1941, when it was described as "a trade center for sheepherders and cowhands; broad-brimmed Stetsons, high-heeled boots, and jangling spurs are commonplace." Gone now are most of the sheep, the city's population has tripled, and spurs are seldom seen.

Vernal is in the valley of Ashley Creek, a perennial stream flowing from the Uinta Mountains and emptying into the Green River near Jensen. The Ashley Valley was initially settled in the early 1870s; its first house was erected by Pardon Dodds, former Indian agent at Whiterocks. Other settlers began arriving soon afterwards, and by 1879—when the Meeker Massacre in Colorado stimulated building of a temporary fort—the valley's population numbered in the hundreds. Both Etienne Provost and Antoine Robidoux were in the area in 1824, and the Dominguez-Escalante expedition passed through in 1776. However, the name of the valley and stream commemorates the visit of General William H. Ashley and a few trapper companions who traversed the Green River downstream from Wyoming to the Uinta Basin in 1825.

After European settlement began during the 1870s, Vernal gradually became the trading center for ranches, farms, and small communities scattered across the eastern basin and mountains, isolated from the rest of the state by long distances and rough roads. In early years it was easier to bring supplies over the Uintas from Wyoming than from Salt Lake City. Not until the railroad was completed through Price in the 1800s did the problem of supply become less critical; but even with improvement of the Nine Mile road and building of the narrow-gauge "gilsonite" railroad, there remained decades of freighting and passenger travel over rough dirt roads.

For many the Utah Field House of Natural History, 235 East Main, (open daily all year) is the most fascinating museum in Utah. An official Utah state park and information center, the museum dates from the 1940s, having gradually expanded its collections and exhibits, today it contains many halls devoted not only to natural history but also to human history, archaeology and anthropology, and an outdoor Dinosaur Garden.

The Old Uintah Stake Tabernacle (Mormon), 5th West and 2nd South, is a large and distinctive brick structure with octagonal cupola. The tabernacle dates from the first decade of the present century (1907) and has functioned since then as a meetinghouse. It is has been renovated and enlarged to serve as an LDS temple.

The Bank of Vernal building (now Zions First National

Red Canyon, where John Wesley Powell floated on his trip down the Green River, can still be seen from the roads near Flaming Gorge – Frank Jensen, UTC

Bank), 3 West Main, gained a modicum of fame as the Parcel Post Bank, so called because the bricks in its facade—four or five tons of them—were shipped from Salt Lake City by parcel post. As described in the 1941 edition, "It was erected in [1916], when freight was $2.50 a hundred pounds and parcel post only $1.05."

- Tours from Vernal -

Turn north in Vernal at 5th West and Main and follow Route 121 (Lapoint Road) to Maeser, one of the older settlements of the Ashley Valley, 3 miles. From a junction 1 mile west of Maeser Center, turn north to Dry Fork Canyon and Red Cloud Loop. Uintah County Park (Merkley Park), 3 miles from Route 121, is in a verdant valley at the confluence of Dry Fork and Ashley Creeks. High on a sheer cliff beside the highway is a full-color painting of the American flag, bearing inscriptions "Remember the Maine" and "Pearl Harbor."

Fort Thornburgh was established in this vicinity in 1881 following the Meeker massacre of 1879. The fort was supplied from Fort Bridger over a primitive trans-Uinta road blazed in 1881 by Judge William A. Carter, a Wyoming merchant. The road was improved by troops and used as a supply route for several years; wagon trains required three weeks each way. Fort Thornburgh was closed in 1884 and the road was gradually abandoned as the Nine Mile route to the railroad at Price was improved. Dry Fork Canyon, nestled between broken cliffs of sandstone, was settled in the late 1870s and at one time contained a modest village population. Few of the original buildings remain. The canyon is renowned as the site of the famed Dry Fork petroglyphs—hundreds of carved and painted pictures on the cliffs, apparently the work of more than one ancient Indian culture. The best known panels are on the McConkie Ranch, 10 miles from Vernal, where the glyphs are inscribed along the north cliffs for two miles.

Near the McConkie Ranch, in a side canyon to the south, are the Peltier Ranch petroglyphs, works of a different style and older vintage. Though considered to be of Basketmaker or Pueblo I age, their actual origin and age are in doubt. Both sites are listed on historic registers and are privately owned.

The Maeser-Dry Fork road continues into the Uinta Mountains as the Red Cloud Loop, traversing scenic canyons, passing through evergreen and aspen woods of the Ashley National Forest, giving access to camp and picnic areas, overlook points, fishing streams, and lakes. The drive joins Route 44 about 21 miles north of Vernal and about 40 miles from Dry Fork. Brush Creek Cave, 6 miles west of the junction with Route 44 (half-mile trail), is a limestone cavern into which Brush Creek disappears.

Northeast from Vernal, a road leads to Rainbow Park (20 miles) and Island Park in Dinosaur National Monument. Another road, partly paved, leads to Diamond Mountain. This road climbs almost 3,000 feet to the rim of Diamond Mountain Plateau at nearly 8,000 feet, then drops abruptly into Jones Hole, a deep gorge that is tributary to Whirlpool Canyon of the Green River. The drive from Vernal affords inspirational views across the Uinta-Dinosaur geological wonderland. Diamond Mountain Plateau was named for "one of the greatest mining swindles in American history," described by the 1941 edition of this book and other publications. In 1871, the swindle's clever perpetrators "salted" a remote area with rough diamonds and other gemstones previously purchased in Europe, then interested wealthy investors and absconded with hundreds of thousands of dollars of investment money.

From the Jones Hole road, at a junction 27 miles from Vernal, turn north off the pavement on a road leading to Crouse Reservoir. The main side road follows Crouse Canyon to the Green River and Brown's Park, crossing the river on a narrow suspension bridge 50 miles from Vernal. Brown's Park is a mountain-girt ranching valley about 25 miles long that extends along Green River from the Red Canyon area in the west (Utah) to Lodore Canyon on the east (Colorado). (See Flaming Gorge National Recreation Area.) Known first as Brown's Hole before renaming by Major Powell, this remote basin still remains one of the most isolated parts of Utah and Colorado. The fabled Wild Bunch and other outlaws used the park as a hideout and base of operations for years, and many

are the tales of outlaw goings-on in the park as well as stories about other eccentric residents. Geologically, Brown's Park is an intermontane valley formed partly by erosion and partly by faulting. From the bridge, roads lead to Colorado and Wyoming, and west to Dutch John, Flaming Gorge Dam, Manila, and Route 44. A short distance from the road to Dutch John, near the mouth of Jesse Ewing Canyon about 10 miles west of the bridge across Green River—watch for directional signs—is the John Jarvie Historical Property. A nostalgic vignette of the frontier West preserved by the Bureau of Land Management, this rustic ranch exhibits an old stone house, a dugout, and other antique structures, as well as a small collection of western artifacts and a cemetery. The house dates from 1888. John Jarvie, who settled in Brown's Park about 1878, operated a store, post office, and ferry at the site. He was murdered in 1909.

The circle distance from Vernal totals about 140 miles. Detailed area information is available from the chamber of commerce and merchants in Vernal. Carry sufficient gasoline, tools, spare tire, food, and emergency equipment when exploring this area; some portions are very remote from the nearest services.

~ Flaming Gorge via Route 44 ~

Route 44 is the main paved access to the mountain, river, and lake country north of Vernal. Beginning about 4 miles from Vernal, a series of 20 interpretive signs along the highway call attention to points of geological interest that can be seen en route. Known as the Drive through the Ages, Route 44 passes through rocks laid down over a billion years. Much of the route is through the Ashley National Forest. Side roads lead east to Diamond Mountain Plateau, connecting with roads to Jones Hole and Brown's Park west to Brush Creek Cave, Red Cloud Loop, Oaks Park and East Park reservoirs, and four forest campgrounds. Two forest campgrounds are beside Route 44, 31 miles from Vernal. Greendale Junction, 35 miles, marks the approximate boundary of Flaming Gorge National Recreation Area.

Steinaker Reservoir, visible from an overlook 4 miles north of Vernal, is an important unit of the Central Utah Project. By storing high flows of Ashley Creek (diverted via a diversion dam and feeder canal), it provides supplemental irrigation water to about 15,000 acres of land in Ashley Valley. The project also provides municipal water for the Vernal area. Steinaker Reservoir is popular for bass and trout fishing, boating, and waterskiing. On its west shore is Steinaker State Park, developed with camping and picnicking facilities, boat ramp, toilets, and swimming beach.

Red Fleet Dam and Reservoir are elements in the Jensen Unit of the Central Utah Project. Surplus flow of Big Brush Creek is stored for municipal, industrial, and irrigation use, as well as for recreation, fish and wildlife, and flood control.

– Dinosaur National Monument via Route 40 –

East of Vernal, Route 40 traverses a thinly populated, semi-arid expanse of low ridges and open valleys, visually dominated by the tortured rock faces of Split Mountain and Blue Mountain. From the highway there is little evidence of the region's wealth of hydrocarbon minerals, deposited by great lakes that occupied the basin during the Eocene epoch of 50 million years ago or so.

At Jensen, 14 miles from Vernal, a highway bridge crosses Green River. This imposing stream, second largest in Utah, flows down from the Wind River Mountains of Wyoming to join the Colorado River in Canyonlands National Park. Its course through Utah is largely a series of grand gorges, interrupted here and there by valleys. The Green has been both a barrier and boon to transportation. The Dominguez-Escalante party forded the Green in 1776 a few miles north of Jensen near the present-day Quarry Visitor Center of Dinosaur National Monument. General Ashley and a few companions floated down the river from Wyoming to the Uinta Basin in 1825. Before the first bridges were built, land travelers found it necessary to ford the river, a hazardous undertaking even in times of low water, or to ferry across. Ferries operated near Jensen until the first bridge was opened in 1911, even longer at Alhandra downstream.

North from Jensen, Route 149 leads 7 miles to the Visitor Center and Quarry of Dinosaur National Monument (see Chapter 2), and to riverside campgrounds of the monument. This is an area of startling geological spectacle, where multi-hued strata have been broken, tilted and folded, then exposed by erosion. Across the river, a mile or so from the Quarry Visitor Center, a grove of cottonwood trees marks the campsite of the Dominguez-Escalante exploring party, who spent three nights here in September 1776. These travelers—among the first Europeans to enter Utah—named the river Rio de San Buenaventura.

Turn south from Jensen 2 miles to Stewart Lake Waterfowl Management Area near the mouth of Ashley Creek. In the vicinity is an impressive stone monument and replica of a ferryboat (Daughters of Utah Pioneers), marking the location of Mau-be Ferry, which operated here for more than 20 years until it was destroyed by an ice jam in 1909. A fair-weather road continues south along the river to the historic ruins of Alhandra Stage Stop and Ferry, about 7 miles from Jensen. Listed on the National Register of Historic Places, this site was located on a toll route connecting Uinta Basin communities with the narrow-gauge railroad at Watson. Travelers went by stagecoach and, later, by auto along the road past Jensen and south to the ferry site. From the ferry the stage passed two additional toll stops before reaching Watson. The ferry operated from 1906 through 1919 until the big bridge at Jensen made it obsolete. This was one of the last stage routes in operation in the United States. The ferry's east-bank terminus is accessible by road leading south from Route 40, across the bridge from Jensen.

East of the river, the massive Blue Mountain (Yampa Plateau) looms ever closer. The uplift's steep flanks are most intriguing, especially those curved monoclinal slopes overlooking the highway, known as Cliff Ridge or Stuntz Ridge, which are the result of folding or flexing of the earth's crust. Blue Mountain is the southeasternmost extension of the Uintas. Near Dinosaur, Colorado, 3 miles east of the Utah line, is the headquarters of Dinosaur National Monument. From here a paved road climbs and winds across the heights of Blue Mountain to Harpers Corner in the monument. (See Dinosaur National Monument.)

UTAH'S NORTHERN TIER

BY MARGARET PETTIS

Swipe a brush loaded with seasons across the northern block of Utah: Draw it down diagonally through the corner of Wyoming. Swing it out across the eastern edge . . . here lies a path of images unique to Utah.

Winter sunrise pushes back the blue shadows sleeping in snowclad crevices of the Raft River Mountains. Breathe in the silence of sage. Walk in the birthplace of clouds. On remote ledges mountain lions blink in winter moonlight, watching for a flick of rabbit ear, a grouse on a juniper bough, a porcupine scratching its way up a bar-

"Making Hay" at the the Jensen Historical Farm, Logan – Frank Jensen, UTC

ren maple, an unwary mule deer snapping through brush. Hawks circle out over Park Valley, where wild horses stream dreamlike across the curvature of the earth.

An early explorer described the more than 200 mountain ranges in the Great Basin as "an army of caterpillars marching to Mexico." Shimmering across the Great Salt Lake, dawn nudges this corner of the Great Basin—the Raft Rivers, Grouse Creeks, the Hogup Mountains—to life.

Spring arranging, rearranging, singing . . . distant lines of Canada geese enter Cache Valley, slipping into the high water of the Bear River. Grebes, herons, avocets, sandhill cranes, loons, eagles—all gather in the rich bottomlands. Jim Bridger and other trappers cached beaver pelts here for trade at their rendezvous with friendly tribes. And in the mountainous country above Logan, Utah's last grizzly bear was slain; among moose, elk, and badger, a heavy monument reminds us of our deeds.

Two wilderness areas offer cornices to the sun: Mt. Naomi conceals limestone sinks, rare orchids, elk, and mountain lion; the Wellsville mountains "rise faster" than any mountain range in the lower 48.

Catching every rivulet, the Bear River deposits all in the remnant of a great inland sea to the west. There, on the migratory bird refuge, time slows for the feathering of nests.

Summer—"make hay . . ."

With a Rich County growing season of little more than two

months, July's haymakers are in a frenzy. Like shredded wheat, great bristled rolls of grass, mounds of sweet hay, and an occasional patterned field of bales tell the story of work in this valley straddling the Wyoming/Utah high desert. Log buildings polished by wind, shaggy grey fence lines soaked by a half century of snow, and tall sage pushed back by the occasional cottonwood, all plot a rugged pioneer settlement.

The sweet plump raspberries ("pick them yourself") and Tahoe blue of austere Bear Lake delight travelers enroute to Yellowstone. Summer cabins and cattle dot the gentle hillsides. Jet skis and John Deere vie for space on the shoreline road. "Make hay . . ."

Autumn below the boulders of Squaw Peak, a rare forest world breathes quietly beneath a dome of bright blue. The wild country of the High Uintas, including Utah's largest Forest Service wilderness, covers three-quarters of a million acres . . . enough territory to host three-fourths of Utah's bird species, give rise to the headwaters of all Utah-born rivers, and shelter bear, cougar, small mammals, and a host of amphibians and reptiles. High and wild, the Uintas preserve a precious past.

Listen for the screech of a goshawk in the dark stands, lie under aspen gold and shimmering, cup a purple gentian along the sedge edges of a pool of lilies. Look! A moose, lips dripping rings of twilight water into a deep pothole. Dark pines crowd the meadow, yellow with frosty helebore and dragonfly grass. In a sudden wind, spruce cones skitter across sparkling pink quartzite. The lusty bugles of wapiti echo through a labyrinth of lodgepole. Clouds string out across the sky . . . September snow!

Sawed in spring snow by railroad-tie hackers, chest-high cottonwood stumps betray human history along the lower stretches of the rivers. Ghosts of fur trappers shoulder pelts beyond the beaver lodge.

To the east, where the Green River flows from Flaming Gorge, rafts of sunburned sailors glide through the land of dinosaurs and gargoyles of stone telling tales of the planet.

"We All Have Work" – Tom Olson

The Central Valleys: Utah's Heartland

– Utah, Carbon, Emery, Sanpete, Sevier, Piute, Beaver, Millard, Iron, and Garfield Counties –

CENTRAL UTAH IS AN AREA OF GREAT TOPOGRAPHIC VARIETY, EXTENDING FROM UTAH VALLEY (THE GREAT BASIN) ON THE WEST TO CASTLE VALLEY AND THE COMMUNITIES OF CARBON AND EMERY COUNTIES ON THE EAST, WITH HIGH PLATEAUS IN BETWEEN. IT INCLUDES UTAH'S COAL COUNTRY, PARTS OF THREE NATIONAL FORESTS, LAKES, RIVERS, AND ASPEN-SHROUDED MOUNTAIN RANGES.

WHAT'S MORE, THIS IS AN AREA OF GREAT HISTORICAL INTEREST. SPANISH FORK CANYON, ONE OF THE PRINCIPAL THOROUGHFARES, WAS PART OF THE ARDUOUS TRAIL FOLLOWED BY THE 1776 DOMINGUEZ ESCA-

Butch Cassidy, one of early Utah's more notorious citizens – USHS

LANTE EXPEDITION IN SEARCH OF A DIRECT OVERLAND ROUTE BETWEEN SANTA FE, NEW MEXICO, AND MONTEREY, CALIFORNIA. THE EXPEDITION EVENTUALLY TRAVELED TO THE NORTHERN REACHES OF UTAH VALLEY BEFORE TURNING AROUND UNDER THE THREAT OF WINTER.

MORE RECENTLY, IN 1897, OUTLAWS BUTCH CASSIDY AND ELZY LAY MASTERMINDED THE ROBBERY OF A PAYROLL AT A NOW-DEFUNCT MINING CAMP NEAR THE TOP OF THIS CANYON. IT WAS REPUTEDLY CASSIDY'S FIRST ROBBERY IN HIS HOME STATE OF UTAH AND ADDED TO HIS ALREADY

"PEOPLE OUT WEST REMEMBER WHEN IMPORTANT THINGS WERE SETTLED VIOLENTLY, AND THEY REMEMBER THE WIDE DRY WASTES BEFORE THE MOUNTAIN WATER WAS CAPTURED AND PUT TO USE. EVEN NOW, THE DRY SPACES, WHERE THE JACKRABBITS HOP THROUGH THE BRUSH AS THICK AS MITES ON A HEN, ARE ALWAYS THERE, WAITING TO TAKE OVER; DRYNESS HUGS THE GREEN FIELDS, PUSHING IN, ONLY THE IRRIGATION DITCHES KEEPING IT AT BAY."

– Virginia Sorenson –
"Where Nothing is Long Ago"
in Where Nothing is Long Ago:
Memories of a Utah Childhood

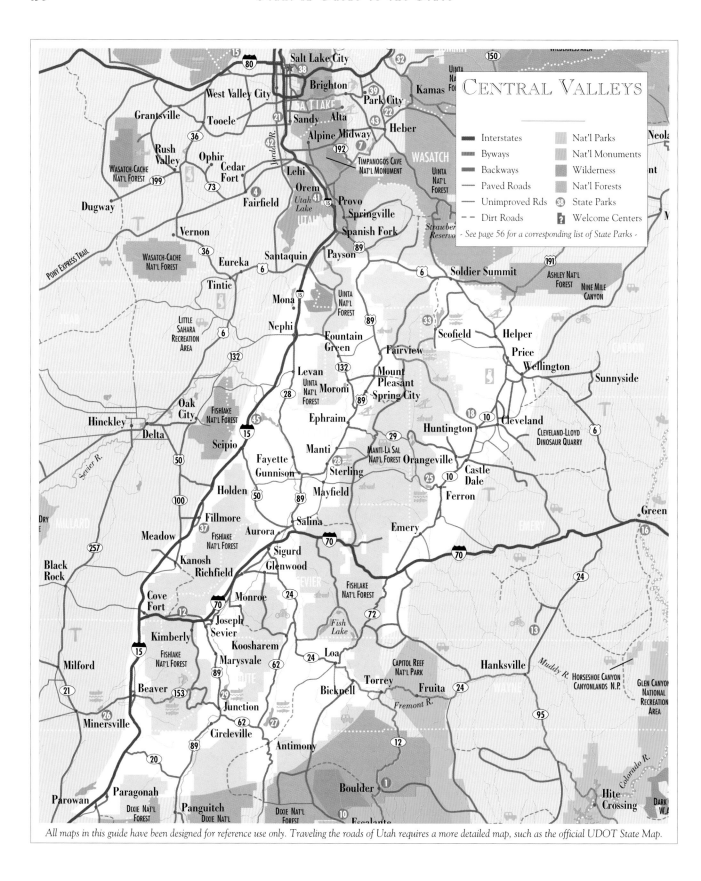

CENTRAL VALLEYS

Interstates		Nat'l Parks	
Byways		Nat'l Monuments	
Backways		Wilderness	
Paved Roads		Nat'l Forests	
Unimproved Rds		38	State Parks
Dirt Roads		?	Welcome Centers

- See page 56 for a corresponding list of State Parks -

All maps in this guide have been designed for reference use only. Traveling the roads of Utah requires a more detailed map, such as the official UDOT State Map.

burgeoning reputation as the "Robin Hood of the Inter-mountain West." Not that all of this area's history is linked to colorful characters and their exploits. Travelers in search of well-preserved history would do well to travel Route 89 through Sanpete Valley, one of the state's prime agricultural regions. The small towns here project a bucolic charm, and many of the homes, stores, and churches have been preserved and restored, giving visitors a sense of what the valley was like half a century ago.

Finally, those in search of panoramic vistas might consider Route 89, a winding highway connecting a series of small agricultural towns, including Marysvale, Junction, and Circleville. The towns of Piute County (one of the state's smallest and least populated counties) exude rustic charm and are ringed by massive plateaus. Route 89 offers an alternative to I-15 if one is bound for Zion National Park, Kanab, and the North Rim of the Grand Canyon.

COAL COUNTRY

Spanish Fork to Price via Route 6

Between the mouth of Spanish Fork Canyon and Price, 65 miles away, Route 6 passes through one of the longest sustained stretches of canyon and mountain terrain of any highway in Utah.

Spanish Fork Canyon in its lower reaches was the route of the Spanish Dominguez-Escalante exploring party of 1776, which is how it received its name. The canyon extends from Utah Valley to rolling plateau summits of the Soldier Summit area, a distance of about 30 miles.

About five miles east of the canyon's mouth, turn north into the canyon of Diamond Fork, a tributary of Spanish Fork. Unpaved roads give access to forest campgrounds and popular fishing waters, one branch leading to Springville via the forks of Hobble Creek Canyon, another leading to Strawberry Reservoir. Diamond Fork Canyon was on the route followed by the Dominguez-Escalante party of 1776 and thereafter by trappers, explorers, and settlers.

Thistle gives little hint that it was once a bustling community during the era of steam railroading prior to World War II. The town received national attention after it was inundated in a huge landslide in the early 1980s. Since then, little has been rebuilt.

At 18 miles from Thistle (6 miles west of Soldier Summit), where Clear Creek and Soldier Creek join the main canyon, a roadside park marks the site of a former railroad settlement known as Tucker. Tucker was settled during the l870s and 1880s as a railroad camp, and for years thereafter it was a rail station—a point where cattle and sheep were shipped to market. Today, nothing is left of the original buildings.

South from the roadside park at Tucker, an unpaved road winds up canyons, through dense forests, and across alpine meadows, climbing to heights approaching 11,000 feet. This is Utah's famed Skyline Drive. The full length can be driven for only a few months during late summer and fall; however, a number of east-west roads between Sanpete and Castle Valleys provide easy access at various points. This route is well described in Ed Geary's excellent book on the plateau country of south-central Utah, *The Proper Edge of the Sky*.

Soldier Summit (7,440 alt.), a cluster of roadside businesses, marks the highest point on Route 6 in Utah and also the highest mainline railroad pass in the state. Streams flowing westward from this area drain into the Great Basin; those flowing east join the Green and Colorado Rivers.

Colton Junction lies in a broad summit valley in the headwaters area of the Price River. Technically, the area is a zone of transition between the Wasatch Plateau, rolling away to the south, and the Roan (Tavaputs) Plateau stretching off toward Colorado on the east; the distinction, however, is not apparent to the eye. Colton, known first as Pleasant Valley Junction, was born during the l880s as a railroad camp. Several buildings are all that remain to mark the site. Turn south from Colton Junction to Scofield Reservoir (12 miles) and the town of Scofield (16 miles).

Scofield Reservoir, formed by the headwaters of the Price River, lies in an alpine bowl called Pleasant Valley. It is a popular fishing and boating lake, its shores lined with cabins, resorts, and campgrounds. Scofield Lake State Recreation Area (open May–October) has facilities for camping, picnicking and boating.

Scofield, 17 miles from Route 6, is an old coal mining community shut in by mountain slopes. At one time its population approached 2,000, most of them employed in the area coal mines. Several thousand other people lived nearby in Clear Creek, Winter Quarters, and throughout the valley.

At Winter Quarters, a mile or so from Scofield, was what is

reportedly Utah's first commercial coal mine, opened in 1877; it provided the base for a community that thrived for several decades. It was also the site of Utah's worst mine disaster, in 1900, when 199 miners perished in an explosion.

South of Scofield is Clear Creek, 5 miles, where coal mine workings and a few buildings mark the site of a town that once boasted a population of more than 500. Founded in 1900 as a company town, Clear Creek contained numerous homes, a large hotel, school, churches, a mine, and business buildings. Its decline began in the 1930s and 1940s with increased mining costs and decreasing demand for coal.

East of Colton Junction, Route 6 dips and climbs across the Roan (Tavaputs) Plateau, following the Price River to the head of Price Canyon and then down to its mouth in Castle Valley. Six miles from Colton Junction, a paved road forks to the east, connecting Route 6 with Route 191 at the Bamberger Monument.

Price Canyon drops 2,000 feet in about 10 miles, serving as a divide between the Wasatch Plateau to the south and the Roan (Tavaputs) Plateau to the east. Price Canyon has been the route of transport for most of Utah's coal production since the early 1880s, when the D&RGW mainline was completed. During that century, hundreds of millions of tons of coal have passed through the canyon by train and truck.

In the canyon's upper reaches, a side road forks west and south from Route 6 to Price Canyon Recreation Site (BLM), 4 miles, an area with picnicking and camping facilities.

Castle Rock is one of two prominent battlements on either side of the canyon, together forming Castle Gate, a famed landmark until highway construction in the 1960s destroyed some of Castle Rock and the original gate effect.

Castle Gate (6,150 alt.), named for the castellated formations originally guarding the entrance to the valley, survived floods, explosions, and a historic outlaw raid to become an outstanding coal mining camp. Nothing is left of yesterday's bustling town, but coal mining operations in the vicinity are among the largest of their type in Utah.

In 1897 Butch Cassidy and his associates pulled off a daring payroll robbery here, an account of which is related in Pearl Baker's *The Wild Bunch at Robbers Roost* and other books about outlaw activity in the area.

North from Castle Gate, Route 191 climbs over the Roan Plateau, then between the colored cliffs to Duchesne (44 miles). The route, which ascends to 9,100 feet and may be closed at times in winter, is notable for its alpine and canyon scenery. About 7 miles from Castle Gate, at the junction with the cutoff road from the head of Price Canyon, is Bamberger Monument, erected about 1917 by convicts from the state prison who had worked on the construction of Route 191. The monument was named for Simon Bamberger, Utah's governor at the time. It has been renovated in recent years by local citizens.

Turn west from the vicinity of Helper to the Spring Canyon group of coal mining towns. Here, forming the largest concentration of ghost towns in Utah, are the remains of Peerless, Spring Canyon (Storrs), Standardville, Latuda, Rains, Mutual, and Little Standard. These communities waxed and waned between World War I and the 1950s and 1960s. The capsule histories of these towns and others that have died are given by Stephen L. Carr in the *Historical Guide to Utah Ghost Towns*.

Helper, at the mouth of Price Canyon where lines of great terraced cliffs stretch away to either side, has a rich mining and railroad history, although the economy has diversed somewhat in the last two decades.

Helper's Civic Auditorium on Main Street is a civic center with auditorium, meeting rooms, and a library. The auditorium houses the Western Mining and Railroad Museum, which includes a gift shop, informative displays, a 1917 railroad caboose, and vintage mining equipment. Tours are available upon request.

Turn east from Helper to Kenilworth, a mining camp on a high bench at the base of a cliff. Just east of the highway, 2 miles south of Helper, is Spring Glen, a residential and farming village. In this vicinity also is the Carbon Country Club and Golf Course.

Turn west from Route 6, 2 miles south of Helper, to the abandoned coal mining towns of Coal City, National, and Consumers. Fairly intact buildings and mine workings mark the sites of communities that once housed several hundred residents and flourished during the 1920s and 1930s.

Price

Price (8,822 pop.), the Carbon County seat, is the largest city in southeastern Utah. According to the 1941 edition of this book, Price was "a moneyed town, with modern buildings, numerous cafes, saloons, and behind-the-scenes gambling houses. If there is a touch of coal dust in the air, it is a dust that means cash, and local people do not give it too much time to settle." The same description could apply today with little change, except that today there is more "coal dust" in the air than ever before, and promise of even greater amounts in future. Many new buildings have been added, including schools, an enlarged college campus, a hospital, and other business buildings.

Price has been the coal capital of Utah since the 1890s; and for much of that time it was also the coal capital of the western United States. During the past hundred years the scores of mines in the Price area have yielded about 400 million tons of coal totaling more than a billion dollars in value.

Price was originally settled as a Mormon agricultural community, and in its early years it resembled most other Utah communities of the 19th century. However, where most others remained predominantly Mormon and agricultural for some decades after founding, the cultural identity of Price began to change within a short period. As coal mining operations expanded following the completion of the mainline railroad between Colorado and Salt Lake City in 1883, new residents of differing cultural and racial backgrounds began to settle in the region. By the time of World War I Price had become the residential or trading capital for thousands of Utah's "new immigrants." Over a period of several decades, gentile Anglos, Japanese, Chinese, Finns, Italians, Greeks, and southern Slavs (Serbs, Croats, Slovenes), Syro-Lebanese, and Armenians settled here, as did Chicanos, African Americans, Native Americans, and others. It is reported that a WPA survey of the 1930s found former residents of 32 different nations as patrons of one pool hall in Helper.

Today, the area's ethnic diversity is celebrated with its annual Greek Days celebration during the second weekend in July and International Days in August.

- Price Attractions -

The Price Municipal Building, 200 East Main, was constructed in 1938–39 as one of the largest buildings in Utah built with WPA funds. The main lobby is encircled on all four walls by a mural depicting scenes from the history of Carbon County, including 82 figures in lifelike representations. This mural was created by Lynn Fausett, a native of the area.

The College of Eastern Utah, 451 East 400 North, is a two-year community college, offering a broad selection of courses. Current enrollment is about 2,300, and its campus has become an attractive complex of modern buildings.

The Prehistoric Museum (College of Eastern Utah), located on the north side of the Price Municipal Building, has a reputation as one of the finest of its kind in the West. Among the more celebrated exhibits here is the mounted skeleton of a giant Allosaurus known as "Al," the fossil bones of which were taken from the Cleveland-Lloyd Dinosaur Quarry south of Price. The museum also houses an exemplary collection of prehistoric artifacts, including cultural relics of the Fremont Indians who inhabited eastern Utah about 700 years ago, and the cast skeleton of a Columbian mammoth discovered in the late 1980s in nearby Huntington Canyon.

The Hellenic Orthodox Church, 61 South 200 East, is considered "a monument to the faith, culture, and industry of the early Greek immigrants in the West." The register description on the National Register of Historic Places reads, "Beautiful icons, stained glass windows, and a massive brass and crystal chandelier enhance the interior of the church."

Notre Dame de Lourdes Catholic Church, 200 North Carbon Avenue, was constructed under the leadership of Father Alfred F. Giovannoni and dedicated in 1923. According to the National Register of Historic Places, "The church played a significant role in uniting the various groups of the county as the Italians, Slovenians, Croations, French, Basque, Northern European and American Catholics found a common bond in the church."

MORMON COUNTRY

Castle Valley

Castle Valley is that vast basin extending east and south from the mouth of Price Canyon, located between cliff-faced highlands on the west and north, and the domed uplift of the San Rafael Swell on the east. South of Price, Route 10 winds at the base of great cliffs, enormously rich in coal and gashed by deep canyons. Route 10 connects most of the valley's communities. Side roads lead west to coal camps, coal mines, and power plants, mountain lakes and streams, forests, and eventually the Sanpete Valley. Other roads lead east from Route 10 to desert farms, the Cleveland-Lloyd Dinosaur Quarry, and the naked rock panoramas of the San Rafael Swell.

Turn west on Route 122, 6 miles south of Price, to

Hiawatha, Wattis, and Mohrland, important coal mining centers. Wattis and Mohrland are now largely deserted as communities. Hiawatha remains a functioning, viable community, perhaps Utah's least changed and best preserved example of a coal mining town of World War I vintage. Homes, buildings, and yards are maintained with care.

For nearly 100 years until the 1970s, Huntington was a quiet town dependent on agriculture and to some extent on coal mining. The town's quiet character was profoundly changed by the construction of the area's first huge coal-fired electric generating plant, built in Huntington Canyon by the Utah Power and Light Company. Construction brought hundreds of engineering and construction workers into Castle Valley beginning in 1970 and continuing for years thereafter, followed by plant personnel and several hundred miners.

Also nearby is Huntington State Park, a 200-acre reservoir beside Route 10, 2 miles north of Huntington, with developed facilities for camping, picnicking, and boating. Open April to November.

Turn west via Route 31 to Huntington Canyon, the site of a large electric generating complex, recreation areas, streams, lakes, and forests. Route 31 climbs through Huntington Canyon, an imposing gorge enclosed between tremendous cliffs, to the summit of the Wasatch Plateau at 9,000 feet, where it intersects Skyline Drive then descends to Fairview in Sanpete Valley. The Huntington Canyon Power Complex, 9 miles west of Huntington, was built during the 1970s as the first of its size in Utah.

Turn east from Route 10 via Route 155 to Cleveland, Elmo, the Desert Lake Waterfowl Reserve and the Cleveland-Lloyd Dinosaur Quarry (18 miles). At the quarry, the Bureau of Land Management maintains interpretive and picnicking facilities at the site of what is reputedly the nation's largest dinosaur graveyard. The quarry is in the Morrison formation of Jurassic age (about 140 million years ago), similar to that at Dinosaur National Monument. Since the 1920s, thousands of fossilized bones have been removed, most of them during the 1960s under a program headed by Dr. W. Lee Stokes of the University of Utah, a nationally known paleontologist/geologist. The quarry is noted for its remains of the Allosaurus, a large carnivorous dinosaur.

Castle Dale and Vicinity

Castle Dale, seat of Emery County, is a solid town with prosperous farms and well-fed livestock. Founded in the 1880s, this was a quiet, largely agricultural community for the first 90 years of its existence. But the last 20 years marked a decided change in the town's character as the Utah Power and Light Company built the state's largest complex of coal-fired electric generating plants. Within a few years Castle Valley's population increased dramatically as hundreds of construction workers, operating personnel, and miners arrived with their families. Emery County's assessed valuation increased more than 20 times in a decade, and it was necessary to spend millions of dollars for expanded services and facilities.

Despite profound social change and great population growth in recent years, Castle Dale has managed to maintain a degree of traditional charm, grace, and dignity.

The Emery County Museum, 93 East 100 North, offers visitors the opportunity to inspect a store stocked with items early settlers might have purchased. The museum includes a vintage lawyer's office and schoolroom, tack and tool displays, and an art gallery.

The Museum of the San Rafael, 64 North 100 East, includes a paleontology room with life-size dinosaurs rotating on a central platform, and exhibits featuring the Indian culture of the San Rafael Swell.

Turn west from Castle Dale via Route 29 to Orangeville, a farming and residential community at the mouth of Straight Canyon. The town was settled in 1877 and named for Orange Seely (Seeley), a man who weighed more than 320 pounds.

Route 29 continues up Straight Canyon to Joe's Valley, a mountain basin ringed by forested slopes, containing the popular recreation site Joe's Valley Reservoir. From the lake, an unpaved road leads north to Huntington and Cleveland reservoirs and Huntington Canyon. The North Horn Road ends at The Rim, a dizzying cliff-edge viewpoint nearly 3,000 feet above Orangeville. The panorama from this overlook is superlative, encompassing much of Castle Valley, the San Rafael Swell, and the great cliff front that extends 200 miles in a grand semicircle from Emery northward to the Price area, and then eastward into Colorado. From Joe's Valley, Route 29 continues west, crossing the plateau's summit at Skyline Drive, then switchbacking down to Ephraim.

Turn east from Route 10, 2 miles north of Castle Dale, to the San Rafael Swell. The road is unpaved but maintained; avoid if wet. Route 10 continues southward through Castle Valley to Ferron, Emery, and Fremont Junction at I-70.

Ferron is a pleasant, tree-shaded agricultural community. Like its neighbors to the north and south, Ferron was settled by Mormons. The massive construction and mining expansion of recent years has brought profound change to the community. Naked desert spreads away toward the San Rafael Swell on the east; Ferron Canyon's broad mouth opens to the west. Millsite Reservoir nearby provides water for irrigation as well as for the huge Hunter power complex near Castle Dale. Of special historic interest is the former Presbyterian Church and "Cottage," dating from 1907, which served until 1942 as a church school, parsonage, and dormitory.

Turn west from Ferron through Ferron Canyon to Ferron Reservoir, 25 miles, a modest lake in a setting of alpine beauty, which is popular for fishing. Beyond the reservoir the road continues to an intersection with Skyline Drive and onward to Mayfield. Every weekend after Labor Day, Ferron celebrates its annual Peach Days, one of the oldest community celebrations in the state.

Emery still retains a picturesque "cow town" atmosphere of rustic homes and rows of Lombardy poplars. The town was settled in 1881 and pioneers bored a 1,240-foot tunnel to tap Muddy Creek for irrigation water.

Fremont Junction, 74 miles from Price, marks the intersection of I-70, Route 10, Route 72, and an unnumbered, unpaved road leading into Capitol Reef National Park (Cathedral Valley).

Sanpete Valley
Fairview to Manti via Route 89

Southbound Route 89 separates from Route 6 in Spanish Fork Canyon at Thistle, formerly an important railroad point. The Thistle area is important geographically because it marks a transition between the Rocky Mountain Province (Wasatch Range) and Colorado Plateau Province (High Plateaus). Rock formations are dramatically twisted in this vicinity.

Route 89 follows Thistle Creek southward between high mountains on either side. Tiny Birdseye was named for a local deposit of Birdseye marble, a beautiful decorative stone. Loafer Mountain (10,687 alt.) stands above the town and valley.

The Indianola Valley, 6,000 feet high and cold, was settled in 1864. One mile north of the Indianola turnoff, a marker beside the highway tells of the massacre of six members of the Given family in 1865 during the Black Hawk Indian War. Much of the valley is devoted to grain and alfalfa and livestock production.

South of Indianola Valley the highway passes over a ridge marking the divide between Thistle Creek drainage (emptying into Great Salt Lake) and Sanpitch River drainage (emptying into Sevier Lake).

The Sanpete Valley, which is transversed by Route 89 for 50 miles, is one of Utah's prime agricultural regions. Perhaps more than any part of the state, it retains a flavor of the pioneer past in its tree-shaded towns, quaint old houses, rustic outbuildings, and pastoral landscape. The first European settlers arrived here in 1849, two years after the first Mormon pioneers arrived in Utah. Settlement continued through the 1850s, giving the area the distinction of being one of the earliest Mormon colonies in the state. Scandinavian surnames, abundant here, reveal the origin of many of its settlers.

Cradled between mountains to the east and west, Sanpete Valley widens south of Fairview, then narrows again near Sterling where the Sanpitch River leaves Sanpete and enters the Sevier Valley. The great Wasatch Plateau, known locally as Manti Mountain, forms the eastern horizon, rising in places to more than 11,000 feet; streams provide water for most of the valley's communities. Sanpete is a corruption of Sanpitch (Sampitches, Sampichya, Sanpuchi), the original name of the native Utes.

Fairview, a farming and commercial center in the upper valley, was settled in 1859 by pioneers from Mt. Pleasant who were attracted by meadows of wild hay. Fairview probably contains more early-day barns and outbuildings than any other town in Utah, as well as numerous 19th-century houses. A large percentage of these structures are historically and architecturally noteworthy.

The Fairview Museum of History and Arts, housed in a former stone schoolhouse and dating from 1900, features historical relics, Indian artifacts, local craftwork, and art. The museum displays sculptures and sculpture models by noted Utahn Avard Fairbanks. The replica of an ancient Columbian mammoth, which was uncovered in the area in 1988, is a recent addition.

Turn east from Fairview on Route 31 to Fairview Canyon, Skyline Drive, Huntington Canyon, and Huntington in Castle Valley. This scenic mountain canyon drive crosses the spine of Wasatch Plateau, a part of the High Plateaus subdivision of the Colorado Plateau Province. The plateau's western side is a great sloping whaleback, plunging beneath the Sanpete and Sevier Valleys; its eastern face overlooks Castle Valley in one of western America's most captivating escarpments.

Skyline Drive intersects Route 31 near the head of Fairview Canyon, extending north to Tucker on Route 6 and south to Mayfield, Ferron, and Salina Canyon. For much of its length the drive winds through the Manti-La Sal National Forest at elevations of 9,000 to 11,000 feet, skirting glacial basins and deep canyons, passing through aspen and evergreen groves and grassy meadows that flaunt displays of wildflowers in late spring and summer. Views sweep thousands of feet downward onto the farms and towns of the Sanpete Valley, then to the west over ranks of mountain ranges. Eastward, the alpine panorama consists of deep canyons, cliffs, and forested mountain slopes, with an intermittent blue lake as accent. The road is unpaved, rough in spots, and open along its full length of more than 100 miles for only a few months (July to early October). Access, however, is convenient, with a number of roads crossing the drive from west to east, connecting Sanpete towns with communities in Emery County.

Mt. Pleasant, a spacious community of unusually broad streets, has an economy based on agriculture, commerce, and education. The town dates from the late 1850s when settlers from Ephraim established a new community on the site. It contains a number of 19th-century buildings of note and some later ones of interest. In 1979 the commercial district of 44 buildings was listed in the National Register of Historic Places because of its well-preserved architectural and commercial significance, and because it is "a fascinating documentary record of the commercial vigor of rural Utah in the decades from 1890 to 1910." Some of these buildings date from the 1870s.

Older homes of interest include the Morten Rasmussen House, 417 West Main, built in 1875 (Federal style); the Alma Staker House, 81 East 300 South, "one of the two best extant examples of Creek Revival-inspired 'temple form' vernacular house type in Utah"; the William Seely Home, 150 South State, built in 1861, a two-story stuccoed adobe residence with 12 rooms and basement; the James Hansen Home, 382 West Main, built in 1861–62. The Old Pioneer Museum (Daughters of Utah Pioneers) displays historic relics.

Also in Mt. Pleasant is the Wasatch Academy, a private school founded in 1875 and today the oldest continuously operating secondary school in the state. Its founder, Dr. Duncan J. McMillan, was a Presbyterian minister who had come west for his health and arrived in Mt. Pleasant as one of the first non-Mormon residents. The academy is an interdenominational, nonprofit, coeducational, boarding and day school, offering a wide range of courses and activities for grades 9 through 12. It has both state and national listing as an outstanding historical site.

Turn west from Mt. Pleasant 7 miles to Moroni. The town was named for the angel Moroni, a person from the Book of Mormon who is said to have revealed to Joseph Smith the golden plates bearing the characters from which Smith translated the Book of Mormon. The town was settled as a farming community in 1859 and has been a major turkey-raising, processing, and feed-milling center for more than 50 years. Moroni has several significant structures from the past century, including a 100-year-old opera house that is being restored.

Turn north from Moroni 8 miles via Route 132 to Fountain Green, an agricultural community founded in 1859 and at one time widely recognized for its long-fiber wool. Prior to America's entry into World War I, the quantity produced here, with the high price of wool, made Fountain Green one of the wealthiest towns per capita in the nation.

Turn west from Moroni several miles to Wales and Freedom, hamlets on the foothills of the Gunnison Plateau (Sanpitch Mountains). Wales is Utah's first coal mining colony, settled in 1859 by Welsh converts to the Mormon Church. Several miles north from Freedom, a steep unpaved road climbs into Maple Canyon. The narrow gorge is heavily wooded with maples. The canyon's most unusual feature is Box Canyon, a dead-end gorge from 500 to 700 feet deep, half a mile long, and so narrow that in places a person can touch both walls at the same time. The walls overhang in places, blocking out the sky and giving a dungeon-like effect. Be aware, however, that falling rocks are a hazard.

Turn south from Mt. Pleasant 4 miles to Spring City, a bucolic village 4 miles east of Route 89. Spring City was settled and resettled during the 1850s and 1860s, its people having been forced to move during the Indian wars of that period. The leader of the first two groups of settlers was James Allred, a bodyguard of Joseph Smith, and the town's first name was Allred's Settlement. At one time it was on the main highway and a busy railroad, and prosperity was its lot—hence, the town's unusually high number of impressive buildings. Today the town has a reputation for pastoral, nostalgic charm. Many of its older log, adobe, frame, and stone buildings are being preserved and restored. Today, Spring City is developing a reputation as an arts community.

The Mormon Ward Chapel, strikingly original in design, dates from 1902. City Hall, built in 1893 of oolitic limestone, served initially as a school. The Orson Hyde Home, Main and C Streets, dates from the 1850s. The house was the residence of Orson Hyde, Mormon apostle and pioneer leader of the Sanpete Valley. The Spring City Public School, dating from 1899, was converted to a museum in 1981 by the Daughters of Utah Pioneers. The proceeds from Heritage Days, held annually over the Memorial Day weekend, are donated to the restoration of this school.

East from Spring City an unpaved road climbs steeply to the top of the Wasatch Plateau, intersecting Skyline Drive and the plateau's highest point–11,300-foot South Tent.

Ephraim is an educational, agricultural, and commercial center. It is the home of Snow College, a state institution with an enrollment of about 2,500 students that offers lower-division college and technical courses. Founded in the 1880s as a

Mormon academy, the school underwent successive stages as a private junior college, state junior college, and branch of the state Agricultural College. In addition to education, Snow College offers plays, concerts, and lectures.

Ephraim dates from 1854 when it was settled by families from nearby Manti, who built a fort where they lived until 1860. Their first years were troubled by killing frosts and grasshoppers. Later years rewarded their efforts with bountiful harvests of grain, and wealth in the form of sheep, cattle, turkeys, and other agricultural products.

Ephraim is notable, along with Manti, Spring City, and other Sanpete Valley communities, for its distinctive 19th-century architecture. Visitors should drive the side streets to view the unusual older homes made of stone, logs, adobe, and frame, dating back more than a century. On Main Street (which is listed as a Historic District on the National Register of Historic Places) is a large two-story stone structure known as the United Order Co-op Mercantile Institution. This building dates from 1864 and was the first home of Snow College. The building is now home to the Sanpete Trade Association, and locally produced items are sold here. The Main Street Historic District also features about 30 other buildings of architectural and historic significance, which together "trace the steps of Ephraim's journey from Farm Village to Commercial City" during the late-19th and early-20th centuries. Side streets display a fascinating array of architecture from long-gone years. The Ephraim Town Hall and Jail (Old Jail House), 38 East Center, was built about 1875 and served many functions during the intervening years; it is now a private residence. The Canute Peterson Home, 10 North Main, dates from about 1869. The Hansen Sparks Home, 75 West 1st North, was built in 1862 of rock and adobe (now stuccoed).

Turn east from Ephraim on Route 29 (improved but not fully paved), which winds steeply to the summit of Wasatch Plateau where it intersects Skyline Drive at about 10,000 feet altitude. The Lake Hill Campground has improved facilities for camping and picnicking. East of Skyline Drive the road descends through valleys and canyons past Joe's Valley Reservoir to Orangeville. Route 29 is paved from the reservoir to Orangeville.

Manti and Vicinity

Manti, the Sanpete County seat and one of the oldest

Old stone Mormon pioneer home in historic Spring City – Frank Jensen, UTC

Mormon settlements in Utah, was settled in November 1849. In 1851 Manti was among the first five settlements incorporated by the State of Deseret. Many people lived in dugouts in Temple Hill during the first winter, while men on snowshoes pulled sleds loaded with supplies from wagons that could not break through the heavy snows to the village. Next spring those settlers living in the hill found themselves competing for space with hordes of rattlesnakes, but not a person was bitten. Brigham Young visited in 1850, at which time the name of the valley was changed from Sanpitch to Sanpete and the village was named Manti, after a city mentioned in the Book of Mormon.

The Manti Temple occupies a commanding position overlooking the valley from a low hill. Of strikingly unusual architecture, the temple is central Utah's dominant man-made landmark. Construction began in 1877 on a site dedicated by Brigham Young a few months before his death, and was completed in 1888. The temple is used for sacred ordinances and ceremonies; only Mormons in good standing are admitted, but a visitors' center is open to the public.

Manti, like Ephraim, has built a modest industrial base, though its economy is diversified with agriculture, trade, and tourism. The popular Mormon Miracle Pageant, a religious drama held on the temple grounds each July, attracts an estimated 30,000 attendees per night during its annual run.

Manti's buildings are both architecturally and historically interesting. There are numerous well-preserved examples from the 19th century—homes, churches, public and commercial buildings—most of them tastefully maintained. Visitors should make a point of driving the side streets, for in few parts of western America is there such a display of original and distinctive early-day architecture. Many of the buildings are listed on national and state historic registers.

Turn east from Manti through Manti Canyon on an improved but not fully paved road to the summit of the Wasatch Plateau and a junction with Skyline Drive at more than 10,000 feet altitude (Manti-La Sal National Forest). En route, 5 miles from Manti, is the Manti Community Camp, open June–September, with camping and picnic facilities, and trailer spaces.

Sterling is a pleasantly open town at the mouth of Six-mile Canyon in the narrowing southern end of Sanpete Valley. Turn east from Sterling to Palisade State Park (2 miles), a recreational development on the shore of an attractive reservoir. East of Palisade Lake, the road continues up Sixmile Canyon to the Wasatch Plateau.

South of Sterling 6 miles via Routes 89 and 137 is Mayfield, a secluded village on Twelvemile Creek, surrounded by tall trees, mountains, and hills.

East of Mayfield an improved but unpaved road climbs through Twelvemile Canyon to the heights of Wasatch Plateau, Skyline Drive, Ferron Reservoir, and Ferron in Castle Valley. Mayfield is the most convenient southern terminus of Skyline Drive, though networks of fair-weather forest roads crisscross the southern plateau, connecting the drive with Salina Canyon and Emery. In the upper reaches of Twelvemile is the Aspen Giants Scenic Area where some of the largest known quaking aspen grow. This is a region of great white cliffs, culminating in the prominent white knob known as Musinia.

Sevier Valley
Gunnison to Richfield via Route 89

Gunnison, a commercial and agricultural center near the confluence of the Sanpitch and Sevier Rivers, was founded in 1860 and named for Captain John W. Gunnison, a United States topographical engineer who gained popularity with the Mormons by writing a book about them that they considered more objective than most.

Northwest from Gunnison, Route 28 passes through semiarid valleys and forests of pygmy evergreens to Interstate 15 at Levan. At 5 miles, just off the highway, is the village of Fayette, named after Fayette, New York, where the Mormon Church was founded by Joseph Smith in 1830.

Centerfield is a farming community noted for the length of its main street (Route 89), along which the town stretches for more than three miles. Until recent years, when the costs of processing sugar beets have increased to the point where their production became uneconomical here, it was an important sugar center and the site of the largest sugar refinery in central Utah.

Four miles west of Centerfield near the Sevier River is the former site of a cooperative Jewish colony known as Clarion. Beginning in 1911, about 75 Jewish families from eastern states moved into the valley, each acquiring 40 irrigated acres around a central commissary, schoolhouse, and community well.

Crops were bountiful the first year or two, but harvests began to decline and financial problems developed. Gradually the settlers drifted away, and by 1920 nothing remained.

South of Gunnison-Centerfield, the highway follows the eastern foothills of Sevier Valley. The Wasatch Plateau retreats to the east and finally terminates at Salina Canyon. On the west, subdued and ordinary earth colors give way to the glorious vermilions and pastels of the Aurora Cliffs (Pahvant Plateau), surmounted by a great cone known as the Red Pyramid. Beyond Salina to the south is a cluster of weird badland cones or gypsum hills, and rising behind these are the dark and massive hulks of other high plateaus—the Sevier, Fish Lake, and Tushar—all climbing to summits of more than 11,000 feet. The Sevier River flows in lazy meanders through the green fertile valley.

Salina is a commercial center for livestock, produce, coal, salt, and highway travel. It is strategically situated in Sevier Valley at the mouth of Salina Canyon at the junction of Route 89 with I-70, which connects Denver and points east with Las Vegas and Los Angeles. Salina was first settled in 1864, vacated during the Indian troubles of the 1860s, and resettled in 1871. Scattered about the city are a number of structures of historical and architectural interest, including an old rock meetinghouse-schoolhouse (1864) and a steepled Presbyterian church (1864) now used as a residence.

Turn east from Salina to Salina Canyon, route of Interstate 70. Salina Canyon is one of the oldest routes in historic times, an important link in the famed Spanish Trail, followed not only by trading and exploration caravans of New Mexicans from about 1830 or earlier years—prior to Mormon settlement—but also by mountain men, government surveyors, and military troops. The trail had various branches in Utah, but the main route between Santa Fe and Los Angeles apparently followed Salina Canyon into the Sevier Valley, then south along the Sevier River to the low divide (Bear Valley) between the Tushar Plateau and Markagunt Plateau, where it veered westward into the Great Basin. Another branch appears to have left Salina Canyon in its upper reaches, passing by Fish Lake into Grass Valley, down Grass Valley to East Fork Canyon, then to the Sevier Valley near Junction and Circleville where it joined the main trail.

The canyon and highlands surrounding Salina also serve as summer range for cattle and sheep. Roads lead north and south into the Fishlake and Manti-La Sal National Forests, giving access to ranchers, rangers, and recreationists. Route 72 offers stunning views across the eastern desert and provides access to Thousand Lake Mountain, Cathedral Valley, Fremont, and the area surrounding Capitol Reef National Park.

North of Salina a few miles is Redmond, formerly on Route 89 but now isolated by highway realignment. It is most noted for being the site of a large salt-mining operation north of town where a reddish-brown rock salt is quarried from an open pit and sold in blocks.

Turn west from Salina via Route 50 through open valleys to Scipio and the junction with I-15. Eight miles west of Salina, forking from Route 50, an unpaved but maintained forest road climbs onto the Pahvant Range (Plateau) and winds southward along the plateau's summit through the Fishlake National Forest. This is a scenic mountain-forest drive at 8,000 to nearly 10,000 feet, resembling the better known and longer Skyline Drive detailed earlier. The drive affords glimpses downward over the Sevier Valley and into a network of deep canyons opening out into the valley. Viewpoints also afford panoramic glimpses of Pahvant Valley and the Sevier Desert to the west. The road skirts the base of Red Pyramid, Mt. Catherine, White Pine and Sunset Peaks, which are among the highest summits on the plateau at more than 10,000 feet. Toward the south, forks descend to Richfield and Elsinore; more primitive spurs lead off to the west and south. Travelers are advised to check on the road's condition in advance with the offices of the Fishlake National Forest in Richfield.

Sigurd is a small village about 12 miles south of Salina, several miles east of the highway. It is the site of two gypsum-processing mills that utilize local deposits in the manufacture of plasterboard and other building products.

Turn east from Sigurd Junction via Route 24 to Fish Lake, Wayne County, Capitol Reef National Park, Hanksville, Lake Powell, and other points in south-central Utah.

Richfield and Vicinity

Richfield is the seat of Sevier County and the commercial capital of a vast mountain-valley region. Agriculture is the region's main enterprise (livestock, alfalfa, grain, etc.), but Richfield's economy receives important support also from trade, manufacturing, mining, and other industries. It is a major highway stop, the site of federal and state government offices, and the home of Sevier Valley Tech, a state vocational school.

Richfield was first settled in January 1864 by people who spent their first winter enduring primitive conditions. The first name for Richfield was Omni, which was a Book of Mormon character, and Fort Omni was built of rock in 1865. The site of this fort is marked by a bell campanile at First North and Second West.

The Paiute ATV Trail—with access points at Richfield, Beaver, Fillmore, Fremont Indian State Park, Kanosh, Paiute State Park, Marysvale, and Circleville—is a 300-mile-loop trail that can be explored by ATV enthusiasts, hikers, mountain bikers, and equestrians. The topography on the trail varies; not all segments are designed for all types of use. Check with the Fishlake National Forest at Richfield, or with local state park offices for information and a brochure.

The Ralph Ramsay Home, 5757 East 200 North (just east of the county courthouse), dates from 1873–74. Its builder, Ralph Ramsay, carved the original eagle for Salt Lake City's famed Eagle Gate. The Young Block, at the corner of Center and Main streets, is termed "the most architecturally significant commercial building in Sevier County." It dates from 1907. Both the Ramsay Home and Young Block are listed on the National Register of Historic Places. The Daughters of Utah Pioneers Relic Hall, 340 West 500 North, exhibits pioneer relics and artifacts.

Turn east from Richfield via Route 119 to Glenwood and the junction with Route 24 leading to Capitol Reef National Park. En route, climbing the valley's eastern slopes, the road passes through the Rainbow Hills, which display a spectrum of bright and varied colors and, from their heights, provide an engaging panorama of the Sevier Valley and the mountains surrounding it.

Glenwood is a quiet, sleepy village—a mixture of the old and new. In some respects its pioneer history is most unusual. Like a number of other Mormon communities in the 1870s, the village at least partially experimented with President Brigham Young's United Order. Livestock herds were owned by the cooperative, as were grain fields and industries such as the sawmill, woolen mill, gristmill, tannery, lumber-finishing mill, molasses mill, and so on. Each worker, despite the kind of work performed, received the same pay, and at the end of the year all debts and accounts receivable were canceled. The Glenwood experiment was reportedly successful in many ways, but as with Orderville it was broken up mainly by outside influences and internal friction.

The Joseph Wall Gristmill, a fortress-like building with a mansard roof and sturdy walls of black lava rock and brick, is listed in the National Register of Historic Places. A relic of the United Order days, the mill was built about 1874 and saw continued use for some 75 years.

THE HIGH PLATEAUS

Sevier Plateau via Route 89

The Sevier Plateau is only one of the High Plateaus visible from the Richfield vicinity. In every direction one can view tabular highlands, from the Wasatch on the northeast, clockwise to the Fishlake, then the Sevier (close to Richfield and therefore the dominating mass), on to the summits of the Tushar in the southwest, and finally to the Pahvant's rainbow-hued slopes on the west. Other High Plateaus are out of view: the Aquarius (Boulder Mountain), Thousand Lake Mountain, the Paunsaugunt and Markagunt, and the rugged, remote Kaiparowits Plateau.

All of the plateaus are based on sedimentary deposits that have been raised and lowered over millions of years by crustal forces, and the jagged edges of some are the result of great faults or breaks in the earth's surface.

In addition to faulting, the plateau province has been shaped by extensive volcanic activity over great lengths of time. Nearly every product of volcanic eruption is evident in this region, including trachyte, rhyolite, and basalt, and some lavas have issued from the earth in very recent times. The sum of vast erosion, faulting, and volcanic activity make this a region of great interest to the geologist.

Monroe, several miles east of Route 89, is situated in a secluded cove at the southern end of the valley. Behind it rise the Sevier Plateau's highest peaks, 6,000 feet above. Monroe has increasingly become a residential area for commuters and retired people.

Monroe is one of Utah's showplaces for 19th-century and early-20th-century architecture; numerous older buildings here have been thoughtfully restored, maintained, and are still occupied. On Main Street a log cabin built in 1866–67 serves as a pioneer relic hall. An old Presbyterian church built of stone in the 1880s has been preserved as a home. The Old Monroe City Hall, a square structure of stone blocks, still stands. These are only a few of Monroe's historic buildings, many of distinguished Victorian architecture, others of more humble logs, stone, and frame.

Monroe Canyon, between castellated walls southeast of town, is the site of Monrovian Park, an improved picnic area and playground in the Fishlake National Forest. Beyond the park the unpaved road climbs steeply in zigzags up the mountainside to the summit of the Sevier Plateau at 10,000 feet or more, affording views over the Sevier Valley, the Tushar peaks, and seemingly a good part of central and southern Utah. The road continues through the Fishlake National Forest, across open alpine meadows and through groves of aspen and evergreens, finally descending to Koosharem in the Grass Valley. Summit peaks rise above the drive to more than 11,000 feet. This route, as with most of the area's alpine drives, is particularly dramatic in late September–early October, when autumn colors are at their best.

Elsinore is a farming and trading community located among fields of alfalfa and grain. It was settled in 1874–75 and named by Danish colonists for the site of Hamlet's castle in Denmark; for a time its founders lived communally in the United Order experiment of that period. A pioneer log cabin dating from 1876 is preserved on the church lot. Other distinctive buildings include a number of early rock structures and the two-story White Rock School, built in 1897–98 and restored in 1976.

Joseph and Sevier are small highway villages at the south end of the valley, near the Route 89-Interstate 70 junction. Both date from pioneer days, and several aged buildings attest to their antiquity. Other structures, not so old but of architectural interest, include the old Joseph Schoolhouse (1894–1904) and the Sevier LDS Chapel (1928–33), a quaint rock structure now privately owned. Two miles north of Joseph, beside the highway, the Parker home is a distinguished residence of stone blocks with dormer windows and a tower, stained-glass windows, large porch, and ornate wood decoration. It is included on state and national registers of historic places.

Turn west from Sevier Junction via Interstate 70 through Clear Creek Canyon to I-15 at Cove Fort. Clear Creek Canyon is a narrow pass with jagged, curiously eroded palisades of igneous rock. In this canyon near Exit 17 on I-70 is Fremont Indian State Park—created in 1987 to protect the remains of the largest Fremont village in Utah, home to approximately 150 occupants—which was uncovered during interstate construction here in 1983. The park includes handicap-accessible trails, rock-art panels, and an informative visitor center with interpretive materials.

From an exit 5 miles west of Sevier Junction, an unpaved, steep, and winding forest road meanders southward along the canyon of Mill Creek, climbing to the site of Old Kimberly, 8 miles, beneath the majestic peaks of the Tushar. The road continues on through the dense aspen and evergreen growth of the Fishlake National Forest to Marysvale, 16 miles from Kimberly, climbing to 10,000 feet or so. A lusty turn-of-the-century mining town, Kimberly today exhibits little to remind the visitor of its heyday: a few crumbled or crumbling buildings, waste deposits, and new mining buildings. Kimberly, center of the Gold Mountain Mining District, dates from 1888 when gold was discovered.

In 1981, highway construction obscured the turnoff from I-70. This unpaved loop drive from I-70 to Marysvale, though usually well maintained, is steep and narrow, clinging to mountainsides thousands of feet above the canyon floor—not for those who are afraid of heights. Inquire locally or at the Fishlake National Forest offices about road conditions.

Marysvale Canyon, route of Highway 89 between Sevier Junction and Marysvale, cuts through masses of igneous rock, twisting and turning in tight curves south of Sevier, then opening and straightening somewhat near the Big Rock Candy Mountain. This brightly colored hill, painted in vivid yellow and chocolate hues, was the inspiration for the popular folk song "The Big Rock Candy Mountain," and provided the central image in the novel of the same name by Wallace Stegner. A resort provides lodging, food, fuel, and souvenirs.

Marysvale is a picturesque town in the canyon of Pine Creek, overshadowed by the peaks of the Tushar and Sevier Plateaus. The mines in this area have produced large quantities of valuable minerals, including gold, lead, silver, copper, and uranium.

West from Marysvale, unpaved but maintained roads climb steeply into the Tushar Mountains, providing access to mine workings, the site of Old Kimberly (see above), and heights of more than 10,000 feet in the area of the loftiest peaks.

Panoramic views are superb, but these roads are not for the timid. Take water and inquire locally about conditions, or at the Fishlake National Forest in Richfield or Beaver, where maps are available.

The Tushar Plateau is more commonly known as the Tushar or Beaver Mountains and has the highest peaks in Utah with the exception of a few in the Uinta and La Sal ranges. The name Tushar is derived from T'shar (Paiute), meaning "white" and referring to the plateau's light-colored peaks.

South of Marysvale, Route 89 follows the Tushar foothills, hundreds of feet above the trough of the Sevier River to the east. Peaks loom overhead to 12,000 feet and more, and across the valley the Sevier Plateau stretches from north to south.

The Piute Reservoir, one of central Utah's largest bodies of water, backs up behind a dam on the river east of the highway. Piute Lake State Beach offers facilities for boating, camping, and picnicking.

Junction, the seat of Piute County near the confluence of the south and east forks of the Sevier River, is the political center of a little-populated farming and livestock region. Piute County is one of Utah's smallest, least populated, and most mountainous, with an economy based largely on agriculture, trade, and mining. The Piute County Courthouse in Junction dates from 1902-3. The town hosts the Piute County Fair in late summer.

Turn west from Junction via Route 153 to the Tushar Plateau, Puffer Lake, and Beaver. The road is unpaved but well graded for about half the distance to Beaver; parts of it, particularly east of Mt. Holly Resort, are closed in winter. From Junction it climbs steeply up City Creek Canyon to expansive 10,000-foot-high flats near the plateau's highest summits. The panoramic views from this road are among Utah's best, and it offers convenient hiking access to the naked Tushar spine, highest in southern Utah. Climbing these summits is not particularly difficult, though loose rock may be hazardous.

South of Junction 2 miles, turn east on Route 62 to Kingston, Otter Creek Lake, Antimony, and Grass Valley.

Kingston, 2 miles east of Route 89 via Route 62 at the mouth of East Fork Canyon, displays little of its historic past. The community from which the present town took its name was located a mile or so to the west, receiving its name from the King family of Fillmore, who led its founding as a communal settlement in the 1870s. For a number of years the commu-

nity practiced the Mormon United Order. There was a community dining hall, cattle herd, fields, gristmill, woolen factory, and tannery.

Route 62 passes through East Fork (Kingston) Canyon, a scenic gorge confined between volcanic battlements eroded into exotic shapes. Otter Creek Lake State Beach is popular for boating, fishing, and camping.

Antimony is an agricultural village named for a nearby deposit of antimony ore; originally it was known as Coyote. Route 22, unpaved part of the distance south of Antimony, connects with Route 12 near Bryce Canyon.

Route 62 veers northward from Otter Creek Junction, passing through the spacious expanse of Grass Valley to Greenwich, Koosharem, and Burrville. This is wide-open ranching country, located between the Sevier and Aquarius uplifts, the home of eagles, ravens, and hordes of jackrabbits.

Circleville lies in the Circle Valley, almost surrounded by rugged and massive plateaus towering to more than 11,000 feet. Agriculture is the main industry, as it has been since the first days of settlement, though highway travel and trade support the economy.

Circleville's main claim to fame (and one which irritates some local people) is that it was the childhood home of Robert LeRoy Parker, better known as the outlaw Butch Cassidy. Butch was one of the West's most celebrated badmen around the turn of the century when he and the Wild Bunch robbed trains and banks and rustled cattle. Although one of their most publicized hideouts was in the wild and almost inaccessible canyon country near Hanksville, Butch and the Wild Bunch operated over much of the West. Cassidy's exploits have been told and retold in books and articles, and in a film starring Robert Redford and Paul Newman. The old Parker homestead, marked by a log house where Butch visited his family in later years, is beside the highway about 2 miles south of town.

South of Circleville, Route 89 again plunges into a narrow canyon formed in volcanic rock of somber hue; and known as Circleville or Panguitch Canyon. This was the route for some decades before 1850 of the Old Spanish Trail between Santa Fe and Los Angeles (see Salina Canyon above). Of more immediate interest was the journey of John Charles Fremont and his compatriots, who passed through this canyon in the winter of 1853–54. This was during Fremont's ill-fated Fifth

Expedition, and at that time he and his party were in desperate straits after a terrible journey across the Green River desert and through the Grass, Sevier, and Circle Valleys. When they reached the Tushars, deep in snow, none of the men had any shoes, only stockings or moccasins of rawhide, and their food supply was almost exhausted. By the time they finally reached Parowan on the west side of the plateaus, the men had lived on horse meat for more than 50 days, had been without food of any kind for two days, and one of their number had perished from exposure.

Route 89 continues south into Panguitch (see Chapter 8); Route 20 leads west to I-15. The southern end of Panguitch Canyon opens into the upper Sevier Valley.

Fishlake Plateau
via Route 24

Route 24 branches southeast from Route 89/I-70 near Sigurd and passes through mountainous terrain for 60 miles. From an altitude of 5,300 feet at Sigurd, it climbs gradually through canyons and flatlands to Grass Valley at 7,000 feet, climbs Fish Lake Pass at 8,400 feet, then descends to 7,000 feet again in Rabbit Valley.

Route 119, east from Richfield, is an alternate approach to Route 24. Passing near Glenwood, this route ascends by switchbacks into the brightly colored Rainbow Hills, and offers high-level overviews of the Sevier Valley, the Tushar peaks and the Pahvant front across the valley.

About 20 miles from Route 89/I-70, the highway enters Grass Valley, a deep and narrow basin. Only a few hundred people live in this valley bottom that stretches for more than 30 miles; it is ranching country for the most part, and at nearly 7,000 feet is too high for most crops. Koosharem Reservoir, formed along Otter Creek, is popular for trout fishing.

On the west side of the highway, 1 mile south of Koosharem Reservoir, is a stone-and-bronze marker commemorating a peace treaty of 1873 that ended long-lasting hostilities between settlers and local Indians.

Route 62 branches southward not far from the monument, and leads to Burrville, Koosharem, and Greenwich, the upper valley's communities. These villages typify the rural isolation of Utah's past and still retain a rustic atmosphere. Interesting points include early structures of logs, bricks, and frame, some dating from the 1870s and 1880s, as well as a youth camp

development of modern vintage. The Amusement Hall in Koosharem, built in 1914, has served as a community center ever since. In Greenwich, a picturesque brick building beside the highway, complete with bell and belfry, was dedicated in 1906 and has served as schoolhouse, Mormon chapel and Relief Society meetinghouse, and tourist information center. Route 24 leaves Grass Valley by way of the "Fish Lake grade," a climb of more than 1,500 feet. The Fish Lake Pass or Summit (8,400 alt.) marks the division between Piute and Wayne Counties, and also the approximate separation between Fishlake Plateau, rising 2,000 feet higher to the north, and the Awapa Plateau, which stretches away in heaving swells toward the south. The Awapa is grazing country, the home of numerous pronghorn antelope.

Two miles west of Fish Lake Pass, Route 25 branches from the main highway and climbs to Fish Lake (7 miles), one of Utah's most popular fishing and outdoor recreation areas. Route 25 is designated as one of Utah's Scenic Byways.

Public facilities at Fish Lake include lodges, cabins, restaurants, groceries and supplies, boat rentals, guides, public campgrounds, and picnic areas. Numerous summer homes are clustered near the lake. Fish Lake, as its name implies, is a popular fishery for rainbow and lake trout.

In a volcanic basin caused by faulting, Fish Lake is a scenic jewel measuring five miles in length, nearly a mile in width, at about 8,800 feet altitude. On either side, steep slopes rise more than 2,000 feet to summits of 11,000 feet or more. The lake is fed by half a dozen streams; its overflow water drains into Johnson Valley Reservoir at the north, the source of the Fremont River. The autumn foliage here is spectacular.

The Fishlake Plateau, of which the "Hightop Plateau" containing Fish Lake is but a part, is a rugged lava-covered highland measuring some 30 by 25 miles in extent, heavily utilized for livestock grazing.

The Fish Lake Pass provides the first bird's-eye view of the Wayne Wonderland to the east—tantalizing glimpses of rainbow colors, far-off peaks, and strange rock forms. Majestic uplifts loom in the distance: Thousand Lake Mountain on the north, the Aquarius on the south. Route 24 dips and climbs across the almost treeless Awapa, finally dropping more than a thousand feet into Rabbit Valley.

Rabbit Valley is a circular basin at 7,000 feet. The valley was settled by Europeans during the 1870s. Wayne County's oldest towns are in the valley, which is so high and has such a short growing season that agriculture is limited mainly to raising livestock, garden vegetables, potatoes, feed crops such as alfalfa, and some dairying. Water is comparatively plentiful here, allowing for the sprinkler irrigation of thousands of acres.

Loa is the Wayne County seat. It was settled in the mid-1870s and named after the Mauna Loa volcano on the Hawaiian Islands. Its landmark building, an attractive rock structure with a terraced steeple, is the Wayne Stake Tabernacle, built between 1906 and 1909. The Wayne County Courthouse, dating from 1938–39, displays a collection of polished rocks, the work of Dr. A. L. Inglesby of Fruita.

Turn north 5 miles to Fremont, named for the Fremont River that flows nearby. The Fremont area, the first to be settled by Europeans in Rabbit Valley during the 1870s, retains an aura of rural quaintness. Meriting an off-highway drive is Worthen's Merc, an old-fashioned country store (now closed) built of more than 70 varieties of stone. Also of historic interest is the old Fremont church house, built of local volcanic rock about 1902–7 and restored in the 1970s for public functions.

Northwest of Fremont at Brian Springs is the Loa Fish Hatchery, a state installation that produces fingerling trout for transplanting to waters throughout Utah. Open to visitors.

Turn north from Fremont via Route 72 to the heights of Fishlake Plateau and Thousand Lake Mountain. Side roads give access to productive fishing spots such as Mill Meadow, the Forsyth and Johnson Valley reservoirs, Fish Lake, the Fremont River, and smaller streams. Seven miles from Fremont a side road climbs eastward between high peaks to the eastern shoulder of Thousand Lake Mountain, to the Elkhorn Guard Station and Campground. Scenic views from this road, encompassing a wild panorama of Canyonlands and Utah's Painted Desert to the east, are superlative. Cathedral Valley and the South Desert (Capitol Reef National Park) occupy the middle ground beyond a plunging foreground of brushy meadows interspersed with groves of aspen and evergreens.

Several miles before reaching Elkhorn, unpaved branch roads drop from the mountain into Cathedral Valley and to Baker Ranch, joining eventually with I-70 at Fremont Junction, or with Route 24 east of Fruita (see Capitol Reef National Park).

Route 72 continues across rolling highlands to I-70 at Fremont Junction, with panoramic glimpses to the east resembling those from the Elkhorn road.

Bicknell, on a bench at the base of Thousand Lake Mountain and painted cliffs, overlooks an expanse of Fremont River marshes in the valley below. The southern view is dominated by Aquarius Plateau (Boulder Mountain). Bicknell has blossomed with new homes and commercial buildings, leaving limited evidence of its 19th-century past. Among those that remain are the old brick (now stuccoed) Mormon Relief Society Building (1897–99) and a quaint two-story stone building across the street, built about 1900, which served for many years as a store.

Bicknell was settled during the 1870s, although its first location was several miles south in the valley near the river. For 40 years or so the town bore the name Thurber, after a pioneer leader. The town became Bicknell in 1916 in return for a library offered by Thomas Bicknell, an Easterner, to any Utah town that would take his name. Thurber, and Grayson in San Juan County, accepted. Thurber got half of the library and the name Bicknell; Grayson got the other half and became Blanding, the maiden name of Bicknell's wife.

Turn east from Route 24, 1 mile south of Bicknell, to the Sunglow Recreation Area (Fishlake National Forest), a camping and picnic area nestled 1 mile from the highway in a circular amphitheater formed by high red cliffs. From Route 24, 3 miles south of Bicknell near the Fremont River, a road forks to the south.

Drive on this road to the Bicknell Bottoms of the Fremont River, a popular waterfowl hunting area. Near the road is the J. Perry Egan Fish Hatchery, a state wildlife unit.

The side road continues across the almost treeless expanses of Parker Mountain and eventually drops down through forests and canyons to Escalante, about 50 miles from Bicknell. En route, side roads lead onto the heights of Parker Mountain, to Posey Lake, Hell's Backbone, and the 11,000-foot summit of Boulder Mountain, also known as the Aquarius Plateau. The plateau's remarkably flat summit, known as Boulder Top, is a rolling tableland of perhaps 50 square miles, formed of dark lava and rimmed by steep cliffs.

Most of Boulder Top exceeds 10,000 feet in elevation, with summits in excess of 11,000 feet; Bluebell Knoll, highest of all, is 11,328 feet. Lava boulders are scattered everywhere. Stands of Engelmann spruce and fir cloak much of the

Fish Lake is a sportsman's paradise nestled between high mountain slopes of aspen and stands of fir – Frank Jensen, UTC

summit, interspersed with meadows of arctic tundra and numerous small lakes and ponds. The extensive evergreen growth is very unusual for such an altitude, and the Aquarius bears one of the highest forests in the world.

The junction of Route 24 with the aforementioned side road coincides with a narrow gateway between Thousand Lake Mountain and the Aquarius, carved by the Fremont River. Explorer-scientists of the 1870s applied the name Red Gate to this colorful portal between the High Plateaus and the red rock desert of Canyonlands.

Route 24 continues east to Teasdale, Torrey, Capitol Reef National Park, Notom, Lake Powell, and other attractions. Route 12 east of Torrey climbs south over Boulder Mountain toward Grover, Boulder, Escalante, and Bryce Canyon National Park.

JUAB AND PAHVANT VALLEYS

Santaquin to Parowan via I-15/Route 91

From Santaquin Junction southward, the highway passes over a low ridge marking the drainage divide between the Utah Valley and the Juab Valley. The huge bulk of Mt. Nebo forms the eastern horizon for 20 miles, cresting near Mona, 7,000 feet higher than the valley at their base. The Nebo massif marks the southwestern terminus of the Rocky Mountain Province in Utah.

The small town of Mona, cradled near the center of the valley, has been bypassed by the highway. Mona Reservoir extends along the valley floor to the north. Nephi is the seat of Juab County and a regional commercial center. The town's varied economy is based on tourism, farming, small manufacturing, trading, and a little mining. Nephi's noted Ute Stampede, held every year in July for over half a century, features a parade and a popular rodeo.

Part of the old Salt Creek Fort, dating from the 1850s, is preserved in the city park. The original fort, built of gravel, mud, and straw, enclosed nine blocks with 12-foot walls. Among the more compelling sites in Nephi are the 25-room Whitmore Mansion (1898–1900), 106 South Main, a three-story edifice of brick and stone; and the Booth House, 94 West 300 South, a late 19th-century Victorian residence (both on the National Historic Register).

East from Nephi, Route 132 winds through scenic Salt

Creek Canyon to Fountain Green, Moroni, and Route 89 in the Sanpete Valley. Salt Creek Canyon forms the boundary between the Rocky Mountain and Colorado Plateau provinces in Utah. Six miles east of Nephi, a paved side road forks north from Route 132 into the Uintah National Forest and the alpine heights of the Nebo massif. This is the Nebo Loop Road, a popular scenic drive that can be accessed either here, near Santaquin, or in Payson. The Bear Canyon-Cottonwood-Ponderosa Forest campground complex (Uintah National Forest), 11 miles and 12 miles from Nephi, is near this road. In the vicinity of the turnoff of the Nebo Loop Road from Route 132 is a picturesque alcove of eroded forms, corridors, and chambers.

West from Nephi, Route 132 leads to Leamington and to Route 6 at Lynndyl. South of Nephi, I-15 skirts a sloping terrace known as Levan Ridge. Extending both north and south of Levan, this foothill terrace provides a bountiful harvest of dry-land (nonirrigated) grain. Only a few places in Utah are suitable for dry-land agriculture.

Levan is a farming village at the junction of Routes 78 and 28. Side streets still proffer nostalgic glimpses into Utah's small-town rural past, with tree-shaded yards and modest homes of varied styles, weary outbuildings, and tottering fences, some a hundred years old or more. The impressive Mormon chapel, a registered historic site, dates from 1904.

Turn south from Levan via Route 28 to Gunnison and Route 89 in the Sevier Valley, passing through an area of widespread dry-farms with expansive views of the Great Basin. The Sevier Bridge Reservoir is glimpsed en route, filling the valley of the Sevier River for many miles. Route 28 carries a heavy volume of truck traffic, including mammoth trailers loaded with coal from Salina Canyon, and trucks piled high with plaster wallboard from the gypsum mills at Sigurd.

The Sevier Bridge Reservoir, known more popularly as Yuba Dam Lake, is a fluctuating body of water that may extend 15 miles upstream at times. Near the dam, several miles from the highway, the State Division of Parks and Recreation maintains the Yuba Lake State Recreation Area, developed with facilities for camping and boating.

Scipio is near the junction of I-15 and Route 50. An agricultural town, Scipio has a pleasant location in Round Valley under the nestling peaks of the Canyon, Valley, and Pahvant Mountains. The area's hillsides and bottomlands support herds of livestock and fields of hay and grain.

Turn south from Scipio Junction via Route 50 to Salina and the junction there with Route 89 and I-70. En route the highway passes through a sparsely settled countryside of scattered farms and rangelands.

West of Scipio Junction, the highway surmounts Scipio Pass, a low divide between the rugged Canyon Range to the north and the Pahvant Range or Plateau to the south. At the summit of Scipio Pass, a monument commemorates the passage here in 1776 of the Dominguez-Escalante expedition.

Interstate 15 drops from Scipio Pass into the Pahvant Valley, the bed of ancient Lake Bonneville. Pahvant Butte, the crater of an inactive volcano, juts from the floor of the valley.

Holden, an agricultural village with pioneer origins, now marks the junction of I-15 with Route 50. Route 50 veers northwest to Delta and a junction there with Route 6.

Fillmore and Vicinity

Fillmore is the seat of Millard County and the largest community along the highway between Nephi and Cedar City, a distance of nearly 200 miles. No longer is it the town of 50 years ago, when " 'Levi's, five-gallon hats, and peg-heeled cowpunchers' boots are common habiliments" and "saddled cayuses hitched outside" were common sights along main street. Yet, though dress and transportation have changed, Fillmore still remains a commercial center for a vast farming and livestock region.

Fillmore was named and designated as the seat of territorial government in 1851, even before the town had been settled, when the townsite was personally selected by Governor Brigham Young and other dignitaries. The Pahvant Valley was chosen as the capital site because of its location in the approximate center of the vast Utah Territory, which at that time extended about 800 miles from the Sierra Nevada on the west to the Rocky Mountains on the east, and 400 miles from north to south.

The Territorial State House State Park is maintained by the State Division of Parks and Recreation as a museum and visitor center. A curious two-story, red-stone structure in the central city park, the Old State House served as Utah's first territorial capitol, and is one of the very few public buildings of its age still standing in Utah. It was designed by Truman O. Angell, architect of the Salt Lake Temple and Tabernacle, and

was intended to be a large domed structure with four wings in the form of a cross.

However, only one wing—the present State House—was actually completed. This housed the Fifth Session of the territorial legislature in December 1855. Only two brief sessions were actually held in the building; thereafter, the legislature moved from Fillmore to Salt Lake City for the remainder of its business. Today, one of Utah's best rose gardens is located next to the building. There is also an adjacent picnic area.

Examples of noteworthy architecture abound in Fillmore, a number of sites remarkable enough for inclusion on national and state historic registers. Among them are the Huntsman-Nielsen Home, 155 West Center, built in 1871–75 of red brick and sandstone; the Edward Partridge Home, built in 1871, and the Rock Schoolhouse on the northeast corner First South and First West, built in 1867.

Turn east from Fillmore to Chalk Creek Canyon, a popular camping and hunting locale.

On the flat valley floor west of Fillmore, Meadow, and Kanosh is an extensive area of diversified igneous phenomena, now dormant but active in fairly recent ages. Known as the Millard Volcanic Field, the area includes the grand volcanic crater of the Pahvant Butte as well as less imposing craters, lava fields, hot springs, and ice caves representing eruptions occurring over a long period of time.

South of the Fillmore interchange, I-15 passes across the valley floor several miles west where Route 133, the former highway, takes a more circuitous route through Meadow and Kanosh. West of Kanosh at the south end of Pahvant Valley, I-15 bisects the imposing Black Rock Volcanic Field.

Kanosh is a small farming town that received its name from the Indian leader. Settled in 1859, Kanosh was known first as Corn Creek. Near here lived Chief Kanosh and his band of Pahvants, Kanosh was their leader during the early decades of Mormon colonization. Many intriguing tales have been told about this remarkable man. One recites how he refused to leave his house to greet Brigham Young in his carriage, insisting that protocol demanded that Brigham Young dismount and enter his home for the meeting. A number of Pahvants continue to reside on the Kanosh Indian Reservation near Meadow and Kanosh.

South of Pahvant Valley the highway enters a rugged region of low, dark volcanic hills covered with pinyon pines

The Territorial State House served as Utah's first territorial capitol, and is one of the very few early pioneer public buildings still standing – Mel Lewis, UTC

and cedars. The massive slopes of the Tushar Range or Plateau soon come into view, high above Cove Fort.

Cove Fort was a welcome way station on the Salt Lake City-Los Angeles road for a hundred years after it was built in 1867. For the past 10 or 15 years, however, it has been bypassed by most travelers, who glimpse it from a distance. Interstates 15 and 70 join in the vicinity of the old fort, which is near the western entrance to Clear Creek Canyon.

East from Cove Fort Junction, I-70 winds through rugged terrain to a junction with Route 89 at Sevier. Belknap and Baldy Peaks loom in startling majesty from one viewpoint, while intricately sculptured volcanic cliffs also help to make this stretch of highway a very scenic drive.

Just a few miles south of Cove Fort in the eastern foothills is Sulphurdale, the site of sulphur-mining operations since the 1880s when sulphur was used in gunpowder and sugar refining.

Beaver is the center of a farming, ranching, and mining district, and the seat of Beaver County. In recent years it has attracted a significant number of retirees.

Mormons settled Beaver in 1856, raising sheep and soon establishing a big woolen mill. About 1870 the discovery of rich mineral deposits in the San Francisco Mountains west of Beaver started to bring hordes of miners and camp-followers into the district; by 1871 friction between Mormon and non-Mormon, coupled with fear of Indians and the lack of law and order, caused both sides to ask for federal troops. Four companies of soldiers camped in tents on the Beaver River in May 1872 where they remained until the following year, when a number of black rock buildings were erected at the mouth of Beaver Canyon, two miles east of the city. In 1874 this post was named Fort Cameron in honor of Colonel James Cameron, veteran of the battle of Bull Run near Manassas, Virginia, during the Civil War. For years its 250 soldiers maintained the peace in Beaver.

Beaver is a showplace of early Utah architecture, so rich in unusual and distinctive buildings that it is considered a historic district. Among the 200 historic buildings is the Old Beaver County Courthouse, a towered structure with clock and bell built of brick on a massive lava-rock foundation. The building dates from the 1870s and 1880s and was used as a public office and court building for almost a hundred years. Today, the courthouse functions as a pioneer museum, art gallery, and auditorium for live theater.

Turn east from Beaver via Route 153 into Beaver Canyon and onto the heights of the Tushar Mountains. En route at the mouth of the canyon, the road threads through an attractive area of new housing, past the municipal golf course, and the well-kept racetrack. For many decades Beaver Canyon and the Tushars (also known as the Beaver Mountains) have been one of southern Utah's favorite fishing, hunting, and camping regions. The Fishlake National Forest has developed a number of camping and picnicking facilities at Kent's Lake, City Creek, Mahogany Cove, Anderson Meadow, and other alpine sites. Puffer Lake and Otter Creek State Park are popular for fishing. Densely wooded except for rocky peaks and crests, this mountain region is the highest and most rugged in southern Utah, with several summits topping 12,000 feet. East of Puffer Lake, Route 153 (unpaved) passes over the high passes of the high Big Flat crest at more than 10,000 feet, then drops in tight turns to Junction and Route 89.

Located 20 paved miles east of Beaver, Elk Meadows is a winter sports and residential development nestled in an alpine canyon. Runs here climb as high as 10,400 feet. The mostly intermediate runs are served by two double chairs, one triple chair, one poma lift, and one T-bar.

South of Beaver, I-15 crosses sagebrush flats, pinyon-draped foothills, and wide valleys before descending into the Parowan Valley. The Old Spanish Trail entered the Parowan Valley several miles south of the Beaver-Iron county line. Along this old trail, Fremont's battered band of explorers came to Parowan in February 1854.

Route 20 forks east from I-15 at a junction 17 miles south of Beaver, threading a broken region of canyons, valleys, and low mountains, connecting with Route 89 near Panguitch.

Paragonah, settled in 1852, is an agricultural town between red and brown cliffs on one side and the Parowan Valley on the other. Its residents grow alfalfa and grain, and raise livestock. Archaeologists have explored local Indian remains at various sites for decades. Numerous pit houses and granaries were uncovered and many artifacts found, including tools, weapons, and pottery. Some of these items are on display at Southern Utah University in Cedar City. SUU also has excavated at Summit, a few miles south of Parowan. The area's Indian culture flourished between A.D. 700 and 1150.

Parowan, the seat of Iron County, is southern Utah's oldest permanent settlement. Visitors see it as a blend of new and old homes situated at the base of juniper-capped red cliffs and overlooking the broad Parowan Valley. It is the center of a large livestock and farming industry and also a bedroom community for Cedar City. Parowan displays some noteworthy buildings of architectural and historical value, including the following Historic Register sites: a rock church erected in 1862, now one of Utah's oldest standing chapels, used as a relic hall; the Third Ward Meeting House, built in 1915–16 in Prairie School style; and the Jesse Smith Home, just west of Main on First South, built of adobe in 1856–57.

Turn east from Parowan via Route 143 to Route 148 to Parowan Canyon, Brian Head Resort, Cedar Breaks National Monument, and the junction with Route 14. Parowan Canyon is a colorful alternate route to Cedar Breaks, Brian Head, and other points on the lofty, forested Markagunt. It winds through lovely forests and red rocks to the 10,000-foot heights of the plateau. En route is Vermilion Castle Forest Campground (Dixie National Forest), with improved facilities for camping and picnicking. Side roads lead to Yankee Meadows Reservoir, Panguitch Lake, and numerous smaller lakes on the plateau.

Turn west from Parowan via improved road to the Parowan Gap, a deep narrow gorge cut through the Red Hills. Listed in the National Register of Historic Places, it is the site of remarkable Indian petroglyphs on its walls. This rock art was incised over approximately 1,000 years.

Poplars frame the old pioneer gristmill, which served the Mormon farming hamlets scattered along the Fremont River – John P. George, UTC

The People of the Valley

by Edward A. Geary

Above my desk hangs an enlarged print of a photograph taken by the Utah documentary photographer George Edward Anderson in 1898. In the foreground, an irrigation canal winds its slow way around a blue shale hill. The middle ground is occupied by a river-bottom farm made up of small plots of cropland, orchard, and pasture spread like a patchwork quilt around the farmer's new-built two-story brick house. Behind the house, and repeating its truncated pyramidal shape on a vastly larger scale, rises Gentry Mountain, a promontory of the Wasatch Plateau, ascending in a rhythmic series of horizontal ledges and steep talus slopes to a sharp-edged horizon. This picture has been much admired and widely exhibited as a photographic adaptation of the panoramic style of nineteenth-century American landscape painting. But whenever I raise my eyes to look at it, my immediate impression is simply

a feeling of rightness. This is how the world was meant to look! For this is the valley where I grew up, with its gray-blue hill, naked rocks, cottonwood-shaded streams, intensely green irrigated fields, and always the dominating mountain ridgeline giving definition to the land, a proper edge to the sky.

Not far away from the scene photographed by Anderson, in a farm village laid out like a checkerboard on the prickly-pear flat, two brothers, "old-batches," lived in a corner house half hidden by a wilderness of overgrown lilac bushes and yellow roses. By reputation, they had spent their entire lives in the valley, going out and back each day to their farm a mile or so north of town and shuffling across Main Street in the evening to spend an hour at Klecker's beer joint. I remember the story told by the local miller about the younger of these brothers once being invited to accompany a friend on a day's trip to the M&O Ranch in Salina Canyon, about eighty miles away. The next evening one of the fellows at Klecker's asked him what he thought of his adventure. He replied, "Well, if the world goes as far the other way as it goes that way, it is a mighty big place."

That story has the ring of folklore and has no doubt been told about other provincials in other places. But I like to think of it as really happening to that old man I remember. I can recall a time in early childhood when I believed that the visible horizon of our valley marked the actual limits of the earth within which even such remote places as Salt Lake City and Los Angeles were somehow contained. In time, of course, I learned that there were other valleys and other mountains beyond our own. Later still I found that there were people who live entirely without mountains to shape their world, though my imagination has never been able to take this in. Indeed, I spent the first half of my life discovering that the world was much bigger than I thought and the second half discovering that it is not so big after all. Wherever I have gone—and not least in the great urban center—I have found that most people, like the people I grew up with, like myself, are essentially provincials and hold the conviction that their own province is the world's center point.

Still, I have found few people as strongly attached to a particular landscape as those who grew up on the mountain-girt valleys of Utah. They may travel the world, master foreign tongues, make decades-long careers in places far distant from their native towns, but they remain first and last Sanpeters or Dixieties or Cache Valley folk. For example, the late Utah governor Scott Matheson spent the greater part of his life in Salt Lake City, but he was buried back home in Parowan because that is where the Mathesons come from. I know a couple who have been disputing for the forty-odd years of their marriage whether they will be laid to rest in her family plot in the Manti cemetery or his in Star Valley, Wyoming—never mind the fact that hey have never lived, as a couple, in either place.

The peculiar pull of this landscape is partly the result of natural conditions and partly, I am convinced, the product of a deliberate design. When Mormon settlers spread beyond the Wasatch Front oasis, especially those who went south, they went of necessity to more difficult (though also, I would maintain, more beautiful) environments. Every location that had a living stream and a patch of arable land was planted with a village or a town, depending on the flow of the creek and the acreage that could be embraced by the irrigation canal. The settlers, "called" to fulfill a religious mission by redeeming the waste places of Zion, had to struggle with the hard land until they fell in love with it, and both the struggle and the love became the heritage of succeeding generations.

In 1888, the Utah Commission—established by Congress to wean the Mormons from their theocratic and polygamous ways and bring them into the American mainstream—filled a report explaining their failure to accomplish their goals. They had run up against an insurmountable barrier in the Utah geography. The Mormons had occupied all of the arable valley land, appropriated the available water. The commission report ruefully declared that "those who hold the valleys . . . own and hold Utah, and nature has fortified their position more strongly than it could be done by any Chinese wall or artificial defense." I suspect, however, that this entrenchment was not only a product of accommodation to the natural conditions but also reflected a deliberate policy on the part of the Great Colonizer, Brigham Young. For the thirty years he lived in Utah, he dispersed his followers among the valleys in the very kind of small tightly-knit communities that were most likely to breed a sense of belonging. He was determined to plant his people so deeply in the valleys of the mountains that they could never be rooted out. And we never have been.

Call of the River – Tom Olson

Chapter 7

Utah's Canyonlands and the Colorado Plateau

– Carbon, Emery, Garfield, Grand, San Juan, Uintah, and Wayne Counties –

T HE SOUTHEASTERN REGION OF UTAH, BOUNDED BY THE UINTA BASIN ON THE NORTH AND THE STATES OF COLORADO AND ARIZONA ON THE EAST AND SOUTH, EXTENDS WEST TO INCLUDE THE RED ROCK DESERTS OF GLEN CANYON NATIONAL RECREATION AREA, CAPITOL REEF NATIONAL PARK, AND THE SAN RAFAEL SWELL.

THE AREA INCLUDES THREE NATIONAL PARKS: CAPITOL REEF, ARCHES, AND CANYONLANDS. MOUNTAIN RANGES— THE HIGH LA SALS, THE BLUE ABAJOS, AND THE HENRY MOUNTAINS— ARE VISIBLE FOR LONG DISTANCES IN THE DRY AIR OF THE COLORADO PLATEAU. LAKE POWELL,

Rochester Creek's petroglyph "Rainbow Panel" – François Camoin

FORMED BY IMPOUNDING THE WATERS OF THE COLORADO RIVER BEHIND GLEN CANYON DAM, IS THE SECOND-LARGEST ARTIFICIAL LAKE IN THE UNITED STATES. MAJOR TOWNS INCLUDE GREEN RIVER, MOAB, MONTICELLO, BLANDING, BLUFF, HANKSVILLE, AND TORREY. THREE BIG RIVERS—THE SAN JUAN, THE GREEN, AND THE COLORADO—HAVE PLAYED AN IMPORTANT PART IN SHAPING THE TOPOGRAPHY AND THE POLITICS OF THIS CORNER OF UTAH.

"THE SPELL OF THE DESERT COMES BACK TO ME, AS IT ALWAYS WILL COME. I SEE THE VEILS, LIKE PURPLE SMOKE, IN THE CANYONS, AND I FEEL THE SILENCE. AND IT SEEMS THAT AGAIN I MUST TRY TO PIERCE BOTH AND GET AT THE STRANGE WILD LIFE OF THE LAST AMERICAN WILDERNESS—WILD STILL, ALMOST, AS IT EVER WAS."

- Zane Grey -
"Foreword" from The Rainbow Trail

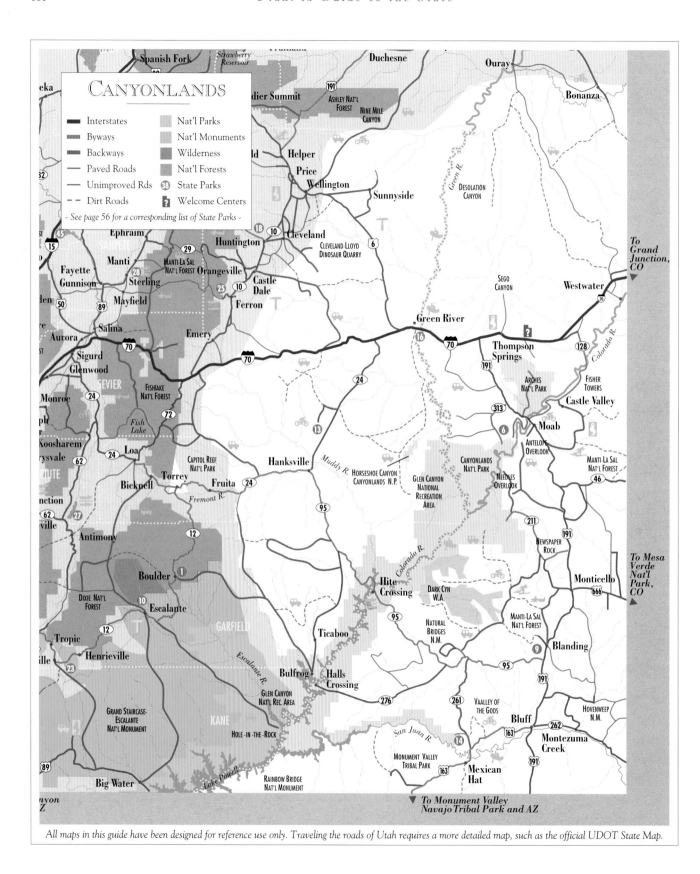

CANYONLANDS

▬▬▬ Interstates	▨ Nat'l Parks
▬▬ Byways	▨ Nat'l Monuments
▬▬ Backways	▨ Wilderness
— Paved Roads	▨ Nat'l Forests
— Unimproved Rds	🅃🅃 State Parks
- - - Dirt Roads	🅿 Welcome Centers

- See page 56 for a corresponding list of State Parks -

THE GREEN AND COLORADO RIVERS

The Green River is one of Utah's two largest rivers. It originates in the Wind River Mountains of Wyoming and joins the Colorado more than 100 miles below the town that bears its name. "Beckoning with one hand and thumbing its nose with the other, [the Green River] lures the riverman," says the 1941 edition of this book. "It is a wolf in sheep's clothing, hiding behind a bland and limpid surface its turbulent upstream past, and giving no hint of its crashing, thrusting, downstream future."

Trappers used sections of the river in the 1820s, but if they reached the junction of the two rivers, it has not been recorded. The first man to attempt the Green appears to be General William H. Ashley, who went downstream almost to Green River, Utah, in 1825. The name, "D. Julien," with the date 1836, appears several times on the walls of the canyons of the Green River, but little is known of his trip.

The one-armed Major John Wesley Powell may not have been a good manager, but there can be no question of his daring. He made two assaults upon the rivers, one in 1869, the other in 1871. Without maps or charts, Powell made his way along the Green and Colorado to the Grand Canyon. Leaving Green River, Wyoming, May 24, 1869, Powell set out with four boats and a crew of nine. The boats passed uneventfully through U-shaped Horseshoe Canyon, and Kingfisher Canyon.

In Lodore Canyon, Powell had his first accident, resulting in the loss of a boat. The men were saved, but it was thought that all the barometers, which were on this boat, had been lost. Powell sent two men through the rapids to the still-intact cabin the next day, and they returned triumphantly with the barometers and a three-gallon keg of whisky. Powell, because he had only one arm, almost lost his life in Split Rock Canyon (see Dinosaur National Monument).

At the junction of the Uinta, Powell went to visit the Indian reservation at Whiterocks, and Frank Goodman left the party. He had been on the boat that was lost, and Powell intimates that he had lost his nerve, but the Major was not always fair to the men who left him. Above Stillwater, Powell gazed upon "a strange, weird, grand region. The landscape everywhere, away from the river, is of rock—cliffs of rock; tables of rock; plateaus of rock; terraces of rock; crags of rock—ten thousand strangely carved forms. Rocks every-where, and no vegetation, no soil, no sand . . . a whole land of naked rock, with giant forms carved on it; cathedral shaped buttes, towering hundreds or thousands of feet; cliffs that cannot be scaled, and canyon walls that shrink the river into insignificance, with vast, hollow domes, and tall pinnacles, and shafts set on the verge overhead, and all highly colored—buff, gray, red, brown, and chocolate; never lichened; never moss-covered; but bare, and often polished."

The 1941 account neglected to include Powell's passage through Desolation Canyon north of town, where the Green has cut one of the deepest and most magnificent river canyons in America. This stretch of the Green has gained increasing popularity with boaters. The canyon is included in the National Register of Historic Places, which describes it as follows:

THE 1869 EXPEDITION OF 11 MEN AND FOUR BOATS STARTED FROM THE POINT ON THE GREEN RIVER WHERE IT IS CROSSED BY THE UNION PACIFIC RAILROAD [WYOMING]. IN DESOLATION CANYON THE MEN SAW A HERETOFORE UNEXPLORED AREA OF THE UNITED STATES AND WERE CONFRONTED BY DANGERS AND NATURAL WONDERS, FRIGHTENING AND AT THE SAME TIME AWE-INSPIRING. HERE THE MEN GAVE ENDURING NAMES TO MOUNTAINS, RAPIDS, STREAMS, AND OTHER NATURAL LANDMARKS THAT NEVER BEFORE HAD BEEN SEEN BY WHITE MEN. EXCEPT FOR AN OCCASIONAL ABANDONED RANCH, DESOLATION CANYON IS VIRTUALLY UNCHANGED FROM ITS APPEARANCE IN 1869. THERE ARE NO PERMANENT RESIDENTS OF THE CANYON.

The Colorado River originates in the Colorado Rockies and flows 1,400 miles west before it reaches the Pacific Ocean at the Gulf of California, though so much water is impounded and diverted by the intervening states that only a thin sluggish salty flow actually reaches the Pacific. It is the second longest river in the 48 contiguous states outside the Mississippi River system; the Rio Grande is longer but carries less water. The Colorado River and its tributaries drain parts of seven western states—one-twelfth of the area of the 48 states or 242,000 square miles (almost three times the area of Utah). Its drainage basin is 900 miles in length and from 300 to 500 miles wide. If the drainage basin were not so arid, the river would have a much greater volume.

In Utah, with very few exceptions, the main Green and Colorado Rivers are almost completely entrenched in steep-walled canyons. Though the Colorado-Green river system drains almost half of the entire state, less than 10 percent of Utah's people reside within its basin.

The Colorado above its junction with the Green was

known as the Grand until 1921, when the name was changed. From Moab downstream to the junction, a distance of 68 miles, the river's flow is almost unobstructed, making it navigable (usually) by powered craft during spring runoff months. At other times it is more suited to rafts or jet-powered craft. Upstream the river is popular for pleasure boating in rafts, canoes, or kayaks.

Much farther upstream, just west of the Utah-Colorado line, Westwater Canyon offers a challenging white-water experience. Here in this 17-mile canyon there are nearly a dozen rapids, several of which compare with the most dangerous cataracts of Grand or Cataract Canyons. The cliffs of Westwater Canyon are partially formed of dark metamorphic gneisses, nearly two billion years in age, the oldest exposed rocks in eastern Utah. They represent the exposed Precambrian spine of the ancient Uncompahgre Uplift. BLM rangers are on duty at the canyon's launch point south of Harley Dome from April through October. Permits and reservations are required; these and boating information may be obtained at BLM offices in Moab.

The following history is quoted from the 1941 edition:

ALMOST WITHOUT EXCEPTION, EXPLORATIONS OF THE COLORADO RIVER BY BOAT HAVE STARTED AT SOME POINT ON THE GREEN. IN 1889, HOWEVER, FRANK M. BROWN LED A PARTY DOWN THE UPPER COLORADO RIVER TO MAKE A PRELIMINARY SURVEY FOR A "WATER-LEVEL" RAILROAD ROUTE FROM COLORADO TO CALIFORNIA. THE PARTY SET OUT FROM GRAND JUNCTION, COLORADO, AND REACHED THE CONFLUENCE OF THE COLORADO AND THE GREEN WITHOUT MISHAPS. BELOW THE JUNCTION, BROWN WAS SWEPT TO HIS DEATH IN THE SOAP CREEK RAPIDS. THE REORGANIZED PARTY CONTINUED TO NEEDLES, CALIFORNIA, REPORTING THE ROUTE IMPRACTICAL BECAUSE OF PERIODIC FLOODS.

THE UINTA BASIN

The Uinta Basin is not, strictly speaking, a basin at all, since its runoff waters eventually reach the ocean by way of the Green and Colorado Rivers, or would if the Colorado still reached the ocean instead of being reduced to a salty trickle by agricultural irrigation when it finally reaches the Gulf of California. The basin is a vast and largely roadless stretch of arid land without a single major settlement. There is no paved road between 191 near the west boundary of the basin and the Colorado line on the east, nor between Route 40 on the north and Interstate 70 at the south end of the basin, except for two fairly short stretches of pavement leading south from Route 40. Route 88, about halfway between Roosevelt and

Vernal, takes the traveler to Ouray, the Ouray National Wildlife Refuge, and the northern end of the oddly shaped Uintah and Ouray Reservation. After Ouray, it splits into two unpaved roads, one leading east to the town of Bonanza and the other continuing south as the Seep Ridge Road, which crosses the East Tavaputs Plateau and eventually intersects a network of unimproved primitive roads that rejoin I-70.

Route 45, the other paved road, leaves 40 at Naples and heads through some unpopulated country until it comes to Bonanza. A short distance south of Bonanza the pavement stops and the road continues south, eventually crossing into Colorado north of Baxter Pass. This was the route of a narrow-gauge railroad from Mack, Colorado, to the Gilsonite mines at Dragon and Rainbow. Gilsonite is an asphalt-like mineral found in commercial quantities only in the Uinta Basin. It was named after Samuel Gilson, who encouraged its commercial development. A more complete description of Dragon, Rainbow, and the related ghost towns of Ignatio and Watson, can be found in Stephen L. Carr's book *The Historical Guide to Utah Ghost Towns.* (For more on the Ouray National Wildlife Refuge, Ouray, and Bonanza, see Chapter 5.)

THE BOOK CLIFFS
Green River via Route 6

Southeast of Price, Route 6 traverses an arid region of low bluffs and shallow washes, its drab desolation relieved here and there by the greenery of farms, streamside vegetation, and a scattering of stunted evergreens. Even the great Book Cliffs, looming to the north as a facade for high plateaus, do little to break the monotony of this wasteland; despite their magnitude, they are but bare rock of somber hue. Yet the impression for many travelers is one of grandeur, conveying a powerful sense of the inconceivable ages involved in the building up and tearing down of earth's crust in this region.

The Book and Roan Cliffs to the north and east give no hint to the traveler of the mineral wealth they contain. These great ramparts form one of the most impressive series of escarpments in America, extending in a 200-mile semicircle from Emery to Price to Colorado. Buried in the cliffs are layers of bituminous coal, rock asphalt, and oil shale. Farther north, their rocks contain tar sands, Gilsonite, and liquid petroleum.

Wellington (5,400 alt.) is a farming, trade, and residential center. Turn south from Wellington a short distance to wells that have produced most of Utah's natural carbon dioxide gas for many years.

North from Route 6, at a junction 3 miles east of Wellington, a paved road leads 13 miles to the modern coal mining complex of Soldier Creek Mining Company. North from the mine, the road (now unpaved but suitable for passenger cars) continues over a summit into Nine Mile Canyon. Winding along the canyon bottom for some 20 miles, the main road exits Nine Mile through Gate Canyon. Eventually it enters the grand expanse of the Uinta Basin, crossing 20 miles or so of open badlands before joining Route 40 two miles west of Myton and about 70 miles from its southern terminus at Route 6. Surmounted here and there by snowcapped peaks that hint of others not seen, the bulk of the Uinta Mountains stretches across the northern horizon for a hundred miles.

This route is one of Utah's fascinating side road drives, not only because of exceptional scenery but for its glimpses into the romantic past. Ranch buildings, corrals, and farm equipment are scattered along the valley floor. Cattle graze by the hundreds in fields of alfalfa. This was the main route of travel for 40 years between the Uinta Basin and the railroad at Price, a lifeline over which wagons, stages, buggies, mounted riders, and myriad livestock traveled in endless parade. Most of the land-rush settlers of 1905–6 used this route. First improved as a main road during the 1880s by army troops from Fort Duchesne, the route was only gradually replaced in early decades of this century by the Uintah Railway and improved roads through Indian Canyon and Daniels Canyon. Few original mementos of early freighting days have been preserved.

Of special interest to visitors are Nine Mile Canyon's Indian antiquities, more particularly its numerous petroglyphs or rock etchings, which can be seen on smooth rock faces beside and near the road for 20 miles or more. A detailed folder describing the location of points of interest in the canyon is available from the Carbon County Travel Council, 625 East 100 North, Price, Utah 84501. Remember: antiquities are protected by federal and state laws. The canyon is listed on the state Register of Historic Places because of its outstanding Indian antiquities.

At Sunnyside Junction, 17 miles from Price, turn east on Route 123 to East Carbon City and Sunnyside.

East Carbon City (6,000 alt.), formerly known as Dragerton, was a commercial and residential center for large coal mines operated at Sunnyside by Kaiser Steel Corporation and at Horse Canyon by U.S. Steel. The community flows imperceptibly into Sunnyside. In earlier years, many of the area's miners and their families lived within Whitmore Canyon at old Sunnyside, but this was gradually replaced by newer communities outside the canyon.

The Sunnyside mines produced more than 50 million tons of coal. Kaiser Steel became a lessee operator in 1942 during World War II, and later purchased the local mines. Most of the mines have been closed for at least ten years; the Sunnyside Mine closed in 1993. Up-canyon from Sunnyside, the road continues in steep switchbacks onto upper levels of the West Tavaputs (Roan) Plateau with lush alpine meadows and forests, entering private lands and terminating at the dizzy rim of a gorge that plunges 5,000 feet into Desolation Canyon.

Turn south from East Carbon City via Route 124 to Columbia (6,400 alt.), a tree-shrouded village high on a hillside, built in the early 1920s as a model town to house miners supplying coking coal to the Columbia Steel Plant at Ironton. From the Columbia turnoff, Route 124 continues five miles to the Horse Canyon (Geneva) Mine of the U.S. Steel Corporation. Dating from 1942–43 during World War II, the Geneva mine was developed to provide coking coal for the huge Geneva Works at Orem as well as other markets. Beyond the mine, an unpaved road climbs steeply up Horse Canyon and over a shoulder of imposing Patmos Head (9,851 alt.) into Range Valley, one of the deepest and most spectacular side gorges of Green River's Desolation Canyon.

Woodside (4,600 alt.) is now only a stop on the highway beside the Price River. Originally Woodside was a farming community known as Lower Crossing, first settled in the 1880s. According to Stephen L. Carr, there were vegetable and turkey farms, and it was a center for cattlemen, sheepmen, and railroaders. By World War I it had become a modest community with shops and a school; then, with drought, changes in railroad operations, and the fading of livestock operations, the town disappeared.

South of Woodside the Book Cliffs pinch closer to the rise of the San Rafael Swell, with the Beckwith Plateau looming high above, an aerial island enclosed by canyons and cliffs. Beckwith, chronicler to the Gunnison expedition of 1853, described the scene:

THIS MOUNTAIN WALL . . . IS VERY IRREGULAR; DEEP RAVINES AND GORGES EXTEND BACK INTO IT, GIVING IT . . . THE APPEARANCE OF AN UNFINISHED FORTIFICATION, ON A SCALE WHICH IS PLEASING TO THE IMAGINATION, AND CONTRASTS THE WORKS OF MEN STRONGLY WITH THOSE OF NATURE. . . . DESOLATE AS IS THE COUNTRY OVER WHICH WE HAVE JUST PASSED, AND AROUND US, THE VIEW IS STILL ONE OF THE MOST BEAUTIFUL AND PLEASING I REMEMBER TO HAVE SEEN. AS WE APPROACHED THE RIVER YESTERDAY, THE RIDGES ON EITHER OF ITS BANKS TO THE WEST APPEARED BROKEN INTO A THOUSAND FORMS—COLUMNS, SHAFTS, TEMPLES, BUILDINGS, AND RUINED CITIES COULD BE SEEN, OR IMAGINED, FROM THE HIGH POINTS ALONG OUR ROUTE.

Four miles from Woodside a dirt road forks west, winding through the northern breaks of the Swell to Buckhorn Flat and Castle Dale, paralleling closely in places the route of the Old Spanish Trail. The route was also used as a cutoff for considerable travel between Castle Valley and central Utah and points east, even after the railroad was built to Price.

Green River

Green River (4,100 alt.) occupies both banks of the stream after which it is named. Today it is a sprawling, bustling, growing community, but its people are realistic about future prospects because the town's hundred-year history has been one of alternating growth and decline—growth from railroading, cattle and sheep, farming, uranium and oil, highway construction, land development, a missile base, tourism, and river recreation—contrasted with the bust when boom conditions changed.

New Mexicans, traveling the Old Spanish Trail in the 1830s and 1840s, crossed the Green River at a ford several miles north of the present highway. Their ford, an Indian crossing, was used in ensuing years by the Gunnison survey party (giving birth to the name Gunnison's Crossing, used for many years thereafter), and by countless other travelers until the railroad was completed in the early 1880s.

The town's history to 1940 was summarized in the first edition of this book:

SETTLED IN 1878, THE TOWN WAS A MAIL RELAY STATION BETWEEN SALINA, UTAH, AND OURAY, COLORADO, UNTIL THE RIO GRANDE WESTERN RAILROAD ENTERED IN 1882. WITH THE COMING OF THE RAILROAD, A SHORT-LIVED LAND BOOM HIT THE LITTLE SETTLEMENT. IN AN INTERVIEW CHRIS HALVERSON STATED THAT HE AND HIS BROTHER CAUGHT 180 BEAVER THE FIRST WINTER, SELLING THE HIDES FOR 50¢ TO $1.50. PROSPECTORS FOUND GOLD IN THE REGION, BUT IT WAS "FLOUR" GOLD, TOO FINE TO SIFT OUT. EASTERN FARMERS TRIED TO IRRIGATE WITH WATER FROM THE GREEN RIVER. THE RIVER WAS HARD TO HANDLE—IT STILL IS—AND CROP AFTER CROP FLOODED OUT. THE FEW WHO SUCCEEDED TOOK LAND ALONG SMALL STREAMS THAT COULD BE CONTROLLED. MELON-GROWING BEGAN IN 1917, BUT IT WAS NOT UNTIL 1926 THAT LOCAL MELONS REACHED NEW YORK CITY, WHERE THEY HAVE SINCE COMMANDED PREMIUM PRICES.

The town's melons have been appreciated by epicures ever since and may be obtained from roadside stands in season.

On the east side of the river, between 1963 and 1979, a large missile testing operation was active at the Utah Launch Complex. Employing hundreds of workers at times, the complex was the principal off-range facility of the White Sands Missile Range. During its operational life it supervised the assembly, testing, and firing of several hundred Athena and Pershing missiles between Green River and White Sands, 400 miles away.

Green River State Park, on the west bank of the river, is a 50-acre public development featuring camping facilities, toilets, showers, water, fireplaces, boat ramp, and dock. Open year-round. This unusual park is the starting point for private and commercial boating tours through the canyons of the Green and the rapids of Cataract Canyon below the confluence with the Colorado, exiting at Hite Marina on Lake Powell.

The John Wesley Powell River History Museum at 885 East Main in Green River displays replicas of the various kinds of boats used to explore the rivers of the West, including the one in which Powell made the first European exploration of the Colorado River canyons.

THE SAN RAFAEL SWELL

A classic geological phenomenon, the San Rafael Swell is an oval-shaped uplift that has been so severely eroded over time that its inclined flanks form a saw-toothed ridge or reef completely encircling a central elevated core, known by early geologists as Red Amphitheater but today called Sinbad Country. Nature has sculptured the Swell's multicolored rocks into a multitude of strange forms. The Swell is remarkable also because it exhibits within a compact area many of the landscape and structural characteristics of the much larger Canyonlands region.

In 1941 the interior of the Swell was isolated and remote, little visited by anyone other than stockmen. Since then, Interstate 70 has been built, crossing the Swell from east to west, cutting it almost exactly in half. Yet much of it, away from the highway, remains almost as unknown to the public at large as it was in 1941.

Clouds float over the San Rafael River, as viewed from the Wedge Overlook, San Rafael Swell – Frank Jensen, UTC

The Swell North of I-70

Buckhorn Flat, an expansive flat lying between Red Plateau (Cedar Mountain) and the San Rafael River-Buckhorn Wash breaks, is traversed by the access road from Castle Dale. The flat is notable for having been a route of transport for 150 years, first as a section of the Old Spanish Trail and the route of American explorers following that trail, then as a freighting and mail route between Colorado, Green River, and Castle Valley towns. It was also the original proposed route of the D&RGW Railroad west from Green River in the early 1880s (more than $200,000 was spent in surveying and grading in the vicinity before the route was abandoned) and the escape route of Butch Cassidy and Elza Lay after the Castle Gate robbery of 1897. In later years it was

the main route of travel from Castle Dale into the interior of the Swell.

The Wedge Overlook (junction 13 miles along the main road east of Castle Dale, then 8 miles south from the junction) affords a series of panoramic views from the upper edge of the spectacular San Rafael gorge, 600 feet above the winding river. The topography is one of naked rock, painted in shades of red, carved into a maze of steep-walled canyons, cliffs, and some of Utah's most splendid freestanding buttes.

Buckhorn Draw or Wash is a deep red-rock gorge cut into the northern flank of the Swell. The draw extends some ten miles from Buckhorn Flat (15 miles east of Castle Dale) southeastward to its mouth in the interior of the Swell at the San Rafael River. In its upper reaches, the draw is shallow, but it deepens rapidly and its walls grow higher until they exceed a thousand feet at the river. In its ten-mile course the draw descends through 75 million years of geological history, from late Jurassic rocks at the upper end to early Triassic at the river. In rock structure and erosional characteristics, Buckhorn Wash resembles numberless other gorges of Canyonlands, but it is more easily accessible than most, marvelous by any standards, a cameo masterpiece that more than repays visitation.

Beside the road, about halfway through the draw, was a badly vandalized panel of prehistoric Indian cliff art. Mingled with and at times superimposed upon the Indian art were the names of travelers of historic times. Residents of Emery County retained art conservator Constance Silver to restore the panel. The canyon also contains pictographs (painted rock art) as well as a cave that served as shelter for prehistoric peoples. Buckhorn's antiquities are listed on the National Historic Register.

Clustered at the mouth of Buckhorn Wash is a majestic group of sandstone buttes, a miniature Monument Valley. These include Windowblind Peak, stateliest of all at more than 1,500 feet, as well as Assembly Hall and Bottleneck peaks. The river is crossed by a picturesque suspension bridge, and on the south bank of the river is an improved campground developed by the BLM.

The San Rafael River, named by New Mexicans traveling the Old Spanish Trail, is the combined product of Huntington, Cottonwood, Ferron, and other smaller streams. It empties into the Green River after slicing a series of deep and narrow canyons through the Swell. West of the mouth of Buckhorn Wash, its gorge can be viewed from The Wedge (see above). East of the mouth of Buckhorn Wash, it flows alternately through open country and entrenched chasms, one of which—the Black Box—is hundreds of feet deep and very narrow with almost sheer walls. Here the river cuts through the Swell's most ancient rocks, corresponding to those found at the upper levels of Arizona's Grand Canyon. East of Buckhorn Wash a primitive road follows the river along its north bank, leading to the Red Canyon and Spring Canyon labyrinth of cliffs and canyons. The road also gives access to the rim of Black Box.

South of Buckhorn Wash the road continues through high, open grazing country with widespread vistas across a broken

wonderland, finally joining I-70 at Sinbad Interchange some 44 miles from Castle Dale. Rough side roads lead off toward the Black Box, Mexican Mountain, and other parts of the Swell's rugged interior, known generally as Sinbad Country. South of I-70 the main access road continues on to Temple Mountain, Hondoo (Muddy River) country, and Route 24.

The Swell South of I-70

Route 24 parallels the San Rafael Reef, marking the eastern boundary of the San Rafael Swell. The Reef is a strikingly eroded monoclinal ridge of steeply inclined rocks of Jurassic age. All around is the sandy San Rafael Desert, apparently a wasteland but long used for cattle grazing. At Temple Mountain Junction (24 miles from Interstate 70), dirt roads fork west to Goblin Valley and Sinbad-Hondoo country, and east to Robbers Roost, Glen Canyon National Recreation Area, and Canyonlands National Park. Robbers Roost has gained widespread notoriety from legend, myth, and the writings of such authors as Zane Grey, Charles Kelly, and Pearl Baker. Its history is summarized in the files of the National Register of Historic Places:

NUMEROUS OUTLAWS BOTH VISITED HERE AND MADE THIS THEIR HEADQUARTERS. SOME OF THEM WERE BUTCH CASSIDY (ROBERT LEROY PARKER), THE SUNDANCE KID (HARRY LONGABAUGH), KID CURRY, HARVEY LOGAN, BILL CARVER, MATT WARNER, ELZA LAY, TOM AND BILL MCCARTY, BEN KILPATRICK, JOHN CARTER (C. L. "GUNPLAY" MAXWELL), "BLUE JOHN" (JOHN GRIFFITH), AND "SILVER TIP" (JAMES F. HOWELLS). THESE AND OTHERS USED THIS AREA AS A HIDEOUT WHILE EVADING THE LAW. THE AREA WAS USED FOR THIS PURPOSE FROM 1875 UNTIL 1905. THIS PARTICULAR SPOT AFFORDED EXCELLENT PROTECTION FROM SURPRISE AS WELL AS PROVIDING GOOD POTABLE WATER. MANY OF THE HORSES RUSTLED BY THE OUTLAWS WERE HELD HERE UNTIL THEY COULD SAFELY BE SOLD IN GRAND JUNCTION OR DURANGO, COLORADO. THE CATTLE THAT WERE RUSTLED WERE HELD UP ON ROOST FLATS UNTIL THEY TOO COULD BE SOLD. NOT A SINGLE LAWMAN ENTERED THE ROOST TO CAPTURE ANY OF THE OUTLAWS.

Since its outlaw days the Roost has been used as a cattle range, in particular by the Biddlecome family (of which writer Pearl Baker was a member) and the Ekker family, related to the Biddlecomes by marriage.

Horseshoe Canyon (now a part of Canyonlands National Park), in the area of Robbers Roost, is known for its Indian rock art. This vast wedge between the Green and Dirty Devil Rivers is rather gently contoured for the most part; its gorges are not too apparent from the road. Close to the rivers, however, where Lands End Plateau breaks away in a sinuous vertical wall known as the Orange Cliffs, gentle contours dissolve into a confusing maze of steep-walled canyons, cliffs, buttes, and numberless smaller erosional forms. In complexity and red-rock grandeur, this region matches any other part of Canyonlands. Part of the area is the Land of Standing Rocks, western counterpart of the Needles, which together form one of the world's strangest landscapes: the inner Junction country where the Green and upper Colorado Rivers join near the head of Cataract Canyon. (See also Glen Canyon National Recreation Area and Canyonlands National Park.)

From a base south of Temple Mountain Junction and east of Gilson Buttes, army missile tests were conducted during the 1960s. A temporary camp was occupied by hundreds of artillery troops training in the firing of solid-propellant Pershing missiles from Utah to White Sands Missile Range in New Mexico, 400 miles away.

The San Rafael Reef is prominently visible from the east from I-70, Route 6, or from Route 24, which parallels the reef between I-70 and Temple Mountain Junction. Its incised whaleback slope is toward the east; high cliffs form its broken western face inside the Swell. I-70 passes through one of the reef's canyons just south of the canyon of the San Rafael River, and the road to Temple Mountain passes through another. Some of the reef's canyons harbor excellent examples of prehistoric Indian rock art.

Temple Mountain, a prominent and distinctive butte visible for many miles, juts high above the crest of San Rafael Reef. Temple Mountain has been known since early years of the century as a rich repository of vanadium and uranium. It is said that uranium used in the first atomic bomb came from there, and it was the scene of extensive mining during the uranium rush of the 1950s. Today the butte and abutting cliffs are pocked with tunnels and shallow caves (danger, use care!); these and assorted ruins attest to former glory days. The area is reached by a short paved road from Route 24 from junction 21 miles north of Hanksville, the side road passing through San Rafael Reef in a short but narrow gash of a canyon. In this canyon, high on the north wall and visible from the road, is a small panel of prehistoric Indian pictographs, somewhat vandalized but still of interest.

Goblin Valley State Park, on the eastern outer flanks of the Swell, was created to protect one of the most extraordinary concentrations of eroded rocks in America. The valley—

actually a long, narrow, shallow basin enclosed between low but fantastically sculptured cliffs extending for miles—contains countless chocolate-colored "goblin" rocks of varying size. Many of the rocks are freestanding and precariously balanced, and the valley floor consists of soft mudstone and sand that retain the impressions of feet and tires.

The main side road continues north from Temple Mountain, rising with a bulge of the Swell's cliff-ringed interior. This great amphitheater, 30 miles long from north to south and 15 miles wide, has long been known locally as Sinbad Country, though the name's origin is unknown. Since pioneer days it has been utilized for stock grazing, and until recent years it was not uncommon to see wild horses in the area. It is now a favored backcountry hiking area.

Hondoo-Muddy River Country is easily reached from Interstate 70 (Sinbad Interchange) or Route 24 (Temple Mountain); the unpaved road is suitable for passenger cars in dry weather. In general the area resembles that at the mouth of Buckhorn Wash (above), consisting of giant cliffs, deep canyons, and great buttes. Yet it differs in erosional design and coloring, and perhaps exhibits a wider variety of natural forms. The access road forms a loop, beginning near Family Butte, which may be traveled in either direction, in both cases descending rather precipitously from the heights of Sinbad Country into the drainage maze of Muddy River (more technically Muddy Creek). Scenic views along the way are superb. About halfway along the loop at imposing Tomsich Butte—the site of sporadic uranium mining dating from rush years of the 1950s to the present time—the Muddy enters the interior of the Swell through a deep canyon. Cliffs here are a thousand feet high or more, beautifully sculptured and painted in subdued hues. Hondoo Arch, at the top of a cliff across the river from Tomsich Butte, is the dominant feature.

Fremont Junction to Colorado via I-70

Known as the "Main Street of America," Interstate 70 was almost an afterthought in planning the interstate highway system in Utah. The highway bisects the nation in an east-west line from Washington, D.C., to Cove Fort, Utah, where it joins Interstate 15 and continues to southern California.

Interstate 70 parallels the Book Cliffs from Green River to the Colorado line. From Fremont Junction, the highway bisects the rocky fastnesses of the San Rafael Swell, a wild and broken country hardly known to the outside world before the highway came. Initial construction of the San Rafael segment began in the 1960s, with formal opening of 70 miles of two east-west lanes in late 1970. At that time the state Department of Highways proclaimed it the "longest section of new interstate through previously untouched territory to be opened in this century."

Nine miles east of Fremont Junction, the highway passes through Devil's Canyon in one of the most scenic stretches of road on the interstate system. The San Rafael Swell stretches north and south of the road—primitive, unsettled, much as it was before Utah was inhabited.

Between Green River and the Colorado line, the road passes through low ridges and across barren plains, with the Book Cliffs to the north. Almost the only signs of human habitation are at Crescent Junction, Thompson, and Cisco.

Crescent Junction (4,800 alt.) is at the junction of I-70 with Route 191, which leads south to Moab. A single service station marks the intersection.

Thompson Springs (5,100 alt.), now located away from the highway, is a small ranching center, formerly a railroad watering point and highway stop.

Turn north from Thompson to Sego Canyon Indian Writings (3 miles) and the ghost town of Sego (5 miles). A group of prehistoric pictographs and petroglyphs, badly vandalized, is on the cliffs beside the road. Sego, a coal mining town that is now deserted, had a population of 200 in 1940 and more than twice that many in prior decades.

Cisco (4,400 alt.), now bypassed by the highway, consists of a few houses and corrals. According to the 1941 edition of this book, Cisco "was built . . . by the Denver & Rio Grande Western Railroad to serve sheep and cattle ranchers."

Cisco was the temporary home of Charles A. Steen, the storied uranium millionaire, and his family when he first hit pay dirt at the Mi Vida mine south of Moab. At that time (1952) the Steens were flat broke, living in a tar-paper shack and ready to call it quits.

In the general vicinity of Cisco is one of Utah's most interesting historical inscriptions, carved on a smooth rock face in 1837 by Antoine Robidoux, a trapper-trader who was en route to the Uinta Basin to establish the first permanent settlement by whites in Utah. The translated inscription (written in French) reads: "Antoine Robidoux passed here 13

November 1837 to establish a trading house on the Vert (Green) or Winte (Uinta) River."

South from Cisco, Route 128 descends to the canyon of the Colorado River, which it follows to Moab. This route provides views of some of the most stirring river, red rock, and mountain scenery in Utah, and is the longest riverside scenic drive along the Colorado for hundreds of miles.

Harley Dome, 6 miles west of the Colorado line, takes its name from a geological structure that contains natural gas having a rich helium content. The wells were capped in the l920s and set aside in a federal reserve, and though regulations now allow commercial production, this has not taken place. Helium also has been found near Woodside, west of Green River. A road leads south from Harley Dome to the embarkation area of Westwater Canyon, where boaters launch their craft for downstream expeditions through a series of exciting rapids.

SPANISH VALLEY
Moab and Vicinity via Route 191 South

The peaks of the La Sal Mountains loom ever higher as the traveler approaches the Colorado River. Immediately to the east, the ragged slopes of the Salt Valley Anticline form a dramatic horizon, breaking away in places to reveal the rock sculptures of Arches National Park. Drab, monotonous plains on the west become transformed, almost imperceptibly, into a shattered region of blocky buttes and mesas, and grand cliffs painted in rainbow colors. Here, for the first time in this area, the unique personality of Canyonlands—that central core of the vast Colorado Plateau Province—becomes apparent.

West of the highway near the Moab airport, connecting with 191 and with Route 313 leading to Dead Horse Point and Canyonlands National Park, a complex of fair-weather dirt roads gives access to cliff-edge viewpoints, gorges, and a marvelous world of red-rock forms, of natural bridges and arches, buttes and pinnacles, spires, goblin rocks, and other erosional curiosities. This strange region—a rugged peninsula between the Green and Colorado Rivers attracts increasing numbers of off-road vehicles as its adventure opportunities become better known. Many miles of the area's dirt roads may be negotiated by ordinary pickup trucks or even passenger cars.

Route 313 forks west from Route 191 at a point 21 miles south of Crescent Junction and 13 miles north of Moab. This hard-surfaced, all-weather road climbs through Seven-mile

*Reflections along the
Colorado River west of Moab
– François Camoin*

Canyon to open flats at nearly 6,000 feet altitude, leading to Dead Horse Point State Park and Island in the Sky, the north district of Canyonlands National Park, both 20-odd miles from Route 191.

The entrance to Arches National Park is near the south end of Moab Canyon, 5 miles north of Moab, marked by a Visitor Center and other park buildings (see Arches National Park in parks section for details). The park's main attractions are above and behind the east wall of the canyon, reached by a steeply switchbacking access road that affords choice overviews of the Colorado River, Moab, Spanish Valley, and the La Sals.

One mile south of the park entrance is the junction with Route 279, a paved highway following the north bank of Colorado River downstream to a potash mine, and from there as an unpaved road to White Rim Drive, Shafer Trail, and Canyonlands National Park. The large industrial plant near the junction is the uranium reduction plant of Atlas Corporation, which has processed much of the area's uranium production since the mid-1950s. The mill was built at a cost of $8 million by Charles A. Steen, the uranium king, to process ore from his Mi Vida mine; later it was purchased by Atlas Corporation. It is now being torn down, and the mildly radioactive remains of what was once a thriving industrial site are being carted away.

A long highway bridge, built in 1954 to replace a one-lane bridge, crosses the Colorado River. This in turn replaced ferryboats operated since the 1880s. Travelers on the Old Spanish Trail, and others before the ferry was built, crossed the river several hundred yards downstream (west) from the bridge. This was a hazardous, sometimes fatal undertaking.

From the south end of the bridge, Route 128 leads upstream to Castle Valley, Fisher Towers, Dewey Bridge, and I-70 at Cisco interchange.

Moab

Moab (4,000 alt., 4,488 pop.), seat of Grand County, is the commercial center of an extensive mining and livestock country. Since 1930 or so, Moab has achieved considerable importance as a center for scenic and recreational attractions, as well as a reputation for being a regional cultural center (the visual and performing arts, crafts, museum, etc.). For 30 years it was the uranium capital of Utah, and the onetime home of

Charles A. Steen, whose mansion home is now a restaurant, can be seen from the highway north of town, atop a knoll.

In the 1941 edition of this book, Moab was described as having "a small business district, selling everything from hay and gasoline to malted milk and liquor—the only 'legal' liquor in the county. Squat red adobe houses stand neighbor to more pretentious firebrick houses. In the evening neon lights illuminate the business district, but after midnight, except on Saturdays, the town does a complete blackout." Since then the city's business district has expanded greatly, sprawling mainly north and south along the highway, and residential areas have sprouted across the valley floor. Much of this expansion dates from the 1950s when Moab became a uranium boomtown. Charlie Steen (see below) was not the first prospector to find uranium in the Moab vicinity, by any means, nor the only large operator. The uranium rush following World War II had been gaining momentum throughout the entire Four Corners region for several years before his bonanza strike. But the Mi Vida find was of such magnitude that it drew worldwide attention, serving as a beacon for thousands of hopeful prospectors and tens of thousands of penny stock speculators. Moab rode the uranium wave to its crest in the late 1950s, then descended to more stable levels in the 1960s. The city never has returned to anything resembling its pre-uranium rusticity.

Tourism as an industry was stimulated by the creation of Canyonlands National Park and the advancement of Arches from national monument to national park. River boating has increased in popularity over the years. Several commercial tour operations are based in Moab, offering tours by boat, four-wheel-drive vehicles, airplane, and helicopter. Moab advertises itself as a jeeping capital. The Chamber of Commerce sponsors an annual Jeep Safari on Easter weekend, which attracts as many as 200 jeeps, and also a Four-Wheeler Campout on Labor Day. The city has also become a nationally known center for mountain bikers.

Ascending the broken sandstone ledges east of Moab are several popular trails suitable for trail bikes and other off-road vehicles. Passing through scenic red-rock terrain high above Moab they provide spectacular views of valleys, river, canyons, and myriad exotic erosional forms. One branch tops out on Porcupine Rim, 2,000 feet above Castle Valley. Another spur is the Moab Slickrock Bike Trail, a ten-mile marked route across stretches of naked slickrock to bird's-eye overlooks.

High on a red hill beside the highway north of town is the modernistic mansion built by Charlie Steen, uranium multimillionaire, whose rags-to-riches-and-back-again story has been the stuff of legend for three decades. The home was built by Steen and his wife M. L. in the mid-1950s, shortly after Charlie's discovery of the Mi Vida bonanza 30 miles south of Moab. He and his family resided there for about ten years until he moved to Nevada and built an elaborate mansion near Reno. During their residence in Moab, the Steens hosted lavish parties at the mansion, often attended by Hollywood celebrities and other dignitaries.

The Dan O'Laurie Museum, 185 East Center, contains exhibits having to do with the history, archaeology, geology, and economy of the area. Among its permanent exhibits are Indian artifacts, mineral specimens, and gemstones. The museum also has a gallery that displays the work of local artists.

Moab's historical background was summarized in the 1941 edition of this book, as follows:

THE FIRST ATTEMPT TO SETTLE MOAB VALLEY CAME IN 1855, WITH ESTABLISHMENT OF A MISSION IN THE ELK MOUNTAINS (NOW THE LA SALS). ADVANCE PREPARATIONS WERE MADE IN 1854, WHEN FIVE WAGON-LOADS OF PROVISIONS WERE CACHED IN THE VALLEY. THE FOLLOWING SPRING, THE CHURCH CALLED FORTY-ONE MEN TO ESTABLISH THE MISSION. THE GROUP LEFT GREAT SALT LAKE CITY IN MAY, TAKING WITH THEM FIFTEEN WAGONS, THIRTEEN HORSES, SIXTY-FIVE OXEN, SIXTEEN COWS, TWO BULLS, ONE CALF, TWO PIGS, TWELVE CHICKENS, FOUR DOGS, FLOUR, WHEAT, OATS, CORN, POTATOES, PEAS, FIVE PLOWS, TWENTY-TWO AXES, AND OTHER TOOLS.

By mid-July the men had planted crops and built a stone fort. They held friendly meetings with the Indians, converted and baptized some of them.

During late September, Indians killed three of the Mormons in a series of sudden attacks and set fire to haystacks and log fences. The missionaries abandoned the fort the next morning "without eating breakfast." They departed so hurriedly that water was left running in the irrigation canal from Mill Creek. Water continued to run through this ditch year after year until eventually it carved an arroyo twenty-five feet deep.

The next settlers were probably two brothers, George and Silas Green, who brought 400 cattle into the valley about 1875. They were apparently killed by Indians. In the summer of 1877 two prospectors, William "Nigger Bill" Granstaff, a mulatto, and a French-Canadian known only as "Frenchie"

took possession of the fort and laid claim to the valley. In 1878 A. G. Wilson made a trade with Frenchie for his land, but when he returned with his family the following spring, the Frenchman had traded the same land to Walter Moore, and had left the valley. The mulatto, however, remained until 1881. In that year the settlers had their last trouble with the Indians. A canyon outside Moab was named for Granstaff, but in line with contemporary sensitivity it is now known on the maps as "Negro Bill Canyon."

A post office was established in 1879, and a committee chose the Biblical name Moab for the town. Grand County was created in 1890, and Moab was named the county seat.

~ Dead Horse Point State Park ~

Dead Horse Point State Park perches atop the rim of the Orange Cliffs escarpment, a magnificent line of sheer wingate sandstone cliffs that trace a serpentine boundary of perhaps 500 miles around the inner Junction Country where the Green and upper Colorado Rivers merge. In 1941 the point was on the edge of a "howling wilderness," hardly marked by man and little known even to natives. Today it is a state park with a visitor center and campground. The river below is traversed by hundreds of boats, the roads by thousands of vehicles, and the eastern foreground includes some large mineral evaporation ponds. Despite intrusion by the works of men, the view from Dead Horse Point remains one of Utah's soul-stirring erosional panoramas.

The origin of the name of Dead Horse Point is probably a better index to its character than any description. A band of wild desert ponies was herded onto the point, the best of the "broomtails" were culled for "cow service," and the rest were left to return to the range. Confused by the peculiar topography of the point, the horses wandered around in circles, and eventually died of thirst in full view of the Colorado River, half a mile away but straight down.

Visitors are sternly cautioned to keep back from the rim. Several persons have been killed by falling over the edge—a vertical drop of 400 feet or so.

Turn south from Route 313, 8 miles north of Dead Horse Point, to Island in the Sky, the north district of Canyonlands National Park, separated from other sections of the park by fearsomely rugged terrain. (See Canyonlands National Park for further details.)

- Potash Railroad -

South of the junction with Route 313, Route 191 continues toward Moab through a region of high red cliffs and breaks. It is paralleled on the west by the "Potash Railroad," a spur of the D&RGW Railroad, especially built in the 1960s to service the potash mine of Texasgulf Inc., downriver from Moab. Toward the east are the strange rock forms of Arches National Park, and remnants of the old highway can be seen nearby, more closely following the route of Moab's pioneers through Moab Canyon.

Moab Canyon is formed along a prominent fault, or break, in the earth's crust, which raised the rock formations on the west and lowered the corresponding strata on the east, separating identical rocks on either side of the canyon by 2,000 feet or more.

Route 279 (the Potash Road) forks from Route 191 near the remains of the Atlas Uranium Mill and follows the north bank of the winding Colorado to a potash mining operation, 15 miles from Route 191. Hikes may be taken into secluded side canyons and to picturesque natural arches, several of which can be seen from the road. Other attractions include dinosaur tracks and prehistoric petroglyphs. The pavement ends at the potash operation; this is the recommended road terminus for passenger cars. However, the dirt road beyond may be passable by ordinary vehicles for some miles farther, as it climbs higher above the river. (See Canyonlands National Park.) This unpaved extension is not without its hazards. Some years ago newspapers reported the death of a woman who, after dark, had stepped from her car and immediately dropped over the edge of a high cliff.

- Scenic Drive Downriver to Kane Creek -

West from Route 191 in Moab, the Kane Creek access road leads through the river canyon's portal, then downstream along the Colorado's south bank, giving access to dramatically scenic cliff and canyon country that includes Moab Rim, Land Behind the Rocks, and Lockhart Basin. This is a popular area for off-road vehicles because roads are unpaved beyond the first four miles or so. Shallow streams must be forded; there are steep grades in places; and road surfaces may not be suitable at times for passenger car use. Normally, however, ordinary cars may be driven to Hurrah Pass.

At the Portal, according to the 1941 edition of this book,

"the Colorado pierces towering cliffs that surround the valley, and begins its long imprisoned journey through canyons thousands of feet deep. Along the route are natural bridges, arches, windows, buttes, pinnacles, monuments—a continuous, constantly-changing display of strange and remarkable formations carved in naked red rock."

About one mile inside the Portal, a very steep and rough side road (suitable only for off-road vehicles) winds up the cliff, topping out in Land Behind the Rocks, now a wilderness study area (also see below), with grand rim views of the river and its gorge, Moab and Spanish Valley, the La Sal Mountains, Arches, rims and mesas to the north, and the unearthly landscape of Behind the Rocks. Though relatively short (six miles one way), the drive is rewarding in scenic thrills.

About 4 miles from Route 191 the pavement ends as the road leaves the river gorge and turns south into Kane Creek Canyon. Near this point, Pritchett Canyon enters from the southeast. This narrow scenic gorge is the route of an off-road vehicle trail leading into Land Behind the Rocks, a compact but exceptionally rugged region of slickrock fins and domes and labyrinthine drainage channels, a maze of strange and beautiful erosional forms. Much of the area is difficult or impossible of access even to hikers. So rugged is it that one of its largest known arches was not discovered until 1970, and then only through aerial sighting. Behind the Rocks is bounded on the east by the sheer line of cliffs forming Spanish Valley's western face; on the other side its boundary is the gorge of Kane Creek. The area contains a dozen or so natural arches and bridges, best known of which is Pritchett Arch. The easiest access to Behind the Rocks is from Route 191, 13 miles south of Moab.

The main Kane Creek drive continues through a deep, serpentine gorge that is narrowly confined for the first few miles, then widens out. Spur roads lead to Hurrah Pass, a high ridge between Kane Creek Canyon and that of the Colorado; to Amasa Back, Chicken Corners, and Jackson Hole. Two longer trails extend southward from the Kane Creek Drive. One traverses the length of Kane Creek Canyon to Route 191 at Kane Springs rest area, 15 miles south of Moab. This is a distance of about 13 miles from the Hurrah Pass Junction. The other, much longer road (about 50 miles in length), known as Lockhart Basin Trail, loops around from Hurrah Pass to the south, following a broad terrace between the Colorado and a long line of towering cliffs, finally joining Route 211 (the Needles access road) near the Sixshooter Peaks.

– Scenic Drive Upriver to I-70 –

Route 128 to Castle Valley, Fisher Tower, Cisco, and La Sal Mountain Scenic Loop forks from Route 191 at the river, 3 miles north of Moab; it winds beside the Colorado for more than 30 miles. In places the road is confined between the river on one side and a high cliff on the other.

At a junction 16 miles from Route 191, turn south on paved road into Castle Valley, a pastoral basin cupped between high cliffs on two sides, the river and La Sal Mountains on the other two. Until recent years it was wide-open ranching country, and signs of human occupancy were scarce.

Just beyond the remnants of Castleton, a former mining town, the road divides. One fork leads eastward across the high slopes of the La Sals and drops into the Dolores River gorge en route to the historic mining town of Gateway, Colorado. The other road winds across the range's western shoulder to Route 191 and Moab as the La Sal Mountain Scenic Loop. Both drives offer superb alpine scenery and stirring panoramic views across the red wonderland of Canyonlands. From the Gateway road—which is graveled over most of its length but may be unsuitable for conventional autos at times—fair-weather dirt spurs (recommended for off-road vehicles or pickup trucks) lead to Adobe and Fisher mesas, which provide bird's-eye views of Castle Valley, Richardson Amphitheater and Fisher Valley. Another side road leads to Polar Mesa, connecting through Thompson Canyon with Fisher Valley and points beyond (see continuation of State 128 river drive below). Still other forks from the Gateway road lead into Beaver Basin and across Taylor Flat to a junction with the Geyser Pass Trail (below). It is recommended that detailed maps and guidebooks be obtained before traveling this sometimes confusing network of La Sal roads.

The La Sal Mountain Scenic Loop (partially paved) switchbacks south from Castleton to Harpole Mesa, overlooking Pinhook Valley, Castle Valley, the Colorado's gorge, and Arches National Park. Lyman Duncan wrote that "historic old Pinhook was the last battleground of Indians and whites [in the area] and still later the site of a mining boomtown. To the east winds the buggy road and trail leading into a beautiful little mountain retreat known as Miners Basin, the last hold-out of miners and prospectors in the La Sal Mountains. To the west, valley-like Pinhook is enclosed by a long sharp ridge known as Harpole Mesa, where Indians ambushed a posse of whites in 1881, killing ten men in the battle that followed.

Miners Basin was the site of frenetic activity during turn-of-the-century years, when it is said that as many as 200 persons resided there during summer months. The basin had a post office, restaurants and saloons, store, and other establishments. Gold was found but not in bonanza quantities, and the town was short-lived. Sporadic mining activity still continues.

Other side roads lead from the main loop drive to Warner and Oowah Lakes (forest campgrounds, fishing). The Sand Flats Trail leads back to Moab.

Geyser Pass (10,600 alt.), between Haystack Mountain and Mount Mellenthin, leads to Route 46 and Paradox, Colorado, and La Sal Pass. The main road eventually joins Route 191 south of Moab. The main loop road, open only from spring to late fall, usually is suitable for ordinary passenger cars (much of it is paved), but vehicles with high clearance and/or four-wheel-drive are recommended for side road travel.

From the Castle Valley turnoff, Route 128 continues upstream along the Colorado's canyon, which widens out into Professor Valley, with a serpentine alcove on the south known as Richardson Amphitheater. The Fisher Towers are visible for miles, a cluster of dark red spires rising from the soaring 2,000-foot-high south wall of the valley.

Just west of the short spur leading to the base of Fisher Towers (22 miles from Route 191), another unpaved side road winds south into the forbidding gorge of Onion Creek, following the creek along its tortuous path through one of the most fantastic areas of rock erosion in Utah.

Travelers with time and appropriate vehicles (conventional autos are not recommended) may continue through Fisher Valley to a complex of backcountry roads leading onto the La Sals in one direction, or in the other direction to Dolores River Overlook, Top-of-the-World Overlook, Powerpole Rim, and Route 128 at Dewey (see below).

Onion Creek's strange forms are carved from the moenkopi and cutler sandstone formations. Its rainbow colors are found mainly in exposed gypsum deposits. Vast quantities of gypsum and other salts were laid down millions of years ago in the Paradox Basin surrounding Moab, then covered by thousands of feet of younger deposits. Underground movement of these fluid minerals, including potash, was responsible for much of the Moab area's tortured terrain, creating or encouraging the creation of faults, anticlines, synclines, grabens, valleys, and canyons. Fisher Valley, Castle Valley, the anticlines of Arches National Park, Spanish and Moab Valleys, Paradox Valley, Upheaval Dome, and the sunken valleys (grabens) of the Needles—all these and more are the result of crustal deformation caused by movement of subterranean salt.

Beyond Fisher Towers, Route 128 continues along the river to Dewey, 31 miles from Route 191, a rustic old ranching hamlet where the road crosses the Colorado on a narrow, one-lane suspension bridge. At Dewey, the Colorado is joined by the Dolores River, which winds its tortuous way to the mother stream through deep and scenic canyons.

A fair-weather side road from Dewey climbs southeast into a rugged area known as Entrada Bluffs. The road crosses ridges and mesas, with a network of forks leading to the Dolores Canyon and Gateway, Colorado; to canyon overviews; Fisher Valley; Polar Mesa; the La Sal Mountains; and other points. It is possible to circle around through Fisher Valley and Onion Creek Canyon, emerging on Route 128 at Fisher Towers (see above). Of special note are two panoramic overview points not far from Dewey, reached from the Entrada Bluffs road. One tops out on Powerpole Rim, more than a thousand feet above the Colorado River and about 7 miles from Dewey. The other, known as Top-of-the-World Trail, leaves the main side road about 5 miles from Dewey and ascends another 5 miles to a high rim at 6,800 altitude, nearly 3,000 feet above the Colorado.

Route 128 continues north from Dewey, leaving the canyons and joining I-70 near Cisco, 47 miles from Route 191. En route, a side road forks west into the Yellowcat mining district.

San Juan Country
Four Corners Area via Route 191 South

South of Moab, Route 191 traverses the Spanish Valley, a semiarid graben or sunken basin thinly vegetated with brush and prickly pear. The valley's name refers to its use as a segment of the Old Spanish Trail from the 1830s to 1850s and perhaps even earlier. East of the highway loom the peaks of the La Sal Mountains, second highest range in the state, among the loveliest alpine groups of America. The La Sals (from the

Spanish word for "salt") were formed by laccolithic doming, the intrusion of igneous rock between underlying sedimentary beds. In this they resemble other island ranges of the Colorado Plateau: the Abajos, Henrys, Navajo Mountain (probably), and Ute Mountain in Colorado. The range is roughly 15 miles long and 6 miles wide, and high mesas radiating from the main mass cover a much larger area. Mount Peale, the highest peak, has an elevation of 12,721 feet. Half a dozen peaks exceed 12,000 feet, and several others are only slightly lower. Forests of pine, fir, and aspen cover the higher slopes; juniper (cedar), scrub oak, and brush grow on the lower slopes. The greater part of the range is included in the Manti-La Sal National Forest.

About 13 miles south of Moab, an unpaved road forks west to rugged, little-known Land Behind the Rocks and panoramic overlooks along the rim of Kane Creek Canyon, Pritchett Canyon, and junction with the Colorado River drive.

Several hundred yards along the highway from Kane Springs is Hole-in-Rock. In 1945, in the side of a great sandstone bluff, sculptor A. L. Christensen undertook the task, almost singlehandedly, of excavating 50,000 cubic feet of rock to create a cavern home and business establishment with 5,000 square feet of floor space. After his death in 1957, Gladys Christensen and other family members continued to exhibit the "mansion" as a visitor attraction and memorial. Both A. L. and Gladys are buried nearby. Open all year. Gift and rock shop, snack bar, tours.

Across the highway from Hole-in-Rock, a rough four-wheel-drive road enters Kane Creek Canyon and follows that gorge northward to the Colorado River and to Moab.

La Sal Junction, 22 miles from Moab, marks the junction of Route 191 with paved Route 46 leading east to Naturita and other points in Colorado. The junction is a popular wayside stop for ranchers, miners, and truckers.

Turn east on Route 46 to La Sal (7,125 alt.), a small ranching community settled in the 1930s when Old La Sal, 12 miles east, was abandoned because of frequent floods. La Sal is headquarters for Redd Ranches, a vast livestock operation that ranges thousands of sheep and cattle over a huge expanse of public and private land in Utah and Colorado. For years the town was almost synonymous with Charlie Redd, more than any other person its founder and vital spark for decades.

South of La Sal Junction, 1 mile, is another junction with

an unpaved road leading to Looking Glass Rock, a large opening in a rock dome (2 miles from Route 191). Wilson Arch, 3 miles south of La Sal Junction, beside the highway, is a sandstone wall through which a large opening has been eroded.

In Dry Valley, at a junction 11 miles south of La Sal Junction, a road leads westward across a wide expanse of gradually rising flats to the Canyon Rims Recreation Area (U. S. Bureau of Land Management). The access road is paved for the 22-mile distance to Needles Overlook, graded and maintained to two other developed areas to the north: Hatch Point Campground and Anticline Overlook.

The Canyon Rims area features aerial observation points along the rim of Hatch Point, a great peninsula with ragged edges, about 20 miles long but only a few miles wide. Circumscribed by precipitous cliffs up to 2,000 feet high, the Point is one among several islands of the Junction Country rock platforms jutting from the mainland, connected only by narrow causeways and surrounded by thin air. The Point's eastern rim overlooks Hatch Wash and Kane Creek Canyon, while its southern rim is formed by a chasm known as Hart's Draw. Its western edge, affording the grandest panorama, is a sinuous escarpment that serves as an outer wall of the Colorado's inner basin.

Viewpoints from the rim of Hatch Point are limited only by personal inclination, hiking ability, and time. Needles Overlook and other spots along the west rim overlook the heart of Canyonlands National Park, that unbelievably rugged Junction Country where the Green and Colorado Rivers meet, a weird region of naked rock where seeing is not necessarily believing. (See Canyonlands National Park.)

The Bureau of Land Management has developed a campground at Wind Whistle, beside the main side road 5 miles from Route 191. At Needles Overlook are picnic tables. There are camping units and a nature trail at Hatch Point Campground. Picnic tables, interpretive exhibits, and trails have been provided at Anticline Overlook, which some believe affords the finest overview of any rim point in the Canyonlands region.

East from Route 191 in the vicinity of the Canyon Rims junction, other side roads lead to Lisbon Valley and Big Indian mining districts, the location of enormously rich uranium mines, and the site of oil wells and copper deposits.

Nowadays, many of Utah's cowboys spend their time herding dudes – UTC

In 1952, at Big Indian, Charlie Steen found the bonanza uranium lode (Mi Vida—"My Life") that made him a multimillionaire. Other uranium mines such as that of Rio Algom began operations in the vicinity, making this Utah's single most productive uranium district over a period of decades. In the south end of Dry Valley, at the junction of Route 191 and Route 211 (13 miles north of Monticello), the bulbous symmetrical dome of Church Rock flanks the highway on the east, Sugar Loaf mound on the west. The latter, according to the 1941 edition, resembles a "gigantic loaf of bread. Its top is hollowed out by erosion, and in pioneer days teamsters stretched tarpaulins inside the depression to catch rain water for their horses."

– Newspaper Rock and Canyonlands –

Paved Route 211, main access to the south district of Canyonlands National Park, leads westward through a gap in a ridge, down into Indian Creek Canyon—past Newspaper Rock, Dugout Ranch, and the Sixshooter peaks—to pavement's end in the Needles. The decrepit wooden buildings beside Route 211 in the vicinity of the main highway are remnants of the former Home of Truth Colony, a religious community founded in 1933 by Mrs. Marie M. Ogden.

West of Photograph Gap, 3 miles from Route 191, Route 211 descends into Indian Creek Canyon, a grandly scenic sandstone gorge. Its sculptured walls, beautifully colored and surmounted by wondrous erosional forms, enclose an oasis of lush streamside vegetation and alfalfa fields. Indian Creek flows from the Abajo Mountains, a perennial stream that provides water for ranches along its course and, incidentally, for Blanding in the other direction, far to the south via a long diversion tunnel. The walls of the canyon are festooned with well-preserved petroglyphs and pictographs of varying antiquity, the most notable of which are displayed at Newspaper Rock (11 miles from Route 191). Newspaper Rock is a smooth rock face under a protective overhang, bearing at least 350 distinct Indian petroglyphs, some of them superim-

posed on others of earlier vintage. These are of differing age and cultural origin, ranging apparently from the Anasazi period of 800 years ago or more to the Ute era of the past century. Additions by whites also are present, but remoteness has prevented serious vandalism, and Newspaper Rock ranks among the state's archaeological treasures. Nearby is a campground with toilets. Carry drinking water.

About 8 miles farther along the canyon appear the green fields and shady groves of Dugout Ranch, nestled in a superlative setting of red cliffs and finger buttes. Dugout Ranch for many years was the headquarters of S&S (Scorup-Sommerville) Cattle Company, one of Utah's largest cattle empires, whose Canyonlands stock range surely ranks among the most fearsomely rugged and forbidding parts of America. J. A. Scorup was responsible for bulldozing the first vehicle road from Dugout Ranch into The Needles, including in the late 1940s the famed Elephant Hill jeep road that still remains a vehicle challenge more than 30 years later. Cave Spring, now a park attraction, was a Scorup cowboy camp. (See Canyonlands National Park.)

South from Dugout Ranch an unpaved road climbs through Cottonwood Canyon to the 9,000-foot forested heights of Elk Ridge, providing bird's-eye overviews of the

A hidden trapper's cabin in the Abajos is almost just a memory – Mel Lewis, UTC

sublime Salt Creek-Lavender Canyon-Needles maze. The road connects with other unpaved roads leading to Beef Basin, Dark Canyon Primitive Area, the Abajos, Kigalia Ranger Station, Bears Ears, Route 95, Blanding, and Monticello. From this side road a short spur forks north from Cathedral Butte on Salt Creek Mesa to Big Pocket Overlook, 3 miles, atop an aerial peninsula jutting high above an exquisite labyrinth of naked rock—a tangled complex of ridges and slopes, canyons and flats, spires and turrets.

In the vicinity of Dugout Ranch and the Sixshooter peaks, two other canyons are accessible from Route 211. These are Lavender and Davis Canyons, respectively about 3.5 and 7 miles from the ranch junction. Paralleling Cottonwood Canyon on the west, these gorges feature natural arches and other curious erosional phenomena as well as prehistoric Indian ruins.

The west wall of Indian Creek Canyon breaks away to the north of Dugout Ranch and opens out, with a long line of great orange cliffs and blocky buttes forming the distant horizon. Two distinctive buttes, South and North Sixshooter Peaks, rise more than a thousand feet above their bases. Several miles beyond North Sixshooter where Route 211 turns west, an unpaved side road forks northward and goes through Lockhart Basin, a great rock-walled amphitheater formed by the escarpment of Hatch Point, to Hurrah Pass, Kane Creek Canyon, and Moab.

(Passenger cars are not very suitable for the side roads described above, which are rough, rocky, sandy, and subject to washouts—at least in spots. However, four-wheel-drive is not necessarily required. If in doubt, inquire locally. Detailed guidebooks and maps, such as F. A. Barnes' *Canyon Country* series, are advisable for backcountry travel.)

Route 211 continues westward from the Lockhart Basin turnoff into the rock jungle of Canyonlands National Park. (See Parks and Monuments for details.)

South of its junction with Route 211, Route 191 soon leaves Dry Valley and climbs to nearly 7,000 feet where Sage Plain merges into the foothills of the Abajos. Sage Plain, more than a thousand square miles in extent, sweeps eastward into Colorado to Mesa Verde and the peaks of the San Miguel, La Plata, and Ute Mountains. Monotonously level, the vast plain is incised by a network of shallow to deepening channels draining into the canyons of Montezuma, McElmo, and Recapture Creeks, and thence into the San Juan River. It is used as win-

ter range for livestock, and much of it is dry-farmed, with pinto beans and grains being important crops.

Dominating the landscape near Monticello are the Abajo Mountains, or Blue Mountains. Abajo Peak, the highest summit, has an altitude of 11,360 feet, and several other points approach or exceed 10,000 feet. Like the La Sals and Henrys, the Abajos are of laccolithic origin, and almost the entire range is included in the Manti-La Sal National Forest.

Monticello and Vicinity

Monticello (7,050 alt.), seat of San Juan County (Utah's largest county), is a cool green city on the east slope of the Abajos at the headwaters of Montezuma Creek. It was named for Thomas Jefferson's home in Virginia, but the name is pronounced "mon-ti-SELL-o" instead of "mon-ti-CHELL-o" as in the East. Because of altitude, temperatures rarely reach 90 degrees, but winters can be very cold and the summer growing season is short.

Monticello Museum, 80 North Main, contains exhibits of early Indian cultural artifacts and historical relics of San Juan pioneers. Among these are items brought to the area through Hole-in-the-Rock. Also featured are articles having to do with the Home of Truth religious colony (see above).

Turn west from Monticello on a paved road into the Abajo Mountains (see above) and Manti-La Sal National Forest. The pavement ends 5 miles from Route 191 at Dalton Springs Forest Campground (8,200 feet altitude). Tables, toilets, drinking water, trailer spaces; open June to October. About 2 miles beyond is Buckboard Forest Campground (8,600 feet altitude) with similar facilities and season. Reached by the same road is Lake Monticello (fishing, camping). The Abajos also are popular for snowmobiling. A network of unpaved roads crisscrosses the Abajos from this main access road, one looping to the right and back to Route 191 north of Monticello. Another climbs high through Cooley Pass between 11,000-foot peaks and descends the south slope to Blanding. Additional vehicle routes, from rough to primitive, give access to other parts of the range, while many miles of trails invite the hiker and snowmobiler. Inquire locally about details.

East from Monticello, Route 666 crosses sparsely populated Sage Plain into Colorado to Dove Creek, Cortez, Mesa Verde, and Durango, roughly following the route of the Old Spanish Trail.

Between Monticello and Blanding, Route 191 drops nearly

a thousand feet as it crosses the roller-coaster foothills of the Abajos and headwater tributaries of Montezuma and Recapture Creeks.

Route 191 descends into Devil's Canyon, a tributary gorge of Montezuma Canyon where the Manti-La Sal National Forest maintains a public campground and picnic area. Devil's Canyon is described by the U.S. Bureau of Land Management as an "ecologically unique area," habitat for animals such as the Abert squirrel and cougar.

Turn east from Devil's Canyon, and from Recapture Canyon (below), to Alkali Ridge Historical Landmark (10 miles by unpaved road) where archaeologists excavated 13 prehistoric Indian sites in the early 1930s. Here, nearly a thousand years ago, was a long-lived community of Pueblo Indians. Scientists excavated a complex of more than 200 connected rooms, then refilled their diggings to prevent deterioration and vandalism. The site is marked by a monument dedicated in 1965.

Recapture Canyon, 4 miles north of Blanding, is a broad, deep valley through which there is an impressive view of the Abajos. A sawmill flourished for years near the highway. Reputedly, the canyon was named by Peter Shirts, an oft-moving pioneer of southern Utah who settled in the San Juan country in the 1870s. According to Albert R. Lyman, Shirts "was reading a story of Hernando Cortes, and he got a strange idea that Montezuma escaped from Cortes and was recaptured at the creek, which he named Recapture. He also named Montezuma Creek with the same idea in mind."

Blanding and Vicinity
- Edge of the Cedars State Park -

Blanding (6,100 alt.) on White Mesa is an attractive, stable community, the largest in San Juan County, surrounded by fields of hay and grain. Its residents in 1941 derived their livelihood mainly from sheep and cattle. As with Monticello, this is no longer the case. The discovery of uranium, oil, and natural gas in the 1950s at Aneth and other Four Corners locations transformed Blanding and Monticello in particular and San Juan County in general.

The following explanation from Herbert E. Gregoary is excerpted from the 1941 edition of this book:

"BLANDING OWES ITS EXISTENCE TO . . . WALTER C. LYMAN, THE FATHER OF THE IRRIGATION PROJECT THAT BROUGHT THE WATERS OF THE ABAJO MOUNTAINS TO SOME 3,000 ACRES OF FAVORABLY LYING LAND. . . . IN 1905 THE FIRST SETTLERS WHO ARRIVED WERE CHIEFLY THOSE WHOSE FARMS HAD BEEN RUINED BY THE SAN JUAN RIVER AT BLUFF AND THOSE DRIVEN FROM MEXICO BY POLITICAL AND RELIGIOUS PERSECUTION." BLANDING STANDS ON LAND ONCE OCCUPIED BY PREHISTORIC INDIANS, AND RUINS OF ADOBE AND ROCK WERE USED IN CONSTRUCTING SOME OF THE OLDER BUILDINGS. THE TOWN WAS FIRST NAMED GRAYSON, BUT WAS RENAMED IN 1915 WHEN THOMAS W. BICKNELL, AN EASTERNER, OFFERED A LIBRARY TO ANY UTAH TOWN THAT WOULD TAKE HIS NAME. TWO TOWNS, GRAYSON AND THURBER, ACCEPTED. A COMPROMISE WAS ARRANGED WHEREBY THURBER BECAME BICKNELL AND GRAYSON BECAME BLANDING, TAKING THE MAIDEN NAME OF MRS. BICKNELL; THE LIBRARY WAS DIVIDED BETWEEN THEM.

Edge of the Cedars State Park is located in Blanding at 660 West 400 North, on the east rim of Westwater Canyon. It consists of two units: a museum facility built of native stone, and the ruins of a prehistoric Anasazi village adjacent to the museum. The village, accessible by marked trail, was occupied from about A.D. 750 to A.D. 1220 and consists of six residential-ceremonial complexes. The ruins are listed on both state and national historic registers.

Three miles south of Blanding, west of the highway, is Five Kiva Ruin in Westwater Canyon, badly vandalized over the years but recently the subject of technical excavation and reconstruction by the Division of State History. The site was occupied for more than 1,200 years, from the early Basketmaker era near the time of Christ to about A.D. 1250 when it was abandoned by the Anasazi people.

Four miles south of Blanding is the junction with Route 95, Utah's Bicentennial Highway, leading west to Natural Bridges National Monument, Lake Powell, and Hanksville.

Beside the highway, about 5 miles south of Blanding on the east side of the highway, is Posey Monument, erected in recognition of the Paiute Indian War of 1923, said to be the last Indian war in the nation (see Bluff below).

In 1941, along more than 80 miles of highway south of Blanding to Arizona, the total European population was less than 100. With the exception of a few families at Mexican Hat, nearly all of those people lived at Bluff. Population has increased since then, of course—for Indians as well as Europeans—but the region still has one of the smallest population densities in the nation. South of Blanding the highway runs along a flat divide between Cottonwood Canyon on the west and Recapture Canyon on the east. The canyons are not always visible from the road, but at one place they are less than thirty feet apart. The road traverses the southwest corner of Sage Plain, running through miles of gently rolling sagebrush, greasewood, and rabbitbrush.

Paved Route 262 was built in 1958–59 to allow access from Utah to the newly developed Greater Aneth Oil Field, which had been discovered two years previously. Before the new highway was built, oil workers found it more convenient to trade and live in Colorado; afterwards, Utah communities received a larger share of economic benefits. The route passes through a rugged landscape adjoining Montezuma Canyon, into which it descends near the settlement of Montezuma Creek, 23 miles from Route 191. The highway continues from Montezuma Creek through Aneth to the Colorado border, connecting with Route 160 (Navajo Route 1), which gives access to Four Corners Monument, marking the only site in the nation where four states meet at a common point (Utah, Colorado, New Mexico, and Arizona).

– Hovenweep National Monument via Route 262 –

About 8 miles along Route 262 from Route 191 is a junction with an unpaved road leading east to Hovenweep National Monument, Utah's best-known prehistoric Anasazi ruins. (See Hovenweep National Monument.) This region is occupied by Montezuma Canyon and its extensive tributary system as well as the related Recapture-McElmo systems, which drain Sage Plain into the San Juan River, an area of more than 1,000 square miles measuring some 40 by 40 miles in extent. Though not as deeply incised as the canyon country to the west nor scenically as dramatic, these systems are relatively wild. Montezuma Canyon has been identified by the Bureau of Land Management "as a unique area with outstanding archaeological, geological, historical and scenic values." The main canyon itself and some of the side canyons are traversed by fair-weather dirt roads. Parts of the area are habitat for golden and bald eagles, despite several decades of uranium-vanadium development and some scattered canyon ranching operations.

Bluff

South of the junction with Route 262, Route 191 descends from Bluff Bench to the valley of the San Juan River and the rustic frontier village of Bluff. In this descent it leaves the drab, relatively youthful Cretaceous rocks of Sage Plain and enters the more brightly colored older formations typical of the broken Canyonlands country.

Bluff (4,300 alt.) dates from 1880 when it was settled by the Hole-in-the-Rock pioneers (see below). Its history since then has been one of hardship and anguish, poverty and riches, growth and decline, then growth again. The latter period marks Bluff today, as evidenced by a lengthened main street and a motley assortment of modern structures mixed with those of more distant vintage.

In 1941 Bluff consisted of "a score of dusty red houses, built of the soil on which they stand. Five artesian wells provide water for an oasis-like growth of shade trees and fruit orchards. Bluff has an Indian trading post where Navajos are frequent visitors, bringing wool, silver work, goat meat, and handwoven rugs to trade for groceries and clothing." The red brick and stone houses remain as do the Navajos and the lush vegetation. The trading post, when operating, is utilized more by visitors than by the Indians, who prefer the local stores and restaurants. But local color is still a trait of Bluff, including as it does the Navajo Twins buttes at the mouth of Cow Canyon; the Episcopal Mission, quaint pioneer buildings, and dusty streets; Indians in their distinctive dress (less so today than formerly, however), guides offering vehicle and boating tours, roadside trading posts and eating places.

Cemetery Hill is a nostalgic point of interest. "Located in the classic western manner on a bleak gravel hill above our town," Mary Foushee wrote, the cemetery "offers to history and nostalgia buffs a glimpse of the past."

Locomotive Rock, as described by Marian Crawford in the *Deseret News* of March 13, 1948, "stands watch over the first of the brave Hole-in-the-Rock pioneers to die. She lies beneath the rocks, and the wind whispers in the willows and down from San Juan hill. It seems to chant a melody—the San Juan song. 'It's far off the beaten track . . . And we never will come back . . . But we'll find our El Dorado . . . In San Juan.' "

The Mormons of 1880 were not Bluff's only pioneers. Others came years later. Among these was Father Harold B. Liebler, revered "priest with the long hair," who established St. Christopher's Episcopal Mission to the Navajo Indians in 1943. Against great odds, relying mainly on volunteer help and contributions, Father Liebler and a small staff gradually built the mission into an attractive tree-shrouded complex that includes a school, a hogan-shaped chapel, fields, dwellings, kitchen, dining hall, and other facilities. The mission is located on the north bank of the river, two miles east of Bluff via paved road. Visitors are welcome.

Joining both banks of the river a mile east of the mission is a picturesque cable-supported footbridge. Several miles beyond the mission and bridge is Recapture Pocket, an area of strange goblin rock forms.

Bluff's Indian Day Celebration is a colorful happening each year in June or July, featuring Navajo games, horse races, and other events.

Bluff was founded in 1880 by Mormon settlers called by their church to establish a colony on the San Juan River. Their epic journey through the Hole-in-the-Rock, across the Colorado River, and through the slickrock country between the river and Bluff is one of the most amazing episodes in Mormon colonizing history. That tale has been told many times by many writers but in fullest detail by Dr. David E. Miller in *Hole-in-the-Rock*.

The major objective of the San Juan settlement was cultivation of better relations with the Indians, together with the laying of foundations for future permanent Mormon settlements before non-Mormons secured a foothold in the region. There was also the desire for more and better land and the hope that Mormons from the southern states would find the climate more to their liking.

Their ordeal, and that of the main party after crossing the Colorado, was recounted in the 1941 edition (quoted material is from Hoffman Birney's *Zealots of Zion*):

FOUR MEN, SENT AHEAD [FROM HOLE-IN-THE-ROCK] TO FIND THE BEST ROUTE, RETURNED IN TWENTY-FIVE DAYS, A MONTH BEFORE THE CROSSING OF THE COLORADO WAS COMPLETED. ON THE SECOND DAY THEY CAME TO THE SLICK ROCKS, AN AREA OF STEEPLY SLOPED SANDSTONE, IMPOSSIBLE TO AVOID AND APPARENTLY IMPOSSIBLE TO DESCEND; A SCOUT FOLLOWED A HERD OF MOUNTAIN SHEEP ACROSS IT.

THEY WERE FORCED MANY MILES TO THE NORTH BY ROUGH TERRAIN . . . AND THE NECESSITY FOR DISCOVERING A PASS THROUGH THE CLAY HILLS [BIRNEY CONTINUES]. THEY FOUND THAT PASS, THE ONLY ONE IN THE RANGE, BY FOLLOWING ANOTHER DIM TRAIL MADE BY THE ANCIENT INHABITANTS OF THE LAND. . . . EAST OF THE CLAY HILLS . . . LAY A MANYBRANCHED GORGE SO VAST THAT THEY CHRISTENED IT THE GRAND GULCH. . . . ON CHRISTMAS DAY . . . THEY COOKED THE LAST OF THEIR FOOD. THAT CHRISTMAS DINNER WAS "A SLAPJACK OF FLOUR AND WATER BAKED IN A FRYING-PAN."

LATE IN THE ELEVENTH DAY, AFTER FOUR DAYS WITHOUT FOOD, THE MEN STAGGERED INTO A CABIN ON THE PRESENT SITE OF BLUFF. THE FOLLOWING MORNING THEY CONTINUED TO THE SETTLEMENT AT MONTEZUMA, AND AFTER A SINGLE DAY'S REST BEGAN THE RETURN TRIP, WITH A FORTY-EIGHT-POUND SACK OF FLOUR FOR FOOD. WHEN THEY GOT TO THE COLORADO RIVER THEY WERE TIRED AND DISCOURAGED. THE COMPANY, HOWEVER, HAD NO CHOICE BUT TO MOVE FORWARD: HEAVY SNOWS MADE IT IMPOSSIBLE TO RETURN; LACK OF FORAGE MADE IT IMPOSSIBLE TO REMAIN. THEY HAULED LUMBER 60 MILES FROM ESCALANTE TO BUILD A FERRYBOAT, AND BLASTED A ROAD IN THE EAST WALL OF THE CANYON. . . .

TO TELL OF THE JOURNEY OF THAT CARAVAN [WRITES HOFFMAN BIRNEY], WOULD BE VIRTUALLY TO REPEAT THE TALE OF THE SUFFERINGS OF THE FOUR PATHFINDERS AND TO MULTIPLY FIVE-FOLD THE LABOR THAT HAD BEEN NECESSARY TO DESCEND THROUGH THE DREADED HOLE TO THE RIVER. . . . THE HOBBS PARTY MADE THE TRIP IN ELEVEN DAYS; TO COVER THE SAME GROUND WITH HEAVILY-LADEN WAGONS TOOK JUST FIVE TIMES AS LONG—A DAILY AVERAGE OF LESS THAN THREE MILES. . . .

EAST OF ELK RIDGE THE COMPANY DESCENDED INTO THE CANYON OF COMB WASH AND TURNED SOUTH TO THE SAN JUAN RIVER, REACHING THE MOUTH OF COTTONWOOD CREEK IN APRIL, 1880 [BUT NOT BEFORE SURMOUNTING ONE OF THE MOST FORMIDABLE OBSTACLES THEY HAD YET ENCOUNTERED—SAN JUAN HILL—THE ALMOST SHEER, UNBROKEN FACE OF COMB RIDGE. "THEY LEFT THEIR BLOOD THERE," WROTE MARIAN CRAWFORD, "AND BITS OF THEIR CLOTHES, A WAGON OR TWO AND HORSES TOO WEARY TO MAKE THE LAST HARD PULL"]. STILL 15 MILES FROM THE MONTEZUMA SETTLEMENT, [BLUFF] WAS "THE FIRST PLACE THEY HAD FOUND TO STOP AND ALSO THE FIRST PLACE FROM WHICH THEY HAD NO STRENGTH TO GO ON." EXHAUSTION HAD HALTED THE COMPANY AT THE MOST SUITABLE SITE ON THE SAN JUAN RIVER.

Sections of the trail was used for some years afterward for communication between the isolated new community and populated Utah but gradually was abandoned as easier routes were developed. In this century many people have traversed the trail, or portions of it, by jeep, on foot or horseback. Sections of the trail are paralleled today by Route 95 and Route 263. In 1980, the Centennial of San Juan, jeep tours to Hole-in-the-Rock and San Juan Hill were conducted during the year, and commercial guides have offered jeep tours along the pioneer trail for years. The 1941 edition's account continued:

HOFFMAN BIRNEY EVALUATES THE JOURNEY THUS: "IT WAS LABOR BESIDE WHICH THE TOIL OF THE EMIGRANT TRAINS THAT CROSSED THE ENTIRE CONTINENT TO CALIFORNIA AND OREGON WAS CHILD'S PLAY. . . . NOWHERE IN THE HISTORY OF AMERICA IS THERE A MORE IMPRESSIVE EXAMPLE OF THE POWER OF A CREED, OF THE FAITH THAT MOVETH MOUNTAINS, THAN IN THE CONQUEST OF THE HOLE-IN-THE-ROCK AND THE STORY OF THE SAINTS OF THE SAN JUAN."

An act of the Territorial legislature created San Juan County in February 1880 when it had no permanent inhabitants, and leaders of the Mormon company were appointed its officials while still struggling eastward from the Colorado River crossing. Bluff became the county seat and remained so until 1895, when it was removed to Monticello. A few years later, around the turn of the century, it is claimed that those remaining in Bluff had the highest family income of any town in the world. This was a result of boom conditions in nearby Colorado and demand for their livestock. During the first year "about half the population moved away." Yet as the manuscript "San Juan Stake History" records, "somehow, in this wonderful colony which had come through from Escalante whether it could or not, there remained a splendid element of invincibility. When the dissatisfied and disheartened ones moved on to the east, and back to the west, that invincible spirit clenched its jaws the tighter."

With the nearest white settlement more than seventy miles away, the colonists had difficulty with the Paiutes and Navajos. A fort was built to protect women and children, but when Indians stole cattle and horses, the settlers dared do little about it. The most they usually accomplished was to retake the stock. The settlement was not entirely free from Indian trouble until 1923, when Old Posey, chief of the dispossessed Paiutes, died. For twenty years he had done almost everything to make himself unpopular. His career came to an end when he and his band assisted in the escape of two Paiutes who had been arrested for robbing a sheep camp. A posse pursued the Indians for several days, killed one of them, wounded Old Posey, and captured the rest. Old Posey escaped to an abandoned cave in Comb Wash, where he died, his wounds stuffed with weeds, his lifeless face toward the approaching enemy.

More serious were the vagaries of the San Juan River. Time after time the settlers attempted to divert water from the river, but each time the stream rose unexpectedly and flooded the fields. The church sent Francis A. Hammond to act as president of the San Juan Stake. He moved most of the people to Monticello, and stock-raising replaced farming as the primary industry. By 1935 the twenty miles of farmland that existed along the San Juan River in 1880 had been reduced by floods to 200 acres at Bluff. By that time, however, the townspeople had begun to irrigate with water from artesian wells.

Mexican Hat and Monument Valley
via Route 163

Three miles west of Bluff is a junction leading to Sand Island and a public campground (BLM), used by river boaters for launching and disembarking. From this junction the road forks south to Sik-Is Bridge (Bridge of Friendship). The bridge was dedicated in 1971, replacing a heavily used footbridge destroyed in 1970 by floods. Between the campground and bridge, beside the river, a low bluff displays a large panel of petroglyphs.

At Bluff, Route 163 heads east to Montezuma Creek, Aneth, and the Colorado line; to the west it leads to Mexican Hat, the splendid spectacle of Raplee Anticline dominating the landscape. This remarkable structure is "an upfold or arch of stratified rock," so symmetrically eroded that photographs of it are used in geology texts around the world. The anticline is 15 miles long and 1,500 feet high at its crest. Mexican Hat Rock then comes into view, resembling an enormous Mexican sombrero balanced precariously on a tapered base.

Mexican Hat (4,200 alt.) is perched on the north bank of the San Juan River where it emerges from the Raplee Anticline and begins a longer entrenchment downstream through the Goosenecks and other deep gorges to Lake Powell. In 1941 the settlement amounted to little more than the Mexican Hat Lodge, where Norman Nevills had begun in 1937 to offer adventure trips on the San Juan and Colorado.

The area's early background was summarized in the 1941 edition of this book:

THE MUDDY SAN JUAN RIVER, 78.1 MILES, IS SPANNED BY A SUSPENSION BRIDGE. THE RIVER RISES IN THE SAN JUAN MOUNTAINS OF SOUTHERN COLORADO, FLOWS INTO NEW MEXICO . . . ENTERS UTAH NEAR THE FOUR CORNERS, AND FLOWS WESTWARD TO ITS JUNCTION WITH THE COLORADO RIVER NEAR THE ARIZONA LINE. DISCOVERY OF GOLD ALONG THE UPPER TRIBUTARIES OF THE SAN JUAN LED E. L. GOODRIDGE TO MAKE THE FIRST KNOWN BOAT TRIP DOWN THE RIVER IN 1879. HE FOUND ONLY MINOR QUANTITIES OF FLAKE GOLD, BUT "LITTLE STREAMS OF OIL COMING FROM LOOSE BOULDERS" INDUCED HIM TO SEEK FUNDS FOR DEVELOPMENT OF AN OIL CLAIM NEAR THE PRESENT SAN JUAN BRIDGE. THE VENTURE WAS EVENTUALLY FINANCED IN 1907, AND THE FOLLOWING SPRING, GOODRIDGE BROUGHT IN "A GUSHER, THROWING OIL TO A HEIGHT OF 70 FEET." BY 1911 THERE WERE TWENTY-SEVEN DRILLING RIGS IN THE FIELD, A SMALL TOWN HAD SPRUNG INTO EXISTENCE AT GOODRIDGE (NOW MEXICAN HAT), AND A BRIDGE WAS CONSTRUCTED OVER THE SAN JUAN RIVER. MOST OF THE WELLS PRODUCED ONLY A LITTLE OIL AND GAS, AND MANY WERE "DRY HOLES." NONE PRODUCED OIL IN COMMERCIAL QUANTITIES.

From the Colorado line to a point midway between Bluff and Mexican Hat, the river occupies a floodplain half a mile to a mile wide, bordered by low walls. West of Bluff the river follows a meandering canyon to the Colorado River. The airline distance from the head of the canyon to the Colorado is only 63 miles, but the distance by stream is 133 miles. The most closely spaced bends are the Goosenecks (see above), but at the Great Bend the river makes a nine-mile loop and returns to within half a mile of its starting point. At the west end of this loop the Colorado is only 5 miles away, but the San Juan travels 34 miles before the two streams meet. The depth of the canyon varies from a few hundred feet to half a mile.

South of Mexican Hat, Route 163 crosses the San Juan River. Turn southward via this bridge to the Navajo Indian Reservation, where as many as 150,000 Navajos reside in one of the harshest environments in the country. The three-state reservation embraces about 25,000 square miles of red-rock desert, high mesas, plateaus, and mountains, dissected for the most part by stream channels, most of which are dry except for intermittent runoff. Utah's part of the reservation, more than a million acres, amounts to less than 10 percent of the entire reservation, yet it comprises a fourth of San Juan County's area.

- Monument Valley -

"Only one automobile crossed this strip before 1921," said the 1941 edition. Since then the majestic beauty of Monument Valley, straddling the state line ahead, has become known the world over and countless thousands have come to see it. Many more would have come if the valley were not so remote.

Alhambra Rock, 2 miles south of the river, is a jagged black volcanic mass, contrasting with the red of the surrounding country. Monument Pass, 17 miles south of the river, marks the north entrance to Monument Valley, "where maroon buttes and pinnacles rise, like skyscrapers, out of the red desert, and tower nearly a thousand feet [and more] above the valley floor. Between the monuments, distant ranges in Colorado, New Mexico, and Arizona can be seen. Agathlan Peak, a

Sunrise shadows in Monument Valley – François Camoin

metallic blue volcanic spire, stands out in the red Arizona desert . . ."(1941 edition). Route 163 in Monument Pass is flanked by giant fingers and buttes on either side. Beyond is a forest of other enchanted standing rocks. Only a sampling of their names can be given here: Buttes and fingers known as The Eagle, Brigham's Tomb, Natanni Tso, Castle Butte, Big Indian, The Mittens, Mitchell and Merrick, Grey Whiskers, Elephant, Camel, Totem Pole, Three Sisters, Yei-Bichei, Sun's Eye, and Big Hogan; mesas by the name of Oljeto, Sentinel, Eagle, Old Baldy, Pueblo, Wetherill, Spearhead and Hunt; valleys called Windmill, Primrose, and Mystery; canyons and washes named Rock Door, Stagecoach, Eagle Rock, Train Rock, Monument.

John Ford, the Hollywood director famed for his action westerns, is most responsible—at the urging of Harry Goulding—for bringing the beauties of Monument Valley to the attention of the general public, at least in earlier years. Beginning in 1938 with his classic *Stagecoach*, Ford subsequently filmed *My Darling Clementine*, *War Party*, and *She Wore a Yellow Ribbon*—all in the 1940s. Other films were shot at least partially in the valley. These included *Billy the Kid*, *Kit Carson*, *Fort Apache*, *How the West Was Won*, *The Living Desert*, *The Searchers*, and *Cheyenne Autumn*. A false-front Tombstone was built for *My Darling Clementine*.

Monument Valley has been a Navajo Tribal Park since 1959. The following year saw dedication of an attractive Visitor Center-Observatory located four miles east of Goulding's Junction and Route 163, at the entrance to a 14-mile scenic-tour route. Visitors desiring to tour the valley's off-highway attractions must register at the Visitor Center or obtain the services of an authorized guide. *Native subjects expect a photographic fee for posing. Do not photograph Navajos without their permission.*

For many, Monument Valley has always been associated with Goulding's Trading Post. The trading post was established by Harry and Mike Goulding in 1923 and is now listed on the National Register of Historic Places. The Gouldings have been the valley's best-known residents, not only offering crucial trading post services to the Navajos in 30-odd years of dirt-road isolation but also providing lodging and tours for travelers, assistance and comfort to the Navajos in cases of illness and distress, boosterism in promoting the valley's attractions, local color and authentic information for uncounted writers and photographers. According to the 1941 edition of this book, Harry Goulding was called T'pay-eh-nez, or Long Sheep, by the Navajos, "either because he is tall, and owned sheep, when he came into the valley, or because he had many sheep."

– Moki Dugway –

Three miles north of Mexican Hat, route 261 heads toward Route 95 and Hanksville, Caineville, and Capitol Reef National Park. This spectacular road begins as a paved highway and gives little hint of its transformation into a series of dirt and gravel switchbacks called the Moki Dugway as it climbs toward Cedar Mesa. Note: this road is passable in passenger cars when dry but is not recommended for larger recreational vehicles or cars towing trailers.

Goosenecks of the San Juan State Park is 4 miles by paved road (Route 316) from Route 261 at a junction 5 miles north of Mexican Hat. The reserve is an overlook point on the rim of the San Juan River canyon, "one of the world's most magnificent examples of an entrenched meander." According to the 1941 edition, "Here, in a mud-gray canyon [about 1,000 feet] deep, the San Juan makes a series of symmetrical bends, around which it flows six miles to travel an airline distance of one and a half miles. The river is viewed from the north rim as it flows north, then south, then north again, and finally south again, in a series of close-set curves. The center bend is three miles around, but the dividing ridge at its narrowest point is less than 100 yards wide. According to geologists the San Juan once meandered over the surface of a level plain; a slow regional uplift forced the stream to cut deeper and deeper into the plain. Eventually, eons hence, the meanders may cut through, leaving a series of gigantic natural bridges.

Just before Route 261 starts its climb up to Cedar Mesa, an unpaved side road forks northwest into Valley of the Gods, Utah's miniature Monument Valley; the 17-mile drive exits at Route 163 south of Bluff.

Moki Dugway is the name for the steep switchbacks of Route 261 where it climbs the thousand-foot face of Cedar Mesa. The Dugway has been improved since it was bulldozed out of the cliff during the uranium boom of the 1950s but still provides aerial thrills sufficient for most drivers. Views en route are spectacular, sweeping downward into the San Juan canyons and Valley of the Gods, and southward to the jagged skyline of Monument Valley. The rim of Cedar Mesa, at 6,000 feet, is

a thousand feet higher than the terrace forming the floor of Valley of the Gods, which in turn is a thousand feet higher than the river.

Muley Point Overlook, a panoramic viewpoint, ranks for visual impact with better-known Canyonlands overlooks to the north. On the high rim of Cedar Mesa, reached by unpaved road leading about 5 miles from Route 261 at a junction near the top of Moki Dugway, Muley Point offers a geological and scenic spectacle, a bird's-eye sweep across hundreds of millions of years of earth's crustal history, revealed in bare-bones stratigraphic clarity.

Blanding to Hanksville via Route 95 North

Route 95, Utah's Bicentennial Highway (paving was completed in 1976), connects Route 191 near Blanding with Route 24 at Hanksville, more than 125 miles away. In all this distance there is no town, and no services except at Fry Canyon and marinas on Lake Powell. The terrain is wild, an almost pristine landscape of pygmy evergreens, beacon buttes, island ranges, cliff-faced mesas, and seemingly bottomless gorges.

Route 95 was one of the last highways in Utah to be completely paved, its construction having taken place in stages over a period of 70 years or more, from first primitive beginnings as trail segments. Sections near the Colorado River did not see much improvement until after World War II, when much of southeastern Utah was opened by a network of uranium access roads. Originally the route between Blanding and Natural Bridges passed over Elk Ridge near Bears Ears. Segments of the present highway and Route 263 to Halls Crossing parallel sections of the route traversed by the Hole-in-the-Rock pioneers (see Bluff).

Special attractions along Route 95, traveling west from Route 191 near Blanding, include the following (mileages are approximate):

Butler Wash View Area, 11 miles, marks the general locality of an armed encounter between a local white posse and a party of Paiute Indians led by Posey. Posey was shot and later died from the wound, but most of his party escaped. This was in 1923. In the vicinity are prehistoric Indian ruins. A rough, fair-weather road extends south through Butler Wash to Route 163 near Bluff.

Comb Ridge, 14 miles, has been a formidable natural

barrier since pioneer days. The ridge is a long, narrow monoclinal uplift, sloping on the east, cliff-faced on the west, through which builders of Route 95 cut a deep notch for the highway. Looking north along the west face, the steep dugway of the old highway can be seen several miles away. Comb Ridge was a serious obstacle to the Hole-in-the-Rock pioneers, who were almost completely exhausted by the time they reached it (see story under Bluff above).

Mule Canyon Rest Area, 22 miles, is at the site of a partially restored prehistoric settlement complex. A tower and kiva are accessible for public inspection. In the vicinity are seven round towers, known as Cave Towers, which date from late Pueblo times of A.D. 1050 to A.D. 1150. Indian antiquities are a priceless national heritage; there are severe penalties for unauthorized excavation or damage.

Junction with Route 261, 35 miles, leads south to Grand Gulch Primitive area, Muley Point, Moki Dugway, and Mexican Hat. All around is a dense forest of pinyon pine and juniper (cedar) trees. Looming 2,000 feet above the highway on the north is Elk Ridge, surmounted by the landmark twin buttes or knolls known as Bears Ears (9,060 alt.).

Junction with Route 275, 37 miles, Route 275 leads 4 miles to Natural Bridges National Monument. (See Parks and Monuments.) A short distance along Route 275 is a junction with an unpaved route (old Route 95) leading to the heights of Elk Ridge and a network of high-country forest roads in Manti-La Sal National Forest. These pleasant alpine roads fork variously to Dark Canyon Wilderness, Canyonlands National Park, the Abajo Mountains, Blanding, and Monticello, providing access for a motley assortment of stockmen, lumbermen, miners, hunters, hikers, and off-highway tourists. Dark Canyon Wilderness (BLM) incorporates the main gorges and side canyons of three major tributaries of Cataract Canyon— namely Dark, Bowdie, and Gypsum Canyons—grandly imposing gorges that are deep and narrow with unscalable walls for much of their length. The area is popular as a destination for wilderness backpackers.

Junction with Route 276, 43 miles, leads to Halls Crossing Marina on Lake Powell (40 miles from Route 95). This exceptionally scenic paved road parallels the route of the old Hole-in-the-Rock Trail for much of its distance, along the Red House Cliffs and through the Clay Hills via Clay Hills Divide. Rough side roads branch west into the vast reaches of Red

Canyon and south to the San Juan arm of Lake Powell. About 15 miles from the lake, the original pioneer trail (traversable by jeep, or partly so) branches off to Cottonwood Canyon on the opposite side of the lake from Hole-in-the-Rock. Other trails probe the Clay Hills, Moki Canyon, Lake Canyon, and tributary gorges of the San Juan.

About halfway between the junction of Routes 276 and 95 and the end of Route 276 at Halls Crossing is the Grand Gulch Primitive Area, a natural and archaeological preserve of the U.S. Bureau of Land Management, limited to travel on foot or horseback. A tributary of the San Juan, Grand Gulch extends about 50 miles northward from its mouth. Its steep or overhanging walls are impassable to humans except in a few places; countless ledges and crevices contain what is said to be the nation's largest concentration of prehistoric Basketmaker and Pueblo dwellings and storage structures outside of Mesa Verde. The gulch also is rich in rock art. Grand Gulch's culture covered a span of 1,300 years, from 2,000 to 700 years ago. Scenically the gulch is outstanding, remaining virtually a wilderness because of remoteness and difficulty of access.

Halls Crossing Marina is a major facility on Lake Powell across the lake from Bullfrog Marina. First developed by San Juan County financial interests, it is now a unit of ARAMARK, which operates other marinas on the lake. Available: comprehensive boating services such as fuel, repairs, storage, slips and buoys, boat and motor rentals, boating tours. Food, accommodations, supplies, airstrip. From Halls Crossing a vehicle ferry runs across the lake to Bullfrog Marina and the continuation of Route 276. The ferry runs most of the year but may be closed for maintenance or if the level of the lake is too low. (See Glen Canyon National Recreation Area.)

Route 95 west of Route 276 traverses a bench between entrenched White Canyon and the red rampart of the Wingate cliffs. Buttes, curious erosional forms, and the distant peaks of the Henrys accent the broken skyline. Jacob's Chair Butte is named for Jacob Adams, a cowboy who was drowned in a local flash flood. Soldiers' Grave contains the remains of two soldiers killed during the unsuccessful pursuit of raiding Utes in 1884. A little farther is the Happy Jack Mine (few indications except dangerous haulage roads). Happy Jack began as a modest copper mine; then, from about 1949 to 1963, it was one of the most productive uranium mines in Utah, being the source of about 600,000 tons of uranium ore and making a fortune for its owners. Its ore was a complex mixture of pitchblende, iron, copper, aluminum, sulphur, silver, and coal. Uranium content was high.

– Hite Crossing via Route 95 –

Lake Powell (north end) is serviced as a boating recreation area by Hite Marina, located on the lake's east bank several miles south of Route 95. The marina is named for the original settlement and ferry of Hite, now under water, situated on the west side of the lake (formerly the Colorado River). Hite Marina was relocated periodically as the lake rose, being situated first on the west shore at the mouth of North Wash, then later moved to the east shore. It features boating ramp, docking and storage, fuel, boating and fishing supplies, boat rentals, store, airstrip. Lake Powell is crossed in this vicinity by three high bridges—the White Canyon, Colorado River, and Dirty Devil.

About 20 miles south of Hanksville, Route 95 enters the shallow upper end of a deepening gorge known as North Wash, an historic route between Hanksville and Hite (Dandy Crossing) since the 1880s. Until the years following World War II the road was only a wagon trail; but even after the first "improved" road was constructed in 1946 it remained a fair-weather route for another 15 years or more, fording the stream 50 times in a distance of 15 miles. The road was brought to modern standards during the 1960s. Before Lake Powell rose and inundated old Hite in 1964, the road followed the west bank of the Colorado River downstream for six miles from the mouth of North Wash to the ferry site. Today it follows the lake's west shore northward to a bridge crossing of Dirty Devil Bay, then to a bridge crossing of Narrow Canyon, and thence to a bridge crossing of White Canyon.

The Hite Marina of today lies on the east side of the lake, opposite the location of old Hite and the first ferry site. After Hite was inundated in 1964, the ferry was moved up-canyon to the mouth of North Wash, where it remained until the highway and bridges were completed shortly thereafter. The first Hite Marina also was located here until it was moved to the east bank a few years ago. As described in the 1941 edition, Hite was a "town" on the Colorado River with two stone buildings and a population of one. Cass Hite, supposed renegade and former member of Quantrill's Civil War guerrillas, built a rock hovel here in the early 1880s. For years he existed by washing out "flour" gold from the sandbars of the Colorado.

Hite's crossing, which he called "Dandy Crossing," was consistently used by the Indians. It is one of four and perhaps the best natural crossing of the Colorado.

After Cass Hite died, his ranch was abandoned for many years and the crossing was little used until the ranch was revived in 1934 by Arthur and Della Chaffin. Chaffin's prompting of state officials was responsible for the first improved road through North Wash to Hite and across the river in White Canyon, a total distance of 70 miles, which he and a small crew of men bulldozed in a short time and at small cost. Chaffin himself built the first motorized ferry, dedicated with the new road in September 1946.

– Bullfrog via Route 276 –

In the upper reaches of North Wash, 26 miles south of Hanksville, Route 276 branches from Route 95 southward to Bullfrog Marina-Resort and Lake Powell (42 miles). Mt. Hillers looms high to the west, and the two peaks of the Little Rockies (Mt. Holmes and Mt. Ellsworth) are geological and scenic curiosities beside the highway on the east. The landscape is a colorful tangle of steep-walled gorges, slickrock slopes, distorted strata, and picturesque erosional forms.

About 12 miles north of Bullfrog, beside the highway, is the community of Ticaboo, Utah's "most totally planned" community of recent times. Ticaboo came into being during the late 1970s but is now something of a ghost town.

From a junction about 5 miles north of Bullfrog Marina, an unpaved road forks west. This exceptionally scenic route (washboard, dusty, and rough in places) threads its way along the rims of yawning gorges and across far-spreading flats to Grand Gulch (Halls Creek Canyon), Waterpocket Fold, Burr Trail, Circle Cliffs, Route 24, and Capitol Reef National Park.

Bullfrog Marina is the largest recreation development on the north end of Lake Powell. (See Glen Canyon National Recreation Area.) It features launching ramp, campground, stores and service station, boating services and supplies, lodging and meals, airport, boat tours and houseboat rentals.

ROBBERS ROOST

The Henry Mountains

At the junction 9 miles south of Hanksville, turn west on an unpaved road toward the Henry Mountains, past Fairview Ranch. The road climbs steeply into deep canyons on the east slope of Mt. Ellen (11,615 alt.), highest and largest of the Henry peaks. In midsummer it may be possible to cross Mt. Ellen over a high pass via the right-hand road; otherwise it is necessary to follow a lower route around the peak to Penellen Pass, where the main east-west route connects Route 95 with the Waterpocket Fold road.

Many miles of fair-weather roads crisscross the Henrys, connecting the three northern peaks, giving access to Bromide Basin, the site of old Eagle City, Wolverton, Starr Springs, etc. Detailed maps should be obtained before setting out.

The Henrys consist of five isolated peaks: Mt. Ellen (11,615 alt.), Mt. Pennell (11,371), Mt. Hillers (10,723), Mt. Holmes (7,930) and Mt. Ellsworth (8,235), all named by the Powell surveys. Known as the Little Rockies, the latter two peaks stand prominently beside the Bullfrog highway; the others are much higher and more massive. The Henrys are noted as the last mountains in the 48 contiguous states to be formally named and placed on official maps. They were "discovered" in 1869 by the river party led by Major John W. Powell, who called them initially the Unknown Mountains, later applying the name of Professor Joseph Henry of the Smithsonian Institution. (New Mexican travelers, Mormon explorers, fur trappers, and others surely knew of them before that; they are prominent landmarks visible for a hundred miles.) The mountains are composed of igneous material; but they are not volcanoes and originally this igneous material was buried under sedimentary rocks into which it had intruded as magma (molten lava), pushing up as laccolithic uplifts. During the intervening 60 or 70 million years since this process began, the overlying sedimentary formations have been removed from most of the higher elevations, but they still encircle the peaks in places as deformed, contorted beds that are clearly visible.

Since at least the 1870s the Henrys have been known to contain gold deposits, and the peaks have been intensively prospected. But they are stubborn yielders, and few if any gold miners ever struck it rich. The peaks were considered a source of the fine gold in the sandbars of Glen Canyon; their creekbeds have been placered and their ore beds mined and probed for a hundred years or more. Eagle City was their principal boomtown, but it survived only a few years during the 1890s and is hardly evident today.

At 19 miles from North Wash Junction a sign marks the turnoff to Starr Spring Recreation Site, 3 miles, a shady BLM campground in a verdant setting on the historic site of Starr Ranch, which flourished as a major cattle operation for some years after its founding in the 1890s.

Hanksville

Hanksville (4,300 alt.) was long one of Utah's most isolated communities; it did not see its first paved access road until 1959. Today, though Hanksville is the hub of highways leading in three directions, it remains physically remote from large centers of population.

According to the first edition of this book, Hanksville "was used, in the eighties and nineties of the last century, as a rendezvous for the Robbers Roost gang. The gang held sway over all the territory south and east of Hanksville; some people welcomed them in the small settlements, perhaps because the outlaws were good spenders. The large cattle companies were their chief victims." Since that was written, numerous books, articles, and a major Hollywood film production have described Butch Cassidy, Robbers Roost, and the Wild Bunch.

Waterpocket Fold via Route 24

East of Caineville, Route 24 makes its way west to the Waterpocket Fold and Capitol Reef National Park, passing through a desolate, haunting landscape of clays, muds, and "pinto" hills. As described in the first edition, crumbling "spires and monuments have fallen; broken and buried, they make softly-clothed mounds in a wasteland. . . . The late afternoon sun paints the dunes, mesas, and mountain walls in delicate mirage-like pastels." Known generally as Blue Valley, the river valley between Caineville and Hanksville has witnessed attempts at settlement, and several modest communities actually survived for a few years until floods and other factors proved fatal. One of these, known as Giles, is marked by a ruined rock structure beside the highway about 12 miles east of Caineville.

Near Factory Butte, one of Utah's grandest buttes and a regional landmark—at a junction about 10 miles west of Hanksville—an unpaved side road leads north to Salt Wash on the flank of the San Rafael Swell.

Fair-weather roads continue through a tortured landscape into Muddy River Canyon and along the south flank of San Rafael Reef to Wild Horse Butte, Goblin Valley, and Route 24 north of Hanksville. Inquire locally as to passability.

Caineville (4,600 alt.) is a ranching and farming hamlet that stretches for several miles between the Fremont River and the highway. A larger village existed here for several decades in the late 1800s and the early years of this century. The climate is agreeable and the soil productive, but the river is uncooperative and has a discouraging tendency to wash away fields and orchards with little warning. Because of this, most residents moved elsewhere after a particularly disastrous flood in 1909. South 1 mile is the Elijah Cutler Behunin Cabin, a log structure built about 1883 as the first building in Caineville. An unpaved side road, formerly the main highway, winds along the fantastically sculptured, tilting whaleback slope of Caineville Reef, overlooking the river and stately palisades of South Caineville Mesa, and eventually meets the paved highway 3 miles west of Caineville.

Turn north from Route 24 on the western outskirts of Caineville on an unimproved road to Capitol Reef National Park (Cathedral Valley) and other points of unusual scenic and geologic interest. (See Capitol Reef National Park.)

East of the park, Route 24 enters a landscape like no other in Utah or perhaps in America. Colors change from vivid shades of red to rusts, buffs, tans, and shades of bluish gray and purple. This is Utah's Painted Desert. In place of the ancient rocks of Jurassic and Triassic age that form the sheer cliffs and domed slopes of Capitol Reef, younger and softer rocks appear, and these crumble more easily to mud, clay, or low cliffs and ledges. The exception is in the immediate vicinity of Caineville, where relatively young rocks—massive Cretaceous formations a thousand feet thick—are lifted above the land in majestic cliffs, the faces of Caineville Mesa and Factory Butte.

Side roads just east of the park give access to scenic areas north and south of the highway. From Route 24, the Notom Road branches 9 miles east of the park visitor center at Fruita, paralleling the east flank of the Waterpocket Fold and providing access to the park's southern extension. (See Capitol Reef National Park.)

From Route 24, the River Ford Road branches 12 miles east of Fruita (3 miles east of the Notom turnoff), crosses the Fremont River in a normally shallow ford (if unsure, test it by wading!), then winds through rugged canyons and across widespreading flats to Cathedral Valley and northern reaches of Capitol Reef National Park.

The section of Route 24 west of Caineville is one of the prettiest stretches of highway to be found in Utah. It follows the Fremont River until it enters Capitol Reef, passes the visitors' entrance to the park, and continues into the town of Torrey.

Though not included within the park, the "breaks" of Thousand Lake Mountain near Torrey are worthy of inclusion among the foremost scenic wonders of Utah. Here the grand uplift has erupted into a complex of yawning canyons, stepped cliffs and ledges, great buttes and mesas. Cliffs of brown-red moenkopi formation at the bottom are sculptured into flying buttresses and fluted columns, giving the effect of cathedrals in places, or of Egyptian temples, or mile after mile of upright mummy figures. Seemingly every color of the rainbow is represented here in this kaleidoscopic area known as Torrey Breaks.

The red rock desert, 15 miles of State 24 east of Torrey Breaks, is included within Capitol Reef National Park, described in the Parks and Monuments chapter.

Summer storm approaching the Waterpocket Fold – Frank Jensen, UTC

Beauty All Around

by Deenise Becenti

Traveling across the southern stretch of Utah—from the stirring sandstone castles of Monument Valley to the haunting ruins of Hovenweep—stories of independence and evidence of fortitude gleam through many miles of this wondrous, mysterious country.

Beauty before me.
Beauty behind me.
Beauty all around me.

Phrases of a Navajo prayer truly describe this country that times seemed to have locked into a pioneer past, a place where ranching and farming continue to exist as the keys to survival. It's a rustic area where a colorful history weaves together stories of the cultures and people who have become part of the land.

This part of the state is easy to ignore once you've seen the panoramic beauty of Arches National Park near Moab and Canyonlands National Park northwest of Monticello. From inside a car, southeastern Utah looks isolated and barren. People who live here have heard many times others describing their homeland as a "desolate nothing." Yet, once a visitor gets past the unsettled hills and miles of empty highways, each isolated home represents survival. Each family has a deep-rooted history that has kept them here for many generations.

Southeastern Utah is as much up and down as across. Distances "as the crow flies" matter only to the crows because you can't get there from here. Looking in one direction, a canyon opens up before you. Turning in another direction, a snow-capped mountain humbles you. While, in a third direction, the San Juan River beckons you with the promise of life.

The San Juan, which slices across southern Utah, looks much the same as any other western river. But more than any other river in the state, it flows with culture and tradition. The Navajo people who live in San Juan County have a deep respect for the river they call Dine'Bi'Tooh ("The People's Water," serving as the lifeblood for the communities).

Utah Navajos consider this land their home, a place where their ancestors fought to stay alive. Consider the story of K'aa' Yel'lii' (One who Carries Arrows), a legendary Navajo warrior who stood in the forefront of tribal headsmen.

Navajo Nation Councilmen Andrew Tso and Mark Maryboy describe K'aa' Yel'lii' as a fearless protector of his people. When the two give a historical picture of this warrior, they start from the beginning, recounting the Navajo creation story. Tribal members are taught that the land they live on was prepared for them by the Holy People, living on the four sacred mountains surrounding the 25,000-square-mile reservation, an area that sprawls across northeastern Arizona and northwestern New Mexico and southeastern Utah.

The Holy People were the earliest educators, showing the first people survival techniques and teaching them sacred songs and prayers. The people were instructed to pass these teachings on to the next generation. K'aa' Yel'lii' must have heard these stories sometime during the early to mid-1800s because through the Navajo nation's darkest years, he endured, leaving a legacy for tribal members living in southeastern Utah.

In 1864, during the American Civil War, the U.S. Cavalry initiated a campaign to force Navajos to live in a military compound in eastern New Mexico. Thousands of men, women, and children were forced to walk hundreds of miles to their destination, where they were to remain for an undisclosed amount of time. U.S. soldiers were dispatched to gather the people to begin the horrific journey later known as the Long Walk.

There are many stories of Navajos who eluded soldiers, hiding in the hills and mountains throughout the Southwest and moving whenever necessary. K'aa' Yel'lii' was one of these nomads. During the years of Navajo captivity, he kept his small band in southeastern Utah, hiding out in the isolated canyons. After the treaty of 1868 was signed and the leaders of the tribe agreed to be peaceful, Navajos were allowed to return to their aboriginal homelands. The people from Utah eventually found their way back home. K'aa' Yel'lii' was there to greet them.

This story represents a small facet of the extensive histories that are part of southeastern Utah. Each community—Blanding, Monticello, Bluff, and Mexican Hat—has places offering information on local points of interest. There's Monument Valley, to name one famous example: it has served as the spectacular backdrop for countless western movies, television commercials, and magazine advertisements. There's also Hovenweep National Monument, which provides a glimpse of how one ancient group of people adapted to the land. There's Goosenecks State Park, which offers some of the finest scenic views of the San Juan River. The must-see list is long: Canyon Rims Recreation Area, Looking Glass Arch, Natural Bridges National Monument, the Valley of the Gods, and Rainbow Bridge National Monument.

To see all this is to stop.
This area deserves a look, an inquiry.

"People traveling through our part of the country should

know that it's one of the most culturally rich areas of the state. I invite people to stop and take a long look at what this area has to offer," says Mark Maryboy, a member of the Navajo Nation Council, who is also a San Juan County com-

missioner. "There's no other place I would rather be."

He knows. Just like K'aa' Yel'lii' and many others, Maryboy's family had the opportunity to live anywhere else, but they chose to stay here. To them, "this is the place."

Tending sheep near Red Mesa on the Navajo Indian Reservation, an area that at times seems to be locked into a pioneer past – Stephen Trimble

Under the Boulder Rim – Tom Olson

Utah's Dixie and the Grand Staircase

– Kane, Washington, Iron, Garfield, and Wayne Counties –

COLOR COUNTRY IS OFTEN THE NAME GIVEN TO THE SOUTHWEST CORNER OF UTAH, AN AREA THAT INCLUDES THREE NATIONAL PARKS, BRYCE CANYON, ZION, AS WELL AS LAKE POWELL, CEDAR BREAKS, THE NEW GRAND STAIRCASE-ESCALANTE NATIONAL MONUMENT, AND A NUMBER OF UNIQUE STATE PARKS. IT IS AN AREA CUT BY DEEP CANYONS AND RIVERS, UNTIL RECENTLY ONE OF THE MOST INACCESSIBLE SECTIONS OF THE STATE. IT IS A PLACE OF EXTRA-ORDINARY BEAUTY AND DIVERSITY, SPARSELY POPULATED, GIVEN TO UNPREDICTABLE SHIFTS OF WEATHER, RICH IN HISTORY, MYTH, AND LORE. HERE IS LOCATED

Negotiating Zion's North Fork of the Virgin – Tom Till, UTC

GLEN CANYON, LOST UNDER THE WATERS BEHIND THE GREAT DAM; HERE THE POET AND ADVENTURER EVERETT RUESS DISAPPEARED UNDER MYSTERIOUS CIRCUMSTANCES; IT WAS HERE ALSO THAT THE SETTLERS OF BLUFF UNDERTOOK THEIR EXTRAORDINARY TREK ACROSS THE COLORADO TO FOUND A NEW CITY.

INTERSTATE 15 CROSSES THE WESTERN EDGE OF THE COLOR COUNTRY ON THE WAY TO LAS VEGAS AND LOS ANGELES; ROUTE 89 PARALLELS THE INTERSTATE TO THE EAST, LEADING INTO ARIZONA AND THE GRAND

"WHITE AND CRIMSON, OR BLACK AND YELLOW AND BLUE-BEHIND HER AND AHEAD AND AROUND HER—SPEWED IN FANTASTIC VIOLENCE, IN EVERY SHADE AND NUANCE, THE COLORS OF THIS UNREAL LANDSCAPE GLITTERED WITH SUCH INTENSITY THAT SHE CLOSED HER EYES AND FOR A MOMENT HER BREATH CLUNG IN HER THROAT. SHE FELT HEMMED IN WITH UNTAMED, IMPONDER-ABLE FORCES. THIS LAND WAS AS DIFFERENT FROM THE GENTLE VALLEYS OF THE NORTH AS SHE IMAGINED HELL WOULD BE FROM HEAVEN."

- Maurine Whipple -
from The Giant Joshua

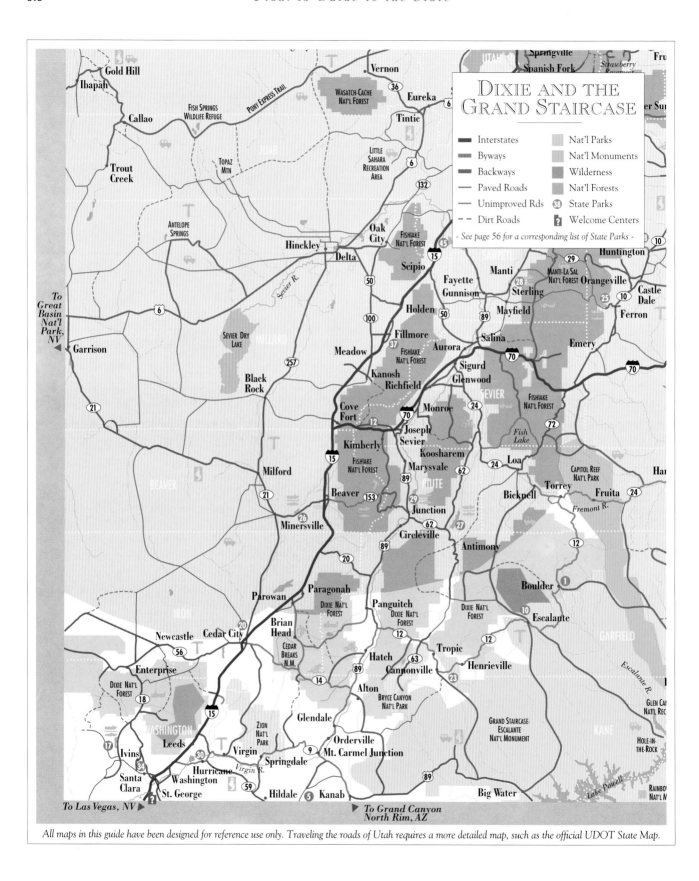

DIXIE AND THE GRAND STAIRCASE

▬▬ Interstates		Nat'l Parks
▬▬ Byways		Nat'l Monuments
▬▬ Backways		Wilderness
— Paved Roads		Nat'l Forests
— Unimproved Rds	38	State Parks
- - Dirt Roads	🅿	Welcome Centers

- See page 56 for a corresponding list of State Parks -

All maps in this guide have been designed for reference use only. Traveling the roads of Utah requires a more detailed map, such as the official UDOT State Map.

Canyon; and Route 12, perhaps the most scenic of Utah's paved roads, heads east from Route 89 to Escalante, Boulder, and eventually, after a spectacular drive over Boulder Mountain, to the town of Torrey and Capitol Reef National Park.

CEDAR CITY ENVIRONS

Cedar City

Cedar City is a regional capital, and until the 1970s, it was the largest city in the state south of Utah Valley and one of the oldest. An attractive community, Cedar City has a diversified economy based on travel, tourism and recreation, trade, agriculture, manufacturing, mining, education, and government. The town was settled in 1851 by English, Scottish, and Welsh emigrants to provide iron products.

Iron mines to the west provided a major economic boost to the city for decades following World War II, though production has fallen gradually in the last four decades. Tourism and recreation have been important to Cedar City since the 1920s; for decades the city was a center to which thousands of tourists would come by rail each year, then board buses for tours of the area's national parks and monuments. Passenger trains no longer come to Cedar City, but tourism is still an important industry. Still standing is the historic Union Pacific Railroad Depot on Main Street, built in 1922–23 as the end of a spur line. Among the first passengers to disembark at the new depot was President Warren G. Harding, a sightseeing tourist.

Among Cedar City's distinctive buildings are the Hunter Home, 76 East Center, a two-story red-brick house built in sections from 1866 to 1924; the George L. Wood Cabin, built in 1851 by an original settler and reputed to be the first log cabin erected in southwestern Utah; and the Mormon First Ward Chapel (Old Rock Church) near the corner of Main and Center, an imposing steepled building of varicolored native stone built during the 1930s; Cedar City's old town clock is in the tower.

Southern Utah University, on a tree-shaded campus of 100 acres in the heart of the city, is a four-year institution of higher learning. SUU was founded in 1897, and it existed under various names as a branch of the University of Utah and Utah State University until 1965, when it became an inde-

pendent institution. Bachelor degrees are offered in numerous fields, with certificates in many others; special emphasis is placed on vocational programs. The college owns and operates a 1,000-acre farm west of Cedar City and a 3,700-acre ranch in the mountains to the east. Of particular interest on the main campus are the library (featuring the Palmer Room of Western History and John Seymour Special Collections); the William R. Palmer Indian Museum; the Braithwaite Fine Arts Gallery; and the Adams Memorial Theater. The latter is an authentic full-size replica of an Elizabethan playhouse, used for productions of the nationally known Utah Shakespearean Festival and named in honor of Fred Adams, founder and longtime director of the festival. Held every year since 1962, the festival runs from July through September. Currently, three Shakespearean plays are presented in the Adams Memorial Theater and three classical or contemporary productions are staged in the indoor Randall L. Jones Theater.

In connection with the plays, the Festival offers seminars, backstage tours, Renaissance concerts, Elizabethan dancing and music, a "Renaissance Feaste," art exhibits, and other activities. From its very humble beginnings, the Utah Shakespearean Festival has grown to the point where tickets are in great demand; theater aficionados schedule their summer vacations around the festival, and more than 60,000 people attend annually.

The Iron Mission State Park, located on North Main (Route 130) near City Park, is a museum with artifacts documenting the history of southern Utah, particularly Cedar City. For history buffs, a collection of more than 100 horse-drawn vehicles, including wagons, coaches, buggies, and sleighs, is the highlight of the park. Most of these vintage vehicles were collected by the late Gronway Parry, a Cedar City resident and pioneer of southern Utah's tourist transportation industry.

Route 56 is the main access highway. From this route several miles west of Cedar City, paved roads fork northwest to Iron Springs and Desert Mound, sites of large open-pit iron mine operations.

Points East of Cedar City

Route 14 forks east from downtown Cedar City, climbing between the steep walls of Cedar (Coal Creek) Canyon to Dixie National Forest and the heights of the Markagunt Plateau (Cedar Mountain). Route 14 joins Route 89 at Long

An ancient ponderosa frames a weathered sandstone butte near Cedar Breaks
— Mel Lewis, UTC

Valley Junction, 41 miles from Cedar City.

The Markagunt is one of the highest and most massive of southern Utah's high plateaus. Less rugged than most highlands, blessed with lakes and streams, and cloaked with pleasant, open forests of aspen and evergreens, the Markagunt is a recreation retreat and vacation homesite.

Route 14, an officially designated scenic byway, and side roads such as Routes 148 to 143 (north to Parowan) give access to several points of interest:

Zion Overlook is a parking area beside Route 14 in the upper reaches of Cedar Canyon. The forested Kolob Terrace, an intermediate platform into which the canyons of Zion National Park have been cut, is visible below. In late September–early October when aspen highlight the Kolob panorama with gold, the view is spectacular.

Cedar Breaks National Monument at 10,000 feet altitude is one of the nation's highest national monuments. (See Parks and Monuments for more description.)

Brian Head Ski and Summer Resort is near Cedar Breaks, 29 miles from Cedar City via Route 14/Route 143, or 12 miles from Parowan via Route 143. At an altitude of 10,000 to 11,000 feet, Brian Head offers plentiful winter snow and varied slopes. The resort was developed originally as a winter attraction but has since gained popularity as a year-round recreation center offering a variety of lodging and dining facilities, shops, horseback riding, hiking and mountain biking trails, and other amenities. Brian Head offers five triple and one double chair for skiers.

Brian Head Peak (11,315 alt.) is one of the highest points in Utah that can be reached by passenger car. Its summit overlooks Cedar Breaks, the Brian Head resort, and much of southern and western Utah, with distant glimpses of Nevada and Arizona. Accessible (usually) from July to October.

Navajo Lake is a favorite fishing, camping, and picnicking spot. The Dixie National Forest maintains a campground on the south shore where boats, lodging, fuel, and limited supplies are provided by a private resort.

Cascade Falls, a picturesque waterfall, can be reached by road and a short nature trail from Navajo Lake on Route 14 near Duck Creek.

Duck Creek Village is in a delightful forest of aspen and evergreens beside the highway several miles east of Navajo Lake. A pond is well known among anglers and the surrounding area is popular with snowmobilers and cross-country skiers. A nearby summer home area was the shooting locale for movies, including *My Friend Flicka* and *How the West Was Won*.

Strawberry Point is an overview atop the Pink Cliffs rim, reached by driving 9 miles of unpaved road from a junction 5 miles east of Duck Creek pond. From here the vista extends across a broken landscape of cliffs and canyons, far south into the Arizona Strip, and westward to the grand forms of Zion National Park. A remarkable natural bridge is found just below the point.

VIRGIN RIVER VALLEY

St. George via I-15 South

South of Cedar City, I-15 ascends gradually to a drainage divide marking the south rim of the Great Basin and the north rim of the Virgin River system. According to the 1941 edition of this book, "Mormon colonization south of this point in early times was characterized as 'going over the Rim,' and in colloquial usage the same phrase came to connote violent death." The mountain front on the east becomes steeper as the highway proceeds south into the Virgin River Valley, changing rapidly into a great cliff near Pintura. This front marks the Hurricane Fault, a 200-mile break in the earth's crust, which has upraised the strata to the east and dropped corresponding rocks to the west, forming a strata offset of thousands of feet—perhaps as much as 14,000 feet in places. To the west, the dark volcanic Pine Valley Mountains climb ever higher to summits of more than 10,000 feet. The hamlets of Hamilton Fort, Kanarraville, and New Harmony are near the highway.

Hamilton Fort displays a few very old houses as evidence of its being one of the oldest inhabited sites in this region. Settled in 1852, the village has had at least four different names: Shirts Fort, Fort Walker, Sidon, and Fort Hamilton.

Kanarraville nestles against colorful red-and-gray cliffs, commanding a fine view of valleys and mountains to the west. It was founded during the early 1860s and named after the local Paiute chief Kanarra. Cattlemen here organized the Kanarra Cattle Company, a huge cooperative that ranged its livestock over much of southern Utah.

New Harmony is an attractive farming village. Its spectacular eastern horizon is formed by the Hurricane Fault scarp and the Finger Canyons of Zion National Park's Kolob section. The location of New Harmony's predecessor, Fort Harmony—marked by foundation stones—lies two hundred yards south of Route 144 to New Harmony, one mile west of I-15. The site is listed on the National Register of Historic Places.

Two miles south of the New Harmony turnoff is a junction with a paved side road leading east into the Kolob Canyons (Finger Canyons) section of Zion National Park. Climbing and winding, this road leads to high viewpoints overlooking giant red cliffs and grand gorges.

Interstate 15 in this vicinity traverses the upper slopes of Ash Creek Canyon between the Hurricane Fault scarp and Pine Valley Mountains. Before the era of paved roads, broken lava made this area (known as the Black Ridge) one of the roughest stretches of road between north and south. In 1856 Peter Shirts surveyed a road south from Fort Harmony through the forbidding Black Ridge area and down Ash Creek Canyon. Leap Creek near Pintura was an especially serious obstacle because of its depth and steep walls. Shirts jokingly proposed to "leap across," and forever afterward the crossing has been known as Peter's Leap. For several years Dixie pioneers traveled the Shirts route, and portions may still be followed on foot. The route is listed on the state historic register. Eighty years before Shirts, the Dominguez-Escalante party had followed roughly the same route.

At Pintura, a fruit-growing village, the altitude is 4,000 feet—much lower than Cedar City's 5,800 feet, yet higher than the 2,800 feet of St. George. Pintura, a Spanish word meaning picture or painting, was applied to the town in 1925.

Four miles south of Pintura at Anderson Junction, Route 17 forks south to Toquerville, LaVerkin, and a junction with Route 9 leading to Hurricane and to Zion National Park.

Toquerville is a tree-shaded community where new and old contrast attractively. The town was settled in 1858 and named for Toquer, chief of the local Paiutes.

Among Toquerville's interesting old buildings are the following, all listed on historic registers: the Naegle Winery, a massive two-story structure built of stone in 1866, used as a residence for a large polygamous family (upper floors) and winery (basement); the Old Mormon Church and Tithing Office, a combined meetinghouse, school, and social hall dating from the years between 1866 and 1879; and the Spilsbury Home, a stuccoed adobe building.

Four miles south of Anderson Junction is the turnoff to Leeds, Silver Reef, and the Red Cliffs Recreation Site.

Leeds is an unassuming town beside the highway, which reportedly has the longest growing season in southern Utah. Leeds has a wild and romantic history. Only a mile from old Silver Reef, the village was a trade center for hundreds of miners during the boom years of the 1870s and 1880s, providing them with a powerful beverage called Dixie wine. These prosperous days, however, passed away with the ore deposits at Silver Reef; today only some aged red houses commemorate them. It is said that many of these old buildings in Leeds would assay high in silver, since they were built of silver-bearing sandstone taken from the reef.

West of Leeds 1.5 miles is Silver Reef, a combination of empty foundations and new homes. In its 19th-century heyday, Silver Reef was a prosperous mining camp. Two remaining antique buildings are of special note: the Rice Bank and the Wells Fargo & Company Express Building. The latter was built in 1877 of red sandstone, ashlar blocks, and rubble. It is currently used as an art gallery and museum, and is listed on the National Register of Historic Places.

At Leeds, a freeway turnoff gives access to the Red Cliffs Recreation Site, a camping and picnicking area with rest rooms, water, and fireplaces. From the campground, a half-mile Desert Wilderness Trail introduces visitors to cacti, juniper, shrubs, pinyon pine, mesquite, yucca, and numerous other plants.

Interstate 15 descends into the Virgin River Valley, known more commonly as Dixie—the lowest-altitude region in Utah. The name Dixie was applied because of the region's warm climate, suitable for growing cotton. The area is known for Zion Canyon and tributary gorges; rainbow cliffs, warm springs, and vast sand dunes; mesas, buttes, plateaus, and mountain ranges. For nearly a century, agriculture and livestock were the most important economic factors in Dixie. Today, however, tourism, recreation, manufacturing, trade, and services for the large number of retirees are rapidly expanding industries in the area.

At Harrisburg Junction, 7 miles south of Leeds, Route 9 forks east to Hurricane, LaVerkin, and Zion National Park.

Quail Creek Reservoir, 14 miles north of St. George, inundated much of the old townsite of Harrisburg. The dam, completed in 1985, gave way in 1989, flooding downriver homes and causing millions of dollars of damage. The dam has since been reconstructed, and Quail Creek is a popular fishing, camping, and recreation site.

Washington is no longer the "leisurely group of red adobe and red brick houses" described in the 1941 edition of this book. From I-15 it resembles a sprawling mobile-home annex of nearby St. George. Washington's pioneer heritage is apparent from side streets and old Route 91, now a frontage road that passes through the town as Telegraph Street. The most imposing structure is the Old Cotton Factory, a massive three-story stone building dating from the 1860s.

St. George

St. George (pop. 38,950) was established in 1861 by 300 Mormon families who received a call to found a mission so that the Saints would have a local source of cotton. The town was named in honor of George Smith, a Mormon apostle.

This growing metropolis "stands at the heart of Utah's Dixie, and is known for its long hot summers and mild winters." As in 1941, it is marked by the white Mormon temple, "which rises dazzlingly above red soil, green trees and lawns, and trim red houses of adobe and brick." But today, the great temple competes for attention with a forest of high billboards, and "trim red houses of adobe and brick" are much less apparent in contemporary St. George than they were in 1941 or even 10 or 20 years ago. The city's population was 3,600 in 1940 and 7,100 in 1970. By 1990 it had grown to about 30,000 and is increasing at a rapid rate.

The county seat of Washington County, St. George is a regional capital—the largest city along the route of I-15 between Utah Valley on the north and Las Vegas on the south, a distance of nearly 400 miles. Dixie's climate, the mildest in Utah during winter months, attracts tourists and many part- and full-time residents. The climate is hardly a new phenomenon, of course, but it is probably the main reason for the phenomenal growth of recent years, in combination with red-rock scenery, a healthy economy, ease of transportation, a mobile population, a larger retired population, higher retirement incomes, and the preference of many urban dwellers for a less stressful living environment.

Also of considerable importance is the influence of the Mormon temple in St. George, which is a magnet for thousands of Latter-day Saints. The most obvious result has been

Brigham Young spent the winter months in St. George – Frank Jensen, UTC

the explosion of St. George's commercial district and new residential suburbs in nearly every direction. St. George and its sister communities of the Virgin River Valley no longer doze lazily in the Dixie sun and dream of their rural pioneer past. They have been yanked rudely into the hectic current of mainstream America. To a marked degree they have become—or are becoming—miniature models of Las Vegas, Salt Lake City, or even Los Angeles. At the same time, it must be pointed out that deliberate effort has been made to keep some development as architecturally attractive and environmentally compatible as possible.

Architectural buffs can discover many worthwhile structures by driving or walking the side streets. A number of these are listed on historic registers. A Walking Tour brochure describing many historical buildings is available from the chamber of commerce. The modern campus of Dixie College also is of interest.

The Mormon temple, between 200 and 300 East and 400 and 500 South, is one of Utah's most photogenic buildings. It was the first temple completed in Utah and is the oldest temple still in use. The construction of this temple was a work of sacrifice requiring six years of great devotion. Mormons from northern Utah were called on 40-day missions to work here, while those in the south gave one day in ten as tithing labor. Seventeen thousand tons of rock were quarried by hand and hauled by ox team; large timbers were freighted overland some 80 miles from Mount Trumbull near the Grand Canyon. Church members contributed food, made the carpets, and did the decorating. The temple was dedicated five months before the death of President Brigham Young.

The Mormon tabernacle, Main and Tabernacle Streets, is a handsome steepled edifice built of red sandstone. It has a four-faced clock on a square tower, surmounted with a slender white wooden steeple. Construction required more than ten years, beginning in 1863. Glass was shipped from New York City to southern California by boat, then brought to St. George by wagon. The clock and bell were purchased by public subscription and served the entire town thereafter. Considered to be one of the most beautiful of Utah's older buildings, the tabernacle is listed on historic registers.

Brigham Young's Winter Home and Office, 200 North and 100 West, was completed in 1873 and used as a winter residence by the LDS Church president until his death in 1877. It is now maintained by the LDS Church, with public tours conducted by missionaries. Listed on historical registers.

Dixie College is a two-year community college run by the state of Utah. The college's nearly 5,000 students pursue associate degrees in the humanities and social sciences, business and trades, natural sciences, and the arts. The college was established in 1911 as a church institution, the St. George Stake Academy, and later renamed Dixie

Normal School and Dixie Junior College. Its present name was adopted in 1970.

McQuarrie Memorial Hall (Pioneer Museum), adjoining the old courthouse to the north, is a comprehensive exhibit of early-day relics of the Dixie region. The red brick building, completed in 1938, is a gift of Mrs. Hortense McQuarrie Odlum.

St. George Area Tours

Santa Clara; Utah Hill, Arizona; and Las Vegas, Nevada

Until the opening of I-15 through the Virgin River Gorge in 1973, this was the main route between Utah and Las Vegas/southern California. The highway now gives access to a fast-spreading complex of new housing subdivisions between St. George and Santa Clara.

Santa Clara has participated in the area's recent residential boom and is now becoming a suburb of St. George. Its historical heritage remains evident in the older part of town, described by this book's 1941 edition as "a clustering group of light brown adobe, red sandstone, and modern brick houses shaded by green trees."

The Jacob Hamblin House in Santa Clara is a well-preserved reminder of what the area was like in 1862 when it was built. Jacob Hamblin is well known for befriending the Indians when he settled in this area. He and his family lived in this rock dwelling for about seven years during the 1860s. Free tours are available from 9 A.M. until dark.

Turn north from a junction immediately west of Santa Clara to the hamlet of Ivins and Snow Canyon State Park, an area of intricately sculptured, beautifully colored sandstone cliffs, dunes of fine red sand, Indian rock art, and other interesting features. Snow Canyon is popular for camping, hiking, and photography. The access road connects with Route 18 north of St. George, forming a loop. The park has an improved campground with showers, a picnic area with tables, drinking water, rest rooms.

Tuacahn, located at the south entrance of Snow Canyon State Park, is an outdoor amphitheater with a capacity of 1,900. In the summer of 1995 a musical drama titled *Utah!* was performed under the stars by a cast of 80 actors. In addition, the complex includes Native American history exhibits and offers backstage tours and a Dutch oven dinner.

An improved road traverses the narrow valley of the Santa

Clara River to Gunlock Lake State Park (boating, camping, fishing, water sports). The road continues to a junction with Route 18 at Veyo. Gunlock is a farming and ranching village named for "Gunlock Bill" Hamblin, sharpshooting brother of Jacob Hamblin. The Santa Clara River Valley was the route of the Old Spanish Trail, south from Mountain Meadows, and of travelers en route to and from southern California.

Route 91 crosses the Beaver Dam Mountains over a 4,600-foot summit, then descends to Arizona over the steep Utah Grade, a long, sustained incline that presented a formidable obstacle to heavy trucks and cars for many years. The lowest point in Utah at 2,100 feet above sea level is on Beaver Dam Wash just west of the highway where it crosses the Arizona line. In 1980 the Beaver Dam slopes became a focus of bitter controversy caused by federal classification of the area's desert tortoise as an endangered species, which restricted livestock grazing. Though the desert tortoise is found elsewhere, this is its only habitat in Utah.

Pine Valley, Mountain Meadows, and Enterprise

North from St. George, Route 18 skirts the upper edge of Snow Canyon State Park, a deep, sculptured sandstone gorge accessible by circular road between Route 18 and Old Route 91 near Santa Clara. Short spurs from Route 18 give dramatic overviews of the canyon. The village of Veyo is famous for a spring-fed swimming pool. From here, Route 18 climbs north between the Pine Valley and Bull Valley mountains to Enterprise and an eventual junction with Route 56. At Central, 6 miles north of Veyo, is a junction with a side road leading east into Pine Valley. The name of the entire mountain range came from this area at the headwaters of the Santa Clara River, as did that of the village of Pine Valley. Steep slopes topped with evergreens loom high above to crests of 10,000 feet and more. Pine Valley is a charming cluster of rustic dwellings, some of which date from pioneer days when the mountains produced timber for the settlements of southern Utah. The area has long been a livestock and recreation center. Pine Valley's lovely wooden chapel is one of Utah's oldest church buildings in continuous use. It was built in 1868 by Ebenezer Bryce, a former shipwright and the person for whom Bryce Canyon was named. The chapel is listed on the National Register of Historic Places. Nearby is Pine Valley Lake, popular for fishing, and the site

of an improved campground maintained by the Dixie National Forest. Other national forest picnicking-camping developments are also nearby.

The Mountain Meadows Massacre Historic Site is a pleasant open valley about half a dozen miles north of the turnoff to Pine Valley. The Meadows were a well known stop on the Old Spanish and California Trails, a place where southbound caravans would make final preparations for the long desert trek ahead. The meadows' fame (or infamy) derived from the slaughter in 1857 of about 120 eastern emigrants by an alliance of Mormons and Indians. Seventeen small children were spared and lived with local families for two years. Ultimately, with government assistance, they were reunited with relatives in Arkansas. Although many of the details are unclear, the massacre was apparently prompted by Mormon anxieties about persecution, and inadequate communication between church leaders in Salt Lake and southern Utah settlers.

Attempts by the federal government to apprehend and punish the participants failed as the tight-knit Mormon society closed ranks and protected its members. Almost 20 years after the massacre, John D. Lee was the only person held responsible for the tragic incident. Following two trials, he was executed by a firing squad at the scene of the crime. Today, a granite monument commemorates the site.

Arizona and Nevada via I-15 South

Interstate 15 south of St. George, within Utah, measures only nine spectacular miles. From there to Las Vegas, a distance of slightly more than 100 miles, the terrain consists of profound gorges, rugged mountain ranges, and one of America's most forbidding deserts. The highway parallels the Virgin River for about 40 miles south of St. George. Almost all of this canyon route is in Arizona and represents one of the lengthiest (nearly ten years) and most challenging feats of road construction in the history of the rural interstate system. Numerous bridges and trestles were required, as well as earth movement on an enormous scale and 2,000 tons of explosives. Quicksand and falling rocks were serious hazards. Total cost of the 30 miles of I-15 in Arizona—the most difficult stretch—approached $50 million, with one four-mile segment costing about $15 million.

Bloomington, several miles south of St. George via I-15, was Utah's first planned resort community.

Zion National Park and Vicinity

At Harrisburg Junction on I-15, take the Zion National Park/Hurricane exit. The road soon cuts through a rocky ridge, the Virgin Anticline, and drops down to a crossing of the Virgin River. All around is a geological wonderland of cliffs and mesas, volcanic cones, buttes, and mountains. The rise of Red Sand Mountain fills the southern view.

Hurricane was established in 1906, two years after irrigation water first became available from the Hurricane Canal. The story of the Hurricane Canal is an epic in Utah history. Beginning in 1893 and continuing for 11 years, the people of Dixie dug and blasted a canal from the Virgin River's cliffs that was eight feet wide, four feet deep, and nearly eight miles long. The first water flowed through the canal in 1904, making agriculture possible for the first time. The canal is listed on the National Register of Historic Sites. Much of Hurricane's growth in recent years is due to the influx of part-time residents and retirees who enjoy the mild climate.

Hurricane received its name from an episode of the early 1860s when Erastus Snow and others, descending a cliff on a makeshift road, were assaulted by a fierce wind. Snow exclaimed, "Well, that was a hurricane! We'll call this place Hurricane Hill." Here in 1776 the Dominguez-Escalante expedition crossed the Virgin River, naming it Rio Sulfureo because it consisted "in great part of hot and sulphurous water." Apparently they did not realize that this was only a condition.

East from Hurricane, Route 59 climbs Hurricane Ledge and passes through open country near the foot of the Vermilion Cliffs to Colorado City, Pipe Spring National Monument, Fredonia, and Route 89-A. Before the late 1950s and early 1960s, this was an unpaved road. Improvement was accelerated by the building of Glen Canyon Dam and the need for a new route from Los Angeles that would reduce heavy truck traffic through Zion National Park.

The route has long been used as a travel corridor by Indians and more recently by settlers. Portions of it were paralleled by the Dominguez-Escalante expedition of 1776. After the settlement of Dixie in the 1850s until the completion of the Zion-Mt. Carmel highway in 1930, it was the only feasible all-year route from east to west in this region. It was the general route for great herds of sheep and cattle en route to the vast Arizona Strip. The colonists of Kane County traveled to and from St. George over the route, including newlyweds (hence,

the name "Honeymoon Trail").

South from Hurricane, an unpaved road winds along the foot of Hurricane Ledge into Arizona. From this road, about 8 miles south of Hurricane, a side road forks west to Fort Pearce Wash and Old Fort Pearce. Old Fort Pearce exhibits the walls of a rock fort built in 1866–67 by Mormons during the Black Hawk Indian War, when Navajos from east of the Colorado River were raiding southern Utah's pioneer communities and stealing livestock.

Fort Pearce Wash and nearby springs were commonly used by both Native American and Euro-American travelers of the time. The fort never saw battle, though for decades it served as a watering and roundup center for livestock. For ages the area had been an Indian campsite, and Indian artifacts were common at one time.

Between Hurricane and LaVerkin, Route 9 crosses the Virgin River over a high bridge. Directly to the east is the mouth of Timpoweap Canyon, by which the river has cut through the Hurricane Fault (Ledge). Far down in the canyon's mouth is a popular bathing resort that utilizes water from hot mineral springs. The Virgin is the normally shallow, muddy sculptor of Zion, giving little hint that such a small stream could be the architect of such geological grandeur. Dixie's pioneers, however, knew what it could do in raging flood. The Virgin rises principally in the upper reaches of the Markagunt Plateau-Kolob Terrace and empties into Lake Mead near Overton, Nevada. It drains an area of about 11,000 square miles, with a total length of approximately 150 miles. The name is a corruption of the Spanish *Rio Virgen*.

La Verkin, like neighboring Hurricane, is nestled beneath the crumbling ledges of the Hurricane Fault. LaVerkin was settled in 1898 after a canal across the canyon from the Hurricane Canal was completed. A tunnel 900 feet long was required, and serious leaking occurred for years. This problem eventually was remedied by the building of flumes and extensive use of concrete. As at Hurricane, water allowed the cultivation of orchards, vineyards, and fields. The name La Verkin derives from the Spanish *La Virgen* (Virgin).

Route 9 east of LaVerkin winds in switchbacks up the Hurricane Ledge and "tops out" at the foot of Hurricane Mesa. Between 1954 and 1962 this flat-topped mesa was the scene of Air Force experiments designed to test the effectiveness of ejection seats in jet aircraft. Aircraft conditions were simulated by attaching dummies to sleds and ejecting them at high speeds from the edge of the mesa.

Virgin is a small farming village, one of the oldest in this part of Utah. Virgin dates from 1858 when it was settled by a group under young Nephi Johnson. He is also credited with being the first Euro-American to enter and explore the Zion Canyon. Like its neighbors in this region, Virgin City suffered terribly from disease, raging floods, and crop failures.

North from Virgin, a partially paved road climbs up the canyon of North Creek to the Kolob section of Zion National Park and onto the 8,000-foot heights of Kolob Terrace, exiting on I-15 near Cedar City or climbing to Route 14 on the Markagunt Plateau. The route is outstandingly scenic with views of giant cliffs, buttes, and gorges—in particular the tremendous face of West Temple, Great West Canyon, Spendlove Knoll, and the red-walled mesas of the Kolob Canyons area. Side roads and trails lead east and west into the park and farther north to the headwaters of the park's great canyons. This road is the main access to summer homes and ranches on the Kolob.

Rockville is a tree-shaded riverside village under the jagged rocky peaks and thirsty talus slopes of lower Zion Canyon, its residents tending fruit orchards and a few sandy fields along the valley floor. Rockville is an old settlement dating from 1862. For several decades between 1880 and 1900 the village prospered, and today it is still one of the most substantial communities in the area. In early days the people grew cotton, made sorghum from cane, and produced silk. On the main street (Route 9) is a historic building known as the Deseret Telegraph and Post Office. The compact wood-frame structure was built in the 1870s and served for years as an office of the church-owned Deseret Telegraph Company, which linked all of Utah and Mormon settlements in nearby states with over 1,000 miles of wire. Adjoining the frame building is a red sandstone house built by Edward Huber in 1864 as a residence for the postmaster and telegraph operator.

Some Rockville residents dry-farm Big Plain south of Smithsonian Butte and Zion Canyon, part of a mesa that extends from the Zion region far south to the breaks of Grand Canyon. The graded road leading to this picturesque tableland is very steep, but it affords magnificent views of the cliffs and temples of Zion. At Big Plain Junction, the road joins Route 59 from Hurricane.

Forking from this road across the river bridge is a 3-mile spur leading west to the well-known ghost town of Grafton. Here a brick church and several distinctive old houses stir memories of the past. Grafton was settled in the 1860s and managed to overcome floods and other difficulties through the years, surviving until the 1920s. Grafton has been a locale for western movies, including *Butch Cassidy and the Sundance Kid*. The church, built in the 1880s, is a registered historic site.

Springdale is only a mile from the entrance to Zion National Park. The town's agricultural history is hardly apparent today. The main street is lined with motels, service stations, restaurants, and stores. A big-screen theater exhibits various dramatizations of the area's history. East of the park the highway crosses the Kolob Terrace, densely wooded with pygmy evergreens, to Route 89 at Mt. Carmel Junction. The forbidding gorge of Parunuweap Canyon is visible to the south. Far above on the north is the rim of the Markagunt. (See Zion National Park for description of Route 9 within the park.)

LONG VALLEY AND SEVIER VALLEY SOUTH

South of Circleville, Route 89 follows the narrow canyon of the Sevier River, which was cut through a mass of igneous rock. This was the path followed prior to Mormon settlement by travelers along the Old Spanish Trail between New Mexico and California, and by the exhausted exploring party of John Charles Fremont in the fierce winter of 1853–54. Emerging from the canyon's confines, the old trail curved westward through low passes toward Paragonah and the Great Basin, leaving the High Plateaus through which it had passed for many miles.

About 15 miles north of Panguitch, the highway enters the upper Sevier River Valley. Hay fields carpet the valley floor, where livestock seemingly outnumber people. Toward the west, the grand Tushar mass has given way to low open valleys and isolated peaks, which blend southward into the Markagunt Plateau. On the east, the Sevier Plateau's volcanic crest has been eroded into a jagged profile not ordinarily seen in the plateau country. This ruggedness is gradually succeeded east of Panguitch by the brilliant sedimentary coloring of the Paunsagunt Plateau.

This high valley and its extension southward beyond Hatch were settled by Mormon pioneers in the 1860s. The Black Hawk Indian troubles caused abandonment of the first settlements between 1866 and 1871. Since then the area's economy has been based largely on livestock and feed crops, timber harvesting, highway travel, and seasonal recreation.

Panguitch is the seat of Garfield County. Summer tourism supports a number of motels, restaurants, and service stations. In winter, commercial activity slows considerably. Panguitch is notable for the distinctive brick architecture of its early homes and outbuildings, and for the original facades of some of its turn-of-the-century Main Street commercial structures.

Panguitch was settled in 1864. The original founders, a few families from Parowan and Beaver, suffered through a snowy first winter. The settlement expanded to about 70 families in 1865. The following year Indian troubles led the settlers to build a fort, which they abandoned the same year when they left the valley. New settlers returned five years later; they found the fort and original buildings intact.

Turn west from Panguitch to Panguitch Lake (21 miles), a popular fishing and summer home area. Private resorts and a public campground support fishing, boating, camping, riding, and other outdoor activities. On the Markagunt Plateau at an elevation of more than 8,000 feet, the lake measures about one square mile in area. Unpaved roads lead from the lake to Yankee Meadows Reservoir, Cedar Breaks, Mammoth Creek, and Route 14. Panguitch Lake Campground, with camping and picnicking facilities, is open from June to October.

South of Panguitch, Route 89 continues along the Sevier Valley, which narrows somewhat and climbs rapidly in elevation. At 7 miles from Panguitch is the junction with Route 12, leading to Bryce Canyon National Park, Escalante, Boulder, the Circle Cliffs, Hole-in-the-Rock, Lake Powell, and other parts of Color Country.

Hatch overlooks the river bottoms and the pink Sunset Cliffs of the Paunsagunt Plateau. Hatch was settled in the early 1870s as a ranch and named for the founding family.

The upper Sevier Valley from Hatch to Long Valley Junction is alpine country, with ponderosa pines, sagebrush, and pygmy evergreens. The Long Valley Junction marks the drainage divide between the Sevier system, which drains north and then west into the Great Basin, and the Virgin, which drains into the Colorado River (Lake Mead) and finally the Gulf of California. The Sevier and its headwater streams such as Asay and Mammoth Creeks provide water for the valley.

Long Valley Junction is marked by a store and service station. Turn west from here on Route 14 to Cedar City (40 miles), Cedar Breaks National Monument, and Brian Head Resort. The highway crosses the forested summit of the Markagunt Plateau, a popular recreation area that offers fishing, hunting, skiing, camping, and sightseeing.

South of Long Valley Junction, Route 89 descends into Long Valley through forested and gently contoured terrain, the headwaters of Virgin River's East Fork. Marked side roads lead several miles east to the farming town of Alton at the foot of pink-and-white cliffs. The Johnson Canyon/Alton Amphitheater Backway provides a close view of the Pink Cliffs on the back side of Bryce Canyon.

Glendale is a pleasant farming, mining, and tourist community strung out along the highway in the narrow upper valley. The little town was founded in 1864 as Berryville by Mormon settlers from northern towns. It was fortified as a stockade and used for protection by Long Valley residents during the Navajo Indian troubles of 1865 and 1866. The town was renamed in honor of Glendale, Scotland, the former home of one of its settlers.

Orderville, largest of the Long Valley communities, was one of the principal sites of the Mormon United Order experiment, though little physical evidence of this period remains. Today its economy relies primarily on agriculture and providing tourist services.

Orderville's early inhabitants lived for more than a decade in an idealistic communal society created "to insure unity in moral, material, and spiritual life." After the disastrous financial crisis of 1873, a number of Mormon communities followed the advice of their leaders in establishing cooperative societies. Orderville became the United Order center for Long Valley and, at least partly because of its geographic isolation, continued the experiment longer than any other Mormon community. From 1875 to about 1886, its people (who numbered 543 in 1877) worked cooperative farms, orchards, dairies, stockyards and sheep herds, blacksmith and carpenter shops, a bakery, a sawmill, a gristmill, a molasses mill, a silk industry, a bucket factory, a woolen factory, a cooper shop, and a tannery. The members pooled their wealth, ate at a common table, and met morning and evening for worship. All proceeds were turned into a common storehouse and shared by everyone according to need.

The venture was abandoned as the result of cumulative difficulties. Young men and other new members could not obtain stock in the company. Anti-polygamy legislation forced leaders into hiding. The death of Brigham Young in 1877 weakened the church's commitment to the program. Booming mines brought prosperity to other towns in southern Utah, prompting dissatisfaction among Orderville's envious youth. Finally, church leaders recommended that the Orderville program be disbanded, and between 1884 and 1889 its property was transferred to private ownership. Thus ended a period of trial in applied idealism.

Mt. Carmel is an agricultural village nestled beneath the Elkhart Cliffs. Called Winsor when it was first settled, the village was later renamed Mt. Carmel after a mountain in Palestine. The famous western painter Maynard Dixon lived at Mt. Carmel for several years during the early 1940s and his ashes were scattered here. The Mt. Carmel School and Church, on Route 89, was built in 1923–24.

Mt. Carmel Junction is at the junction of Route 89 and Route 15, which gives access to Zion National Park via the Zion-Mt. Carmel tunnel. South and west of here, the Virgin River's East Fork enters Parunuweap Canyon.

South of Mt. Carmel Junction, Route 89 ascends a high bench at the base of the beautiful White Cliffs. Grand vistas stretch in all directions, particularly westward to the towers and temples of Zion National Park.

At 4 miles, a paved road leads south to Coral Pink Sand Dunes State Park (11 miles), a colorful basin filled with dunes of fine pink sand eroded from the surrounding cliffs and ridges. This is a popular area for photography, picnicking, camping, and off-road vehicle use. Moviemakers have used the area as a filming location. The side road continues south across the state line into the Arizona Strip, connecting with the highway between Kanab and Hurricane. The park offers campsites, showers, rest rooms, water, and camper and trailer loops.

Route 89 descends into the lovely canyon of Kanab Creek, known here as Three Lake Canyon, with its colored cliffs and intriguing displays of cross-bedded sandstone, remnants of ancient desert dunes. A roadside lake has been featured in numerous films.

Kanab Creek begins in the southern reaches of the Paunsaugunt Plateau, beneath the Pink Cliffs of Bryce, gradually increasing its canyon in depth until it joins the Colorado through one of the deepest tributary gorges of the Grand Canyon. Side canyons in this area contain interesting cliff dwellings and rock art.

Five miles north of Kanab on the Kanab Canyon Road, the Best Friends Animal Sanctuary provides homes for neglected, abused, and otherwise unwanted animals, including dogs, cats, and horses. The 100-acre site houses as many as 1,500 animals at a time.

Kanab and Vicinity

Kanab is the seat of Kane County and the commercial center of a vast farming, livestock, timber-harvesting, moviemaking, and recreation area. In recent years a number of retirement and vacation homes have been built nearby.

Kanab is a Paiute word meaning "place of the willows." In the vicinity are sand dunes, prehistoric Indian sites, majestic cliffs and canyons, mountains, valleys, forests, deserts, and far-spreading plains. The wide variety of natural scenery is ideal for moviemaking, and the Kanab area has been used since the 1920s as locale for several hundred film and television productions.

For decades Parry's Lodge on Kanab's main street has been a beacon for film aficionados; a multitude of Hollywood celebrities have stayed here, including Robert Taylor, Frank Sinatra, Dean Martin, Sammy Davis Jr., Maureen O'Hara, Ava Gardner, and Wallace Beery.

Kanab dates from the mid-1860s. The town served as field headquarters for the Powell-Thompson topographic survey of northern Arizona and Utah that lasted six years from 1871, and Zane Grey lived here in 1912 while writing his novel *Riders of the Purple Sage*. For many years Kanab was perhaps the most isolated town in America. Cut off from the east by the gorges of the Colorado, it could be reached from the west only by a rough dirt road from the Virgin River settlements. The 23-mile journey from Orderville on the north required four harrowing days; north of Orderville the mountain passes were closed by snow for almost half the year.

Side streets in Kanab reveal interesting examples of 19th-century architecture. Of special note is the Heritage House Museum, 100 South Main, a restored historic home with period furniture and Anasazi Indian artifacts.

South of Kanab, Alternate Route 89 leads to Fredonia and other points in Arizona, including the Grand Canyon's North Rim, the vast Arizona Strip, the Kaibab Forest, House Rock Valley, Marble Canyon (Navajo) Bridge, and Lee's Ferry.

Fredonia is located in Arizona's Coconino County, the second largest county in the 48 contiguous states. Its name derives from "free dona" or free women, applied because Mormon refugees from federal anti-polygamy laws were among its first settlers during the 1880s.

From Fredonia, roads give access to the Arizona Strip, a sparsely populated part of Arizona between the Utah line and the Grand Canyon. The Strip has long been used as a travel corridor. Ranchers have grazed their cattle there since the 1860s, and during the great cattle days from 1900 to 1914 as many as 20,000 head of cattle were counted at the roundups held at Pipe Spring and Canaan Ranch. Pipe Spring National Monument features a frontier rock fort dating from the 1870s, when it was built to safeguard an important source of water. Arizona 389 crosses the Arizona Strip along the majestic Vermilion Cliffs. It becomes Utah 59 at the state line.

GRAND STAIRCASE

Kanab to Page, Arizona, via Route 89 South

East of Kanab, Route 89 follows the Vermilion Cliffs through open country. Northward through occasional breaks in the red rampart, the eye catches glimpses of other cliffs, a Grand Staircase rising in giant steps of white, gray, and finally pink—the Pink Cliffs of Bryce Canyon National Park. Southward, the Kaibab Plateau (Buckskin Mountain in this vicinity) becomes lost in distance toward the concealed North Rim of the Grand Canyon. Here and there, strange buttes and promontories appear. Route 89 from Kanab to Page and south into Arizona dates from the late 1950s when it was built to connect the Glen Canyon dam site with urban centers. The stretch east of Kanab in Utah was completed in 1958; sections in Arizona were completed at a later date. In 1959 it was designated as U.S. 89, while the highway south of Kanab—the original U.S. 89—was redesignated as Alternate U.S. 89.

North from Route 89 (8 miles east of Kanab) is Johnson Canyon, which has been used for more than a hundred years as a stock range. A spiderweb of dirt roads branch off to penetrate the broken land between the Paunsaugunt Plateau, the Paria River, and the Vermilion Cliffs; the main road continues on to Alton. Among the canyon's attractions are ranch buildings (the valley was settled during the 1870s), an old western movie set, and Eagle Arch, an unusual rock formation.

Turn north from Route 89 (about 35 miles east of Kanab) to Old Paria Townsite, reached by a 6-mile dirt road. Here, Mormon pioneers established a farming community in the late 1860s and early 1870s. Known first as Pahreah (muddy water), after the normally small stream from which water was taken, the town prospered for a decade or so. Then as a series of floods in the 1880s and later years proved disastrous; most people gradually left, and by the turn of the century, only a handful remained. A few ruins, several old houses, and a forlorn cemetery are all that remain of the original settlement. Modern moviemakers constructed a false-front western set near the old town.

Forming the eastern skyline in this vicinity is a high, north-south trending ridge known as the Cockscomb (Coxcomb). Road crews working on Route 89 encountered a formidable challenge in cutting a roadway through the ridge several miles southeast of the Old Paria turnoff, where it is more than a thousand feet high. Technically, the Cockscomb is but one section of a giant earth flexure or fold known as the East Kaibab Monocline, which extends about 150 miles from the vicinity of Bryce Canyon southward into Arizona.

An interesting part of the monocline is Cottonwood Canyon, formed along the uptilted layers of the flexure; the road between Cannonville and Route 89 follows this canyon.

Five miles south of the Old Paria turnoff, where Route 89 begins to ascend the west slope of the Cockscomb in Fivemile Valley, an unpaved road leads southward into upper House Rock Valley. At 4 and 8 miles from the highway, trails lead from the road into the western arm of Paria Canyon/Vermilion Cliffs Wilderness Area. Hikers must register at the Office of U.S. Bureau of Land Management in Kanab or at the visitor center, where weather information and a brochure with map are available. Wilderness hiking routes here feature narrow passageways, natural windows, and dramatic scenic forms. The most challenging and exciting of all is Buckskin Gulch, an exceptionally narrow, 400-foot-deep tributary of the Paria, which can be hiked along its 12-mile course from the Dive to its confluence with the Paria, 7 miles downstream from the Paria trailhead. The average width of the gulch is less than 15 feet, and ropes may be necessary to descend two drops caused by rock falls. In only one spot is it possible to climb out of the canyon. Floods are a hazard and mud is a problem; hikers must register and obtain the latest weather information from rangers before attempting the Buckskin hike.

East of the Cockscomb, the highway descends into the valley of Paria River, an area of sand and wild rock erosion. Hardly a sign indicates that, a hundred years ago, a fair-sized community existed here. This was Adairville, founded in the 1870s but gradually abandoned because of flooding.

Turn south from Route 89 at the sign (43 miles from Kanab) to the Paria Canyon/Vermilion Cliffs Wilderness Area. Drive 3 miles over an unpaved road to White House Ruins, site of an old homestead where cars may be parked and visitors must register. From this point, hikers descend the awesome Gorge of the Paria River to Lee's Ferry, Arizona. The 35-mile route follows the river, and frequent wading is necessary; one 5-mile stretch known as the Narrows has such steep walls that there is no escape route in case of flash flood, which is why hikers must check with rangers before embarking. From four to six days are recommended for the hike, and highlights include natural arches, Indian antiquities, springs, seeps and pools, rock slides, narrow side canyons, old ruins, and ranches. Warmer months are the most comfortable; winter is too cold for wading. Danger of floods from upstream rain is greatest in July, August, and September. Obtain required permits not more than 24 hours in advance from BLM District Office in Kanab or the visitor center.

Three miles east of the Paria River crossing, an unpaved road leads north to Cannonville, Kodachrome Basin, and Bryce Canyon National Park. Turn north on this road through the rugged, colorful, lonely Paria River-Cottonwood Canyon country.

Big Water, formerly Glen Canyon City, is a rather nondescript settlement of mobile homes, trailers, frame buildings, and other more-or-less permanent structures. The town dates from the late 1950s, the beginnings of Glen Canyon Dam, when land speculation in the area was rampant. The dreams of its founders were not realized.

North from Big Water, an unpaved road crosses Wahweap Creek and ascends Lone Rock Canyon to Nipple Bench.

The corrugated Kaiparowits Plateau, north of Big Water, has long been regarded as one of Utah's last wilderness frontiers, though a network of dirt roads makes much of it reasonably accessible; stockmen have used it as rangeland for a hundred years; oil is produced in quantity; and it is known to contain immense reserves of coal. Despite local familiarity, the 1,500-square-mile region is noteworthy as a wilderness because of its complete lack of permanent inhabitants, its labyrinthine system of steep-walled canyons, and its

The crossbedded sandstone of the Paria Vermilion Cliffs Wilderness are ancient pertrified sand dunes colored a rainbow of hues – Frank Jensen, UTC

formidable cliffs. Much of the plateau can be seen in overview from the rim of Bryce Canyon, its surface appearing deceptively unbroken from that distant vantage point.

In September 1996, President Bill Clinton declared the creation of the Grand Staircase-Escalante National Monument, encompassing 1.7 million acres of the Vermilion Cliffs, the Grey Cliffs, and the Kaiparowits Plateau. Unusual for a national monument, the area will be administered and managed by the Bureau of Land Management rather than the National Park Service. For more information on the Grand Staircase-Escalante National Monument, contact the Bureau of Land Management, Cedar City Office, 176 East D.L. Sargent Drive, Cedar City, UT 84720, (435) 586-2401.

As Route 89 approaches the Utah-Arizona line, the land becomes more rugged and spectacular. Grand buttes and lines of cliffs appear, and looming over all is Navajo Mountain, a regional landmark, sacred to the Indians of the region. Finally the waters of Lake Powell come into view, set in an unearthly landscape of bright color and anguished rock forms. This is Glen Canyon country, gouged out over countless centuries by the Colorado River and its tributaries. Less than half a century ago, it was an almost inaccessible wild land; today it is visited by millions of recreationists and highway travelers.

Glen Canyon Visitor Center and Lake Powell

The dam, bridge, visitor center, and Page are in Arizona; most of Lake Powell is in Utah. This giant water-storage and power-generating development became a reality in the decade between 1956 and 1966. Construction began in 1956, shortly after Congress passed the Colorado River Storage

View from Bryce Canyon National Park looking east into Bryce Valley and the pioneer communities of Tropic, Cannonville, and Henrieville – Frank Jensen, UTC

Project. The dam, bridge, and visitor center are startling sights when first viewed; so is the blue lake stretching away to the north in a weird landscape of bare rock. They seem out of place and inappropriate in this strangest of wild lands, hundreds of miles from the nearest metropolitan area. Statistics alone are worth noting:

The dam is 710 feet high above bedrock, 583 feet above the original riverbed; the power plant cost $70,000,000, and contains eight generating units with a peak capacity of nearly a million kilowatts; the bridge is the world's highest steel-arch bridge, 700 feet above the river at the base of the dam.

The Carl Hayden Visitor Center, perched on the west rim of the canyon above the dam, was dedicated in September 1968 and named in honor of Arizona Senator Carl Hayden. It provides exhibits, an information desk, and self-guided tours through the dam and power plant.

Lake Powell is the huge body of water impounded behind Glen Canyon Dam. Although the dam itself is in Arizona, the greater part of the lake is in Utah. The lake was named for Major John Wesley Powell, who led the first exploratory expeditions through canyons of the Colorado River system in 1869 and 1871, and applied names to many of its landscape features, including Glen Canyon. The lake is 186 miles long, filling almost the entire Glen Canyon basin upstream into Cataract Canyon. Its incredibly indented shoreline totals about 2,000 miles. On the lake are several major marina-resort developments (Wahweap, Bullfrog, Halls Crossing, and Hite) and a smaller marina near Rainbow Bridge; all of these except Wahweap are in Utah. (See Chapter 2: Glen Canyon National Recreation Area.)

Page, Arizona, on a bench overlooking the dam site from the east, was built by the federal government as a construction town. In 1956 when project construction began, the nearest community of moderate size was Kanab, 76 miles away. Within several years, several hundred new homes had been built, as well as a sewer and water system, schools, and a hospital. By 1959 the town had about 5,000 residents. A number of motels, restaurants, shops, and services make it one of the largest highway centers between Flagstaff and Kanab, a distance of 200 miles.

Highway 12

From the junction with Route 89 seven miles south of Panguitch, Utah Highway 12 crosses the Sevier Valley and enters Red Canyon, a miniature of Bryce with similar erosional forms and the same exquisite colors. Red Canyon is cut into the Paunsaugunt Plateau.

Emerging from Red Canyon after a few miles, the highway enters a broad upland known variously as Panguitch Hayfield, Emery Valley, and John's Valley. Unpaved side roads lead north and south into little-visited parts of the Dixie National Forest. At 14 miles is Bryce Junction, a center of motels, stores, service stations, and the Bryce Canyon Airport.

Bryce Canyon and Vicinity

Turn south to Ruby's Inn Lodge and Resort (1 mile), a tourist complex with lodging, meals, supplies, fuel, and other services. Almost immediately thereafter the road enters Bryce Canyon National Park. (See Chapter 2.)

Turn north on Route 22 through the broad valley of the Sevier River's East Fork to Widtsoe, Antimony, and Otter Creek State Park, a popular summer and winter fishing destination. This partly paved, improved road offers views of southern Utah's plateau country.

At 11 miles from Bryce Junction, an unpaved road climbs east to Pine Lake in the Dixie National Forest, a very popular recreation area with a campground nearby. A rough road continues about 4 miles to the upper levels of the Table Cliff Plateau (10,300 alt.), an extension of the Aquarius Plateau. A short trail leads from road's end to Powell's Pink Point at the plateau's southern tip, where a sweeping view unfolds—a view extending into surrounding states on a clear day.

Widtsoe marks the junction of an unpaved road leading east through the Dixie National Forest, climbing over a 9,000-foot pass, and joining Route 12 near Escalante. Until the early 1950s or so, this was the main route between Bryce Canyon and Escalante.

Route 12 continues eastward from Bryce Junction, dropping from the plateau at 7,600 feet into Bryce (Paria) Valley more than a thousand feet lower. En route it passes through outriggers of the park's colorful rock formations. In Bryce Valley are the attractive communities of Tropic, Cannonville, and Henrieville. Tropic, largest and youngest of the valley's towns, is nestled beneath the pink cliffs of Bryce. The town's name came from the early settlers' contention that the climate here was much warmer than in nearby Panguitch.

Cannonville, settled in 1876, was named for early Mormon leader George Q. Cannon. It was locally known as Gunshot, the settlers maintaining that it was not large enough to be called a cannon.

Henrieville is a farming community in a small valley, strung along the highway like a necklace. For some years, beginning in the 1930s, scientists made this town a base for expeditions into the Kaiparowits Plateau. The town was settled during the 1870s and named for James Henrie of Panguitch. There are no businesses, but the old town school, built in 1881, currently functions as a senior citizens center and town hall.

South from Cannonville, a road leads to Kodachrome Basin State Park, Grosvenor Arch, and Cottonwood Canyon, joining Route 89 about 47 miles east of Kanab. From this maintained route, other unpaved roads give access to Bull Valley Gorge and other remarkable points in the rugged Paria River Valley, as well as to the canyons and broken slopes of the Kaiparowits Plateau.

Kodachrome Basin State Park, 8 miles from Cannonville, was established to preserve an area of unique geological phenomena, erosional forms, and color combinations. Its most unusual features are a group of upright, cylindrical spires or "chimneys" of different color and material than the rock from which they project. One explanation for their origin is that they were geyser plugs—tubes filled with more resistant material than the encasing rock, remaining behind when the surrounding matrix eroded away. The spires, however, represent only a part of the basin's weird erosional forms and picturesque cliffs, all painted in a spectrum of soft and vivid colors. The park's facilities include an improved campground, water, tables, rest rooms and a dump station.

An article in *National Geographic* in September 1949 titled "Motoring into Escalante Land" applied the name Kodachrome Flat to the area formerly known as Thorny Pasture. The National Geographic Society's expedition also applied the name Grosvenor—in honor of the society's president, Dr. Gilbert Grosvenor—to a superb double arch in the same general area. Grosvenor Arch is sculptured from a cream-colored cliff, standing as a superb buttress. Secluded in a small cove, the great arch lies a mile from the main side road, about 10 miles east of Kodachrome Basin

Past the turnoff to Kodachrome Basin, the road descends into Cottonwood Canyon, a highly scenic gorge that it follows

for the next 15 miles or so. Cottonwood Canyon, the route of Cottonwood Creek, parallels the axis of the East Kaibab Monocline (Cockscomb), a major flexure or fold in the earth's crust; Cottonwood Creek empties into the Paria River near the lower end of the deep Shurtz Gorge; from that point the road parallels the river for most of the remaining distance to Route 89, which it meets some 47 miles from Cannonville and about the same distance east of Kanab.

Route 12 continues from Cannonville to Henrieville through picturesque Bryce (Paria) Valley. East of Henrieville it enters the canyon of Henrieville Creek, ascending rather gently to a summit (about 7,400 feet) marking the divide between the Paria and Escalante drainage. Along the way there are breathtaking views of Table Cliff Plateau and the weird badland "breaks" known as The Blues that fan out from beneath its upper ramparts. Beyond the drainage divide, which also marks the general separation between Aquarius and Kaiparowits Plateaus, Route 12 descends Upper Valley. Here in the headwaters of the Escalante River, the terrain opens up, expanding at the town of Escalante into the desert vastness of the Escalante River Basin.

Seven miles west of Escalante, a cluster of petroleum tanks marks the unpaved road leading south into Upper Valley Oil Field, a moderate oil producer. The road continues south through the broken Kaiparowits Plateau, skirting the eastern slopes of Canaan Peak and threading between the upper ends of deep canyons. Branches of the increasingly rough road lead to Grosvenor Arch and Cannonville, Collett Canyon, Glen Canyon City, and Route 89. Detailed maps and prior consultation with knowledgeable sources are wise precautions before attempting these roads; an area office of the U.S. Bureau of Land Management is located in Escalante.

Five miles west of Escalante, two roads lead northward from the highway: one follows Birch Creek, then passes across the summit of Escalante Mountains to Widtsoe; the other leads to Barker Reservoir in the Dixie National Forest.

Two miles west of Escalante, turn north a short distance to Escalante State Park, a thousand-acre preserve displaying the fossilized remnants of ancient trees. This is one of Utah's most accessible and impressive natural exhibits of petrified wood, in a setting of multicolored chinle (Sleeping Rainbow) rocks. The park has a public campground with rest rooms.

*Pluge pool in the upper
Escalante River drainage
– François Camoin*

Escalante

Escalante is 47 miles from Bryce Junction, 61 miles from Route 89. No longer the "horse town" described in the first edition, where "people ride on horseback from one part of town to another, and newsboys deliver papers on horseback," Escalante does retain an aura of frontier isolation, though this is not as apparent as it was only a few years ago. The town was settled in 1875 by Mormon pioneers and called Potato Valley for a species of wild tuber. It was later renamed after the river, which in turn was named by one of the Powell expeditions in honor of Francisco Silvestre Velez de Escalante, the Spanish missionary and explorer.

Until recent decades, Escalante was isolated by poor roads, and its people relied primarily on farming, stock raising, and lumbering for economic support. These activities remain important, but highway travel, tourism, and government employment have diversified the economic base.

Escalante still boasts a number of historical buildings, some dating from the late 19th century. Their age is not always obvious, however; adobe or log construction may have been camouflaged with plaster or wood. Many of the town's red brick homes were built before the turn of the century. A Daughters of Utah Pioneers Museum, open in the summer, is located in the center of town.

Turn south from Escalante on an unpaved road into Alvey Wash, a deep canyon, the road eventually climbing to high benches and ridges of the Kaiparowits Plateau at 6,000 and 7,000 feet. In every direction from the road are arroyos and deepening canyons, which become tremendous steep-walled gorges as the road continues south toward the Glen Canyon breaks. Side roads exit through the forks of Collett Canyon to the east and lead off to the left and right; the main road meanders south over the Smoky Mountain, offering overviews of the Lake Powell country, then descending into Warm Creek Canyon and finally exiting at Big Water on Route 89. Maps and road information are available from BLM area offices in Escalante or Kanab.

Turn north from Escalante into the Dixie National Forest and the canyon of Pine Creek, paralleling the tilted, eroded flanks of the Escalante Anticline, through which the Escalante River has carved a narrow channel. This river canyon is popular for scenic hiking. The main road (unpaved and rough in

spots but maintained; closed in winter) continues north across a 10,000-foot terrace of the Aquarius Plateau to Bicknell and Loa. At 15 miles is Posey Lake, a popular fishing and camping spot surrounded by forested mountain slopes. At 14 miles (1 mile east of Posey Lake), a side road leads east to Hells Backbone and Boulder. This also is an unpaved forest road, closed in winter, steep in places, perhaps rutted and corrugated in places, but generally suitable for passenger cars. As described on page 340 of the book's first edition, Hells Backbone "is a knife-edged ridge with a bridge on top spanning a streamless crevice no wider than the bridge itself. On both sides are precipitous walls that drop hundreds of feet, with Death Hollow on one side and Sand Creek Canyon on the other. For years the residents of Boulder carried mail and packed provisions along this ridge."

Hikers may traverse Death Hollow downstream to the Escalante River (22 miles), then upstream to Escalante (8 miles) or downstream to Route 12 (7 miles). This is a strenuous trek, passing through deep pools and forbidding narrows, requiring scrambling over rocks or swimming in places. Obtain details from the BLM office in Escalante.

Route 12 east of Escalante passes across undulating flats that afford exciting views south and east across the Escalante River Basin. The basin's canyons are not visible, but the grand dome of Navajo Mountain can be seen through the haze, 70 miles to the south at the far end of the majestic east face of the Kaiparowits Plateau. This 2,000- to 3,500-foot rampart, its front almost unbroken, is known as Fifty-Mile Mountain or the Straight Cliffs; also as the Escalante Rim.

- Escalante Canyons -

Five miles east of Escalante, an unpaved but maintained road forks south to Hole-in-the-Rock, the Escalante Canyons (Glen Canyon National Recreation Area), Devil's Rock Garden, Collett Canyon, and other points. Maps and information are available from the offices of the BLM and Glen Canyon National Recreation Area, in Escalante, or elsewhere. The road may be impassable in wet weather.

The road parallels the Straight Cliffs of Kaiparowits, which loom overhead for almost the entire distance. This is the general route of the Hole-in the-Rock pioneers of 1879.

At 9 miles, a road leads eastward to Harris Wash, giving trail access to Escalante River Canyon, George Hobbs Historical

Site, Baker Bench petroglyphs, Silver Falls Canyon, and an intricate network of Escalante side canyons.

At 12 miles or so, just off the road to the west, is the Devil's Rock Garden, an area of exotic rock formations, including Metate Arch, and a group of picturesque standing rocks. A short distance beyond, a dirt road leads west into Collett Canyon and the interior of the Kaiparowits Plateau.

At 34 miles a water tank marks a trailhead; from here a trail leads down Hurricane Wash into Coyote Gulch, a spectacular gorge emptying into Escalante River Canyon. Located in Coyote Gulch are Jacob Hamblin Arch and Coyote Bridge, two impressive natural rock spans. At the mouth, perched hundreds of feet above the canyon floor, is Stevens Arch.

West from here, a rough dirt road climbs part way up the face of the Straight Cliffs and winds southward for about 13 miles, providing views over the rugged country to the east and south. A branch of this road descends to the main road eight miles south of Hurricane Wash, providing a circular loop.

In 1963, at Carcass Wash, 45 miles south of Escalante, a modern-day tragedy occurred. A group of Boy Scouts from northern Utah were en route to Hole-in-the-Rock in an open truck. As the driver tried to shift gears on a grade, the brakes failed. The truck rolled backward 100 feet, then dropped over a high bank. Thirteen were killed and twice as many injured.

South from Hurricane Wash for 15 miles or so, trails from the main road give access to gorges of the lower Escalante system, a labyrinth of deep narrow chasms offering a variety of hiking experiences. Most of the canyon system is a part of the Glen Canyon National Recreation Area. There are numerous natural arches in this area, including Broken Bow, LaGorce, Bement, and Nemo arches. The latter is a reminder of Everett Ruess, a romantic young wanderer-poet from California who vanished in this region in the 1930s. Though his pack animals were located, and the inscribed word "Nemo" discovered on a smooth cliff wall, Ruess had disappeared without further trace. Many local people attributed his disappearance to foul play. Ruess's story is told in W. L. Rusho's thoroughly researched book *A Vagabond for Beauty.*

At about 37 miles, Dance Hall Rock appears to the east. A amphitheater carved out of smooth sandstone, it served the Hole-in-the-Rock pioneers of a century ago as a dance floor.

Hole-in-the-Rock, 52 miles from Route 12, one of Utah's most historic and scenically noteworthy natural sites, is a slot or break in the wall of Glen Canyon, through which Mormon pioneers in 1879 and 1880 lowered their wagons to the river far below, then ferried them across to an even more forbidding country beyond. Even on foot, today, it is a strenuous endeavor to negotiate the narrow, precipitous passageway; the lower reaches of the "hole" are now beneath Lake Powell.

The epic crossing through Hole-in-the-Rock was only one part of a journey that holds an honored place in the annals of the early West. In 1879, 230 members of the Mormon Church from southwestern Utah were called to colonize the southeastern corner of the state. An advance party had been to that region but knew next to nothing about the wild country along the more direct route chosen for the main trek. The journey began in November 1879 with more than 80 wagons and a thousand head of cattle. The colonists had already passed through the new settlement of Escalante and were encamped on the desert near Dance Hall Rock when their fearful predicament became apparent: they were blocked ahead by the sheer wall of Glen Canyon, and they could not retreat to the settlements of central Utah because of mountain snow. They chose to go on. A summary of their trek is included in Chapter 7.

Route 12 continues east and north, descending steep curves to the Escalante River, a modest stream that flows to Lake Powell, about 70 miles to the southeast. From the bridge, a hiking trail leads upstream to Escalante Natural Bridge (2 miles), an appealing arch cut from the south wall. The trail continues upstream to a north side tributary known as Death Hollow (7 miles from the bridge), an extremely deep and narrow gorge extending northward from the river for more than 20 miles to the Hells Backbone road (see above). Death Hollow offers special hiking rewards; check with the BLM office for details. Hikers also have a choice of routes through wild canyons downstream from the bridge.

The Calf Creek Recreation Area (BLM), a mile north of the river bridge via Route 12, is in an oasis beside the clear water of little Calf Creek. Colored cliffs loom overhead. Facilities here include tables, fire pits, drinking water, and rest rooms. Upstream from the campground, a sandy foot trail leads along the canyon floor to Lower Calf Creek Falls (2-3/4 miles), formed by a 126-foot drop in the streambed. Native vegetation along the trail is intriguing; a trail guide is available from the BLM. Also of interest are the ruins of small

Lower Calf Creek Falls, an oasis hidden in the canyons of the Escalante, is a sweet reward for the backcountry hiker – Frank Jensen, UTC

Indian structures and examples of Indian rock art; a pioneer fence; and a miniature natural arch. Upper Calf Creek Falls, 5.5 miles upstream from the parking area, can only be reached by a hike over slickrock from Route 12.

BOULDER COUNTRY

Route 12 climbs out of Calf Creek Canyon in a series of steep curves, topping out on a razorback ridge between deep canyons on either side. The full circle view is literally breathtaking, and in fact some people—especially the drivers—prefer to keep their eyes on the road. Painted mostly in delicate shades of white, buff, and cream, the truly stunning panorama overlooks a landscape of bare rock, which has been molded into the soft contours characteristic of navajo sandstone.

This special beauty of soft curving contours and gentle colors continues to Boulder and beyond. Three miles west of town is the junction with the mountain road to Escalante via Hells Backbone (see above).

Boulder

Boulder, 29 miles from Escalante, is nestled serenely on a sloping shoulder of the Aquarius in an idyllic setting. Fields and buildings blend in harmony with the valley's delightful erosional forms. The town was settled in 1894 and named for the dark volcanic boulders that litter the slopes of lava-capped Boulder Mountain (Aquarius Plateau). The first edition described an interesting segment of its history:

FOR YEARS AFTER SETTLEMENT THE TINY TOWN WAS ISOLATED FROM THE WORLD BY TOWERING WALLS OF SOLID ROCK, 35 MILES BY PACK TRAIN FROM ESCALANTE. A MAN PACKED IN A PICK-UP TRUCK, IN PIECES, REASSEMBLED IT, AND RAN IT EIGHT YEARS WITHOUT A LICENSE; GASOLINE, ALSO "IMPORTED" ON PACK HORSES COST SEVENTY-FIVE CENTS A GALLON. IN 1923, PRESIDENT HARDING SET ASIDE 130 ACRES OF PUBLIC DOMAIN FOR A TOWNSITE, BUT A SURVEY WAS NEGLECTED, AND FOR NEARLY TEN YEARS THE RESIDENTS WERE LEGALLY SQUATTERS, IMMUNE FROM TAXATION.

Visitor facilities include several modest motels, gasoline, groceries, and limited supplies. Also in Boulder is the Anasazi Indian Village State Park, an attractive visitor center-museum that includes the reconstruction of a prehistoric Indian dwelling. It occupies the site of what once was a large frontier community of Anasazi Indians, who probably migrated to the area from northeastern Arizona about A.D. 1050 and remained for about 150 years. The village seems to have been abandoned about the same time as most other Anasazi and Fremont communities throughout the Four Corners region.

The visitor center-museum contains historical and cultural displays, information and publications. A diorama illustrates how the village might have once appeared. Most of the former village, excavated in 1958–59 by the University of Utah and reburied for protection, is not visible. In 1978 a reconstruction of a typical Anasazi dwelling, complete with a variety of building styles, was built behind the museum.

Points North of Boulder

Route 12, formerly known as the Boulder-Grover Road, crosses the eastern shoulder of Aquarius Plateau (Boulder Mountain), reaching 9,200-feet altitude and offering stirring views across a corrugated, rainbow-hued landscape that has few equals for rugged grandeur.

The road's immediate environment is a landscape of evergreens and aspen, with open meadows, streams, and the blue of Lower Bown's Reservoir serving as orientation. Above all looms the Aquarius, a dark volcanic rampart surrounding the 11,000-foot table known as Boulder Top. This is an alpine region of numerous small lakes and one of America's highest evergreen forests. Along the road are three excellent public campgrounds: Oak Creek, Pleasant Creek, and Singletree, each featuring tables, fire pits, rest rooms, and drinking water. Primitive facilities are found at Lower Bown's Reservoir, a popular fishing spot. Rough side roads approach Boulder Top, the plateau's summit; they may not be passable at times. Foot trails also lead to the top.

No writer has described the Aquarius and its views better than Captain Clarence E. Dutton, geologist-explorer of the Powell Survey, who wrote in the classic *Report on the Geology of the High Plateaus of Utah* (1880):

THE AQUARIUS SHOULD BE DESCRIBED IN BLANK VERSE AND ILLUSTRATED UPON CANVAS. THE EXPLORER WHO SITS UPON THE BRINK OF ITS PARAPET LOOKING OFF INTO THE SOUTHERN AND EASTERN HAZE, WHO SKIRTS ITS LAVA-CAP OR CLAMBERS UP AND DOWN ITS VAST RAVINES, WHO BUILDS HIS CAMP-FIRE BY THE BORDERS OF ITS SNOW-FED LAKES OR STRETCHES HIMSELF BENEATH ITS GIANT PINES AND SPRUCES, FORGETS THAT HE IS A GEOLOGIST AND FEELS HIMSELF A POET.

About 30 miles from Boulder, over the east and south shoulders of Boulder Mountain, is the ranching village of Grover, home to the Hale Summer Theatre. From the western outskirts of Grover, an unpaved road forks south. Known as the

North Slope road, this forest route climbs steeply up the shoulder of Boulder Mountain to elevations approaching 10,000 feet. Four-wheel-drive is recommended. The road gives hiking and jeeping access to Donkey and Fish Creek reservoirs and Blind Lake.

Slightly west of the turnoff for the road is a marked spur leading to Teasdale. This route follows the Teasdale Fault west past the Cockscomb Ridge. Teasdale is a tiny town of well-preserved older homes; the white steepled Mormon chapel is a landmark. Today's population includes retirees and summer residents. A district office for Boulder Mountain (Dixie National Forest) is also located here. Roads in the vicinity climb the north slope of Boulder Mountain to lakes and streams. The town can also be accessed via Route 24, from Torrey and Bicknell.

Northward from Teasdale and Route 24 is the full southern face of Thousand Lake Mountain, a stupendous frontal exposure of rainbow cliffs and mountain slopes rising 4,000 feet from the Fremont River to the mountain's crest.

Torrey, at the junction of Routes 24 and 12 east of Teasdale, is situated on a sloping bench, marked by large cottonwood and poplar trees. Torrey's older homes and buildings reflect individuality—an independent nonchalance that is rather uncommon in southern Utah. The town is an increasingly popular site with retirees, vacationers, and urban refugees.

Turn north from Route 24 at Torrey's western outskirts to Sand Creek, Velvet Ridge, Holt Draw, and panoramic viewpoints high on the eastern shoulder of Thousand Lake Mountain. This drive and its branches, extremely rough and steep, penetrate a handsome region of red wingate cliffs, pastel chinle hills, and gently contoured navajo slopes and ledges. Most of the area is within the boundaries of the Fishlake National Forest. One fork winds westward across the Velvet Ridge, an intermediate bench atop the Fluted Wall overlooking the Fremont River and Teasdale, and is named for the ridge's fluorescent chinle mounds. Another fork enters Hell's Hole, a deep cliff-encircled basin. The route up the mountain through Holt Draw is steep and rough, but its higher reaches above Sand and Paradise Flats offer a nice overview of Capitol Reef, the northern Waterpocket Fold, Cathedral Valley and South Desert, the Caineville country, the Henry Mountains, and the San Rafael Swell. This road also provides hiker access to Water Canyon, Deep Creek, and other parts of the Waterpocket Fold where it emerges from the mountain. Hikers should obtain information from Capitol Reef National Park.

About 2 miles east of Torrey, State 24 curves northward and drops into the valley of Sand and Sulphur Creeks, then follows the base of brightly colored cliffs and slopes to Fruita and Capitol Reef National Park. (See Chapter 2). Though not included within the park, the "breaks" of Thousand Lake Mountain near Torrey are a beautiful complex of canyons, cliffs, ledges, buttes, and mesas.

Points East of Boulder

A partially improved road from Boulder gives access to the Circle Cliffs, the Burr Trail and lower Waterpocket Fold (Capitol Reef National Park), the Henry Mountains, and Bullfrog Marina-Resort (Lake Powell). This scenic road is passable most of the year by passenger cars, but the very steep switchback turns of the Burr Trail make passage difficult for large motor homes or vehicles towing large trailers or boats.

The road enters the Circle Cliffs through navajo buttes and mesas, eventually passing into the narrow Long Canyon, which extends for about 7 miles through a highland of red wingate sandstone. Through this sandstone, which forms a rim around the Circle Cliffs amphitheater, other canyons of the Escalante River and Halls Creek systems have been gouged out by nature; they are popular for hiking and backpacking.

The Burr Trail (35 miles from Boulder) is a break or notch in the steep face of Waterpocket Fold. The road descends in tight switchbacks (too angular for large vehicles or long multiple-vehicle combinations), dropping about 800 feet in little more than a mile. From the heights west of the trail, the views are breathtaking—a multicolored landscape of cliffs and canyons, buttes, mesas, plateaus, and mountain peaks. Extending north and south from the top of the trail are Upper and Lower Muley Twist Canyons, gorges that are popular for exploring and hiking. (See Capitol Reef National Park.)

From the bottom (east end) of the Burr Trail, the main Waterpocket Fold road extends north to Route 24, south to park overlooks, and the Bullfrog Resort-Marina on Lake Powell. In either direction the road is suitable for passenger cars but may be rough and should be avoided in wet weather.

"Most any place you go in this wide-open wilderness we call southern Utah … something has gone on there before" – Mel Lewis, UTC

LANDSCAPE AND STORY

BY LYMAN HAFEN

I remember it as a perfect afternoon during one of those serene years before the Beatles and Lee Harvey Oswald stirred everything up. My father drove the family Ford southward down the rutted dirt road that connected St. George with what was left of a pioneer farming village called Bloomington. Mom sat on the passenger side of the front seat shading her eyes against the flashing sun with a magazine. My sister and I, both under the age of eight, sat passively in the back seat.

Before long, Dad pulled off and parked next to a giant split rock. It was a massive brown slab, taller than a house, broken clean down the middle. The two halves of rock gaped open like a monster's mouth, one half standing perpendicular to the horizon, its flat surface facing the Virgin River, which snaked through the tamaracks less than a mile away. The lower half lay square on the ground, its face glaring up at the blue sky.

My sister and I scampered onto the lower slab and began to skip and hop across it. Then, in a sudden and stunning revelation, we saw the writing. The upper rock was covered with lines and circles and curlicues, yellow etchings in the dark brown rock. It was like a giant chalkboard, but none of this writing resembled anything on the board at school. I asked Dad what all those marks were.

"Indian writings," Dad said. This was before the word "petroglyphs" became common among southern Utahns. "They're messages the Indians wrote hundreds of years ago."

"Indians lived here?" I asked.

"They sure did," Dad said.

Mom unpacked our lunch and we chomped on sandwiches as Dad said, "A thousand years ago, maybe an Indian family stopped and had lunch on this very rock."

At that point in my life, my concept of time was yesterday, today, and tomorrow. A thousand years for me was the time between now and Christmas. But our lunch on the Indian rock at Bloomington that day was an introduction to a revelation that would come much later, the understanding that there is more to a place than what you see. There was a dimension to that outing that transcended the ritual picnic. The encounter with ancient symbols etched in the rock enlivened the experience and set it ablaze in my memory. I looked at the cryptic figures long and hard and wondered what they meant. But it wasn't so important what they meant. The significant thing was the fact that they were there, that people of an ancient era had stood on the very spot where I stood and had chiseled their story into the rock.

Most any place you go in this beautiful wide-open wilderness we call southern Utah, someone has already been there—something has gone on there before. And there's likely a story to go with the place. Like the story etched in the giant rock at Bloomington.

The landscape of this region has been lifted and cracked, submerged and shattered, windblasted and flooded over countless eons. Its stories are as old as time. And the landscape is covered with stories, if you look for them. It is the stories that enliven the landscape. The stories flow over this state like a magic life potion.

Not all the stories are written on rocks. Some are written in books, some are pressed as fossils between layers of shale, some are tucked in the back corners of old-timers' minds, and some, lamentably, are blowing in the wind, out of reach.

Many years after that picnic on the Indian rock (which is now in the middle of a modern Bloomington subdivision and can be seen in a little park at the corner of Navajo Drive and Geronimo Road), I became a resident of Bloomington myself. Driving to work each morning I crossed the river bridge below the rugged Shinarump ridge bordering Bloomington's north edge. I drove that ridge a hundred times, never noticing the message engraved on a rock above.

Then, during a hot Saturday afternoon on the back porch, I made one of those discoveries that forever changes the routine. I was reading a book on southern Utah history and came upon a photograph of an inscription on a rock. It was a funny looking plant with branches and leaves. I felt I had seen the image before. The caption revealed that the inscription was made on the ridge above Bloomington, near the confluence of the Santa Clara Creek and the Virgin River.

Ten minutes later I pulled off the freeway at the south end of the river bridge and gazed up at the cliffs. Sure enough, there loomed the inscription high on the ridge. The form of a plant was distinguishable even at that considerable distance, but the letters were too small to read from the road. Yet, from the photo in the book, I knew what they said:

"I was set her to rais cotten March 1858 JACOB PEART."

Sitting behind the wheel of my car, looking up at the century-old message on the rock, I imagined the scene: 19-year-old Jacob Peart—lonely, tired, raggedly dressed. He must have spent many a Sunday afternoon pecking at the rock. This was his message to the world, his legacy. There it was for anyone lucky enough to notice it, for anyone knowledgeable enough to appreciate it. I had passed that dormant, sterile ridge a hundred times. Now it was alive.

Recently I took my kids for a drive to the town of Washington, east of St. George. We turned north on Main Street, passed beneath the swooshing traffic of I-15, and drove up to the water tank on the sandy slopes below a red sandstone ridge. We parked near the tank and began tromping out through the brush, plodding heavily across the deep sand. Within minutes we dropped into a dry-wash bed and not many feet downstream found what we were looking for.

Dinosaur tracks.

"Are they really dinosaur tracks?" my six-year-old asked.

"They sure are," I said. "Can you imagine dinosaurs right here, millions of years ago?"

"Look, Dad! One's going this way, and one's going that way."

We sat on the flat slab of rock, which had once been a bog of mud, and passed the canteen around. The sun beat down like a hot lamp. The kids were mesmerized by thoughts of dinosaurs—right here in their own backyard. Already the landscape was coming alive for them.

I took a swig of water, pulled a shirt sleeve across my sweaty forehead, and said, "Maybe sixty million years ago a family of dinosaurs stopped right here and got a drink."

Biographical Sketches

Editors and Designer

Barry Scholl is a writer and editor who currently serves as the editor-in-chief of *Salt Lake City* magazine. He was born and raised in Salt Lake City and holds degrees from the University of Utah and Westminster College. His work has appeared in many publications, including *High Country News*.

François Camoin is a writer and a photographer. He teaches creative writing at the University of Utah, has published two novels and three collections of short stories, and has photographed images that have appeared in *Utah Holiday, Salt Lake City* magazine, as well as the *Utah Travel Guide*.

Larry Clarkson is president of Clarkson Creative, a Salt Lake City design communications firm. A Utah native, he has won more than 300 design awards, and his writing has been featured in professional publications and *New Genesis: A Mormon Reader on Land and Community*. He is design director of the *Utah Travel Guide*, published by the Utah Travel Council.

Writers

Deenise Becenti, who is Navajo, lives in Gallup, New Mexico, and works as a freelance newswriter. She covers Indian Country stories for KTNN Radio, *The Salt Lake Tribune*, and *National Native News*.

Katharine Coles, an assistant professor of English at the University of Utah, has published two collections of poetry and a novel, *The Measurable World*. She is a recipient of NEA awards for both poetry and fiction.

Edward Geary is a professor of English and associate dean of the College of Humanities at Brigham Young University. He grew up in the eastern Utah town of Huntington. Geary is the author of *The Proper Edge of the Sky*.

Lyman Hafen was born and raised in St. George, and spent many summers on his family ranch in Nevada. A graduate of Brigham Young University, he was a founding editor of *St. George Magazine* and is chairman of the Zion Natural History Association.

Margaret Pettis lives in the Cache Valley town of Hyrum. She has won statewide awards for her teaching and her poetry. An active conservationist, Pettis is the editor of *Bearnet*, a publication devoted to black bears and their habitat. She was named Utah poet of the year in 1992.

Gregory C. Thompson, assistant director for Special Collections, J. Willard Marriott Library, University Archivist and University Historian, University of Utah, received his Ph.D in history from the University of Utah. He is general editor of the *Tanner Trust Fund* book series, University of Utah, and author and editor of numerous book and journal articles.

Stephen Trimble, writer and photographer, lives in Salt Lake City. His books include *The Geography of Childhood: Why Children Need Wild Places* (with Gary Nabhan), *The People: Indians of the American Southwest*, and the award-winning *The Sagebrush Ocean: A Natural History of the Great Basin*.

Photographers

Scott Smith lives and works in Logan, Utah. A widely known photographer of cityscapes and wilderness scenes, his photographs have recently appeared in *Sierra, National Geographic Traveler*, and in his book *Nevada: Magnificent Wilderness*, published by West Cliffe.

Steve Midgley has shot everything from weddings to landscapes. Living in Salt Lake City, he carries his field camera to the wilds of southern Utah by jeep and motorcycle. His work has been published widely, and includes the *Utah Travel Guide*.

Steve Greenwood, a Utah native, is a communications graduate from the University of Utah. Prior to becoming a full-time stock photographer, he worked as a newspaper photographer and in advertising. Greenwood is well known for his beautiful scenic shots of Salt Lake City, northern Utah, and his favorite landmark, Antelope Island. His photographs have appeared in Utah travel industry, *Audubon, Smithsonian* and *Reader's Digest* books, calendars, and publications.

John P. George has been photographing the American landscape for twenty-five years. His expressive images have appeared in almost every major nature publication including *Audubon, National Geographic, Sierra*, and the *Wilderness Society*, and grace more than forty scenic calendars annually. *Seductive Beauty of Great Salt Lake: Images of a Lake Unknown* is his most recent publishing contribution.

Frank Jensen is a photographer beguiled by colors—especially those of the desert Southwest. A native Utahn based in Salt Lake City, he has been a teacher, journalist, photojournalist, and commercial photographer at various times. Over the past twenty-six years his work has been published in a variety of books and magazines, including *Time, Newsweek, Sunset Magazine, Arizona Highways*, and Time-Life Books.

Mel Lewis was "transplanted" to Utah from California in 1946. He worked as an industrial engineer, traveling the western states for more than forty years. Now retired, Lewis enjoys his life in Utah to the fullest, writing and photographing the state, donating much of his work to nonprofit organizations.

Tom Till, resident of Moab, is one of the West's most published photographers. Although best known for his southwestern landscapes, Till's images of landscape, nature, and history subjects depict all fifty states and thirty-five countries on six continents. In 1998 he launched the Tom Till Gallery in downtown Moab.

Artists

Tom Olson lives in Salt Lake City. A graduate of the University of Utah in graphic design, his woodblocks are carved in Utah pine, and he relishes the process of printing each print by hand as much as he does creating the original images.

Brian Glissmeyer lives in Kaysville. A graduate of the University of Utah in design with extensive experience in digital illustration and desktop publishing, he is production manager at Clarkson Creative, a Salt Lake design agency.

INDEX

Abajo (Blue) Mountains/Peak, x, 45, 47, 57, 179, 194, 196, 197, 198, 204
Abraham, 122
Abravanel Hall (Salt Lake City), 74
Academy Square (Provo), 89
Adairville, 225
Adams Memorial Theater (SUU), 213
Adobe: Rock, 112; Mesa, 193
Agathlan Peak, 202
Ajax Underground Store, 114
Albion Basin, 82
Alhambra Rock, 202
Alhandra, 152; Stage Stop and Ferry, 152
Alkali Ridge Historical Landmark, 198
Allen: Canyon, 48; Home and Carriage House (Provo), 89
Allred's Settlement, 163
Alpine: Scenic Drive, 50, 84–86; Junction, 85
Alta, 82, 85, 120
Altamont, 147
Alton: Amphitheater Backway, 222; access to, 224
Alvey Wash, 230
Amalga, 133
Amasa Back, 192
American Fork, 50, 84, 86, 140; Creek/River, 50, 90; Canyon, 50, 84, 85, 86, 142; Boat Harbor, 86
American Museum of Natural History, 33
Amusement Hall (Koosharem), 169
Anasazi: State Park (Boulder), 16, 56; Indian Village State Park, 233
Anderson: Meadow, 175; Junction, 216
Aneth, 198, 199
Angel Arch, 24
Angels Landing, 52, 54
Antelope Flat, 37
Antelope: Island/State Park (Syracuse), 16, 56, 65, 98, 99, 119, 121, 125, 127; Flat, 37; Springs, 124, 125
Anticline Overlook, 195
Antimony, 168, 227
Aquarius Plateau, 29, 166, 168, 169, 170, 172, 227, 228, 230, 233
Arches National Park, 5, 15, 16, 17–19, 179, 188, 190, 192, 193, 194, 208
Arch-in-the-Making, 19
Army Commissary Building (Fairfield), 115
Asay Creek, 222
Ash Creek Canyon, 216
Ashdown Gorge Wilderness Area, 16, 58
Ashley: Falls, 36; National Forest, 35, 37, 57, 144, 147, 148, 151; Valley/Creek, 149, 150, 151, 152
Aspen: Grove, 85; Giants Scenic Area, 164
Assembly Hall: (Salt Lake City), 69; Peak, 186
Atlas Uranium Mill, 192
Aurora Cliffs, 165
Avenues (Salt Lake City), 75
Avon, 96, 131
Awapa Plateau, 169

Bacchus/Junction, 80
Baker: Ranch, 170; Bench petroglyphs, 231
Balanced Rock, 18, 19
Bald Eagle Mountain, 138
Bald Mountain, 138, 144; National Scenic Trail, 144
Baldy Beak, 174
Bamberger Monument, 158
Bank: of Corinne, 105; of Vernal, 149–50
Barker Reservoir, 228
Barrier Canyon, 25
Bates/Batesville, 112
Bauer, 113
Baxter Pass, 182
Bean Life Science Museum (BYU), Monte L., 91
Bear Canyon-Cottonwood-Ponderosa Forest, 172
Bear Lake: State Park/Marina (Garden City), 16, 56, 137; Valley, 93, 131, 132, 133, 135, 136, 137, 153
Bear River: Valley, 12, 13, 81, 96, 105, 106, 123, 131, 133,

134, 137, 143, 153; Mountain Range, 96, 131, 133, 135, 137; Migratory Bird Refuge (Brigham City), 105, 125
Bears Ears Buttes (Elk Ridge), 48, 197, 203, 204
Bear Valley, 165
Beaver, 11, 166, 167, 168, 174, 175, 222; Scenic Byway, 59, 174; Creek/Canyon, 96, 142; County, 103, 155, 174, 175; Mountains, 168, 175; River, 175; Basin, 193
Beaver Dam Mountains/Wilderness Area, 16, 58, 219
Beaver Mountain Ski Resort (Logan), 136; Lodge, 136
Beckwith Plateau, 183
Beebe House (Provo), 89
Beef Basin, 24, 197
Beehive: Point, 36; House (Salt Lake City), 70, 75
Beehives, The, 54
Beesley Home (Provo), 89
Behunin Cabin (Caineville), Elijah Cutler, 207
Belknap Peak, 174
Bement Arch, 231
Beneficial Life Tower (Salt Lake City), 74
Benson Grist Mill (Mills Junction), 112
Berryville, 222
Best Friends Animal Sanctuary, 223
Bicknell, 26, 170, 198, 230, 234; Bottoms, 170
Big: Spring Canyon, 25; Cottonwood Canyon/Scenic Byway, 59, 81, 85, 120, 142; Mountain, 81, 137; Brush Creek, 152; Rock Candy Mountain, 167; Flat, 175; Pocket Overlook, 197; Hogan Butte/Finger, 202; Plain Junction, 221; Water (Glen Canyon City), 225, 230
Big Indian: mining district, 195; Butte/Finger, 202
Bingham: Canyon/Copper Mine, 80, 113; Metals, 113
Birch Creek, 54, 228
Bird Island, 121
Birdseye, 161
Black: Box, 186; Ridge, 216
Black Rock, 116, 124; Station, 118; Volcanic Field, 173
Blacksmith Fork Canyon, 131, 135
Blanding, 22, 38, 42, 45, 47, 48, 170, 179, 196, 197, 198, 203, 204, 208
Blind Lake, 234
Bloomington, 219, 235, 237
Bluebell, 147; Knoll, 170
Blue Mountain, 34, 152
Blue Valley, 206
Bluff, 38, 41, 45, 47, 179, 198, 199–201, 203, 204, 208, 211; Scenic Byway, 59; Bench, 199
Bonanza, 182
Boneta, 147
Bonneville: Salt Flats, 58, 109, 110, 125, 127; Speedway, 110; Basin, 127
Book Cliffs/Mountains, 13, 17, 58, 182–84, 187, 188
Booth House (Nephi), 172
Boston Building (Salt Lake City), 74
Bottle Hollow Junction, 148
Bottleneck Peak, 186
Boulder, 8, 172, 213, 222, 230, 231, 233, 234; Mountain (Aquarius Plateau), 57, 166, 170, 172, 213, 233, 234; -Grover Road, 57; Top, 170, 233; Country, 223–34
Bountiful, 97, 99, 125; -Davis Art Center, 99; Tabernacle, 99; Peak Drive, 99
Bowdie Canyon, 204
Box Canyon, 162
Box-Death Hollow Wilderness Area, 16, 58
Box Elder: Peak, 85, 133; County, 103, 134
Boyd Station, 119
Braithwaite Fine Arts Gallery (SUU), 213
Brereton Home (Provo), 89
Brian: -Panguitch Lake Scenic Byway, 59; Springs, 170
Brian Head Ski and Summer Resort, 31, 175, 215, 222
Bridal Veil Falls, 141
Bridge: Canyon, 49; Mountain, 53, 54
Brigham City, 43, 105, 113, 125, 131
Brigham's Tomb Butte/Finger, 202
Brigham Young Monument (Salt Lake City), 70, 91
Brigham Young's Office: (Salt Lake City), 70; and Winter Home (St. George), 217, 218

Brigham Young University (Provo), 84, 87, 88, 89, 90–91, 92, 134
Brighton/Basin/Ski Area, 81, 82, 142
Brimhall Arch, 30
Bringhurst Home (Springville), 91
Broken Bow Arch, 231
Bromide Basin, 206
Browning: Firearms Museum (Ogden), John M., 94; -Kimball Automobile Museum (Ogden), 94; Theatre (Ogden), 94; Center for the Performing Arts (WSU), Val A., 95; Arms Company (Mountain Green), 97
Brown's Park (Brown's Hole), 33, 34, 36, 37, 127, 151
Brownsville, 93
Brush Creek, 151; Cave, 151
Bryce: Canyon/National Park, 16, 20–21, 27, 31, 168, 172, 211, 219, 222, 223, 224, 225, 226, 227; Natural Bridge, 21; Point, 21; Valley, 226; (Paria) Valley, 227, 228; Junction, 227, 230; Canyon Airport, 227
Buckboard Forest Campground, 197
Buckhorn: Flat, 184, 185; Draw, 185; Wash, 185, 186
Buckskin: Mountain, 224; Gulch, 224, 225
Bullfrog Marina/Resort, 8, 30, 38, 42, 49, 60, 204, 205, 227, 234
Bull Valley: Mountains, 219; Gorge, 227
Bureau of Land Management (BLM), 58
Burnt Station, 119
Burr Trail, 30, 45, 205, 234
Burrville, 168, 169
Butler Wash View Area, 203
Butterfield Canyon/Pass, 113
BYU. See Brigham Young University
Byways, 64, 104, 130, 156, 180, 212

Cable Mountain, 54
Cache: County, 129, 134; County Relic Hall (Logan), 135; National Forest, 135; Cave, 140
Cache Valley, 96, 112, 131–37, 153; Cheese Factory, 133; Bay, 134
Caineville, 28, 30, 203, 206, 207; Mesa, 207; country, 234
Cajon Canyon, 45, 46
Calf Creek: Recreation Area, 45, 231; Canyon, 231
California Trail, 127, 219
Callao, 116, 119, 125
Camel Butte/Finger, 202
Camp Floyd: State Park (Fairfield), 16, 56, 86; Military Cemetery, 115; -Fort Crittenden, 115, 116–17
Camp W. G. Williams Military Reservation, 79
Canaan: Ranch (Pipe Spring), 224; Peak, 228
Candy, 119
Cannonville, 224, 225, 226, 227, 228
Canyon: Rims/Recreation Area, 23, 195, 208; Overlook Trail, 55; Ridge, 122; Mountains, 172, 173
Canyonlands/National Park, 2, 3, 5, 22–25, 38, 42, 152, 170, 172, 179–209, 180, 186, 187, 196, 197, 204, 208
Canyons, The, 138
Capitol Gorge, 28, 29; Dome, 29
Capitol (Salt Lake City): Hill, 56, 71, 75; District, 71–72; Theater, 74
Capitol Reef National Park, 5, 16, 26–30, 122, 161, 165, 166, 170, 172, 179, 203, 205, 206, 207, 213, 234
Carbon: County, 113, 155, 158, 159, 179; Country Club and Golf Course, 158
Carcass Wash, 231
Carnegie Museum, 33
Carrington Island, 121
Cascade: Scenic Drive, 85; Springs, 85; Mountain, 141; Falls, 215
Cassidy Arch, 28
Castle: Rock, 140, 157; Gate, 147, 158, 185; Valley, 155, 157, 158, 159–61, 162, 164, 184, 185, 190, 193, 194; Dale, 160, 161, 184, 185, 186; Butte, 202
Castleton, 193
Cataract Canyon, 22, 24, 25, 38, 40, 41, 42, 182, 184, 187, 204, 227
Cathedral: Valley, 29–30, 161, 165, 170, 207, 234;

Junction, 30; in the Desert, 61; of the Madeleine (Salt Lake City), 75, 76; Butte, 197
Causey: Junction, 96; Reservoir, 96
Cave: Spring, 25, 196; Towers, 204
Cedar: City, 11, 13, 31, 44, 52, 57, 58, 87, 124, 173, 175, 213, 215, 221, 222, 226; Breaks National Monument, 16, 31–32, 54, 59, 175, 211, 214, 215, 222; Mesa, 22, 203; Springs, 37; Mountain Range, 54, 115, 127; Mountain, 185, 213; Canyon, 213, 215
Cedars State Park, 198
Cemetery Hill (Bluff), 199
Centerfield, 164, 165
Centerville, 97, 99
Central Heartland/Valleys, 2, 156
Centre, 114
CEU. See College of Eastern Utah
Chaffin Bar, 61
Chalk Creek Canyon, 140, 173
Charleston, 142
Chase: Home Museum of Utah Folk Art (Salt Lake City), 77; Mill (Salt Lake City), Isaac, 77
Chesler Park, 24
Chessmen Overlook, 32
Chicken Corners, 77
Children's Museum of Utah (Salt Lake City), 75
Chimney Rock, 29
Chocolate Fountain, 51
Church Rock, 195
Circle Cliffs, 30, 44, 58, 205, 222, 234
Circle Valley, 168, 169
Circleville, 157, 165, 166, 168, 221
Cisco, 188, 190, 193, 194
City: Hall (Spring City), 163; Park (Cedar City), 213
City Creek: Canyon/Memory Grove (Salt Lake City), 71; Canyon (Junction), 168; (Fishlake N. F.), 175
Civic Center Park (Springville), 91
Clarion, 164
Clarkston, 133; Creek, 133; Mountain, 133
Clark-Taylor Home (Provo), 89
Clay Hills, 200, 204; Divide, 204
Clearfield, 97
Clear Lake, 123; Creek, 157, 158; Creek Canyon, 167, 174
Cleveland: -Lloyd Dinosaur Quarry/Reservoir (Price), 159, 160; access to, 160
Cliff Ridge (Stuntz Ridge), 152
Clifton, 119
Clover, 114
Coal: Country, 157–59; City, 158; Creek Canyon, 213
Coalville, 140
Cockscomb, 45, 224, 225; Ridge, 234
Cohab Canyon, 28; Trail, 29
College of Eastern Utah, 159
Collett: Art Gallery (WSU), 95; Canyon, 228, 230, 231
Colorado Plateau/Province (High Plateaus), 3, 10, 11, 24, 161, 162, 172, 179–209
Colorado River, 3, 17, 18, 19, 21, 22, 23, 24, 25, 31, 38, 39, 41, 42, 44, 45, 49, 52, 60, 61, 129, 148, 152, 157, 179, 181–82, 184, 187, 188, 189, 190, 191, 192, 193, 194, 195, 200, 203, 205, 211, 220, 222, 226, 227; Storage Project, 40; Scenic Byway, 59; Basin, 145
Colton, 147, 157; Junction, 157, 158
Columbia, 183; Steel Plant (Ironton), 183
Comb: Ridge, 48, 200, 203, 204; Wash, 200, 201
Confluence Overlook, 24
Confusion Range, 125
Conger Range, 125
Connecticut, 44, 93
Consumers, 158
Converse Hall, 77
Cooley Pass, 197
Cool Spring, 46
Coon Peak, 112
Copperton, 80, 113
Coral Pink Sand Dunes State Park (Kanab), 16, 56, 223
Corinne, 105, 106, 114, 123, 141; City Hall, 105
Cottonwood: peaks, 65; Campground, 135; Canyon/Creek, 186, 196, 197, 198, 200, 204, 224, 225, 227, 228
Council Hall (Salt Lake City), 71
Courthouse Towers, 18
Court of the Patriarchs, 54

Cove Fort, 120, 167, 174, 187; Junction, 174
Cove of Caves, 18
Cow Canyon, 199
Coyote: Gulch, 231; Bridge, 231
Crater Springs Health Resort, 124
Crescent Junction, 188
Crossing of the Fathers, 41
Crossroads Plaza (Salt Lake City), 72, 74
Crouse Canyon/Reservoir, 151
Croyden, 97
Crystal Cave/Crystal Ball Cave, 125
Curlew Valley/Junction, 107
Cutler: Mansion (Lehi), Thomas, 86; Dam/Reservoir, 133

Daggett County, 36, 129
Dalton Springs Forest Campground, 197
Dance Hall Rock, 45, 231
Dandy Crossing, 41, 60, 205. See also Hite Crossing
Danger Cave, 10, 111, 121
Daniels Canyon, 141, 145, 183
Dark Canyon/Wilderness Area, 16, 47, 48, 58, 197, 204
Daughters of the Utah Pioneers Museum: Alpine, 85; Springville, 91, Spanish Fork, 92; Ogden, 95; Mt. Pleasant, 192; Richfield, 166; Escalante, 230
Davis: Canyon, 24, 197; County, 63, 93, 97–99, 140
Dead Horse Point/State Park (Moab): 16, 23, 56, 188, 190, 191
Death Hollow, 230, 231
Dee Events Center (WSU), 95
Deep Creek, 29, 119, 120, 234; Mountain Range, 58, 119, 127; Valley, 119; Reservoir, 141, 142. See also Ibapah
Deer: Creek State Park (Heber), 16, 56, 140; Valley, 138
Delle, 108
Delicate Arch, 14, 15, 18, 19
Delta, 120, 122, 124, 173; Center (Salt Lake City), 65, 74
Denver & Rio Grande Railroad Depot (Salt Lake City), 74
Deseret, 6, 124; Peak/Wilderness Area, 16, 58, 112; State of, 65, 164; Depot, 114; Telegraph and Post Office (Rockville), 221
Desert: Lake Waterfowl Reserve, 160; Mound, 213
Desolation Canyon, 147, 181, 183
Detroit Mining District, 124
Devil's: Garden, 17, 18, 19, 44, 45; Slide, 97; Cave, 135; Canyon, 188, 198; Rock Garden, 230, 231
Dewey: Bridge, 190; town of, 193, 194
DeWitt Campground/Cave, 135
Diamond: Fork, 91, 157; Mountain/Plateau, 151
Dinosaur: National Monument, 32–35, 129, 145, 151, 152, 160, 181; Garden (Vernal), 149
Dirty Devil: Bridge/Canyon/Bay, 22, 25, 42, 205; River, 27, 41, 186, 205. See also Fremont River
Dividend, 120
Dixie: (Virgin River Valley), 2, 59, 211–36; National Forest, 57, 175, 213, 215, 219, 227, 228, 230, 234; College (St. George), 218; Normal School/Junior College (St. George), 218
Doll House, 25
Dolores River/Overlook/Canyon, 193, 194
Donkey Reservoir, 234
Donner-Reed Memorial Museum (Grantsville), 112
Double Arch, 18, 19
Double-O Arch, 19
Douglas Mountain, 34
Dove's Nest, 51
Dragon, 182
Draper, 65, 79
Driggs Home (Pleasant Grove), Benjamin W., 87
Druid Arch, 25
Drum Range, 124, 125
Dry Fork: Canyon/Creek, 58, 150; petroglyphs, 150–51; town of, 151
Dry Valley, 195, 197
Duchesne: County, 129, 147; town of, 140, 142, 145, 147, 158, 181; Canyon/River, 142, 144, 145, 147, 148, 149
Duck Creek/Village, 215; pond, 215
Dugout Ranch, 196, 197
Dugway: Proving Ground (Grantsville), 108, 112, 114, 115, 116, 117, 118; town of, 115, 118; Pass, 124
Dunderberg Butte, 124
Dutch John, 35, 36, 37, 151
Dutchman Flat, 85

Eagle: Gate (Salt Lake City), 71, 166; Butte/Finger, 202; Rock Canyon, 202; Mesa, 202; City, 206; Arch, 224
East: Rim/Trail, 54; Temple (Zion N. P.), 54, 55; Creek Lake, 97; Park Reservoir, 151; Fork (Kingston) Canyon, 165, 168; Carbon City, 183; Kaibab Monocline (Cockscomb), 224, 228
East Canyon: State Park (Morgan), 16, 56, 81; Reservoir, 81, 97, 137; resort, 97; access to, 137; Creek, 138
Eccles: Canyon Scenic Byway, 59; Community Art Center (Ogden), 95; Home (Logan), David, 135
Echo: Park, 33, 34; town of, 96, 97, 139, 140; Canyon, 140; Church-School, 140; Dam/Reservoir, 140
Eden, 96; Canyons, North and South, 137
Edge of the Cedars State Park (Blanding), 16, 56, 198
Egan Fish Hatchery, J. Perry, 170
Eggertsen Home (Provo), 89
Egyptian: Queen, 18; Theatre (Park City), 138
Elaterite Basin, 25
Elberta, 92, 120
Elephant: Hill, 24, 196; Butte/Finger, 202
Elkhart Cliffs, 223
Elkhorn, 170; Guard Station and Campground, 170; Meadows, 175
Elk Ridge, 47, 48, 196, 200, 203, 204
Elmo, 160
Elsinore, 165, 167
Elton Tunnel, 113
Elwood, 105
Emerald Pools/Trail, 54
Emery: County, 155, 160, 162, 179, 186; County Museum, 160; town of, 160, 161, 164, 182; Valley, 227
Emigration Canyon, 5, 78, 79, 81, 100, 109, 137
Emory, 140
Ensign Peak (Salt Lake City), 71
Enterprise, 219
Entrada Bluffs, 194
Ephraim, 160, 162, 163, 164; Town Hall and Jail, 163
Episcopal: Church of the Good Shepherd (Ogden), 95; Mission (Bluff), 199
Eroded Boulder House, 46
Escalante: State Park, 16, 56, 228; Canyons/River/Basin, 38, 41, 42, 44, 45, 58, 228, 229, 230–33, 234; town of, 44, 170, 172, 200, 201, 213, 222, 227, 228, 230, 231, 233; Mountains, 228; Anticline, 230; Rim, 230; Natural Bridge, 231
Eskdale, 119, 125
E. T. City, 112
Eureka, 92, 114, 120, 121
Exchange Place (Salt Lake City), 74
Executive Mansion (Salt Lake City), 75
Eyring Physical Science Center (BYU), 91

Factory Butte, 206, 207
Fairfield, 86, 114, 115, 116, 117
Fairview, 160, 161, 162; Museum of History and Arts, 161; Canyon, 162; Ranch, 205
Fairy Castle, 21
Fairyland, 21
Family Butte, 187
Family History Library (Salt Lake City), 70
Farmington: Bay, 97; town of, 99; Canyon, 99
Father Time's Jewel Box, 51
Faust: Station, 114, 117; Ranch, 117
Fayette, 164
Federal (Salt Lake City): Office Building, 71, 72; Heights, 75
Ferron, 161, 162, 164; Canyon, 161; Reservoir, 161, 164; stream, 186
Fiery Furnace, 19
Fifty-Mile Mountain, 230
Fillmore, 13, 166, 168, 173
Fins, The, 25
First Presbyterian Church (Salt Lake City), 75
Fish Creek Reservoir, 234
Fisher: Towers, 190, 193, 194; Mesa, 193; Valley, 193, 194
Fish Lake, 13, 165, 169, 170, 171; -Johnson Valley area, 57; Pass/Summit, 169
Fish Springs, 116, 119, 124; Range, 118; Station, 118; National Wildlife Refuge, 118
Fishlake: National Forest, 57, 122, 165, 166, 167, 168, 170, 175, 234; Scenic Byway, 59; Plateau, 165, 166, 169

Five Kiva Ruin, 198
Fivemile: Pass, 117; Valley, 224
Flagstaff Mountain, 138
Flaming Gorge: National Recreation Area, 33, 35–37, 57, 150, 151–52, 153; Dam, 35, 36, 37, 151; Lake/Reservoir, 35, 37, 127, 145; Lodge, 35; -Uintas Scenic Byway, 59
Flint Trail, 25
Fluted Wall, 234
Forbidding Canyon, 49
Forest Service Information Center (Ogden), 94
Forsyth Valley Reservoir, 170
Fort: Buenaventura State Park (Ogden), 16, 56, 94; Crittenden/Camp Floyd, 115; Thornburgh, 140, 150; Duchesne, 147, 148, 149, 183; Robidoux/Fort Winty, 148; Omni, 166; Cameron, 175; Hamilton, 215; Walker, 215; Hamilton, 215; Harmony, 216; Pearce Wash, 220
Fort Douglas (Salt Lake City), 13, 78, 113; Military Museum, 78; Post Cemetery, 78
Fountain Green, 162, 172
Four Corners: Area, 190, 194–203, 233; Monument, 199
Four Mile Bench, 45
Francis, 142, 147
Franklin Quest Field (Salt Lake City), 74, 75
Freedom, 162
Fremont: Indian State Park (Sevier), 16, 56, 166, 167; River (Dirty Devil)/Canyon: 26, 27, 28, 29, 41, 170, 172, 176, 207, 234; town of, 29, 30, 165, 170; Junction; 161, 170, 187, 188; church house, 170
Fruita, 26, 27, 28, 170, 207; Schoolhouse, 29
Fruitland, 145
Fry Canyon, 47, 203
Frying Pan Trail, 28
Fugal Blacksmith Shop (Pleasant Grove), 87

Gallivan Utah Center (Salt Lake City), John W., 72, 74
Gandy, 125
Garden: of Eden, 18; City, 136, 137
Garfield, 80; County, 155, 179, 211, 222
Garland, 133
Gate Canyon, 183
Gateway to the Narrows Trail, 55
Geneva Works of United States Steel Corporation, 87
Gentry Mountain, 176
Geyser Pass/Trail, 193
Giles, 206
Gilson Buttes, 187
Glass Mountain, 29
Glen Canyon: National Recreation Area, 38–41, 42, 49, 60, 179, 186, 187, 204, 205, 227, 230, 231; Dam, 38, 40, 49, 179, 220, 224, 225, 227; access to, 40, 41, 47, 206, 211, 227, 231; City, 225, 228; country, 226; Visitor Center (AZ), 226; breaks, 230
Glendale, 222
Glendinning Home (Salt Lake City), 75
Glenwood, 166, 169
Goblin Valley, 8, 186, 206; State Park (Hanksville), 16, 56, 187
Gold Hill, 119
Golden: Spike National Historic Site, 16, 43, 105, 106; Spike Empire, 94, 105; Throne, 29; Gate Mill, 115
Goodyear Cabin (Ogden), Miles, 95
Goosenecks, 29, 48, 203; State Park (Mexican Hat), 16, 56, 208
Goshen, 92, 120; Valley, 120
Goshute (Gosiute) Indian Reservation, 120
Goulding's Junction/Trading Post, 202
Government Creek Station, 117
Grafton, 221
Grand: View Point/Overlook, 23; Gallery, 25; Wash/Narrows, 28
Grand Canyon/National Park/North Rim: 20, 38, 41, 42, 54, 157, 181, 182, 186, 211, 213, 218, 221, 223, 224
Grand Gulch, 30, 200, 205; Primitive Area, 47, 48, 204; Plateau, 58. See also Hall's Creek Canyon
Grand Staircase-Escalante National Monument, 44–45, 211–36, 224–33
Granite: Mountain Record Vaults, 82; Flat Campground, 85; Mountain, access to, 116, 118
Grantsville, 108, 112

Grass Valley, 165, 167, 168, 169
Grassy Mountains, 108
Grayson, 198. See also Blanding
Great Arch of Zion, 55
Great Bar (Stockton Bar), 113
Great: Basin, 2, 3, 4, 10, 11, 12, 31, 66, 81, 103, 106, 117, 120, 121, 123, 126, 127, 145, 153, 155, 157, 165, 172, 215, 221, 222; West White Throne, 52, 54; West Wall, 54, 55; West Canyon, 55, 221; Bend, 201
Great Plains, 127
Great Salt Lake, 3, 4, 5, 10, 11, 12, 13, 43, 65, 66, 72, 79, 80, 83, 89, 93, 95, 98, 103, 105, 107, 108, 109, 110, 111, 112, 114, 117–25, 118, 119, 121, 123, 125, 126, 127, 131, 134, 153, 161; Valley, 12; State Park (Salt Lake City), 16, 56, 108, 123; Desert: 99, 105–7, 107–20, 108, 111, 116, 118, 119, 120–25, 123, 124, 125, 127; Resorts, 123, 125
Greater Aneth Oil Field, 199
Greendale Junction, 35, 37, 151
Greenwich, 168, 169
Green River: State Park, 16, 56, 184; Overlook, 22, 23; River, 22, 23, 24, 25, 32, 33, 34, 35, 36, 37, 41, 42, 44, 60, 129, 147, 148, 149, 150, 151, 152, 153, 157, 179, 181–82, 183, 186, 187, 188, 191, 195; Junction, 38; town of, 38, 179, 181, 182, 184, 185, 188; desert, 169
Greenwich, 168, 169
Grey: Whiskers Butte/Finger, 202; Cliffs, 226
Grosvenor Arch, 45, 228
Grotto Campground/Picnic Area, 54
Grouse Creek Mountains, 107, 157
Grover: -Boulder Highway, 29; access to, 172, 233
Guardian Angels, 55
Guardsman's Pass, 82, 142
Gunlock/Lake State Park (St. George), 16, 56, 219
Gunnison: Massacre Monument, 124; Plateau, 162; town of, 164, 165, 172
Gunnison's: Island, 121; Crossing, 184
Gunshot, 228
Gypsum: Sinkhole, 29; Canyon, 204

Hackberry Canyon, 45
Hailstone: Junction, 140, 142; recreation area, 142
Hale Summer Theatre (Grover), 233
Hall's Creek Canyon/Valley, 30, 234
Halls Crossing/Marina, 38, 41, 42, 49, 204, 227
Hamblin, Jacob: House (Santa Clara), 218; Arch, 231
Hamilton Fort, 215
Hanksville, 8, 22, 26, 38, 42, 48, 122, 165, 168, 179, 187, 198, 203, 205, 206
Hanna, 142, 145, 147
Hansen: Cave, 50; Planetarium (Salt Lake City), 72; Home (Mount Pleasant), James, 162
Hans Flat, 25; Ranger Station, 25
Hardware Ranch, 96, 131
Harley Dome, 182, 188
Harpers Corner: Scenic Drive, 32, 34; Viewpoint, 34; town of, 152
Harpole Mesa, 193
Harris: Fine Arts Center (BYU), Franklin S., 90; Wash, 230
Harrisburg: Junction, 216, 220; old townsite of, 216
Hart's Draw, 195
Hastings Cutoff, 110
Hatch, 20, 221, 222; Point, 195, 197; Point Campground, 195; Wash, 195
Hayden: Visitor Center (Lake Powell), Carl, 38, 227; Peak, 144
Haystack Peak/Mountain, 119, 193
Health Sciences Center (U of U), 78
Heber: City, 85, 105, 140, 141, 145; Valley, 83, 140, 141, 143; Valley Airport, 141; Valley Railroad Depot, 141; Pioneer Village/Railroad Museum (Heber City), 141
Hellenic Orthodox Church (Price), 159
Hell's: Backbone, 170, 230, 231; Hole, 234
Helper, 147, 158; Civic Auditorium, 158
Henefer, 81, 97, 137
Henrieville, 226, 227, 228; Creek, 228
Henry Mountains, 29, 30, 40, 41, 42, 58, 179, 194, 197, 205–6, 234
Henry's Fork, 36; Park, 145
Heritage House Museum (Kanab), 223
Herriman, 113

Hiawatha, 160
Hickman Natural Bridge, 29
Hidden: Canyon, 54; Peak, 82
Hideout Canyon Overview, 37
High: Uintas/Wilderness Area, 1, 16, 57, 58, 129, 144–45, 146, 147, 153; Plateaus, 5, 81, 107, 122, 161, 162, 165, 166–72, 221
Highline Trail, 144–45
Hightop Plateau, 169
Highway 12 Scenic Byway, 59
Hill Air Force: Base (HAFB), 97, 99; Aerospace Museum, 99; Range, 108
Hill/Wendover/Dugway Range Complex, 108, 111
Hinckley, 122, 124
Hite Crossing/Marina, 38, 41, 42, 60, 61, 184, 205, 227
Hobble Creek/Canyon, 90, 91, 157
Hobbs Historical Site, George, 230–31
Hogle Zoo/Zoological Gardens (Salt Lake City), 78, 79, 81
Hogup Mountain Range/Cave, x, 10, 125, 153
Holden, 173
Hole-in-Rock, 194
Hole-in-the-Rock, 38, 41, 45, 197, 199, 200, 203, 204, 222, 230, 231
Hole-in-the-Wall, 19
Holiday Park, 142
Holnan/Ideal Basic Industries, 97
Holt Draw, 234
Home of Truth Colony, 196
Hondoo: (Muddy River) Country, 186, 187; Arch, 187
Honeycomb Canyon, 82
Honors Library of Living History (Salt Lake City), 71
Hop Valley, 55
Horse: Canyon, 24, 183; Pasture Plateau, 54
Horseshoe Canyon, 25, 36, 181, 186
Hotel: Utah (Salt Lake City), 70; Roberts (Provo), 89
Hot Plug, 124
House: Hosting Center (BYU), Thomas, 90; Range, 124, 125; Rock Valley, 223, 224
Hovenweep: National Monument, 16, 45–46, 199, 208; Castle/House, 46
Howell, 107
Hoytsville, 140
Hungerford Academy (Springville), 91
Hunt Mesa, 202
Hunter Home (Cedar City), 213
Huntington: State Park, 16, 56, 160; access to, 162; Canyon Scenic Byway, 59, 159, 160, 162; Canyon Power Complex, 160; Reservoir, 160; stream, 186
Huntsman: Center (U of U), 78; -Nielsen Home (Fillmore), 173
Huntsville, 95–96, 137
Hurrah Pass, 192, 197; Junction, 192
Hurricane, 52, 216, 220, 221, 223; Fault (Ledge), 215, 216, 220; Canal, 220; Ledge, 220; Mesa, 220; Wash, 231
Hutchings Museum of Natural History (Lehi), John, 86
Hyde: Park, 131; Home (Spring City), Orson, 163
Hyrum: State Park (Hyrum City), 16, 56, 131; town of, 131; Dam/Reservoir, 131

Ibapah, 119, 120
Ignatio, 182
Indian: Peaks, 13; Canyon/Scenic Byway, 59, 147, 183; Creek Canyon, 196, 197
Indianola Valley, 161
Iron Springs, 213
Inspiration Point, 21
Intermountain Power Project, 122
International Peace Garden (Salt Lake City), 75
Ioka, 147
Iosepa, 115, 116
Iron: Mission State Park (Cedar City), 16, 56, 213; County, 103, 155, 175, 211
Ironton, 183; Works (Springville), 91
Island: in the Sky, 22, 23–24, 25, 190, 191; Park, 34, 35, 151
Ivins, 218

Jackson Hole (Kane Creek), 192
Jacob's Chair Butte, 204
Jarvie Historical Property, John, 151
Jensen, 32, 33, 149, 152; Historical Farm, Ronald V., 133
Jeremy Ranch, 138

Jericho, 121; Junction, 121
Jesse Ewing Canyon, 151
Joe's Valley, 160; Reservoir, 160, 163
Johnson: Valley Reservoir, 169, 170; Canyon, 222, 224
Johnson's Pass, 114, 118
John's Valley, 227
Jones Hole: Fish Hatchery/Creek, 34; access to, 151
Jones Theater (SUU), Randall L., 213
Jordan River: State Park, 16, 56, 75; access to, 65, 68, 75, 79, 83, 90; Narrows, 79, 83; Temple, 79
Jordanelle State Park (Heber), 16, 56, 140, 142
Joseph, 167; Schoolhouse, 167
Joseph Smith Memorial Building (Salt Lake City), 70, 72
Joshua Tree Road (Dixie), 59
Joy, 124
Juab: County, 103; Valley, 172–75
Junction: Country, 22, 24, 25, 42, 191, 195; town of, 157, 165, 168, 175

Kachina Bridge, 48
Kaibab: Forest, 54, 223; Plateau, 224; East, Monocline (Cockscomb), 224, 228
Kaiparowits Plateau, 225, 226, 228, 230, 231
Kamas, 140, 142, 143, 144
Kanab, 38, 44, 52, 157, 223, 224, 225, 227, 228, 230; Scenic Byway, 59; Creek, 223
Kanarraville, 215
Kane: Creek/Canyon, 192, 194, 195, 197; Springs, 192, 194; County, 211, 220, 223
Kanosh, 13, 166, 173; Indian Reservation, 173
Kapairowits Plateau, x, 41, 44, 45, 166
Kaysville, 97, 99
Kearns, 80
Keeley Canyon, 45
Keigley Quarry (Payson), 87, 92
Keith Mansion (Salt Lake City), David, 75
Kelseh Home (Springville), 91
Kelton, 107, 125
Kenilworth, 158
Kennecott: Building (Salt Lake City), 72; Bingham Copper Mine Visitors Center (Copperton), 80, 113; Minerals Company (Salt Lake Valley West), 80; smelter, 108; Copper Refinery, 123
Kent's Lake, 175
Kigalia Ranger Station, 197
Kimball: Art Center (Park City), 138; Junction, 138, 139–40; Stage Stop, 140
Kimberly, 167
Kingfisher: Creek-Park Canyon, 36; Canyon, 181
Kingsbury Hall (U of U), 78
King Sisters Home (Pleasant Grove), 87
Kings Peak, 144
Kingston, 168; Canyon, 168
Klondike Bluffs, 18, 19
Knight Block (Provo), 89
Knightsville, 120
Kodachrome Basin State Park (Cannonville): 16, 44, 56, 225, 227, 228
Kokopelli Mountain, 58
Kolob: Canyon, 52, 216, 221; Arch, 55; Finger Canyons/Road Scenic Byway, 55, 59, 216; Section, 55, 216, 221; Terrace, 55, 215, 220, 221
Koosharem, 13, 167, 168, 169; Reservoir, 169

Lagoon: Amusement Park/Pioneer Village (Farmington), 97, 99; Opera House, 99
LaGorce Arch, 231
Lake: Mountains, 88; Point, 108, 114, 123; Point Junction, 108, 112; Monticello, 197; Fork Canyon, 145, 147; Hill Campground, 163; Canyon, 204
Lake Bonneville, 3, 81, 93, 105, 107, 108, 110, 113, 116, 117, 119, 122, 123, 124, 127, 134, 173
Lake Powell, 15, 22, 25, 27, 30, 38, 39, 40, 41, 42, 47, 48, 49, 60, 61, 165, 172, 179, 198, 203, 204, 205, 211, 222, 226, 227, 230, 231, 234
Lakeside, 108; Mountains, 108
Laketown: Scenic Byway, 59; town of, 93, 137
Land Behind the Rocks, 192, 194
Land of Standing Rocks, 24, 25, 41, 187
Lands End Plateau, 186
Landscape Arch, 19

Lark, 113
La Sal Mountains, 11, 17, 18, 19, 45, 57, 168, 179, 188, 190, 191, 192, 193, 194, 197
Last Chance Canyon, 61
Latuda, 158
Lava Point, 54
Lavender Canyon, 24, 197
LaVerkin Creek, 55; town of, 216, 220
Layton, 97
LDS Business College (Salt Lake City), 75
LDS Church: Complex, 65, 69–71; Office Building, 67, 71; Administration Building, 70; Block, 70–71
Leamington, 122, 172
Leap Creek, 216
Leeds, 216
Lee Library (BYU), Harold B., 90
Lee's Ferry (AZ), 38, 40, 41, 42, 60, 61, 223, 225
Legion Park, 113
Lehi, 84, 86
Lehman Caves National Monument, 125
Leota, 149
Levan, 164, 172; Ridge, 172
Lewiston, 134
Liberty, 96; Park (Salt Lake City), 77
Linwood, 36
Lion House (Salt Lake City), 70, 75
Lion's Club Park (Provo), 89
Lisbon Valley, 195
Little: Hole, 37; Bridge, 48; Zion, 53; Sahara Recreation Area, 58, 121; Cottonwood Canyon/Scenic Byway, 59, 66, 69, 81, 82, 85, 120; Mountain, 81, 99; Valley, 106; Yellowstone, 118; Bear River, 131; Standard, 158; Rockies, 205, 206
Lizard Rock, 25

Loa, 26, 30, 170, 230; -Hanksville Scenic Byway, 59; Fish Hatchery (Brian Springs), 170
Loafer Mountain, 92, 161
Lockhart Basin/Trail, 192, 197
Locomotive: Springs State Waterfowl Management Area, 107; Rock (Bluff), 199
Lodore: Canyon of, 32, 33, 34, 151, 181; Gates of, 33, 34
Logan, 1, 131, 133, 134–35, 153; Canyon/River/Scenic Byway, 59, 133, 134, 135–37; Tabernacle, 134; Temple, 134
Lone Peak Wilderness Area, 16, 58; access to, 85
Lone Rock Canyon, 225
Long Canyon, 234
Long Valley/Junction, 31, 213, 215, 221–24
Looking Glass Rock/Arch, 195, 208
Lookout Pass, 117
Lost Creek State Park (Morgan), 16, 56; Canyon/Reservoir, 97
Low Junction/Pass, 108
Lower: Brown's Reservoir, 29, 233; Muley Twist Canyon, 30, 234; Crossing, 183; Calf Creek Falls, 231, 232
Lucerne Valley, 36, 37
Lucin: Cutoff, 43, 95, 107, 100, 123; town of, 110
Lyric Theater (Logan), 135
Lynndyl, 122, 172

Maeser, 149, 150; Center, 150
MagCorp magnesium plant (Rowley), 112
Magna, 80
Mahogany Cove, 175
Main Street: (Salt Lake City), 71, 73; Historic District (Park City), 138; Historic District (Ephraim), 163
Mammoth, 120, 121; Creek, 222
M&O Ranch (Salina Canyon), 177
Manila, 35, 36, 37, 151
Manti: -La Sal National Forest, 47, 57; 162, 164, 165; 194, 197, 198, 204; Division, 57; ZCMI Mercantile building (Salt Lake City), 78; town of, 161, 163–64, 177; Mountain, 161; Temple, 164; Canyon, 164; Community Camp, 164
Maple Canyon, 162
Marble Canyon, 41, 42; (Navajo) Bridge, 223
Markagunt Plateau, 31, 55, 59, 165, 166, 175, 213, 220, 221, 222
Marmalade District (Salt Lake City), 71
Marriott: Library (U of U), J. Willard, 78; Center (BYU), 90

Marysvale, 157, 166, 167, 168; Canyon, 167
Massachusetts, 5
Mau-be Ferry, 152
Maughan's Fort, 134
Mayfield, 161, 162, 164
Maze, The, x, 22, 23, 25; Overlook, 25
McConkie Ranch, petroglyphs on, 150–51
McCune Mansion (Salt Lake City), 71
McCurdy Historical Doll Museum (Provo), 89
McElmo Creek/Canyon, 45, 197, 199
McKay Home (Huntsville): Angus, 96; David O., 96
McKee Springs, 35
McQuarrie Memorial Hall (St. George), 218
Meadow, 173
Memorial Park (Pleasant Grove), 86
Memory Grove (Salt Lake City), 71, 72, 75
Mendon, 131
Mercur, 114, 115
Merkley Park, 150
Merrick Butte/Finger, 202
Metate Arch, 231
Methodist Church (Corinne), 105
Mexican: Hat, 38, 47, 48, 49, 198, 202, 203, 204, 208; Mountain, 186
Mexico, 12, 153, 198
Middle: Cave, 50; Canyon (Oquirrh Mountains), 113
Midvale, 68, 80
Midway, 82, 85, 141–42
Milford, 13, 124
Millard: Canyon/Benches, 25; County, 103, 120, 122, 155, 173; Volcanic Field, 173
Mill Creek Canyon, 81, 167; access to, 191
Mill Meadow, 170
Mills Junction, 112
Millsite State Park (Ferron), 16, 56; Reservoir, 161
Mineral Canyon, 24
Miner's Mountain, 28, 29; Basin, 193
Minersville State Park (Minersville), 16, 56
Mirror Lake/Scenic Byway, 59, 143, 144, 145
Mitchell Butte/Finger, 202
Mittens Butte/Finger, 202
Moab: 3, 5, 6, 8, 17, 18, 22, 24, 38, 58, 60, 179, 182, 188, 189, 190–91, 192, 193, 194, 197; Canyon, 18, 190, 192; Slickrock Bike Trail, 190; Rim, 192
Mohtland, 160
Moki: Dugway/Switchbacks, 8, 48, 203, 204; Canyon, 204
Mona, 172; Reservoir, 172
Monroe, 166; Canyon, 167
Monrovian Park, 167
Montana, 94, 135
Monte Cristo: Campground, 96; access to, 131; Summit/Peak, 96, 137
Monterey, 124
Montezuma Creek/Canyon, 45, 119, 197, 198, 199; access to, 200
Monticello: 8, 22, 47, 179, 195, 197, 198, 200, 201, 204, 208; Museum, 197
Monument: Valley, 1, 9, 47, 49, 61, 186, 202–3, 208; Basin, 23; Pass, 202; Canyon/Wash, 202
Monuments and Parks, 16
Moon Lake (Lake Fork Canyon), 147
Morgan: County, 63, 96–97, 103; town of, 81, 96–97; Valley, 99
Mormon: -Donner Pioneer Trail, 81; Rock Chapel (Farmington), 99; Country, 159–66; Ward Chapel (Spring City), 163; First Ward Chapel (Cedar City), 213. See also LDS Church/Complex
Moroni, 6, 162, 172
Morton Salt Company (Salt Lake Valley West), 79
Mother Earth's Lace Curtains, 51
Mount: Naomi/Wilderness Area, 16, 58, 153; Olympus Wilderness Area, 16, 58; Timpanogos, 50, 81, 83, 84, 85, 86, 87, 140; Kinesava, 54; Joseph, 109; Agassiz, 144; Pleasant, 161, 162; Catherine, 165; Holly Resort, 168; Mellenthin, 193; Peale, 194; Ellsworth, 205, 206; Holmes, 205, 206; Pennell, 206; Ellen, 206; Hillers, 206; Trumbull, 218
Mount Carmel, 52, 221, 223; Junction, 52, 223
Mount Nebo: Wilderness Area, 16, 58; Loop, 57, 172; access to, 81, 84, 113, 120, 172
Mountain: West, 12; of the Sun, 54; Green, 97; Home, 147

Mountain Dell, 81, 137; Canyon/Reservoir, 137
Mountain Meadows, 13, 219; Massacre Historic Site, 219
Moyle Home and Tower (Alpine), 85
Muddy: Creek, 161; River, 186, 187; River Canyon, 206
Mukuntuweap National Monument, 53
Mule Canyon Rest Area, 204
Muley: Point Overlook, 48, 203; Twist Canyon, 30;
   Point, access to, 204
Municipal Building and Gardens (Ogden), 94
Murphy's Point Overlook, 23
Murray, 68
Museum of: Church History and Art (Salt Lake City),
   70; Fine Arts (U of U), 78; Natural History (U of U),
   78; Art (BYU), 90; the San Rafael (Castle Dale), 160
Music Temple, 61
Musinia, 164
Mustang Ridge, 37
Mutual, 158
Mystery: Canyon, 61; Valley, 202
Myton, 147, 183

Naegle Winery (Toquerville), 216
Naples, 182
Narrow Canyon, 25, 42, 205
Narrows: (Capitol Reef N. P.), 28, 29; Trail (Zion N. P.),
   55; (Paria River), 225
Natanni Tso Butte/Finger, 202
National, 158
Natural: Bridges National Monument, 16, 47–48, 60, 198,
   203, 204, 208; History Museum (WSU), 95
Navajo: Indian Reservation/Tribal Park, 3, 202, 209;
   Arch, 19; Loop Hike, 21; Mountain, 40, 49, 194, 226,
   230; Lake, 57, 215; Twins Buttes, 199
Neck, The, 23
Needles, 22, 23, 24–25, 187, 193, 194, 195, 196, 197
Negro Bill Canyon, 191
Nemo Arch, 231
Neola, 148
Nephi, 6, 121, 122, 172, 173
New Harmony, 52, 55, 215–16
Newgate Mall (Ogden), 94
Newhouse Building (Salt Lake City), 74
Newspaper Rock, 196
Newton, 131, 133; Dam/Reservoir, 133
Nine Mile Canyon, 147, 148, 183
Nipple Bench, 225
Nordic Valley Ski Area, 96
North: Window, 19; Creek (Zion N. P.), 54, 55, 221;
   Wash/Junction, 61, 205, 206; Tract, 122
Norton Hall of Minerals (U of U), 77
Notch Peak, 124, 125
Notom, 29, 172
Notre Dame de Lourdes Catholic Church (Price), 159
Not Zion, 53

Oak: City, 122; Creek, 122; Creek Campground, 233
Oakley, 142
Oaks Park Reservoir, 151
Observation Point, 54
Ogden, 1, 43, 58, 63, 87, 92–95, 96, 97, 125, 133;
   River/Scenic Byway, 59, 93, 96; City and County
   Building, 94; Hall, 94; Mall, 94–95; Union
   Depot/Station, 94; -Weber Convention and Visitors
   Bureau Information Center, 94; Canyon, 95–96;
   Nature Center, 95; Tabernacle, 95; Temple, 95;
   Valley, 95, 96, 131; Air Logistics Center, 99
O'Laurie Museum (Moab), Dan, 191
Old: Spanish Trail, 41, 165, 168, 175, 184, 185, 186, 190,
   194, 197, 219, 221; Ute Crossing, 41; Deseret Village
   (Salt Lake City), 78, 79; Bell School (Pleasant Grove),
   86; Presbyterian Church (Springville), 91; Pony
   Express and Stage Trail, 114, 116–20, 123; Stagecoach
   Inn (Fairfield), 115; City Hall and Fire Station
   (Ophir), 114; Cache County Courthouse (Logan),
   135; Jardine Juniper (Logan Canyon), 135; Ephraim's
   Grave (Logan Canyon), 136; Town (Park City), 138;
   Midway School, 142; Uintah Stake Tabernacle
   (Vernal), 149; Pioneer Museum (Mount Pleasant),
   162; Kimberly, 167; Monroe City Hall, 167; Beaver
   County Courthouse, 175; La Sal, 194; Baldy Mesa,
   202; Mormon Church and Tithing Office

(Toquerville), 216; Cotton Factory (Washington),
   217; Paria Townsite, 224
Old Fort: Utah (Provo), 89; Deseret, 124; Pearce, 220
Old River Bed: Station, 117; access to, 118, 123, 124
Oljeto Mesa, 202
Olpin: University Union (U of U), A. Ray, 78;
   Home (Pleasant Grove), 87
Omni, 166
Onaqui Mountain Range, 114
Onion Creek, 193; Creek Canyon, 194
Oowah Lake, 193
Ophir: City Hall, 106; town of, 114, 115; Canyon, 114
Oquirrh Mountain Range, 65, 79, 80, 112, 113, 127
Orange (Wingate) Cliffs, 23, 25, 38, 41, 42, 187, 191
Orangeville, 160, 163
Orderville, 6, 166, 222–23
Oregon Trail, 109
Orem, 86, 87, 140, 183
Organ, The: (Arches N. P.), 18; (Zion N. P.), 54
Otter Creek: State Park/Beach (Antimony), 16, 56, 168,
   175, 227; Junction, 168; Lake, 168, access to, 169
Ott Planetarium (WSU), 95
Ouray: National Wildlife Refuge, 149, 182; Reservation,
   182
Overland Canyon, 119
Owachomo Bridge, 47, 48
Oyler Mine, 28

Page (AZ), 38, 42, 49, 224, 226, 227
Pahvant: Valley, 121, 123, 124, 165, 172–75; Butte (Sugar
   Loaf Mountain), 124, 173; Plateau/Range, 165, 166,
   169, 172, 173. See also Sevier Desert
Painted Desert, 28, 170, 207
Paiute: ATV Trail, 57, 166; State Park, 166
Palisade: State Park (Sterling), 16, 56, 164; Lake, 164
Palmer: Indian Museum (SUU), William R., 213; Room
   of Western History (SUU), 213
Panguitch, 20, 21, 169, 175, 221, 222, 227; Lake, 57, 175,
   222; Canyon, 168, 169; Campground, 222; Hayfield,
   227
Panorama Point, 29
Parade of Elephants, 19
Paradise, 96, 131; Tithing Office, 131; Flats, 234
Paradox: Basin, 193; Valley, 194
Paragonah, 175, 221
Paria: Canyon/Vermilion Cliffs Wilderness Area, 16, 58,
   224, 225; View, 21; (Lee's Ferry), 41; access to, 45;
   River, 224, 225, 228; River Valley, 227
Park: Avenue, 18; Building (U of U), 78; Valley, 107,
   153; Meadows, 138
Park City/Ski Area, 82, 86, 120, 138–39, 142
Parker: Home (near Joseph), 167; Mountain, 170
Parks and Monuments, 15–61
Parley's: Canyon/Summit, 81, 137; Park, 138, 139
Parowan, 31, 169, 177, 215, 222; Canyon/Gap/Valley, 175
Parry's Lodge (Kanab), 223
Partition Arches, 19
Partridge Home (Fillmore), Edward, 173
Parunuweap Canyon, 221, 223
Patmos Head, 183
Paul Bunyan's Woodpile, 121
Paunsaugunt Plateau, 20, 166, 221, 222, 223, 224, 227
Payson, 63, 84, 87, 91, 92, 172
Peek-a-boo: Arch, 30; Canyon, 45
Peerless, 158
Pelican Lake, 148–49
Peltier Ranch, petroglyphs on, 150
Penellen Pass, 206
Peter's Leap, 216
Peterson Home (Ephraim), Canute, 163
Pete's Mesa, 25
Photograph Gap, 196
Pilot Peak, 108, 110, 111
Pine: Tree Arch, 19; Creek/Canyon, 55, 142, 167, 230;
   Lake, 219, 227
Pine Valley: Mountains/Wilderness Area, 16, 58, 215,
   216, 219; town of, 57, 219
Pineview Dam/Reservoir, 96
Pinhook Valley, 193
Pink Cliffs, 20, 31, 45, 215, 222, 223, 224
Pintura, 215, 216

Pinyon Ridge, 145
Pioneer: Register, 28–29; Cabin (Provo), 89; Memorial
   Building (Provo), 89; Mother Monument and
   Memorial Fountain (Springville), 91; Museum
   (St. George), 218
Pioneer (Salt Lake City): Memorial Museum and
   Carriage House, 71; Park, 74; Mural, 78; Theatre
   Company (U of U), 78; Trail State Park, 79
Piute: State Park (Junction), 16, 56; County, 155, 157,
   168, 169; County Courthouse, 168; Lake State Beach,
   168; Reservoir, 168
Platts House (Salt Lake City), John, 71
Pleasant Creek, 28; Canyon, 29; Campground, 233
Pleasant Grove, 50, 84, 86–87; Canning Plant, 87;
   Town Hall, 87
Pleasant Valley/Junction, 157
Plymouth, 105
Pogu Lake, 11
Point: Supreme, 31, 32; of the Mountain, 79, 83, 84;
   Lookout, 117
Polar Mesa, 193, 194
Pole Line Pass, 142
Pony Express Trail. See Old Pony Express Trail
Pool Creek Canyon, 34
Pope, The, 21
Portal, 192
Posey: Lake, 170, 230; Monument, 198
Potash, 24; Scenic Byway, 59; Railroad, 192
Potato: Hollow, 54; Valley, 230
Powder Mountain Ski Resort, 96
Powell: Art Gallery (Ogden), Myra, 94; River History
   Museum (Green River), John Wesley, 184
Powell's Pink Point, 227
Powerpole Rim, 193, 194
Prehistoric Museum (CEU), 159
Presbyterian Church and "Cottage" (Castle Dale), 161
President's Circle (U of U), 78
Price: 57, 92, 147, 148, 149, 150, 157, 158–59, 160, 161,
   182, 183, 184; Canyon: River, 157, 158, 183;
   Recreation Site, 158; Municipal Building, 159
Primrose Valley, 202
Pritchett: Arch, 192; Canyon, 192, 194
Professor Valley, 193
Promised Valley Playhouse (Salt Lake City), 72
Promontory, 43; Trail, 43; Summit, 43, 123; Point, 105,
   106, 125; Mountain Range, 106, 123
Prospector Square Convention Center (Park City), 138
Providence, 131
Provo: 1, 57, 84, 86, 87–90, 134; Canyon/River, 59, 81, 83,
   84, 85, 86, 88, 90, 141, 142, 143, 144, 145; Tabernacle,
   89; Third Ward Chapel, 89; Temple, 95
Pueblo Mesa, 202
Puffer Lake, 168, 175

Quail Creek State Park/Reservoir (St. George), 16, 56,
   216, 217
Quarry Visitor Center/Dinosaur National Monument, 32,
   33, 34, 152
Quayle House (Salt Lake City), Thomas, 71

Rabbit Valley, 169, 170
Raft River Mountains, 57, 107, 153
Railroad Village Museum (Heber City), 105
Rainbow: Point, 21; Park, 34, 151; Hills, 166, 169;
   town of, 182
Rainbow Bridge National Monument, 16, 42, 49, 208
Rains, 158
Ramsay Home (Richfield), Ralph, 166
Randlett, 149
Randolph, 137
Range Valley, 183
Rasmussen House (Mount Pleasant), Morten, 162
Recapture: Creek/Canyon, 197, 198, 199; Pocket, 200
Reclining Camel, 51
Red: Rock Pass, 134; Cloud Loop, 150, 151; Pyramid, 165;
   Gate, 172; Hills, 175; Amphitheater, 184; Plateau,
   185; House Cliffs, 204; Mesa, 209; Cliffs Reacreation
   Site, 216; Sand Mountain, 220
Red Butte Garden (U of U), 78
Red Canyon: (Lake Powell), 42; (Buckhorn Wash, 186);
   access to, 204, 227

Red Canyon (Flaming Gorge), 35, 36, 37, 150, 151;
    Overlook, 35, 37; Lodge, 35; Visitor Center, 35, 37
Red Fleet: State Park (Vernal), 16, 56; Dam/Reservoir, 152
Redd Ranches, 194
Redmond, 165
Reed Trading Post, 148
Refrigerator Canyon, 54
Relief Society Stake Meeting Hall (Ogden), 95
Rendezvous Beach (Bear Lake), 137
Reno, 191
Rhode Island, 44
Rhodes Valley, 142
Rice Bank (Silver Reef), 216
Richardson Amphitheater, 193
Rich County, 129, 137, 153
Richfield, 26, 57, 58, 164, 165–66, 167, 169
Richmond, 131, 133, 134
Ridge Trail, 85
Riley Canyon, 121
Rim: Road, 20, 21; Overlook, 29; The, (Castle Valley) 160
River Ford, 30
Riverside, 105
Roan (Tavaputs) Plateau, 157, 158, 182, 183
Robbers Roost: (Hanksville), 38, 42, 186, 205–7;
    (Antelope Springs), 125
Rock: Cliff Recreation Area, 142; Creek Canyon, 145,
    147; Schoolhouse (Fillmore), 173;
    Door Canyon/Wash, 202
Rockport: State Park (Wanship), 16, 56, 143; Lake,
    access to, 143
Rockville, 221
Rocky Mountains/Province (Wasatch Range), 2, 36, 81,
    117, 127, 129–153, 144, 161, 172, 173
Roosevelt, 147, 148, 182
Rose Springs Fort. See Batesville
Rosette, 107
Round: Station, 119; Valley, 172
Rowley, 108; Junction, 108, 115
Ruby's Inn Lodge and Resort, 21, 227
Ruin Canyon, 45, 46
Rush Valley, 112, 113, 114, 116, 117, 121; access to, 113;
    Bay, 113; City, 114; Station, East, 117

Sage Plain, 45, 197, 198, 199
Salem, 91, 92
Salina: Canyon, 162, 164, 165, 168, 172, 177; town of,
    173, 184
Saltair, 125
Salt: Wash, 19, 206; Valley Anticline, 19, 188;
    Palace/Convention Center (Salt Lake City), 68, 72,
    74; Desert, 109, 110, 111, 112
Salt Creek, 24; Canyon, 172; Fort (Nephi), 172; Mesa,
    197; -Lavender Canyon-Needles maze, 197
Salt Lake: Valley, 12, 44, 65–79, 79–80, 81–82, 83, 84,
    108, 109, 113, 117, 119, 131, 137; Temple, 63, 66, 67,
    68, 69, 70, 79, 91, 173; County, 63, 65, 68, 80, 81, 97;
    Tabernacle, 66, 69, 173; Theater, 66; Visitors Bureau,
    68; Art Center, 72, 74; Collegiate Institute, 77;
    Cutoff, 107
Salt Lake City: 1, 6, 7, 10, 27, 56, 57, 58, 65, 66, 68–69, 80,
    82, 87, 91, 92, 93, 94, 97, 100, 103, 107, 110, 113, 114,
    115, 119, 122, 123, 127, 135, 137, 138, 144, 149, 150,
    159, 166, 173, 174, 177, 191, 217, 219; International
    Airport, 65, 79, 125; Hall, 71; and County Building,
    72; Public Library, 72
San Juan: County, 12, 48, 170, 179, 197, 198, 200, 202,
    204, 208, 209; Country, 194–205; River, 38, 41, 42, 45,
    47, 48, 179, 198, 199, 200, 201, 202, 203, 204, 208; Hill,
    199, 200; State Park, 203
San Rafael: Swell, 58, 159, 161, 179, 183, 184–88, 206,
    234; Gorge, 185; River, 185, 186, 187; Desert, 186;
    Reef, 186, 187, 206
Sand: Canyon, 34; Bench Trail, 54; Wash Launching
    Site, 147; Flats/Trail, 193, 234; Creek/Canyon,
    230, 234
Sanpete: Valley, 11, 157, 159, 160, 161–64, 172; County,
    155; Trade Association (Ephraim), 163
Sanpitch: River, 161, 164; Mountains, 162; access to, 163
Santa Clara: River/Valley, 13, 218–19; town of, 218, 219;
    Creek, 236
Santaquin: 91, 92, 120, 172; Peak, 92; Junction, 172

Satan, 19
Sausage Rock, 18
Sawtooth National Forest, 57
Scenic Byways and Backways, 59
Scipio, 165, 172; Junction, 173; Pass, 173
Scofield: Lake State Recreation Area, 16, 56, 157;
    access to, 88, 158; Reservoir, 157
Seagull Monument (Salt Lake City), 69
Sego, 188; Canyon Indian Writings, 188
Seely Home (Mount Pleasant), William, 162
Sentinel: The, 54, 55; Mesa, 202
Settlement Canyon, 113
Seven-mile Canyon, 188, 190
Sevier: River/Valley, 11, 57, 120, 122, 124, 161, 162,
    164–66, 167, 168, 169, 172, 221–24, 227; Bay, 117, 188;
    Desert, 120, 121, 123, 165; (Dry) Lake, 122, 123, 124,
    161; County, 155, 165, 166; Valley Tech, 166; town of,
    167; LDS Chapel, 167; Bridge Reservoir, 172; Plateau,
    165, 166–69, 221
Seymour Special Collections (SUU), John, 213
Shafer: Canyon, 23; Trail, 23, 25, 190
Sheep Creek: Bay, 36; Canyon Geological Area, 37;
    Cave, 37; -Hideout Canyon Overview, 37
Shepherd Union Building (WSU), 95
Shinarump Ridge, 236
Shinob Canyon, 28
Shirts Fort, 215
Shivwits, 13
Shurtz Gorge, 228
Sidon, 215
Sigurd, 165, 169, 172; Junction, 165
Silent City, 21
Silver: Flat Reservoir/Lake, 85; Island Range, 111; City,
    120, 121; Creek Canyon, 139; Creek Junction, 139,
    140; Reef, 216; Falls Canyon, 231
Simpson, 117
Sinbad: Country, 184, 186, 187; Interchange, 186
Singing Rock, 28
Singletree Campground, 233
Sipapu Bridge, 47, 48
Six-mile Canyon, 164
Sixmile Ranch, 119
Sixshooter Peaks, 193, 196, 197
Skull: Crack Forest Campground, 96; Valley/Indian
    Reservation, 109, 115, 116, 127; Rock Pass, 124
Skyline Drive, 157, 160, 161, 162, 163, 164, 165
Sleeping Rainbow Ranch, 28
Slickrock Mountain, 58
Slide, The, 24
Smith and Morehouse Reservoir, 142
Smithfield, 131, 133; Canyon, 133; Canyon Forest
    Campground, 133
Smith Home: (American Fork), 86; (Provo), 89; (Cedar
    City), Jesse, 175
Smithsonian: Institution, 33, 46, 206; Butte, 221
Smoky Mountain, 230
Smoot Home (Provo), Reed, 89
Snake: Creek Canyon, 85, 142; Valley, 125;
    River/Country/Drainage, 131, 134
Snow: Canyon State Park (St. George), 16, 56, 218, 219;
    College (Ephraim), 163
Snowbasin Ski Resort, 96
Snowbird, 82
Snowville, 105, 107
Snyderville, 138
Soap Creek Rapids, 182
Soldier: Creek/Dam, 145, 157; Summit, 157; Creek
    Mining Company, 183
Soldiers' Grave, 204
Solitude Ski Area, 82
Sonoran Desert, 59
South: Window, 19; Willow Canyon, 112; Tent, 163
Southern: Pacific causeway, 108, 121, 123; Utah
    University, 175, 213
Southwest, American, 6
Sowiette Park and Pioneer Museum (Provo), 89
Space Science Library/Museum (Salt Lake City), 72
Spanish: Bottom, 25; Valley, 188–94
Spanish Fork: River, 90; town of, 91, 92, 157; Canyon, 92,
    155, 157, 161
Sparks Home (Ephraim), Hansen, 163

Spearhead Mesa, 202
Spectra Point, 32
Spectrum (USU), 135
Spendlove Knoll, 221
Spillway Boat Ramp, 37
Spilsbury Home (Toquerville), 216
Split Mountain: Canyon/Gorge, 32, 34; access to, 152
Split Rock Canyon, 181
Spooky Canyon (Storrs), 45, 158
Spring: Canyon, 29, 158, 186; Lake, 92; Glen, 158
Spring City, 162, 163; Public School, 163
Springdale, 52, 53, 221
Springville, 84, 88, 91; Museum of Art, 91
Square Tower Canyon, 46
Squaw: Butte, 24; Flat Campground, 25; Flat Scenic
    Byway, 59; Peak/Trail, 91, 153
St. George, 1, 5, 11, 13, 52, 54, 215, 216, 217–18, 219, 220,
    235, 236; Temple, 217, 218; Tabernacle, 218;
    Stake Academy, 218
St. John/Junction, 114
St. John's Episcopal Church (Logan), 135
St. Lawrence Catholic Church (Heber City), 141
St. Mark's Episcopal Cathedral (Salt Lake City), 75
Stagecoach: Inn (Fairfield), 86; Canyon/Wash, 202
Staker House (Mount Pleasant), Alma, 162
Standardville, 158
Standing Rocks, 23
Stansbury: Island, 108, 121, 127; Mountain Range, 108,
    112, 114, 115, 127
Starr: Springs/Recreation Site, 206; Ranch, 206
Starvation: State Park (Duchesne), 16, 56; Reservoir,
    145; Lake State Beach, 145
State (Salt Lake City): Antiquities Office, 74; Historic
    Preservation Office, 74; Arboretum of Utah, 78
Stateline Hotel and Casino (Wendover), 111
Steamboat Rock, 33, 34
Steinaker State Park/Reservoir (Vernal), 16, 56, 151, 152
Sterling, 161, 164
Stevens Arch, 231
Stewart: Carillon Tower (WSU), 95; Library (WSU),
    152; Lake Waterfowl Management Area, 152
Stillwater, 181
Stockton: Bar (Great Bar), 113; access to, 114, 120
Straight Canyon, 160
Straight Cliffs, 45, 230, 231
Strawberry: Reservoir/River, 57, 91, 141, 145, 157; Valley,
    148; Point, 215
Strike Valley Overlook, 30
Stronghold House, 46
Stuntz Ridge, 152
Sugar Loaf, 195
Sugarville, 122, 123
Sulphur Creek, 28; Canyon, 29, 234
Sulphurdale, 174
Summerhays Planetarium (BYU), 91
Summit: County, 63, 129, 140; House (Park City), 139;
    peaks, 167
Sun Dance Cave, 135
Sundance/Resort, 50, 83, 84, 85, 86
Sunglow Recreation Area, 170
Sunnyside/Junction, 183
Sunrise Point, 21
Sunset: Point, 21; Pass, 25; View, 32; Peak Overlook,
    113; Peaks, 165; Cliff, 222
Sun's Eye Butte/Finger, 202
Sutherland, 122, 123
SUU. See Southern Utah University
Swazey Peak, 125
Swett Ranch, 37
Syracuse, 125

Tabiona, 147
Table Cliff Plateau, 227, 228
Talmage House (Provo), 89
Tantalus Basin, 29
Tavaputs Plateau, 3, 17, 145, 147, 149, 157, 158, 182, 183
Taylor: Canyon of Green River, 23; Flat, 193
Teasdale, 172, 234; Fault, 234
Temple: of Isiris, 21; Mountain/Junction, 22, 186, 187; of
    Sinawava, 53, 54, 55; Square (Salt Lake City), 65, 66,
    67, 68, 69–70, 71, 74, 75; Fork, 136; Hill (Manti), 164

Territorial State House (Fillmore), 16, 56, 173, 174
Thatcher Home (Logan), Joseph, 135
Third Ward Meeting House (Cedar City), 175
This Is the Place State Park (Salt Lake City), 16, 56, 78, 81, 100, 101
Thistle, 157, 161; Creek, 161
Thomas Range, 124
Thompson, 188; Springs, 188; Canyon, 193
Thorny Pasture, 228
Thor's Hammer, 21
Thousand Lake Mountain/Plateau, 27, 29, 30, 165, 166, 169, 170, 172, 207, 234
Three: Gossips, 18; Patriarchs, 54; Sisters Buttes/Fingers, 202; Lake Canyon (Kanab Creek), 223
Thurber, 198. See also Bicknell
Tibble Fork Reservoir, 85
Ticaboo, 61, 205
Timber Top, 55
Timpanogos: Wilderness Area, 16, 58; Cave National Monument, 16, 50–51, 84, 85, 86; Cave, 50, 51; Cave Visitor Center, 85
Timpie: Springs State Waterfowl Management Area, 115; Junction, 115
Timpooneke Campground, 85
Timpoweap Canyon, 220
Tintic: Mining District, 92, 120; Mountains, 120, 121; Valley, 121
Tomsich Butte, 187
Tony Grove Lake, 136
Tooele: County, 103, 107, 111, 112; town of, 108, 112, 113, 116, 121; Valley, 108, 112, 113, 127, 133; County Courthouse, 112–13; Army Depot (Grantsville), 112, 113, 114
Topaz: Mountain/range, x, 122, 123, 124; War Relocation Center, 123
Top-of-the-World Overlook, 193, 194
Toquerville, 216
Torrey, 5, 26, 27, 28, 29, 172, 179, 207, 213, 234; Breaks, 29, 207
Totem Pole: (The Maze), 25; (Monument Valley), 202
Tower Arch, 19
Towers of the Virgin, 54, 55
Tracheyte Creek, 61
Tracy Aviary (Salt Lake City), 77
Trail of the Ancients Scenic Byway, 59
Train Rock Canyon/Wash, 202
Tree of Life, 106, 110
Tremonton, 43, 133
Trolley Square (Salt Lake City), 77
Tropic, 20, 226, 227
Trout Creek, 119, 125
Tuacahn, 218
Tucker, 157, 162
Tule (Tuilia) Springs, 112
Turret Arch, 19
Tushar Mountains/Plateau, 165, 166, 167, 168, 169, 174, 175, 221
Twelvemile Canyon/Creek, 164
25th Street Historic District (Ogden), 94
Twilight Canyon, 61
Twin: Peaks Wilderness Area, 16, 58; Towers, 46

U-Bar Ranch, 148
Uinta: Mountains, x, 3, 11, 13, 32, 81, 83, 129, 134, 137, 142, 143–53, 168, 183; Basin, 3, 13, 34, 84, 141, 142, 143, 145, 147, 148, 149, 152, 179, 182, 183, 188; Crest Fault, 37; Canyon, 145, 148
Uintah: National Forest, 57, 85, 91, 172; County, 129, 149, 179; County Park, 150; Reservation, 182
Uncompahgre Uplift, 182
Union Pacific Railroad Depot/Station: (Salt Lake City), 74, 75; (Logan), 135; (Cedar City), 213
Union Pacific Rail Trail State Park (Park City), 16, 56
United Order Co-op Mercantile Institution (Ephraim),163
University (Salt Lake City): of Utah, 33, 40, 49, 77–78, 111, 148, 160, 213, 233; Research Park, 78
Unjoined Rock, 18
U of U. See University of Utah
Upalco, 147
Upheaval Dome, 23, 194

Upper: Muley Twist Canyon, 30, 234; Valley Oil field, 228; Calf Creek Falls, 233
Urban Corridor, 2; 63–101; Central, 65–81; Southern, 83–92; Northern, 92–99
USU. See Utah State University
Utah: Lake/State Park/Boat Harbor, 11, 16, 56, 79, 83, 84, 86, 87, 88, 89, 119; Field House/Natural History State Park (Vernal), 16, 56, 149; County, 63, 88, 155; Travel Council (Salt Lake City), 68–69, 71; Media Center (Salt Lake City), 74; Arts Council (Salt Lake City), 75; Museum of Natural History (U of U), 77; County Building, 89; Wool Pullery (Mills Junction), 112; Launch Complex (Green River), 184
Utah State: Capitol (Salt Lake City), 71–72; Heritage Foundation (Salt Lake City), 71; Historical Society (Salt Lake City), 74; Fair Grounds (Salt Lake City), 79; Prison (Point of the Mountain), 79; Railroad Museum (Ogden), 94; University (Logan), 134, 135, 213
Utah Valley, 81, 83–92, 113, 115, 120, 145, 155, 157, 172, 213, 217; State College, 87; Convention and Visitors Bureau, 89
Ute Reservation, 148

Valley: of the Gods, 48, 203, 208; Mountains, 172
Velvet Ridge, 234
Vermilion: Cliffs, 44, 45, 220, 224, 226; Castle Forest Campground, 175
Vernal, 32, 33, 34, 35, 58, 140, 145, 147, 148, 149–50, 151, 152, 182; Temple, 149; tours from, 150–52
Vernon, 114
Veterans: Memorial State Park (Bluffdale), 16, 56; Medical Center (Salt Lake City), 78
Veyo, 219
Virgin Anticline, 220
Virgin River, 52, 55, 221; Narrows, 52, 55; Valley (Dixie), 54, 215–21; Gorge, 218, 219, 220, 222, 236

Wah Wah Range, x
Wahsatch, 140
Wahweap: Marina (AZ), 38, 42, 49, 227; Creek, 225
Wales, 162
Wall: Arch, 19; of Windows, 21; Street, 21; Gristmill (Glenwood), Joseph, 166
Walton Canyon, 96
Wanship, 140, 143; Dam, 143
Warm Creek Canyon, 230
Warner Lake, 193
Wasatch: Mountains/Range/Front, x, 3, 5, 6, 8, 11, 32, 50, 57, 63, 65, 71, 78, 79, 81, 83, 84, 85, 87, 91, 93, 95, 96, 99, 105, 107, 109, 113, 119, 127, 129, 131, 133, 135, 137–43, 44, 161, 177; Mountain State Park (Midway), 16, 56, 85, 141, 142; -Cache National Forest, 57, 81, 82, 112, 131, 133, 135, 144; County, 63, 129, 141; Stake Tabernacle (Heber City), 141; Plateau, 145, 157, 158, 160, 161, 162, 163, 164, 165, 166, 176; Academy (Mount Pleasant), 162
Washington: Square (Salt Lake City), 72; County, 211, 217; town of, 217, 236
Watchman, 53
Water Canyon, 29, 234
Water Hole Flat (Sunset Pass), 25
Waterpocket Fold, 27, 29, 30, 45: 205, 206–7, 234
Watkins-Coleman Home (Midway), 142
Watson, 152, 182
Wattis, 160
Wayne: Wonderland, 27, 169; County, 122, 165, 169, 170, 179, 211; County Courthouse (Loa), 170; Stake Tabernacle (Loa), 170
Weber: County, 63, 92–96, 97, 140; River/Canyon/Valley, 83, 93, 94, 95, 96, 97, 109, 131, 138, 139, 140, 142; County Memorial Park, 96; State University (Ogden), 95
Webster Junction, 134
Wedge Overlook, 185, 186
Weeping Rock, 54
Welfare Square (Salt Lake City), 75
Wellington, 147, 182, 183
Wells Fargo Express Building (Silver Reef), 216
Wellsville: Mountains Wilderness Area, 16, 58, 131, 133,

153; Canyon, 131, 133; Cone, 133; town of, 133, 134
Wendover, 3, 10, 13, 80, 103, 105, 106, 107, 108, 109, 110, 111, 116, 119, 120, 125; Air Force Base, 108, 111
West: Desert, 1, 6; District, 22; Rim/Trail/Viewpoint, 54, 55; Temple (Zion N. P.), 53, 54, 55, 221; Valley City, 80; Mountain, 113
Western Mining and Railroad Museum (Helper), 158
Westminster College (Salt Lake City), 77
Westwater Canyon, 182, 188, 198
Wetherill Mesa, 202
Wheeler Historic Farm (Salt Lake Valley South), 79
Whirlpool Canyon, 32, 34, 151
Whirlwind Valley, 124
White: Rim, 22, 23; Rim Trail, 23, 190; Canyon, 42, 48, 60, 204, 205; Cliffs, 45, 223; Community Memorial Cahpel (Salt Lake City), 71; Valley, 124–25; Sand Dunes, 121; River, 149; Pine, 165; Rock School (Elsinore), 167; Mesa, 198; House Ruins, 225
Whiterocks, 147, 148, 149, 181
Whitmore: Mansion (Nephi), 172; Canyon, 183
Widtsoe, 227, 228
Wildcat Canyon, 55
Wild Horse: Mesa, x; Bar, 61; Butte, 206
Wildwood, 50
Wilkinson Student Center (BYU), 90
Willard Bay State Park (Brigham City), 16, 56
Willow: Springs Station (Callao), 119; Creek Canyon, 147
Wilson Arch, 195
Wilson's Health Resort, 118
Wind: Caves, 135; Whistle, 195
Windmill Valley, 202
Windowblind Peak, 186
Windows Reef, 18
Windows, The, 18–19
Wingate (Orange) Cliffs, 23, 204
Winn Home (Lehi), 86
Winter Quarters, 157
Witches Castle, 135
Wolf: Ranch, 19; Creek Resort, 96; Creek Pass, 142, 145, 147
Wolverine Petrified Forest, 45
Wolverton, 206
Wood Cabin (Cedar City), George L., 213
Woodland, 122, 147
Woodruff, 96, 137
Woodside, 183, 184, 188
Worthen's Merc (Fremont), 170
WSU. See Weber State University

Yampa: River, 32, 33, 34; Bench, 34; Plateau, 34, 152
Yankee Meadows Reservoir, 175, 222
Yei-Bichei Butte/Finger, 202
Yellowstone: Canyon, 145, 147; National Park, 153
Young Block (Richfield), The, 166
Yuba: State Park (Nephi), 16, 56; Dam Lake, 172; Lake State Recreation Area, 172

ZCMI Center (Salt Lake City), 72, 74
Zion: National Park, 16, 20, 27, 31, 52–55, 157, 211, 215, 216, 220–21, 223; Lodge, 52, 54; Canyon, 53, 54, 55, 216, 221; National Monument (Kolob Section), 53, 55, 216; Stadium, 53, 55; Park Scenic Byway, 59; Overlook, 215
Zion-Mount Carmel: Highway/Switchbacks, 53, 54, 55; tunnel, 55, 223
Zion's Bookstore (Salt Lake City), Sam Weller's, 69